Academic Services
Library Services

IMPLEMENTING THE URUGUAY ROUND

Implementing the Uruguay Round

JOHN H. JACKSON
and
ALAN O. SYKES

CLARENDON PRESS · OXFORD
1997

Oxford University Press, Great Clarendon Street, Oxford OX2 6DP
Oxford New York
Athens Auckland Bangkok Bombay
Buenos Aires Calcutta Cape Town Dar es Salaam
Delhi Florence Hong Kong Istanbul Karachi
Kuala Lumpur Madras Madrid Melbourne
Mexico City Nairobi Paris Singapore
Taipei Tokyo Toronto
and associated companies in
Berlin Ibadan

Oxford is a trade mark of Oxford University Press

Published in the United States
by Oxford University Press Inc., New York

British Library Cataloguing in Publication Data
Data available

Library of Congress Cataloging in Publication Data
Implementing the Uruguay Round/John H. Jackson and Alan O. Sykes.
p. cm.
Includes bibliographical references and index.
1. Uruguay Round (1987–1994). 2. Foreign trade regulation.
3. Tariff—Law and legislation. I. Jackson, John Howard, 1932–
II. Sykes, A. O.
K4603 1987.I49 1997
341.7'54—dc21 96–53051
ISBN 0–19–826236–1

1 3 5 7 9 10 8 6 4 2

Typeset by Cambrian Typesetters, Frimley, Surrey
Printed in Great Britain on acid-free paper by
Bookcraft Ltd., Midsomer Norton, Somerset

CONTENTS

TABLE OF CASES

EUROPEAN COURT OF JUSTICE

GERMANY

ITALY

JAPAN

TABLE OF NATIONAL LEGISLATION

BELGIUM

BRAZIL

CANADA

GERMANY

JAPAN

KOREA

SPAIN

SWITZERLAND

UK

US

1

INTRODUCTION AND OVERVIEW

John H. Jackson and Alan O. Sykes

1.1 THE NATURE OF THE PROJECT

The treaty creating the World Trade Organization is perhaps the most important development in international economic law since the Bretton Woods Agreement. The broad scope of the WTO Agreements, from trade in goods to trade in services to intellectual property to investment, along with the newly created Dispute Settlement System to administer them, has the potential to transform international economic relations in many ways. But the extent of this transformation will rest chiefly on the faithful implementation of new international legal obligations in the domestic law of each member country, and on the ability of WTO members to pursue further fruitful negotiations on a range of issues. This book is the culmination of a two-year project to examine this task of negotiating the Uruguay Round Agreements and implementing these historic accords in national law.

Our focus is not on the substance of the final Agreements, nor on the details of the multilateral negotiations that preceded them, but on the constitutional processes at the national level that facilitate or impede international negotiation and the implementation of international accords. The objective is to understand better the effect of different governmental structures and rules about the domestic effect of international law on the ability of nations to negotiate and to implement international obligations.

The project resembles in many ways a smaller project undertaken over fifteen years ago at the conclusion of the Tokyo Round. Professors Jackson, Jean-Victor Louis, and Matsuo Matsushita reviewed the implementation of the Tokyo Round Agreements in Europe, Japan and the United States.[1] The present volume expands and elaborates on the type of analysis developed there, extending it to new areas and to new issues.

Each of the following chapters, save the last, is an invited contribution from an author with expertise in the law of a particular WTO member nation (or group of nations). We invited each author to undertake a broad assessment of the interface between their national political systems and the

---

[1] See J. H. Jackson, J.-V. Louis and M. Matsushita (eds.) *Implementing the Tokyo Round* (1984).

international law of the World Trade Organization/General Agreement on Tariffs and Trade system. We provided some guidance in this task, encouraging all the authors to address a common set of issues and to indicate how they were handled in their respective legal systems (see pages 5–6 and Appendix A). From this set of papers, we hope that readers will develop some important comparative insights on a range of matters, such as the way that different domestic constitutional structures influence the negotiation of international agreements, the significance of different rules about the status of international law in the domestic legal system for the level of compliance with international obligations, the consequences of 'subsidiarity' and 'federalism' for the international economic order, the way that the design of the domestic legal system (and related matters such as the standing of private parties to enforce international accords) can affect implementation and compliance, and many other matters. The concluding chapter of the book suggests some tentative thoughts about such issues, but we emphasize that the most important pay-off to this project lies not so much in what the present volume contains as in the work that we hope it will stimulate among international legal scholars.

Although we provided the participating authors with considerable guidance in their task, we also left them with the freedom to pursue the issues that are special or unique to their national jurisdictions. The choice of countries to examine in the study was somewhat arbitrary, although we did seek to include the major players in the trading system. We also sought to include a cross-section of other countries, varying by size, geography and level of economic development. The result is a series of chapters covering the European Union, Belgium, Germany, Japan, the United States, Canada, Australia, Switzerland, Korea, Costa Rica and Brazil.

The papers were first presented at a conference sponsored by the Centre for Interdisciplinary Research at the University of Bielefeld, in Bielefeld, Germany in 1995. We are immensely grateful to the Centre and to Prof. Dr Meinhard Hilf for organizing the conference. We are also deeply grateful to the Thyssen Foundation for additional financial support.

1.2 THE HISTORY OF THE WTO/GATT SYSTEM

The treaty establishing the World Trade Organization was the culmination of over fifty years of effort toward the development of an international institution to govern and discipline world trade. These efforts begin with the Bretton Woods Conference of 1944, where the Allied leaders agreed to create three post-war institutions: the World Bank, the International Monetary Fund and the International Trade Organization. As an intermediate step toward the creation of the ITO, the major non-communist developed countries entered the General Agreement on Tariffs and Trade in 1947. Although efforts to create the ITO proceeded to the point of a draft charter, the US Congress refused to accept it. As a consequence, the GATT—conceived as a temporary measure—remained in force for nearly fifty years.

The GATT gradually evolved from a document into an institution, and a number of subsequent multilateral trade negotiations (rounds) were conducted under its auspices. These negotiating rounds were quite successful at reducing tariffs on trade in goods, at least among the developed countries, to the point that over time various non-tariff barriers assumed greater importance than tariffs. An early effort to address one set of these barriers was the 1967 Anti-Dumping Code, but the major push toward discipline of non-tariff barriers came in the late 1970s with the Tokyo Round. The resulting agreements on subsidies and countervailing measures, product standards, customs valuation practices, and others were an important step toward disabling nations from frustrating tariff concessions through the use of certain non-tariff measures.

Yet, despite the achievements of the Tokyo Round and modest steps taken afterwards, the GATT remained seriously incomplete in a number of areas. As an institution, its dispute resolution authority was weak. Operating under the consensus rule, a disputant could for many years block the dispute panel process altogether, and could always block authorization for sanctions once a violation had been adjudged. The level of compliance with GATT obligations thus depended on the costs to a country's reputation and any unilateral retaliation that might attend violations, a situation that was far from perfect.

More importantly, the coverage of the GATT was incomplete. It addressed trade in goods, but said nothing about services, or the increasingly important set of issues surrounding various forms of intellectual property protection. And even with respect to trade in goods, many obligations were incomplete or underenforced. Perhaps the most glaring examples involved measures for the protection of beleaguered industries. Largely in disregard of formal GATT obligations, trading nations throughout the world had negotiated a proliferation of 'voluntary restraint agreements' in industries such as textiles and steel, negating the effects of tariff liberalization on an open-ended basis.

These deficiencies in the system prompted another round of negotiations, termed the Uruguay Round, launched in 1986. The agenda was far broader than that of any previous round, and accordingly the negotiations were slow and halting. At a ministerial meeting in Brussels in late 1990, intended to provide a conclusion to the negotiations, a negotiating impasse developed which threatened the success of the Round. In an effort to revive the negotiations, the then Director-General of GATT, Arthur

Dunkel, oversaw the preparation of a tentative draft agreement (the Dunkel Draft) that later served as the basis for ongoing discussion.

Interestingly, the original agenda for the Uruguay Round did not contemplate the creation of a new organization. But there had been some discussion over the history of GATT about the need for such an organization, given that GATT had never been intended to serve that function and that it lacked many features usually found in international organizations. Concrete proposals for a new organization began to surface during the Uruguay Round,[2] and the Dunkel Draft incorporated a draft charter. By the time negotiations were finally completed in 1993, the result was the agreement creating the World Trade Organization. The Treaty establishing the WTO served as an umbrella for a series of annexed agreements on various substantive topics. Any nation joining the WTO was obliged to accept these annexed agreements as well—the major ones being GATT 1994 (trade in goods), the General Agreement on Trade in Services, and the Agreement on Trade-Related Aspects of Intellectual Property Rights. Other annexes concern dispute settlement, a trade policy review mechanism, and a handful of plurilateral (optional) agreements. Further refinements were introduced at Marrakesh, Morocco in 1994 when the Agreement was signed, in most cases subject to subsequent national ratification procedures.

Although the WTO Agreements left open a number of matters for further negotiation later (most importantly, sector-by-sector commitments on services), the achievements were remarkable. For the first time, services and intellectual property were brought within the purview of the GATT system. In the goods sectors, further progress toward eliminating tariffs altogether was made. And with regard to non-tariff barriers, sweeping agreements regarding dumping, subsidies and countervailing measures, product standards and regulations, and other matters were concluded. The voluntary restraint problem was addressed in a comprehensive safeguards agreement, and the thorny issues facing the agricultural and textile sectors were addressed in separate agreements as well. Institutionally, the WTO represents a dramatic reorganization of the GATT, with an end to the consensus rule and thus a serious prospect of centralized dispute resolution backed by a credible threat of sanctions. The judicialization of the system was further enhanced by the creation of an automatic right of appeal to a standing appellate body. Excerpts from a brief summary of the agreements on each topic, prepared by the GATT Secretariat, follows at the end of this chapter as Appendix B.

The breadth and depth of these accords poses a formidable problem of

---

[2] See J. H. Jackson, *Restructuring the GATT System* (1990).

implementation at the national level for both the original WTO members and those that may join in the future. Excluding the national schedules of individual product and service commitments, the text exceeds 500 pages. When the national schedules are added, its length grows to approximately 26,000 pages! The agreements are filled with ambiguities and omissions—deliberate and unintended—that will challenge WTO members for decades, and may well affect the course of future negotiations. Much of the implementation process will turn on national constitutional rules and legislative processes. Such matters, and their implications for international economic relations generally, are the primary focus of this book.

1.3 THE HEART OF THE INQUIRY: THE INTERFACE BETWEEN THE WORLD TRADE ORGANIZATION AND NATIONAL LEGAL SYSTEMS

The domestic legal system of each member nation affects the WTO system at three stages—negotiation, ratification and implementation. During the negotiation phase (whether during the Uruguay Round or during future negotiations under WTO auspices), the structure of the national legal system determines who has the power to negotiate on behalf of each member. This determination in turn affects the negotiating stance of the member through, *inter alia*, its impact on the access of pertinent interest groups to the negotiating process. The national legal system also controls the power of the negotiators to make offers and to accept offers from others, and thus affects the credibility of each member's negotiating position and perhaps other strategic matters as well.

During the ratification phase, the national legal system determines who will have the authority to block the results of the agreement or impede its implementation. Although no such entity exercised its veto after the completion of the Uruguay Round negotiations, the possibility of such a veto was a constant factor during the negotiating process. Thus, as a practical matter, the national structure of the ratification process plays a critical role not so much after the negotiations are complete, but while they are ongoing.

Finally, during the implementation phase, the national legal system can have a profound impact on the extent to which the international obligations are faithfully followed. Among the critical issues here are the status of the international obligation in domestic law, and the structure of the domestic judicial system that enforces domestic law.

In designing this project, we asked each of the authors to focus on these matters, with greater or lesser emphasis according to their own judgment. Appendix A contains the guidelines that were sent to each author prior to the preparation of their initial drafts. The discussion at Bielefeld led us to further focus the inquiry, and in the end we asked each author to consider the following three sets of issues:

1. *The constitutional and statutory structure of negotiation by national representatives*: topics under this rubric might include, *inter alia*, the competence of the European Community to negotiate on behalf of Member States; the past and future role of European Union Member States in WTO negotiations; the formal and informal role of interest groups in the negotiation process; the formal and informal role of legislative bodies in the negotiation process; the 'fast track' and its analogues in other nations; and the practical consequences of all of these matters for past and future negotiations.

2. *The application of the WTO agreements in domestic law*: topics under this rubric might include, *inter alia*, the legal status of the international agreement in domestic law, including, in cases of direct applicability, the priority of international law in relation to domestic statutes; the ability of various interested parties to 'invoke' international law on their behalf; the question of what practical difference direct application/ invocability or its absence makes in each nation; historical/political/ economic explanations for direct application/invocability or its absence country by country; the effect of the WTO Agreement on subsidiary governments (federalism issues); the 'indirect' application of the international agreement as a device for statutory construction; and the existence and consequences for implementation of the WTO agreements of domestic concerns about 'sovereignty'.

3. *The interface, now and in the future, between national law and the WTO dispute resolution process*: topics under this rubric might include, *inter alia*, the status of WTO dispute panel reports in international and national law, and the ability of private parties to encourage and participate in WTO complaints by their national governments.

The chapters that follow are the result of this exercise. In the final chapter, we will return to these issues, and attempt to draw some comparative lessons from the papers along with some speculations about their implications for what has happened so far under the WTO and what may happen in the future.

APPENDIX A
GUIDELINES FOR AUTHORS

The objective of this project is to examine the national legal and constitutional problems involved in the implementation of the results of international negotiations on trade. We are interested in understanding how different national legal systems operate, how the design of these legal systems may affect the international commitments that a nation undertakes, and how different legal systems may be more or less efficacious in implementing international obligations domestically. To this end, we are interested in a series of subordinate questions, including:

1. What are the existing legal and constitutional constraints on the development of international trade policy? How did they affect the negotiating position of national negotiators and the commitments ultimately made?
2. How was the Uruguay Round 'single package' treaty ratified and then implemented in the national legal system of each of the entities examined?

Additional factors bearing upon the overall study include:

1. The legal authority of the negotiators to make offers.
2. The legal authority or procedure for the negotiators to accept the international commitments of the agreement (as distinguished from implementation in domestic law.)
3. The legal authority or procedure for implementing the international commitments of the agreement through changes in domestic law.
4. The prospects for successful domestic implementation of various Uruguay Round accords, and the reasons for any difficulty in this respect.
5. Changes or adjustments needed in national governmental systems to accommodate current or prospective trade agreements.
6. The legal relationship between the international law of the Uruguay Round agreements and the laws in the national systems—for example, will the multilateral trade negotiation agreements be self-executing? Will they have a direct effect?
7. The role of private litigants in implementing and enforcing Uruguay Round accords internationally and domestically.
8. The role of legislative bodies in formulating, negotiating, and implementing international trade initiatives, as well as public and citizen participation.
9. The role of judicial procedures in implementing national rights and obligations, and the design of judicial tribunals, including measures to insulate them from political pressures.
10. The perceived burden of the Uruguay Round accords on 'sovereignty', and the attendant implications for the willingness of governments to enter future trade negotiations.
11. The effect of the Uruguay Round accords on subsidiary governments—provinces, states, localities—and its consequences.

In considering these issues, we hope to sharpen the understanding of the legal constraints, to suggest to all nations new approaches to implementation that might not otherwise have been considered, and to examine whether there might exist in the differences between the national structures certain potential dangers that could make further negotiations difficult or impossible.

APPENDIX B
SUMMARY OF THE URUGUAY ROUND AGREEMENTS
PREPARED BY GATT SECRETARIAT[3] [EXCERPTS]

The Final Act of the Uruguay Round: a summary

The Final Act Embodying the Results of the Uruguay Round of Multilateral Trade Negotiations is 550 pages long and contains legal texts which spell out the results of the negotiations since the Round was launched in Punta del Este, Uruguay, in September 1986. In addition to the texts of the agreements, the Final Act also contains texts of Ministerial Decisions and Declarations which further clarify certain provisions of some of the agreements.

The following summarizes . . . the Final Act. These summaries are intended to provide an informal guide to the agreements and have no legal status.

The Final Act covers all the negotiating areas cited in the Punta del Este Declaration with two important exceptions. The first is the results of the 'market access negotiations' in which individual countries have made binding commitments to reduce or eliminate specific tariffs and non-tariff barriers to merchandise trade. These concessions are to be recorded in national schedules which will form an integral part of the Final Act. The second is the 'initial commitments' on liberalization of trade in services. These commitments on liberalization are also to be recorded in national schedules.

Agreement establishing the World Trade Organization

The agreement establishing the World Trade Organization (WTO) envisages a single institutional framework encompassing the GATT, as modified by the Uruguay Round, all agreements and arrangements

---

[3] *GATT Focus Newsletter*, Dec. 1993.

concluded under its auspices and the complete results of the Uruguay Round. Its structure will be headed by a Ministerial Conference meeting at least once every two years. A General Council will be established to oversee the operation of the agreement and, ministerial decisions on a regular basis. This General Council will itself act as a Dispute Settlement Body and a Trade Policy Review Mechanism, which will concern themselves with the full range of trade issues covered by the WTO, and will also establish subsidiary bodies such as a Goods Council, a Services Council and a TRIPs Council. The WTO framework will ensure a 'single undertaking approach' to the results of the Uruguay Round—thus, membership in the WTO will entail accepting all the results of the Round without exception.

General Agreement on Tariffs and Trade 1994

. . .

Agreement on Agriculture

The negotiations have resulted in four main portions of the Agreement; the Agreement on Agriculture itself; the concessions and commitments Members are to undertake on market access, domestic support and export subsidies; the Agreement on Sanitary and Phytosanitary Measures; and the Ministerial Decision concerning Least-Developed and Net Food-Importing Developing countries.

Overall, the results of the negotiations provide a framework for a long-term reform of agricultural trade and domestic policies over the years to come. It makes a decisive move towards the objective of increased market orientation in agricultural trade. The rules governing agricultural trade are strengthened which will lead to improved predictability and stability for importing and exporting countries alike.

The agricultural package also addresses many other issues of vital economic and political importance to many Members. These include provisions that encourage the use of less trade-distorting domestic support policies to maintain the rural economy, that allow actions to be taken to ease any adjustment burden, and also the introduction of tightly prescribed provisions that allow some flexibility in the implementation of commitments. Specific concerns of developing countries have been addressed including the concerns of net-food importing countries and least-developed countries.

The agricultural package provides for commitments in the area of market access, domestic support and export competition. The text of the Agricultural Agreement is mirrored in the GATT Schedules of legal commitments relating to individual countries (as noted in the section of this paper that describes the Uruguay Round Protocol).

. . .

Agreement on Sanitary and Phytosanitary Measures

This agreement concerns the application of sanitary and phytosanitary measures—in other words food safety and animal and plant health regulations. The agreement recognizes that governments have the right to take sanitary and phytosanitary measures but that they should be applied only to the extent necessary to protect human, animal or plant life or health and should not arbitrarily or unjustifiably discriminate between Members where identical or similar conditions prevail.

In order to harmonize sanitary and phytosanitary measures on as wide a basis as possible, Members are encouraged to base their measures on international standards, guidelines and recommendations where they exist. However, Members may maintain or introduce measures which result in higher standards if there is scientific justification or as a consequence of consistent risk decisions based on an appropriate risk assessment. The Agreement spells out procedures and criteria for the assessment of risk and the determination of appropriate levels of sanitary or phytosanitary protection.

It is expected that Members would accept the sanitary and phytosanitary measures of others as equivalent if the exporting country demonstrates to the importing country that its measures achieve the importing country's appropriate level of health protection. The agreement includes provisions on control, inspection and approval procedures.

. . .

Agreement on Textiles and Clothing

The object of this negotiation has been to secure the eventual integration of the textiles and clothing sector—where much of the trade is currently subject to bilateral quotas negotiated under the Multifibre Arrangement (MFA)—into the GATT on the basis of strengthened GATT rules and disciplines.

. . .

While the agreement focuses largely on the phasing-out of MFA restrictions, it also recognizes that some members maintain non-MFA restrictions not justified under a GATT provision. These would also be brought into conformity with GATT within one year of the entry into force of the Agreement or phased out progressively during a period not exceeding the duration of the Agreement (that is, by 2005).

. . .

Agreement on Technical Barriers to Trade

This agreement will extend and clarify the Agreement on Technical Barriers to Trade reached in the Tokyo Round. It seeks to ensure that technical negotiations and standards, as well as testing and certification procedures, do not create unnecessary obstacles to trade. However, it recognizes that countries have the right to establish protection, at levels they consider appropriate, for example for human, animal or plant life or health or the environment, and should not be prevented from taking measures necessary to ensure those levels of protection are met. The agreement therefore encourages countries to use international standards where these are appropriate, but it does not require them to change their levels of protection as a result of standardization.

Innovative features of the revised agreement are that it covers processing and production methods related to the characteristics of the product itself. The coverage of conformity assessment procedures is enlarged and the disciplines made more precise. Notification provisions applying to local government and non-governmental bodies are elaborated in more detail than in the Tokyo Round agreement. A Code of Good Practice for the Preparation, Adoption and Application of Standards by standardizing bodies, which is open to acceptance by private sector bodies as well as the public sector, is included as an annex to the agreement.

Agreement on Trade-Related Investment Measures

The agreement recognizes that certain investment measures restrict and distort trade. It provides that no contracting party shall apply any TRIM inconsistent with Articles III (national treatment) and XI (prohibition of quantitative restrictions) of the GATT. To this end, an illustrative list of TRIMs agreed to be inconsistent with these articles is appended to the agreement. The list includes measures which require particular levels of local procurement by an enterprise ('local content requirements') or which restrict the volume or value of imports such an enterprise can purchase or use to an amount related to the level of products it exports ('trade balancing requirements').

The agreement requires mandatory notification of all non-conforming TRIMs and their elimination within two years for developed countries, within five years for developing countries and within seven years for least-developed countries. It establishes a Committee on TRIMs which will, among other things, monitor the implementation of these commitments. The agreement also provides for consideration, at a later date, of whether it should be complemented with provisions on investment and competition policy more broadly.

Agreement on Implementation of Article VI (Anti-Dumping)

Article VI of the GATT provides for the right of contracting parties to apply anti-dumping measures, i.e. measures against imports of a product at an export price below its 'normal value' (usually the price of the product in the domestic market of the exporting country) if such dumped imports cause injury to a domestic industry in the territory of the importing contracting party. More detailed rules governing the application of such measures are currently provided in an Anti-Dumping Agreement concluded at the end of the Tokyo Round. Negotiations in the Uruguay Round have resulted in a revision of this Agreement which addresses many areas in which the current Agreement lacks precision and detail.

In particular, the revised Agreement provides for greater clarity and more detailed rules in relation to the method of determining that a product is dumped, the criteria to be taken into account in a determination that dumped imports cause injury to a domestic industry, the procedures to be followed in initiating and conducting anti-dumping investigations, and the implementation and duration of anti-dumping measures. In addition, the new agreement clarifies the role of dispute settlement panels in disputes relating to anti-dumping actions taken by domestic authorities. On the methodology for determining that a product is exported at a dumped price, the new Agreement adds relatively specific provisions on such issues as criteria for allocating costs when the export price is compared with a 'constructed' normal value and rules to ensure that a fair comparison is made between the export price and the normal value of a product so as not to arbitrarily create or inflate margins of dumping.

. . .

Agreement on Rules of Origin

The agreement aims at long-term harmonization of rules of origin, other than rules of origin relating to the granting of tariff preferences, and to ensure that such rules do not themselves create unnecessary obstacles to trade.

The agreement sets up a harmonization programme, to be initiated as soon as possible after the completion of the Uruguay Round and to be completed within three years of initiation. It would be based upon a set of principles, including making rules of origin objective, understandable and predictable. The work would be conducted by a Committee on Rules of Origin in the GATT and a technical committee under the auspices of the Customs Co-operation Council in Brussels.

Until the completion of the harmonization programme, contracting parties would be expected to ensure that their rules of origin are transparent; that they do not have restricting, distorting or disruptive effects on international trade; that they are administered in a consistent, uniform, impartial and reasonable manner, and that they are based on a positive standard (in other words, they should state what *does* confer origin rather than what does not).

An annex to the agreement sets out a 'common declaration' with respect to the operation of rules of origin on goods which qualify for preferential treatment.

. . .

Agreement on Subsidies and Countervailing Measures

The Agreement on Subsidies and Countervailing Measures is intended to build on the Agreement on Interpretation and Application of Articles VI, XVI and XXIII which was negotiated in the Tokyo Round.

Unlike its predecessor, the agreement contains a definition of subsidy and introduces the concept of a 'specific' subsidy—for the most part, a subsidy available only to an enterprise or industry or group of enterprises or industries within the jurisdiction of the authority granting the subsidy. Only specific subsidies would be subject to the disciplines set out in the agreement.

The agreement establishes three categories of subsidies. First, it deems the following subsidies to be 'prohibited': those contingent, in law or in fact, whether solely or as one of several other conditions, upon export performance; and those contingent, whether solely or as one of several other conditions, upon the use of domestic over imported goods. Prohibited subsidies are subject to new dispute settlement procedures. The main features include an expedited timetable for action by the Dispute Settlement Body, and if it is found that the subsidy is indeed prohibited, it must be immediately withdrawn. If this is not done within the specified time period, the complaining member is authorized to take countermeasures.

The second category is 'actionable' subsidies. The agreement stipulates that no member should cause, through the use of subsidies, adverse effects to the interests of other signatories, i.e. injury to domestic industry of another signatory, nullification or impairment of benefits accruing directly or indirectly to other signatories under the General Agreement (in particular the benefits of bound tariff concessions), and serious prejudice to the interests of another member. 'Serious prejudice' shall be presumed to exist for certain subsidies including when the total *ad valorem* subsidization of a product exceeds 5 per cent. In such a situation, the burden of proof is on the subsidizing member to show that the subsidies in question do not cause serious prejudice to the complaining member. Members affected by actionable subsidies may refer the matter to the Dispute Settlement Body. In the event that it is determined that such adverse effects exist, the subsidizing member must withdraw the subsidy or remove the adverse effects.

The third category involves non-actionable subsidies, which could either be non-specific subsidies, or specific subsidies involving assistance to industrial research and pre-competitive development activity, assistance to

disadvantaged regions, or certain type of assistance for adapting existing facilities to new environmental requirements imposed by law and/or regulations. Where another member believes that an otherwise non-actionable subsidy is resulting in serious adverse effects to a domestic industry, it may seek a determination and recommendation on the matter.
. . .

Agreement on Safeguards

Article XIX of the General Agreement allows a member to take a 'safeguard' action to protect a specific domestic industry from an unforeseen increase of imports of any product which is causing, or which is likely to cause, serious injury to the industry.

The agreement breaks major ground in establishing a prohibition against so-called 'grey area' measures, and in setting a 'sunset clause' on all safeguard actions. The agreement stipulates that a member shall not seek, take or maintain any voluntary export restraints, orderly marketing arrangements or any other similar measures on the export or the import side. Any such measure in effect at the time of entry into force of the agreement would be brought into conformity with this agreement, or would have to be phased out within four years after the entry into force of the agreement establishing the WTO. An exception could be made for one specific measure for each importing member, subject to mutual agreement with the directly concerned member, where the phase-out date would be 31 December 1999.

All existing safeguard measures taken under Article XIX of the General Agreement 1947 shall be terminated not later than eight years after the date on which they were first applied or five years after the date of entry into force of the agreement establishing the WTO, whichever comes later.
. . .

In principle, safeguard measures have to be applied irrespective of source. In cases in which a quota is allocated among supplying countries, the member applying restrictions may seek agreement with other members having a substantial interest in supplying the product concerned. Normally, allocation of shares would be on the basis of proportion of total quantity or value of the imported product over a previous representative period. However, it would be possible for the importing country to depart from this approach if it could demonstrate, in consultations under the auspices of the Safeguards Committee, that imports from certain contracting parties had increased disproportionately in relation to the total increase and that such a departure would be justified and equitable to all suppliers. The duration of the safeguard measure in this case cannot exceed four years.

The agreement lays down time limits for all safeguard measures. Generally, the duration of a measure should not exceed four years though this could be extended up to a maximum of eight years, subject to confirmation of continued necessity by the competent national authorities and if there is evidence that the industry is adjusting. Any measure imposed for a period greater than one year should be progressively liberalized during its lifetime. No safeguard measure could be applied again to a product that had been subject to such action for a period equal to the duration of the previous measure, subject to a non-application period of at least two years. A safeguard measure with a duration of 180 days or less may be applied again to the import of a product if at least one year had elapsed since the date of introduction of the measure on that product, and if such a measure had not been applied on the same product more than twice in the five-year period immediately preceding the date of introduction of the measure.

The agreement envisages consultations on compensation for safeguard measures. Where consultations are not successful, the affected members may withdraw equivalent concessions or other obligations under GATT 1994. However, such action is not allowed for the first three years of the safeguard measure if it conforms to the provisions of the agreement, and is taken as a result of an absolute increase in imports.

. . .

General Agreement on Trade in Services

The Services Agreement which forms part of the Final Act rests on three pillars. The first is a Framework Agreement containing basic obligations which apply to all member countries. The second concerns national schedules of commitments containing specific further national commitments which will be the subject of a continuing process of liberalization. The third is a number of annexes addressing the special situations of individual services sectors.

Part I of the basic agreement defines its scope—specifically, services supplied from the territory of one party to the territory of another; services supplied in the territory of one party to the consumers of any other (for example, tourism); services provided through the presence of service providing entities of one party in the territory of any other (for example, banking); and services provided by nationals of one party in the territory of any other (for example, construction projects or consultancies).

Part II sets out general obligations and disciplines. A basic most-favoured-nation (m.f.n.) obligation states that each party 'shall accord immediately and unconditionally to services and service providers of any other Party, treatment no less favourable than that it accords to like services and service providers of any other country'. However, it is recognized that m.f.n. treatment may not be possible for every service activity and, therefore, it is envisaged that parties may indicate specific m.f.n. exemptions. Conditions for such exemptions are included as an annex and provide for reviews after five years and a normal limitation of ten years on their duration. Transparency requirements include publication of all relevant laws and regulations. Provisions to facilitate the increased participation of developing countries in world services trade envisage negotiated commitments on access to technology, improvements in access to distribution channels and information networks and the liberalization of market access in sectors and modes of supply of export interest. The provisions covering economic integration are analogous to those in Article XXIV of GATT, requiring arrangements to have 'substantial sectoral coverage' and to 'provide for the absence or elimination of substantially all discrimination' between the parties.

Since domestic regulations, not border measures, provide the most significant influence on services trade, provisions spell out that all such measures of general application should be administered in a reasonable, objective and impartial manner. There would be a requirement that parties establish the means for prompt reviews of administrative decisions relating to the supply of services.

The agreement contains obligations with respect to recognition requirements (educational background, for instance) for the purpose of securing authorizations, licences or certification in the services area. It encourages recognition requirements achieved through harmonization and internationally-agreed criteria. Further provisions state that parties are required to ensure that monopolies and exclusive service providers do not abuse their positions. Restrictive business practices should be subject to consultations between parties with a view to their elimination.

While parties are normally obliged not to restrict international transfers and payments for current transactions relating to commitments under the agreement, there are provisions allowing limited restrictions in the event of balance-of-payments difficulties. However, where such restrictions are imposed they would be subject to conditions; including that they are non-discriminatory, that they avoid unnecessary commercial damage to other parties and that they are of a temporary nature.

The agreement contains both general exceptions and security exceptions provisions which are similar to Articles XX and XXI of the GATT. It also envisages negotiations to develop disciplines on trade-distorting subsidies to the services area.

Part III contains provisions on market access and national treatment which would not be general obligations but would be commitments made in national schedules. Thus, in the case of market access, each party 'shall accord services and service-providers of other Parties treatment no less favourable than that provided for under the terms, limitations and conditions agreed and specified in its schedule'. The intention of the market-access provision is to progressively eliminate the following types of measures: limitations on numbers of service-providers, on the total value of service transactions or on the total number of service operations or people employed. Equally, restrictions on the kind of legal entity or joint venture through which a service is provided or any foreign capital limitations relating to maximum levels of foreign participation are to be progressively eliminated.

The national–treatment provision contains the obligation to treat foreign service-suppliers and domestic service suppliers in the same manner. However, it does provide the possibility of different treatment being accorded the service-providers of other parties to that accorded to domestic service-providers. However, in such cases the conditions of competition should not, as a result, be modified in favour of the domestic service-providers.

Part IV of the agreement establishes the basis for progressive liberalization in the services area through successive rounds of negotiations and the development of national schedules. It also permits, after a period of three years, parties to withdraw or modify commitments made in their schedules. Where commitments are modified or withdrawn, negotiations should be undertaken with interested parties to agree on compensatory adjustments. Where agreement cannot be reached, compensation would be decided by arbitration.

Part V of the agreement contains institutional provisions, including consultation and dispute settlement and the establishment of a Council on Services. The responsibilities of the Council are set out in a Ministerial Decision.

The first of the annexes to the agreement concerns the movement of labour. It permits parties to negotiate specific commitments applying to the movement of people providing services under the agreement. It requires that people covered by a specific commitment shall be allowed to provide the service in accordance with the terms of the commitment. Nevertheless, the agreement would not apply to measures affecting employment, citizenship, residence or employment on a permanent basis.

. . .

Agreement on Trade-Related Aspects of Intellectual Property Rights, including Trade in Counterfeit Goods

The agreement recognizes that widely varying standards in the protection and enforcement of intellectual property rights and the lack of a multilateral framework of principles, rules and disciplines dealing with international trade in counterfeit goods have been a growing source of tension in international economic relations. Rules and disciplines were needed to cope with these tensions. To that end, the agreement addresses the applicability of basic GATT principles and those of relevant international intellectual property agreements; the provision of adequate intellectual property rights; the provision of effective enforcement measures for those rights; multilateral dispute settlement; and transitional arrangements.

Part I of the agreement sets out general provisions and basic principles, notably a national–treatment commitment under which the nationals of other parties must be given treatment no less favourable than that accorded to a party's own nationals with regard to the protection of intellectual property. It also contains a most-favoured-nation clause, a novelty in an international intellectual property agreement, under which any advantage a party gives to the nationals of another country must be extended immediately and unconditionally to the nationals of all other parties, even if such treatment is more favourable than that which it gives to its own nationals.

Part II addresses each intellectual property right in succession. With respect to copyright, parties are required to comply with the substantive provisions of the Berne Convention for the protection of literary and artistic works, in its latest version (Paris 1971), though they will not be obliged to protect moral rights as stipulated in Article 6b of that Convention. It ensures that computer programs will be protected as literary works under the Berne Convention and lays down on what basis data bases should be protected by copyright. Important additions to existing international rules in the area of copyright and related rights are the provisions on rental rights. The draft requires authors of computer programmes and producers of sound recordings to be given the right to authorize or prohibit the commercial rental of their works to the public. A similar exclusive right applies to films where commercial rental has led to widespread copying which is materially impairing the right of reproduction. The draft also requires performers to be given protection from unauthorized recording and broadcast of live performances (bootlegging). The protection for performers and producers of sound recordings would be for no less than fifty years. Broadcasting organizations would have control over the use that can be made of broadcast signals without their authorization. This right would last for at least twenty years.

With respect to trade marks and service marks, the agreement defines what types of signs must be eligible for protection as a trade mark or service mark and what the minimum rights conferred on their owners must be. Marks that have become well-known in a particular country shall enjoy additional protection. In addition, the agreement lays down a number of obligations with regard to the use of trade marks and service marks, their term of protection, and their licensing or assignment. For example, requirements that foreign marks be used in conjunction with local marks would, as a general rule, be prohibited.

. . .

As regards patents, there is a general obligation to comply with the substantive provisions of the Paris Convention (1967). In addition, the agreement requires that twenty-year patent protection be available for all inventions, whether of products or processes, in almost all fields of technology. Inventions may be excluded from patentability if their commercial exploitation is prohibited for reasons of public order or morality; otherwise, the permitted exclusions are for diagnostic, therapeutic and surgical methods, and for plants and (other than micro-organisms) animals and essentially biological processes for the production of plants or animals (other than microbiological processes). Plant varieties, however, must be protectable either by patents or by a *sui generis* system (such as the breeder's rights provided in a UPOV Convention). Detailed conditions are laid down for compulsory licensing or governmental use of patents without the authorization of the patent owner. Rights conferred in respect of patents for processes must extend to the products directly obtained by the process; under certain conditions alleged infringers may be ordered by a court to prove that they have not used the patented process.

. . .

Part III of the agreement sets out the obligations of member governments to provide procedures and remedies under their domestic law to ensure that intellectual property rights can be effectively enforced, by foreign right-holders as well as by their own nationals. Procedures should permit effective action against infringement of intellectual property rights but should be fair and equitable, not unnecessarily complicated or costly, and should not entail unreasonable time-limits or unwarranted delays. They should allow for judicial review of final administrative decisions. There is no obligation to put in place a judicial system distinct from that for the enforcement of laws in general, nor to give priority to the enforcement of intellectual property rights in the allocation of resources or staff.

. . .

Understanding on Rules and Procedures Governing the Settlement of Disputes

The dispute settlement system of the GATT is generally considered to be one of the cornerstones of the multilateral trade order. The system has already been strengthened and streamlined as a result of reforms agreed following the Mid-Term Review Ministerial Meeting held in Montreal in December 1988. Disputes currently being dealt with by the Council are subject to these new rules, which include greater automaticity in decisions on the establishment, terms of reference and composition of panels, such that these decisions are no longer dependent upon the consent of the parties to a dispute. The Uruguay Round Understanding on Rules and Procedures Governing the Settlement of Disputes (DSU) will further strengthen the existing system significantly, extending the greater automaticity agreed in the Mid-Term Review to the adoption of the panels' and a new Appellate Body's findings. Moreover, the DSU will establish an integrated system permitting WTO Members to base their claims on any of the multilateral trade agreements included in the Annexes to the Agreement establishing the WTO. For this purpose, a Dispute Settlement Body (DSB) will exercise the authority of the General Council and the Councils and committees of the covered agreements.

The DSU emphasizes the importance of consultations in securing dispute resolution, requiring a Member to enter into consultations within thirty days of a request for consultations from another Member. If after sixty days from the request for consultations there is no settlement, the complaining party may request the establishment of a panel. Where consultations are denied, the complaining party may move directly to request a panel. The parties may voluntarily agree to follow alternative means of dispute settlement, including good offices, conciliation, mediation and arbitration.

Where a dispute is not settled through consultations, the DSU requires the establishment of a panel, at the latest, at the meeting of the DSB following that at which a request is made, unless the DSB decides by consensus against establishment. The DSU also sets out specific rules and deadlines for deciding the terms of reference and composition of panels. Standard terms of reference will apply unless the parties agree to special terms within twenty days of the panel's establishment. And where the parties do not agree on the composition of the panel within the same twenty days, this can be decided by the Director-General. Panels normally consist of three persons of appropriate background and experience from countries not party to the dispute. The Secretariat will maintain a list of experts satisfying the criteria.

Panel procedures are set out in detail in the DSU. It is envisaged that a panel will normally complete its work within six months or, in cases of urgency, within three months. Panel reports may be considered by the DSB for adoption twenty days after they are issued to Members. Within sixty days of their issuance, they will be adopted, unless the DSB decides by consensus not to adopt the report or one of the parties notifies the DSB of its intention to appeal.

The concept of appellate review is an important new feature of the DSU. An Appellate Body will be established, composed of seven members, three of whom will serve on any one case. An appeal will be limited to issues of law covered in the panel report and legal interpretations developed by the panel. Appellate proceedings shall not exceed sixty days from the date a party formally notifies its decision to appeal. The resulting report shall be adopted by the DSB and unconditionally accepted by the parties within thirty days following its issuance to Members, unless the DSB decides by consensus against its adoption.

Once the panel report or the Appellate Body report is adopted, the party concerned will have to notify its intentions with respect to implementation of adopted recommendations. If it is impracticable to comply immediately, the party concerned shall be given a reasonable period of time, the latter to be decided either by agreement of the parties and approval by the DSB within forty-five days of adoption of the report or through arbitration within ninety days of adoption. In any event, the DSB will keep the implementation under regular surveillance until the issue is resolved.

Further provisions set out rules for compensation or the suspension of concessions in the event of non-implementation. Within a specified time-frame, parties can enter into negotiations to agree on mutually acceptable compensation. Where this has not been agreed, a party to the dispute may request authorization of the DSB to suspend concessions or other obligations to the other party concerned. The DSB will grant such authorization within thirty days of the expiry of the agreed time-frame for implementation. Disagreements over the proposed level of suspension may be referred to arbitration. In principle, concessions should be suspended in the same sector as that in issue in the panel case. If this is not practicable or effective, the suspension can be made in a different sector of the same agreement. In turn, if this is not effective or practicable and if the circumstances are serious enough, the suspension of concessions may be made under another agreement.

One of the central provisions of the DSU reaffirms that Members shall not themselves make determinations of violations or suspend concessions, but shall make use of the dispute settlement rules and procedures of the DSU.

. . .

2

THE EUROPEAN COMMUNITY AND THE URUGUAY ROUND AGREEMENTS

Confusion and controversy over the competence and conduct of the
European Community in international economic relations: the bittersweet
experience of the Uruguay Round

*Peter L. H. Van den Bossche**

2.1 INTRODUCTION

Controversy and confusion reign with regard to the competence and
conduct of the European Community in the field of international economic
relations. Within and without Europe, questions surrounding the
Community's competence and conduct cause a pervasive feeling of
bewilderment. The fact that *both* the Community *and* all the Member
States of the European Union have joined the newly established World
Trade Organization, the forum par excellence for negotiations on
international economic relations, has certainly added to the potential for
bewilderment. This chapter is meant to achieve a greater understanding of
the internal rules and processes by which the European Community
undertakes international commitments in the field of economic relations.[1]

* Counsellor, Appellate Body Secretariat, World Trade Organization, Geneva, and
Visiting Professor of Law at the University of Maastricht. The author wishes to thank Jacques
Bourgeois, Piet Eeckhout, Tania Friederichs, Pietet Jan Kuijper, Jean-Victor Louis and
Bruno de Witte for their most helpful advice and comments, Joshua Sanderson for his
invaluable research assistance and the Maastrichts Europees Instituut voor Transnationaal
Rechtswetenschappelijk Onderzoek (METRO) for its support. Responsibility for any factual
inaccuracy rests with the author. The opinions expressed in this article are the personal views
of the author.
  [1] A first point of clarification I would like to make relates to the use of the terms European
Community, European Communities and European Union. Throughout this chapter I use the
term European Community.
  The European Parliament as well as leading newspapers systematically use the term
European Union in the context of international economic relations. Occasionally also the
Commission seems to prefer this term. What is permissible for politicians and journalists may,
however, be less acceptable for lawyers. The competence to act in the field of international
economic relations rests specifically with the European Community and not with the
European Union. The Community is, of course, part of the Union, but the latter does not
have international legal personality. The European Union itself can therefore not negotiate or
conclude international agreements or be a member of international organizations. To refer to
the European Union rather than to the European Community as the 'actor' in the context of
international economic relations may be politically convenient but is incorrect.

With this purpose in mind, I will discuss in detail the issues relating to the competence and conduct of the European Community in this field, as they arose in the context of the Uruguay Round of multilateral trade negotiations—the longest, most comprehensive and most difficult trade negotiations in which the Community has participated to date.

The issues relating to *competence* (discussed in Section 2) primarily concern the scope of Article 113 EC on the common commercial policy on the one hand, and the scope and exclusive nature of the Community's implied external competence on the other. Careful attention is given in particular to the issue of the exclusive competence of the Community in the emerging fields of trade in services and trade related aspects of intellectual property rights. It is clear that the competence issues discussed in this chapter are not only of interest to the Community and the Member States. In view of future negotiations on international economic relations, non-member countries obviously have an interest in understanding the limits of the Community's competence in this field.

Section 3 deals with the *conduct* of the European Community in the field of international economic relations. It focuses on the negotiation, conclusion and implementation of the Uruguay Round Agreements by the European Community. This discussion reveals that the process by which the Community negotiates, concludes and implements international agreements concerning economic relations is often complex and 'treacherous'. Again, in view of future negotiations, non-member countries cannot afford to ignore the many issues relating to the conduct of the Community in such negotiations.

The ultimate goal of both Sections 2 and 3, is to show how the rules of the Community on the division of competence between the Community and the Member States, as well as the procedural rules on the conduct of the Community, may affect the process of international negotiations on economic relations. The bittersweet experience of the Uruguay Round negotiations hides many a lesson for future negotiations; and this for the Community institutions and the Member States as well as non-member countries. With such a focus at hand, this chapter will not attempt to

A careful reader of the WTO-Agreement will notice that not the European Community, but the European Communi*ties* is a Member of the WTO (see Art. XI, WTO Agreement). The Marrakesh Final Act of April 1994 was also signed by the European Communi*ties* rather than by the European Community (see Ss. 1.1.1. and 2.2.2.). The reason for this was that, at the time, it was thought that, to the extent the Uruguay Round Agreements concerned matters falling within the scope of the ECSC or Euratom Treaty, these agreements fell outside the competence of the European Community. In the meantime it has become clear that this is not the case. With regard to Euratom matters, see Op. 1/94, para. 24 and with regard to ECSC matters, see Op. 1/94, para. 27 (See S. 1.2.4.). The Uruguay Round Agreements have therefore been concluded by the European Community , and not by the European Communi*ties*, see Council Dec. 84/800, 22 Dec. 1994. (see S. 2.2.5). An amendment of Art. XI, WTO Agreement was, however, no longer possible.

evaluate the substantive results of the Uruguay Round negotiations, or the substance of the further implementing legislation. If reference is made to substantive issues, it is merely to put the issues of competence and conduct in the proper context.[2]

2.2 THE COMPETENCE OF THE EUROPEAN COMMUNITY IN THE FIELD OF INTERNATIONAL ECONOMIC RELATIONS

2.2.1 *The competence issue in the context of the Uruguay Round*

2.2.1.1 A blessed truce (1986–1993)

The division of competence between the European Community and the Member States in the field of international economic relations has always been a controversial issue. This is not surprising. The field of foreign policy, of which the field of international economic relations is an ever more important part, is notorious for being 'the most jealously guarded area of national sovereignty'.[3] The Member States have been openly reluctant to completely surrender their competence over international trade matters to the European Community. This reluctance is nourished and strengthened by the fact that the competence of the Community in the field of international economic relations is—as are many other Community competences—ill-defined in the Treaty of Rome. The European Court of Justice ('the Court') has both clarified and expanded the Community's competence in the field of international economic relations, but it has never defined the scope of this competence with precision.

When the Community agreed, in September 1986, to take part in a new GATT round of multilateral trade negotiations which would, for the first time, also cover trade in services and trade related aspects of intellectual property rights, it was clear that the Community would have to face the vexing issue of the scope of its competence in the field of international economic relations. Fortunately, it managed 'to avoid' the issue until the end of the Uruguay Round negotiations, by pragmatically 'agreeing to disagree' on the scope of its competence, and thus was able to get on with the negotiations. The Punta del Este Ministerial Declaration, launching the Uruguay Round, was approved by both the Council and the

---

[2] For a comprehensive, insightful and entertaining discussion of the substantive issues dealt with during the Uruguay Round and the Community's position on these issues, see Paemen, H. and Bensch, A., *From the GATT to the WTO: the European Community in the Uruguay Round* Publisher and Date.

[3] J. Weiler, 'The European Parliament and foreign affairs: external relations of the European Economic Community', in Cassese, A. (ed.) *Parliamentary Control over Foreign Policy* (1980) 156.

representatives of the Member States 'to the extent that they were concerned', without indicating to what extent that was.[4] In the minutes of the relevant Council meeting, it was explicitly stated that this joint approval did not prejudge the question of the competence of the Community or the Member States on particular issues. Furthermore, it was agreed that the Commission would act as the sole negotiator on behalf of the Community *and* the Member States. In this way, the burning question of the scope of the Community's competence was effectively put on ice until the end of the negotiations.[5] It should be noted, however, that in spite of this blessed truce regarding the division of competence, the competence issue did have a marked influence on the way in which the Commission conducted the negotiations.[6] The competence issue was also reflected in the Community's (successful) demand that both the Community and the Member States would be Members of the WTO.[7]

The Final Act embodying the Uruguay Round Agreements was signed on 15 April 1994 in the Moroccan city of Marrakesh.[8] Pursuant to a decision taken by the Council and the representatives of the Member States at a meeting on 7 and 8 March 1994, the Final Act was signed by the Community as well as the Member States. As appears from the minutes of the March 1994 meeting, the Commission had strongly objected to the fact that the Member States would also sign the Final Act.[9] The Commission held the opinion that the Final Act and its Annexes fell within the exclusive competence of the European Community. The latter opinion was reflected in the Commission's proposal for a Council decision on the approval of the Uruguay Round Agreements.[10] Unwilling to bow to the Council's restrictive interpretation of the scope of the Community's competence, the Commission submitted a request for an Opinion on the competence to conclude the latter agreements to the Court, only a few days before the signing of the Final Act.[11]

---

[4] Op. 1/94 (Competence of the Community to conclude international agreements concerning services and the protection of intellectual property), 15 Nov. 1994, also referred to in the WTO Opinion, [1994] ECR I–5276 at I–5282.   [5] See S. 2.1.1.

[6] See S. 2.1.3.

[7] In view of the Court's later ruling regarding the competence issue in Op. 1/94 (see Ss. 1.2 and 1.3), it was fortunate that the Community had negotiated that the Member States would also be Members of the WTO. For an opposing view, see J. Bourgeois, 'The EC in the WTO and Advisory Opinion 1/94: an Echternach procession', (1995) CML Rev., 763 at 764, where he defines the 'dual' membership as a 'missed opportunity'. In this sense, see also M. Hilf 'The ECJ's Opinion 1/94 on the WTO: no surprise, but wise?', (1995) EJIL, 245 at 258.

[8] See S. 2.2.2.   [9] See n.4 at I–5282.

[10] Proposal for a Council decision concerning the conclusion of the results of the Uruguay Round of multilateral trade negotiations (1986–94), COM(94) 143 final, 1a–9a. See S. 2.2.3.

[11] The request was submitted on 6 Apr. 1994. In addition to articles referred to below, see J. Auvret-Finck, 'Avis 1/94 de la Cour du 15 novembre 1994' (1995) RTDE, 322; and J. J. Feenstra, 'Advies 1/94' (1995) *Informatierecht/AMI*, 132.

2.2.1.2 The request to the European Court of Justice for an Opinion (1994)

Under Article 228 (6) EC, the Council, the Commission or a Member State may obtain an Opinion from the Court as to whether an agreement the Community envisages concluding is compatible with the provisions of the EC Treaty. Where the Opinion is adverse, the EC Treaty must be amended before the agreement may enter into force. In the past, the Court had been repeatedly requested for an Opinion on questions relating to the division of powers between the Community and the Member States (for example, Opinion 1/75, Opinion 1/78 and Opinion 2/91), but all these requests had been submitted well in advance of the signing of the relevant agreement. While only the Spanish Government raised a formal objection of inadmissibility to the Commission's request for an Opinion, the late submission of the request was harshly criticized. The Council seriously doubted whether it was still possible to seek a preliminary Opinion in relation to an 'envisaged' agreement once obligations had been created at the international level—as was the case by the time the Court was able to look at the Commission's request. The French Government criticized the Commission for waiting until the last moment to make its request, especially because the disagreement about the competence of the Community and the Member States had been apparent long before. To some extent this criticism is unfair since both the Community and the Member States had agreed to let the competence issue rest during the negotiations.[12] The Court dismissed both the formal objection of inadmissibility made by the Spanish Government, as well as the doubts expressed by others. According to the Court, it may be called upon to state its Opinion at any time before the Community's consent to be bound by an agreement is finally expressed. Unless and until that consent is given, the agreement remains an envisaged agreement.[13]

The Commission requested the Court for an Opinion, in order to establish whether the Community was competent to conclude the Uruguay Round Agreements alone. As noted earlier, the Commission was of the view that the Community had exclusive powers to conclude the Uruguay Round Agreements, either under Article 113 EC or, in the alternative, the

---

[12] Furthermore, it should be noted that in 1994 the issue of the scope of the Community's external competence was already before the Court, as a result of a request for an Op. on Art. 228 (6) submitted by Belgium in 1992 on the Third Revised Dec. of the Council of the OECD regarding National Treatment (Op. 2/92). Note, however, that this case had received limited attention, and that the Court was clearly hesitant to rule on the issue of the Community's competence in the context of such a 'minor' case. Eventually the Court rendered OECD Op. 2/92 on 24 Mar. 1995, following closely the reasoning set out in WTO Op. 1/94 of 15 Nov. 1994 (see S. 1.4.4).   [13] Op. 1/94, para 12.

doctrine of implied powers.[14] The Council and the eight Member States which submitted observations to the Court did not agree.[15] They took the position that the competence to conclude the Uruguay Round Agreements was shared between the Community and the Member States. Consequently, and pursuant to the decision of 7 and 8 March 1994 referred to above, the Uruguay Round Agreements had been signed as mixed agreements, only a few days after the request for an Opinion was submitted to the Court. The European Parliament also disagreed with the Commission, rejecting the Commission's argument that the Community's exclusive powers to conclude the Uruguay Round Agreements could be based on Article 113 EC.[16]

While the disagreement ran deep between the Commission on the one hand, and the Council, the Member States and the Parliament on the other, it should be stressed that at no point *after* the signing of the agreements in April 1994 was any question raised as to the expediency and necessity of concluding the Uruguay Round Agreements.[17] Unlike in the United States, the ratification debate in Europe was not about whether to conclude the Uruguay Round Agreements, but about who had the power to conclude them: the Community and/or the Member States.[18]

Furthermore, it should be pointed out that the disagreement over competence to conclude the Uruguay Round Agreements did not concern all the Agreements. As a matter of fact, the pivotal Agreement establishing the World Trade Organization, and the important and innovative Understanding on Dispute Settlement, did not raise any particular problems.[19] The focal point of the disagreement was the

---

[14] See Ss. 1.2. and 1.3.

[15] Observations were submitted by the governments of the UK, the Netherlands, France, Germany, Greece, Spain, Portugal and Denmark.

[16] The Parliament objected to the use of Article 113 EC because, in principle, this article did not (even) require the Parliament to be consulted (see S. 1.2.1). While the Commission had made clear that it was of the opinion that the second subpara. of Art. 228 (3) EC applied to the Uruguay Round Agreements, and that the Parliament would thus have to give its assent to these Agreements, the Parliament—presumably out of principle—nevertheless objected to Art. 113 EC.   [17] See Ss. 2.2.3–2.2.5.

[18] In the US the ratification debate concerned the question of whether to conclude the Uruguay Round Agreements, as well as the question of how they should be concluded (by 'treaty' or 'congressional executive agreement').

[19] Note that the Council, and some Member States, pointed out that certain Member States remain competent to conclude and perform agreements relating to certain dependent territories to which the Treaty does not apply, and that therefore the Community could not have exclusive powers to conclude the Uruguay Round Agreements. Moreover, the Portuguese Gov. pointed out that each WTO member is to contribute to the expenses of the WTO (Art. VII, WTO Agreement), and that the Member States of the Community are to acquire the status of original Members (Art. XI:1 WTO). Referring to Op. 1/78, to the Portuguese Gov., this was enough to justify the participation of the Member States in the conclusion of the Uruguay Round Agreements. The Portuguese Gov. also argued that its

competence to conclude the General Agreement on Trade in Services and the Agreement on Trade-Related Aspects of Intellectual Property Rights. In addition, there was also some disagreement on the competence to conclude the multilateral agreements on trade in goods, to the extent that those agreements concerned ECSC products, agricultural products and elimination of technical barriers.[20]

2.2.1.3 The relevance of the competence issue

Given the significance of the Uruguay Round Agreements, the competence question raised in Opinion 1/94 was obviously a weighty one; yet its importance is even greater in view of the fact that some of the Agreements, and in particular the GATS, are primarily intended to constitute a negotiating framework. The WTO, of which both the Community and all fifteen Member States are Members, was conceived as a permanent forum for further negotiations elaborating these (and other) agreements. The answer to the competence question will therefore determine the roles which the Community, on the one hand, and the Member States, on the other, will play in the context of the WTO when future agreements are negotiated and concluded. Furthermore, the issue of competence is obviously not only important to the Community's institutions and the Member States, but also to non-member countries. They need to know whom to talk to, and who eventually decides. Confusion and controversy on this point may not only marginalize the Community, and undermine its negotiating power, but may also lead to the paralysis of the WTO.

constitutional law did not allow it to join an international organization without the approval of the Portuguese Parliament.

I do not dwell on these arguments since they were summarily rejected by the Court. Referring to Op. 1/78 (para. 62), the Court noted that the special position of the Member States referred to above cannot affect the solution of the problem relating to the demarcation of spheres of competence within the Community (see paras. 17–18). With regard to the invocation of Op. 1/78 by Portugal, the Court noted that, given that the WTO is an international organization which will only have an operating budget and not a financial policy instrument, the fact that the Member States will bear some of its expenses cannot of itself justify participation of the Member States in the conclusion of the WTO Agreement (para. 21). Finally, with regard to the argument based on Portuguese constitutional law, the Court reminded us that internal rules of law, even of a constitutional nature, cannot alter the division of international powers between the Member States and the Community as laid down in the Treaty (para. 20).

[20] In its request for an Op. the Commission had also raised the question whether trade in goods subject to the Euratom Treaty fell within the scope of Art. 113 EC. During the proceedings, however, nobody disputed that they did. Neither the Council nor any of the Member States made observations on this question. The Court summarily ruled that they did (see Op. 1/94, para. 24).

2.2.2 The competence of the European Community under Article 113 EC

2.2.2.1 The Court's case law prior to Opinion 1/94

The Treaty of Rome initially conferred express external competence to the Community in Article 113 EEC, with regard to the common commercial policy; in Articles 229 to 231 EEC, with regard to relations with international organizations; and in Article 238 EEC, with regard to association agreements. The Single European Act 1986, and the Maastricht Treaty on European Union of 1992, considerably expanded the number of domains in which the Community had express external competence.[21] The Treaty of Rome, as amended, now confers express external competence to the Community in Article 109 EC with regard to monetary policy; in Article 130m EC, with regard to research and technological development; in Article 130r (4) EC with regard to the environment; in Article 130y EC with regard to development co-operation; and in Article 228a EC with regard to economic sanctions.[22] The Community's competence with regard to commercial policy, as currently laid down in Article 113 EC, is however, still by far the most important express external competence of the Community.

The Treaty of Rome does not define the concept of common commercial policy,[23] and it is not surprising, therefore, that the scope of Article 113 EC has always been the subject of controversy. Article 113 EC provides a non-exhaustive list which merely defines the core, and definitely not the outer limits, of the matters which fall within the concept of commercial policy.[24] In 1973, the Court ruled in the *Massey-Ferguson Case* that, if the customs union was to function properly, then a broad interpretation of Article 113 would be necessary.[25] In Opinion 1/75 (Export Credits), the Court held that the concept of commercial policy had the same content 'whether it is applied in the context of the international action of a State, or to that of the

---

[21] The SEA came into force on 1 July 1987 and the TEU on 1 Nov. 1993.

[22] See generally: F. Dehousse and K. Ghemar, 'Le traité de Maastricht et les relations extérieures de la Communauté européenne', 1994, EJIL, 151.

[23] Art. 113 (1) EC stipulates: 'The common commercial policy shall be based on uniform principles, particularly in regard to changes in tariff rates, the conclusion of tariff and trade agreements, the achievement of uniformity on measures of liberalization, export policy and measures to protect trade such as those to be taken in the event of dumping or subsidies.'

[24] The non-exhaustive nature of the list contained in Art. 113 was confirmed by the Court in Op. 1/78, given 4 Oct. 1979, [1979] ECR 2871, para. 45 and more recently in Case 165/87, *Commission* v. *Council* (commodity coding) [1988] ECR 5545, para. 15.

[25] Case 8/73, *Hauptzollamt Bremerhaven* v. *Massey-Ferguson GmbH* [1973] ECR 897 at 908.

Community'.[26] A few years later, the Court ruled in Opinion 1/78 (Natural Rubber), that it could not restrict Article 113 to an interpretation which would limit the Common Commercial Policy instruments to the 'traditional aspects of external trade'.[27] As the Court aptly observed, 'a "commercial policy" understood in that sense would be destined to become nugatory in the course of time'.[28] Such a restrictive interpretation of the concept of 'commercial policy' would—according to the Court—also 'risk causing disturbances in intra-Community trade by reason of the disparities which would then exist in certain sectors of economic relations with non-member countries'.[29] From this and later case law of the Court, it follows clearly that the concept of commercial policy was considered to be an open and dynamic concept which changed with the needs of time.[30]

In Opinion 1/78, the Court also held that whether an agreement is a commercial policy agreement 'must be assessed having regard to its essential objective, rather than in terms of individual clauses of an altogether subsidiary and ancillary nature'.[31] An agreement could therefore also deal with other matters and still be a commercial policy agreement within the meaning of Article 113 EC. Furthermore, the Court stated that the fact that an agreement may have political ramifications or repercussions on certain sectors of economic policy was not a valid reason to exclude it from the scope of the Common Commercial Policy.[32]

As its broadest statement on the scope of Article 113 EC, the Court held in its judgment of 29 March 1990 in Case C–62/88, *Greece* v. *Council*, that a Regulation which, according to its objective and its content, is intended to regulate trade between the Community and non-member countries, falls within the scope of the Common Commercial Policy, as defined in Article 113 EC.[33] In view of the often vague and fragmented case law of the Court discussed above, it is, however, not surprising that considerable confusion remained with regard to the scope of the Common Commercial Policy.

The Court has been much more articulate with regard to the nature of competence in the field of commercial policy. In Opinion 1/75 (Export Credits), the Court clearly ruled that commercial policy is an exclusive competence of the Community, and that the Member States had lost all

---

[26] Op. 1/75, 11 Nov. 1975, [1975] ECR 1355 at 1362. [27] Op. 1/78, para. 44.
[28] Ibid. [29] Ibid., para. 45.
[30] See e.g. Case 45/86, *Commission* v. *Council* (Generalized System of Preferences) [1987] ECR 1493. [31] Op. 1/78, para. 56.
[32] Ibid., para 49. *In casu*, the building up of stocks of rubber might have a political importance and the sectors of economic policy affected were the supply of raw materials to the Community and price policy.
[33] Case C–62/88, *Greece* v. *Council*, [1990] ECR I–1527, para. 16.

competence to act in this field.[34] As the Court argued, the Common Commercial Policy was introduced 'for the defence of the common interests of the Community, within which the particular interests of the Member States must endeavour to adapt to each other'.[35] The Court further stated that actions of a Member State, attempting to invoke a concurrent power to ensure its own interests, would be quite incompatible with this notion, and would even pose a risk of 'compromising the effective defence of the common interests of the Community'.[36] The competence of the Community in the field of commercial policy was therefore an exclusive competence.[37] There is no room for concurrent competence of the Member States. This exclusivity, as well as the fact that Article 113 EC provides for decision-making by qualified majority without (mandatory) Parliamentary involvement, explains why the Commission was opposed to the Council, the Member States and the European Parliament[38] in the debate over a broad interpretation of the scope of Article 113 EC. Most legal scholars sided with the Commission, and supported a broad definition of the concept of the Common Commercial Policy.[39] In Opinion 1/94 the Court was called upon to further clarify the scope of the Community's competence under Article 113 EC.

2.2.2.2 The scope of the Common Commercial Policy and trade in services

As noted above, the Commission argued in its request for Opinion 1/94 that the GATS fell within the scope of Article 113 EC and should therefore be concluded by the Community alone. This contention was vigorously disputed, as to its essentials, by the Council, the European Parliament, and the Member States which submitted observations to the Court.

In the Commission's view, *any agreement liable to have a direct or indirect effect on the volume or structure of commercial trade was a*

---

[34] Note, however, that a Member State may still be able to act with an explicit authorization of the Community and within the limits of such an authorization (Case 41/76, *Donckerwolcke*, [1976] ECR 1921).   [35] Op. 1/75, at 1363–4.   [36] Ibid.

[37] Also in Op. 1/75 (at 1364), the Court held that, with regard to the division of competence between the Community and the Member States, it was of little importance that the obligations and financial burdens inherent in the execution of the agreement envisaged were borne directly by the Member States. The Court qualified this view in Op. 1/78 (para. 60), ruling that the financing of an agreement by the Member States implied 'their participation in the agreement together with the Community'. The exclusive competence of the Community could not be envisaged in such a case. The latter was, however, an anomaly. See also n. 19.

[38] The Parliament argued that a wide interpretation of the concept of common commercial policy would prejudice its powers, which is incompatible with the constitutional principle of participation by the Parliament, as established in the *Titanium dioxide Case* (Case C–300/89, *Commission* v. *Council* [1991] ECR I–2867).   [39] See S. 1.2.2.

commercial policy agreement and therefore fell within the scope of the Community's exclusive competence under Article 113 EC. The Commission asserted that there was strong support for this very broad definition of the scope of Article 113 EC within the Court's case law,[40] among legal scholars,[41] and in Community practice. Furthermore, it pointed to the links noted by economists between goods and services, and observed the similarities between the GATS and the GATT with regard to the objectives pursued and the policy instruments used.[42]

In Opinion 1/94 the Court acknowledged that—as the Commission had pointed out—in certain developed countries the services sector has become the dominant sector of the economy, and that the global economy was undergoing fundamental structural changes. The trend, as the Court saw it, is for basic industry to be transferred to developing countries, while the developed economies have tended to become the main exporters of services and of goods with a high value-added content. The Court noted that this trend is addressed, for the first time, by the Uruguay Round agreements, which cover both trade in goods and trade in services.[43] Contrary to views expressed by some Member States, but in line with its case law on the concept of the common commercial policy discussed above, the Court thus considered that 'trade in services cannot immediately, and as a matter of principle, be excluded from the scope of Article 113'.[44] This was, however, no reason for celebration for the Commission, because the Court subsequently stated that to establish whether trade in services does

---

[40] See S. 1.2.1.

[41] The Commission acknowledged that certain scholars excluded from the scope of the common commercial policy services provided through the intermediary of an establishment located in the country where the services are rendered. It argued, however, that there was no reason to do so. Regarding the scholarly opinion on the scope of Art. 113 EC I limit myself to a single reference to P. J. G. Kapteyn and P. VerLoren van Themaat, *Introduction to the Law of the European Communities* (Gormley edn. 1990) 781, where it is stated that: 'If negotiations in the GATT take place on matters such as the international provision of services and international establishment . . . and such matters become a permanent concern of the GATT then it is not conceivable that the concept of a common commercial policy would not also embrace these subjects in the long run.'

[42] Note that the purpose of the GATS is the liberalization of trade and that the instruments used to achieve this purpose are traditional instruments of trade policy (MFN treatment, transparency, market access provisions (schedules of specific commitments), national treatment). Many of the key provisions of the GATS have their equivalent in comparable provisions of the GATT.   [43] Op. 1/94, para. 40.

[44] Op. 1/94, para. 41. The Court recalled that in Op. 1/78 (para. 45) it rejected an interpretation of Art. 113 'the effect of which would be to restrict the common commercial policy to the use of instruments intended to have an effect only on the traditional aspects of international trade'. On the contrary, 'the question of external trade must be governed from a wide point of view', as is confirmed by 'the fact that the enumeration in Art. 113 of the subjects covered by commercial policy . . . is conceived as a non-exhaustive enumeration' (Op. 1/94, para. 39).

fall within the scope of Article 113 EC, 'one must take into account the definition of trade in services given in GATS in order to see whether the overall scheme of the Treaty is not such as to limit the extent to which trade in services can be included within Article 113.'[45]

Article I:2 GATS defines trade in services as comprising four modes of supply: (1) cross-frontier supply; (2) consumption abroad; (3) commercial presence; and (4) presence of natural persons.

The Court observed that under the first mode, the cross-frontier supply of services, there is no movement of persons. The service is rendered by a supplier established in one country to a consumer residing in another. The Court argued that, in this sense, cross-frontier supply of services is 'not unlike trade in goods'. Since the latter was undisputedly covered by the Common Commercial Policy, the Court thus concluded that there is no particular reason why such cross-frontier supply of services should not fall within the concept of the Common Commercial Policy.[46] Many transactions in the sectors of banking, insurance, telecommunications and the media constitute such cross-frontier supplies of services, and thus fall within the Community's competence under Article 113 EC.[47]

The other modes of supply of services, however, involve the movement of natural or legal persons, and are therefore quite different from trade in goods. The Court pointed out with regard to the movement of natural persons, that it is clear from Article 3 EC—a provision which distinguishes between 'a common commercial policy' (paragraph b) and 'measures concerning the entry and movement of persons' (paragraph d)—that the treatment of nationals of non-member countries on crossing the external frontiers of Member States cannot be regarded as falling within the Common Commercial Policy.[48] On a more general note, the Court observed that the Treaty contains specific chapters on the free movement of natural and legal persons, and drew the conclusion that those matters therefore do not fall within the common commercial policy.[49] The Court thus ruled that only cross-frontier supply of services, and not the other modes of supply, fall within the scope of Article 113 EC.[50]

With regard to the Community practice to which the Commission referred in support of its position (and, in particular, measures on economic sanctions), the Court stated that these 'precedents' were not conclusive. The suspension of transport services (based on Article 113 EC) was—according to the Court—to be seen as a 'necessary adjunct' to the principal measure, that is, the suspension of trade in goods.[51] At any rate,

---

[45] Op. 1/94, para. 42.   [46] Ibid.
[47] See Hilf, 'The ECJ's Op. 1/94' at 252.   [48] Op. 1/94, para. 46.
[49] Ibid.   [50] Ibid., para. 44.   [51] Ibid., para. 51.

a mere practice of the Council cannot create a precedent with regard to the correct legal basis which is binding on the Community institutions.[52]

The Court also excluded from the scope of Article 113 EC the specific area of services in transport. The Commission had argued that international agreements of a commercial nature in relation to transport fall within the scope of Article 113 EC, and not within the scope of Article 75 EC, the Treaty provision specifically dealing with the common transport policy. The Court disagreed. It observed that the idea underlying the milestone *ERTA* (or *AETR*) judgment[53] is that international agreements in transport matters are not covered by Article 113 EC, but, on the contrary, that competence to conclude such agreements could be derived from Article 75 EC.[54] The Court rejected the Commission's attempt to limit the scope of the *ERTA* judgment to agreements on safety rules, as opposed to agreements of a commercial nature. According to the Court, there is no basis in the latter judgment (or subsequent case law)[55] for such a limitation, and it upheld its decision against the inclusion of transport matters within Article 113 EC.[56]

2.2.2.3 The scope of the Common Commercial Policy and Trade-Related Aspects of Intellectual Property Rights

In its request for Opinion 1/94, the Commission argued that the TRIPs Agreement also fell within the scope of Article 113 EC, and should therefore be concluded by the Community alone. In addition to the arguments it had already advanced in the context of the GATS for a very broad interpretation of the scope of Article 113 EC, it pointed in particular at the close link between intellectual property rights, and trade in products and services, to which these rights applied.

In its Opinion the Court first focused upon the TRIPs rules concerning trade in counterfeit goods, and in particular the rules on the measures applied at border crossing points to enforce intellectual property rights.[57] It observed that these rules have their counterpart in the provisions of Council Regulation (EEC) No 3842/86 of 1 December 1986, laying down measures to prohibit the release for free circulation of counterfeit goods.[58]

---

[52] See Case 68/86, *United Kingdom* v. *Council* [1988] ECR 855, para. 24.
[53] Case 22/70, *Commission* v. *Council* [1971] ECR 263, para. 16. See S. 2.1.3.1.
[54] Op. 1/94, para. 48.
[55] The Court also referred to Op. 1/76 which concerned an agreement on the economic rationalization of the inland waterways sector and was based on Art. 75 EC (see Op. 1/94, para. 50).   [56] Op. 1/94, para. 50.
[57] S. 4, Part III, TRIPs.   [58] [1986] OJ L357/1.

This Regulation was (correctly) adopted on the basis of Article 113 EC,[59] and the Court thus concluded that, since measures of that type can be adopted autonomously by the Community institutions on the basis of Article 113 EC, the Community has exclusive competence to conclude international agreements on such matters on the same legal basis.[60]

With regard to the rest of the TRIPs, the Court acknowledged that—as the Commission had pointed out—there is an undeniable connection between intellectual property rights and trade in goods and services. Intellectual property rights inevitably have an effect on trade, and are, moreover, specifically designed to produce such effects. In the Court's opinion, however, this is not enough to bring such rights within the scope of Article 113 EC since 'intellectual property rights do not relate specifically to international trade; they affect internal trade just as much as, if not more than, international trade.'[61]

Furthermore, the Court observed that the harmonization of national legislation on intellectual property rights, or the creation of new rights superimposed on national rights is—pursuant to Articles 100/100a and 235 EC respectively—subject to voting and procedural rules which are much stricter than the voting procedures stipulated in Article 113.[62] The Community institutions would, however, be able to escape the internal constraints to which they are subject as a result of these voting and procedural rules, if the Community were to be recognized as having exclusive competence under Article 113 EC to enter into agreements with non-member countries for the protection of intellectual property.[63] Such circumvention of the Treaty could not be tolerated by the Court. After having also rejected the Commission's arguments based on Community practice,[64] the Court thus came to the conclusion that, apart from those of its provisions which concern the prohibition of the release into free circulation of counterfeit goods, the TRIPs does not fall within the scope of the Common Commercial Policy.

2.2.2.4 Controversy regarding specific aspects of trade in goods

As already mentioned above, the disagreement with regard to the scope of Article 113 EC was primarily concerned with the GATS and TRIPs; yet

---

[59] Note that in July 1994, the Council amended the legal basis of a Commission proposal for a new Community regulation to boost efforts to control counterfeit products by adding to Art. 113 EC, Art. 100a EC. In Oct. 1994 the Parliament wisely decided to await Op. 1/94 of the Court before stating its position on this proposal (*Europe*, 24/25 Oct. 1994, 7).

[60] Op. 1/94, para. 55.   [61] Ibid., para. 57.

[62] In the case of Arts. 100 and 235 EC, unanimity and the consultation of the European Parliament is required. In the case of Art. 100a EC, the co-decision procedure of Art. 189b EC applies. Art. 113 *juncto* 228 EC merely requires a qualified majority and provides for no Parliamentary involvement unless the second subpara. of Art. 228 (3) EC applies. See S. 2.1.1.   [63] Op. 1/94, para. 60.

[64] For details, see ibid., para. 63 ff.

this was not the only source of contention. With regard to the multilateral agreements on trade in goods ('the multilateral agreements'), there had been general consensus that these agreements fell within the scope of Article 113 EC, and yet nagging disagreement had arisen related to the specific areas of trade in ECSC products, agricultural products and technical barriers. According to the Commission, the agreements covering the latter areas did not require any legal basis other than Article 113 EC, but this opinion was not shared by the Council and the Member States submitting observations.

The latter argued that, pursuant to Article 71 ECSC, the multilateral agreements, to the extent that they concerned ECSC products, should be concluded not by the Community but by the Member States.[65] The Court ruled, however, that Article 71 ECSC only reserves competence to the Member States as regards agreements which specifically relate to ECSC products.[66] Since none of the multilateral agreements specifically relates to ECSC products, the conclusion of these agreements, which encompass all types of goods, is therefore the exclusive competence of the Community, pursuant to Article 113 EC.[67]

With regard to the agreements concerning agricultural products,[68] it was not disputed that the Community had the exclusive competence to conclude these agreements. The disagreement focused on the question of whether Article 113 EC, the common commercial policy provision, or Article 43 EC, the common agricultural policy provision, was the appropriate legal basis for doing so. The Court noted that the agreements concerning agricultural products were not intended to achieve one or more of the common agricultural policy objectives laid down in Article 39 EC. On the contrary, their objectives—as stated in the preamble—are very much in line with the objectives of the common commercial policy as defined in Article 110 EC.[69] Furthermore, the Court stated that the fact

---

[65] Art. 71 ECSC stipulates: 'The powers of the Governments of Member States in matters of commercial policy shall not be affected by this Treaty, save otherwise provided therein.' Also note Art. 232 (1) EC which stipulates: 'The provisions of this Treaty shall not affect the provisions of the Treaty establishing the European Coal and Steel Community, in particular as regards the rights and obligations of Member States.' At first view the combination of these two provisions seems to leave little room for the application of Art. 113 EC.

[66] Op. 1/94, para. 27. It is possible that in the future an agreement specifically dealing with ECSC products will be negotiated in the context of the WTO. In the latter case, the ECSC and not the European Community will be competent. At that point, it will be useful that the European Communit*ies* (including the ECSC), and not merely the European Community, is a Member of the WTO (see n. 1).

[67] Op. 1/94, para. 27. The Court reminded us in this context that it had already held in Op. 1/75 (at 1365), that Art. 71 ECSC cannot 'render inoperative Articles 113 and 114 of the EEC Treaty and affect the vesting of power in the Community for the negotiation and conclusion of international agreements in the realm of the common commercial policy'.

[68] i.e. the Agreement on Agriculture and the SPS Agreement.

[69] Op. 1/94, para. 29 and 31.

that the commitments entered into under these agreements require internal measures to be adopted on the basis of Article 43 EC does not prevent the international commitments themselves from being entered into pursuant to Article 113 EC alone.[70]

Finally, there was the issue of the Agreement on Technical Barriers.[71] The Dutch Government had argued that the powers to conclude this Agreement were shared between the Community and the Member States. It had based this view upon the fact that the Member States continued to have their own powers in relation to technical barriers to trade and this by reason of the optional nature of certain Community Directives in that area, and because complete harmonization has not been achieved, and is not envisaged, in that field. The Court rejected this argument. It noted that, pursuant to the Preamble and Articles 2.2. and 5.1.2. of the Agreement on Technical Barriers, the main objective of the Agreement is to ensure that technical regulations and standards do not create unnecessary obstacles to international trade. Thus follows the conclusion of the Court that such an agreement definitely falls within the scope of Article 113 EC.[72]

The Court therefore sided with the Commission, as regards the Community's exclusive competence under Article 113 EC to conclude all multilateral agreements on trade in goods. It should be recalled, however, that the Court did for the most part reject the Commission's reasoning to bring the GATS and TRIPs under this exclusive competence. Its arguments for doing so are open to criticism. These criticisms will be dealt with in Section 2.2.4. The next section will address the Commission's subsidiary arguments in favour of the Community's exclusive competence to conclude the GATS and TRIPs. As mentioned above, the Commission maintained in the alternative that the Community has exclusive competence to conclude both Agreements by virtue of the doctrine of implied powers.

2.2.3 The scope of the European Community's implied competence in the field international economic relations

2.2.3.1 The Court's case law prior to Opinion 1/94

Apart from the express external competences dealt with above, the European Community also has implied external competences. In the *ERTA* Case the Council had argued that since the Community only has

---

[70] Op. 1/94, para. 29.

[71] It should be noted that the Tokyo Round TBT Agreement had been concluded by the EEC and the Member States jointly. It has been convincingly argued, however, that this was more for political reasons than for reasons related to the substance of this agreement (see J. Bourgeois, 'The Tokyo Round Agreements on Technical Barriers and on Government Procurement', (1982) 19 CMLRev. 5 at 22.   [72] Op. 1/94, para. 33.

such powers as have been conferred on it, authority to enter into agreements with non-member countries cannot be assumed in the absence of an express provision in the Treaty of Rome.[73] In its landmark judgment of 31 March 1971, the Court, however, disagreed with the Council, and ruled that the authority to conclude international agreements

arises not only from an express conferment by the Treaty—as is the case with Articles 113 and 114 for tariff and trade agreements and with Article 238 for association agreements—but may equally flow from other provisions of the Treaty and from measures adopted, within the framework of those provisions, by the Community institutions.[74]

The Court thus held that the Community had implied external competences.[75] A few years later the Court clarified and extended the scope of the implied external competences. In its Opinion 1/76 (Inland Waterway Vessels) it ruled that

whenever Community law has created for the institutions of the Community, powers within its internal system for the purpose of obtaining a specific objective, the Community has the authority to enter into the international commitments necessary for the attainment of that objective, even in the absence of an express provision in that connection.[76]

It is important to note that, while under the *ERTA* judgment internal competence only gives rise to implied external competence when the internal competence has actually been *exercised*, under Opinion 1/76 no prior exercise of the internal competence is required. For the Community to have implied competence to conclude an international agreement, it is merely required that the conclusion of such agreement is *necessary* for the attainment of a Community objective.[77] In its recent Opinion 2/91 (ILO) of 19 March 1993, the Court ruled with regard to the Community's competence to conclude an International Labour Organization Convention:

[73] See n. 53, para. 9.

[74] See n. 53, para. 16. Central in the Court's reasoning is the fact that pursuant to Art. 210 E(E)C the Community has (international) legal personality. On the basis of this provision, placed at the head of the Part of the Treaty devoted to General and Final Provisions, the Court concluded that in its external relations the Community enjoys the capacity to establish contractual links with third countries over the whole field of objectives defined in the Treaty.

[75] With regard to the existence of implied external competence, the *ERTA*-judgment was confirmed by the Court in its 1976 judgment in Cases 3, 4, & 6/76 *Kramer and Bais SNC* v. *The Netherlands* [1976] ECR 1279.

[76] Op. 1/76 (Draft Agreement establishing a European laying-up fund for inland waterway vessels) [1977] ECR 741, para. 3.

[77] Note that the implied external competence of the Community is not confined to the conclusion of international agreements. It also covers the power, with deference to the Treaty, to set up international organizations (Op. 1/76 at 755–6), or to accede to them (*Kramer*, at 1311) and to co-operate in the elaboration of international bodies and to enter into international commitments in that context (*Kramer*, at 1307).

The Community thus enjoys an internal legislative competence in the area of social policy. Consequently, Convention No 170, whose subject-matter coincides, moreover, with that of several directives adopted under Article 118a, falls within the Community's area of competence.[78]

While obviously building on the *ERTA* judgment and Opinion 1/76, it should be noted that Opinion 2/91 (ILO) seems to go a step further. On careful reading of (in particular) paragraph 17 of the Opinion (see above), it appears that the Court's conclusion that the Community has implied external competence depends neither on the exercise of internal competence (the *ERTA* requirement), nor on the necessity of concluding an international agreement (the Opinion 1/76 requirement).[79] Opinion 2/91 thus represents the most radical endorsement so far of the *in foro interno, in foro externo* principle, according to which the external competence of the Community mirrors its internal competence.

The mere existence of implied external competence was, however, seldom contested. Controversy focused mostly on the exclusive nature of this implied competence. Just as for express external competence, implied external competence can be of an exclusive nature. In the *ERTA* judgment, the Court ruled that

each time the Community, with a view to implementing a common policy envisaged by the Treaty, adopts provisions laying down *common rules*, whatever form these may take, the member states no longer have the right, acting individually or collectively, to undertake obligations with third countries which affect those rules.[80]

and that

. . . to the extent to which Community rules are promulgated for the attainment of the objectives of the Treaty, the member states cannot . . . assume obligations which might *affect* those rules or *alter their scope*.[81]

From the *ERTA* judgment it follows that, so long as the Community does not enact any common rules with regard to a given subject matter, the Member States retain the competence to conclude international agreements in this area. This national competence ceases to exist, however, when rules and international agreements concluded by the Member States *affect* or *alter the scope* of the common rules enacted by the Community. The latter is the logical result of the principle of supremacy of Community law.

The *ERTA* judgment was clarified and extended by the Court in its recent Opinion 2/91 (ILO). First of all, the Court held that exclusive competence may not only result from the existence of common rules

---

[78] Op. 2/91, 19 Mar. 1993 (*ILO Convention No. 170 on Chemicals at Work* [1993] 3 CMLR 800 and [1993] ECR I–1061, para. 17.
[79] See also C. W. A. Timmermans, 'Noot bij Advies 2/91', (1994) SEW, 615 at 623.
[80] See n. 53, para. 17. Emphasis added.   [81] Ibid., para. 22. Emphasis added.

adopted within the framework of a common policy (as stated in the *ERTA* judgment), but may also result from common rules unrelated to a common policy.[82] Of at least equal significance, however, is the Court's reasoning in paragraphs 25 and 26 (concerning those provisions of the ILO Convention No 170 which did not merely lay down minimum requirements), in which it is stated that:

While there is no contradiction between these provisions of the Convention and those of the directives mentioned above, it must nevertheless be accepted that Part III of Convention 170 is concerned with an area which is already covered to a large extent by Commmunity rules progressively adopted since 1967, with a view to achieving an ever greater degree of harmonization, and designed, on the one hand, to remove barriers to trade resulting from differences in legislation from one Member State to another and, on the other hand, to provide, at the same time, protection for human health and the environment.
. . .

In those circumstances, it must be considered that the commitments arising from Part III of Convention 170, falling within the area covered by the directives cited above in paragraph 22, are of such a kind as to affect the Community rules laid down in those directives, and that consequently member-States cannot undertake such commitments outside the framework of the Community institutions.

Note that the Court examined in these paragraphs only whether Member State obligations may affect common rules, and not—as in the *ERTA* judgment—whether the Member State obligations may alter their scope.[83] Of more importance, however, is the Court's attempt to clarify the 'affect requirement' of the *ERTA* judgment. Paragraph 25 seems to imply that to fulfil this requirement there is no need for 'a contradiction' between the common rules and the international obligations. For the 'affect requirement' to be fulfilled, the Community rules 'only' need to cover to a large extent the subject area of the international obligations, and this with a view to achieving an ever greater degree of harmonization. It should be noted, however, that the Court ruled in the same Opinion that, to the extent that both the provisions of the ILO Convention and the Community rules (adopted pursuant to Article 118a EC) laid down minimum requirements, the Community rules were not liable to be 'affected' by the Convention.[84] The precise nature of the 'affect requirement' thus remained unclear.

Equally troublesome was the question of the exclusivity of implied external competence derived from the need to conclude an agreement in order to achieve a Community objective (see Opinion 1/76). The Court's case law did not offer much guidance in this respect.

In the context of Opinion 1/94, the Council and the Member States acknowledged that the Community did have implied competence with

---

[82] Op. 2/91, paras. 10 and 11.
[83] Ibid., para. 26. See also para. 18 with regard to provisions of the Convention which merely laid down minimum requirements. [84] Ibid., para. 19

regard to trade in services and trade related aspects of intellectual property. However, they ardently disputed the Commission's claim that this implied competence was of an exclusive nature.

2.2.3.2 Implied competence and trade in services

Regarding the GATS, the Commission contended that there are in fact three possible sources for implied external competence of an exclusive nature:

1. the powers conferred on the Community institutions by the Treaty of Rome at the internal level;
2. the need to conclude an agreement in order to achieve a Community objective; and
3. Articles 100a and 235 EC.[85]

The Court disagreed on all points.

With regard to the Commission's first source of exclusive external competence, the Court firmly held that the Community's exclusive external competence does *not* automatically flow from its powers to lay down rules at the internal level. The Court stressed that even in the field of transport policy this is the case. On the basis of Article 75 (1)(a) EC, which also concerns transport to and from non-member countries,[86] the Court had held in its *ERTA* judgment that 'the powers of the Community [extend] to relationships arising from international law'. However, the Court recalled that it had also ruled in its *ERTA* judgment that Member States only lose their right to assume obligations with non-member countries 'as and when common rules which could be affected by those obligations come into being'.[87] Therefore, it is only in so far as common rules have been established at the internal level that the external competence of the Community becomes exclusive.[88] Many matters regarding trade in services are not (yet) covered by common rules.

Furthermore, the Court noted that, unlike the Treaty chapter on transport which was concerned in the *ERTA* judgment, the chapters on the right of establishment and on the freedom to provide services do not contain any provision expressly extending the competence of the Community to 'relationships arising from international law'.[89] The sole objective of these chapters is to secure within the Community the right of establishment and the freedom to provide services for nationals of Member States.[90] They do not contain any provision on the problem of the first

---

[85] Op. 1/94, paras. 73 and 99.
[86] i.e. regarding that part of a journey which takes place on Community territory.
[87] Op. 1/94, para. 77.   [88] Ibid.   [89] Op. 1/94, para. 81.   [90] Ibid.

establishment of nationals of non-member countries, and the rules governing their access to self-employed activities. The Court therefore concluded that it could certainly not be inferred from these chapters that the Community has exclusive competence to conclude an agreement with non-member countries to liberalize first establishment and access to service markets.[91]

At the Court hearing, the Commission had argued that to leave the Member States the competence to conclude international agreements will inevitably lead to distortions in the flow of services, and will progressively undermine the internal market.[92] The Court was not impressed by this argument. In reply, it stated that the Treaty does not prevent the institutions from arranging concerted actions in relation to non-member countries, nor from prescribing the approach to be taken by the Member States in their external dealings in order to ward off the danger noted by the Commission.[93] The Court noted that this possibility is illustrated by several regulations on transport.[94]

With regard to the Commission's second source for implied external competence of an exclusive nature, that is, the need to conclude an agreement in order to achieve a Community objective, the Court held that the Commission's interpretation of Opinion 1/76—on which the Commission's argument was based—was faulty. Referring to Opinion 1/76, the Commission had argued that whenever Community law has conferred internal powers upon the institutions for the purposes of attaining specific objectives, the exclusive external competence of the Community implicitly flows from those provisions. It is enough—according to the Commission— that the Community's participation in the international agreement is necessary for the attainment of one of the objectives of the Community.[95] The Court, however, gave a much more restrictive interpretation to the rule laid down in its Opinion, and objected to its application to the GATS. According to the Court, Opinion 1/76 related to a situation in which it was not possible to achieve the objective(s) of the Treaty by the establishment of internal legislation, and that in such a specific situation 'it is understandable that external powers may be exercised, and thus become exclusive, without any internal legislation having first been adopted'.[96] Such a specific situation was, however, not present with regard to trade in

---

[91] Ibid., para. 81. On the basis of Art. 113 EC, however, the Community does have the exclusive competence to conclude agreements concerning cross-border supply of services. See S. 1.2.2.

[92] Op. 1/94, para. 78. The Commission thus argued that travellers will choose to fly from airports in Member States which have concluded an 'open skies' type of bilateral agreement with a non-member country and its airline, enabling them to offer the best quality/price ratio for transport.   [93] Ibid., para. 79.

[94] The Court gives some examples in ibid., para. 80.   [95] Ibid., para. 82.

[96] Ibid., para. 85.

services. As the Court noted, the attainment of freedom of establishment and freedom to provide services for nationals of the Member States—both prominent Community objectives—are not 'inextricably linked' to the treatment to be afforded in the Community to nationals of non-member countries or in non-member countries to nationals of Member States of the Community.[97] In other words, to attain the objectives of the Community the GATS was not really *necessary*.

Finally, with regard to the Commission's third source for exclusive external competence, that is, Articles 100a and 235 EC,[98] the Court rejected the Commission's argumentation without much ado. With regard to Article 100a EC (which gives the Community the internal competence to harmonize national legislation) the Court noted that 'an internal power to harmonize which has not been exercised in a specific field cannot confer exclusive external competence in that field on the Community'.[99] With regard to Article 235 EC (the Treaty provision which enables the Community to cope with any lacuna in its powers (both express and implied) for the achievement of its objectives) the Court held that the provision 'cannot in itself vest exclusive competence in the Community at an international level'.[100] Also, in this context 'internal competence can give rise to exclusive external competence only if it is exercised'.[101]

In reaction to an argument advanced by some Member States, the Court stated that, although the only objective expressly mentioned in the chapters on the right of establishment and on freedom to provide services is the attainment of this right or freedom for nationals of the Member States within the Community, it does not follow that the Community is prohibited to use its competence in those fields to specify the treatment which is to be accorded to nationals of non-member countries.[102] Moreover, the Court ruled—referring to its *ERTA* judgment—that:

whenever the Community has included in its internal legislative acts provisions relating to the treatment of nationals of non-member countries, or expressly conferred on its institutions powers to negotiate with non-member countries, it acquires exclusive external competence in the spheres covered by those acts.[103]

---

[97] Op. 1/94, para. 86.
[98] Art. 100a EC stipulates: '1. . . . The Council shall . . . adopt the measures for the approximation of the provisions laid down by law regulation or administrative action in Member States which have as their object the establishment and functioning of the internal market.' Art. 235 EC stipulates: 'If any action by the Community should prove necessary to attain, in the course of the operation of the common market, one of the objectives of the Community and this Treaty has not provided the necessary powers, the Council shall . . . take the appropriate action.'   [99] Op. 1/94, para. 88.
[100] Ibid., para. 89.   [101] Ibid.
[102] Ibid., para. 90. At the request of the Court the Commission had drawn up a list of such acts which the Council had adopted on the basis of Arts. 54 and 57(2) EC. For a discussion of these acts, see Op. 1/94, para. 92–94.   [103] Ibid., para. 95.

Likewise, the Community also has exclusive external competence where the Community has achieved complete harmonization of the rules governing access to a self-employed activity.[104]

As the Commission itself acknowledged, this is not yet the case in all service sectors. The Court thus concluded that the competence to conclude the GATS is not an exclusive competence of the Community, but a competence 'shared between the Community and the Member States'.[105]

2.2.3.3 Implied competence and Trade-Related Aspects of Intellectual Property Rights

With regard to the Community's implied external competence to conclude the TRIPs, the Commission's arguments were very similar to the arguments advanced in the context of the GATS. In support of its claim that the Community has exclusive competence to conclude TRIPs, the Commission relied on:

1. on the existence of legislative acts of the institutions which could be affected if the Member States were jointly to participate in its conclusion;
2. on the need for the Community to participate in the agreement in order to achieve one of the objectives set out in the Treaty; and
3. on Articles 100a and 235 EC.[106]

The Court held in response to the Commission's arguments that the relevance of the reference to Opinion 1/76 was 'just as disputable' in the case of TRIPs as in the case of GATS: unification or harmonization of intellectual property rights in the Community context does not necessarily have to be accompanied by agreements with non-member countries in order to be effective.[107] With regard to Articles 100a and 235 EC, the Court also repeated what it had already stated in the context of its discussion on the GATS, namely that these provisions 'cannot in themselves confer exclusive external competence on the Community'.[108] These internal competences need to be exercised first. With regard to the Commission's first argument in favour of exclusive external competence to conclude the TRIPs, the Court observed that, in some areas covered by the TRIPs, the harmonization achieved within the Community is only *partial*, while in other areas *no* harmonization has been envisaged. Consequently, there was—contrary to what the Commission maintained—little or no

---

[104] The common rules thus adopted would be 'affected' within the meaning of the *ERTA* judgment if the Member States retained freedom to negotiate with non-member countries (ibid. para. 96).   [105] Ibid., para. 98.   [106] Ibid., para. 99.   [107] Ibid., para. 100.   [108] Ibid., para. 101.

danger of Community legislative acts being affected, within the meaning of the *ERTA* judgment, if the Member States were to participate in the conclusion of the TRIPs. Therefore, with regard to the TRIPs, there could be no question of exclusive external competence on the basis of the *ERTA* case law. As it had done with regard to the GATS, the Court thus came to the conclusion that the Community and the Member States are jointly competent to conclude the TRIPs.[109]

2.2.4 Does Opinion 1/94 resolve the competence issue?

2.2.4.1 'Political' constraints

In its Opinion 1/94 the Court has shown itself generous with regard to the Community's exclusive competence relating to trade in goods,[110] but extremely prudent with regard to the latter's exclusive competence to conclude the GATS and TRIPs.[111] While one may disagree with the Court's conclusions and consider its reasoning faulty at points, it must be observed that the division of external competence between the Community and the Member States is in fact 'not susceptible to strict judicial demarcation'.[112] The division of external competence is an issue with political overtones. Therefore, it must be questioned whether the Court *could* have come to substantially different conclusions with regard to the Community's competence to conclude the GATS and TRIPs, than the very cautious and compromising ones reached in Opinion 1/94.

With regard to both the scope of the common commercial policy and the exclusive nature of implied external competence, the Commission took a truly maximalist position. As far as the scope of common commercial policy is concerned, the Council, the intervening Member States and the European Parliament were all strongly opposed to the position of the Commission; not in the least because it led, in their view, to unacceptable, if not absurd, conclusions. While building on the Court's case law and on scholarly support, the Commission overplayed its hand with its very broad

---

[109] Note that before coming to this conclusion the Court felt the need to reject explicitly an argument made by some Member States according to which the provisions of the TRIPs relating to measures to be adopted to secure the effective protection of intellectual property rights fall within some sort of '*domaine reservé*' of the Member States. The Court stressed that this was not the case. The Community is definitely competent to harmonize national rules on the enforcement of intellectual property rights. The Court noted, however, that so far this competence had not been exercised except in Reg. No. 3842/86 concerning counterfeit products. See Op. 1/94, para. 104.   [110] See S. 1.2.4.

[111] See Ss. 1.2. and 1.3.

[112] Trimidas, T. and Eeckhout, P., 'The external competence of the Community and the case law of the Court of Justice: principle versus pragmatism', (1994) 14 YBEL 143–177.

definition of the scope of the common commercial policy.[113] As was observed by the Council, exchange rate fluctuations and differences between wage costs have, in today's world economy, a more significant influence on the volume and flow of international trade than, for example, customs tariff variations. Applying the Commission's definition of the common commercial policy to its full logic, and with a touch of demagoguery, one would thus come to the conclusion: that the Community has exclusive competence under Article 113 EC to regulate the exchange rates of the currencies of the Member States or to implement a salary-fixing policy. In view of the advanced internationalization of national economies, *any* internal or external measure which is adopted in the context of economic relations and is liable to have a direct or indirect effect on the volume or the structure of commercial trade, would therefore—according to the Commission's definition—fall within the scope of the common commercial policy. This is obviously an unacceptable conclusion, for it would totally negate the competence of the Member States in matters of economic policy.

The Council—as well as some of the Member States (France, Denmark and the United Kingdom)—correctly observed that the interpretation advocated by the Commission leads to the transformation of that policy into a common policy on external economic relations.[114] In the context of the 1991 Intergovernmental Conference on Political Union, which eventually led to the Maastricht Treaty on European Union, the Commission had already proposed such a transformation. In the Commission's proposal, initially supported by the Dutch presidency, the common commercial policy was to be replaced by a common policy on external economic relations.[115] The latter policy, which was to fall within the exclusive competence of the Community, would include economic and trade measures in respect of goods, services, capital, intellectual property, investment, establishment and competition. In their observations to the Court, the Council and the Member States referred to above were emphatic in pointing out that this proposal for an extended common commercial policy had previously been rejected, and they strongly criticized the Commission for trying to implement it by means of judicial interpretation. The rejection of the Commission's attempt to modify the scope of the common commercial policy may have been a regretable mistake, but the Court could not possibly ignore the strong political

---

[113] See S. 2.1.2.2. [114] Op. 1/94, I–27.

[115] J.-V. Louis, 'Les relations extérieures de l'Union européenne: unité ou complémentarité', (1994, no. 4 *RMUE* 5 at 7, and M. Maresceau, 'The concept "Common Commercial Policy" and the difficult road to Maastricht', in M. Maresceau (ed.), *The European Community's Commercial Policy after 1992: the Legal Dimension* (1993), 3.

message this rejection entailed.[116] From its conclusions on the scope of the common commercial policy, it is evident that it did not.

Regarding the exclusive nature of the implied external competence, the Court was obviously very conscious of the danger of introducing a common policy on external economic relations in a roundabout way. To conclude that the Community had implied external competence of an exclusive nature to conclude the GATS and TRIPs would definitely have been a big step in that direction. The Court did not want to take that step.

In the post-Maastricht climate, one could hardly have expected to see the Court decide against a vocal majority of the Member States with regard to either the scope of Article 113 EC or the exclusive nature of the implied external competence.[117]

2.2.4.2 Problems of logic?

The above observations help to explain why the Court has been extremely cautious with regard to the Community's exclusive competence to conclude the GATS and TRIPs. While one may 'sympathize' with the Court's final conclusions, it should be observed that the legal reasoning leading to these conclusions is—dare it be said—weak at points. I will limit myself to a few examples.[118] First, the fact that the Treaty provides for a specific chapter on transport policy is seen as grounds for excluding international agreements on transport from the scope of Article 113.[119] The fact that the Treaty also provides for a specific chapter on agricultural policy does not, however, bring the Court to the conclusion that international agreements on trade in agricultural products should be excluded from the scope of Article 113 EC.[120] Secondly, with regard to trade in services, the Court also noted the existence of specific chapters in the Treaty on the free movement of natural and legal persons, in order to exclude most of the GATS from the scope of Article 113 EC.[121] Later in its Opinion, however, the Court observed that these chapters did not contain any provision

---

[116] It should be pointed out that, in the context of the 1991 IGC, the Commission's proposal regarding the Common Commercial Policy was in fact only discussed very briefly. This could lead to the conclusion that one should perhaps not give too much importance to the rejection of the Commission's proposals. On the other hand, one could also see this as a clear indication that the extension of the scope of the Common Commercial Policy was in fact a non-issue for most Member States.

[117] See Hilf, 'The EJC's Opinion 1/94' at 256.

[118] See J. Bourgeois, 'The EC in the WTO and Advisory Op. 1/94' at 776 ff. See also J. Bourgeois, 'L'avis de la Cour de justice des Communautés européennes à propos de l'Uruguay Round: un avis mitigé', (1994) 4 RMUE II. In the latter article Bourgeois talks about 'Schönheitsfehler' (at 20) and the examples given here are partly based on his examples of such 'Schönheitsfehler'.   [119] Op. 1/94, para. 48.

[120] Ibid., para. 28–31. Could this difference be explained by Art. 38 (2) EC?

[121] Op. 1/94, para. 46.

regarding first establishment and access to service markets of nationals of non-member countries.[122] Thirdly, in order to exclude all of the TRIPs from the scope of Article 113 EC, except the provisions on counterfeit products, the Court argued that intellectual property rights do not relate specifically to international trade; they affect internal trade, just as much as, if not more than, international trade.[123] This is correct, but one may wonder whether this is also not the case for other matters, such as technical barriers to trade, which the Court found to be within the scope of Article 113 EC. Fourthly, in the same context, the Court stated that the primary objective of the TRIPs is to strengthen and harmonize the protection of intellectual property on a world-wide scale. On reading the preamble of the TRIPs, however, it appears that the objective of this agreement is 'to reduce distortions and impediments to international trade'. With regard to the Agreement on Technical Barriers to Trade, it ruled on the basis of a similarly worded objective that that agreement falls within the scope of Article 113 EC.[124] Fifthly, the Court excluded the three modes of supply of services involving the movement of natural persons from the scope of Article 113 EC, on the basis of the distinction made in Article 3 between paragraph (b) on commercial policy, and paragraph (d) on measures concerning the entry and movement of persons in the internal market. The latter paragraph, however, primarily concerns visa requirements which fall outside the scope of the GATS.[125] Finally, with regard to the exclusive external competence to conclude the GATS, the Court stated that the attainment of freedom of establishment and freedom to provide services for nationals of Member States is not inextricably linked to the treatment to be afforded in the Community to nationals of non-member countries.[126] This may be the case; however, one cannot help wondering whether past experience does not show that the realization of the freedom to supply services, and the freedom of establishment for nationals of Member States within the Community, is all but facilitated by the existence of Member State rules regarding the supply of services and establishment by nationals of non-member countries?[127]

---

[122] Ibid., para 81.   [123] Ibid., para. 57.

[124] Ibid., para. 33. I do not contest that the TBT Agreement is quite different from TRIPs in that it does not aim to harmonize technical regulations and standards but only deals with the reduction of barriers to trade. TRIPs, however, does the latter too and this the Court ignored.

[125] See S. 1.2.2. The GATS 'Annexe on Movement of Natural Persons Supplying Services under the Agreement' effectively excludes visa requirements from the scope of the GATS. See also T. Trimidas and P. Eeckhout, *supra*. n. 112.   [126] Op. 1/94, para. 86.

[127] When one looks at the field of air transport and the controversy surrounding the 'Open Sky' agreements, it becomes clear that the danger of deflection of trade also exists with regard to services.

It has been suggested that the 'weakness' of the legal reasoning may be explained by the time constraints under which the Court had to deliver its Opinion.[128] In view of the complexity and controversial nature of the subject-matter, as well as the hundreds of pages of observations submitted to it, the Court was faced with a daunting task.

2.2.4.3 Departure from previous case law

In many respects, more troublesome than any alleged weakness in the legal reasoning is the fact that the Court definitely deviated from its established (albeit often open-ended) case law. It is fair to say that the Court's conclusions on the scope of the concept of 'commercial policy' are difficult to reconcile with its case law as discussed above.[129] Referring to Opinion 1/75, the Commission correctly made two points: (1) none of the Member States would seriously maintain that trade in services does not constitute trade; and (2) the agreements which the Community concludes in that regard are not part of commercial policy. Yet the Court excluded most trade in services from the concept of commercial policy.

In Opinion 1/78, the Court had ruled that the non-exhaustive enumeration of subjects covered by Article 113 leaves open the door to the application in a Community context 'of any other process intended to regulate external trade'.[130] In further support for a broad definition of the Common Commercial Policy, the Court had ruled in *Greece* v. *Council* that a regulation intended to regulate trade between the Community and non-member countries falls within the scope of the common commercial policy.[131] On the basis of the two latter cases, it seems that the Court's conclusions should have been different. However, the Court was clearly unwilling to draw the logical conclusion from its case law when it decided on whether the GATS and TRIPs fall within the scope of Article 113 EC.

Regarding the Court's case law concerning the exclusive nature of implied external competence, it should be noted that Opinion 1/94 seems to imply a withdrawal from the liberalization of the 'affect requirement' advanced in Opinion 2/91 (in paragraphs 25 and 26). In order for the 'affect requirement' to be fulfilled, the Court requires *more* than the mere existence of Community rules covering, to a large extent, the subject area of the international obligations.[132]

Furthermore, it should be recalled that the Court gave in its Opinion 1/94 a very restrictive interpretation of its Opinion 1/76, and thus considerably reduced the significance of this Opinion.[133] It has been

---

[128] See Bourgeois: 'L'avis de la Cour de justice' at 20.   [129] Ibid. at 22.
[130] Op. 1/78, para. 45.   [131] Case C–62/88, para. 16.
[132] See Ss. 1.3.2 and 3.   [133] See Ss. 1.3.2 and 1.3.3.

argued that the criterion of 'necessity' in Opinion 1/76, on which the existence of implied external competence of an exclusive nature depended, is now supplemented by a 'proportionality' test, that is, 'even if external action by the EC may be necessary, one should assess whether the aim could not be achieved by a concerted action of Member States'.[134] The 'necessity criterion' of Opinion 1/76 has been turned into an 'otherwise not possible' criterion. It is obvious that, as a result, there are in fact only very few instances in which the Community has implied external competence of an exclusive nature without prior use of internal powers.

2.2.4.4 A clear and workable solution?

All this criticism would carry little weight, however, if the Court's Opinion had brought a clear and workable solution to the battered problem of the division of competence between the Community and the Member States in the field of international economic relations. Alas, it is questionable whether the Opinion achieved this goal. One could argue that by ruling that the Community and the Members States are *both* competent in the field of trade in services and trade-related aspects of intellectual property rights, the Court has in fact laid down a division of competence, which is neither clear nor workable.[135]

At the Court hearing in October 1994, the Commission drew the Court's attention to the problems which will arise, as regards the administration of the GATS and TRIPs, if the Community and the Member States are recognized as sharing competence with regard to the conclusion of these agreements. The Commission expressed the fear that the Member States will, in the context of the WTO (of which they are also members), seek to express their views individually on the matters falling within their competence whenever it proves difficult to find a consensus. This may result in sheer 'cacophony' in the WTO when trade in services or TRIPs are discussed.[136] Moreover, the Commission was concerned that a Court's ruling in favour of shared competence will lead to endless discussions about whether a given matter falls within the competence of the Community (and

---

[134] See Bourgeois, 'The EC in the WTO and Advisory Op. 1/94' at 780–1.

[135] Note that there is a difference between joint or shared competence on the one hand, and parallel competence on the other. In the fields of joint or shared competence, such as trade in services and TRIPs, the Community can eventually obtain exclusive competence when all matters in that field are covered by common internal rules (see e.g. Op. 1/94 (WTO), paras. 77, 95 & 96). In the fields of parallel or concurrent competence, such as development co-operation (Art. 130u EC), the Community's competence will never become exclusive (see Case C–316/91, *Parliament* v. *Council* (Fourth Lomé Convention) [1994] ECR I–625, para. 26.).

[136] For the term 'cacophony', see Bourgeois, 'The EC in the WTO and Advisory Op. 1/94' at 784.

therefore subject to the Community's decision-making procedures), or within the competence of the Member States (and thus in need of a consensus in order to take joint action). The Commission expressed grave anxiety that a possible Court ruling in favour of shared competence will undermine the Community's unity of action *vis-à-vis* the rest of the world, and will greatly weaken its negotiating power.[137]

In the concluding section of Opinion 1/94, the Court acknowledged that the Commission's apprehension was 'quite legitimate'. In line with what the Council had argued, the Court subsequently stated, however, that the resolution of the problem of the division of competence cannot depend on problems which may possibly arise in administering the Uruguay Round Agreements. The Court noted that 'any problems regarding the co-ordination necessary to ensure unity of action where the Community and the Member States participate jointly cannot modify the answer to the question of competence, that being a prior issue.'[138]

Obviously aware of the fact that this was not a very 'helpful' conclusion, the Court then explicitly bestowed on both the Community and the Member States a *duty to co-operate*.[139] Where it is apparent that the subject-matter of an agreement falls in part within the competence of the Community and in part within that of the Member States, it is essential— according to the Court—to ensure close co-operation between the Member States and the Community institutions. This close co-operation is called for in the process of negotiation and conclusion, as well as in the fulfilment of the commitments entered into. In the Court's view, this duty of close co-operation flows from the requirement of unity in the international representation of the Community. The duty to co-operate had already been identified by the Court in Ruling 1/78,[140] and more recently Opinion 2/91 (ILO),[141] yet this duty becomes even more imperative in the context of the Uruguay Round Agreements. This is due to the fact that the Uruguay Round Agreements, and in particular the Understanding on Dispute Settlement, provide for the possibility of cross-retaliation measures.[142] As the Court explained,[143] a Member State duly authorized within its sphere of competence to take cross-retaliation measures, but confronted with the fact that these measures would be ineffective if taken in the field covered by the GATS or TRIPs, would not, under Community law, be empowered to retaliate in the area of trade in goods; since this area falls within the exclusive competence of the Community. Similarly, if the Community were given the right to retaliate in the sector of goods, but

---

[137] These observations by the Commission are summarized in Op. 1/94, para. 106.
[138] Ibid., para. 107.   [139] Ibid., para. 108.
[140] Ruling 1/78 [1978] ECR 2151.   [141] See S. 1.3.1.
[142] Art. 22 DSU.   [143] Op. 1/94, para. 109.

considered it impossible or impractical to do so, it would find it difficult to retaliate in the areas such as those covered by the GATS and TRIPs where competence is partly shared with the Member States. In both situations, only close co-operation between the Community and the Member States offers a solution.

The division of competence in the field of international economic relations, as laid down by the Court in Opinion 1/94, and as recently confirmed in Opinion 2/92 of 24 March 1995,[144] creates more problems than it solves for the Community as an actor on the international stage. Though there may have been—as I pointed out above—no politically realistic alternative to the Court's very cautious and compromisorial solution to the competence issue, it is certainly not, as such, a workable solution. As a matter of fact, with this 'solution' to the competence issue the Court now forces the Community institutions and the Member States back to the negotiating table; with the short-term objective to agree on a code of conduct which would translate the 'duty to co-operate' into specific procedural rules, and the long-term objective to revise the Treaty. Such a revision should provide for a more rational division of competence in the field of international economic relations, and/or prescribe the manner in which to exercise joint competence. The issue of a code of conduct and the need for a Treaty revision will be discussed further in the conclusion of this chapter.

2.3 THE CONDUCT OF THE EUROPEAN COMMUNITY IN THE CONTEXT OF THE URUGUAY ROUND

2.3.1 The negotiation of the Uruguay Round agreements by the European Community

2.3.1.1 The Commission as the sole negotiator

The Uruguay Round negotiations were officially launched by the Punta del Este Ministerial Declaration of 20 September 1986.[145] By that time, however, the international community had already been talking about these negotiations and their possible agenda for almost four years.[146] In

---

[144] Op. 2/92, on the Third Revised Dec. of the Council of the OECD regarding National Treatment.

[145] Bull. EC 9–1986, 1.4.1. For the full text of the Declaration, see ibid., 1.4.4.

[146] At the meeting of the Contracting Parties of the GATT in Nov. 1982, the decision was taken in principle to set up a Preparatory Committee to pave the way for a new round of trade

late 1984, the Commission submitted to the Council a communication concerning a new round of GATT trade negotiations, in which it came out strongly in favour of the opening of such negotiations and outlined the objectives and a possible agenda. After detailed discussions on the basis of this communication, the Council issued a statement on 19 March 1985 in which the Community declared itself fully committed to the launching of such negotiations.[147] The European Council of Heads of State or Government endorsed and stressed the importance of the Council's statement at its meeting in Brussels on 29 and 30 March 1985.[148]

Pursuant to Article 113 (3) EEC:[149]

Where agreements with third countries need to be negotiated, the Commission shall make recommendations to the Council, which shall authorize the Commission to open the necessary negotiations.

---

negotiations (see K. R. Simmonds, 'The Community and the Uruguay Round', (1988), CMLRev. 95 at 96). Later the possibility of a new round of multilateral trade negotiations had received particular attention at the meeting of the OECD Ministers in May 1984, at the London Economic Summit in June 1984 and at the meeting of the Contracting Parties of the GATT in Nov. 1984 (see Bull. EC 3–1985, 2.2.12. and Bull. EC 11–1984, 2.2.52.).

[147] Bull. EC 3–1985, 2.2.12.

[148] Ibid., 2.2.13. In the Conclusions of the European Council it reads: 'The European Council stresses the importance of the decision adopted by the Council of Ministers with regard to all factors which will enable a new round of multilateral trade negotiations to be initiated in Brussels as soon as possible.' (Ibid., 1.2.3).

[149] Note that at the time of the opening and throughout most of the Uruguay Round negotiations, Art. 113 (3) EEC was still applicable. It was only as from the entry into force of the Maastricht Treaty on European Union (1 Nov. 1993) onwards that Arts. 113 (3) and 228 (1) EC apply to the negotiations of international trade and other agreements. The procedure laid down in these Treaty provisions is, however, very similar to the one stipulated in the old Art. 113 (3) EEC. See, however, S. 2.1.3.

Art. 113 (3), first subpara., EC reads:

Where agreements with one or more States or international organizations need to be negotiated, the Commission shall make recommendations to the Council, which shall authorize the Commission to open the necessary negotiations.

The Commission shall conduct these negotiations in consultation with a special committee appointed by the Council to assist the Commission in this task and within the framework of such directives as the Council may issue to it.

The relevant provisions of Art. 228 shall apply.

Art. 228 (1), first subpara., EC reads:

Where this Treaty provides for the conclusion of agreements between the Community and one or more States or international organizations, the Commission shall make recommendations to the Council, which shall authorize the Commission to open the necessary negotiations. The Commission shall conduct these negotiations in consultation with special committees appointed by the Council to assist it in this task and within the framework of such directives as the Council may issue to it.

In exercising the powers conferred upon it by this paragraph, the Council shall act by a qualified majority, except in the cases provided for in the second sentence of paragraph 2, for which it shall act unanimously.

Given the fact that Art. 228 (1) EC seems to apply to *all* international agreements between the Community and non-member states or international organizations, including trade agreements, one could argue that Art. 113 (3) EC is superfluous.

The Commission shall conduct these negotiations in consultation with a special committee appointed by the Council to assist the Commission in this task and within the framework of such directives as the Council may issue to it.

It should be noted, however, that with its 1984 communication on a new GATT round of trade negotiations, the Commission sought neither authorization to open negotiations nor negotiating directives. It merely informed the Council of its intention to have 'exploratory' talks on a possible new GATT round, and for such talks no authorization was required.[150] The Council's statement of 19 March 1985 did, however, give useful guidance and support to the Commission in those pre-negotiation talks.

After more than one year of such talks, at both bilateral and multilateral levels, concerning a new GATT round and the topics which should feature on the agenda,[151] the Commission submitted to the Council a communication on the overall approach to the new GATT round on 28 May 1986.[152] In this communication, the Commission outlined its approach to the negotiations, what it expected from its GATT partners, and the various topics to be discussed. The Commission's communication received the Council's blessing at the latter's meeting on 16 and 17 June 1986, and was transmitted back to the Commission on 19 June 1986 as a document which became known as the *Overall Approach* or the *Vue d'ensemble*.[153] The European Council of Heads of State or Government expressed its agreement with the Council's conclusions at its meeting in The Hague on 26 and 27 June 1986.[154]

Note that in its communication of 28 May 1986, the Commission did not request authorization to open the negotiations, nor did it propose any negotiating directives for the Council to issue. In its conclusions of the meeting of 16 and 17 June 1986 the Council stated in this respect that:

The Commission will be invited to propose formal negotiating directives in the context of Article 113 at a later stage, after agreement has been reached to launch the new round. Meanwhile, however, the Council has considered it appropriate that the Community's general approach to the future negotiations, and its

[150] See J. Bourgeois, 'Trade policy-making in the European Community', in M. Hilf and E.U. Petersmann, *National Constitutions and International Economic Law* (1993), 190 at 191.

[151] See e.g. the quadripartite meeting with the US, Canada and Japan organized in the summer of 1985, where the Community was represented by Mr De Clercq, the Commissioner responsible for external trade (Bull. EC 7/8–1985, 2.3.11.); the special session of the GATT Contracting Parties, 30 Sept.–2 Oct. 1985 (Bull. EC 10–1985, 2.3.6); and the annual session of the GATT Contracting Parties 25–28 Nov. 1985 (Bull. EC 11–1985, 2.3.8.).

[152] SEC(86) 840 and Bull. EC 5–1986, 2.2.1.

[153] *Overall Approach: New Round of Trade Negotiations in Defence of Open Multilateral Trade*, Doc. 7748, PV/CONS 33 EXT. 1 GATT 107. See Bull. EC 6–1986, 2.2.2. For a detailed analysis of *Overall Approach*, see Simmonds, 'Community and Uruguay Round' at 98–101.   [154] Bull. EC 6–1986, 1.1.10 and 2.2.1.

objectives be elaborated further. . . . The Commission's communication . . . is welcomed by the Council and provides the Commission with the necessary orientations.[155]

During the weeks preceding the Ministerial Conference at Punta del Este, as well as at the September 1986 Ministerial Conference itself, the Commission was acting on the basis of the Council's *Overall Approach* of June 1986. Under its direction, the Commission was able to play an active and constructive role in the negotiations which eventually led to an agreement on the aims, the methods and the subjects of the new round of trade negotiations.[156] On 20 September 1986, the Punta del Este Ministerial Declaration, launching a new round of multilateral trade negotiations, was adopted.[157]

At a Council meeting convened in Punta del Este on that same day, the Commission submitted the Punta del Este Declaration for approval, and requested the Council to authorize it to open negotiations. This request presented a serious problem. A number of Member States were of the opinion that some of the issues on the agenda of the Uruguay Round negotiations did not fall within the competence of the Community, and that the negotiations should therefore be conducted by both the Commission and the Member States.[158]

At the Council meeting of 20 September 1986, the Punta del Este Declaration was eventually approved by both the Council *and* by the representatives of the Member States 'to the extent that they were concerned'. While it was explicitly stated in the minutes of the Council meeting that the joint approval of the Declaration did not prejudice the question of competence of the Community or the Member States on particular issues,[159] this joint approval must be seen as a clear indication of the Council's disagreement with the Commission's broad interpretation of the Community's competence. Nevertheless, it was decided at the same time that the Commission would act as the sole negotiator on behalf of the

[155] Bull. EC 6–1986, 2.2.2.

[156] Ibid., 2.2.3. and Bull. EC 9–1986, 1.4.1. as well as Twentieth General Report on the Activities of the European Communities (1986), 300.

[157] Bull. EC 9–1986, 1.4.1.

[158] Note that for the negotiation of (multilateral) mixed agreements, the practice in the mid-80s was that there were either eleven delegations (10 Member States and the Commission) or a 'two-headed' delegation of the Commission and the 'Presidency' of the Council, or a single combined delegation with the Commission representative more often than not acting as a spokesman on Community matters (See E. Stein, in collaboration with L. Henkin, 'Towards a European foreign policy? The European foreign affairs system from the perspective of the United States Constitution', in Cappelletti, M., Seccombe, M., and Weiler, J. (eds.), *Forces and Potential for a European Identity*, Book III, Vol. 1, EUI Integration Through Law Project, (1986), 1 at 43).

[159] Doc 9205/86, PV/CONS 49 GATT 147, 2. See also S. 1.1.1.

Community and the Member States 'in order to ensure the maximum consistency in the conduct of the negotiations'.[160]

The Commission thus negotiated for both the Community *and* the Member States during the whole period of the Uruguay Round, that is from September 1986 to December 1993 (and beyond).[161] The Commission's chief negotiator was the Commissioner responsible for external trade, successively Mr De Clercq from 1986 to 1988, Mr Andriessen from 1989 to 1992 and Sir Leon Brittan from 1993 onwards. The Commissioners responsible for agriculture—Mr Andriessen from 1986 to 1988, Mr MacSharry from 1989 to 1992, and Mr Steichen from 1993 onwards—were also deeply involved in the negotiations. It should be noted that no single Commissioner had the authority to commit the Commission. The Commission operates as a collegiate body, and the negotiating activities of the Commission negotiator(s) therefore needed the support and approval of the full Commission.[162] In practice, however, and mostly for reasons of efficiency, this internal process of approval often involved a smaller group of Commissioners, who followed the negotiations more closely than their colleagues.

In the course of the Uruguay Round the Commission understandably had its fair share of internal conflict.[163] By way of example, one could refer to Commissioner MacSharry's temporary resignation as negotiator for agriculture because of alleged interference from Commission President Delors in the negotiations.[164] Note that, according to the Commission statement closing this 'incident', the accusation against Mr Delors of 'interference' 'made no sense' because as a member of the group of four Commissioners authorized by the Commission to conduct the Uruguay Round negotiations, Mr Delors—like the three others—had not only the right, but the duty to intervene.[165]

Within the Commission administration it was primarily the Directorate-General for External Relations (DG I), and in particular the Uruguay Round Steering Group (headed by Deputy Director-General Paemen) and the Commission delegation in Geneva, which was responsible for the conduct of the negotiations. Specialized Directorates-General, such as the Directorate-General for Agriculture (DG VI) and the Directorate-General

---

[160] Op. 1/94 (see n. 4), at I–5282. It was in this way that the Community and the Member States were able 'to avoid' the issue of competence during the negotiations. See S. 1.1.1.

[161] Also after the substantive stage of the negotiations had been concluded the Commission continued to negotiate on a number of technical issues until 15 Apr. 1994 (see below).

[162] Note that the Commission makes decisions by simple majority vote.

[163] See also T. Oppermann and M. Beise, 'GATT-Welthandelsrunde und keine Ende?', *Europa-Archiv*, Folge 1/1993, at 5.

[164] *Financial Times*, 22 Sept. 1993, 8.   [165] *Europe*, 13 Nov. 1992, 7.

for Customs and Indirect Taxation (DG XXI) obviously played an important role in the negotiations as well.

Although the Commission was the sole negotiator for the Community and the Member States, the latter sometimes joined the Commission at the negotiating table. As a rule, they only did so in the most formal negotiating settings. At the Ministerial conferences, for example, the Member States were always represented, but the statements delivered by their ministers were mostly of a very general and ceremonial nature, and often involved consultation and co-ordination with the Commission.[166] The Member States were not to deviate from the line taken by the Commission on behalf of the Community *and* the Member States. At the formal meetings of the Negotiating Groups, the Member States were also present, but normally did not take the floor.[167] In informal negotiation settings, however, the Member States were not present.[168]

The fact that the Commission was the sole negotiator did not keep the Member States' political leaders from discussing the negotiations with their counterparts in non-member countries. While this was often considered useful to advance the negotiations, occasionally this led to friction between an 'enterprising' Member State and the Commission. The dividing line between helpful discussions with the Community's negotiating partners and entering into parallel negotiations may not always be very clear.[169] Exemplary in this respect was an 'incident' in March 1992 involving Chancellor Kohl. In the run-up to a meeting with President Bush in Camp David, it was suggested by Chancellor Kohl that the Community could accept quantitative limitations on its agricultural exports, in exchange for a 'freeze' by the Americans of their exports to the Community of cereal substitutes.[170] When asked for a reaction, however, the spokesman for the Commission simply said that Chancellor Kohl had no mandate to negotiate for the Community, but that any contributions leading to a compromise

---

[166] See also S. 2.1.2.

[167] As a matter of fact, when France, in the context of discussions in a GATT committee, took a position contrary to that taken by the Commission, it was effectively ignored by the committee's chairman and the other Contracting Parties. While a similar incident did not occur in the context of the Uruguay Round negotiations, the reaction would not have been different.

[168] P. J. Kuijper, 'The EC's Common Commercial Policy: which way the swing of the pendulum?', (1994) ASIL Procs. 294 at 295. It must be noted that in the so-called 'green-room' meetings the Commission was often accompanied by the Member State holding the Presidency of the Council (Ibid.).

[169] It should be noted, however, that during the Round no Member State ever really crossed this dividing line. See also S. 2.1.3.

[170] This idea had reportedly already been discussed with and had the support of President Mitterrand, Commission President Delors, and Prime Ministers Major and Lubbers.

were welcome and could be useful.[171] A few days later Commission President Delors added on a more diplomatic, but no less cautioning tone, that Chancellor Kohl would undoubtedly defend the Community's common position to President Bush.[172] Closing this incident, Chancellor Kohl was careful to point out to the press, at the end of his meeting with President Bush at Camp David, that he had not come to negotiate regarding the Uruguay Round, but simply to express some views and to reaffirm his country's desire to conclude the Round as quickly as possible. Chancellor Kohl stressed that the European Commission was the Community's sole negotiator, and that the former had the complete confidence of the Member States.

It should also be noted that the United States at times tried to circumvent the Commission and negotiate directly with the Member States. Notorious in this respect is President Clinton's failed attempt during the last days of the negotiations to split the Member States among themselves and against the Commission by directly contacting Chancellor Kohl and Prime Ministers Major and Balladur.[173]

2.3.1.2 The relative importance of negotiating directives

While the Commission conducted the negotiations, its freedom to do so was circumscribed in two ways. Pursuant to the second subparagraph of the then applicable Article 113 (3) EEC on the negotiation of trade agreements,[174] quoted above, the Commission had to conduct the negotiations 'within the framework of such directives as the Council may issue to it', and in consultation with a special committee appointed by the Council. With regard to the former 'restriction' of the Commission's freedom to negotiate, it should be noted that negotiating directives issued by the Council may play—and in the past have played—an important role in the negotiations of international agreements, and will then often allow the Commission only limited discretion.[175] In the context of the Uruguay Round, however, the situation was different. As the wording of the second subparagraph of Article 113 (3) EEC suggested,[176] the issuance of negotiating directives was not requisite for the Commission to conduct negotiations, and the Uruguay Round negotiations were a fine illustration

---

[171] *Europe*, 19 Mar. 1992, 7.   [172] *Europe*, 23/24 Mar. 1992, 10.

[173] *The Times*, 15 Dec. 1993, 10.

[174] Art. 228 EEC on the procedure for the negotiation of other agreements remained mute on this point but was in practice subject to a similar rule. As was already noted above, the currently applicable Arts. 113 (3) and 228 (1) EC, provide for the same 'restrictions' on the Commission's freedom to negotiate. See S. 2.1.1.

[175] See Stein, 'Towards a European foreign policy?' at 41.

[176] This provision read '. . . directives such as the Council *may* issue' (Emphasis added).

of this. The Council never adopted *formal* negotiating directives covering all aspects of these negotiations.[177]

It will be recalled that, when the Council adopted its *Overall Approach* in June 1986, it stated that it would invite the Commission to propose formal negotiating directives after agreement had been reached to launch the new round.[178] In its decision of 20 September 1986, authorizing the Commission to open the negotiations, the Council made it clear that it did intend to issue formal negotiating directives, but in fact it failed to do so.[179] The negotiations were started with only the 'informal' negotiating directives laid down in the *Overall Approach* to guide the Commission. With regard to most issues on the negotiating agenda, the Council never, in fact, issued negotiating directives of a more specific and/or formal nature than the general guidelines laid down in the *Overall Approach*.

Throughout the Uruguay Round, the Commission regularly submitted reports to the Council on the progress of the negotiations. The Council would take these Commission reports as an opportunity to discuss the Community's negotiating strategy and, when and where necessary, elaborate somewhat the general guidelines of the *Overall Approach*. On 22 April 1988, for example, the Commission sent a report to the Council which took stock of the state of the negotiations, and looked ahead to the mid-term ministerial conference in Montreal scheduled for December 1988.[180] At its meeting on 25 and 26 April 1988, the Council held a general exchange of views on the Uruguay Round on the basis of the Commission's report, and confirmed the negotiating guidelines it had previously laid down.[181] It will not come as a surprise that it was especially during the final stage of the negotiations that the Commission's progress reports to the Council followed each other at an increasing pace, and that the Council adopted further guidelines for the closing negotiations on the basis of these reports. It should be noted, however, that even at that stage, these guidelines did not take the form of formal negotiating directives.[182] They remained fairly vague, non-controversial policy statements, which allowed

---

[177] In the context of the Tokyo Round, the Council reportedly adopted negotiating directives in Feb. 1975, but subsequently never formally modified them until the end of the negotiations in 1979. The unanimous conclusions adopted by the Council before and during the negotiations apparently served as (informal) negotiating directives. See J.-V. Louis, 'The European Economic Community and the implementation of the GATT Tokyo Round results', in J. Jackson, J.-V. Louis and M. Matsushita, *Implementing the Tokyo Round: national constitutions and international economic rules*, (1984), 21 at 27.

[178] See above.

[179] Doc. 9205/86, PV/CONS 49 GATT 147, 2.

[180] In its report the Commission called upon the Council to reaffirm the negotiating principles already laid down (Bull. EC 4–1988, 2.2.1.).

[181] Ibid., 2.2.2.

[182] See e.g. Bull. EC 7/8–1993, 1.3.105, Bull. EC 9–1993, 1.3.79. and Bull. EC 10–1993, 1.3.86.

the Commission a wide margin of discretion, and had in fact only a limited impact on the negotiations.

In contrast to their relative insignificance with regard to most of the issues on the agenda of the Uruguay Round, the Council's negotiating directives did play an important role in the context of the negotiations on agriculture. These negotiation directives on agricultural trade also constituted amongst Member States the most bitter and hotly debated issue of the Uruguay Round. The internal disagreement on these directives could easily have led to the failure of the Round, and a profound crisis within the European Community. Obviously, there was much disagreement over the substance of the directives to be issued, but of particular interest to us here was the contention over the extent of the Commission's discretion when negotiating a very sensitive issue such as agricultural trade.

It was clear, from the very beginning of the negotiations, that a successful conclusion of the Uruguay Round would be impossible without an agreement on the liberalization of agricultural trade. Agriculture was pivotal, 'not because of an American whim', as many in the Community seemed to believe, but because it was 'the *sine qua non* for many other participants, both developed and developing'.[183] During the first years of the Round, the European Community however, rejected any compromise which questioned the foundations of the common agricultural policy and its high levels of internal support, import restrictions and export subsidies.[184] For a long time, the Council even failed to agree on a negotiating position on the liberalization of agricultural trade, thus calling into question the prospect of serious negotiation continuing on the other fourteen items of the Uruguay Round agenda.[185] The December 1990 Ministerial Conference in Brussels, at which the Uruguay Round negotiations should have been concluded, was therefore doomed to fail; and the December 1991 Dunkel draft Final Act was found unacceptable.[186]

It was not until the Community itself shook the foundations of its common agricultural policy with the radical reform adopted in May 1992 that the negotiations on agriculture had a chance of success. With clear and detailed directives—to negotiate an agreement that would entail no changes to the common agricultural policy that would go further than the internal reform—the Commission could start the negotiations on agriculture in earnest. Eventually, a first breakthrough was realized in the beginning of November 1992, during a meeting in Chicago between Mr MacSharry, the Commissioner responsible for agriculture, and Mr Madigan, his

---

[183] *Financial Times*, 20 Jan. 1992, 14.
[184] G. Koopmann, 'Final curtain for the Uruguay Round?', (Nov./Dec. 1992), *Intereconomics*, 253 at 254.
[185] *Financial Times*, 29 and 30 Oct. 1990.
[186] *Financial Times*, 7 Dec. 1990, 2; *Europe*, 4 Jan. 1992, 5; and *Europe*, 13/14 Jan. 1992, 9.

American counterpart.[187] After a lengthy debate in restricted session on the elements of agreement emerging from the Chicago meeting, the Council confirmed its confidence in Mr MacSharry 'to negotiate with the United States to reach a global and balanced agreement that is compatible with the reform of the common agricultural policy'.[188] While most of the Member States emphasized the urgency of reaching a compromise with the United States and, therefore, had decided not to impede the Community negotiators in their task by subjecting them to further negotiating directives, France expressly pointed out to the Commission that it was negotiating 'in supervised freedom'.[189] Mr MacSharry declared that he did not have the time to study a French document regarding a statistical evaluation denouncing the incompatibility of the Commission's Chicago offers with the reform of the common agricultural policy;[190] this irritated the French Government. France insisted that, before a final agreement was reached with the United States, the Commission would submit a report to the Council to enable the latter to assess the compatibility of the tentative agreement with the reform of the common agricultural policy. In the opinion of Mr Gummer, the British agricultural minister and the Council's president-in-office, there was, however, no need for the Commission to operate in this manner. He pointed out that 'once the negotiations are *concluded*, it will be up to the Council to decide whether [the Commission has] achieved a result acceptable to the Community'.[191]

On 20 November 1992, Mr Andriessen and Mr MacSharry (the Commissioners responsible for external trade and agriculture respectively) announced that they had reached a compromise agreement on agricultural trade with the United States, the so-called Blair House Accord.[192] France, however, immediately reacted by rejecting this agreement as incompatible with the May 1992 reform of the common agricultural policy, and therefore in violation of the negotiating directives given to the Commission.[193] After

---

[187] *Europe*, 31 Oct. 1992, 7. Note that, prior to this meeting the pressure by (some) Member States on the Commission in general and Mr MacSharry in particular was such that Mr Gummer, the British agricultural minister and the Council's president-in-office, stated that 'the Council must deal with the question of how to enable the Community negotiator, Mr MacSharry, to get on with the negotiations under proper conditions. It is not a question of seeking to define a new brief, but of enabling Mr MacSharry to continue his task' (*Europe*, 26/27 Oct. 1992, 5.).   [188] *Europe*, 18 Nov. 1992, 5.   [189] Ibid.

[190] Commissioner MacSharry did, however, say that some of France's conclusions were 'totally absurd' and sometimes even 'fanciful'. Mr Gummer made a similar statement (see *Europe*, 18 Nov. 1992, 5 and *Le Figaro*, 16 Sept. 1993, 2).

[191] *Europe*, 18 Nov. 1992, 8.

[192] *Europe*, 21 Nov. 1992, 7. Of the negotiations leading to the Blair House Accord it was later reported in a leading French newspaper that the UK, holding the Presidency at that time, had sent its Minister of Agriculture to Washington 'pour mettre l'épée dans les reins' of the two members of the Commission who were negotiating the accord and of which the term in office would expire 2 months later (*Le Figaro*, 16 Sept. 1993, 2).

[193] *Europe*, 23/24 Nov. 1992, 6. In its report to the Council of 25 Nov. 1992 on the compatibility of the Blair House Accord with the reform of the common agricultural policy,

a negative vote in the Assemblée Nationale, the French Government announced that it would veto the Blair House Accord if it were voted upon within the Council.

During the first half of 1993, France remained zealously opposed to the Blair House Accord, and repeated its threat to veto it. While in principle the Blair House Accord could be adopted by qualified majority, France claimed that this accord threatened its 'vital interests' and thus implicitly invoked the so-called Luxemburg Compromise to veto it.[194] This invocation of the Luxemburg Compromise, which many thought to be out of use,[195] was quite controversial. However, whether France could or would have eventually vetoed the Accord by invoking the Luxemburg Compromise, will never be known. The other Member States—some of which were also quite critical towards the Accord[196]—wisely decided not to put it to a vote. As a result, however, this pivotal accord on agriculture between the United States and the European Community remained without the approval of the Council. Obviously this situation could not drag on for ever. It had been agreed at the multilateral level, and confirmed by the European Council of Copenhagen, that the Uruguay Round negotiations were to be concluded before 15 December 1993. As already pointed out, any successful conclusion of the negotiations would necessarily include an agreement on agricultural trade.

In an attempt to unblock the situation, the issue of the Council's position regarding the Blair House Accord and future Commission negotiations on agriculture were discussed on 20 and 21 September 1993, at a so-called Jumbo Council meeting of the foreign, agricultural and trade ministers of the Member States.[197] During the weeks preceding this Council meeting, France insisted time and again that the Commission should be instructed to

---

the Commission stated that in certain cases, the compatibility is clear, in other cases assessment is more delicate, but the conclusion is positive on the whole (*Europe*, 26 Nov. 1992, 7). France, however, disagreed with the Commission's analysis (*Europe*, 27 Nov. 1992, 5).

[194] See e.g. *Europe*, 7/8 Dec. 1992, 11.

[195] The French Government itself in the Spring of 1992 declared the Luxemburg Compromise was out of use. In the run-up to the referendum on the Maastricht Treaty in Sept. 1992, however, it took the position that the use of the Luxemburg compromise was not excluded in very exceptional cases (See T. Oppermann and M. Beise, 'GATT-Welthandelsrunde unde keine Ende?', at 8).

[196] In Dec. 1992, Belgium, Italy, Spain, Portugal and Ireland expressed reservations on the Blair House Accord (*Europe*, 7/8 Dec. 1992, 11). On the growing support for the French position during the first half of 1993, see *Le Figaro*, 15 Sept. 1993, II). At the Council meeting of 15 Dec. 1992, the outgoing Commissioner MacSharry tried in vain to convince (with elaborate statistics and figures) all Member States that the Blair House Accord did not go beyond the May 1992 reform of the common agricultural policy (*Europe*, 16 Dec. 1992, 5).

[197] In preparation of this Council meeting, Mr Claes, the Belgian foreign minister and the Council's president-in-office, undertook a tour of the twelve capitals. The week before this Council meeting (11 and 12 Sept. 1993) the foreign ministers also met for an informal Gymnich type of meeting (*Europe*, 11 Sept. 1993, 7).

re-negotiate the Blair House Accord, and to come to an agreement with the United States which would not exceed the reform of the common agricultural policy agreed upon in May 1992.[198] While some Member States came out in support of France's call for a re-negotiation of the Blair House Accord,[199] other Member States, and in particular the United Kingdom, the Netherlands and Denmark, were very much opposed to any revision. They refused to give the Commission directives in this sense. The United States had repeatedly stated that it was not willing to re-negotiate the Blair House Accord,[200] and the latter Member States feared that a Community demand to re-open negotiations might jeopardize the whole Round.[201] The disagreement on the Blair House Accord severely tested the solidarity between the twelve Member States. At the core of this disagreement was the question of which negotiating directives, if any, the Council should give to the Commission and, if it did give any, how much freedom it should continue to give the Commission during these last months of the negotiations. Pouring oil on the fire, Mr Hurd, the British foreign minister, reportedly said that he could not conceive how the Community could continue with the normal transaction of business if it were seen to have caused the collapse of the Uruguay Round.[202] This statement was considered a British threat to paralyse the Community (by imitating the empty-chair tactics last used by General de Gaulle in 1965), if France caused the Round to fail over its refusal of the Blair House Accord.[203] France definitely played for the highest stakes, and the potential for a debilitating crisis was only too real.[204] Not surprisingly, the Jumbo Council meeting of 20 and 21 September 1993 was therefore an event of high drama.

Speaking for the Commission at this Council meeting, Sir Leon Brittan strongly objected to the re-negotiation of the Blair House Accord, and pleaded to the ministers not to tie his hands in future negotiations with the United States.[205] In line with this request, he criticized a Franco-German draft compromise which would, in his opinion, overly restrict his abilities in the forthcoming negotiations by requiring the Commission to seek 'clarifications' on the Blair House Accord. Sir Leon remarked that he needed no further negotiating directives to take into account the French

---

[198] *The Economist*, 18 Sept. 1993, 78.

[199] See e.g. *Le Figaro*, 15 Sept. 1993, II.

[200] The US felt that it had already been too soft on the Community.

[201] While obviously unwilling to endanger the chances of a successful conclusion of the Uruguay Round, the German position with regard to the French demand of a re-negotiation of the Blair House Accord had been somewhat ambivalent. Germany was definitely not very happy with this demand, but in August 1993 Chancellor Kohl nevertheless seemed to echo France's call to re-open the negotiations on agricultural trade (*The Economist*, 4 Sept. 1993, 15).   [202] *Financial Times*, 21 Sept. 1993, 1.

[203] *The Economist*, 25 Sept. 1993, 41.

[204] *Financial Times*, 21 Sept. 1993, 1.   [205] Ibid., 1.

concerns during further negotiations. Such a position provoked a furious reaction from the French foreign minister, Mr Juppé, who reminded Sir Leon that he was a mere *fonctionnaire* who would kindly take his orders from the Council.[206] After more than thirteen hours of continuous discussions, the twelve Member States were eventually able to come to a compromise on the negotiating directives for the Commission.[207] This appeared to give credence to some French objections but, most importantly, it cleared the air and avoided a major crisis in the Community. The text of the compromise was quite precise with regard to what the Commission was to achieve.[208] It was, according to a high ranking Commission official, *une véritable feuille de route*.[209] It should be noted, however, that this compromise did not amount to a mandate to re-negotiate; and that Sir Leon's brief was to explore whether the United States was willing to show new flexibility in interpreting, amplifying or clarifying parts of the Blair House Accord.[210]

During the following weeks, the Commission continued its negotiations with the United States. Though the French Government initially stressed that it would veto any 'clarified' Blair House Accord that would not take its interests fully into account, it gradually showed a willingness to compromise on agricultural trade.[211] On 6 December 1993 the Commission was finally able to reach an agreement with the United States on a 'new' Blair House Accord.[212] One should realize, however, that this 'new' Accord was dearly paid for, in the simultaneous and subsequent negotiations with the United States on industrial tariffs. When defending this compromise agreement before the General Affairs Council of 7 December 1993, Mr Steichen, the Commissioner responsible for agriculture, stated that the 'clarified' Accord met all of the demands put forth by the Jumbo Council.[213] To everyone's

---

[206] *The Economist*, 25 Sept. 1993, 41; *Financial Times*, 22 Sept. 1993, 8; and *Le Figaro*, 22 Sept. 1993, I. 'Une sévère prise de bec avait eu lieu, en effet, entre les deux hommes vers minuit, quand M. Brittan avait refusé un mandat de négotiation trop contraignant à ses yeux et que M. Juppé lui avait rétorqué que c'était aux ministres de décider et non aux commissaires'.

[207] *Europe*, 22 Sept. 1993, 5–6.

[208] Commenting on the compromise reached, Mr Juppé said that 'des orientations précises' had been given to the Commission and that Sir Leon Brittan was to take up the negotiations with Mr Kantor again on the basis of these precise guidelines (*Le Figaro*, 22 Sept. 1993, p. I). As far as Mr Juppé was concerned 'Sir Leon va aux Etats-Unis l'épée dans les reins et nous allons le suivre pas à pas' (Ibid.). The UK Foreign Secretary, Mr Hurd stated, however, that France had not succeeded in tying the hands of the Community's negotiator (Ibid.) Germany agreed (*Financial Times*, 22 Sept. 1993, 1 and 8).

[209] *Le Figaro*, 22 Sept. 1993, I.   [210] *Financial Times*, 22 Sept. 1993, 1.

[211] Ibid., 8. However, Sir Leon therefore had to get some sort of deal for France on agricultural trade. Failure to deliver apparent concessions from the US might still sink the Uruguay Round and embroil the Community in a profound internal crisis (*Financial Times*, 27 Sept. 1993, 6.)   [212] *Europe*, 6/7 Dec. 1993, 7.

[213] *Le Monde*, 8 Dec. 1993, 1 and 22.

relief, France declared that it also found the new arrangements acceptable, yet it insisted that the Community should take *internal* measures to protect its farmers from any further losses in production.[214] As a veteran European diplomat put it, with both distaste and admiration, 'The French have realized they have squeezed as much as they can expect out of the Americans, now they are looking to do the same with their European partners.'[215]

While the difficult French attitude during the negotiations on agriculture could have plunged the Community into a debilitating crisis, one may wonder whether the French obstinance might, at times, have been a useful bargaining chip for the Commission in its negotiations with the United States.

It must be understood, however, that the extremely tense drama, as seen in the crucial negotiations on agriculture, is not a proper representation of the role of the Council in the Uruguay Round negotiations in general. As I noted above, the Council took a less active and steering role in the context of the other issues on the negotiating agenda. Its directives to the Commission did not reach too far beyond the informal general guidelines laid down in the *Overall Approach* of June 1986.[216] This was neither accidental, nor the result of political inability to reach agreement on formal and detailed negotiating directives. In looking for a tool to control the Commission's negotiating activities, the Member States had come to understand that, in the context of negotiations such as the Uruguay Round, negotiating directives were not an appropriate instrument. The highly complicated and often quickly evolving nature of such activities meant that even detailed negotiating directives would inevitably have left much important ground uncovered, and would need frequent adjustment. Most importantly, however, such directives would deprive the Commission of a degree of flexibility which most Member States agreed the Commission needed to negotiate effectively.

2.3.1.3 The crucial role of the 113 Committee

As I mentioned above, there was a second way in which the freedom of the Commission to negotiate was limited. Pursuant to the second subparagraph of Article 113 (3) EEC, the Commission's activities during the Uruguay

---

[214] *Europe*, 9 Dec. 1993, 8.   [215] *Financial Times*, 8 Dec. 1993, 5.

[216] Note that with regard to audio-visual services, the Council defined in early Oct. 1993 the so-called 'Six Objectives of Mons' (*Europe*, 7 Oct. 1993, 9 and 10). The Commission, however, disagreed with the Member States on the ways to achieve these objectives (*Europe*, 15 Oct. 1994, 5). As a matter of fact, the conduct of the negotiations on audio-visual services deserves careful attention. For a detailed analysis, see C. Doutrellepont (ed.), *L'Europe et les enjeux du GATT dans le Domaine de l'audiovisual* (1994).

Round were closely monitored by a special Council committee for trade policy, the so-called 113 Committee. Throughout the Round, this committee of Member States' officials met, as always, at least once a month at the level of Directors-General of external economic relations, and weekly at a lower level.[217] During the busiest periods of the Uruguay Round, the 113 Committee would meet daily when necessary. At the lower level, the composition of the Committee would vary depending on the issues to be discussed.[218] While it usually met in Brussels, the 113 Committee also regularly convened in Geneva, in order to be as close as possible to the Commission's negotiators at crucial moments during the negotiations.

The role of the 113 Committee during the Uruguay Round negotiations was very significant.[219] The close collaboration between the Commission and the 113 Committee was at the core of the Community's negotiating system during the Uruguay Round, and contributed significantly to the Round's eventual success. However, it is important for a correct understanding of the role of the 113 Committee to stress that this committee had in fact only an advisory role. Its task was not to issue binding instructions to the Commission but 'to assist' the latter.

The Committee has been very pointedly described as a 'two-way transmission belt for information' for the Member States and a 'sounding board' for the Commission.[220] One must remember that in most informal negotiating sessions, the Member States would not be present during the negotiations, and therefore it was basically through the 113 Committee (and informal talks with other delegations in Geneva) that the Member States were kept informed about the details of the negotiations.[221] It was also the 113 Committee which offered the Member States a forum to voice their national positions on any of the issues covered by the ongoing negotiations. The Commission, for its part, used the 113 Committee to try out the acceptability of new ideas and tentative negotiation results. The Commission obviously had no interest in achieving results unacceptable to the Council. In the context of the Uruguay Round, the Commission therefore tried to reach a *consensus* in the 113 Committee on all new ideas or tentative results which it submitted. In view of its position on the scope of the Community's competence and the applicability of Article 113 EEC, the Commission could have been satisfied with qualified majority support

---

[217] See Kuijper, 'EC's Common Commercial Policy' at 295.

[218] Note that at the start of the negotiations, the Council explicitly established an ad hoc Committee for Services, which operated in the same way as the 113 Committee and was often referred to as the '113 Services Committee'.

[219] See Kuijper, 'EC's Common Commercial Policy' at 295.

[220] Ibid. The 113 Committee is also referred to as 'the mothers-in-law' (see Bourgeois, 'The EC in the WTD and Advisory Op. 1/94', at 763).   [221] See above.

in the 113 Committee. However, in the light of the Council's rejection of this position, and the fact that it had a mandate to negotiate for both the Community and the Member States, the Commission sought consensus rather than qualified majority support. Obviously, this did not facilitate the negotiations, but this consensus approach within the 113 Committee was very helpful in keeping the Community together throughout the negotiations.

Now and then, a Member State was seen to take positions and voice opinions which were not in line with those of the Commission. Occasionally, a Member State also bluntly and publicly castigated the Commission for the manner in which it was conducting the negotiations on a specific issue. The media seldom failed to report and thicken these incidents. For the sake of brevity, I will mention only two examples.[222] In October 1992, Mr Heseltine, the British Secretary for Trade and Industry and, at the time, the Council's president-in-office, accused Commission President Delors of having French 'sympathies', and not making enough of an effort to iron out the differences relating to agricultural subsidies, which were threatening the outcome of the Uruguay Round.[223] In September 1993, at the height of the debate on the Commission's mandate to re-negotiate the Blair House Accord, Mr Juppé, the French foreign minister, was quoted as saying about Sir Leon Brittan, the chief negotiator, that '*Nous ne vous faisons pas confiance, nous ne vous avons jamais fait confiance, et nous ne vous ferons jamais confiance.* We don't have confidence in you, we have never had confidence in you, and we never will have confidence in you'.[224]

These and other incidents reflect a genuine (mutual) lack of confidence between the Commission and the Member States, in particular over institutional matters and competence. At the same time, however, some of these incidents were definitely orchestrated, either to mollify public opinion back home, or to put pressure on the Commission and/or the other Member States. It is important to observe that such incidents never occurred at any of the negotiating sessions, and that none of the Member States openly challenged the Commission's role as sole negotiator by starting parallel negotiations.[225] The consensus approach of the Commission within the 113 Committee can be credited with this astounding success.

In view of the Commission's steady search for a consensus within the 113 Committee, it is fair to say that the Commission was in fact continually negotiating on two fronts. It was negotiating on the home front with the Member States, and on the external front with the other participants in the Uruguay Round. The latter were not always the more difficult negotiations.

---

[222] For some other examples, see above.   [223] *Europe*, 24 Oct. 1992, 6.
[224] *Le Figaro*, 27 Sept. 1993, 8.   [225] See also S. 2.1.1.

The interests of the Member States were frequently in conflict and difficult to reconcile. The European Community was often split between a free-trading bloc led by Germany and the United Kingdom, and a protectionist-leaning rump led by France. The job of the chief Commission negotiator therefore required 'the skill of juggler and tight-rope walker'.[226] He had to balance the Member States' conflicting interests while following the guidelines and directives issued by the Council. At the same time he had to show non-member countries that he had the flexibility to negotiate and ultimately deliver a deal. It has been said that 'this is a shade more complicated than the hand played by Mr Kantor'.[227]

When there was no consensus within the 113 Committee, the Commission was in fact considerably handicapped in its negotiations with non-member countries. Non-member countries often knew about the absence of consensus within the 113 Committee; and the Commission's negotiating ability was thus curtailed. On the other hand, when a consensus did exist, the Commission often tried to keep non-member countries guessing as long as possible about the nature and the limits of the consensus reached in the 113 Committee. In such a case, putting anything down on paper was intentionally avoided so that the Commission could 'play its hand' as craftily as possible.

For the sake of clarity, I would like to note that the *currently* applicable rules on the negotiation of agreements by the Commission, as laid down in Articles 228 (1) and 113 (3) EC, have not changed much from the rules which were applicable throughout most of the Uruguay Round.[228] However, the rules with regard to Council voting on decisions relating to the conduct of negotiations have become more complex since the entry into force of the Maastricht Treaty. Decisions on the authorization to open negotiations, on negotiating directives, and on the appointment of special '113 type' committees, are in most cases taken by qualified majority.[229] But, the Council acts by unanimity when the negotiations concern an association agreement within the meaning of Article 238 EC, or a field for which unanimity is required for the adoption of internal rules.[230] The opening of negotiations on fiscal matters, the free movement of persons and the rights and interests of employed persons, for example, thus require unanimity in the Council.

2.3.1.4 The position of the European Parliament

Before discussing the conclusion of the Uruguay Round Agreements by the European Community, I would like to make some observations

---

[226] *Financial Times*, 18 Dec. 1993, 8.   [227] Ibid.   [228] See n. 148.
[229] Art. 228 (1) EC, 2nd subpara.
[230] Ibid., 2nd subpara. *juncto* Art. 228 (2) EC.

concerning the role played by the European Parliament during the negotiations.[231] It should be noted that neither in the Treaty provisions applicable until 1 November 1993[232] nor those applicable since that time,[233] is the European Parliament explicitly attributed any role in the context of the authorization of negotiations, the adoption of the negotiating directives or the decisions on the monitoring of the negotiations. However, on the basis of the 1964 Luns-I[234] and 1973 Luns-II[235] procedures, as well as the Solemn Declaration on European Union of the Stuttgart European Council of 1983 (the Stuttgart Declaration),[236] the Parliament is, in practice, involved in the negotiations of international agreements. Though the legal nature of these arrangements is unclear, there is no contention that they carry considerable political weight. Some authors argue that the Parliament is thus able to exert influence on the course of the negotiations.[237] It is both puzzling and unfortunate that neither the Single

---

[231] The influence on the negotiations of the Economic and Social Council, the Community advisory body consisting of representatives of the various categories of economic and social activity, has been so marginal that it does not deserve special attention. It is interesting to note that economic and other interest groups often voiced their concerns through more direct channels. By way of example, one could refer to the numerous statements made by UNICE, COPA and BEUC (see *Europe*, 13/14 Jan. 1992, 14 and *Europe*, 11 Dec. 1993, 15).

[232] Arts. 113 (3) or 228 (1) EEC.

[233] Art. 228 (1) EC and Art. 113 (3) EC.

[234] With regard to association agreements within the meaning of Art. 238 EC, the Council had already agreed (on 25 Feb. 1964) to the so-called Luns-I procedure. Under this procedure, the Parliament can organize a debate before the beginning of the negotiations. More importantly, the Commission will, throughout the negotiations, maintain close contacts with the competent parliamentary committees and inform the latter on the development of the negotiations. Finally, at the end of the negotiations, but before the agreement is signed, the Council confidentially and unofficially will inform the competent parliamentary committees of the substance of the agreement. See Louis, 'EEC and the Tokyo Round', at 32.

[235] On 15 Oct. 1973 the Council agreed with regard to trade agreements within the meaning of Art. 113 EC to the so-called Luns-II or Westerterp procedure (See Bull. EC 5-1982, 2.4.2. and 2.4.3.). Under this procedure, the Council will inform the competent Parliamentary committees before the beginning of the negotiations and the Parliament can organize a debate based on this information. At the end of the negotiation but before the signing, the Council will inform confidentially and unofficially the competent Parliamentary committees of the essence of the agreement. Finally, after the signing but before the conclusion, the Council will officially inform the Parliament of the content of the agreement. The latter does not really concern the Parliament's involvement in the negotiation of the agreements any more since the negotiations are already finished at that point in time. It concerns more the Parliament's involvement in the conclusion of the agreements. See below. Note that under the Luns-II procedure the Commission is not explicitly instructed to inform the competent Parliamentary committees of the progress of the negotiations.

[236] According to the Stuttgart Declaration the European Parliament is to be informed on a confidential and informal basis on all international agreements of significant importance. Subsequent to this Declaration, it has gradually become normal practice for the European Parliament to be briefed throughout the negotiations of an agreement of any significance. See Bull. EC 6–1983, 2.3.7. The Commission will give confidential briefings to the competent Parliamentary committees and in particular the Committee on External Relations.

[237] T. C. Hartley, *The Foundations of European Community Law: an Introduction to the Constitutional and Adminstrative Law of the European Community* (1994), 167. As Hartley

European Act nor the Treaty on European Union amended Article 228 so as to 'associate' the European Parliament to the negotiations of international agreements. It is to be hoped that such a step will be taken in the context of the 1996 Intergovernmental Conference, so that the involvement of the Parliament will have a firmer legal basis than it currently has.[238]

In the context of the Uruguay Round specifically, the Parliament was 'involved' in the negotiations under the Luns-II procedure and the Stuttgart Declaration. Pursuant to the former arrangement, the European Parliament was informed of the impending negotiations prior to the Council's decision authorizing the Commission to open the negotiations. On the basis of this information, the Parliament held a debate and adopted a resolution on the opening of the Uruguay Round on 9 September 1986, in which it outlined its expectations.[239] Under the terms of the Stuttgart Declaration, the Parliament's Committee on External Relations, known as the REX Committee, regularly received confidential briefings from the Commission throughout the negotiations. The Parliament discussed the Uruguay Round in plenary session on many occasions, and adopted a number of Resolutions stating its position on the substance and progress of the negotiations.[240] Apart from holding debates followed by Resolutions, the Parliament also made good use of its right to ask both the Council and the Commission specific questions (oral and written) on the progress of the negotiations.

While perhaps little more than a *fait divers*, it is nevertheless interesting to note that in November 1992, some Members of the European Parliament who belonged to the Green group, who were later joined by MEPs from three other political groups, tabled a motion of censure against the Commission pursuant to Article 144 EEC. They argued that the

points out this is especially true where the agreement cannot be concluded without the assent of the European Parliament.

[238] It should be noted, however, that such parliamentary involvement in the negotiations of international agreements is not customary in many Member States.

[239] Bull. EC 9–1986, 2.4.11.

[240] It serves no purpose to list all Parliamentary Resolutions on the Uruguay Round but by way of example I would like to refer to the resolution of 26 Oct. 1988 on international trade in services in which it welcomed the negotiations on trade in services taking place in the Uruguay Round ([1988] OJ, C309), the resolution of 16 Dec. 1988 on the state of GATT negotiations at the mid-term Ministerial Meeting in Montreal earlier that month, in which it welcomed the substantial progress achieved in many areas while regretting the lack of progress in the field of agriculture ([1989] OJ, C12), the resolution of 11 June 1991 on the renewal of the Multifibre Agreement and the need for a productive outcome in the Uruguay Round negotiations on textiles ([1991] OJ, C183), the resolution of 17 Dec. 1992 on the agreement on agriculture reached between the US and the Community in November 1992 (Blair House Accord) ([1993] OJ, C21) and, as a final example, the resolution of 30 Sept. 1993 on the state of the Uruguay Round negotiations, in which it endorsed the Blair House Accord but called for clarifications, amplifications and additions, and in which it also backed the 'cultural exception' and Europe's desire to preserve and defend its cultural identity ([1993] OJ, C279).

Commission, by agreeing to the Blair House Accord, had gone beyond the mandate entrusted to it by the Council, and had called into question the common agricultural policy as reformed in May 1992.[241] The motion did, not, however, get much support, and the Parliament had no trouble rejecting it.[242]

Finally, it should be noted that the European Parliament was also represented by delegations at the ministerial conferences in Montreal (December 1988), Brussels (December 1990) and Marrakesh (April 1994). The MEPs taking part in the Community's delegation to these conferences had only an observer status and could not actively participate in the negotiations. Nevertheless, the latter gave the Parliament increased access to confidential information on the progress of the negotiations, and gave its 'trade specialists' an opportunity to get to know the Community's top negotiators better. The participation in these meetings encouraged and contributed to a productive dialogue between the Parliament, on the one hand, and the Council and the Commission, on the other.[243]

Whereas the Parliament has obviously monitored the Uruguay Round negotiations carefully, and has made its views known to the Council and the Commission on many issues, its leverage has not been very large with regard to the conduct of the negotiations. Considering the fact that, during the last stages of the negotiations, it should have been clear that the Parliament would eventually have to give its assent to the Uruguay Round Agreements, one might have expected the Parliament to play a more prominent role.[244] It has been stated that further integration of the European Parliament into the negotiation process may lead to 'complicated three-way negotiations among the Council, the Commission and the European Parliament and will *not* make the Community into an easy and incisive negotiator'.[245] Though this may be true in some cases, it would nevertheless be unwise of both the Commission and the Council to try to 'minimize' the involvement of the Parliament in the negotiating process, and take its assent for granted. With regard to the negotiations of Agreements which require the Parliament's assent, I am convinced that, in the future, the European Parliament will become more assertive during the negotiations of such agreements, and exercise greater influence than it did during the Uruguay Round negotiations.

---

[241] *Europe*, 28 Nov. 1992, 14 and *Europe*, 4 Dec. 1992, 5.

[242] *Europe*, 19 Dec. 1992, 13. Such a motion of censure needs a ⅔ majority of the votes cast, representing a majority of the MEPs.

[243] See Report on the proposal for a Council Dec. concerning the conclusion of the results of the Uruguay Round of multilateral trade negotiations (1986–94), PE 208.961/fin, 5.

[244] On the need for the Parliament's assent to the Uruguay Round Agreements, see Ss. 2.2.1. and 2.2.4.

[245] See Kuijper 'EC's Common Commercial Policy' at 297. Emphasis added.

2.3.2 The conclusion of the Uruguay Round Agreements by the European Community.

2.3.2.1 A brief analysis of Article 228 (2) and (3) EC

Since November 1993, international agreements, including agreements such as the Uruguay Round Agreements, shall, *to the extent they fall within the Community's competence*, be concluded by the Council pursuant to Article 228 (2) EC.[246] Most international agreements shall be concluded by qualified majority on a proposal from the Commission.[247] The Council shall, however, act by unanimity when concluding an association agreement under Article 238 EC, and when concluding an agreement concerning a field for which unanimity is required for the adoption of internal rules.[248]

As a general rule, the Council merely needs to consult the European Parliament before concluding an international agreement.[249] The Parliament's opinion is not binding on the Council, and therefore carries little, if any, weight. Moreover, if the Parliament fails to deliver its opinion within the time-limit laid down by the Council, the latter can conclude the agreement without the Parliament's opinion.[250] Note that for trade agreements within the meaning of Article 113 EC, the consultation of the Parliament is not provided for in Article 228 (3) EC or any other Treaty provision, but constitutes a firmly established practice under the Luns-II procedure and the Stuttgart Declaration, both mentioned above.[251] It is a mystery why the Treaty does not provide for parliamentary consultation on trade agreements, especially in view of the limited leverage this right of consultation gives to the Parliament.[252]

As an exception to the general rule, outlined above, some agreements,

---

[246] Note, however, that this provision gives the Council this power to conclude agreements 'subject to the powers vested in the Commission in this field'. The scope of these powers vested in the Commission was the central issue in case C–327/91, *France* v. *Commission*, an Art. 173 action for annulment against an agreement concluded by the Commission with the government of the US concerning the application of competition law. In its judgment of 9 Aug. 1994, the Court ruled on the basis of a restrictive interpretation of the words 'subject to the powers vested in the Commission', that the Commission has only in very exceptional situations—and not in the case in question—the power to conclude an international agreement. In practice, however, there are more situations in which the Commission concludes international agreements, often in the form of exchange of letters. In the field of food aid to developing countries, for example, the Commission concludes since the seventies the supply agreements with the beneficiary countries or international organizations. While of doubtful legality, nobody seems to mind.   [247] Art. 228 (2) EC.

[248] Ibid.   [249] Art. 228 (3), first para., EC.   [250] Ibid.

[251] See S. 2.1.4.

[252] A likely explanation may be the fear of having to involve the European Parliament in the adoption process of even the most technical tariff or sectoral agreement.

however, can only be concluded by the Council after the assent of the European Parliament. As it stipulated in the second subparagraph of Article 228 (3) EC, this is the case for

1. association agreements within the meaning of Article 238 EC;
2. agreements, other than association agreements, establishing a specific institutional framework by organizing cooperation procedures;
3. agreements having important budgetary implications for the Community; and
4. agreements entailing amendment of an act adopted under the co-decision procedure (Article 189b EC).[253]

2.3.2.2 The signing of the Marrakesh Final Act

Seven years and three months after the Uruguay Round negotiations had been launched in Punta del Este, the Trade Negotiations Committee formally closed the negotiations at its meeting in Geneva on 15 December 1993, and adopted the Final Act Embodying the Results of the Uruguay Round of Multilateral Trade Negotiations.[254] Sir Leon Brittan 'agreed' to the Final Act on behalf of the European Community and the Union's Member States. On the same day, the Council unanimously gave its broad approval to the overall package agreed upon in Geneva.[255] During the week preceding the conclusion of the negotiations, the Commission negotiators had been careful to keep the Council promptly informed on the details of the evolving deal.[256]

While 15 December 1993 marked the formal conclusion of the negotiations, it should be noted that further discussions were needed until the end of March 1994, in order to reach agreement on a number of technical issues (relating in particular to market access) which were left pending in December 1993.[257] It was only when these issues were resolved that the Final Act was ready to be signed.

---

[253] Art. 228 (3), third para., EC. Note that the Council and the European Parliament may, in an urgent situation, agree upon a time-limit for the assent.

[254] Bull. EC 12–1993, 1.3.99.

[255] See e.g. *Financial Times*, 16 Dec. 1993, 1 and *Europe*, 16 Dec. 1993, 7.

[256] See e.g. *Europe*, 13/14 Dec. 1993, 5. In his report to the Council of 13 Dec. 1993, Sir Leon stated that: 'The global assessment of the result which can be made at this point, while awaiting the detailed analysis currently being made . . . shows that the major aims which have led Community action over the last seven years of negotiations have been attained in a globally satisfactory way' (Ibid.). The Community's chief negotiator did point out, however, that pressure had to be kept up to obtain acceptable results especially with regard to trade in textiles, financial services, audio-visual services and the establishment of the WTO. At the same Council meeting Mr Steichen set out the results for agriculture.

[257] Among the issues left pending in Dec. 1993 were the schedules of tariff commitments (market access) and the schedules of initial specific commitments in the area of services (see

The Final Act was formally signed on 15 April 1994, at the Ministerial Conference in Marrakesh. As already noted above, the Council and the representatives of the Member States, disregarding strong objections on the part of the Commission, had decided at a meeting on 7 and 8 March 1994 that the Final Act would have to be signed by both the Community and the Member States.[258] Consequently, the Final Act was signed, on the one hand, by Mr Pangalos, the Council's president-in-office, and Commissioner Brittan, on behalf of the European Community and, on the other hand, by representatives of the Member States on behalf of their respective governments. In the run-up to the Conference, the European Parliament had adopted, on 24 March 1994 and after a debate on the report on the Uruguay Round by Mr Stavou, a lengthy Resolution in which it expressed an opinion in favour of the evolving deal.[259]

The signing of the Final Act by the Community and the Members States was, however, not without its problems. It was only in the morning of 15 April 1994 that the Member States managed to iron out their internal dispute over banana imports. The Commission had inserted offers on bananas in the Community's schedule of tariff concessions; and had outlined in the remarks to the schedule the deal on the import of bananas which it had negotiated with Latin-American banana exporting countries. Though France, Spain and the United Kingdom welcomed and supported the deal on the import of bananas, Germany and some other Member States [260] were very much opposed to this deal, since they considered that it could be seen as an implicit recognition of the new regulation on common organization of the market in bananas, the validity of which was being

---

COM(94) 143 final, 1a). These issues were the subject of further discussion (see e.g. *Europe*, 7/8 Feb. 1994, 5, on further negotiations with Japan in order to obtain further tariff concessions for leather, shoes and alcohol, and with other Asian countries over textiles). On 24 Feb. 1994 the Commission submitted the Community's concessions on market access in Geneva but did so with a reservation: the Community lists were only valid if the concessions made by the other countries fully conformed with what was agreed on 15 Dec. 1993 (*Europe*, 25 Feb. 1994, 8). At its meeting of 7 and 8 Mar. 1994, the Council came to the conclusion that the final offers of the US might compromise the expected balance of mutual concessions agreed to on 15 Dec. 1993 and therefore need readjustment of the Community's schedules (*Europe*, 9 Mar. 1994, 9). Eventually the European Community revised slightly downwards its offers on lorries and on copper to meet a decrease in certain American offers (*Europe*, 11/12 Apr. 1994, 5).

[258] The Council reportedly already reached an agreement on this issue at an informal meeting of the trade ministers in Athens on 7 Feb. 1994 (*Europe*, 7/8 Feb. 1994, 5). This agreement was endorsed by the General Affairs Council on 21 Feb. 1994 (*Europe*, 21/22 Feb. 1994, 5). Other sources, however, seem to indicate that the issue had not yet been settled before the meeting of 7 and 8 Mar. 1994 (*Europe*, 5 Mar. 1994, 8).

[259] *Europe*, 25 Mar. 1994, 10. The European Parliament did, however, make several critical remarks concerning, in particular, agriculture, services and the position of developing countries. Note also that Members of the European Parliament took part in the Community delegation to the Marrakesh Conference. See S. 2.1.4.

[260] Belgium, The Netherlands, Denmark, Luxemburg and Ireland.

challenged before the Court. Germany's concern about the consequences of the inclusion of the offers on bananas, and the deal on the import of bananas, was such that it expressed doubts about its willingness to sign the Final Act.[261] While Community officials considered it unthinkable that the signature of the Final Act could at the eleventh hour be jeopardized by this dispute over bananas,[262] there was definitely a feeling of crisis in the air. It was only a few hours before the midday deadline on 15 April 1994, that the Member States reached a compromise which—without resolving the controversy as to its substance—satisfied both Germany and France and their respective allies. Both sides were guaranteed that their conflicting positions on the Community's banana regime would not be affected at this stage by the fact that they had signed the Uruguay Round Agreements.[263]

Another last minute problem arose when all twelve Member States rejected the Commission's suggestion that the European Community and the Member States would sign under a collective rubric.[264] In an embarrassing and futile show of dissension, the Member States insisted that they follow the overall alphabetical order of the list of GATT delegations. As a result, France's signature preceded Gabon's, the Netherlands followed Namibia, and the United Kingdom followed the United Arab Emirates.

Not directly related to the signing itself, but also a source of controversy at the Marrakesh Conference, were the statements Sir Leon Brittan and the Member States' ministers would make, and in particular their emphasis on the need to strive in the future for the inclusion of minimum labour standards in WTO trade provisions. The Commission took the position that the inclusion of such standards in trade provisions should be taken into consideration, but that developing countries should be given guarantees that this will not have protectionist effects.[265] The Council decided, however, that the statement the Commission would make in Marrakesh had first to be approved unanimously by the Council.[266] In reaction, the Commission insisted that the statements by Member States' ministers would be discussed and approved by the Commission.

A clear indication of the fact that the relationship between the Commission and (some of) the Member States regarding international economic relations was likely to remain troublesome in the future, was given by Mr Longuet, France's industry minister. In the context of the

---

[261] *Europe*, 15 Apr. 1994, 6. In reaction to the German objections to the offers on bananas, France threatened to block the adoption of the agreement on public procurement.

[262] Ibid., 6.   [263] *Europe*, 16 Apr. 1994, 6.

[264] *Financial Times*, 14 Apr. 1994, 5. In the official GATT list of delegations the Member States and the European Communities were also grouped together.

[265] *Europe*, 11/12 Apr. 1994, 5. The Commission also maintained that it will not question differences in salaries between rich and poor countries.

[266] *Europe*, 21/22 Feb. 1994, 5.

Marrakesh Conference, the latter had a high profile bilateral meeting with Mr Kantor *before* Sir Leon Brittan had a chance to meet the American trade negotiator, and afterwards informed the assembled press of France's position on the major issues in international economic relations. When questioned on the admissibility of this exercise in freelance diplomacy, the French minister pointed out that the Member States were entitled to act independently in all these areas which were not covered by the Community's exclusive competence. He openly admitted, however, that he would have a difficult time stating exactly what does and what does not fall within the scope of this exclusive competence.[267]

2.3.2.3 The Commission's proposal on the conclusion of the Uruguay Round Agreements

By signing the Final Act, the Community and the Member States agreed to submit the Uruguay Round Agreements to their competent authorities for approval and final conclusion, in accordance with their respective procedures.[268] Pursuant to the first subparagraph of Article 228 (3) EC, international agreements are concluded by the Council *on a proposal* from the Commission. On the very day the Final Act was signed, the Commission therefore adopted a 'Proposal for a Council decision concerning the conclusion of the results of the Uruguay Round of Multilateral Trade Negotiations', and submitted this proposal to the Council.[269] The Commission thus formally recommended the Council to adopt:

1. the WTO Agreement and its Annexes 1 to 4;
2. the ministerial declarations and decisions included in the Final Act;
3. the Understanding on Commitments in Financial Services; and
4. the Bovine Meat Agreement with Uruguay.

In line with the position it had consistently taken, and which was also reflected in its request for an Opinion to the European Court of Justice, the Commission suggested in its proposal that the Council should conclude all Uruguay Round Agreements on the basis of Article 113 EC.

Furthermore, it indicated that, pursuant to the second subparagraph of Article 228 (3) EC, the Uruguay Round Agreements would need the assent of the European Parliament. The latter was in fact hard to dispute. The Uruguay Round Agreements, and in particular the pivotal WTO Agreement, obviously established a specific institutional framework. It

---

[267] *Financial Times*, 14 Apr. 1994, 5.
[268] By signing the Final Act they also agreed to adopt the Ministerial Declarations and Decisions.   [269] COM(94) 143 final.

could also have been argued that the Uruguay Round Agreements have 'important budgetary consequences' due to the reduction in tariff revenue, and therefore need the assent of the Parliament. However, it was and still is very disputed *how* important these budgetary consequences really have to be in this context. The latter was therefore not advanced as a reason for seeking the Parliament's assent.

2.3.2.4 The assent of the European Parliament to the Uruguay Round Agreements

In its Resolution of 19 January 1994, which was adopted after having been informed by the Commission of the conclusion of the negotiations, the European Parliament had called upon the Council to submit the Uruguay Round Agreements to it as soon as possible, so it could apply the assent procedure before the European Parliament elections of June 1994. The MEPs, who for years had followed the Uruguay Round negotiations, understandably wanted to finish the job, by giving Parliament's assent to the Agreements. However, the Council failed to submit the request for assent to the Parliament until October 1994,[270] and the outgoing Parliament was therefore—in the absence of a request thereto—unable to give its assent. This did not prevent the Parliament, during the closing months of its term, from adopting a number of resolutions in which it both expressed its generally positive reaction to the Uruguay Round results, and made critical observations on some specific issues.[271]

The reason for the delay in the submission of the request for assent was to be found in the disagreement among the Member States regarding the correct legal basis for the Council decision to conclude the Uruguay Round Agreements.[272] Pursuant to Article 189a EC, unanimity was required to change the legal basis proposed by the Commission and this unanimity could not be found. While most Member States strongly disagreed with the

---

[270] *Europe*, 5 Oct. 1994, 6–7.

[271] See European Parliament Resolution, 24 Mar. 1994, on the Uruguay Round results in general [1994] OJ, C114/25, European Parliament Resolution, 9 Feb. 1994, on the introduction of a social clause in the unilateral and multilateral trading system [1994] OJ, C61/89 (see also *Europe*, 10 Feb. 1994, 14) and European Parliament Resolution, 24 Mar. 1994, embodying the recommendations of the European Parliament to the Commission concerning negotiations in the Trade Negotiations Committee of the GATT on an agreement on a Trade and Environment Work Programme [1994] OJ, C114/35.

[272] There has been some discussion on whether it would not suffice to obtain the assent of the Parliament on the agreements only and not also on the Council's decision on the conclusion of the agreements. Somewhat surprisingly, the REX Committee of the Parliament was in favour of such a 'restricted request' for assent. The Legal Service of the Council, however, objected to this. (See further: Kuijper, P.-J., 'The conclusion and implementation of the Uruguay Round results by the European Community', (1995) 6 EYIL 222–244, at 229.

Commission's choice of Article 113 as the sole legal basis, Belgium reportedly sided with the Commission. It made little sense to ask the Parliament for its assent on the unamended Commission proposal, because the Council would then be obliged to repeat its request for assent once the legal basis was modified. The Council remained deadlocked on the issue of the appropriate legal basis until the beginning of October 1994, when the Member States in the Council decided—by way of compromise solution, and subject to change in the light of the impending Opinion 1/94—to add Articles 43, 54, 57, 66, 75, 84 (2), 99, 100, 100a and 235 EC to the legal bases already provided for in the Commission's proposal. Furthermore, it was explicitly stated that the results of the Uruguay Round would be concluded as a mixed agreement. Unanimous agreement on a modified Commission proposal having been reached, the Council was finally able to ask the European Parliament for its assent on 4 October 1994.[273]

At the first plenary session after the Court's decision in Opinion 1/94, and with the deadline for ratification of 31 December 1994 rapidly approaching, the European Parliament gave its assent to the Uruguay Round Agreements and the proposal for a Council Decision concerning the conclusion of the Agreements on 14 December 1994.[274] Having regard to its favourable resolution of 24 March 1994 adopted in the run-up to the Marrakesh Conference, as referred to above, and the report of Mrs Randzio-Plath of the REX Committee,[275] as well as to the opinions of other Parliamentary committees,[276] the Parliament gave its assent by an overwhelming vote of 327 for, 65 against and 13 abstentions.[277] This vote clearly reflected the widespread support for the Uruguay Round Agreements. Nevertheless, the Parliament made it quite clear, during the debate that preceded the vote and in a resolution adopted the day after,

---

[273] *Europe*, 5 Oct. 1994, 6.

[274] Since the official request for assent was submitted so late, the European Parliament was not given much time to consider the Uruguay Round Agreements and the proposal for a Decision on the conclusion of these agreements. It should be noted, however, that the agreements were of course not unknown to the Parliament. It had already adopted a number of Resolutions on them (see above). Also note that in the context of the Tokyo Round, the European Parliament had not been able to discuss the results of the Round in detail at all. It only had a few days to study the final report on the negotiations before it was to give its opinion (Louis, 'EEC and the Tokyo Round', 42–3).

[275] Report on the proposal for a Council Dec. concerning the conclusion of the results of the Uruguay Round of multilateral trade negotiations (Rapporteur: Mrs. Randzio-Plath), A4–0093/94, PE 208.916/fin.

[276] See Opinions of the Committees on Foreign Affairs, Security and Defence Policy, Budgets; the Environment, Public Health and Consumer Protection; Development Co-operation; and Institutional Affairs. These Opinions were all annexed to the report of the REX Committee (A4–0093/94, PE 208.961/fin and A4–0093/94, PE 208.961/fin, annexes 1 & 2).

[277] [1995] OJ, C18/53. Note that the assent procedure requires an absolute majority of the members or—in Dec. 1994—265 votes.

that its enthusiasm was somewhat qualified at points.[278] The Parliament emphasized, for example, the need for the WTO to link trade issues to environmental, social, consumer and animal protection issues [279] and—of more interest to us here—its own ambition to be closely 'involved' in all activities of the WTO. It considered it to be essential for the Council, the Commission *and* the Parliament to negotiate a code of conduct accurately defining the role of the Community (and the Member States) in the WTO.[280] It also stressed the need for the rule of decision-making by qualified majority on common commercial policy matters to be upheld, as well as the need for the Community to act as one within the WTO, even in areas which are not exclusively the responsibility of the Community.[281] The Parliament also expressed the wish to be represented at the biennial meetings of the WTO's Ministerial Conference by a delegation with observer status, and to be constantly and fully informed by the Commission between meetings.[282] Finally, and not surprisingly, the Parliament insisted that any decision taken within the context of the WTO would require its assent pursuant to the second subparagraph of Article 228 (3) EC.[283]

In his reaction to the criticism voiced during the debate preceding the Parliamentary vote, Sir Leon Brittan, speaking for the Commission, promised that the Parliament would play a role in the work of the WTO, the legal basis of which should be the same as that for the Uruguay Round.[284] He added, however, that the 1996 Intergovernmental Conference should clarify and strengthen the Parliament's role on international negotiations.[285] He also stressed that, in the light of Opinion 1/94, it was now necessary to work together on a code of conduct respecting the principle of Community unity in international representation. Referring to the Community's unfortunate experience in the Food and Agricultural Organization, he stated that a lack of union among the Member States at

---

[278] European Parliament Resolution of 15 Dec. 1994 on the conclusion of the Uruguay Round and the future activities of the WTO, [1995] OJ, C18/165.

[279] European Parliament Resolution, 15 Dec. 1995, paras. 23–9. See also the interventions of Mrs Randzio-Plath, Mr Cassidy, Mr De Clercq and Mr Pimenta during the debate on 14 Dec. 1994 (*Europe*, 16 Dec. 1994, 11–12).

[280] European Parliament Resolution, 15 Dec. 1994, para. 4.

[281] Ibid., paras. 5, 12 & 13. The European Parliament called on the Member States to accept the Commission as the sole representative of the 'Union' in all the areas of activities of the WTO (para. 13).

[282] Ibid., para. 16. It will be recalled that the European Parliament took part in the Community's delegation to all Ministerial conferences of the Uruguay Round negotiations (see above). The Parliament also insisted on the greatest possible transparency of the WTO's activities.   [283] Ibid., para. 16.

[284] This seems to imply that the Parliament would be asked for its assent on all decisions taken within the WTO since the legal basis for the Parliament's role in the Uruguay Round was the second subpara. of Art. 228 (3) EC.

[285] *Europe*, 16 Dec. 1994, 11.

international level is dangerous, and may be exploited by others.[286] He expressed full support for Parliamentary representation in the Community's delegation to the meetings of the WTO Ministerial Conference,[287] and the belief that meetings and hearings should be organized in order to ensure the full participation of the Parliament. In his opinion, this involvement is not only 'right' but also 'helpful'.[288] The Commissioner stated that 'he did not see why, if Mickey Kantor says he must absolutely do or ask what Senator so-and-so is pushing him to do, he could not say the same thing about requests from MEPs'.[289]

As the final vote on the assent indicated, there was within the Parliament a small minority opposed to the Uruguay Round Agreements. This group was predominately made up of the Greens, the ultra-right National Front, and French Socialists.[290] One of the more colourful opponents was Sir James Goldsmith, who accused the REX Committee of acting as a lobbyist and agent for importers, and of selling out Europe's industry and agriculture. Another member opposed to the agreements, Mr Lang, a former French Minister of Culture, condemned the GATT system which he believed sanctions American hegemony and the economic, banking and industrial dominance of multinational companies. For him it was therefore 'no and no' again to the Uruguay Round Agreements.[291] Such views were, however, held only by a few.[292]

2.3.2.5 The conclusion of the Uruguay Round Agreements by the Council

On 19 December 1994, five days after the Parliament's assent, the Council reached a political agreement on the conclusion of the Uruguay Round Agreements, and on 22 December 1994 it formally adopted Council Decision 94/800/EC, concerning 'the conclusion on behalf of the European Community, as regards matters within its competence, of the Agreements

---

[286] Ibid., 12.

[287] Questioned on the same point, Mr Eekhoff, President-in-office of the Council, also came out in support of Parliamentary representation in the Community's delegation to the meetings of the WTO Ministerial Conference (*Europe*, 15 Dec. 1994, 13.)

[288] *Europe*, 15 Dec. 1994, 12. Note that the position of Sir Leon on Parliamentary involvement deviates from the 'traditional', more reserved position of the Commission.

[289] Ibid., 12

[290] *Europe*, 14 Dec. 1994, 11. The Greens asked for the vote to be postponed because they felt that it would not be right to give assent without knowing exactly what the Uruguay Round agreements would mean for e.g. social matters or the environment.

[291] *Europe*, 16 Dec. 1994, 12.

[292] Note that on 23 Nov. 1994 the Social and Economic Committee also delivered a positive opinion on the proposed Decision to conclude the Uruguay Round Agreements.

reached in the Uruguay Round multilateral negotiations (1986–94)' ('the Decision on the conclusion').[293] At the same time the Council also adopted the implementing legislation, which I discuss below.[294]

As proposed by the Commission, the Decision on the conclusion concerned the WTO Agreement and its Annexes 1 to 4, the ministerial declarations and decisions and the Understanding on Commitments in Financial Services which appear in the Uruguay Round Final Act, and, finally, the bilateral Agreement Bovine Meat with Uruguay. Sharply departing from the Commission's proposal, however, the Decision on the conclusion was based on Articles 43, 54, 57, 66, 75, 84 (2), 99, 100, 100a, 113 and 235 EC, in conjunction with the second subparagraph of Article 228 (3) EC, and explicitly indicated that not all matters covered by the agreements and acts concerned are within the competence of the Community.[295] While hardly surprising, it is interesting to note that the Council obviously felt the need to include in the preamble of the Decision a fairly elaborate justification of the legal bases invoked, as well as of the fact that the agreements were also to be concluded by the Member States.[296] The Council first of all recalled the general rules concerning the Community's external competence. It stated that the competence of the Community to conclude international agreements does not derive only from explicit conferral by the Treaty, but may also derive from other provisions of the Treaty, and from acts adopted pursuant to those provisions by Community institutions. It further stated that where Community rules have been adopted in order to achieve the aims of the Treaty, Member States may not, outside the framework of the common institutions, enter into commitments liable to affect these rules or alter their scope.[297] The Council then observed that a portion of the commitments contained in the Uruguay Round agreements falls within the competence of the Community under Article 113 EC, and that of the remainder of the commitments *some* affect Community rules adopted on the basis of Articles 43, 54, 57, 66, 75, 84 (2), 99, 100, 100a and 235 EC, and could therefore only be entered into by the Community alone. Finally,

---

[293] [1994] OJ, L336/1.

[294] See S. 2.2.3.

[295] See Arts. 1 (1), 2 (1) and 3 (1) of Council Dec. 94/800/EC, [1994] OJ, L336/2.

[296] Council Dec. 94/800/EC is reportedly the first decision on the conclusion of an agreement in which it is made explicit that this is an agreement for which the Community is competent only in part and that it is therefore concluded as a mixed agreement (See Kuijper, 'Conclusion and implementation of the Uruguay Round results' at 234–5). Kuijper considers this preambular justification of legal bases undesirable (ibid., 235).

[297] The Council apparently ignored the fact that Op. 1/94 (and before that Op. 2/91 too), dropped the words 'or alter their scope' from the ERTA formula. See S. 1.3.1.

it felt the need to justify in particular the use of Articles 100 and 235 EC, and the absence of Article 73c EC among the legal bases.[298]

It has been argued that, in view of the Court's Opinion 1/94, Articles 43, 99 and 100 EC should not have been mentioned among the legal bases for the Council's Decision.[299] In view of the rapidly approaching deadline for ratification, the Council was, however, unwilling to open the debate on the detailed and technical implications of the Opinion 1/94.

With regard to the WTO Agreement and the agreements annexed to it, the Council authorized its President to designate the person empowered to deposit the instruments of ratification with the Director-General of the GATT, in order to bind the European Community with regard to that portion of the agreements falling within its competence. It had been decided that the Community and the Member States would deposit their respective instruments of ratification simultaneously. By mid-December 1994, Germany, the UK, Ireland and Luxemburg had already completed their national procedure for approval of the Uruguay Round Agreements.[300] France and Belgium were expected to do so on 20 and 22 December 1994, respectively. Greece, Denmark and the Netherlands were also about to complete their national procedures for approval. While both Spain and Portugal had made their approval conditional on the results of the Fisheries Council of December 1994 and a Community statement on Textiles respectively, they both approved the Agreements in time.[301] Eventually, the European Community and the Member States deposited the instruments of ratification on 30 December 1994. Note, however, that this deposition gave rise to a small incident when the Council Secretariat insisted, against the objections of the Commission, that the instruments of ratification would be deposited in Geneva by *both* representatives of the

---

[298] With regard to the first, the Council pointed out that the Uruguay Round Agreements affect Council Dir. 90/434/EEC of 23 July 1990 on the common system of taxation applicable to mergers, divisions, transfers of assets and exchanges of shares concerning companies of different Member States, and Council Dir. 90/435/EEC of 23 July 1990 on the common system of taxation applicable in the case of parent companies and subsidiaries of different Member States. These two directives were based on Art. 100 EC. With regard to Art. 235 EC, the Council stated the Uruguay Round Agreements affect Council Reg. (EC) No. 40/94, 20 Dec. 1993, on the Community trade mark. With regard to Art. 73c EC, the Council observed that no act in Community law had yet been adopted on the basis of this provision. It has been observed, however, that Art. 73c in fact seems to found both an autonomous and a contractual Community power to act in the field of free movement of capital to or from non-member countries involving direct investment, establishment, the provision of financial services or the admission of securities to capital markets (Kuijper 'Conclusion and implementation of the Uruguay Round results' at 234–5).

[299] Ibid., at 234.

[300] Strictly speaking, the Member States should only have given their approval to that portion of the Uruguay Round Agreements that fell within their competence. However, most Member States did not bother to qualify their approval in this way.

[301] *Europe*, 17 Dec. 1994, 8.

Commission and the Council Secretariat. Austria, Finland and Sweden, which joined the European Union on 1 January 1995, deposited their instruments of ratification during the last days of 1994 as well.

2.3.3 The implementation of the Uruguay Round Agreements by the European Community

To comply with its international commitments under the Uruguay Round agreements, the Community had to implement these agreements in Community law.[302] Some aspects of the latter agreements did not need any implementation, since Community legislation was already in conformity with the relevant provisions of the agreements. With regard to many other aspects, however, the Community had to adopt new or amend existing Community legislation, and had to do this in most cases before 1 January 1995, the date on which the agreements were to enter into force. It should be noted, however, that some of the additions or amendments to Community law, referred to as implementing legislation, were in fact not explicitly required by commitments undertaken by the Community under the Uruguay Round Agreements, but were additions and amendments on which some Member States had insisted in return for their approval of the agreements. This was particularly true for the March 1994 amendments to the Community's legislation, concerning commercial defence instruments.[303] The latter legislation in fact pre-dated the signing of the Final Act, and therefore the undertaking of any international commitment.

2.3.3.1 The March 1994 Regulations on the strengthening of the Community instruments of commercial defence

During the last stages of the negotiations France, supported by its habitual Southern European allies in trade matters, had insisted on the strengthening of Community's trade defence instruments.[304] Germany, the United Kingdom and the Netherlands were opposed to such a strengthening, and they strongly objected to the link between a decision on the latter and the approval of the results of the Uruguay Round.[305] In view of the French insistence, and in order not to jeopardize the conclusion of the Uruguay

---

[302] For an overview of the implementing legislation, see also S. Griller, 'The common commercial policy instruments after the Uruguay Round—with some implications for Austria', in F. Breuss (ed.), *The World Economy after the Uruguay Round*, (1995), 269.
[303] Note also that in order to ensure the support of Portugal, the Council also decided, on 15 Dec. 1993, on aid for the restructuring of the Portuguese textile industry (*Europe*, 16 Dec. 1993, 7).   [304] *Financial Times*, 8 Dec. 1993, 5.
[305] *Europe*, 9 Dec. 1993, 7.

Round negotiations, Germany eventually dropped its longstanding objections against tougher trade defence instruments.[306] Simultaneously with its unanimous approval of the results of the negotiations on 15 December 1993, the Council agreed *by qualified majority* to strengthen the Community's trade defence instruments by making it easier for the Community to decide to act against dumping and subsidized imports and to invoke safeguard measures.[307] Giving effect to this decision, the Council adopted on 7 March 1994 four regulations stipulating a first series of changes to the Community's trade policy measures and concerning in particular:

1. a new Community import procedure, including an improved safeguard clause;[308]
2. amendments to the rules of anti-dumping and countervailing duty procedures in order to speed up these procedures;[309]
3. other improvements in the decision-making procedure in antidumping and other unfair trade cases;[310] and
4. a new procedure for the management of Community quota.[311]

It should be noted, however, that with the adoption of these four regulations, the work on the implementation of the Uruguay Round

---

[306] *Financial Times*, 16 Dec. 1993, 1.

[307] The Council approved a Belgian compromise with Franco–German amendments. The UK and the Netherlands voted against. See *Europe*, 16 Dec. 1994, 7. The link between the approval of the global results of the Round and the strengthening of the trade policy instruments had been politically agreed to at the European Council meeting of 11 & 12 Dec. 1993. During the General Affairs Council on 13 Dec. 1993, Mr Juppé referred to the gentlemen's agreement on this issue reached at the European Council. Mr Hurd was reportedly somewhat perplexed over this commitment and Mr Claes, the president-in-office, suggested he contact Mr Major for confirmation (*Europe*, 13/14 Dec. 1993, 5). The Mar. 1994 amendment makes it easier for the Community to act against dumping and subsidized imports and to invoke safeguard measures. The Commission's preliminary decisions to impose anti-dumping and countervailing duties are made definitive by a simple majority vote. Commission action can therefore no longer be blocked by a 'qualified' minority of free-trade-leaning countries. To block Commission use of safeguard measures against imports from countries with which the Community has preferential arrangements now requires a qualified majority. See *Financial Times*, 16 Dec. 1993, 1.

[308] Council Reg. (EC) No 518/94, 7 Mar. 1994, on common rules for imports and repealing Reg. (EEC) No 288/82, [1994] OJ, L67/77. Note that this regulation was repealed by Council Reg. (EC) No 3285/94, 22 Dec. 1994, [1994] OJ, L349/53. See below.

[309] Council Reg. (EC) No 521/94, 7 Mar. 1994, on the introduction of time-limits for investigation procedures carried out against dumped or subsidized imports from countries not members of the European Community and amending Reg. (EEC) No 2324/88, [1994] OJ, L66/7.

[310] Council Reg. (EC) No 522/94, 7 Mar. 1994, on the streamlining of decision-making procedures for certain Community instruments of commercial defence and amending Reg. (EEC) No 2641/84 and 2423/88, [1994] OJ, L66/10.

[311] Council Reg. (EC) No 520/94, 7 Mar. 1994, establishing a Community procedure for administering quotas, [1994] OJ, L66/1.

Agreements and the legislative changes *required* by the Agreements had not even started in earnest.

2.3.3.2 The Commission's October 1994 proposals for implementing legislation

To implement the Uruguay Round Agreements, the Commission submitted to the Council on 5 October 1994 a total of 10 proposals for additions and amendments to Community legislation 'necessitated' by Uruguay Round Agreements:[312] four proposals concerning commercial defence instruments,[313] two proposals concerning agriculture,[314] two proposals on TRIPs,[315] one proposal concerning pre-shipment inspection,[316] and one proposal concerning textiles.[317] At the same time, the Commission submitted a proposal on the simultaneous entry into force of all the other proposals mentioned here.[318]

The form in which the Commission submitted its draft implementing legislation to the Council was somewhat of a surprise. In the Ministerial Declaration of Punta del Este of September 1986, it was explicitly stated at

---

[312] Provision was made for a proposal on changes to the Common Customs Tariff necessary as a result of the agreed reduction in customs tariffs (see COM(94) 414 final, 13–14), but this proposal was not included in COM(94) 414 final and was eventually not submitted to the Council. See below.

[313] The proposals for Council Regs. on protection against dumped imports from countries not members of the European Community; protection against subsidized imports from countries not members of the European Community; common rules for imports, repealing Reg. (EC) No 518/94; the strengthening of the common commercial policy, in particular with regard to protection against illicit commercial practices and adverse trade effects suffered by Community enterprises, and to the exercise of the Community's rights under international trade rules (COM(94) 414 final, at 158–207, 209–304, 305–31, and 332–57 respectively).

[314] The proposals for a Council Reg. on the adjustment and transitional arrangements required in the agricultural sector in order to implement the agreements concluded during the Uruguay Round of multilateral trade negotiations, COM(94) 414 final, 42–7 and annexes, 53–155, and for a Parliament and Council Reg. amending Council Reg. (EEC) No. 1576/89 laying down general rules on the definition, description and presentation of spirit drinks and Council Reg. (EEC) No 1601/91 laying down general rules on the definition, description and presentation of aromatized wines, aromatized wine-based drinks and aromatized wine-product cocktails following the Uruguay Round of the multilateral trade negotiations, COM(94) 414 final, 49–51.

[315] Proposals for a Council Reg. concerning certain measures to be taken to implement the Agreement on TRIPs in relation to certain modifications of Council Reg. (EC) 40/94 on the Community trade mark, COM(94) 414 final, 363–5, and for a Council Dec. concerning certain measures on the extension of the legal protection of topographies of semiconductor products to persons from a country of the WTO, COM(94) 414 final, 366–7.

[316] Proposal for a Council Dir. on pre-shipment inspection for exports from the Community, ibid., 15–23.

[317] Proposal for a Council Reg. amending Council Reg. (EEC) No 3030/93 of 12 Oct. 1993 on common rules for imports of certain textile products from third countries, Ibid., 27–31.

[318] Ibid., 12–13.

the Community's insistence that 'the launching, the conduct and the *implementation* of the outcome of the negotiations shall be treated as parts of a single undertaking'.[319] Throughout the negotiations, the Council stressed that the result of the Uruguay Round should be a 'comprehensive and balanced outcome' and the Commission insisted that only a global assessment of the result would allow the Uruguay Round's contribution to the Community to be fairly judged.[320] One could have expected that, in order to reflect and underscore the political unity and indivisibility of the Uruguay Round results, all implementing legislation would be laid down in a single legislative act.

When the time had come to draft the necessary implementing legislation, however, the Commission considered it impractical to propose to the Council to adopt all the necessary implementing legislation as a single legislative act. Adopting all implementing legislation in one single act would have a number of serious drawbacks. First of all, such a single legislative act would obviously require a combination of legal bases. Each legal basis would stipulate its own decision-making procedure, but to adopt the single legislative act, the most demanding and laborious procedure would have to be followed. In practical terms, this would mean that for all implementing legislation the co-decision procedure and unanimity in the Council would be required.[321] Secondly, it would complicate the discussion of the proposed implementing legislation in the various Council committees, and further elongate the time-pressed process of approval of the proposed implementing legislation.

At the Council meeting of 15 April 1994 in Marrakesh, the Member States insisted, however, that the Commission should propose the implementing legislation as a single package.[322] This position reflected feelings of mutual distrust, as well as the need to stress—for the 'benefit' of critics and sceptics back home—that the Uruguay Round agreements were a package deal in which the good elements compensated for the bad ones. Reluctantly, the Commission agreed to do so. As Kuijper states, the Commission 'did not believe that it should do as a matter of law what the Council normally does as a matter of politics, namely build legislative packages'.[323]

---

[319] Bull. EC 9–1986, 17 and COM(94) 414 final, 4. Emphasis added.

[320] COM(94) 414 final, 4. The single undertaking approach was eventually reflected in the WTO Agreement which required as a condition of membership of the newly established WTO the acceptance of all multilateral trade agreements (Arts. XI and XII WTO Agreement).

[321] C. W. A. Timmermans, 'L'Uruguay Round: sa mise en oeuvre par la Communauté européenne', (1994) 4 RMUE 176.   [322] *Europe*, 16 Apr. 1994, 6.

[323] See P. J. Kuijper, 'Conclusion and implementation of the Uruguay Round results' at 240. In the explanatory memorandum annexed to the proposals submitted to the Council in

Conscious of the problems the adoption of a single implementing act would give rise to, the Commission looked for a way to mitigate them. Consequently, it submitted to the Council in October 1994, in one single document, all the substantive proposals for implementing acts, held together by a proposal for a Council act on the simultaneous entry into force of the substantive proposals. This decision would embody, in legal form, the political unity of the result of the Uruguay Round.[324] The substantive proposals, all on their own appropriate legal bases, could be discussed separately in the competent Council committee(s), and would each be adopted following the respective procedures. The draft decision on the simultaneous entry into force stipulated Article 113 EC as the appropriate legal basis, and could thus be adopted by qualified majority. The latter was obviously not to the liking of some Member States, who would have preferred this decision to be taken by unanimity. Instead of changing the legal basis to Article 235 EC, however, the Council eventually dropped the proposed decision for the simultaneous entry into force, and abandoned the whole idea of a single legislative package to implement the Uruguay Round results. Instead, a political agreement was reached, to decide at the same time and by unanimity, on both the Decision on the conclusion of the Uruguay Round Agreements and all the legislative acts implementing these Agreements.[325] In the end, therefore, the Council did what it should have done all along, namely 'build a political package instead of requiring the Commission to go through all kinds of legal contortions'.[326] One cannot but regret, however, that while much of the implementing legislation could have been adopted by qualified majority, the Council, in disregard of the Treaty, agreed that unanimity would be needed for the adoption of all implementing legislation. It is hard to say to what extent this influenced the implementing legislation adopted, but it is unlikely that it did not have any influence.

2.3.3.3 The European Parliament's involvement in the adoption of the implementing legislation

At the end of October 1994, the Commission's proposals for additions and amendments to Community legislation necessitated by Uruguay Round Agreements were forwarded to the European Parliament. All but one of

---

Oct. 1994, the Commission gives the impression, however, that it was at its own initiative that it proposed at the Council meeting of 15 Apr. 1994 that the implementing legislation be presented as a whole in the form of a single legislative act (COM(94) 414 final, 4).

[324] COM(94) 414 final, 4–5.
[325] See Timmermans, 'L'Uruguay Round' at 176.
[326] See Kuijper, 'Conclusions and implementation of the Uruguay Round results' at 241.

the proposals were submitted to the European Parliament for its opinion, although the Council was under no legal obligation to do so in respect to the proposals based on Article 113 EC alone.[327] One proposal, however, was based on Articles 43 and 100a EC, and therefore submitted to the Parliament for its approval in accordance with the co-decision procedure of Article 189b EC.[328] The Parliament was very dissatisfied at the fact that these proposals, regarding the legislative changes required by the Uruguay Round Agreements—almost 370 pages of text—had been submitted to it so late that a proper debate on these proposals was made virtually impossible.[329] Nevertheless, on 14 December 1994, the Parliament—simultaneously with its assent to the Uruguay Round Agreements—did provide its opinion on, and, in one case, its approval to the proposed implementing legislation.

Cognizant of the time constraints on the whole ratification and legislative implementation process, the Parliament delivered its opinion in the shortest time possible. The Parliament suggested merely a few amendments to the proposed implementing legislation. These amendments concerned: (1) the annual information for the Parliament on implementing measures; (2) the setting at thirteen months (rather than eighteen months) of the maximum duration of anti-dumping enquiries; and (3) a change in the notion of 'Community interest' for justifying protective measures, in order to take account of 'all interests involved', including those of workers and consumers.[330] It should be recalled that the Council is free to disregard the Parliament's opinion (and often does), but whether in reaction to the opinion or not, it should be noted that the Council did bring down the maximum duration of anti-dumping inquiries to fifteen months.[331]

With regard to the proposal based on Article 43 and 100a EC, and therefore subject to the co-decision procedure laid down in Article 189b EC, it should be noted that this complex, multiphased procedure normally takes months to complete. The Parliament, however, succeeded in squeezing the two required readings of the proposal into *one week*.[332]

---

[327] The proposals relating to pre-shipment inspection, textiles, safeguards, common rules on imports were based on Art. 113 EC alone.

[328] The proposal for a Parliament and Council Reg. amending Reg. (EEC) No. 1576/89 laying down general rules on the definition, description and presentation of spirit drinks and Council Reg. (EEC) No. 1601/91 laying down general rules on the definition, description and presentation of aromatized wines, aromatized wine-based drinks and aromatized wine-based cocktails following the Uruguay Round of the multilateral trade negotiations

[329] European Parliament Resolution, 15 Dec. 1994, on the conclusion of the Uruguay Round and the future activities of the WTO, ([1995] OJ, C18/165, para. 8).

[330] Ibid.

[331] Art. 6 (9), Council Reg. (EC) No. 3283/94, 22 Dec. 1994, on protection against dumped imports from countries not members of the European Community, [1994] OJ, L349/11. Compare the Commission proposal, (see COM(94) 414 final, 188).

[332] See Kuijper, 'Conclusion and implementation of the Uruguay Round results' at 241.

Although this highly technical proposal was all but controversial, this was nevertheless quite an achievement, and indicative of the awareness in the Parliament of the importance of completing the ratification and implementation process before the end of the year.

2.3.3.4 The adoption of the implementing legislation by the Council

After the Parliament had given its opinion or approval to the proposed implementing legislation on 14 December 1994, it was up to the Council to adopt the implementing legislation. The Commission's proposals were, however, still the subject of reserves by various Member States.[333] In particular, the Commission's proposal for the new so-called trade barriers instrument, the successor of the 'new commercial policy instrument', met with serious objections of principle from some delegations. Central to the proposal was the introduction of a 'third track', under which Community exporters could prompt the Community to react against objectional or illicit foreign trade practices that affect them in non-member-country markets.[334] Belgium, Spain, France, Greece, Italy and Portugal globally endorsed the proposal; but Germany, Luxemburg and the Netherlands were fundamentally opposed, and Denmark and the United Kingdom considered it to be premature.[335] The opponents argued that the adoption of this measure could be seen by the trading partners as a sign that the Community was not totally committed to comply with and implement the Uruguay Round results.[336] The opponents warned the other Member States that if this proposal was maintained, the timely adoption of all other proposals, as well as the approval of the Uruguay Round Agreements themselves, would be put at risk.

The differences between the Member States which still had to be resolved by mid-December did not, however, only concern the proposal on the trade barriers instrument. There were a host of other points of contention of a more technical nature, including anti-dumping (and especially the circumvention of anti-dumping duties, the definition of the interest of the Community, the suspension of anti-dumping measures, and the duration of the inquiries), subsidies (and especially the minimum level of subsidies below which no anti-subsidy measures could be taken), safeguards (and in particular the conditions under which safeguard

---

[333] *Europe*, 16 Dec. 1994, 11.

[334] For a detailed analysis of the Commission's proposal, see COM(94) 414 final, 333–57.

[335] *Europe*, 12/13 Dec. 1994, 8. The position of Ireland was not clear and Sweden and Finland reportedly sided with Germany, Luxemburg and the Netherlands.

[336] This could in turn have negative consequences on the willingness of some third countries to ratify the Uruguay Round Agreements. See *Europe*, 12/13 Dec. 1994, 8.

measures could be taken), agriculture (and the distribution of responsibilities between the Council and the Commission in this field), pre-shipment
inspection (and the necessity and the form of Community legislation on
this matter) and textiles (and especially the use of safeguards in this
sector).[337]

In spite of this impressive list of outstanding issues, the Council reached
an overall political agreement on 19 December 1994.[338] After having
finalized the texts, it formally adopted, on 22 December 1994—at the same
time as the Decision on the conclusion of the Uruguay Round agreements—
the implementing legislation.[339] The latter included four regulations
amending the Community's commercial defence instruments,[340] two
regulations on agriculture,[341] a regulation on pre-shipment inspection,[342] a
regulation concerning the Community trademark,[343] a regulation on textile
products,[344] and a decision on the legal protection of semiconductor
topographies.[345] It is beyond the scope of this chapter to discuss each of the
amendments and additions to existing Community trade law. Each of these
implementation acts requires a chapter of its own. Let me merely point out
that, with regard to the most controversial of the Commission's proposals—
the proposal for the trade barriers instrument—the Council finally did
follow the Commission, albeit with substantial modifications to the latter's
proposal.

[337] For a detailed picture of the outstanding problems, see ibid., 8–9.

[338] *Europe*, 23 Dec. 1994, 10.

[339] [1994] OJ, L349. Note, however, that this issue of the Official Journal was only
published in Feb. 1995, weeks after much of the implementing legislation contained therein
had entered into force!

[340] Council Reg. (EC) No. 3283/94, 22 Dec. 1994, on protection against dumped imports
from countries not members of the European Community [1994] OJ, L349/1–21; Council
Reg. (EC) No. 3284, 22 Dec. 1994, on protection against subsidized imports from countries
not members of the European Community [1994] OJ, L349/22–52; Council Reg. (EC) No.
3285/94, 22 Dec. 1994, on the common rules for imports and repealing Reg. (EC) No. 518/94
[1994] OJ, L349/53–70; and Council Reg. (EC) No. 3286/94 of 22 Dec. 1994 laying down
Community procedures in the field of commercial policy in order to ensure the exercise of the
Community's rights under international rules, in particular those established under the
auspices of the WTO ([1994] OJ, L349/71–78).

[341] Council Reg. (EC) No. 3203/94, 22 Dec. 1994, on the adjustment and transitional
arrangements required in the agricultural sector in order to implement the agreements
concluded during the Uruguay Round of multilateral trade negotiations, [1994] OJ, L349/105.

[342] Council Reg. (EC) No. 3287/94 on pre-shipment inspection for exports from the
Community, [1994] OJ, L349/79–82.

[343] Council Reg. (EC) No. 3288/94, 22 Dec. 1994, amending Reg. (EC) No. 40/94 on the
Community trade mark for the implementation of the agreements concluded in the
framework of the Uruguay Round, [1994] OJ, L349/83–84.

[344] Council Reg. (EC) No. 3289/94, 22 Dec. 1994, amending Reg. (EEC) No. 3030/93 on
common rules for imports of certain textile products from non-member countries [1994] OJ,
L349/85–104.

[345] Dec. 94/824/EC on the extension of the legal protection of topographies products to
persons from a Member of the WTO [1994] OJ, L349/201.

It should be noted that, apart from the implementing legislation adopted by the Council, the Commission also adopted a number of acts which fell within the scope of regulatory powers delegated to it. As such the Commission adopted, on 20 December 1994, a regulation amending the new combined nomenclature, together with the corresponding rates of duty of the Common Customs Tariff, as changed by the GATT 1994.[346] Likewise, the Commission amended its Regulation No 2454/93 of 2 July 1993, laying down provisions for the implementation of the Community's Customs Code.

The implementing legislation adopted during the closing days of 1994 primarily concerned measures necessary as from 1 January 1995, the date of the entry into force of the Uruguay Round Agreements. Other measures, such as legislation implementing the Agreement on Government Procurement (which only had to be implemented by the end of 1995), and the publication of the agricultural tariffs rates (which only applied as from 1 July 1995), were postponed. The exception was the legislation implementing the TRIPs agreement, Council Regulation (EC) No 3288/94. The Council could have waited for the adoption of this regulation until the end of 1995, but it chose not to do so.

2.3.4 The application of the Uruguay Round Agreements by Community and Member State courts

Finally, I would like to comment briefly on an issue which has not yet been touched upon in this chapter, and which concerns the 'invocability' of the Uruguay Round Agreements in Community and Member State courts. Will it be possible for citizens and companies to invoke the provisions of the Uruguay Round Agreements in proceedings before a Community or national judge? It is clear that the recognition of direct effect and therefore the private 'enforcability' of the Uruguay Round Agreements would contribute notably to both the effectiveness and the significance of these Agreements.

However, in the preamble of its December 1994 Decision on the conclusion of the Uruguay Round Agreements, the Council stated that these agreements are, *by their nature*, not susceptible to being invoked in Community or Member State courts.[347] In its proposal for a Council decision on the conclusion of the Uruguay Round Agreements, the Commission had also denied direct effect to these Agreements.[348] In

---

[346] Comm. Reg. (EC) No. 3115/94, 20 Dec. 1994, amending Annexes I and II to Council Reg. (EEC) No. 2658/87 on the tariff and statistical nomenclature and on the Common Customs Tariff [1994] OJ, L345/1. Initially the Commission had considered submitting a proposal to the Council to amend the Common Customs Tariff (see above).
[347] Council Dec. 94/800/EC, 22 Dec. 1994, [1994] OJ, L336/2.
[348] COM(94) 143 final, 7a.

justification of its position, it argued that it was already known that the United States and many other of the Community's trading partners would explicitly rule out the invocability of the Agreements in national courts, and that if the Community would not deny direct effect to these Agreements, 'a major imbalance would arise in the actual management of the obligations of the Community and other countries'.[349] It should be noted, however, that it is not up to the Council or even less the Commission to decide on the invocability of the Uruguay Round Agreements. Eventually, it is for the European Court of Justice to decide whether the provisions of the Uruguay Round Agreements can be invoked in Community and national courts.[350]

The Court has consistently stressed that the effects of an international agreement in the Community legal order must be determined by reference to the nature and objectives of the agreement in question.[351] With regard to the GATT, the Court has always held that while the provisions of the GATT have the effect of binding the Community, they cannot be invoked directly in court.[352] Most recently, the Court held in its judgment of 5 October 1994, in the so-called *Banana Case*,[353] that in assessing the effect of the GATT in the Community legal system, the spirit, the general scheme and the terms of the GATT must be considered.[354] The Court noted that according to its preamble, the GATT is based on the principle of negotiations undertaken on the basis of 'reciprocal and mutual advantageous arrangements', and is characterized by the great flexibility of its provisions; in particular those conferring the possibility of derogation, the measures to be taken when confronted with exceptional difficulties and the settlement of conflicts between the contracting parties.[355] In previous judgments the Court had concluded, on the basis of these features of the GATT, that an individual within the Community cannot invoke GATT

---

[349] Ibid., 5a.

[350] Note that to the extent that the provisions of the Uruguay Round Agreements do not concern a matter falling within the competence of the Community, the invocability is an issue to be settled under Member State law.

[351] See the Court's judgments in Case 104/81 *Kupferberg* [1982] ECR 3641, para. 17 and in Case 12/86 *Demirel* [1987] ECR 3719

[352] See e.g. Cases 21–24/72 *International Fruit Company* [1972] ECR 1219, and more recently in Case 70/87 *Fediol* [1989] ECR 1781 and in Case C–69/89 *Nakajima* [1991] ECR I–2069. See for criticism on this case law of the Court e.g. E.-U. Petersmann, 'Applications of GATT by the Court of the EC', in (1983) CMLRev. 397, and more recently M. J. Hahn and G. Schuster, 'Zum Verstoss von gemeinschaftlichem Sekundarrecht gegen das GATT', (1993) *Europarecht* 261.

[353] Case C–280/93, *Germany* v. *Council* (Bananas) [1994] ECR I–4973. In the context of an Art. 173 EC action for annulment, Germany had submitted that compliance with GATT is a condition of the lawfulness of Community acts regardless of any question of direct effect of the GATT and that the Council Reg. (EEC) No. 404/93, 13 Feb. 1993 on the common organization of the market in bananas, infringes certain basic provisions of GATT (para. 103). [354] Case C–280/93, para. 105.

[355] Ibid., para. 106, and further developed in para. 107 (dispute settlement) and para. 108 (escape clause measures).

provisions in a court to challenge the lawfulness of a Community act, and in the *Banana Case* it confirmed this conclusion.

At the heart of the *Banana Case*, however, was not the issue of direct effect, but rather the question of whether a Member State could bring an Article 173 EC action for annulment against a Community regulation based upon the fact that this regulation violated the provisions of the GATT. This question is obviously of great importance to the impact GATT obligations have on Community legislation and measures. The Community's trade policy would definitely be more congruent with GATT law if a Member State could challenge the legality of Community legislation or measures which are not in compliance with GATT rules. However, the Court ruled in the *Banana Case* that the features of the GATT which excluded the direct effect of GATT provisions, also preclude the Court from taking GATT provisions into consideration to assess the legality of a Community regulation, challenged under Article 173 EC.[356] The special features noted above show that the GATT rules are not unconditional, and that an obligation to recognize them as rules of international law which are directly applicable in the domestic legal systems of the contracting parties cannot be based on the spirit, general scheme or terms of the GATT.[357] As an exception to this general rule, the Court can, however, review the legality of Community legislation or measures from the point of view of the GATT rules if the Community intended to implement a particular obligation entered into within the framework of the GATT, or if the Community act expressly refers to specific provisions of the GATT.[358]

Will the Court come to a similar conclusion with regard to the Uruguay Round Agreements? The answer to this question depends on whether the Court will conclude that the GATT and the Uruguay Round Agreements share the special features which led the Court to decide that GATT provisions could not—generally speaking—be invoked in Community and national courts. There is, however, major disagreement on what conclusion the Court should reach.[359]

While controversial, there is good reason for the Court to grant direct effect to provisions of the Uruguay Round Agreements, as well as to allow actions for annulment under the first paragraph of Article 173 EC. First of all, one cannot but note that the rules and obligations laid down in the

[356] Case C–280/93, para. 109.

[357] Ibid., para. 110.

[358] See Case 70/87, *Fediol* v. *Commission* [1989] ECR 1781 and Case–69/89 *Nakajima* v. *Council* [1991] ECR I–2069.

[359] Even with the Legal Service of the Commission, opinions are divided. See e.g. on the one hand, P.-J. Kuijper, 'The new WTO Dispute Settlement System: the impact on the Community', in J. Bourgeois (ed.), *The Uruguay Round results: a European Lawyer's Perspective*, European Interuniversity Press, Brussels, 1995, 87–114 and on the other hand,

Uruguay Round Agreements allow for less flexibility than did the GATT. This is particularly well illustrated by the Agreement on Safeguard Measures, which has introduced stricter rules with regard to use of such measures, and has prohibited so-called grey-area measures.[360] Of even greater importance, however, are the new rules on dispute settlement. Unlike the dispute settlement system under the GATT, the Uruguay Round Agreements provide for a virtually complete judicial system of dispute settlement, so that there is no longer any practical possibility of the losing party blocking the adoption of the panel report.[361] It is true that the losing party can, instead of implementing the panel report, choose to offer compensation, or to bear retaliation measures, but it is argued that these alternatives are now highly regulated. It has also been argued convincingly that the possibility of withdrawal after authorized retaliation, as provided for in Article XXIII GATT, is no longer operative.[362]

It must be understood, however, that a decision to grant direct effect, or allow Article 173 actions, could place the Community in an unfavourable position in relation to trading partners which do not grant direct effect. Unlike these trading partners, the Community would—directly or in-directly—face actions before Community and Member State courts if it would not honour its commitments under the Uruguay Round Agreements. The Court will therefore definitely come under a lot of 'political' pressure to reject the invocability of the Uruguay Round agreements in Community and national courts. It will be (and has already been) forcefully argued that as long as the Community has not shown in any way its intention to implement a specific provision of the Uruguay Round Agreements, it should not be obliged to do so by its courts.[363]

2.4 CONCLUSIONS

The Uruguay Round has been a bittersweet experience for the European Community. There is reason for joy and satisfaction in view of the fact that—in spite of considerable internal strife and conflict of interests—the

Timmermans, 'L'Uruguay Round', at 177. For other contributions to this debate, see P. Mengozzi, 'Les droits des citoyens de l'Union européenne et l'applicabilité directe des accords de Marrakech', (1994) RMUE, 165, and W. Meng, 'Gedanken zur Frage unmittelbarer Anwendung von WTO-Recht in der EG', in U. Beyerlin (ed.), *Recht zwischen Umbruch und Bewahrung—Festschrift für Rudolf Bernhardt*, (1995), 1063.

[360] Ibid.
[361] See Kuijper, 'New WTO Dispute Settlement System'. Note, however, that pursuant to Art. IX WTO the final word on the interpretation of the Uruguay Round agreements rests with the Ministerial Conference, the quintessential political organ (Timmermans, 'L'Uruguay Round' at 178). [362] Ibid.
[363] Timmermans, 'L'Uruguay Round', 175–183 and Mengozzi, 165–174. Note that if the Community does show its intention to implement a specific provision of the Uruguay Round Agreements, it is possible under the *Fediol* and *Nakajima* case law, to invoke this provision in the context of an Art. 173 action.

Community did hold together, and was thus able to achieve a successful and favourable conclusion of the Round. It also succeeded, albeit barely, in ratifying the Uruguay Round Agreements and adopting the necessary implementing legislation in time. There is, however, also plenty of reason for disappointment and frustration. In conclusion, I will discuss some of the lessons that may be drawn from the Community's Uruguay Round experience for future negotiations, in particular within the WTO.

The controversy regarding the competence to conclude the Uruguay Round Agreements has led the Court to clarify the scope of the Community's competence in the field of international economic relations in general, and in the new areas of trade in services and the protection of intellectual property in particular. In its prudent and compromising Opinion 1/94, the Court generously ruled that the Community has exclusive competence with regard to all Uruguay Round Agreements on trade in goods but—cognizant of 'political' constraints, and willing to depart from previous case law—concluded that the Community and the Member States have joint competences with regard to the GATS and TRIPs. Rejecting the Commission's broad—and to some extravagant—interpretation of the Community's exclusive competence under Article 113 EC, the Court held that 'only' cross-frontier supply of services (including many transactions in the sectors of banking, insurance, telecommunications and the media), and rules concerning the release into free circulation of counterfeit goods fall within the scope of common commercial policy. With regard to the Community's implied competence in the fields concerned, the Court gave a restrictive interpretation to its previous case law, and insisted that the implied competence in these fields is only of an exclusive nature, to the extent that international commitments undertaken by the Member States would 'affect' common rules already laid down by the Community. However, many matters relating to trade in services and the protection of intellectual property are not yet covered by common rules. Therefore, the Community's exclusive competence, whether express or implied, concerns only a limited number of matters in these fields. The Member States retain competence with regard to many matters. In this sense the Opinion fits in well with a recent line of rulings, in which the Court has tended towards understanding and protecting the (legitimate) interests of the Member States, and therefore did not really come as a surprise.[364]

While the legal reasoning of the Court did not, perhaps, always convincingly support the conclusions it arrived at, Opinion 1/94 made it clear who was competent to conclude the Uruguay Round Agreements. At the same time, however, it is obvious that the division of competence laid down by the Court may seriously complicate future negotiations. Is it a workable division of competence?

---

[364] M. Hilf, 'The ECJ's Opinion 1/94' at 245.

As the Commission had pointed out to the Court, this division of competence is likely to give rise to endless discussions on whether a given matter falls within the competence of the Community or within the competence of the Member States. Disagreement about the division of competence will persist primarily as a result of lingering confusion about the scope of the Community's exclusive implied competence. Recurrent internal disagreement on competence will obviously weaken the standing and the effectiveness of the Community in international negotiations.

Furthermore, it should be noted that, with regard to matters which are within the competence of the Member States, the latter may—whenever consensus cannot be found—be very tempted to express their views individually on these matters, in particular in the context of the WTO, of which they are also members. This would, however, seriously undermine the Community's unity of action *vis-à-vis* the rest of the world, and therefore greatly compromise its negotiating power. In order to mitigate this most unfortunate consequence of the division of competence laid down in Opinion 1/94, the Court bestowed upon both the Community and the Member States a duty to co-operate. The Court ruled that where the subject-matter of an agreement falls in part within the competence of the Community and in part within that of the Member States, it is essential to ensure close co-operation between the Member States and the Community institutions during the negotiation, the conclusion and the implementation of the agreement. The duty to co-operate also exists, and is obviously important, in the context of the dispute settlement system. However, the Court has not made any effort to clarify this duty, and has left this task to the Community institutions and the Member States. They will have to reach agreement on a code of conduct in which this duty to co-operate is translated into specific procedural rules.

At the start of the Uruguay Round, the Council and the Member States had agreed that the Commission would act throughout the Round as the sole negotiator for both of them. It will be recalled that they decided to do so 'in order to ensure the maximum consistency in the conduct of the negotiations'. Reflecting the same concern, the Member States, the Council and the Commission confirmed on 6 May 1994 the Commission's role as sole negotiator with regard to negotiations on services. Under the so-called 'Code of Conduct on Post-Uruguay Round Negotiations on Services', which was agreed upon for an unlimited period, the Commission remains the sole negotiator for all questions related to services, yet the Member States' representatives will now attend *all* meetings. This specific code of conduct has been very useful, but it obviously does not supplant the need for an all-encompassing arrangement on the Commission's authority to negotiate within the context of the WTO, as well as on the representation of Member States in dispute settlement cases.

Negotiations on such a general code of conduct between the Member

States, the Council and the Commission had already begun before the Court took a decision in Opinion 1/94, and imposed a duty to co-operate. Fearing that the Community would not be able to ratify the Uruguay Round agreements before the 31 December 1994 deadline, an attempt was made during the summer of 1994 to reach a political agreement on the conduct of the Member States and the Commission within the framework of the WTO. In the case of an agreement, the Commission would have dropped its request to the Court for an Opinion, in order to ensure a timely ratification of the Uruguay Round Agreements. In early October 1994 it became clear, however, that it would not be possible to reach a consensus on a general code of conduct. There was serious opposition to the proposed code in the Commission as well as in the Council. In the latter instance, Belgium continued to hold out for a Court ruling to decide the competence issue once and for all.

The discussions on a general code of conduct have been veiled in secrecy. It seems, however, that the initial enthusiasm has totally withered away and that very little progress is being made. On the basis of the arrangement applicable throughout the Uruguay Round and the May 1994 Code of Conduct on Services, as well as the failed draft for a general code of conduct, one can identify some of the key elements of a possible general code of conduct. Such a code of conduct will undoubtedly entrust the Commission with the task to speak and negotiate on behalf of the Community *and* the Member States in the WTO. The Member States will not be entitled to speak in the WTO except when explicitly provided for in the code. The Commission will definitely have to inform the Member States in advance of the time and place of all WTO discussions and negotiations, and will have to facilitate the attendance of the Member States or (preferably) the Member State holding the Presidency. The Commission will also have to circulate promptly to the Member States any text produced by the WTO Secretariat or any other WTO Member, which has not been sent to the Member States directly. A code of conduct is also likely to include a provision requiring the Commission to call, at the request of any Member State, for a temporary break in the negotiations or discussions in the WTO in order to allow for consultation and further co-ordination between the Commission and the Member States. A future code will definitely require that the positions taken or actions undertaken by the Commission in discussions and negotiations in the WTO result from a common decision. More problematic, however, is what such a code will stipulate for the situation when no common decision can be agreed upon. In the failed draft code of conduct, it was stated that when no common decision can be agreed upon, 'it may be decided at an appropriate level by consensus that each Member State will be free to present its own position'. In case there is no consensus to allow Member States to present their own positions, it would—according to the failed draft code—be for 'the Commission, after consulting with the Member States and guided by their wishes [to present] its assessment reflecting in a balanced way the range of views held'. After such an assessment, Member States would be allowed to present their own positions. A future code of conduct will probably also stipulate that the Member States will act and speak on their own behalf on adminstrative and budgetary measures, although they may be asked to avoid taking divergent positions so far as possible. With regard to the dispute settlement procedure, it should be noted that, according to the failed draft code, a dispute settlement procedure introduced against one of the Member States is a matter of concern to the Community as a whole; and the Commission and the Member State concerned will co-operate as closely as possible in preparing the defence before the WTO Panel. Conversely, the nullification or impairment of a benefit of a Member State shall also be a matter of concern to the Community as a whole. The introduction of a dispute settlement procedure will be done in accordance with the relevant Community procedures, and the Commission and Member States concerned will co-operate as closely as possible in preparing dispute settlement cases.

A general code of conduct along these lines should minimize the dangers that the shared competences of the Community and the Member States in the field of international economic relations would seriously undermine the Community's unity of action *vis-à-vis* the rest of the world, and would greatly weaken its negotiating power.

It should be noted that in Opinion 1/94, the Court not only left it up to the Community institutions and the Member States to negotiate a code of conduct translating the duty to co-operate into specific procedural rules, but it also side-stepped the question of the legal basis for such a duty to co-operate. Before the entry into force of the Maastricht Treaty, Article 116 EEC obliged the Member States to proceed within the framework of international economic organizations in respect to all matters relating to the common market only by *common action*. On the Commission's proposal, the Council was to decide by qualified majority on the scope and implementation of such common action. This Article 116 EEC would have been the perfect legal basis for a code of conduct but, unfortunately, it was deleted by the Maastricht Treaty. The main objection to Article 116 EEC was that it provided for qualified majority decision-making even where the exercise of internal Community competence required unanimity.

Neither a duty to co-operate laid down in the Treaty, nor a code of conduct translating this duty into procedural requirements will, however, mitigate yet another serious drawback of the division of competence as laid down in Opinion 1/94. By recognizing that the Community and the Member States have shared competence in the field of services and TRIPs, the Court is, as it were, 'guilty of complicity' in the *de facto* substitution of supranational decision-making with intergovernmental decision-making in regard to trade matters which fall within the competence of the

Community. Since many trade negotiations will cover both Community matters and Member State matters, the results of these negotiations will require the approval of *both* the Community and the Member States. The consequence for those Community matters which are dealt with in the agreement reached is that qualified majority voting will thus, in many cases, be replaced by a *de facto* requirement of consensus. This will obviously have a negative impact on the effectiveness of the Community in international negotiations. Consensus among the Member States is never easy to find, especially in view of the great divide between the free-trading bloc of northern Member States, led by Germany and the United Kingdom, and the southern protectionist-leaning coalition led by France.

Initially it was thought that during the Intergovernmental Conference on the Revision of the Maastricht Treaty (1996–97), the current division of competence between the Community and the Member States in the field of international economic relations would be unlikely to be altered significantly. It was said that a renewed Commission initiative for a common policy on external economic relations stood even less of a chance of being accepted than the previous attempt in 1991. The Commission under the Santer presidency took in general a cautious approach to the Intergovernmental Conference so as to avoid accusations of Brussels power-grabs. The most one could expect of the Intergovernmental Conference, it seemed, was that it would address the issue of the co-operation between the Community and the Member States in fields of shared competence. The introduction of a provision similar to Article 116 EEC, but without its main flaw, would give a clear legal basis to the duty of co-operation, and help to ensure that shared competences do not undermine the Community's unity of action *vis-à-vis* the rest of the world and thus weaken its negotiating power. Somewhat unexpectedly therefore, the division of competence between the Community and the Member States in the field of international economic relations did, however, appear on the agenda of the Intergovernmental Conference. Better still, at present the Community's competence in the field of external economic relations is considered to be 'one of the most important issues' on the agenda of the Conference.[365] The European Commission has called for an extension of the Community's exclusive common commercial policy powers. The Commission is urging the Member States to update Article 113 EC so that Europe can negotiate with one clear voice on services, investment and TRIPs and unanimity would no longer be required for the conclusion of agreements on these issues.[366] This Commission proposal immediately provoked opposition among sovereignty-conscious Member States led by the United Kingdom

---

[365] See the statement of Mr. N. Dorr, chair of the Group of Personal Representatives of the Ministers of Foreign Affairs, *Europe*, 18 October 1996, p. 3.

[366] See in this respect the passionate appeal of Sir Leon Brittan in the *Financial Times* of 11 November 1996, p. 16.

and France. Also Germany and Spain reacted coolly.[367] However, it is said that few Member States think that there is no need at all to revise Article 113 EC and that a mere code of conduct would be enough. Whether the Member States will be successful in coming to an agreement on the extension of the scope of Article 113 EC will largely depend on whether the negotiators will be able to allay deeply rooted fears that amendments to Article 113 EC would lead to a general extension of the Community's powers. This will not be an easy task to accomplish.

The effectiveness of the Community in international trade negotiations also depends on the division of powers between the Community institutions involved in the negotiation and conclusion of international agreements. For the Commission to negotiate efficiently on behalf of the Community (and the Member States) it needs a certain degree of freedom. Non-member countries should be able to look upon the Commission as the institution truly empowered to negotiate and 'deliver a deal'. If they have to worry at each stage of the negotiations whether or not the Commission has the support of the Member States, negotiations with the Community would become strenuous. The experience of the Uruguay Round has taught us that close co-operation and constant dialogue between the Commission and the Council's advisory 113 Committee can contribute significantly to the successful completion of negotiations. Conversely, the issuance of formal and detailed negotiating directives by the Council may frustrate, rather than facilitate, a happy end to negotiations. Such directives tie the hands of the Commission, and thus deprive it of a degree of flexibility it needs to negotiate effectively. In very sensitive negotiations, formal and detailed negotiating directives may be difficult to avoid, but they are unlikely to be very helpful. This is illustrated most clearly in the Uruguay Round negotiations on agriculture. It is interesting to note that the interplay between the Council and the Commission was not substantially different during the Uruguay Round than it was during the Tokyo Round. As during the Uruguay Round, the Article 113 Committee also played a pivotal role in the Tokyo Round. Negotiating directives, however, were arguably more important during the Tokyo Round than the Uruguay Round.[368]

When one compares the role of the European Parliament in the negotiation and conclusion of the Uruguay Round Agreements to its role in the context of the Tokyo Round, it becomes clear that the Parliament has made considerable progress.[369] In the future, the Parliament will play an even more important role in both the negotiation and conclusion of international trade agreements. The Parliament has claimed—and Sir Leon Brittan seemed to support this claim—that all agreements negotiated in the context of the WTO should be submitted to the Parliament for its assent. While one may understand the Parliament's desire to submit the

---

[367] *Financial Times*, 5 September 1996, p. 2.
[368] J.-V. Louis, 'EEC and the Tokyo Round' at 61–2.   [369] Ibid., at 63.

international economic relations of the Community to a healthy degree of democratic control, there is no legal basis in the Treaty for such an expanded use of the assent procedure. Furthermore, one should note that increased involvement of the European Parliament will not facilitate the negotiation and conclusion of international agreements. How important a role the Parliament will play, will depend to a large degree on the interpretation that is given to the concept 'agreements having important budgetary implications for the Community'. Not surprisingly, the inter-pretations of this concept differ considerably. In order to avoid *ex post* challenges by the Parliament of the validity of international agreements, it is therefore indispensable to clarify this concept. The Intergovernmental Conference of 1996 would be a good occasion to do so.

With regards to the implementation of international trade agreements, it should be pointed out that the implementation is subject to the Community's complicated and demanding internal legislative procedures, and that therefore a swift implementation should not be taken for granted.[370] The fact that Community legislation implementing the Uruguay Round Agreements was adopted in time should, therefore, be seen as a major achievement; one which was possible only because all Community institutions shared the political will to implement the agreements in time. It is to be hoped that the 1996 Intergovernmental Conference will lead to a much-needed simplification of the legislative procedures.

Finally, it should be noted that the Court *may* decide that provisions of the Uruguay Round Agreements (and future agreements concluded within the context of the WTO) can be invoked in Community and Member State courts. This would put the Community at a disadvantage *vis-à-vis* its main trading partners, who are unlikely to recognize such invocability. At the same time, however, it would limit the Community's ability to deviate from its commitments under the international trade agreements, and thus inspire confidence in the Community.

From the bittersweet experience of the Uruguay Round, one may conclude that the Community is unlikely to be an easy partner in international trade negotiations in the years to come. Confusion and controversy over the Community's competence and conduct in inter-national economic relations, which have troubled the Community and the Member States during the Uruguay Round, will persist. Unless the Community clarifies the scope of its competence in external economic relations, and fine-tunes procedures for the exercise of competence in this field, the Community is in danger of remaining an enigmatic and somewhat unpredictable negotiating partner, enfeebled by internal discord.

---

[370] When compared to the procedures at place at the time of the Tokyo Round (see Louis, 'EEC and the Tokyo Round'), it is evident that the situation has become more problematic as a result of the reforms introduced by the SEA and the TEU.

3

BELGIUM

*Piet Eeckhout**

3.1 INTRODUCTION: THE PROCESS OF CREATING A SYSTEM OF 'CO-OPERATIVE FEDERALISM'

At the outset it is essential to give a brief survey of the current structure of the Belgian state and to highlight the main features of the latest constitutional changes, in particular in relation to the conduct of external relations.

Since the seventies the structure of government has been subject to a process of near continuous amendment and adaptation. That process is mainly inspired by the relationship, tense at times, between the various linguistic communities (mainly the Dutch-speaking part of the population, living in Flanders, and the French-speaking part, living in Wallonia, with Brussels being predominantly French-speaking). The tensions between those communities have always resonated in the country's domestic politics; some might even say that those politics have tended to exacerbate them. On the other hand it has always proved possible to find a negotiated settlement of outstanding differences, although at the cost of creating an extremely complex system of devoluted government.

In recent years that process seems to have reached a more definitive stage.[1] Through the latest amendment of the Constitution[2] the country is henceforth a federal state, composed of 'communities' and 'regions' (Article 1; I shall also refer to these as sub-federal entities). The mix of communities and regions is one of the peculiarities of the system. The

* Professor, Universities of Ghent and Brussels; Chambers of Advocate General F. G. Jacobs, European Court of Justice.
The author wishes to express his thanks to Anne-Marie Van den Bossche, Elisabetta Montaguti, Bertrand de Crombrugge, Jean-Victor Louis, Chris Timmermans, Marc-André Gaudissart and Peter Van den Bossche for their very helpful comments.

[1] See e.g. *La Constitution fédérale du 5 mai 1993* (1993); *Les réformes institutionnelles de 1993: vers un fédéralisme achevé?* (1994); A. Alen and L.-P. Suetens (eds.), *Het federale België na de vierde staatshervorming* (1993); F. Delpérée (ed.), *La Belgique fédérale* (1994); B. Seutin and G. Van Haegendoren, *De nieuwe bevoegdheden van Gemeenschappen en Gewesten* (1994).

[2] That amendment dates from 5 May 1993. For a newly co-ordinated version of the Constitution see *MB*, 17 Feb. 1994 at 4054.

communities are language-based (the Flemish community, the French community and the small German community); the regions are territorially-based (the Flemish region, the Walloon region and the Brussels' region) (Articles 2 and 3). The distinction reflects the history of the process of devolution of powers, which started off with aspirations for linguistic and cultural autonomy leading to the creation of the communities. Cultural and educational policy are still the latter's main competences. It may be added that although there are only three communities there are four language areas: the Dutch, the French, the German and the bilingual language area of Brussels (Article 4). The creation of the regions was a further step, accompanied by a transfer of more economically and geographically orientated competences.[3] At the Flemish level the distinction between region and community is no longer significant, as there is a single assembly (Vlaams Parlement) and government (Vlaamse Regering). That is not the case for the French-speaking part of the country, however, where community and region continue to have separate assemblies and governments. There is also some form of assembly and government for the Brussels' region. The exercise of community-based competences in Brussels is too complex for this survey.

All those assemblies, to which should be added the federal Chamber of Representatives and the Senate where the communities and regions are to some extent represented, have full legislative powers in the areas of their competence. There is no hierarchy of norms.[4] Conflicts of norms can only be settled by modification of the legislation or by annulment for lack of competence. Annulment can only be decided by the Cour d'arbitrage, the Belgian constitutional court, which has jurisdiction over competence disputes and over the enforcement of the principles of equal treatment of all Belgian citizens and freedom of education. Although that does not amount to a full constitutional review, the Cour d'arbitrage has managed to construe its jurisdiction quite broadly.[5]

The conduct of external relations has constantly been the subject of debate during the process of constitutional reform, but it was only at the latest stage that major changes were made.[6] Before, external relations had

---

[3] The regions currently have partial or full competence in areas such as environmental and water policy, agricultural policy, economic policy, public works, and public transport.

[4] See J.-V. Louis, 'La primauté, une valeur relative?', (1995) *Cahiers de droit européen* 23–8.

[5] See e.g. L.-P. Suetens, 'De invloed van het Arbitragehof op het grondwettelijk recht' (1993–94) *Rechtskundig Weekblad* 1313–18.

[6] See e.g. M. Leroy and A. Schaus, 'Les relations internationales', in *Les réformes institutionnelles de 1993*, 26–70; M. Mahieu, 'Fédéralisme et relations extérieures' (1994) *Administration publique* 223–32; R. Ergec, 'La réforme de l'État—les relations internationales', (1994) *Journal des tribunaux* 837–40; G. Craenen, 'België en het buitenland—De

remained almost entirely within the competence of the Crown (that is, the central government). The latest version of the Constitution provides, however, that the communities and the regions have full external powers in the areas of their competence, including treaty-making powers. In view of those powers, it has been said that as regards external relations the system is confederal, rather than federal.[7] To ensure some degree of unity (or federal loyalty) it is none the less provided that the Crown directs the country's external relations (Article 167). That principle is translated into a number of mechanisms which allow the federal government to intervene in certain cases where sub-federal entities make improper use of their external relations powers. It is, for example, possible for the federal government to 'substitute' decision-making by sub-federal entities where the latter fail to implement certain international commitments properly (in particular EC commitments).[8]

It is also obvious that in a small country like Belgium such an advanced devolution of powers may prove to be artificial in many areas, and that it is often difficult to fit in with the practical necessities of decision-making. Those problems are countered by a unique feature of the federal system: the conclusion of so-called co-operation agreements between various governmental entities.[9] By concluding such agreements, which in some cases amounts to a constitutional requirement, those entities manage to co-ordinate their policies in certain areas. Because of this unique feature of the Belgian system, it has been called a system of co-operative federalism. Such co-operation agreements are also a vital instrument in the field of external relations, as will be shown below.

As regards external trade the division of competences is not clear-cut.[10]

nieuwe regeling van de buitenlandse betrekkingen', in *Het federale België* 59–105; F. Ingelaere, 'De nieuwe wetgeving inzake de internationale betrekkingen van de Gemeenschappen en de Gewesten' (1993) *Tijdschrift voor Bestuurswetenschappen en Publiek Recht* 807–20 and 'De Europeesrechtelijke raakvlakken van de nieuwe wetgeving inzake de internationale betrekkingen van de Belgische Gemeenschappen en Gewesten' (1994) *Sociaal-Economische Wetgeving* 67–82; J. van Ginderachter, 'Les compétences internationales des Communautés et des Régions en Belgique' (1993) *Studia diplomatica* 85–92; Y. Lejeune, 'La conduite des relations internationales', in *La Belgique fédérale*, 313–57; various contributions in (1994) No. 1 *Revue belge de droit international*, see in particular also the annexes containing the main constitutional texts at pp. 284–352 (only in French).

[7] R. Ergec, 'La Réforme de l'Etat' 840. J. Erauw speaks of the Balkanization of Belgian foreign policy, see 'Balkanisering in het buitenlands beleid' (1995) No. 2 *Tijdschrift Rechtsdocumentatie en-informatie*, pp. 193–4.

[8] See Art. 16 (3) of the Special Law of 8 Aug. 1980 on institutional reform, as amended by the Special Law of 5 May 1993 on the conduct of international relations by the communities and the regions, *MB*, 8 May 1993, at 10559.

[9] On the legal status of such agreements, see R. Moerenhout and J. Smets, *De samenwerking tussen de federale Staat, de Gemeenschappen en de Gewesten* (1994) 123–86.

[10] The problem of the division of competences between the European Community and the Member States in the area of external trade is not discussed here; see Chap. 2. It is obvious

The regions now have competence over export promotion, with the exception of export credits, which remain within the province of the federal authorities. The latter is also the case for what is called policy on quotas and licensing.[11] Given that the federal authorities are responsible for safeguarding the free circulation of goods and the Belgian economic and monetary union, a lot of external trade issues remain within their competence. It should, however, be noted that regional and community-based competences in the areas of protection of the environment, agriculture, state aids, and cultural policy may be affected by external trade issues.[12]

This paper first examines the role played by Belgium in the Uruguay Round negotiations. It then analyses the procedures which were followed for the ratification and implementation of the World Trade Organization Agreement. The status of the Agreement in the domestic legal order and the future representation of Belgium in the WTO are examined in separate sections. Those subjects are both three-dimensional (and therefore more lively, but paradoxically also more intangible) because of the impact of EC law and policies. The paper then addresses the question whether certain mechanisms of the Belgian constitutional system are exportable.

3.2 POSITION AND ROLE IN THE NEGOTIATIONS

Belgium played only a small role in the negotiations in view of the fact that the EC Commission negotiated for the Community and its Member States, under the supervision of the EC Council. The Belgian impact could therefore only be indirect, through the medium of the EC institutions.

It seems that Belgium almost never took a high profile on any of the major negotiating issues. That may be explained by the traditional Belgian attitude in EC decision-making, which is an attitude of consensus-seeking, and by the lack of interest in public opinion for international trade matters. The Belgian authorities did side somewhat with the French in criticizing the Blair House Accord. Perhaps the most outspoken position was taken on audio-visual services, considered to come within the province of the communities, which are competent for cultural matters. The Belgian

---

that even for matters where the EC has exclusive competence the question of the Belgian internal division of competences arises. The answer to that question determines which Belgian authorities have competence to participate in EC decision-making, in particular in the Council of Ministers.

[11] Art. 6 (1) (VI), first para. of the Special Law of 8 Aug. 1980 on institutional reform, as amended by the Special Law of 16 July 1993, *MB*, 20 July 1993.

[12] See generally C. Darville-Finet, 'Le commerce extérieur—les principales étapes du nouveau paysage institutionnel' (1994) *Revue belge de droit international* 164–83.

negotiating position in that area was therefore decided by those communities,[13] the French community strongly insisting on protecting Europe's
audio-visual industry against US imports. Under the Belgian presidency of
the EC Council (July–December 1993) an informal Council meeting on
those issues was held in Mons in October 1993, where the ministers for
cultural affairs took a firm view on the question of European protection,
pleading for the introduction of a cultural-exception clause in the General
Agreement on Trade in Services.[14] As is well-known, the EC did not
manage to have such a clause inserted.

Belgium also took a stand in the so-called Banana War. It is one of the
Member States which voted against the adoption of the common market
organization,[15] and it put up resistance against the framework agreement
which the Commission negotiated with Latin American countries a couple
of weeks before the signature of the Final Act.[16] It appears that it
continued to voice its opposition to that agreement until the Council
concluded the WTO Agreement (22 December 1994), and the dislike of
the banana regime continues. The sensitivity of the issue is well illustrated
by the debate on the ratification of the WTO Agreement in the Chamber
of Representatives, where after a protracted discussion the Minister for
External Trade exclaimed: '*Je ne tiens pas à passer la soirée sur le régime
des bananes!* (I am not keen on spending the evening on bananas!)'[17]

The role played by Belgium in behind-the-scenes diplomacy is probably
not to be underestimated, in particular since Belgium held the presidency
of the EC Council during the last months of the negotiations (July–
December 1993). That presidency was generally characterized as particularly effective, among other things because of the successful conclusion of
the Uruguay Round. One of the main achievements was that the Belgian
presidency apparently managed to contain French opposition against the
agricultural package of the Round.[18]

It must also be noted that Belgium attempted to obtain, in the course of

---

[13] See the Senate External Relations Committee Report, Sess. 1994–95, *Documents du
Sénat* No. 1211–12, at 85. See however also J.-F. Neuray, 'Compétence de la Communauté
française en matière de relations extérieures', in C. Doutrelepont (ed.), *L'Europe et les
enjeux du GATT dans le domaine de l'audiovisuel* (1994) 83–6, on the problems in defining the
Belgian position.

[14] See F. Dehousse, 'Exception culturelle ou spécificité culturelle?', in C. Doutrelepont
(ed.), *L'Europe et les enjeux du GATT*, 123–5.

[15] See Reg. 404/93 [1993] OJL47/1.

[16] Germany has requested the Opinion of the ECJ under Art. 228 (6) ECT on the
compatibility of the framework agreement with the ECT. The Court held in Op. 3/94 that
since the conclusion of the WTO Agreement by the Community the request for an Opinion
had lost its object, because the framework agreement was no longer envisaged but concluded.

[17] Annales PLEN 1994–95 Session, 19–538.

[18] See 'Parijs wacht op geruststellende toezeggingen van Washington', *Financieel
Ekonomische TIJD*, 22 Sept. 1993.

the Uruguay Round negotiations, a ruling by the European Court of Justice on the Community's competence in such areas as services and investment: in 1992 it requested an Opinion from the Court, pursuant to Article 228 of the Treaty, on the Community's competence to participate in the Third Revised Decision of the Organization for Economic Co-operation and Development on national treatment. The Court, however, did not deliver that Opinion until 24 March 1995,[19] after having handed down Opinion 1/94 on the Community's competence to conclude the WTO Agreement.[20]

3.3 APPROVAL, RATIFICATION AND IMPLEMENTATION

The Federal Minister for External Trade signed the Final Act in Marrakesh, after having been so authorized by the competent federal and sub-federal authorities. It may be worth mentioning that there was even a dispute between the EC Commission and the Member States over the order of signing the Final Act. The Commission wished the Member States to sign under the heading 'European Communities', whereas the Member States wanted to sign in dispersed alphabetical order. The latter formula prevailed.[21]

In terms of external competence the WTO Agreement is a 'mixed' agreement, not only in the context of the division of powers between the European Community and its Member States, but also in the Belgian internal sphere. Since the latest amendments to the Constitution the communities and regions have treaty-making powers in the areas of their competence. Treaties come in to effect after approval by the competent assembly (Article 167 (3) of the Constitution). Where the competence for concluding an international agreement is mixed, ratification of the agreement is conditional upon approval by all the competent assemblies (in some cases up to nine). In the case of the WTO Agreement, approval was required by seven federal and sub-federal assemblies.[22] It may be pointed out that each of those assemblies approved the entire WTO Agreement, and did not indicate for which matters they are competent.[23]

It is obvious that such a complex system of concluding international

---

[19] [1995] ECR I–521.   [20] [1994] ECR I–5267.   [21] See also Chapter 2.

[22] i.e. the Senate and the Chamber of Representatives at the federal level (the federal Act of Approval is not yet published), the Flemish Council (now Flemish Parliament), the Walloon Regional Council, the Brussels' Regional Council, the French Community Council, and the German Community Council (see *MB* 21 Mar. 23 Feb. 7 Feb. 14 Feb. 23 Mar. 1995 at 6306, 4131, 2717, 3239, and 6595 respectively).

[23] cf. the different course followed by Germany, see Chapter 4.

agreements requires some co-ordination.[24] The basic principles of such co-ordination are laid down in a co-operation agreement concluded between the various governmental authorities.[25] According to that agreement the so-called Interministerial Conference on Foreign Policy, where both the federal government and the sub-federal governments are represented, is the main vehicle for co-ordination. The decision, for example, on how many approvals were required in the case of the WTO Agreement was taken by that conference.

The terms of the co-operation agreement have also led to an official statement made by the Kingdom of Belgium and published in the *Official Journal*.[26] In that statement Belgium announces the way it intends to proceed in future when concluding mixed agreements (that is, those for which both the European Community and the Member States are competent). There will only be one Belgian signature appended, with a statement referring to the communities and regions where such an indication is imposed by Belgian constitutional law. Belgium also confirms that the whole Kingdom as such will be bound by the provisions of those agreements, and that the Kingdom as such will bear full responsibility for compliance, with regard to both the European Community and the other contracting non-member countries. It appears that the statement was inspired by concern in other Member States regarding the country's international capacity.

The process of approving the WTO Agreement was relatively smooth. The debates held in the various assemblies show that there was no fundamental opposition to the Agreement, except from the side of the Greens, which represent less than 10 per cent of the electorate. The issues on which a lot of concern was none-the-less expressed across the political spectrum were the relationship between trade and environment and between trade and labour policies. It was felt that on those issues the current WTO Agreement lacks substance.[27]

---

[24] The system whereby multiple approvals are required for some agreements has existed since the 1980 constitutional reform, and has in some cases given rise to problems. The Lomé III Convention, for example, was ratified by Belgium very late in the day, and in the absence of certain approvals which were required under constitutional law (see M. Maresceau, 'Belgium', in F. G. Jacobs and S. Roberts (eds.), *The Effect of Treaties in Domestic Law* (1987) 9–11). A proposal to attribute the right of approval of mixed agreements exclusively to the reformed Senate was unfortunately not accepted, see R. Ergec, 'La réforme de l'Etat' 839.

[25] Co-operation agreement of 8 Mar. 1994, not yet published. The agreement has to be approved by the various competent assemblies but is provisionally applied.

[26] [1995] OJ C157/1.

[27] See e.g. the debates in Chamber of Representatives, Annales PLEN 1994–95 Session, 18–531 to 18–548 and 19–561 to 19–592.

That concern was shared by the federal government. In its proposal for the Act whereby the Senate and the Chamber of Representatives were to approve the Agreement it inserted a provision stating that the date on which Belgium was to deposit the instruments of ratification was to be decided by the Council of Ministers, on the basis of an assessment of progress made as regards the introduction of social and environmental provisions in the European Community's Generalized System of Preferences (Article 2 of the Act). The federal government explained that that provision was intended to put pressure on the negotiations in the EC Council on the reform of the GSP. Judging from the outcome of those negotiations the Belgian Government's efforts had some success. The reformed GSP contains a special incentive arrangement for countries implementing certain International Labour Organization conventions and certain environmental standards. That arrangement is due to operate as from 1 January 1998.[28] The reformed GSP also provides that preferences may be temporarily withdrawn in certain cases of forced labour or prison labour.[29] The Belgian Government was apparently satisfied with those results since the ratification instruments were deposited at the end of December 1994.

It may be added that there was some discussion, especially in the Senate, on whether Article 2 of the Act of approval of the WTO Agreement was in accordance with the rules of the Constitution. The Conseil d'État had issued a negative opinion on that question, taking the view that it is not possible for the legislature to instruct the federal government, through an act of approval, to take additional action such as that set out in the contested provision, in particular since the regions have competence in the areas of protection of the environment and social policy.[30] The Senate and the Chamber of Representatives none the less approved the provision.

As regards implementation of the WTO Agreement most of the work is done by the European Community, and not by the individual Member States. The Minister for External Trade made it known that at the Belgian level only TRIPs required some implementation: the Benelux Convention on trade marks and national legislation concerning patents had to be revised.[31]

---

[28] See Arts. 7 & 8 of Reg. 3281/94, applying a four-year scheme of generalized tariff preferences (1995–98) in respect of certain industrial products originating in developing countries [1994] OJ L348/1.

[29] Art. 9.

[30] For the discussion see *Documents du Sénat* 1211–2 (1994–95) at 51–60. The opinion of the *Conseil d'État* is reproduced in the appendix to those *Documents*.

[31] Chamber of Representatives, Annales PLEN 1994–95 Session, 19–548.

3.4 STATUS OF THE WTO AGREEMENT IN THE DOMESTIC LEGAL ORDER

The exact status of the WTO Agreement in the domestic legal order is a complex issue. The Agreement was concluded both by the European Community and by the Member States. On the division of competences there is the guidance provided by Opinion 1/94 of the European Court of Justice,[32] but it can certainly not be said that that Opinion resolves all issues of competence.[33] In many areas it is therefore not clear whether the Community or the Member States have competence, although it is probably safe to say that, except for the areas of exclusive Community competence, the Community and the Member States have concurrent competence for most parts of the WTO Agreement.[34] The question, however, is whether the status of the Agreement in the domestic legal order depends on the exact division of competences.

It is not clear to what extent decisions of the European Court of Justice on the interpretation and the effect of the Agreement will extend to the entire Agreement. Under current case law the Court would not seem to be precluded from taking the view that it has sole authority to determine whether the WTO Agreement, as a mixed agreement in the Community law sense of the term, is capable of having direct effect.

In *Haegeman* v. *Belgium* the Court said that the 1961 association agreement with Greece (a mixed agreement) was an act of one of the institutions of the Community, since it was concluded by the Council under Articles 228 and 238 of the EC Treaty.[35] The provisions of the agreement formed an integral part of Community law, and the Court accordingly had jurisdiction to give preliminary rulings concerning their interpretation.[36] In *Hauptzollamt Mainz* v. *Kupferberg*, relating to the 1972 free trade agreement between the EEC and Portugal (which was not, however, a mixed agreement) the Court held that where the Member States took measures to implement certain provisions of that agreement they fulfilled

---

[32] See n. 20.   [33] See Chap. 2.

[34] That view is supported by a passage in Op. 1/94 where the Court rejected the argument that the provisions of TRIPs relating to measures to be adopted to secure the effective protection of intellectual property rights fell within the exclusive competence of the Member States. The Court held (para. 104): 'If that argument is to be understood as meaning that all those matters are within some sort of domain reserved to the Member States, it cannot be accepted. The Community is certainly competent to harmonize national rules on those matters, in so far as, in the words of Art. 100 of the Treaty, they "directly affect the establishment or functioning of the common market".'

[35] Art. 228 contains the procedure for concluding agreements; Art. 238 deals with association agreements (i.e. 'agreements establishing an association involving reciprocal rights and obligations').

[36] Case 181/73 [1974] ECR 449, paras 2–6 of the judgment.

'an obligation not only in relation to the non-member country concerned but also and above all in relation to the Community which has assumed responsibility for the due performance of the agreement'.[37] The Court added:

It follows from the Community nature of such provisions that their effect in the Community may not be allowed to vary according to whether their application is in practice the responsibility of the Community institutions or of the Member States and, in the latter case, according to the effects in the internal legal order of each Member State which the law of that State assigns to international agreements concluded by it. Therefore it is for the Court, within the framework of its jurisdiction in interpreting the provisions of agreements, to ensure their uniform application throughout the Community.[38]

The question is whether the Court would be prepared to adopt the same reasoning in the case of a mixed agreement, where the Member States implement provisions considered to be outside the Community's competence. In *Demirel* v. *Stadt Schwäbisch Gmünd*, where provisions concerning free movement of workers in the 1963 association agreement with Turkey were in issue, the Court declined to decide the point by holding that those provisions came within the Community's specific competence for concluding association agreements.[39] In *Sevince* the question subsequently arose whether the Court also had jurisdiction over decisions adopted by the Association Council under the same mixed agreement with Turkey. The Court referred to previous rulings, including *Haegeman* and *Demirel*, and held that such decisions also form an integral part of the Community legal system. It added:'

Since the Court has jurisdiction to give preliminary rulings on the Agreement, *in so far as it is an act adopted by one of the institutions of the Community* . . . it also has jurisdiction to give rulings on the interpretation of the decisions adopted by the authority established by the Agreement and entrusted with responsibility for its implementation.[40]

The Court also referred to the above-quoted passage of *Kupferberg* concerning the requirement of uniform interpretation.[41] It no longer mentioned the fact that the provisions of the agreement on free movement, which the decisions of the Association Council aimed to implement, came within the Community's competence. Finally, in *Kus* the German Government attempted to persuade the Court to reverse its ruling in

---

[37] Case 104/81 [1982] ECR 3641, para. 13 of the judgment.
[38] Para. 14.
[39] Case 12/86 [1987] ECR 3719, paras 6–12 of the judgment.
[40] Case C–192/89 [1990] ECR I–3461, para. 10 of the judgment (emphasis added). See also Case 30/88 *Greece* v. *Commission* [1989] ECR 3711, paras 12 and 13.
[41] See text at n. 37.

Sevince, by arguing among other things that the decisions of the Association Council on free movement dealt with matters coming within the competence of the Member States, and thus were not acts of a Community institution. The Court however saw no reason to go back on *Sevince* and did not even answer the German arguments.[42]

It is probably arguable under Community law that the effect of the WTO Agreement in the Community's legal order, as well as its effect in the legal orders of the Member States, should be governed by uniform principles, applied by the European Court of Justice.[43] It has to be borne in mind that those legal orders are not like watertight compartments[44] but are intertwined and integrated. Differences in interpretation and application of the WTO Agreement would be difficult to sustain; even if they only related to matters coming within national competence there would always be a risk of spill-over to Community law.[45] Moreover, on one view the entire WTO Agreement could be regarded as an act of one of the institutions (the Council) in terms of the above case law: the Council concluded it as a whole.[46] The qualification in *Sevince* ('in so far as it is an act adopted by one of the institutions of the Community')[47] might therefore be regarded as irrelevant.

It may be added that the Council indicated in the preamble of the decision whereby it concluded the Agreement that the Agreement is not susceptible to being directly invoked in Community or Member States courts.[48] The reference to the latter courts seems to imply a preference for a uniform domestic legal status throughout the Community.

From the perspective of the Member States, on the other hand, it could however be argued that, to the extent that the Member States have competence over certain WTO matters, the position of the Agreement in the domestic legal order is determined by the relevant national rules. The attitude of Belgian courts towards international agreements is quite receptive, inspired as it is by the principles of Community law regarding

[42] Case C–237/91 [1993] ECR I–6781, para. 9.

[43] cf. F. Castillo de la Torre, 'The Status of GATT in EC Law, Revisited' (1995) *JWT* 68; M. Hilf, 'Statement on the scope and exclusiveness of the common commercial policy—limits of the powers of the Member States', in J. Schwarze (ed.), *Discretionary Powers of the Member States in the Field of Economic Policies and their Limits under the EEC Treaty* (1988) 93 (with other references).

[44] cf. the doctrine which prevailed in Canada pursuant to the case law of the Judicial Committee of the Privy Council, see Chap. 7.

[45] In Op. 1/94 (para. 109) the Court of Justice emphasized that the duty of co-operation between the Member States and the Community institutions in the administration of a mixed agreement 'is all the more imperative in the case of agreements such as those annexed to the WTO Agreement, which are inextricably interlinked, and in view of the cross-retaliation measures established by the Dispute Settlement Understanding'.

[46] See Dec. of 23 Dec. 1994 [1994] OJ L336/1.   [47] See text at n. 40.

[48] See n. 40.

primacy and direct effect.[49] In the leading *Le Ski Case* the Cour de cassation decided that the primacy of treaty rules is inherent in their international law character, and that such rules, provided they have direct effect, prevail over rules of domestic law.[50] Belgian courts have almost never failed to implement that approach, and the condition of direct effect does not seem to be a real hurdle for applying international agreements. Belgian courts could, however, also be expected to abide by a ruling of the Court of Justice on the effects of the WTO Agreement, even if that ruling denied direct effect.[51]

Recently, a new player entered the Belgian judicial field. The Cour d'arbitrage, which has jurisdiction to annul legislative acts for breach of the constitutional rules on the division of competences, on equal treatment, and on freedom of education, has decided in judgments of 1991 and 1994 that its jurisdiction extends to acts approving international agreements. It interprets that jurisdiction as covering the contents of those agreements.[52] Although the Cour d'arbitrage ruled that such review is not an exception to the primacy of international agreements in the Belgian legal order, it is difficult to interpret it in any other way.[53] However, the new case law is not surprising in that it is developed by a constitutional court. One can see the difficulty for such a court to declare that treaty rules, which become binding on the country concerned by virtue of the completion of a procedure laid down in the constitution, subsequently prevail over the rules of that constitution. Similar problems exist in other jurisdictions in the case of the primacy of EC law.[54]

---

[49] For an overview see Maresceau, 'Belgium', in *The Effect of Treaties in Domestic Law* 14–27.

[50] Cass., 27 May 1971, (1971) *Journal des tribunaux* 460; (1971) *Cahiers de droit européen* 560. For an English translation see [1972] CMLR 330.

[51] It may be less certain whether the courts of other Member States would also be prepared to follow. In Germany, e.g., there is much insistence on granting direct effect to GATT since the Banana War.

[52] Cour d'arbitrage, 16 Oct. 1991, No. 26/91 and *MB*, 23 Nov. 1991 at 26325; 3 Feb. 1994, No. 12/94 and *MB*, 11 Mar. 1994 at 6137; 26 April 1994, No. 33/94 and *MB*, 22 June 1994 at 7034. Those judgments sparked off a vivid debate, see J. Velu, 'Toetsing van de grondwettigheid en toetsing van de verenigbaarheid met verdragen' (1992–93) *Rechtskundig Weekblad* 487–516; C. Naômé, 'Les relations entre le droit international et le droit interne belge après l'arrêt de la Cour d'arbitrage du 16 octobre 1991', (1994) *Revue de droit international et de droit comparé* 24–56; J. Van Nieuwenhove, 'Over internationale verdragen, samenwerkingsakkoorden en "Établissement". Enkele kanttekeningen bij de arresten 12/94, 17/94 en 33/94 van het Arbitragehof' (1994–95) *Rechtskundig Weekblad* 449; Ph. Brouwers and H. Simonart 'Le conflit entre la Constitution et le droit international conventionnel dans la jurisprudence de la Cour d'arbitrage' (1995) *Cahiers de droit européen* 7; P. Popelier, 'Ongrondwettige verdragen: de rechtspraak van het Arbitragehof in een monistisch tijdsperspectief' (1994–95) *Rechtskundig Weekblad* 1076–80.

[53] See J.-V. Louis 'La primauté'.

[54] See in general Th. de Berranger, *Constitutions nationales et construction communautaire*, (1995) LGDJ. On the recent judgment of the *Bundesverfassungsgericht* on the Maastricht

The practical effect of this case law may however be rather less important. The Cour d'arbitrage will no doubt endeavour to find that there are no inconsistencies between agreements to which Belgium is a party, and the Constitution.[55] For the WTO Agreement in particular it is difficult to see in what way its provisions could be contrary to the above-mentioned constitutional rules.

3.5 REPRESENTATION IN THE WORLD TRADE ORGANIZATION

The representation of Belgium in the WTO, and in particular the authority to conduct future negotiations, are also clouded by the presence of mixed competences. Belgium is a founding WTO Member, and it has its own representation in the WTO, but for matters within the competence of the European Community it can only act indirectly, through its impact on EC decision-making. That would be no problem if the division of competences were clear cut. Again it must be emphasized that that is not the case, in spite of Opinion 1/94.[56] The Community institutions and the Member States are working on an arrangement covering their representation and future negotiations, but apparently there are no results yet.[57] As things stand today, it is therefore necessary to look at both EC decision-making and independent Belgian decision-making. Matters are further complicated by the fact that in both cases the Belgian internal division of competences may affect decision-making. It has been observed that federal states often have difficulties in committing themselves internationally.[58] In the case of the representation of Belgium in the WTO there is a double layer of federalism: within the country, and in its relationship with the EC.

5.1 EC decision-making

The role which Belgium may play through its impact on EC decision-making is governed by the ordinary rules of Community law. However, to the extent that the communities or the regions are competent for matters discussed or decided by the EC Council there is the problem of how to reach decisions on the Belgian position to be defended in the Council. That problem is addressed by a co-operation agreement on the representation of Belgium in the Council of Ministers, which was concluded between the

Treaty of European Union see e.g. M. Herdegen, 'Maastricht and the German constitutional court: constitutional restraints for an "ever closer union" ' (1994) CMLRev 235–49.

[55] cf. Van Nieuwenhove 'Over internationale verdragen' at 457.
[56] See n. 34. [57] See Chap. 2.
[58] See M. Leroy and A. Schaus, 'Les relations internationales', in *Les réformes institutionnelles*, at 55.

federal government, the communities, and the regions on 8 March 1994.[59] That agreement contains rules on co-ordination, in advance of Council meetings, and on actual representation. For Council meetings where the matters under discussion come within the competence of the communities or the regions a rotation system was set up: each competent government will in turn occupy the Belgian seat in the EC Council. The Minister representing Belgium can only act on the basis of a previously agreed position decided between the competent governments.

It may be expected, however, that in a lot of cases involving EC Council decision-making on WTO matters the federal government will have competence. The problem of internal co-ordination will therefore not often arise, except for issues transcending the classical trade policy domain, such as the relationship between trade policy and cultural, environmental and social policy.

5.2 Belgian autonomous decision-making and representation

Belgian autonomous decision-making on WTO matters and its representation in the WTO are governed by a co-operation agreement dated 30 June 1994, concerning the representation of Belgium in international organizations whose activities concern mixed competences.[60] That agreement covers the WTO. Under that agreement the communities and the regions may be represented in the Permanent Representation of Belgium. A system of permanent concertation is provided for, mainly in the framework of the Interministerial Conference on Foreign Policy. There are rules on internal decision-making, on the constitution of Belgian delegations and on how the Belgian position should be defended at meetings of an international organization. Whether those rules will be effective in producing an efficient participation of Belgium in the WTO remains to be seen. The procedures are complicated and will require a lot of pragmatism in implementing them.

5.3 Exportable constitutional mechanisms?

Other contributions to this volume show that federal states often have difficulties in ensuring implementation of international trade agreements by sub-federal entities. In the Belgian system such difficulties should be avoided through the fact that the communities and the regions have full treaty-making powers in the areas of their competence, which means that the external and internal powers are parallel. It may be expected that,

---

[59] *MB*, 17 Nov. 1994 at 28209.   [60] *MB*, 19 Nov. 1994 at 28706.

where communities or regions enter into certain international commitments, they will also faithfully implement those commitments. It is doubtful however whether such a radical solution, more confederal than federal in character, would be acceptable for other constituencies.

It may be more useful to examine whether the substitution mechanism is exportable.[61] That mechanism makes it possible for the federal authorities to substitute decision-making by the communities or the regions where the latter fail to implement international commitments. The substitution mechanism may only be set in motion under strict conditions. The lack of implementation first has to be decided by an international or supranational court of law (arguably including a WTO Panel). The failing region or community has to be associated to the procedure leading to that decision. The federal government may then call upon the failing region or community to act, for which it has to give a term of three months, except in urgent cases. Where after that term there is still no implementation the federal authorities may act and take implementing measures. Such measures cease to be valid when the communities or regions implement the decision of the international or supranational court of law.

The substitution mechanism explains why it was possible for the federal government to issue the above-mentioned statement on mixed agreements, which states that the Kingdom will bear full responsibility.[62] It is also interesting to note that the mechanism, by attributing a decisive role to international judicial procedures, may lead to 'special effects' of WTO Panel decisions in the domestic legal order.

But perhaps more important is the question whether another Belgian constitutional device, the so-called co-operation agreement, is exportable, in particular to the relationship between the European Community and its Member States. Opinion 1/94 on the competence to conclude the WTO Agreement confirms the long-existing trend towards mixed external action.[63] Most of the significant agreements concluded by the Community are mixed agreements. In the Food and Agriculture Organization, until recently the only world-wide organization where the Community was a *de iure* full member, both the Community and its Member States have full membership rights. In the General Agreement on Tariffs and Trade there used to be a *de facto* exclusive membership of the European Community, at least as regards questions of substance, but the Member States appear adamant to claim a role of their own in the WTO. Such mixed external action is of course not always easy to manage.[64] With regard to mixed

---

[61] See text at n. 8.　　　　　　　　　　　　　　　　　　　　[62] Ibid.

[63] cf. J.-V. Louis, 'Les relations extérieures de l'Union européenne: unité ou complémentarité' (1994) *Revue du Marché Unique Européen*, No. 4 at 5–10.

[64] It might be expected that, in those areas where the EC, which is the vehicle for an advanced co-operation between the Member States, acts externally, it replaces the Member

agreements, the question of their legal status in the various legal orders (Community and national) is discussed above.[65] Even more difficult, however, is organizing the day-to-day co-operation between the Community and the Member States in an international organization such as the WTO. In Opinion 1/94 the Court emphasized that there is a duty of close co-operation,[66] without however suggesting how that duty should be implemented. In the FAO, where the Community and the Member States can only exercise their membership rights on an alternative basis, the co-operation is organized on the basis of an arrangement between the Council and the Commission.[67] The European Commission claims that the Community is not given the chance to play a role of its own, and brought a case against the Council before the European Court of Justice. In its judgment of 19 March 1996 the Court ruled, to some surprise, that the internal arrangement was binding on the Council and the Commission, and reference was made to the duty of co-operation which exists in cases of mixed competence.[68] The judgment would appear to be crucial for the WTO 'code of conduct' which is under negotiation in the Community[69] and which, once adopted, would also have to be regarded as binding on the Community's institutions.

It might none the less be useful to amend the EC Treaty so as to create a formal legal instrument in the area of external relations which might be comparable to the Belgian co-operation agreement. In the Belgian context co-operation agreements are used, among other things, for the joint exercise of mixed external competences.

In the Community context such an instrument, whether or not named co-operation agreement, would have to meet the following requirements. It should be concluded between the competent Community institutions (Council, Commission, European Parliament where relevant) and the Member States. It should lay down the rules and mechanisms governing the joint exercise of external competence. Provided that it is broadly in conformity with the division of competences between the Community and

States. That conception is however too integrationist for the post-Maastricht Community, so it appears. Where the Community acts externally, the Member States tend to look at it as a separate entity, and not merely as the vehicle for their co-operation.

[65] See Sect. 4.

[66] See n. 8.

[67] cf. A. Tavares de Pinho, 'L'admission de la Communauté économique européenne comme membre de l'Organization des Nations unies pour l'alimentation et l'agriculture (FAO)' (1993) *Revue du Marché commun et de l'Union européenne* 656–73; R. Frid, 'The European Economic Community—a member of a specialized agency of the United Nations' (1993) *European Journal of International Law* 239–55.

[68] Case C–25/94, not yet published, paras 48 and 49.

[69] See 'Editorial comments: The aftermath of Opinion 1/94 or how to ensure unity of representation for joint competences' (1995) CMLRev. 385–390.

the Member States it should not itself be the subject of detailed review by the European Court of Justice. By contrast, the Court should be given jurisdiction to review the observance of the agreement, at least for certain significant matters.

It is not suggested that the introduction of such a new legal instrument will resolve all problems of co-ordination, but it would at least give a firm legal basis to the mixed external action of the Community and its Member States.

3.6 CONCLUDING REMARKS

The negotiation, ratification and implementation of the WTO Agreement show that from the Belgian perspective there are two, related areas which present difficulties.

There is the new Constitution, giving full external powers to the communities and the regions in the areas of their competence. That leads to a multiplication of ratification procedures in the case of wide-ranging agreements such as the WTO Agreement. Ratification requires close co-ordination, as will also the negotiation of future agreements or the definition of the Belgian position in the organs of international organizations. The new approach towards the conduct of the external relations of Belgium will be tested in the years to come.

There is, however, not only the internal division of competences, but also the division of competences between the Community and the Member States, which are all WTO Members. There will have to be an arrangement on how the respective competences will be exercised, and it is worth examining whether the example of Belgian co-operation agreements could be transposed to the EC setting.

It would seem that our post-modern societies are increasingly characterized by a proliferation of rules and legal systems, as the present contribution illustrates. It is the task of lawyers to find mechanisms to interconnect all those systems as efficiently as possible. From that perspective, the implementation of the WTO Agreement has broader significance than its economically-oriented content might suggest.

4

NEGOTIATING AND IMPLEMENTING THE URUGUAY ROUND: THE ROLE OF EC MEMBER STATES—THE CASE OF GERMANY

*Meinhard Hilf**

4.1 INTRODUCTION AND OVERVIEW

Among the now fifteen Member States of the European Community, Germany is the one most dependent on international trade in goods and services.[1] The Uruguay Round Agreements have met with Germany's full and unequivocal support.

According to Article X of the Agreement Establishing the World Trade Organization, Germany has become a founding Member of the WTO as it has been a Contracting Party to the General Agreement on Trariffs and Trade since 1953. Moreover, for the first time the European Community has—in addition to its Member States—acquired the formally recognized status of a Member of the WTO as is analysed in detail in Chapter 2.

This joint WTO membership raises some legal questions. The WTO Agreement provides no clarification as to the internal distribution of powers between the European Community and its Member States with respect to their obligations as Members of the WTO. In theory, since both the European Community and its Member States signed the Agreement, they would each appear to be responsible for the entire fulfillment of any obligations arising from their membership. In practice, however, the joint WTO membership of the European Community and its Member States is not thought to change any of the established practices which had previously allowed the European Community to act within the GATT in accordance with its evolving exclusive internal competence under Article 113 of the Treaty Establishing the European Community relating to the Common Commercial Policy. Under the text of the GATT and most of its side agreements, the European Community was not visible, but it had become

* Professor, University of Hamburg.
[1] Germany accounted for 12.4% (1994) of the world trade in goods, the entire EC for 40% (domestic and foreign trade). Cf. BT–Drs. 12/17655 (*neu*), 340; *Der Fischer Weltalmanach* (1995), 870.

generally recognized that it could act in accordance with the powers attributed to it by the ECT, even with respect to all other Contracting Parties. There was no pressure upon the European Community and its Member States to clarify the internal dividing line of their respective powers. In the same vein, concurrent membership was admitted in the WTO under the assumption that the European Community and its Member States would find an acceptable *modus operandi* for playing an active and reliable part in the operation of the WTO, as they did previously within the GATT. The European Court of Justice in its Advisory Opinion of 15 November, 1994 has clarified some disputed aspects as to the extent of the European Community's external powers. The main ruling of the Court was that trade in services and the protection of intellectual property do not fall under the exclusive power of the European Community but are concurrent powers of both the European Community and its Member States. Thus, even in the future, pragmatism will survive; this is certainly not to the benefit of the European Community itself, which finds itself in constant teeter-tottering discussions with its Member States as to the conduct of its policies. Member States tend to cling to their sovereignty and to their international identity, seeking to maintain their seat at the international table. Currently, discussions are underway to create an internal Code of Conduct to ensure that, as during the negotiations under the Uruguay Round, the European Community and its Member States will continue to act effectively in the safeguard of their interests when operating within the WTO.

Looking at Germany, with its role determined on the one hand by its own constitution, and on the other hand, by the limitations on the exercise of its sovereign powers under the ECT, one will discover unresolved legal problems at this three-sided interface of the national, European and international legal order. In the following, the role of Germany within the negotiations under the Uruguay Round is evaluated in Section 2. Particular aspects regarding Germany's signature, the Act of Consent by the German Parliament, and ratification are examined in Section 3. The resulting measures of implementation will be discussed in Section 4, leading to some general conclusions and perspectives in Section 5 which will underline the important role EC Member States are still playing within the WTO framework as they do, of course, within the European Community itself.

4.2 NEGOTIATIONS

4.2.1 Foreign relations powers under the German Constitution

There is no specific Chapter in the German Constitution—the Grund-gesetz—governing foreign relations powers. Article 32, paragraph 1 GG provides that foreign relations are within the jurisdiction of the Federation (*Bund*) without, however, specifying to what extent such powers are vested in the executive or legislature. According to the case law of the Federal Constitutional Court, the Federal Government (*Bundesregierung*) has the primary responsibility as to the conduct of foreign relations.[2] The two Houses of the Parliament, that is the Bundestag and the Bundesrat, may only intervene in cases expressly provided for in the Constitution such as that in Article 59, paragraph 2 GG, requiring an Act of Consent to conclude certain treaties. These are treaties which regulate the overall political relations of the Federal Republic with other states or international organizations, or treaties which may concern certain matters of legislation, such as the protection of intellectual property. The WTO and the other Uruguay Round Agreements clearly met these constitutional requirements.

More recently, the Federal Constitutional Court has enlarged the scope of the involvement of the Bundestag in foreign affairs by requiring a consenting vote in two relevant cases, concerning the final stage for the European Monetary Union,[3] and the participation of German troops in peace-keeping operations within NATO or the UN.[4] This does not, however, affect the overall responsibility and power of the Federal Government for negotiating treaties.

4.2.2 Negotiating the WTO: the role of the Federal Government

The Federal Government is represented by one of its members in the EC Council. In strict legal terms, that representative is not acting under the authority of the German Constitution. The composition of the EC Council is regulated in Article 2 of the Merger Treaty (1965) and its authority derives only from the terms of the ECT. In practice, however, the member of the Council delegated by the Federal Government has ample opportunity and the undisputed obligation to consider German interests within the EC Council's deliberations.

The German Federal Government also had opportunities to affect the course of negotiations outside of the EC Council. As has been shown in Chapter 2, negotiations on behalf of the European Community and—in the case of mixed agreements such as the WTO—of its Member States are entrusted under Article 113 EC to the European Commission acting according to the guidelines of the Council (that is, according to the Council's directives).[5] The Commission is 'assisted' by a special committee (the so-called 113 Committee) appointed by the Council. Since not all

---

[2] BVerfGE 68, 1.   [3] BVerfGE 89, 155.
[4] BVerfGE 87, 173.   [5] Art. 113 para. 3 EC.

WTO negotiations came undisputably within the scope of Article 113, the Council, the Commission and the Member States agreed to a 'Code of Conduct' which allowed the Commission to continue negotiating in strict co-ordination with the Council and the Member States via the 113 Committee. In this Committee—as well as in the Council—the German Economic Department (*Bunderministerium für Wirtschaft*) and the Foreign Office (*Auswärtiges Amt*) supported the Commission in effectively handling the negotiations. This may have helped to fend off particular interests of some other EC Member States which might have endangered the final conclusion of the Uruguay Round.[6]

4.2.3 The role of the German Parliament

During the Uruguay Round negotiations the Federal Government communicated on a regular basis with the relevant Parliamentary committees as well as with the Federal Parliament as a whole, that is the Bundesrat and the Bundestag. The Government provided all the required documentation and took positions with regard to all questions which were tabled by members of both Houses. There were also a number of rather short debates within Parliament leading to resolutions supporting the general negotiating line of the Government. One of the issues raised was the situation in the audio-visual sector. This was of interest to the German Länder, which wanted to avoid any interference with their respective public policies regulating this sector. The relevant agreement, the General Agreement on Trade in Services, does not impose any such limitations.[7] Overall, the Federal Government noted with some satisfaction that no major arguments had been raised by either of the two Houses against the final results of the Uruguay Round.

Since 1993 the Federal Government is bound to co-operate even more closely with the Parliament on the basis of the newly inserted Article 23, paragraph 2–7 GG, which refer to all matters relating to the European Union. A special Act of Parliament sets out in detail the obligations of the Federal Government in order to allow both Houses to take positions on all matters on the agenda of the European institutions. In some cases, relating mainly to the powers of the Länder, the Federal Government may even be bound to follow the line for negotiation laid down by the Bundesrat.[8] With respect to the negotiations leading to the conclusion of the WTO

[6] See the Report of the Federal Executive of 24 May 1994 to the German Parliament, accompanying the Draft Act of Consent BT–Drs. 12/7655.

[7] See BT–Drs. 12/17655 (*neu*), 342.

[8] See Act of 12 Mar. 1993 on the collaboration of the Federation with the Länder in matters concerning the EU, BGBL. I, 313 f. Cf. Borchmann, 'Neue Bund-Länder-Vereinbarung über die Zusammenarbeit in Angelegenheiten der EU' (1994), 5 EuZW 172; V. Neller, 'Die "neue Ländermitwirkung" nach Maastricht' (1994), 29 EuR 216.

Agreement this recent 1993 Act did not, however, have any impact as the main results had already been achieved prior to its adoption.

As the Federal Government was only participating indirectly in the negotiating process, which was conducted primarily by the EC Commission, it is safe to say that the overall involvement of the German Parliament was only minimal. Whether this is true with regard to the other national parliaments cannot be confirmed in this context. It may only be assumed that the Uruguay negotiations were 'far away' and displayed such a degree of detailed technicality that it would have been difficult anyhow for any national parliament of the EC Member States to try to influence the world-wide negotiations among the then 124 negotiating states. In any case, the European Parliament is in a better position to influence the Commission's position in ongoing negotiations. Within the European Parliament the interests of the peoples of all Member States are represented and can be voiced collectively. The national parliaments cannot effectively keep an eye on the Commission. Though the Treaty on European Union[9] as well as the '*Rapport d'étape* (interim report)' of the Reflection Group (24 August, 1995), on the Intergovernmental Conference of 1996, both highlight the necessity of a greater involvement of the national parliaments in European affairs, it seems that in the realm of international negotiations there may be only very limited prospects for such involvement.

4.2.4 Interest groups

Interest groups are highly effective in detecting the centres of power and decision-making. Those groups interested in the outcome of the Uruguay Round provided the Federal Government as well as the Parliament with their views and recommendations. They probably did even more to try to influence the EC Commission and the members of the European Parliament. To promote the interests of German industry, the most efficient way still seems to address the respective department of the Federal Government. On the European level, however, interest groups have to organize themselves in order to bring together the opinion of 'the European industry'. This requires compromises of various sorts.

4.3 SIGNATURE, ACT OF CONSENT AND RATIFICATION: UNRESOLVED DIVISION OF POWERS AND TIME-CONSTRAINTS

4.3.1 Internal procedure

The internal procedure leading to the ratification by Germany was overshadowed by the then still unresolved question of the division of

[9] See annexed Declaration No. 13, Declaration on the role of national Parliaments in the European Union.

powers between the European Community and its Member States. Whereas all the Member States conceded that the Uruguay Round Final Act was to be considered as a mixed agreement, the Commission maintained its position that all aspects under the agreement would be covered by the exclusive powers of the EC under the ECT. Yet the EC Council decided on 7 March 1994 to have signatures by both the European Community and its Member States,[10] and the EC Commission asked the European Court of Justice for an Opinion on 6 April 1994.

The Federal Government was of the opinion that all areas covered by the GATS and the Agreement on Trade-Related Aspects of Intellectual Property Rights fell within the powers of the Member States as well as all tariff concessions made with respect to products covered by the European Coal and Steel Treaty. As is well known from Opinion 1/94, rendered on 15 November 1994, however, all the above mentioned views of the Federal Government turned out to be 'wrong' or, to put it less harshly, not to be in line with the opinion of the European Court. Had the Government waited for the Court's opinion, the internal ratification procedure would have been different.[11] The Federal Government, however, had no choice but to introduce the internal procedure for providing the necessary parliamentary consent to the ratification without waiting for the outcome of the Court's proceedings. Being faced with general government elections in October 1994, and thus with no Bundestag in session after August 1994, the Federal Government had to try to get the consent of the outgoing Bundestag before the end of July 1994. The other Chamber, the Bundesrat, being a permanent institution representing the Länder, does not suffer the effects of the principle of discontinuity which does away with all unfinished business of an outgoing Bundestag.

Thus, the burden of the unresolved question of the division of powers between the EC and its Member States imposed upon the Federal Government and the unusual time-constraints may explain some of the following quite unusual aspects of the internal procedure leading to Germany's ratification of the Uruguay Round Agreements.

4.3.2 Signature on 15 April 1994

As agreed by the EC Council together with the Representatives of the Member States, Germany signed the Uruguay Round Agreements at

---

[10] This was confirmed by a decision of the Federal Executive of 15 Mar. 1994.

[11] For the solution found by the ECJ see M. Hilf, 'The ECJ's Opinion 1/94 on the WTO—no surprise, but wise?' (1995) 6 EJIL 245 and J. Bourgeois, 'The EC in the WTO and Advisory Opinion 1/94: an Echternach procession' (1995) 32 CMLRev. 763 as well as Chap. 2.

Marrakesh on 15 April 1994 along with the other EC Member States. No declaration was made as to the division of powers between the European Community and its Member States. And no such declaration was asked for by the other signatories: it was presumed that the European Community and its Member States[12] would continue operating according to prior GATT practice.

The only unilateral declaration made by the Federal Government was related to the access of bananas to the EC market. Following the famous *Bananas Case*,[13] the EC Commission had signed an agreement with the Central American states, except Guatemala, improving the market access for bananas originating from these countries. The Federal Government did not consider these measures to be sufficient enough to liberalize trade in bananas and therefore made a declaration with respect to the internal protocol of the EEC Council reserving its legal position as to this dispute. This declaration, however, is not part of the Marrakesh documents.[14]

4.3.3 Act of Consent by Parliament

Due to the agreed time-frame for the entering into force of the WTO by 1 January 1995, the internal procedure for asking the consent of both Houses of the Parliament turned out to be a struggle with time and paper. The Marrakesh documents comprise some 26,000 pages. They are drafted in English, French and Spanish and could not have been transmitted to the Parliament without a German translation. The official German text which would appear in the *Official Journal* was not, however, to be expected before October 1994.[15] Therefore the Federal Government had to find ways and means to start the parliamentary deliberations without waiting for the official translation. Under the normal constitutional procedures the Government can save time by having a bill initiated by the Parliament itself. However, this possibility is not open in the case of Acts of Consent to international treaties.[16] Except where the Constitution otherwise provides, the Federal Government is solely responsible for dealing with all matters of foreign affairs. It is considered to be within the discretion of this power also to determine the right moment to introduce a bill for the act of consent to an international treaty. Therefore the Federal Government initiated the ratification proceedings by choosing an urgent procedure under Article 76, paragraph 2, 3rd sentence GG and introduced the Bill for

---

[12] See differently in the case of UNCLOS in 1982.
[13] Case C–280/93, *Germany* v. *Commission* [1994] ECR I–4973.
[14] See BT–Drs. 12/7655 (*neu*), 349 as well as Case C–280/93, n. 13.
[15] See now [1995] OJ L336/2; German is one of the official languages of the EC according to Art. 248 ECT.
[16] See Art. 76 GG and the relevant commentaries.

the Act of Consent to the Uruguay Round Agreements with the Bundesrat on 29 April 1994. The important questions were: to what extent did the Federal Government have to ask for the Parliament's consent? Should it be for the entire text signed at Marrakesh or only for those parts which were considered to be covered by the powers still in the hands of the Member States? Moreover, would it be sufficient to submit these Uruguay Round texts accompanied by a provisional translation, risking that such a translation might diverge from the official translation provided by the European Community at a later stage?

4.3.3.1 Selective introduction of texts

The proposed bill, sent to the Bundesrat on 24 May 1994, asked for the consent of both Houses to ratify all the agreements which had been signed at Marrakesh. However, not all these agreements were submitted to the Parliament. The Federal Government was of the opinion that only some of the Marrakesh agreements were covered by powers still retained by the EC Member States and although consent for all was requested, only those latter agreements were transmitted to the Houses. The agreements were transmitted in their English version accompanied by an 'in-house' translation in German. The respective agreements were:

1. The Final Act, together with the Agreement on the Establishment of the WTO;
2. the Protocol concerning the GATT 1994;
3. List L XXX concerning Tariff Concessions falling under the ECSC Treaty;
4. the GATS, including the lists of the binding agreements made by the European Community;
5. the TRIPS Agreement; and
6. the Understanding on Rules and Procedures Governing the Settlement of Disputes.

With respect to all other agreements the Federal Government thought it sufficient to simply inform the Parliament of their content in its Explanatory Memorandum,[17] on the basis of which the Bundesrat had already given its opinion on 10 June 1994.[18] Finally, the Federal Executive on 16 June 1994, distributed to both Houses 'for their information' texts falling, in its view, exclusively under the powers of the EC.[19] These texts

---

[17] See BT–Drs. 12/7655 (*neu*) 348.
[18] The opinion of the Bundesrat is given before this House's final consent at a preliminary stage of the proceedings. The opinion is then communicated to the Bundestag for discussion.
[19] See BT–Drs. 12/7986.

comprised 585 pages, and they were transmitted only in the English version together with a translation into German.

From a merely formalistic point of view this separation of texts can be criticized: Germany, having signed the entire range of Agreements, could be held responsible for the fulfilment of each one of them. This follows from the very nature of mixed agreements in relation to which no declaration as to the dividing line of the respective powers of the European Community and its Member States is given to the other signatories. However, it has to be taken into account that all the Uruguay Round Agreements are published in the *Official Journal*. Thus, as far as the internal legal order of the European Community is concerned, those agreements falling under the exclusive powers of the European Community can bind all the Member States pursuant to Article 228, paragraph 7 ECT.[20] However, since Germany is a member of the WTO and has signed all the Uruguay Round Agreements, it must also ratify them all in order to be bound under public international law as well. Consequently, as has been indicated above, the Federal Government had asked for the Parliament's consent to *all* the Uruguay Round Agreements and, indeed, the final Act of Consent refers to all of them.

4.3.3.2 Authentic texts and translation

The Uruguay Round Agreements are equally authentic in English, French and Spanish.[21] The interpretation and application of the agreements have to be based on all of these three versions in order to resolve divergencies between them. This rule follows from Article 31 of the Vienna Convention on the Law of Treaties (1969). Again, under strict construction, the consent of any parliament would have to be given to all of these three versions. Nonetheless, it may be assumed that for practical reasons most states restrict their internal procedure of consent to one authentic text and, if necessary, to a translation in their official language. State practice in this regard differs.[22] The fact that the Federal Government limited the texts submitted to the Parliament to the English text and a translation in the German language can therefore hardly be criticized.[23] The translation of the agreements falling under the competence of Germany was at first an 'in-house translation', as the EC Commission was not yet in a position to prepare a German text of all the agreements to be published in the *Official*

---

[20] 'Agreements concluded under the conditions set out in this Article shall be binding on the institutions of the Community and on Member States.'

[21] See the final clause following Art. XVI of the WTO Agreement.

[22] See M. Hilf, *Die Auslegung mehrsprachiger Verträge* (1973), 188 f.

[23] Cf. BT–Drs. 12/7655 (*neu*).

Journal.[24] In June 1994, however, a revised 'in-house translation' was prepared and transmitted to the services of the EC Commission which did not object to it and seemed, thus, to have approved it.[25] Such translations are necessary and they are common practice in order to allow members of parliament to understand the nature and impact of all the obligations to which their consent was required. They are all the more important for any authority applying the respective agreements as well as for any interested natural or legal person. The general principle of due process requires that any obligation or right imposed or conferred by public authorities must be expressed in the official language of the given state. However, the translated versions are not binding and should not be considered as being the authoritative text to be applied. The obligations entered into by Germany cannot be affected by the fact that its Parliament had given its internal consent without having seen the authentic versions in French and Spanish. Nor can they be affected by the fact that the Parliament formed its initial opinion only on the basis of those agreements which were first selected by the Federal Government as being covered by the remaining powers of the EC Member States. At the time of the final vote and the authentification of the Act of Consent by the Federal President on 30 August 1994 all the texts of the Marrakesh Agreements had been given to the Parliament even though this was for the sole purpose of information. The vote was almost unanimous in the Bundestag[26] as well as in the Bundesrat.[27]

4.3.3.3 Publication

The German Act of Consent was finally published on 9 September, 1994.[28] This voluminous document contains the Act consenting to all the Marrakesh Agreements and lists the amendments which had to be made to existing German legislation (see below, Section 4.4). It publishes, however, only the texts of those agreements which the Federal Government thought to be within the powers of the Federal Republic. These texts are reproduced first in their authentic version in English. Annexed to this is a translation in German apparently approved by the services of the EC-Commission. The other agreements, which were considered to be covered by the exclusive powers of the EC, were not published; the reader is

---

[24] See [1995] OJ L336/2.

[25] See BR–Drs 12/7984 of 16 June 1994.

[26] Two adverse votes were given by PDS/Linke Liste; cf. *Verhandlungen des Bundestages*, 12. Wahlperiode, Stenographische Berichte, Band 175, 237. Sitzung, 20870 (C).

[27] The Bundesrat gave its final vote on 8 July 1994; see *Verhandlungen des Bundesrates* 1994, Stenographische Berichte, 380 (B).

[28] BGBL. II, 1438–1764.

advised to look at the publication in *Official Journal* for their text. For information on tariff concessions, as well as binding agreements and exceptions from the most favoured nation clause of the GATS made by other WTO Members, readers are referred to the WTO Secretariat in Geneva. These referrals seem to be unavoidable since at the time the Parliament's consent was given not all such concessions and binding agreements had been made. In these circumstances, referrals of this kind seem to be acceptable even though each such concession or binding agreement, mostly falling under the competence of the EC anyhow, may have a considerable impact on trade.

4.3.3.4 Ratification

It had been agreed that the EC and its Member States should only become Members of the WTO concurrently as neither the EC alone, nor the Member States severally, could perform the entire range of agreements. In fact, on 1 January 1995 all documents of ratification had been deposited, not all at the same time, but all being effective at the same date.[29] Thus a 'depot-ballet' of ratification documents was avoided, especially in a situation in which the EC would not have become a Member other than together with all its Member States.

4.3.3.5 Assessment of the procedure

The procedure leading to the final ratification by Germany may be noteworthy in various aspects. First of all, the Federal Government had to manœuvre under a number of unusual circumstances. As indicated above, the Government was working within a very tight time-frame since the act of ratification had to be deposited by 1 January 1995. From 15 April to 30 August 1994 the Federal Government managed to steer the voluminous documents through the required procedure. As will be shown in Section 4.4 and as has been confirmed by the Opinion of the European Court, only a few modifications have been necessary to the German legal order as by far the major part of powers involved is vested in the European Community.[30] In addition, it is accepted practice under constitutional law that no

---

[29] Most of the instruments had been deposited on 30 Dec. 1994. Greece's acceptance is good as of the date of signature as the representative of Greece had not made any reservation requiring subsequent ratification by Parliament. For Austria and Sweden, the new Member States of the EC, the WTO Press Release of 28 Aug. 1995 indicates the 6 Dec. and 22 Dec. 1994 respectively.

[30] The President of the EC Commission Delors estimated that about 80% of all legislation in the economic field will finally have to be taken by the EC: see Bull. EC7/8–1988, 124.

amendments can be made to international treaties such as the Marrakesh Agreements.[31]

Therefore it is not astonishing that this procedure did not elicit a major interest within the German Parliament. Consequently the Federal Government could afford to take the many procedural risks alluded to above. One of the other important risks concerned the unresolved question of the respective powers of the European Community and its Member States. The Federal Government initiated the procedure before knowing what the European Court would decide as to the respective powers of the European Community and its Member States in this field. Opinion 1/94 confirmed the opinion of the Federal Government that the entire package did not fall under the exclusive competence of the European Community. But the Court did not share the assessment of the Federal Government that tariff matters relating to the ECSC products would fall under the power of the Member States.[32] Nor did it share the view that the GATS and TRIPS were entirely covered by the competence of the Member States. Thus in retrospect it appears that the Federal Government had erred without, however, any detrimental effect, as its Parliament had given its consent to all agreements resulting from the Uruguay Round. However, the final publication in the *Journal of Federal Legislation* (*Bundesgesetzblatt*) does not reveal clearly which agreements are still covered by the remaining powers of the Member States.

4.4 IMPLEMENTATION IN GERMANY

The successful outcome of this rather unique procedure was due to the fact that the Uruguay Round Agreements required hardly any amending legislation within the German legal order. Legislation of the Länder, in particular, did not have to be amended at all. The Federal Executive included in the text of the bill for the Act of Consent proposals for the amendment of the following four legislative acts:

1. Paragraph 206 of the Act regulating the Profession of Lawyers (*Bundesrechtsanwaltsordnung*) had to be adapted to Article II para. 1 of the GATS by deleting the requirement of reciprocity in order to allow the free establishment of lawyers. Lawyers from other GATS Members will thus be allowed to become members of the German bar and to practise law, but only in regard to the legal order of their home country and to questions of public international law. For lawyers from non-EU

---

[31] Cf. § 82 of the Rules of Procedure of the Bundestag.
[32] This was, however, the prevailing opinion under the GATT.

or non-GATS countries the requirement of reciprocity is maintained.[33]

2. With respect to the Act regulating the Profession of Legal Consultants other than lawyers (*Rechtsberatungsgesetz*, Article 1, Section 1), citizens of GATS Members may act as consultants as far as their home country law is concerned. This would include the law of the European Community only where the home country is one of the Member States of the European Community.

3. A minor change relates to patents having been granted by the former German Democratic Republic. Those patents were protected for a period of only eighteen years, whereas Articles 33 and 70 paragraph 2 of the TRIPs now provide for a period of twenty years. The respective amendment made to the so-called *Erstreckungsgesetz*, however, only relates to patents which were still valid on 31 December, 1995, the date at which TRIPs had to be implemented. The Federal Government is of the opinion that from 1996 onward TRIPs will be directly applicable so that any change to the existing legislative rules on the period of protection would be superfluous.[34]

4. Finally Section 10 of the Act relating to Economic Accountants (*Wirtschaftsprüferordnung*) had to be amended in order to withdraw the requirement of reciprocity. The Federal Government as well as the EC Commission were convinced that the most-favoured-nation treatment in Article II para. 1 of the GATS would be acceptable as there had been sufficient binding agreements undertaken by most of the important GATS Members. Thus a sufficient level of access of economic accountants seemed to exist throughout the Member States of the GATS.

These amendments to federal legislation have been accepted without further discussion. During the legislative procedure two more amendments had been added to the bill which, however, had no link at all to the WTO. The only reason for adding these amendments to the WTO package was that the implementing bill was one of the last to be passed before the summer recess of the outgoing Bundestag.[35]

A few further adaptations to the German legal order were necessary, but could be brought about by either issuing executive regulations in the case of tariffs relating to ECSC products[36] or by just considering the respective agreements as being directly applicable. This is the case, according to the

---

[33] See BT–Drs. 12/7655 (*neu*), 7.

[34] See BT–Drs. 12/7655 (*neu*), 345.

[35] Cf. Arts 8 and 9 of the Act of Assent of 30 Aug. 1994 concerning amendments to the Federal Act for Notaries (*Bundesnotarordnung*) and to the Act relating to the procedure in administrative courts (*Verwaltungsgerichtsordnung*).

[36] Cf. s. 6 para. 2 of the Act on the Administration of Customs Duties (*Zollverwaltungsgesetz*), BT–Drs. 12/7655 (*neu*), 340.

opinion of the Federal Government, in regard to those rules under TRIPs which lend themselves 'according to their wording' to such an application (unambiguous time-limits, national treatment or most-favoured-nation treatment).[37]

This concept of direct applicability is remarkable as the European Court has ruled that at least GATT law shall not be considered as being directly applicable in the legal order of the EC.[38] And the EC Council has extended this concept to the WTO by setting out in the considerations of the Regulation accepting the Uruguay Round Agreements that those Agreements will not be considered as being directly applicable.[39] In the recent *Bananas Case* the Federal Government had taken the EC Council to court arguing that the recent regulation on a market organization for bananas[40] was in conflict with a number of applicable GATT rules. The Court, however, did not accept this concept and did not allow the Federal Republic to challenge the EC Regulation on that ground.[41] It is beyond the scope of this contribution to discuss this restrictive ruling.[42] But it seems difficult to reconcile the non-direct applicability of WTO law within the legal framework of the European Community, which in case of conflict with the law of any Member States shall prevail, and the concept of direct applicability as proposed by the Federal Executive and obviously endorsed by the German Parliament. Especially in the event of a breach of WTO law by the European Community or in the event of cross-retaliation, which may eventually cover the entire range of Uruguay Round Agreements, these divergent positions with respect to direct applicability must be kept in mind. However, it may be assumed that any considerable measure of cross-retaliation is to be based on acts of the respective legislatures. Thus the German legislature may at any time revoke the status of WTO law as directly applicable.

Finally, as to the financial impact of the WTO Agreements, there is no specific balancing requirement with respect to the annual budget. Losses by tariff reductions accrue in their entirety to the budget of the European

---

[37] Cf. BT–Drs. 12/7655 (*neu*), 337 and esp. 345.
[38] See Case C–280/93 at 5072 (n. 13 above); cases 267/81–269/81, *Amministrazione delle Finanze dello Stato* v. *Società Petrolifera Italiana SpA and SpA Michelin Italia* [1983] ECR 801 at 830; case 9/73, *Schlüter* v. *Hauptzollamt Lörrach* [1973] ECR 1135 at 1157.
[39] See EC Council Dec. 22 Dec. 1994, [1994] OJ L336/2.
[40] [1993] OJ L47/1.
[41] See Case C–280/93, n. 13 above. However, the Lower Finance Court of Hamburg, by a decision of 19 May 1995, (1995) 6 EuZW 413, again held GATT law as being directly applicable and referred this question to the ECJ (still pending).
[42] See M. Hilf 'The role of national courts in international trade relations' in E.-U. Petersmann (ed.), *International Trade Law and the GATT–WTO dispute settlement systems* (1997, forthcoming) and in general J. H. Jackson, 'Status of treaties in domestic legal systems: a policy analysis' (1992) AJIL 310.

Community. The budget of the German Federation and of the Länder will be minimally affected by slightly higher contributions to the administrative costs of the WTO and by the extension of UN privileges to the civil servants of the WTO under Article VII of the Agreement.[43]

4.5 CONCLUSIONS AND PERSPECTIVES OF GERMANY'S WTO MEMBERSHIP

At a time when the WTO has only just begun its operations it may be premature to draw conclusions about the impact of the WTO membership on EC Member States. But some observations may be suggested here for further assessment.

1. There is an astonishing gap between the rather minimal effects of WTO rules on the German legal order and Germany's role in respect to rule-making within the WTO. Within Germany's legal order only minor adaptations have been necessary.[44] In spite of—or due to—the Opinion of the European Court, the most important powers lie with the European Community (especially under the Common Commercial Policy and in regard to transfrontier services). Within the European Community, Germany is backing every effort to liberalize the world's trading order and can exercise a considerable influence on the positions taken by the European Community. Though the code of conduct for organizing the joint WTO membership of the European Community and all its Member States has still to be adopted, it is safe to say that no EC position will be taken which may be incompatible with the major interests of any one of its Member States.

   It is an open question to what extent Germany as one of the EC Member States will be able to negotiate or to take part in dispute settlement proceedings if in some cases only German interests or powers are in question and there is no common position of the European Community. It is, however, the position of the Federal Government to avoid such situations which could undermine the standing of the European Community within the WTO. This supports the requirements formulated by the European Court that the EC Member States should together with the European Community strive for a high degree of coherence and solidarity.[45]

2. The role of the German Parliament seems to be rather reduced given its distance from the decision making process within the WTO. It remains

---

[43] See BT–Drs. 12/7655 (*neu*), 8.   [44] Op. 1/94 15.11.1994, ECR I–5267.
[45] Cf. Op. 1/94 at 5419 f. (n. 44 above).

to be seen to what extent the European Parliament will be able to make up for this failure by controlling and thus lending legitimacy to the EC Commission's negotiations and conduct within the WTO.[46]

3. Germany's membership of the WTO alongside that of the European Community indicates the continuing desire of Germany to uphold its status as a sovereign entity in international trade relations. Although the EC Member States are no longer in a position to influence negotiations within the WTO without the European Community, their presence at the table still underlines their need to assert their international identity.[47] This often leads to a loss of efficiency and operability on the side of the European Community. It assures, however, that all Member States' interests are taken into account and are present within the operations of the WTO, thus also assuring a continuing legitimation of and support to the European Community by its Member States.[48]

[46] See n. 6.

[47] See at the same time the references to the 'international' and the 'european' identity of the European Union in the Preamble and in Art. B TEU respectively.

[48] See J. H. H. Weiler, 'The external legal relations of non-unitary-actors: mixity and the federal principle', in D. O'Keeffe & H. G. Schermers (eds.), *Mixed Agreements* (1983), 35.

5

CONSTITUTIONAL PROBLEMS INVOLVED IN IMPLEMENTING THE URUGUARY ROUND IN JAPAN

*Yuji Iwasawa**

5.1 INTRODUCTION

The Uruguay Round of multilateral trade negotiations were concluded in 1993 after more than seven years of intensive discussion. It was a bold Round; the topics for negotiations included new areas which had not been dealt with by the General Agreement on Tariffs and Trade 1947—services, Trade-Related Intellectual Property, and Trade-Related Investment Measures—and the areas which had given exceptional treatment under GATT 1947—agriculture and textiles. The number of participating countries in the Round was far greater than that for the Tokyo Round. The organizational structure of the GATT was reviewed, and a new international organization called the World Trade Organization was eventually created. The implications of the Uruguay Round for the world economy, including the economy of Japan, is enormous.

The purpose of this contribution is to analyse constitutional problems involved in implementing the Uruguay Round in Japan. What was the process in Japan of concluding and implementing the Uruguay Round Agreements? What problems were involved in it? Those are the main focus of this contribution. It is not the purpose of this contribution to describe all the measures taken by Japan to implement the Uruguay Round. In Section 4, however, implementing measures in some of the important areas for Japan will be examined.

* LL.B. (Tokyo), LL.M. (Harvard), S.J.D. (Virginia). Associate Professor of International Law, Department of International Relations, University of Tokyo. The present contribution draws upon the author's previous articles, including 'Implementation of international trade agreements in Japan', in M. Hilf & E.-U. Petersmann (eds.), *National Constitutions and International Economic Law* (1993), 299 and 'The relationship between international law and national law: Japanese experiences', (1993) 64 BYIL 333.

5.2 TREATY-MAKING PROCESS IN JAPAN

5.2.1 Approval of treaties by the Diet

5.2.1.1 Process of approval

Article 73 (3) of the Japanese Constitution provides that the Cabinet has
the authority to '[c]onclude treaties' on the condition that 'it shall obtain
prior or, depending on circumstances, subsequent approval of the Diet
[Japanese Parliament]'. Different procedures apply for the passage of
statutes (Article 59) and approval of budgets (Article 60). The difference is
most conspicuous when the upper house (House of Councillors) and the
lower house (House of Representatives) reach conflicting conclusions. In
the approval of budgets, where no agreement is reached through a joint
committee of both houses, the decision of the lower house simply prevails
(Article 60 (2)). The Constitution provides that this streamlined procedure
for the approval of budgets is also to be used for the approval of treaties
(Article 61).[1] Thus, procedurally it is easier to conclude a treaty than to
enact a statute, let alone to amend the Constitution.[2] When approving a
treaty no statute is enacted, as is commonly done in many European
countries. The cabinet simply submits an agenda item concerning the
approval of a treaty to the Diet, which then approves the item by majority
vote.

  Japan is a parliamentary democracy; the cabinet is formed on the basis
of a majority in the lower house of the Diet. Since the Liberal Democratic
Party controlled both houses of the Diet in most of the postwar period,
approval of treaties by the Diet has not been a problem in the past. In
1993, however, the LDP lost its parliamentary majority for the first time in
almost forty years, and since that time the Cabinet has been formed on a
coalition of political parties. As a result, the passage of treaties in Japan
has become more complicated and difficult. However, unless the Cabinet
loses the support of the ruling parties—which is highly unlikely—the treaty
will gain the approval of the Diet. In fact, it is the practice of the
Government to submit a treaty to the executive committees of the ruling
parties and secure their approval before it sends it to the Diet. This

---

[1] Only in some instances a decision of the lower House prevailed in approval of a treaty,
e.g., the 1960 Treaty of Mutual Co-operation and Security, 1 Jan. 1960, Japan–US, 373
UNTS 179. See Kazuo Yamanouchi, *Seifu no Kenpō Kaishaku [Interpretations of the
Constitution by the Government]* (1965), 240.
[2] Constitutional amendments must be proposed by a ⅔ majority of each House of the Diet,
and be submitted to a people's referendum. Art. 96, Kenpō.

practice ensures the approval of the treaty, as long as the members of the Diet vote along the party line. And, in most cases, they do.

When the Marrakesh Agreement Establishing the World Trade Organization was submitted to the Diet, the Government was formed by a coalition of the LDP and the Social Democratic Party of Japan with the chairman of the SDPJ, Tomiichi Murayama, as Prime Minister. The combination was a peculiar one, because the SDPJ was the leading opposition party—a fervent one—when the LDP dominated Japanese politics. They now co-operate in support of the Cabinet. When the Uruguay Round negotiations were being conducted, the LDP was in power and the SDPJ was part of the opposition camp most of the time. In July 1993, the LDP lost power and a non-LDP coalition government was formed with the leader of the Japan New Party, Morihiro Hosokawa, as Prime Minister. The SDPJ was the largest political party and a key member of the coalition.

As the Uruguay Round negotiations approached a conclusion, Japan faced a decision to open its rice market. The question of rice was the single most important issue for Japan in the Round. The Hosokawa government was forced to make the decision to open its rice market, or to refuse to do so and thereby bring the Uruguay Round negotiations to a collapse. In December 1993, at the very last moment in the negotiations, Prime Minister Hosokawa decided to accept the minimum access formula proposed by the Chairman of the Market Access Group. Most of the political parties forming the coalition regarded the Prime Minister's decision as unavoidable. The SDPJ was in a difficult position because many of its members represented farming constituencies. The party was faced with the dilemma of accepting the Prime Minister's decision, or refusing it and thereby disintegrating the non-LDP coalition government only several months after it came into being. In the end, the SDPJ gave priority to maintenance of the coalition framework, and accepted the opening of the rice market. The LDP also found it difficult to accept Hosokawa's decision readily, having an even larger group of members representing farmers' interests within itself. The LDP, however, had the advantage of being on the opposition at that time. Thus, the President of the LDP, Yohei Kono, was able to make remarks highly critical of the coalition government's attitude toward rice.

The coalition government collapsed in 1994, because a group within the coalition led by the Shinseito (Japan Renewal Party) and the Komeito (Clean Government Party) tried to alienate the SDPJ. The LDP, which had strong cravings to return to power, persuaded the SDPJ to form a new joint coalition. The LDP occupied many of the important posts in the new Cabinet, including the post of Foreign Minister for its President, Kono. The LDP, however, allowed the SDPJ Chairman, Murayama, to head the cabinet. It was this new coalition government which undertook the task to push the WTO Agreement through the Diet. Kono, as the Foreign Minister, had to defend the Agreement which he himself had criticized when it was signed by the Hosokawa government less than a year before. Although both the LDP and the SDPJ had high stakes in protecting Japan's rice market, they could not put the success of the Uruguay Round at risk on the issue of Japanese rice alone. Under these circumstances, they persuaded the Japanese bureaucrats to adopt an Outline of Counterplan in Agriculture in October 1994, with a total budget of over US$6bn., to be spent over the next six years, to alleviate the hardship of Japanese farmers adversely affected by the opening of the rice market. Armed with that Counterplan, the coalition government submitted the WTO Agreement to the Diet. The ruling parties—the LDP and the SDPJ combined—had an easy majority in the Diet. And, the size of the Counterplan was sufficiently large to allay the fears of those members who represented the interests of farmers.

Most of the opposition parties were not in a position to denounce the Government for proposing ratification of the WTO Agreement which they themselves had decided to accept. In power in December 1993, they were the ones responsible for accepting the Agreement on behalf of Japan. Under these circumstances, only the Japan Communist Party, which was not a member of the non-LDP coalition in December 1993, could plausibly oppose ratification of the WTO Agreement in the Diet, and they did, as will be explained later.

5.2.1.2 Subsequent approval

It is the normal practice of the Japanese Government to obtain the approval of the Diet *before* Japan becomes bound by a treaty. In the Diet, the Government has expressly accepted the view that approval should, in principle, be sought in advance.[3] If a treaty requires ratification, the Government normally obtains the approval of the Diet before ratifying it. To date, there have been eleven cases in which the Government has, exceptionally, sought subsequent approval of the Diet. In the field of international trade, the conclusion of an international agreement is often considered urgent. Thus, the Government has sought subsequent approval for some agreements on trade. Five of the eleven cases mentioned above relate to the GATT, including the Protocol of Terms of Accession of Japan

---

[3] See e.g., HR, Standing Comm. for House Management, 20 Apr. 1960, 34th Diet, 26 Giin'un'eiiinkaigiroku 4 (1960) (remarks of the Director General of the Cabinet Legislation Bureau).

to the GATT, the treaty by which Japan acceded to the GATT.[4] As for the WTO Agreement, the lower house approved it on 1 December 1994; and the upper house followed on 8 December. The Government submitted an instrument of ratification of the WTO Agreement on 27 December 1994. Thus, the approval of the Diet was obtained before Japan ratified the WTO Agreement.

If a treaty fails to gain the subsequent approval of the Diet, the treaty is invalid under Japanese law, because the treaty fails to fulfil the requirement of Article 73 (3) of the Japanese Constitution. It must be asked whether, in such a case, the treaty's validity under international law is affected as well. The question is much discussed by constitutional scholars, and several different conclusions have been suggested.[5] Now that Japan has ratified the Vienna Convention on the Law of Treaties,[6] the critical question must be whether the failure to gain Diet approval can be invoked by the Japanese Government as a ground of invalidity of a treaty under Article 46 of the Convention. It is probably difficult to consider the violation to be 'manifest' when the Government believes it can gain subsequent approval but the approval is in fact refused by the Diet. In the eleven cases where subsequent approval was sought, approval was in fact given; thus, the question remain theoretical so far.

5.2.1.3 Power of the Diet to amend a treaty

It is a subject of much controversy whether, under the Japanese Constitution, the Diet has the power to 'amend' a treaty on approving it. The Government holds the view that the Diet has no power to amend a treaty but can only approve or reject it.[7] Scholarly opinion is divided, with a majority asserting that the Diet has no power to amend a treaty.[8] Under the Japanese Constitution, it is the Government which has the power to make treaties; the Diet is only given the power to 'approve' a treaty submitted by the Government. Given the circumstances, the Diet probably should not be considered to have the power to change the wording of a treaty and impose the new text on the Government. The Diet, however,

---

[4] For details on approval of the GATT by the Diet, see Iwasawa, 'Implementation of international trade agreements', 302–3.

[5] See e.g., Y. Higuchi et al., Chūshaku Nihonkoku Kenpō [Commentary on the Japanese Constitution] (Vol. 2, 1988), 1096–8. The Government takes the view that the validity of the treaty is unaffected. M. Orita, 'Practices in Japan concerning the conclusion of treaties', (1984) 27 JAIL 52 at 62.

[6] Vienna Convention on the Law of Treaties, 23 May 1969, 1155 UNTS 331, came into force 27 Jan. 1980 (for Japan 1 Aug. 1981).

[7] See e.g., Orita, 'Practices in Japan', 62.

[8] See generally Higuchi et al., Japanese Constitution, 1093–6.

should be able to attach conditions to the treaty's approval, to propose understandings, declarations, or reservations to the treaty, or to amend reservations proposed by the Government.[9] In the United States, a fast-track procedure was devised for the conclusion of trade agreements to shield the results of trade negotiations from encroachment by Congress. The confrontation between the Cabinet and the legislature is not so acute in Japan, since it is a parliamentary democracy; therefore, there is no comparable procedure in Japan. It is possible that when the Government makes compromises in trade negotiations, the Diet, especially the upper house, will denounce the Government. However, since the Cabinet is formed on the basis of the majority in the lower house, it is hardly likely that the Diet will amend a treaty submitted by the Government.

With regard to the WTO Agreement, most opposition parties were not in a position to criticize the government, except the JCP, for the reasons explained above. The JCP attacked the government, *inter alia*, for making excessive concessions in agriculture, in particular, in opening Japan's rice market to foreign rice. They argued for renegotiation of the whole package. They cited the example of the United Nations Convention on the Law of the Sea and argued that renegotiation was possible.[10] Murayama and Kono stressed that the WTO Agreement was in the process of being ratified in most states, including the United States and the European Union, and that it was impossible to renegotiate the Agreement at that stage.[11]

5.2.2 Treaties and executive agreements

In spite of the clear mandate of Article 73 (3) of the Constitution, it is established that not all international agreements need to be approved by the Diet. The Cabinet can conclude international agreements without Diet approval under the power to '[m]anage foreign affairs' provided for in Article 73 (2). These agreements are called 'executive agreements' and

---

[9] Ibid at 1095. T. Abe, *Kenpō [Constitutional Law]* (2nd edn. 1991) 274. T. Fukase, 'Kokkai no Jōyaku Shōninken' ['The power of the Diet to approve treaties'], in *Enshū Kenpō [Seminars on Constitutional Law]* (1984), 458 at 465–8.

[10] HR, Special Comm. on the WTO Agreement, 131st Diet, Sekai Boeki Kikan Setsuritsu Kyotei to ni kansuru Tokubetsu Iinkaigiroku (No. 3) at 43–4 (17 November 1995); (No. 8) at 41 (29 November); (No. 10) at 14 & 16 (1 December); HC, Special Comm. on the WTO Agreement, 131st Diet, Sekai Boeki Kikan Setsuritsu Kyotei to ni kansuru Tokubetsu Iinkai Kaigiroku (No. 4) at 37 (5 December 1995); (No. 5) at 34 (6 December); (No. 6) at 34 (7 December); (No. 7) at 17 (8 December) (remarks of members of the JCP).

[11] HR, Special Comm. on the WTO Agreement, *supra* note 10 (No. 3), at 43–4; (No. 10), at 14; HC, Special Comm. on the WTO Agreement, *supra* note 10 (No. 4), at 37; (No. 5), at 34–5; (No. 6), at 34 (remarks of Murayama & Kono).

usually take the form of an exchange of notes. It is the Government which decides whether an international agreement is a 'treaty', which requires Diet approval, or an 'executive agreement', which can be concluded by the Cabinet alone. The Government's view, however, has often been challenged in the Diet.

As its explanation on the distinction between treaties and executive agreements was not necessarily consistent, the Government enunciated a 'unified view' before the Diet in 1974. According to the Government, three categories of international agreements require the approval of the Diet as treaties. The first category is international agreements which contain 'statutory matters'. This category includes the following three subsets of agreements: (1) international agreements which require the enactment of new statutes; (2) international agreements which require the maintenance of existing statutes; and (3) international agreements which affect the sovereignty of the state, and thus modify the power of the legislature as well (for example, those which transfer a territory). The second category is international agreements which deal with 'financial matters'. The third category is international agreements which are deemed politically important, in the sense that they provide a fundamental legal framework for a relationship between Japan and another state, or amongst states in general; as such they require ratification. On the other hand, the following agreements need not be approved by the Diet, but can be concluded by the Government alone as executive agreements: (1) agreements concluded within the scope of a treaty already approved by the Diet; (2) agreements concluded within the scope of domestic laws and regulations; and (3) agreements concluded within the scope of budgetary appropriations.[12] The Government's unified view has, in principle, found support among scholars.[13] However, the first category of executive agreements— agreements concluded 'within the scope of' a treaty—is vague and imprecise. It should be understood to mean agreements concluded under a specific provision of a treaty authorizing the Government to conclude further agreements, or agreements concluded for the implementation of a treaty.[14]

Many international trade agreements are concluded as treaties with Diet approval. The Protocol of Terms of Accession of Japan to the GATT was

---

[12] HR, Foreign Affairs Comm., 20 Feb. 1974, 72nd Diet, 5 Gaimuiinkaigiroku 2, (1984) 27 JAIL 102 (statement by Foreign Minister Ohira). See also Orita, 'Practices in Japan', 57–60.

[13] I. Sato, 'Kokkai no Jōyaku Shōninken to Kōkan Kōbun ['The power of the Diet to approve treaties and exchanges of notes'], (1976) 19 *Jochi Hogaku* 135. K. Sato, *Kenpō* [*Constitutional Law*] (3d edn. 1995), 175. S. Yamamoto, *Kokusai Hō* [*International Law*] (new edn. 1994), 106–9.

[14] cf. I. Sato, 'The power of the Diet', 155–6.

approved by the Diet, albeit subsequent to its signature.[15] Most of the
Tokyo Round agreements, namely those on tariff reduction, subsidies,
anti-dumping, import licensing, and customs valuation, were also approved
by the Diet. Numerous bilateral trade agreements have also been approved
by the Diet. Treaties on commerce and navigation, including those with
the United States (1953) and the United Kingdom (1963), and treaties on
investment protection, including those with Egypt (1978) and China
(1989), were approved by the Diet. On the other hand, some multilateral
trade agreements have been concluded as executive agreements without
Diet approval. For example, the 1974 Multifibre Arrangement was not
approved by the Diet. Some Tokyo Round agreements, namely those on
dairy products and bovine meat, were likewise concluded as executive
agreements.

Bilateral trade agreements relating to particular products, notably
voluntary restraint agreements, have been concluded as executive agreements, including the Japan–US Agreement on Textile Trade of 1972 and
the Japan–US Agreement on Semiconductor Trade of 1986. In 1971, it was
debated in the Diet whether the Government could conclude the
Agreement on Textile Trade with the United States without Diet approval.
The Government took the view that it could, and concluded the
Agreement as an executive agreement.[16] In the *Japan–US Textile
Agreement litigation*, the plaintiff, the Japan Fibre Industry Association,
challenged the Agreement, arguing that it was unconstitutional because it
had not been approved by the Diet. The Government replied that it did not
need Diet approval because it had been concluded on the basis of the
powers granted to the Government by existing domestic laws and
regulations. Unfortunately, the case was later withdrawn and no decision
was given by the court on this issue.[17] In response to arguments of some
legislators that Diet approval was necessary for the Textile Agreement, the
Director General of the Cabinet Legislation Bureau stated in the Diet that
international agreements that were not directly applicable (self-executing)
did not need to be submitted to the Diet because they were enforced
through domestic laws.[18] This sweeping explanation was obviously not

---

[15] A Foreign Ministry official explains that the GATT was approved by the Diet because it
was an international agreement falling into the second type of the first category—agreements
requiring the maintenance of existing statutes. Orita, 'Practices in Japan', 58 n. 12.

[16] Exchange of Notes Constituting an Agreement Confirming the Arrangement Relating to
Trade in Wool and Manmade Fibre Textiles, 3 Jan. 1972, Japan–US, 898 UNTS 33.

[17] For details on the litigation, see Nihon Sen'i Sangyō Renmei, *Nichibei Sen'i Kyōtei
nikansuru Gyōsei Soshō Kiroku* [*Records of the Administrative Litigation Concerning the
Japan–US Textile Agreement*] (1974).

[18] HC, Budget Comm., 9 Nov. 1971, 67th Diet, 7 Yosan'iinkai Kaigiroku 15, 18 (remarks
of the Director General of the Cabinet Legislation Bureau).

acceptable to the Diet. Under such a theory, many important agreements could be concluded as executive agreements. This line of reasoning was later dropped by the Government, as is evident from the brief submitted in the *Japan–US Textile Agreement litigation* and the unified view proclaimed by the Government in the Diet.

Professor Matsushita has suggested that the Government could have chosen not to submit the Tokyo Round agreements to the Diet, on the basis that they were agreements concluded for the implementation of a treaty already approved by the Diet—namely the GATT.[19] The power of the Government to conclude agreements for the implementation of a treaty without Diet approval should be acknowledged only when such agreements spell out minor details of an administrative or technical nature for the implementation of the treaty. Most of the Tokyo Round Agreements covered new issues not dealt with by the GATT, and are very specific and detailed. It is difficult to characterize them as mere agreements relating to the implementation of the GATT.

The WTO Agreement was approved by the Diet, as it is an international agreement which contains 'statutory matters' (an agreement which requires the enactment of new statutes or the maintenance of existing statutes), and one which is deemed politically important in the sense that it provides a fundamental legal framework for a relationship amongst states in general. Among the plurilateral trade agreements annexed to the WTO Agreement in Annexe 4, the Agreement on Government Procurement was submitted to the Diet after the WTO came into existence, and was approved by the Diet on 31 May 1995. In contrast, the International Bovine Meat Agreement and the International Dairy Agreement were concluded as executive agreements without Diet approval on 27 January 1995. These agreements succeeded similar agreements drawn up in the Tokyo Round, which were concluded by Japan as executive agreements. The same procedure was used for the new agreements.

5.2.3 Implementation of treaties in Japan

5.2.3.1 Publication of treaties

Article 7 of the Constitution provides that '[t]he Emperor, with the advice and approval of the Cabinet, shall [p]romulgat[e] treaties.' Thus, when the Diet approves a treaty and the Cabinet ratifies it, the treaty is promulgated in the *Official Gazette* under the name of the Emperor and the Cabinet.

---

[19] J. H. Jackson, J.-V. Louis, & M. Matsushita, *Implementing the Tokyo Round: National Constitutions and International Economic Rules* (1984), 85.

When Japanese is not one of the authentic languages of the treaty—which is usually the case with multilateral treaties—an authentic text (usually in English) is promulgated in the *Official Gazette* together with a Japanese translation. By virtue of 'promulgation', a treaty is *incorporated* into Japanese law and acquires the force of law. Nevertheless, the treaty retains its character as international law; it is not *transformed* into national law. Executive agreements, on the other hand, are published in the *Official Gazette* by way of 'notification' by the Ministry of Foreign Affairs. Those agreements which do not affect the rights or obligations of Japanese nationals are often not published.[20]

Japan submitted an instrument of ratification of the WTO Agreement to the GATT on 27 December 1994. Next day, on 28 December, it was promulgated in the *Offical Gazette* as Treaty No. 15. A Japanese translation was published together with the English authentic text.[21] The WTO Agreement contains many agreements in its annexe, one of which is the General Agreement on Tariffs and Trade 1994 (GATT 1994). GATT 1994, in turn, provides that it consists of the provisions of GATT 1947 (the original GATT). Therefore, the Foreign Ministry published the provisions of GATT 1947 in the *Official Gazette* by way of 'notification'.[22] The International Bovine Meat Agreement and the International Dairy Agreement were published in the *Official Gazette* on 14 February 1995.[23] The Agreement on Government Procurement provided that it would enter into force on 1 January 1996—one year later than the other agreements. Japan ratified it on 5 December 1995, and promulgated it in the *Official Gazette* as Treaty No. 23 on 8 December 1995.[24]

5.2.3.2 Implementation of treaties

As will be explained, treaties have the force of law and prevail over statutes in Japan. Nevertheless, if there is any conflict between a treaty and domestic law, the Government strives to amend the domestic law before it enters into the treaty. If there is no domestic law giving effect to the treaty, the Government usually attempts to have laws and regulations enacted to

---

[20] S. Hayashi, 'Jōyaku no Kokunaihōjō no Kōryoku ni tsuite' ['On domestic effects of Treaties'], (1963) 7 *Hogaku Kyoshitsu (1 Ki)* 34 at 37.

[21] Marrakesh Agreement Establishing the WTO, Treaty No. 15, *Kanpo* [*Official Gazette*], Spec. Iss. No. 243, at 13 (28 Dec. 1994).

[22] Foreign Ministry Notification No. 749, *Kanpo*, Spec. Iss. No. 242, at 57 (28 Dec. 1994).

[23] Foreign Ministry Notification No. 114 & 115, *Kanpo*, Speci. Iss. No. 26, at 1, 3 (14 Feb. 1995) (signed by Japan 27 Jan. 1995).

[24] Agreement on Government Procurement, Treaty No. 23, *Kanpo*, Spec. Iss. No. 233, at 28 (8 Dec. 1995).

give effect to the treaty. Sometimes the Government takes no special measures to implement the treaty, on the theory that it has the force of law and is capable of regulating the matter directly in Japan. This was the technique used for such treaties as the 1910 Brussels Convention Respecting Assistance and Salvage at Sea. Even if a treaty is capable of regulating the matter directly, a special statute is sometimes enacted, rephrasing the text of the treaty in Japanese legal terms and adding some new provisions. This technique was used for such treaties as the 1924 Brussels Convention Relating to Bills of Lading. No special measure needs to be enacted, if domestic law giving effect to the treaty already exists and there is no conflict between the treaty and the law. As a result, corresponding domestic law usually exists for any treaty, and it normally suffices to apply the domestic law. Nevertheless, the question of direct applicability of treaties remains, because if there is a conflict between a treaty and a statute, the treaty is to be given priority.

When Japan entered into the GATT, no special measure was taken to implement it. In contrast, when Japan entered into the Tokyo Round agreements, it made extensive revisions to its domestic laws and regulations, in order to bring them into conformity with the agreements. For example, the Customs Tariff Law, and the Cabinet Orders concerning countervailing and anti-dumping duties, were amended to implement the Subsidies Agreement and the Anti-Dumping Agreement.[25]

The WTO Agreement likewise required extensive revisions of domestic laws and regulations. The revisions of law on agriculture were most extensive. With respect to trade of rice, the Food Control Law was abolished and the New Staple Food Law was enacted.[26] With respect to other agricultural products, the Special Measures Law on Subvention to Producers of Processed Milk, the Agricultural Products Price Stabilization Law, the Raw Silk Price Stabilization Law, and the Silk and Sugar Price Stabilization Agency Law were revised.[27] With respect to tariffs, the Customs Tariff Law, the Tariff Special Measures Law, and the Tariff Law were revised.[28] The following laws were revised in the area of patent and

---

[25] For details on the revisions made by Japan to implement the Tokyo Round agreements, see M. Matsushita & T. Schoenbaum, *Japanese International Trade and Investment Law* (1989), 99–121.

[26] Law for Stabilization of Supply–Demand and Price of Staple Food, Law No. 113, *Kanpo*, Spec. Iss. No. 26, at 5 (14 Dec. 1994).

[27] Law Revising a Part of the Special Measures Law on Subvention to Producers of Processed Milk, Law No. 119, *Kanpo*, Spec. Iss. No. 242, at 3 (28 Dec. 1994). Law Revising a Part of the Agricultural Products Price Stabilization Law, Law No. 114, *Kanpo*, Spec. Iss. No. 26, at 15 (14 Dec. 1994). Law Revising Parts of the Raw Silk Price Stabilization Law and the Silk and Sugar Price Stabilization Agency Law, Law No. 115, *Kanpo*, ibid. at 15.

[28] Law Revising Parts of the Customs Tariff Law and Other Laws, Law No. 118, *Kanpo*, Spec. Iss. No. 241, at 1 (28 Dec. 1994).

copyright to implement the TRIPs Agreement and the General Agreement on Trade in Services: the Copyright Law, the Patent Law, the Utility Model Law, the Design Law, the Trade Mark Law, the Unfair Competition Prevention Law, the Patent Attorneys Law, and the Law Concerning International Applications Made Pursuant to the Patent Co-operation Convention.[29] With respect to service trade, the Wireless Telegraphy Law, the Foreign Attorneys Law, and the Welfare Pension Insurance Law were also revised.[30] In addition to these laws, a number of Cabinet Orders and Regulations were revised as well.[31]

Measures to implement the Agreement on Government Procurement were taken in late 1995, because the Agreement did not enter into force until January 1996. Cabinet Orders were revised in November 1995 and a Headquarter to Promote the Settlement of Complaints on Government Procurement was established by a decision of the Cabinet in December 1995. Some of the most important features of the measures taken by Japan to implement the Uruguay Round will be examined in detail below (see Section 4).

5.3 POSITION OF TREATIES IN JAPAN

5.3.1 Validity (force of law) of treaties in Japan

According to the prevailing view, treaties[32] concluded by Japan and published in the *Official Gazette* have the force of law in Japan. Article 98 (2) of the Japanese Constitution provides: 'Treaties concluded by Japan and established laws of nations shall be faithfully observed.' A majority of scholars take the view that treaties have the force of law in Japan through this Article. It is self-evident that international law must be observed on the international level. If that is what Article 98 (2) means, it is of little use.

---

[29] Law Revising Parts of the Copyright Law and the Law Providing for Exceptions to the Copyright Law for the Implementation of the Universal Copyright Convention, Law No. 112, *Kanpo*, Spec. Iss. No. 26, at 4 (14 Dec. 1994). Law Revising Parts of the Patent Law and Other Laws, Law No. 116, ibid. at 16.

[30] Law Revising a Part of the Wireless Telegraphy Law, Law No. 71, *Kanpo*, Spec. Iss. No. 96, at 16 (16 June 1993). Law Revising a Part of the Special Measures Law on Legal Works by Foreign Attorneys, Law No. 65, *Kanpo*, Spec. Iss. No. 122, at 91 (29 June 1994). Law Revising a Part of the National Pension Law and Other Laws, Law No. 95, *Kanpo*, Spec. Iss. No. 211, at 5 (9 Nov. 1994).

[31] Some of the implementing measures were published in *Kanpo* together with the WTO Agreement on 28 Dec. 1994. Other measures preceded the promulgation of the WTO Agreement.

[32] The term 'treaty' is used in the sense in which it is used in international law, referring to all international agreements, not just those approved by the Diet.

Therefore, the purpose of this provision must be in ordering the residents and officials in Japan to observe international law. In other words, the effect of the provision is to give international law the force of law in Japan. The proponents of this view also base their arguments on the following facts:

1. international law was given the force of law under the former Constitution of 1889;
2. Article 73 (3) of the Constitution requires approval of treaties by the Diet; and
3. Article 7 (1) requires promulgation of treaties by the Emperor.[33]

The Government has consistently taken the position that treaties have the force of law in Japan through Article 98 (2) of the Constitution. Japanese courts have endorsed that view as well.[34] Some statutes contain explicit provisions giving priority to treaties (for example, Article 3 of the Tariff Law). Those provisions merely have a declaratory effect. Those executive agreements which are published in the *Official Gazette* also acquire the force of law in Japan by virtue of Article 98 (2). In other words, executive agreements are 'treaties' within the meaning of Article 98 (2), even though they are not 'treaties' in the sense used in Article 73, and do not need to be approved by the Diet.[35] The Government also subscribes to the view that published executive agreements have the force of law in Japan.[36] It is established that customary international law is a part of the law of the land.

It is clear that the WTO Agreement has the force of law in Japan. So did the Tokyo Round Agreements. As for GATT 1947, there were some problems because the Protocol of Accession of Japan to the GATT was promulgated in the *Official Gazette* together with the schedules of concessions in 1955, but the GATT itself was not published until 1966. Despite non-publication of the GATT until 1966, a Japanese court recognized domestic validity of the GATT in 1961.[37]

---

[33] See e.g., T. Miyazawa, *Zentei Nihonkoku Kenpō* [*The Constitution of Japan*] (completely revised edn. 1978), 808; I. Sato, *Poketto Chūshaku Zensho Kenpō* [*Pocket Commentary Book: The Constitution*] (Vol. 2, 1984) 1289–90; S. Kyozuka, 'International enforcement and application of treaties in Japan', (1968) 12 JAIL 45 at 50–3.

[34] See e.g., Judgment of 28 June 1977, Sup. C., 31 Minshu 511, (1980) 23 JAIL 174.

[35] Higuchi *et al.*, *Japanese Constitution*, 1493. Miyazawa, *Constitution of Japan*, 808.

[36] Hayashi, 'Domestic effects of treaties', 39. S. Yachi, 'Kokusai Hōki no Kokunaiteki Jisshi' ['Domestic implementation of international rules'], in T. Tanaka & K. Hirobe (eds.), *Yamamoto Soji Sensei Kanreki Kinen: Kokusai Hō to Kokunai Hō* [*Commemorating the Sixtieth Birthday of Professor Soji Yamamoto: International Law and National Law*] (1991), 109 at 113.

[37] Judgment of 30 May 1966, Kobe District Court, 3 Kakeishu 519 at 524–5. For details of the case, see Iwasawa, 'Relationship between international law and national law', 313.

5.3.2 Application of treaties in Japan

5.3.2.1 Direct applicability of treaties

Even if treaties have the force of law in Japan, they are not necessarily directly applicable. Japanese scholars of international and constitutional law have recognized the distinction between 'self-executing' and 'non-self-executing' treaties.[38] According to the conventional usage of the term, while self-executing treaties can be applied directly without further legislative or other measures to implement them, non-self-executing treaties cannot be directly applied, but must be implemented by legislative or other measures. Japanese courts have tended to apply a treaty without examining its direct applicability once they confirmed that the treaty had the force of law in Japan by virtue of Article 98 (2). The courts have refused to apply a treaty in some instances, although they have rarely used the term 'non-self-executing'. On refusing to apply a treaty, the courts usually did not engage themselves in a detailed explanation as to why it was not directly applicable. Starting from the late 1980s, Japanese courts have rendered some noteworthy judgments concerning the direct applicability of international law. In those judgments, precision of a treaty provision was considered as an important criterion in determining its direct applicability.[39] As for executive agreements, one author has contended that they cannot be self-executing.[40] However, the direct applicability of executive agreements should not be denied categorically. Those executive agreements which have been published acquire the force of law in Japan. As long as a provision of a published executive agreement is sufficiently precise, there is no reason to deny its direct applicability. If executive

---

[38] See generally Y. Iwasawa, *Jōyaku no Kokunai Tekiyō Kanōsei: Iwayuru 'self-executing' na Jōyaku ni kansuru Ichi Kōsatsu* [*Domestic applicability of treaties: What are self-executing treaties?*] (1985).

[39] Judgment of 2 Mar. 1989, Sup. C., 35 Shomu Geppo 1754 at 1760–1 (stating that Art. 9 of the International Covenant on Economic, Social and Cultural Rights 'does not provide for a concrete right to be granted to individuals immediately'), aff'g Judgment of 19 Dec. 1984, Osaka High Court, 35 Gyoshu 2220 at 2282–3. Judgment of 5 Mar. 1993, Tokyo High Court, 811 Hanta 76, (1994) 37 JAIL 129 (declaring: 'If a customary international rule is not minutely detailed as to the substantive conditions on the creation, existence, and termination of a right, the procedural conditions on the exercise of the right, and moreover, the harmony of the rule with the existing various systems within the domestic sphere, and so forth, its domestic applicability cannot but be denied'), aff'g Judgment of 18 Apr. 1989, Tokyo District Court, 1329 Hanji 36, (1989) 32 JAIL 125, (1990) 29 ILM 391.

[40] Y. Murakami, 'Waga Kuni niokeru Jōyaku oyobi Kanshū Kokusai Hō no Kokunaiteki Kōryoku' ['Domestic effects of treaties and customary international law in Japan'], (1969) 680 *Toki no Horei* 18 at 24, 26 n. 20, and 28.

agreements could not be directly applicable, it would become difficult to manage foreign affairs speedily and effectively.[41]

The domestic status of resolutions of international organizations is not clear. The United Nations Security Council resolutions imposing economic sanctions on member states, such as Southern Rhodesia, South Africa, and Iraq, have been published in the *Official Gazette* by way of notification of the Foreign Ministry. The issue of their legal force in Japan has not arisen because these resolutions have been implemented by Cabinet and ministerial Orders. An argument can be made that internationally binding resolutions of international organizations have the force of law in Japan.[42] With respect to decisions of the Organization for Economic Co-operation and Development, the Japanese Government has specifically denied their direct applicability, declaring in the Diet that they 'will not be executed in a self-executing manner but will all be implemented within the scope of laws'.[43]

5.3.2.2 Direct applicability of the GATT/WTO Agreement

5.3.2.2.1 General Agreement on Trade and Tariffs

5.3.2.2.1.1 Kobe Jewelry Case *of 1966*
GATT 1947 was invoked in the *Kobe Jewellery Case*. In this case, the Kobe District Court interpreted Article 8 (3) of the GATT, which provides that '[n]o contracting party shall impose substantial penalties for minor breaches of customs regulations or procedural requirements'. The court explicitly acknowledged the superiority of treaties over statutes, but concluded that the Article did not apply to substantial breaches of law such as an evasion of tariffs.[44] One can argue that the court *sub silentio* assumed the direct applicability of Article 8 (3) of the GATT.

5.3.2.2.1.2 Japan–US Textile Agreement Litigation *of 1971*
In the *Japan–US Textile Agreement litigation* initiated in 1971, the plaintiff presented arguments relying heavily on the GATT. The plaintiff, the Japan Fibre Industry Association, argued that the 1972 Japan–US Textile Agreement and the export denial that could be made under it were contrary to GATT 1947. According to the plaintiff, the Agreement, a VRA, was inconsistent with Article 11 of the GATT prohibiting quantitative restrictions. The plaintiff withdrew the claim three years later

---

[41] Yachi, a Foreign Ministry official, also believes that there is no reason to deny the direct domestic effect of executive agreements. Yachi, 'Domestic implemention of international rules', 113.

[42] See *infra* text accompanying notes 83–84.

[43] HR, Foreign Affairs Comm., 18 Mar. 1964, 46th Diet, 11 Gaimuiinkaigiroku 4–8 (statement of Foreign Minister Ohira).

[44] Judgment of 30 May 1966, Kobe District Court, 3 Kakeishu 519.

because the Multifibre Arrangement was concluded in 1974 and the circumstances in fibre trade changed substantially.

5.3.2.2.1.3 Kyoto Necktie Case *of 1990*

In the *Kyoto Necktie Case*, the Kyoto District Court denied the direct applicability of GATT 1947 in 1984, and the Supreme Court seems to have endorsed the decision in 1990. In 1976, the Raw Silk Price Stabilization Law was amended, giving the Japan Silk Business Corporation an exclusive right to import raw silk from abroad. As a result, the domestic price of silk in Japan soared to about twice that of the world market price. The necktie fabric producers in Kyoto brought a lawsuit against the Japanese Government, demanding compensation for the losses. The plaintiffs argued that the Law, which had prohibited any person other than the Japan Silk Business Corporation from importing raw silk from abroad, was contrary to Article 17 (1) (a) and Article 2 (4) of GATT 1947.[45] The Kyoto District Court dismissed the plaintiffs' claims in 1984, stating:

The exclusive importership and the price stabilization system under consideration . . . are designed to protect the business of raw silk producers from the pressure of imports for a while. It has the same substance as an emergency measure permitted under Article 19 of the GATT . . . Besides, violations of the GATT provisions cited by the plaintiffs will result in the violating country being forced to rectify them, suffering such disadvantages as the following: the [violating] country will be confronted with a request for consultation from other contracting parties, or will have retaliatory measures taken. The violations cannot be interpreted to have any more effects. Accordingly, the court cannot hold that the provisions under consideration are contrary to the GATT and therefore null and void, and that the enactment of such law was unlawful.[46]

Thus, the court in effect denied the domestic applicability of the GATT as a whole.

The plaintiffs appealed to the Osaka High Court, but the court dismissed the appeal in 1986. The court strangely distorted the arguments of the appellants and summarily dismissed them.[47] The appellants appealed further to the Supreme Court, arguing that 'statutes which contravene the GATT are illegal *per se* and do not have the force of law in Japan.' In their opinion, the holding of the Kyoto District Court 'confused the question of

---

[45] Art. 17 (1) (a) provides: 'Each contracting party undertakes that . . . a [State] enterprise shall . . . act in a manner consistent with the general principles of non-discriminatory treatment prescribed in this Agreement.' Para. (b) states that '[the above provision] shall be understood to require that such enterprises shall . . . make any such purchases or sales solely in accordance with commercial considerations', including price, quality, and availability. Art. 2 (4) stipulates that 'If any contracting party establishes . . . a monopoly of the importation of any product . . ., such monopoly shall not . . . operate so as to afford protection on the average in excess of the amount of protection provided in the Schedule.'

[46] Judgment of 29 June 1984, Kyoto District Court, 31 Shomu Geppo 207 at 234.

[47] Judgment of 25 Nov. 1986, Osaka High Court, 634 Hanta 186.

effective measures among states for fulfilment of treaties, on the one hand, and the question of legal validity, on the other, and was thus incorrect.'[48] The Supreme Court dismissed the appeal in 1990. On the question of the GATT, the court simply stated: 'The decision of the lower court [Osaka High Court] on this point can be approved in the light of the court's reasoning. In the decision of the lower court we find no violation of law as alleged by the appellants.'[49] Thus, one may conclude that the Supreme Court approved the decision of the Kyoto District Court, at least in principle.

The Kyoto District Court denied the direct applicability of the GATT simply because the GATT had its own dispute settlement mechanism. This reasoning of the court is difficult to accept. Even if a treaty provides for an international procedure to ensure its fulfilment, one should not readily conclude that the treaty is not directly applicable in domestic law. When the international procedure is accessible only to states, and not to individuals—as is the case with the GATT/WTO Agreement—one must be especially careful in concluding that it is not directly applicable. If it is not directly applicable, no remedy is available to individuals either on the international plane or on the national plane. In the 1972 *Banque de Crédit International Case*, the Supreme Court of Switzerland concluded that the European Free Trade Association Treaty was directly applicable, in particular, because the treaty did not provide for a procedure accessible to individuals.[50] In the 1982 *Kupferberg Case*, the European Court of Justice held that a trade agreement between the European Economic Community and Portugal was directly applicable in the European Community, and stressed: '[T]he mere fact that the contracting parties have established a special institutional framework for consultations and negotiations *inter se* in relation to the implementation of the agreement is not in itself sufficient to exclude all judicial application of that agreement.'[51] In the 1963 *Van Gend & Loos Case*, the same court had rightly pointed out that '[t]he vigilance of individuals concerned to protect their rights amounts to an effective supervision in addition to the [system of international] supervision [established by the EEC Treaty].'[52] Japanese courts have held that the International Covenant on Civil and Political Rights is directly applicable, even though it has its own enforcement mechanism.[53] The judgment of the

---

[48] Judgment of 6 Feb. 1990, Sup. C., slip op.

[49] Judgment of 6 Feb. 1990, Sup. C., 36 Shomu Geppo 2242 at 2245.

[50] Judgment of 13 Oct. 1972, Tribunal fédéral, BGE 98 Ib 385 at 388 (Switz).

[51] *Hauptzollamt Mainz v. Kupferberg, [1982] ECR 3641 at 3664.*

[52] *Van Gend & Loos v. Nederlandse Administratie de Belastingen*, [1963] ECR 1 at 10.

[53] The ICCPR provides for a reporting procedure, an interstate communication procedure, and an individual communication procedure. Only the first of these procedures applies to Japan, because it has not made a declaration in accordance with Art. 41, nor ratified the

Kyoto District Court is inconsistent with the decisions of the courts on the ICCPR.

None the less, if the international procedure is very flexible and leaves states room to settle disputes on grounds of political expediency, overriding the strict terms of the treaty, the treaty's direct applicability may be denied. If domestic courts apply a treaty setting forth a political procedure, the courts will interfere with the foreign affairs prerogative of the Government. Such practices, in turn, may defeat the purpose of establishing a political procedure. The question then is whether the GATT/WTO dispute settlement procedure is so political that its direct applicability must be denied on that ground. In the 1971 *International Fruit Company Case*, the European Court of Justice pointed out 'the great flexibility of [the GATT's] provisions, in particular those conferring the possibility of derogation, the measures to be taken when confronted with exceptional difficulties and the settlement of conflicts between the contracting parties' in denying its direct applicability in the European Community.[54]

However, the GATT dispute settlement procedure was quasi-judicial in reality, and resembled arbitration more than negotiation. It became a normal practice in the GATT to establish panels for the settlement of disputes, and these panels proceeded in a court-like manner. The disputes were not settled merely on the basis of political expediency. The procedure was not as political as alleged to be, and should not have been considered as an obstacle to recognizing the direct applicability of the GATT.[55] Treaties rarely establish rigid judicial enforcement mechanisms. If the political nature of an international procedure is too readily recognized, few treaties will be domestically applicable.

Professor Jackson recognized that 'many clauses of GATT read as though they were meant to be directly applicable as domestic law', but denied their self-executing character because of the Protocol of Provisional Application, the language of which, he believed, was 'that of commitment to apply GATT, not language of immediate application'. Professor Jackson highlighted the fact that in the Protocol the governments undertook to apply the GATT subject to certain conditions.[56] The word

Optional Protocol to the Covenant. In 1994, the Osaka High Court expressly recognized the direct applicability of the ICCPR, stating that 'the [ICCPR], in principle, has the self-executing character and is susceptible to direct application in domestic law in view of its contents'. Judgment of 28 Oct. 1994, Osaka High Court, 1513 Hanji 71 at 86.

[54] *International Fruit Co.* v. *Produktschap voor Groenten en Fruit*, [1972] ECR 1219 at 1228.

[55] See E.-U. Petersmann, 'Application of GATT by the Court of Justice of the European Communities', (1983) 20 CMLR 397 at 429–34.

[56] J. H. Jackson, 'The General Agreement on Tariffs and Trade in United States domestic law', (1967) 66 *Mich. L. Rev.* 249 at 285–6. See also R. Hudec, 'The legal status of GATT in the domestic law of the United States', in M. Hilf *et al.* (eds.), *The European Community and GATT* (1986), 187 at 200–1.

'undertake', however, does not necessarily indicate the intent of the parties to make the treaty not directly applicable. Jackson also believed that 'the draftsmen of the Protocol did not intend a self-executing effect'[57] and cited a statement of an American delegate in the drafting of the Protocol.[58] The statement, however, is far from clear.[59] The grandfather clause of the Protocol, which preserved the existing national laws inconsistent with the GATT, was also sometimes alleged to negate the GATT's direct applicability.[60] The grandfather clause, however, could not obstruct the direct application of the GATT in an area where no conflicting law existed, or where conflicting law had been enacted after the Protocol entered into force. The Supreme Court of Italy has made an explicit statement to this effect.[61] In the light of these considerations, it was submitted that the direct applicability of the GATT should not be denied in its entirety, and that its direct applicability must be examined according to the terms of each GATT provision.[62]

5.3.2.2.2 World Trade Organization Agreement

The WTO Agreement is more likely to be regarded as directly applicable than the original GATT of 1947. Unlike GATT 1947, the WTO Agreement is neither applied 'provisionally', nor does it contain a 'grandfather clause'. In addition, the dispute settlement procedures are much more judicialized and no longer as 'flexible' as they were claimed to be under GATT 1947.[63] One must note that the Austrian Constitutional Court held in 1990 that Article 2 of the 1979 Subsidies Agreement concluded in the Tokyo Round was 'directly applicable'.[64] However, if a

---

[57] Jackson, 'GATT in US domestic law', 286. See also Hudec, 'Legal status of GATT', 200–1.

[58] '[P]rovided there is simultaneous publication and entry into force of the document, there would be no objection if there were differences in the actual time at which they were put provisionally into force, provided there was a date before which that must be done . . .' UN Doc. EPCT/TAC/PV.4, at 22 (1947).

[59] In the US most GATT articles were 'proclaimed' by the President. As a result, the GATT as proclaimed by the President was treated by US courts as directly applicable. The GATT was considered as superior to state law, but inferior to federal statues, because its effect stemmed from a President's proclamation. See Hudec, 'Legal status of GATT', 199–216; Jackson, 'GATT in US domestic law', 280–311.

[60] cf. *International Fruit Co.* (n. 54) at 1231, 1242 (opinion of Advocate-General Mayras).

[61] Judgment of 7 Jan. 1975, Corte Cass., (1976) 2 IYIL 385 at 387–8.

[62] Iwasawa, 'Implementation of international trade agreements'.

[63] W. Meng, 'Gedanken zur Frage unmittelbarer Anwendung von WTO-Recht in der EG', in U. Beyerlin *et al.* (eds.), *Recht zwischen Umbruch und Bewahrung: Völkerrecht, Europarecht, Staatsrecht: Festschrift für Rudolf Bernhardt* (1995), 1063 at 1084–5.

[64] Judgment of 30 Nov. 1990, VfGH, (1991) 5 *Wirtschaftsrechtliche Blätter* 230 (Aust.). For commentaries on this judgment, see T. Eilmansberger, 'Zur unmittelbaren Anwendbarkeit des GATT-Subventionskodex', (1991) 5 *Wirtschaftsrechtliche Blätter* 214; F. Zehetner, 'Ist der GATT-Subventionskodex wirklich "unmittelbar anwendbar"?', (1991) 18 *Österreichische Zeitschrift für Wirtschaftsrecht* 81 (criticizing the conclusion of the Court).

statute excludes the direct applicability of the WTO Agreement (for example, Article 102 (c) of the US Uruguay Round Agreements Act of 1994), the direct applicability of the WTO Agreement must be denied.

In the *Nakajima Case*, the European Court held that an anti-dumping regulation of the European Community violated neither Article 2 (4) nor Article 2 (6) of the 1979 Anti-Dumping Agreement. In doing so, the court emphasized that the applicant had not urged the court to recognize the direct applicability of the said provisions.[65] Despite the court's caveat, it is important to note that the court recognized its competence to exercise judicial review and scrutinize whether EC regulations were in conformity with the Anti-Dumping Agreement.[66] In approving the conclusion of the WTO Agreement, the Council of the European Union stated: '[B]y its nature, the Agreement establishing the World Trade Organization, including the Annexes thereto, is not susceptible to being directly invoked in Community or Member State courts' (Preamble).[67] These questions— whether the statement binds the European Court, and whether it excludes not only the direct applicability of the WTO Agreement, but also the court's competence to exercise judicial review in the light of the WTO Agreement—remain to be decided by the court.[68]

There is no provision in the Japanese implementing legislation comparable to Article 102 (c) of the US Uruguay Round Agreements Act of 1994, or the paragraph in the Preamble to the Decision of the EU Council. The issue of whether the WTO Agreement is directly applicable in Japan was not addressed in the deliberations of the Japanese Diet. Under the circumstances, it is up to the courts to decide this issue in Japan. Government officials have acknowledged that tariff concessions contained in the WTO Agreement are to be applied directly in accordance with Article 3 of the Tariff Law, which provides that 'if a treaty contains a special provision on tariffs, that provision shall be applied'.[69] In addition, those provisions stipulating that the WTO shall be accorded legal

---

[65] Case C–69/89, *Nakajima* v. *Council*, [1991] I ECR 2069 at 2177–81. See also Case C–188/88, *NMB* v. *Commission*, [1992] ECR 1689 at 1735 & 1739–41.

[66] For an analysis of the role the GATT can play in the judicial review of the secondary law of the European Community, see generally M. J. Hahn & G. Schuster, 'Zum Verstoß von gemeinschaftlichem Sekundärrecht gegen das GATT: Die gemeinsame Marktorganisation für Bananen vor dem EuGH', (1993) 28 *Europarecht* 261.

[67] Council Dec. 94/800/EC [1994] OJ L336/1, preamble.

[68] See Meng, 'Frage unmittelbarer Anwendung von WTO-Recht'; P. J. Kuijper, 'The New WTO Dispute Settlement System: the impact on the European Community', (1995) 29 JWT 49 at 62–5.

[69] T. Yamazaki, 'Uruguai Raundo Gōi wo uketa Kanzei Kankei Hō Kaisei no Gaiyō: Tokushu Kanzei Seido no Kaisei wo Chūshin to shite' ['An outline of the amendment of the laws relating to tariffs to implement the Uruguay Round agreement: the amendment the special tariff system'] (1995) 561 NBL 22 at 22; (the author is an official of the Customs and Tariff Bureau, the Ministry of Finance).

personality, and that the WTO and its officials shall be accorded such privileges and immunities as are necessary for the exercise of its functions (Article 8), are to be applied directly in Japan, since they have not been implemented in the Japanese legislation. Direct applicability of other provisions of the WTO Agreement remains unclear. Theoretically, it is possible to apply those provisions that are precise and complete. However, when individuals challenge the conformity of Japanese law to the WTO Agreement before the courts, it is unlikely that the courts will declare the law to be null and void, especially because the direct applicability of the WTO Agreement is denied in the United States and possibly also in the European Union, the two major trade partners of Japan. The courts can avoid deciding on the claim by denying the direct applicability of the WTO Agreement, by calling it a 'political question', or by allowing the legislature a wide discretion in implementing the WTO Agreement.

5.3.3 Rank of treaties

5.3.3.1 Treaties and statutes

Article 98 (2) of the Japanese Constitution provides only that treaties and established laws of nations 'shall be faithfully observed'. It does not specify the rank international law holds in the Japanese legal order. As for the relationship between treaties and statutes, treaties are generally regarded as ranked the higher. Treaties prevail over statutes, no matter when a statute is enacted; a treaty prevails even when an inconsistent statute is enacted later. Scholars have reached this conclusion for the following reasons:

1. the Constitution makes internationalism one of its basic tenets;
2. Article 73 (3) of the Constitution requires approval of treaties by the Diet; and
3. the phrase that treaties 'shall be faithfully observed' implies that they are higher than ordinary statutes.[70]

The Government adopted this view during the drafting stage of the Constitution, and it has been generally accepted by the courts as well. Japanese courts have regarded GATT 1947 as being ranked higher than statutes. In the *Kobe Jewellery Case*, in interpreting the GATT, the Kobe District Court declared: 'The principle of faithful observance of treaties

---

[70] E.g., S. Kiyomiya, *Kenpō* [*Constitutional Law*] (3rd edn. 1979) 449; Miyazawa, *Constitution of Japan*, 814; Y. Takano, *Kenpō to Jōyaku* [*Constitutions and Treaties*] (1960), 209–13.

. . . is understood to proclaim the superiority of treaties.'[71] Thus, there is no doubt that in Japan the WTO Agreement is ranked higher than statutes and prevails over them.

The rank of executive agreements is rarely discussed. Some commentators seem to presume that they have the same rank as treaties.[72] However, one of the grounds for giving superiority to treaties over statutes—that treaties are approved by the Diet—is lacking as far as executive agreements are concerned. An executive agreement concluded by the Government alone on the basis of domestic laws and regulations, or within the scope of budgetary appropriations, should not be given a rank higher than statutes enacted by the Diet; their rank should be equal to orders and regulations issued by the Government. Only an executive agreement concluded based on a treaty may be given the same rank as a treaty.[73]

5.3.3.2 Treaties and the Constitution

As for the relationship between treaties and the Constitution, scholarly opinions are sharply divided into those who regard treaties as higher than the Constitution ('the treaty supremacy theory'), and those who regard the Constitution as higher than treaties ('the constitutional supremacy theory'). The treaty supremacy theory was strongly advocated by some of the most influential scholars immediately after the Second World War, when the mood of internationalism was very strong.[74] Starting from the late 1950s, however, when the constitutionality of the Japan–US Security Treaty became an intense political issue, the validity of this theory came into serious doubt, and support for the theory dwindled. Today, most scholars support the constitutional supremacy theory. They stress that, under the Japanese Constitution, it is easier to conclude a treaty than to enact an ordinary statute, not to speak of revising the Constitution. Therefore, the view giving superiority to treaties would, in effect, make a revision of the Constitution easy and infringe the principle of the sovereignty of the people.[75] The Government also supports the constitutional supremacy

[71] Judgment of 30 May 1966, Kobe District Court, 3 Kakeishu 519.

[72] e.g., N. Ashibe, *Kenpōgaku I: Kenpō Sōron [A Study of Constitutional Law I: General Discussion]* (1992), 90; Higuchi *et al.*, *Japanese Constitution* 1493 & 1500; Miyazawa, *Constitution of Japan*, 808 & 814.

[73] See Abe, *Constitutional Law*, 279; Hayashi, 'Domestic effect of treaties', 39. Cf. Yachi, 'Domestic implementation of international rules', 113 (suggesting that all executive agreements should be ranked lower than statutes).

[74] e.g., Hogaku Kyokai (ed.), *Chūkai Nihonkoku Kenpō [Commentaries on the Japanese Constitution]* (Vol. 2, 1954), 1482–4; Miyazawa, *Constitution of Japan*, 814–8.

[75] e.g., K. Hashimoto, *Nihonkoku Kenpō [The Constitution of Japan]* (rev. edn. 1988), 680–1; Higuchi *et al.*, *Japanese Constitution*, 1500–1; Kiyomiya, *Constitutional Law*, 450–2; I. Sato, *Pocket Commentary*, 1290–3; Takano, *Constitutions and Treaties*, 207–9.

theory, at least with respect to 'bilateral political or economic treaties'.[76] In 1959, the Supreme Court endorsed the constitutional supremacy theory in the *Sunagawa Case*.[77]

5.3.4 Judicial review of treaties

Under the Japanese Constitution, courts unquestionably have the power to review the formal constitutionality of a treaty; that is, courts can determine whether a treaty was concluded and promulgated in accordance with the procedure prescribed in the Constitution. What is more problematic, and thus much discussed by constitutional scholars, is whether the courts can review the substantive constitutionality of a treaty—that is, whether courts can find a treaty to be inconsistent with the Constitution in substance and declare it to be null and void under Japanese law. The views of constitutional scholars differ greatly on this point.

The proponents of the treaty supremacy theory, of course, deny that treaties are subject to judicial review, because, in their view, treaties rank higher than the Constitution. Among the adherents of the constitutional supremacy theory, there is yet another division of views. Some scholars contend that even though the Constitution is ranked higher than treaties, courts are barred from reviewing treaties and declaring them unconstitutional.[78] In contrast, other scholars recognize the possibility of judicial review of treaties. The latter view is held by many constitutional lawyers in recent years.[79] Article 81 of the Constitution empowers the Supreme Court to review the constitutionality of any 'law, order, regulation or official act'. It is argued that treaties may be equated with 'law' under Article 81 as far as their domestic validity is concerned.

In the *Sunagawa Case* of 1959, the Supreme Court reviewed the formal constitutionality of the Administrative Agreement concluded between Japan and the United States under the Japan–US Security Treaty. The

---

[76] The Government seems to distinguish between three kinds of treaties and takes the position that some treaties prevail over the Constitution while others do not: treaties which represent 'established laws of nations' prevail over the Constitution; treaties which concern 'a matter of vital importance to the destiny of a nation such as a surrender document or a peace treaty' prevail over the Constitution; while the Constitution prevails over 'bilateral political or economic treaties'. See Yamanouchi, *Interpretations of the Constitution*, 247–8.

[77] Judgment of 16 Dec. 1959, Sup. C., 13 Keishu 3225, (1960) 4 JAIL 103, 32 ILR 43. See *infra* text accompanying n. 80.

[78] e.g., Kiyomiya, *Constitutional Law*, 375.

[79] e.g., Ashibe, *Study of Constitutional Law*, 94–5; Higuchi *et al.*, *Japanese Constitution*, 1233–6; N. Kobayashi, *Kenpō Kōgi* [*Lectures on Constitutional Law*] (new edn., 1981), 531–3; I. Sato, *Pocket Commentary*, (Vol. 2), 1047–51 (changing his view from the previous edition); K. Sato, *Constitutional Law*, 313–4; Takano, *Constitutions and Treaties*, 215–25. Some scholars, such as Takano and Kobayashi, believe that only 'self-executing' treaties are subject to judicial review. For criticisms of this view, see Iwasawa, *Domestic applicability of treaties*, 52–4, 332–3.

Agreement had not been approved by the Diet. The court held the Agreement to be constitutional, stating that it was concluded on the basis of the delegation contained in Article 3 of the Security Treaty. As for the substantive constitutionality of the Security Treaty, the Supreme Court declined to engage in such a review, stating: 'The Security Treaty . . . must be regarded as having a highly political nature . . . Consequently, the legal decision concerning its constitutionality has a character unsuitable in principle for review by a judicial court.' The court, however, suggested that it would exercise a review power if a treaty's 'unconstitutionality or invalidity is obvious'.[80]

In the *Japan–US Textile Agreement litigation*, the plaintiffs argued that the 1972 Japan–US Textile Agreement was unconstitutional for both formal and substantive reasons. As the case was later withdrawn, no answer was given on these points by the court. If the Government concludes an international trade agreement without Diet approval as an executive agreement, even though it should have been approved by the Diet, then there is a possibility that the court will declare its irregularity. The possibility of a court finding an international trade agreement unconstitutional in substance is much smaller. Japanese courts use lower standards of scrutiny in reviewing constitutionality of statutes of a socio-economic nature. A restriction of this nature is found unconstitutional only when 'it is obvious that the legislature overstepped the power of discretion and that the legal measure of restriction is excessively unreasonable.' This requirement is very difficult to meet. Under the circumstances, it is hardly imaginable that an international trade agreement will be held unconstitutional by a court.

5.3.5 Effects of WTO Panel Reports in Japanese courts

GATT/WTO Panel Reports are often considered to be non-binding by Japanese commentators. This is a view taken by a number of scholars outside Japan as well. Since panels have never used the term 'ruling' in their reports, it has been argued that their reports are recommendations, and, as such, non-binding even on the parties concerned.[81] In violation complaints, however, findings of the panel that one party has violated the WTO Agreement arguably become rulings of the Dispute Settlement Body, and, as such, binds the parties concerned. Even if they may not be characterized as rulings, when the DSB officially finds violations of the WTO Agreement and requests one party to bring its measures into conformity with the Agreement, it must be the party's legal duty to do so.

---

[80] Judgment of 16 Dec. 1959, Sup. C., 13 Keishu 3225, (1960) 4 JAIL 103, 32 ILR 43.
[81] e.g., T. Flory, *Le GATT: Droit international et commerce mondial* (1968), 68–71.

Parties have legal rights and obligations under the WTO Agreement. The findings of the DSB are merely declaratory of existing rights and obligations under a binding treaty. The conclusion that Panel Reports bind the parties concerned also finds support in Article 31 (3) of the Vienna Convention on the Law of Treaties, which commands that 'any subsequent practice . . . which establishes the agreement of the parties' be taken into account in interpreting a treaty.[82]

If WTO Panel Reports are not legally binding on the international plane, they are without question non-binding on Japanese courts under Japanese law. If they are binding on the international plane, it must still be questioned what effects they may have on Japanese courts under Japanese law. Article 98 (2) of the Japanese Constitution provides that 'treaties concluded by Japan' and 'established laws of nations' shall be faithfully observed. The status of resolutions of international organizations and judgments of international courts in Japan is not clear. One could argue that internationally-binding resolutions of international organizations and judgments of international courts are also binding under Japanese law. They may be considered to fall within 'treaties' under Article 98 (2) because their binding character stems from treaties. Since the basic treaty which had established the international organization has acquired validity in Japan, this validity is arguably automatically extended to binding decisions adopted by the organization.[83] Alternatively, one can argue that all forms of international law acquire domestic legal force in Japan through Article 98 (2). This interpretation conforms to the spirit of Article 98 (2) which requires the residents and officials of Japan to faithfully observe international law.[84]

Reports of organs of the International Labour Organization have frequently been invoked before Japanese courts, and the legal status of the reports has become a subject of controversy. ILO organs have often expressed in their reports views critical of the Japanese restrictions of trade union rights in the public sector, especially the prohibition of strikes by public employees. Paradoxically, Japanese courts have tended to rely on the ILO reports in justifying restrictions on trade union rights. When they expand these rights, they have done so solely on the basis of constitutional interpretation without mentioning the ILO reports.[85] In the *Agriculture &*

---

[82] For further discussion on the binding character of WTO Panel Reports, see Y. Iwasawa, *WTO no Funsō Shori* [*Dispute Settlement of the World Trade Organization*] (1995), 135–8.

[83] See B. Conforti, *International Law and the Role of Domestic Legal Systems* (1993), 36–40.

[84] cf. Kazuya Hirobe, 'Art. 98 Para. 2 of the Constitution of Japan and the domestic effects of Resolutions of the United Nations Security Council' (1993) 36 JAIL 17 at 32.

[85] For details on the Japanese courts' treatment of the ILO reports, see Iwasawa, 'Relationship between international law and national law', 381–5.

Forestry Trade Union Case of 1973, the Supreme Court held that the Japanese prohibition of strikes by public employees was entirely constitutional due to their special status. In this judgment the court used the reports of the ILO organs selectively, and concluded that it was internationally recognized as acceptable to treat public employees differently from other employees.[86] In 1985, in dismissing arguments based on ILO reports, the Fukuoka District Court stated:

[T]he views of the various ILO organs [concerning Convention No. 87 and Convention No. 98] are nothing but calls to the governments to make arrangements in domestic laws in accordance with the object of the ILO Conventions. One cannot conclude that they have become sources of law as legally binding standards in interpreting and applying the Conventions, *unlike a final decision of the International Court of Justice rendered in cases of doubts or disputes over the interpretation of a Convention (ILO Charter Article 37 (1) & (2))).*[87]

This statement of the court is noteworthy, because the court implied that a final decision of the ICJ would become a binding interpretative standard for Japanese courts. However, not only was it *obiter dicta*, but also the italicized part was deleted later by the Fukuoka High Court when it approved the lower court's decision in 1991.[88] In any case, rulings of the DSB deserve to enjoy a stronger authority in Japanese courts than recommendations of the ILO organs, because rulings of the DSB are legally binding on the parties concerned, and because they are final, with no further recourse to the ICJ available for the interpretation of the WTO Agreement.

Thus, if the WTO Agreement is directly applicable in Japan, then one could argue that WTO panel reports should be used as authoritative standards for the interpretation of the WTO Agreement by Japanese courts. It is doubtful, however, that Japanese courts would use panel reports as delineating binding standards for the interpretation of the WTO Agreement, and invalidate trade restrictions imposed by Japanese laws. The courts might regard panel reports as non-binding, deny the direct applicability of the WTO Agreement, characterize the question as a 'political' one, or give the legislature a large discretion to avoid judicial review. In the *Kyoto Necktie Case*, the appellants alleged in their brief to the Supreme Court that 'it was determined in the GATT panel consultations of 1979' that the sole importership and the price stabilization system

---

[86] Judgment of 25 Apr. 1973, Supr. C. Grand Bench, 27 Keishu 547 at 554 & 556, translated and reprinted in part in H. Tanaka, *The Japanese Legal System: Introductory Cases and Materials* (1976), 806.

[87] Judgment of 26 Dec. 1985, Fukuoka District Court, 32 Shomu Geppo 2145 at 2179–80.

[88] Judgment of 26 Dec. 1991, Fukuoka High Court, 639 Rohan 73, aff'd, Judgment of 8 Apr. 1993, Sup. C., 639 Rohan 12.

under the Raw Silk Price Stabilization Law violated the GATT.[89] The Supreme Court summarily dismissed their arguments.[90] WTO panel reports may be invoked in various situations. Japanese courts may find it easier to use the WTO Agreement and panel reports as aids in interpreting Japanese domestic trade laws, or as evidence supportive of a conclusion reached though the interpretation of the laws. For this purpose any panel report could be of relevance; Japan need not even be a party to the case.

5.4 IMPLEMENTING THE URUGUAY ROUND

The purpose of this section is not to describe all the measures taken by Japan to implement the Uruguay Round, but to focus upon some of the more important ones. In the following subsections, the implementing measures taken by Japan in the areas of agriculture, countermeasures, and safeguard measures will be examined.

5.4.1 Agriculture

5.4.1.1 GATT Panel Report in the *Twelve Agricultural Products Case*

Japan maintained quotas on twenty-two agricultural products as of 1986. In 1986, the United States filed a complaint with the GATT with respect to twelve of them. In a panel report adopted by the GATT in 1988, it was found that the import restrictions regarding ten of the products were contrary to the prohibition of quantitative restrictions provided for in Article 11. With respect to the two remaining products—dried leguminous vegetables and groundnuts—the restrictions were found to be unjustified, because Japan had not been able to provide sufficient evidence to the contrary; they were not necessarily found to be inconsistent with the GATT.[91] In 1988, Japan and the United States agreed on concrete measures to implement the panel report. Japan agreed to expand the quotas with respect to the two products, the restriction of which had been found unjustified but not necessarily inconsistent with the GATT. Of the other ten products, Japan agreed to eliminate quotas with respect to eight by 1990. As for the remaining two products—dairy products and starch— Japan was unwilling to eliminate the quotas. Japan agreed to abolish

---

[89] Judgment of 6 Feb. 1990, Sup. Ct., slip op. The appellants were probably referring to the *Thrown Yarn Case*. Import Restriction of Thrown Silk Yarn, BISD 24S/107 (1978). In this case, however, no determination was made by the GATT, but the dispute was settled by bilateral consultations.

[90] Judgment of 6 Feb. 1990, Sup. C., 36 Shomu Geppo 2242.

[91] Restrictions on Imports of Certain Agricultural Products, BISD 35S/163 (1988).

quotas on some dairy products, including ice cream and frozen yoghurt, but merely expanded quotas on other dairy products. With respect to starch, Japan merely improved the tariff quota system for corn used for the production of starch. And, in order to compensate for the refusal to eliminate the quotas on these two products, Japan reduced tariffs on other agricultural products.

One of the major issues in this case was whether the GATT permitted maintenance of import restrictions made effective through state trading. The issue had enormous implications on the import of rice into Japan, because rice was also a state trading item. Japan argued that prohibition of quantitative restrictions as provided for in Article 11 (1) of the GATT did not apply to state trading. The panel rejected this argument, noting that the wording of Article 11 (1) was comprehensive enough to comprise restrictions made effective through an import monopoly. This interpretation would make it difficult for Japan to justify its ban on the import of rice under the GATT. Consequently, Japan was reluctant to agree on the adoption of the panel report by the Contracting Parties. Japan stated at a session of the Contracting Parties that it was ready to accept adoption of the panel report except for the parts concerning certain dairy products and starch, and state trading. Many states opposed Japan's position on the ground that partial adoption of a panel report should not be established as a precedent. Under the circumstances, Japan agreed to the adoption of the entire report, provided that the Council put on record the statement of the Japanese representative.[92] A month later, a panel report in the Canadian *Import of Alcoholic Drinks Case* containing the same interpretation on state trading was placed before the Council for adoption. Japan again demanded that the Council record Japan's understanding that the Council's adoption of the report would not establish a generally applicable interpretation of the provisions relating to state trading.[93] It was a hollow cry by Japan, however, for panel reports acquire legal force once adopted by the Council. Objections to the interpretations by the panel recorded in the Council minutes do not necessarily prevent the panel report from constituting a part of GATT law.

5.4.1.2 Tariffication of rice

The import of rice was the single most important issue for Japan in the Uruguay Round. In the Uruguay Round negotiations on agriculture, the United States made a proposal to replace all border measures other than tariffs with tariffs, and also to reduce the tariffs (so-called tariffication). No

---

[92] GATT Doc. SR.43/4, at 1–7 (Dec. 1987). SR.43/6, at 1–3 (Dec. 1987). C/M/217, at 17–25 (Feb. 1988).
[93] C/M/218, at 5 (Mar. 1988).

exception was to be allowed; the importation of rice to Japan was also to be included. The Dunkel Draft, presented in December 1991, incorporated the idea of 'tariffication without exception'.[94] Since Japanese farmers formed a powerful political group in the Japanese political scene, the Japanese Diet could not but put up a slogan of allowing no foreign rice into Japanese markets. Under such circumstances, it became the prime objective of Japan to reject the 'tariffication without exception' proposed by Arthur Dunkel, the Director-General of the GATT, and obtain an exception for Japanese rice. The Japanese Government came up with a food security argument, and stressed that the Japanese rice was unique. On the other hand, however, the panel report in the *Twelve Agricultural Products Case* made painfully clear that if Japan did not make compromises in the Uruguay Round, the United States would certainly file a complaint in the GATT dispute settlement procedures against Japan, and Japan would lose. The Japanese Government feared that, in that scenario, immediate tariffication would be required on conditions not necessarily favourable to Japan.

Even though the Uruguay Round negotiations were, in principle, multilateral ones, the import of rice was essentially a bilateral issue between Japan and the United States. In January 1993, a new administration came into power in the United States. The Clinton Administration was more flexible than the previous one with regard to tariffication of border measures on agriculture. In October 1993, at the last stage of Uruguay Round negotiations, Japan and the United States came to a compromise on the issue of rice importation. According to the compromise, tariffication would be postponed for six years. In return, Japan would allow a minimum access of 4 per cent in the first year, and this amount would be gradually increased to 8 per cent in six years. This compromise allowed the Japanese Government and politicians to argue that they had succeeded in rejecting the 'tariffication without exception' formula and making Japanese rice an exception. For the United States, on the other hand, tariffication was achieved anyway—albeit with a delay of six years—and a practical gain was obtained by forcing Japan to allow 4–8 per cent of minimum access. When the compromise was leaked to the press, the Japanese Government kept denying that such a compromise had been struck with the United States.

The compromise was presumably transmitted to the Chairman of the Market Access Group by the end of November, and the Chairman indicated a sketch of a draft agreement to the Japanese Government on 7 December 1993. Prime Minister Hosokawa stressed that the Government had achieved postponement of tariffication for six years, and expressed a

---

[94] Draft Final Act Embodying the Result of the Uruguay Round of Multilateral Trade Negotiations, GATT Doc. MTN.TNC/W/FA (20 Dec. 1991).

view that the draft did not contradict the resolutions adopted by the Diet. On 8 December, however, it was revealed that the Chairman's draft contained conditions which had yet to be reported. First, additional concessions would be required if tariffication was to be postponed after six years. Secondly, reduction of tariffs would proceed behind the scene during the six years; that is, if Japan decided to accept tariffication in six years, the tariff rate applied to Japan would be 15 per cent lower than the original tariff rate which would have been applied to Japan in the first year. The revelation made it more difficult for Prime Minister Hosokawa to accept the WTO Agreement. Nevertheless, the political parties forming the coalition, except for the SDPJ, decided to accept the WTO Agreement before too long. Only the SDPJ could not decide until the very last moment. In the end, it went along grudgingly, attaching greater importance to the maintenance of the coalition than to closing the Japanese market to foreign rice.

Even some politicians within the ruling coalition parties were critical of the way the Hosokawa government handled the rice problem. Japanese farmers had strong connections with the LDP and the SDPJ, but not with the Japan New Party and the Shinseito in which Prime Minister Hosokawa had his base of power. Under the circumstances, the Hosokawa government presumably failed to consult the farmers' associations on the rice problem in a sufficient manner, and to convince them that the acceptance of the WTO Agreement was unavoidable. Although Japanese political leaders claimed that they were not aware of the conditions attached to the Chairman's draft proposal, it was speculated that at least some bureaucrats were. The process of Japan's acceptance of the WTO Agreement has proven yet again that Japan is run by bureaucrats, rather than by politicians.

5.4.1.3 Enactment of the New Staple Food Law

The acceptance of the WTO Agreement forced Japan to revise legislation on the production and distribution of rice. The Government abolished the 1942 Food Control Law and enacted the Law for Stabilization of Supply-Demand and Price of Staple Food (known as the New Stape Food Law). The new Law came into full effect in November 1995. The former Food Control Law was enacted during the Second World War. It provided for a planned system with rigorous control of sale and distribution of rice by the Government. Farmers were bound to sell rice only to the Government. Collectors of rice were designated by the Government, and wholesalers and retailers were licensed by it; they acted, in effect, as government agents. Rice was rationed to consumers at prices determined by the Government. Other ways of distribution were prohibited. Application and enforcement of the Law gradually became flexible; a new category of 'voluntarily marketed rice' was created in 1969, and rationing of rice was abolished in 1981. Nevertheless, since the basic idea underlying the Food Control Law remained rationing of rice, room for deregulation was limited.

The New Staple Food Law purports to rationalize rice distribution by strengthening market principles and deregulation. Rice producers are no longer obliged to sell rice to the Government. Rice is divided into three categories: government-marked rice; voluntarily marketed rice; and other rice. The Government draws up an annual basic plan with a forecast of rice supply and demand, and notifies rice producers of their standard amount of rice production. The rice produced in accordance with the standard amount—orderly marketed rice—must be sold through specified channels as voluntarily marketed rice or government-marketed rice. Other rice can be sold freely, provided that the quantities are notified to the Government. The Government purchases government-marketed rice only from farmers participating in the production adjustment programme. In other words, while the sale of rice to the Government was an obligation under the old law, under the new law it is a right given only to farmers complying with the Government's production adjustment programme. The rest of the rice produced in accordance with the standard amount is distributed by the private sector as voluntarily marketed rice. Thus, while voluntarily marketed rice was an exception under the old Law, it is the primary category of rice under the new Law.

The new Law diversifies distribution channels and promotes competition in distribution. Dealers handling orderly marketed rice have only to be registered; they are no longer designated or licensed. The old system of limiting the number of wholesalers and retailers was discarded. Prices of rice are designed to reflect its supply and demand more accurately than before. The Voluntarily Marketed Rice Price Formation Centre was set up; it uses tenders to help form 'index prices' of voluntarily marketed rice. Prices of government-marketed rice are to reflect the price trend of voluntarily marketed rice. The Government handles minimum access imports and administers stockpiles through the management of government-marketed rice. To what extent the minimum access—4 per cent in the first year and rising to 8 per cent in the sixth year—affects rice distribution in Japan is yet to be seen.

5.4.1.4 Impact of the Uruguay Round on agricultural products other than rice

The basic negotiation strategy of Japan in the Uruguay Round was to avoid tariffication of rice at all cost. Agricultural products other than rice were used to compensate for postponing the tariffication of rice. In other words, producers of agricultural products other than rice were sacrificed for producers of rice. Japan refused to eliminate quotas on dairy products and starch when the panel in the *Twelve Agricultural Products Case* requested Japan to do so in 1988. In the Uruguay Round negotiations, however, Japan agreed to eliminate quotas on these two products as compensation for postponing tariffication of rice. Japan committed itself to replacing border measures on dairy products and starch with tariffs. In addition, Japan accepted tariffication of wheat, barley, beans, peanuts, devil's-tongue, raw silk, and cocoons. Importation of these products were subject to quantitative restrictions under the 1949 Foreign Exchange and Foreign Trade Control Law. Accordingly, this Law and the Customs Tariff Law of 1910 were revised to achieve tariffication of the above products. Tariff quotas have been introduced in place of quantitative restrictions. Even though tariffication was thus achieved for these products, the first tariff applied to the tariff quota and the tariff equivalent for the amount exceeding the tariff quota was sufficiently high that it was unlikely that import of these products would increase rapidly.

The Special Measures Law on Subvention to Producers of Processed Milk was revised to allow persons other than the Livestock Industry Promotion Corporation to import dairy products if they pay tariff equivalents. In a similar vein, the Raw Silk Price Stabilization Law and the Silk and Sugar Price Stabilization Agency Law were revised to allow persons other than the Silk and Sugar Price Stabilization Agency to import raw silk if they pay tariff equivalents. The Agricultural Products Price Stabilization Law was revised to enable the Government to sell starch in a flexible manner. Japan committed itself to lower tariffs on citrus fruits and beef to a significant extent in six years. Thus, the impact of the Uruguay Round is likely to be felt more strongly by farmers producing citrus fruits and beef.

5.4.2 Countermeasures and safeguard measures

5.4.2.1 Countermeasures under the Dispute Settlement Understanding

According to the Dispute Settlement Understanding, if a member of the WTO fails to implement recommendations and rulings of a panel, the party having invoked the dispute settlement procedures may request authorization from the DSB to suspend the application of concessions or other obligations under the covered agreements. Japan amended the Customs Tariff Law to give domestic authority for countermeasures authorized by the DSB. The unique feature of the Japanese system of countermeasures is that it is not uniform, but consists of two sub-systems: one on retaliatory tariffs administered by the Ministry of Finance under the Customs Tariff Law; and the other on quantitative restrictions administered by the Ministry of International Trade and Industry, under the Foreign Exchange and Foreign Trade Control Law. Japan only changed the former system by revising the Customs Tariff Law. The new Article 6 of the Customs Tariff Law, entitled Retaliatory Duty, provides:

In the case where it is considered necessary to protect benefit accrued to Japan directly or indirectly under the [WTO Agreement] or attain the objective of the WTO Agreement, a duty . . . may be imposed upon any imported product which is exported from . . . any country referred in the following paragraph, in addition to customs duty chargeable at an applicable rate in the Annexed Tariff . . . within the scope of approval prescribed in the following subparagraph, in accordance with a Cabinet Order, and with the country and products specified:

(1) Country of the Member of the World Trade Organization, where there are circumstances to be considered to nullify or impair the benefit accruing to Japan directly or indirectly under the WTO Agreement or to impede the attainment of any objective of the WTO Agreement; Authorization of the DSB to suspend the application to such country of concessions or other obligations prescribed under the provision of Article 2 of the [Dispute Settlement Understanding]
. . .

With regard to any imported products which are exported from . . . any foreign country which treats any . . . article of Japan . . . less favourably than any . . . article of any other country, a duty may be imposed upon such imported products, in addition to customs duty chargeable at an applicable rate in the Annexed Tariff . . . in accordance with a Cabinet Order, with products specified. *However, this provision does not apply in a case which should be entrusted to procedures of the DSB in accordance with paragraph 1 of the preceding Article* [emphasis added].

A Cabinet Order on retaliatory tariffs was promulgated on 28 December 1994, the same day that the Law was revised.[95] The order provides, *inter alia*, that the Minister of Finance consults the Advisory Council on Tariff Rate on taking a retaliatory measure under Article 6 of the Law. Paragraph 2 of Article 6 is to be applied, in principle, to states which are not members of the WTO. The last sentence of paragraph 2 suggests that the WTO dispute settlement procedures should be exhausted before Japan takes a retaliatory measure against a member of the WTO for matters covered by the WTO Agreement.

Retaliatory measures in the form of quantitative restrictions on export and import of goods may be taken under the Foreign Exchange and Foreign Trade Control Law. Article 48 (Permission of Export) and Article

---

[95] Cabinet Order No. 418, *Kanpo*, Spec. Iss. No. 242, at 20 (28 Dec. 1994).

52 (Approval of Import) of the Law are sufficiently wide in scope that no revision was considered necessary. Neither the Customs Tariff Law nor the Foreign Exchange Law contains provisions to co-ordinate actions taken by MOF under the Customs Tariff Law, and actions taken by MITI under the Foreign Exchange Law. When Japan takes retaliation, MOF and MITI are expected to consult each other to administer the separate procedures in a synchronized manner. Japan has yet to create an agency like the US Trade Representative, which co-ordinates retaliation policies. The rivalry between ministries is so strong that it is not likely that such an agency will be created in Japan in the near future.

Even though the DSU allows cross-sectoral retaliation, Japanese laws do not allow the Government to make full use of different means of retaliation. If benefits accruing to Japan under the WTO Agreement, including the General Agreement on Trade in Services and TRIPs, are nullified or impaired, Japan can take countermeasures in the area of trade in goods, imposing retaliatory tariffs or quantitative restrictions on goods. In other words, Japan can resort to cross-sectoral retaliation in trade in goods for nullification of benefits in trade in services or intellectual property. Before the Customs Tariff Law was revised, Japan could impose retaliatory tariffs only against discrimination in the trade of goods. The scope of retaliation was thus expanded—but only to that extent. The Japanese Government is still not given domestic authority to take cross-sectoral retaliation in other directions; it is not authorized to take countermeasures in trade in services or intellectual property for nullification of benefits in trade in goods.

5.4.2.2 Safeguard measures

5.4.2.2.1 General safeguard measures

In parallel with the system for countermeasures, Japan's system of safeguard measures is divided into two sub-systems: one on emergency duties administered by MOF under the Customs Tariff Law; and the other on quantitative restrictions administered by MITI under the Foreign Exchange and Foreign Trade Control Law. Article 9 (Emergency Duties) of the Customs Tariff Law was revised and expanded, and a revised Cabinet Order Concerning Emergency Duties was promulgated on 28 December 1994.[96] Since the old Customs Tariff Law had no provision on

---

[96] Cabinet Order No. 417, *Kanpo*, Spec. Iss. No. 242, at 18 (28 Dec. 1994). Unofficial English translation of Japanese laws relating to safeguard measures may be found in Notification of Laws, Regulations and Administrative Procedures Relating to Safeguard Measures: Japan, WTO Doc. G/SG/N/1/JPN/2 (June 1995).

investigation, it was theoretically possible for the Government to take emergency measures without investigating the matter. The revised Article sets out detailed procedures for investigation, using the procedures for anti-dumping and countervailing duty investigation as models. An investigation for emergency duties can be initiated only by the Government; complaints by domestic industries are not allowed. When either the Minister of Finance, the Minister of International Trade and Industry, or the Minister in charge of the affected industry believes that an investigation needs to be initiated, he or she notifies the other two Ministers and the three Ministers make decisions in consultation. The Minister of Finance has to consult the Advisory Council on Tariff Rate on taking emergency measures. The revised Customs Tariff Law and the Cabinet Order effectively implement the Safeguard Agreement. The period for which emergency duties are imposed is limited to four years and may be extended up to eight years. No emergency action can be taken again to a product that has been subject to such action for a period equal to the duration of the previous measure, subject to a non-application period of at least two years. An emergency measure imposed for a period more than one year must be progressively liberalized. In certain cases, provisional measures lasting less than 200 days may be imposed.

Until 1994, the legal basis for safeguard measures in the form of import quotas were provided by Article 52 (Approval of Import) of the Foreign Exchange and Foreign Trade Control Law, and the Import Trade Control Order (Cabinet Order No. 414 of 1949). They were not fully compatible with Article 19 of the GATT, because they did not explicitly require that a product was being imported in such increased quantities as to cause serious injury to domestic producers before an emergency action was taken by the Government. The defect of the laws did not cause problems, because Japan did not resort to safeguard measures in those days. The Japanese Government repaired this defect in implementing the WTO Agreement. MITI published a Regulation Concerning Emergency Measures against an Increase of Import of Goods on 28 December 1994, setting out procedures for safeguard measures taken under Article 3 (1) of the Import Trade Control Order in the form of import quotas.[97] Article 2 of the Regulation provides that when MITI imposes import quotas on goods for the reason that the import of the goods causes or threatens to cause serious injury to domestic industry, it shall do so in accordance with Articles 3 to 20 of the Regulation. These Articles correspond to the provisions of the Safeguard Agreement. The Regulation contains some provisions co-ordinating actions

---

[97] Regulation Concerning Emergency Measures against an Increase of Import of Goods (MITI Notification No. 715), 1554 *Kanpo* 9 (28 Dec. 1994).

by MITI and MOF. When the Minister of International Trade and Industry intends to initiate an investigation under the Regulation, he or she notifies the Minister of Finance and the Minister in charge of the affected industry. The Minister in charge of the affected industry may request the Minister of International Trade and Industry to initiate an investigation.

5.4.2.2.2 Safeguard measures in the textile trade

Even though the Japanese textile industry pressured MITI to take safeguard measures under the Multifibre Arrangement, MITI kept refusing to do so until 1994. However, in May 1994, after the WTO Agreement was signed, MITI changed its policy and decided to set up procedures for safeguard measures on textiles. On 5 December 1994, before Japan ratified the WTO Agreement, MITI published and put into force a Regulation Concerning Emergency Measures against an Increase of Import of a Textile Product.[98] The procedures may be used for safeguard actions either under the MFA or under the WTO Agreement on Textiles and Clothing. The Agreement on Textiles and Clothing contains a specific transitional safeguard mechanism which can be applied to products not yet integrated into GATT 1994. The procedures for safeguard measures in the textile trade is different from the procedures for general safeguard measures in that a domestic industry suffering serious injury may make a request to MITI to take safeguard measures. Otherwise, the two procedures are similar. For example, the procedures for safeguard measures in the textile trade also contain detailed provisions for investigations and a requirement to maintain an interval before repeated actions are taken for the same product.

In February 1995, only a few months after the Regulation went into effect, the Japan Spinning Association made a request to MITI to take safeguard measures on No. 40 count class cotton yarn. The same Association, together with the Japan Federation of Cotton and Rayon Textile Industry Associations, made another request on poplin broad textiles made of cotton. MITI initiated safeguard investigations on these two products in April 1995,[99] and decided not to take action in November 1995. While MITI acknowledged that these two products were imported in increased quantities in some periods during the preceding three years and that serious injury had been caused to domestic producers, it pointed out that import was on the decrease in recent months.[100]

---

[98] Regulation Concerning Emergency Measures against an Increase of Import of a Textile Product (MITI Notification No. 667), *Kanpo*, Spec. Iss. No. 227, at 1 (5 Dec. 1994).

[99] MITI Notification 232 (poplin broad textiles made of cotton), MITI Notification No. 233 (No. 40 count class cotton yarn), 1630 *Kanpo* 3 (21 Apr. 1995).

[100] MITI Notification 668 (poplin broad textiles made of cotton), MITI Notification No. 669 (No. 40 count class cotton yarn), 1772 *Kanpo* 10 (15 Nov. 1995).

5.5 CONCLUSION

Japan is a parliamentary democracy; the Cabinet is formed on the basis of a majority in the Diet. Consequently, there is little tension between the Cabinet and the Diet. The LDP has controlled a majority in the Diet for most of the post-war period. Thus, the Cabinet has been able to secure Diet approval of treaties without too much difficulty. In 1993, the LDP lost its parliamentary majority, and the cabinet has been formed on a coalition of political parties since then. As a result, treaty-making by Japan has become more complicated than before. Nevertheless, unless the Cabinet loses the support of the ruling parties, the treaty will gain the approval of the Diet. When the Cabinet submitted the WTO Agreement to the Diet for approval in 1994, most of the opposition parties were not in a position to criticize the Government for proposing ratification of the WTO Agreement, because those parties were in power in 1993 and were responsible for accepting the WTO Agreement for Japan. Given such circumstances, only the JCP could oppose the ratification of the WTO Agreement.

Treaties have the force of law in Japan by virtue of Article 98 (2) of the Japanese Constitution. They override statutes enacted by the Diet, even if the statutes are later in time. It is thus indisputable that the WTO Agreement has the force of law and prevails over statutes in Japan. What is unclear is whether the WTO Agreement is directly applicable in Japan. The Kyoto District Court denied the direct applicability of GATT 1947 in the *Kyoto Necktie Case* in 1984, and the Supreme Court apparently approved it in 1990. The issue of whether the WTO Agreement is directly applicable was not addressed in the deliberations of the Diet. Thus, it is up to the courts to decide it. Government officials have acknowledged that tariff concessions contained in the WTO Agreement are to be applied directly. The application of the WTO Agreement in this manner is anticipated by Article 3 of the Tariff Law. In addition, the provisions concerning the legal personality of the WTO and the privileges and immunities of the WTO and its officials must be applied directly, since they have not been implemented in the Japanese legislation. Direct applicability of other provisions remains unclear. Theoretically, it is possible to apply those provisions that are precise and complete. However, when individuals challenge the conformity of Japanese law to the WTO Agreement, it is unlikely that Japanese courts will declare the law to be null and void, especially because the direct applicability of the WTO Agreement is denied in the United States and possibly also in the European Union.

The WTO Agreement required considerable revisions of Japanese laws and regulations. The revisions of law on agriculture were most extensive.

In particular, the Food Control Law was abolished and the New Staple Food Law was enacted. The New Staple Food Law rationalizes rice distribution by strengthening market principles and deregulation.

The political scene of Japan changed dramatically during the negotiation, ratification, and implementation process of the WTO Agreement. In July 1993, at the last stage of the Uruguay Round negotiations, the LDP lost power and a non-LDP coalition government was formed. The coalition collapsed in 1994 and the LDP returned to power with the help of the SDPJ. Thus, it was the successive LDP governments which conducted the Uruguay Round negotiations, and the non-LDP coalition government which accepted and signed the WTO Agreement, and the LDP-SDPJ coalition government which ratified and implemented it. The trade policies of Japan remained essentially the same all through this political turmoil. The negotiation, ratification, and implementation of the WTO Agreement by Japan has proven yet again that Japan is run by bureaucrats, rather than by politicians.

IMPLEMENTATION OF THE URUGUAY ROUND RESULTS IN THE UNITED STATES

*David W. Leebron**

6.1 INTRODUCTION AND OVERVIEW

The Uruguay Round of multilateral trade negotiations constitutes one of the most ambitious efforts at international lawmaking and institution building since the establishment of the United Nations, and it is at least arguably the only one of such efforts that was fully and promptly implemented by the United States.[1] In this context, it is hardly surprising that the implementation of the results by the United States was both controversial and complex.[2] Between the 1979 completion of the Tokyo Round and the completion of the Uruguay Round, international trade agreements had moved from obscurity to front page news and political drama in the United States.[3] Not only was the substance of the agreements attacked, but also the procedure for their implementation in the United States. This consisted of objections both to the fast-track process for adopting the implementing legislation (as undemocratic) and to the failure

* Professor of Law, Columbia University. I thank Merit Janow, John Jackson, and Michael Young for comments, and Elizabeth Jane Williamson, Kevin Huff, Keith Hwang, Daniel Schneiderman, Eva Valik, and Juliet Wong for valuable research assistance.
[1] Cf. ITO (to be established pursuant to Havana Charter of 1948; Congress did not actually reject the ITO but members signalled that it would not be accepted); ICCPR, S. Exec. Doc. E, 95th Cong., 2nd Sess. 3, 999 UNTS 171 (1966), adopted by the UN Gen. Ass. on 19 Dec. 1966 (signed by US on 5 Oct. 1977, transmitted to the Senate 23 Feb. 1978, ratified by US 8 Sept. 1992); ICESCR, S. Exec. Doc. D, 95th Cong., 2nd Sess. 3, 993 UNTS 3 (1967) adopted by the UN Gen. Ass. 16 Dec. 1966. (signed by US 5 Oct. 1977, not yet ratified by US); The UNCLOS, UN Doc. A/CONF. 62/122. (7 Oct. 1982), reprinted in (1982) 21 ILM 1261 (opened for signature on 10 Dec. 1982, 117 states and two other entities became signatories. Supplemental Agreement adopted by UN Gen. Ass. on 28 July 1994. UNCLOS entered into force on 16 Nov. 1994 and was transmitted to the Senate for its advice and consent on 6 Oct. 1994; not yet ratified).

[2] That the Uruguay Round Agreements were extremely controversial is illustrated not only by the contentious tone of the public debate, but also by the final vote. Although the vote approving the agreements and the implementing legislation was by an overwhelming majority (288 to 146 in the House of Representatives, 140 Cong. Rec. H11535–6 (29 Nov. 1994) and 76 to 24 in the Senate, 140 Cong. Rec. S15379 (1 Dec. 1994)), it did not approach the nearly consensus vote for the implementing legislation of the Tokyo Round agreements.

[3] The tone of high-stakes political drama had in fact been set by the approval of NAFTA in 1993.

to present the agreements as a treaty, which would have required approval by a two-thirds vote in the Senate rather than a majority of both Houses of Congress.

As with the Tokyo Round, the defining element in the negotiation and implementation of US trade commitments was the allocation of authority between the executive and legislative branches of governments. In the United States, the independence of the legislature is further complicated both by a relatively weak party system and comparatively strong values of federalism.[4] Another distinctive feature is the role of private parties in the administrative and remedial process. Although Congress continues to place emphasis on the administrative process and private sector initiative in both opening foreign markets and defending American producers from unfair trade practices, it is notably less enthusiastic about providing either foreign exporters or domestic importers means to challenge American trade barriers within the United States' domestic legal system. Thus, as we shall see, Congress has sought to minimize the remedies (including defences) available to those groups.

One theme dominated the debate over the Uruguay Round Agreements in the United States, and this was sovereignty. In this context, 'sovereignty' primarily meant autonomy to determine various aspects of US policy. The sovereignty concerns had many manifestations, and these are analysed in detail below. Here I point out only that the sovereignty claims were made with respect to both the federal government and, under the name of federalism, state governments. Many provisions of the implementing legislation are specifically aimed at limiting the status and import of the Uruguay Round Agreements in domestic law, and exercising close supervision over the new World Trade Organization and its dispute settlement process. These provisions are particularly important since they are the sole basis for implementing and applying the Uruguay Round Agreements in US domestic law, and in general are more restrictive than the law which applied to the General Agreement on Tariffs and Trade of 1947 and the subsequently adopted amendments and multilateral codes.

Other important issues concerned the role of environmental protection and labour rights in international trade relations. Ultimately, these issues resulted in the failure to include a renewal of the 'fast-track' legislative procedure for trade agreements in the implementing legislation. The ability of the United States to pursue unilaterally a market-opening trade policy outside the WTO framework was also an important concern. Rather than repealing, or at least weakening, Section 301 of the Trade Act of

---

[4] As elaborated below, federalism (in the sense of decentralizing power to the states) as a political value plays a more important role than the limited legal constraints federalism places on the implementation of trade agreement obligations.

1974—as many of the United States' trading partners had hoped—the implementing legislation aims to strengthen and expand it, as has been the case in virtually all major trade laws since Section 301 was originally adopted as part of the Trade Act ('the 1974 Act').

This chapter proceeds as follows. Section 2 addresses general issues relating to the authorization, negotiation, and approval of the Uruguay Round Agreements. The basic allocation of negotiating and implementing authority, both as a constitutional and statutory matter, is described. In this connection, I very briefly outline the historical development of United States trade law since the original GATT. The section concludes with an analysis of the negotiating authority and legislative procedure applicable to the Uruguay Round. Section 3 looks to specific elements in the Uruguay Round Agreements Act of 1994. It begins with an overview of the implementing legislation, and proceeds to analyse the major issues that generally affected the implementation of Uruguay Round obligations into domestic law. In particular, constraints on challenges to domestic law and the implementation of dispute settlement are examined. Section 4 considers US participation in the WTO, and the present negotiating authority of the US President within the WTO.

6.2 NEGOTIATION AND IMPLEMENTATION

6.2.1 Authority to enter into trade agreements

6.2.1.1 Constitutional allocation of powers

Both the President and the United States Congress exercise aspects of foreign relations powers, and the history of United States trade law is to a great extent the history of the allocation of power between these two branches of government. While the President (or his delegate) is the exclusive representative of the United States in international dealings, Congress must generally approve or implement any agreements which touch on its legislative powers.

There are five basic procedures through which the United States can negotiate and implement international trade commitments.[5] One is the negotiation of an international treaty that is ratified pursuant to the

---

[5] See J. H. Jackson, W. Davey and A. Sykes, *Legal Problems of International Economic Relations* (3rd ed. 1995), 118; Restatement (Third) of the Foreign Relations Law of the US, s. 303; J. H. Jackson, 'US constitutional law principles and foreign trade law and policy', in Meinhard Hilf and E.-U. Petersmann, eds., *National Constitutions and International Economic Law* (1993), 65, 73.

Constitutional provision which requires the approval of two-thirds of the United States Senate. Secondly, the President may be authorized pursuant to the terms of such a treaty to enter into additional agreements.[6] A third method is for the President to enter into a 'sole executive agreement' under his inherent power over foreign affairs, without authorization or participation by Congress. This process has generally not been used for trade agreements, as the Constitution specifically provides that Congress shall have the powers to 'lay and collect . . . Duties' and to 'regulate Commerce with foreign Nations.'[7] Thus, in order to negotiate and implement trade agreements, the President generally requires some co-operation from Congress. This can take the form either of the delegation by Congress of authority to the President, or Congressional approval and legislative implementation of the terms of the agreement after it is concluded. These two methods of entering international trade agreements fall under the rubric of Congressional–executive agreements, which involve the participation of both Houses of Congress and the President.

The Congressional–executive agreement is by far the most dominant means by which the United States enters international agreements.[8] In one form, the Congress fully authorizes the President in advance to enter into certain agreements, and those agreements become both binding international commitments of the United States and part of its municipal law without further action by Congress. This was the process followed both in the Reciprocal Trade Agreements Act of 1934 and in general for tariff reductions negotiated under the GATT. Alternatively, Congress may or may not authorize the President to negotiate particular agreements, but

---

[6] Similar power might flow from Congressional approval of an executive agreement. In the context of the Uruguay Round, Congress sought to restrain the President from entering into certain agreements pursuant to the WTO agreements, but these appeared to be exceptions to the President's authority to enter into additional agreements. See p. 240 infra (discussing restraints on entering an agreement on rules of origin and an extension of 'green light' subsidy provisions).

[7] US Constitution, Art. I, s. 8. Although Congress cannot on its own enter into international agreements, it can unilaterally adopt legislation establishing tariffs and other aspects of trade policy. Such legislation would either have to be signed by the President, or Congress would have to override a veto by a two-thirds vote of both houses.

[8] See S. O'Halloran, *Politics, Process, and American Trade Theory* (1994), 72 (indicating 85% of all international agreements entered into by the US were pursuant to authority delegated by Congress to the President); Jackson, Davey and Sykes, *Legal Problems*, at 118–19 (noting that in the period since the Second World War, over 90% of US international agreements have been executive agreements rather than treaties, and that 97% of the executive agreements were 'effected through statutory authority of some kind'); Memorandum to Ambassador Michael Kantor, US Trade Representative, from Walter Dellinger, 29 July 1994 (State Dept. reports that about 95% of international agreements entered into between 1946 and 1993 were executive agreements, 'the overwhelming majority of which were based at least in part on Congressional legislation, principally legislation delegating to the President the authority to conclude international agreements').

any agreements negotiated by the President are subsequently implemented into municipal law by legislative action of Congress, which requires a majority approval of both Houses.[9] As part of such implementing legislation, Congress 'approves' the agreement and authorizes the President to ratify it. This was the process by which the Tokyo Round agreements on non-tariff barriers, as well as more recent bilateral and regional free trade agreements, were implemented.

Given the long history of Congressional–executive agreements in the area of trade policy,[10] including most recently the North American Free Trade Agreement,[11] it seemed well settled that trade agreements need not be approved as treaties by the Senate.[12] Thus it was somewhat surprising when this issue emerged as part of the debate over the Uruguay Round Agreements. Despite the fact that the vast majority of foreign economic agreements in this century have been implemented either as Congressional–executive agreements or sole executive agreements,[13] an argument was made that the Uruguay Round agreements were required to be approved as a treaty by a two-thirds vote of the United States Senate. Two types of arguments were made for this requirement, both intended in part to distinguish past US practice. One was that the United States' sovereignty was significantly affected by the creation of the WTO and the reform of the dispute settlement process. The other was that the Uruguay Round Agreements had a significant impact on state powers.

Although prominent scholars joined on both sides of this fray,[14] the

[9] Since the President has negotiated the agreement, I put aside the question of a possible Presidential veto of implementing legislation. Ordinarily, legislation can be adopted over the President's veto by a two-thirds vote of both the House and Senate. It is doubtful, however, that Congress could effectively enter into an international agreement without supporting action by the President, and any attempt to do so would probably be regarded as beyond Congressional power.

[10] The historical emergence of the Congressional–executive agreement is traced in B. Ackerman and D. Golove, 'Is NAFTA constitutional?' (1995) 108 Harv. L. Rev. 799.

[11] The negotiation of NAFTA was authorized by the Omnibus Trade and Competitiveness Act 1988, and implemented by the NAFTA Implementation Act of (1993).

[12] See, e.g., M. S. McDougal and A. Lans, 'Treaties and Congressional–executive or Presidential agreements: interchangeable instruments of national policy (parts 1 and 2)', (1945) 54 Yale LJ 181, 534; Restatement (Third) s. 303, comment e (1986) ('The prevailing view is that the Congressional–executive agreement can be used as an alternative to the treaty method in every instance. Which procedure should be used is a political judgment . . .').

[13] A prominent exception to the use of Congressional–executive agreements is bilateral investment treaties, which are approved by the Senate as treaties.

[14] On the scholarly level, the debate was largely through a series of letters and testimony from Professor Tribe of Harvard, Professor Ackerman of Yale, and Walter Dellinger, a Duke University Professor of Law now serving as Assistant Attorney-General, Office of Legal Counsel. A group of Constitutional and international law scholars also filed a letter in support of the view that the Uruguay Round Agreements could be approved as a Congressional–executive agreement. Memorandum of Law from Professors Bruce Ackermann, Abram Chayes, Kenneth Dam, Thomas Franck, Charles Fried, David Golove, Louis Henkin, Robert

procedural question received comparatively little serious attention by the legislators.[15] Senator Helms made a motion that the Uruguay Round Agreements should be submitted to the Senate as a treaty, but then agreed to withdraw it.[16] Hours before the final vote, the most distinguished academic supporter of the view that the agreements had to be ratified as a treaty at least partially recanted.[17] For present purposes, it is unnecessary to reach any definitive conclusion regarding this important question. It is unlikely that a court would ever reach the question of whether the agreements should have been approved as a treaty, and if it should decide that question it is improbable (but far from impossible) it would strike down over a half century of Congressional and executive practice.[18] More important perhaps, the resolution of this question would probably have little effect on the United States' implementation, as the specific provisions enacted by Congress to implement Uruguay Round obligations would still constitute valid laws of the United States. Indeed, there are very few contexts in which the issue could be raised.[19] The most obvious would be in a special proceeding by the Attorney General to strike down a state law as violative of the Uruguay Round Agreements.[20]

Hudec, John H. Jackson, Harold H. Koh and Myres McDougal to Members of Congress and Executive Branch Officials (11 Nov. 1994). See also Letter of Professor Richard Parker to Senator Robert Byrd (9 Aug. 1994). Professors Tribe and Ackerman subsequently published scholarly presentations of their views—see B. Ackerman & D. Golove, 'Is NAFTA constitutional?', and L. H. Tribe, 'Taking text and structure seriously: reflections on free-form method in Constitutional interpretation', (1995) 108 Harv. L. Rev. 799 and 1221 respectively.

[15] The issue was mentioned a number of times in the House and Senate debates, but did not receive extended consideration.

[16] Proposal of Helms Amendment No. 2458, 103rd Cong., 2d Sess., 140 Cong. Rec. S10574, S10582. Withdrawal of the amendment at 140 Cong. Rec. S10591.

[17] Memorandum from Laurence H. Tribe to Sen. George J. Mitchell et al. (28 Nov. 1994). In an article published several months later, Professor Tribe forcefully elaborated his views, and stated that the Senators who quoted this statement as an 'abandonment' of the view the WTO Agreement must be ratified as a treaty had 'an incorrect understanding of what [he] had said'. Tribe, 'Taking text and structure seriously', at 1303 n. 47.

[18] Still, the courts have of late shown a willingness to rediscover 'exiled' Constitutional doctrines. See L. Greenhouse, 'The nation: past masters; blowing the dust off the Constitution that was', N.Y. Times, 28 May 1995, s. 4, at 1, col. 1. For the most prominent recent example of a case disinterring doctrines presumed dead, see United States v. Lopez, 115 S.Ct. 1624 (1995) (finding Congress's power under the Commerce clause did not extend to prohibiting the possession of guns near schools).

[19] As noted below, the implementing legislation prevents any private litigant from using the Agreements to challenge any federal or state law. It is possible, but unlikely, that a court would reach the question in the context of whether to interpret a federal or state law in accordance with Uruguay Round obligations. The most likely context in which a court might decide the issue is in a challenge by the US under s. 102 (b) (2) of the URAA to state law that conflicts with the Uruguay Round Agreements, but not with any specific provision of the URAA itself.

[20] See discussion at p. 228.

6.2.1.2 Statutory authorization and delegation of power: a brief history

That the authority to negotiate and implement trade agreements incorporates aspects of both Presidential and Congressional powers under the Constitution does not resolve how the power to influence that negotiation and implementation is allocated and exercised. United States trade law is exceedingly complex, in part because it embodies the shifting division of power between the legislative and executive branches of government, and in part because the United States tends to place greater emphasis on the role of private firms and groups.[21] Indeed, to some extent Congress appears to have limited executive freedom of action by assuring participation of private sector interests in the trade agreements process. In virtually every Trade Act of the last century, Congress has placed some combination of substantive and procedural constraints on the President to enter into trade agreements and conduct trade policy. Our focus here is necessarily on the last two major legislative trade actions that frame the Uruguay Round: the Omnibus Trade and Competitiveness Act of 1988,[22] which provided the negotiating authority, and the URAA,[23] which implemented those agreements into United States law. Nonetheless, it is worthwhile at least for purposes of comparison to outline briefly the major developments in United States trade law as it pertains to the negotiation and implementation of international agreements.[24]

Prior to 1934, United States trade policy was largely within the province of Congress. Tariff lines were specifically established by statute, although often with alternative punitive tariffs and sometimes flexible tariffs designed to offset production cost advantages. The United States generally adopted the position that its tariffs were non-negotiable. The President,

---

[21] See J. H. Jackson, 'United States law and implementation of the Tokyo Round negotiation,' in J. H. Jackson, J.-V. Louis and M. Matsushita (eds.), *Implementing the Tokyo Round: national constitutions and international economic rules* 139 (1984); H. H. Koh, 'Congressional controls on Presidential trade policy-making after *INS v. Chadha*', 18 NYUJ.Int'l L. & Pol. 1191, 1225–33. In other countries, such influence is typically mediated through political parties. In the US, individual legislators, particularly chairmen of important congressional committees, can wield significant power and influence over the formulation and approval of legislation.

[22] Pub. L. No. 100–418, 102 Stat. 1107 (1988).

[23] Pub. L. No. 103–465, 108 Stat. 4809 (1994).

[24] Obviously, the discussion here must of necessity gloss over the details and subtleties. For more exhaustive treatments, see R. A. Pastor, *Congress and the Politics of US Foreign Economic Policy: 1929–1976* (1980); S. D. Cohen, *The Making of United States International Economic Policy* (4th ed. 1994); I. M. Destler, *American Trade Politics* (2nd ed. 1992); S. C. Schwab, *Trade-offs: Negotiating the Omnibus Trade and Competitiveness Act* (1994); Jackson, 'United States law' and O'Halloran, *Politics*.

pursuant to Congressional authority, entered into most-favoured-nation agreements with other nations. As these agreements contained only the conditional version of the clause prior to 1923, and the President's tariff negotiating authority was in any event extremely limited, the agreements generally had little trade liberalizing effect. Congress vacillated between liberal and protectionist policies, culminating in the notoriously protectionist Smoot–Hawley tariffs of 1930.[25]

Congressional log-rolling on behalf of domestic industries desiring economic protection was soon widely recognized as a disaster. The RTAA[26] was the first major step in the delegation of trade policy authority away from Congress to the President, although prior legislation had delegated narrower ranges of negotiating authority.[27] The RTAA authorized the President to enter into reciprocal trade agreements for the reduction of tariffs. Although the tariff-cutting authority was broad and deep (various amendments to the RTAA authorized cuts up to 40 or 50 per cent), Congress kept some control through short authorization periods, usually one to three years. This was the authority under which the GATT was entered into in 1947, although the status of that agreement in United States law has been disputed.[28] The following four GATT negotiating rounds were also under the authority of the RTAA and its extensions.

The Trade Expansion Act of 1962,[29] which provided the negotiating authority for the Kennedy Round, established some of the principle structures of current United States trade law, although most have since been significantly revised. Prior to the Trade Expansion Act ('the 1962 Act'), the lead agency in international trade negotiations had been the State Department. Many in Congress viewed the State Department as insufficiently concerned about domestic economic interests.[30] The 1962 Act created the position of Special Representative for Trade Negotiations to be the chief representative in international trade negotiations.[31] In an attempt to exercise greater Congressional supervision, the 1962 Act also required that two representatives from both the House and Senate be accredited as members of the US delegation.[32] The President was required to seek the advice of the Tariff Commission on the effects of proposed tariff reductions or duty-free treatment, and to hold public hearings.[33] The

[25] Pub. L. No. 71–361, 46 Stat. 590 (1930).
[26] Pub. L. No. 73–316, 48 Stat. 943 (1934).
[27] For a good overview of US tariff history and the Congressional enlargement and restriction of Presidential authority, see O'Halloran, *Politics*, 76–109.
[28] See text, and sources cited at n. 6.
[29] Pub. L. No. 87–794, 76 Stat. 872 (1962).
[30] See Pastor, *Congress and the Politics of US Foreign Economic Policy*, 112.
[31] S. 241.   [32] S. 243.
[33] Ss. 221–4. This provision was carried over to the 1974 Act, ss. 131–4, and the Omnibus Trade and Competitiveness Act of 1988, s. 1111, with modifications.

negotiating authority was apparently still limited to tariff reductions (of 60 per cent, with greater reductions authorized for products on which a duty of not more than 5 per cent already applied and products of which the United States and European Economic Community accounted for more than 80 per cent of world export value).[34] Although the Act provided no clear authority to negotiate non-tariff barriers, the United States agreed during the Kennedy Round to an agreement on dumping and to repeal the 'American Selling Price' provision that required duties on certain products be calculated on the basis of US prices.[35] Congress refused to enact the agreements on non-tariff barriers,[36] and also failed to renew the President's tariff negotiating authority when it expired in 1969.

As the next negotiating round was contemplated, it became clear both that non-tariff barriers would be the central issue and that the United States could not credibly negotiate if it could not provide, in the wake of the Kennedy Round failures, some greater assurance that any agreements negotiated would be approved by Congress. The 1974 Act[37] was the most important revision of the Congressional–executive allocation of trade policy-making authority since 1934. For the first time it explicitly authorized the President to enter into agreements on non-tariff barriers. The price of this broader authority was a requirement that the President consult throughout the negotiations with Congress and private sector advisory committees, and that any agreement entered into be implemented by Congressional legislation.[38] For present purposes, the most important specific aspects of the 1974 Act were the establishment of the 'fast-track' process for the approval of trade agreements and the placement of the Office of the Special Representative for Trade Negotiations (which later became the United States Trade Representative) within the Executive Office of the President.[39] The fast-track process, which is discussed below, provided for expedited consideration, without amendment, of bills to implement trade agreements on non-tariff barriers.[40] Congress significantly expanded the role and powers of the STR, and added two deputies, who

---

[34] Ss. 201, 202 and 211.

[35] This provision dated back to 1922. See F. W. Taussig, *The Tariff History of the United States* (8th ed. 1931) 475. It was a violation of the terms of the GATT itself, but permitted under the 'grandfather' provision of the Protocol of Provisional Application.

[36] Subsequently the President did implement the Anti-Dumping Agreement through administrative action, but not the agreement regarding the American Selling Price.

[37] Pub. L. No. 93–618, 88 Stat. 1978 (1975).

[38] Ss. 102(e), 131–135.   [39] S. 141.

[40] See Sect. 2.2.2. The House had intially proposed a legislative veto, which would provide that any agreement negotiated would be adopted unless either House of Congress voted by a majority to disapprove it. The Supreme Court declared the legislative veto unconstitutional in *INS* v. *Chadha*, 462 US 919 (1983). Although the legislative veto was not used to approve trade agreements, it was adopted in several other contexts in the 1974 Act. See Koh, 'Congressional Controls', at 1207 (identifying six legislative vetoes in the 1974 Act).

were also to hold ambassadorial rank and be confirmed by the Senate. The number of members of Congress to be accredited as part of the United States' Trade Delegation was increased from four to ten.[41] The 1974 Act also included the now-famous Section 301, which authorized the President, upon his own initiative or private complaint, to take unilateral action against certain foreign countries whose actions are determined to burden or restrict United States trade.

The results of the Tokyo Round were implemented five years later by the Trade Agreements Act of 1979.[42] Congress was apparently content with the operation of the fast-track authority during the Tokyo Round.[43] It amended the provision of the 1974 Act simply by replacing 'five-year period' with 'thirteen-year period', thereby extending the fast-track authority for non-tariff barriers until 3 January 1988.[44] That provision expired a little more than a year after the Uruguay Round was launched in September of 1986.

The Trade and Tariff Act of 1984[45] was less important for present purposes than the two major trade bills that preceded it, or the two that followed it, but it did represent significant assertions of Congressional control over trade policy. Congress required that in order to be eligible for the fast-track procedure, the President was required to notify the principal House and Senate committees of the trade negotiations at least sixty legislative days prior to the date he notifies Congress of his intent to enter into a trade agreement. During the sixty day period, if either Committee voted to disapprove the negotiations, any implementing legislation would be denied fast-track treatment.[46] The Trade and Tariff Act (the 1984 Act) also gave prominence to negotiating objectives in the areas of services, direct investment, and intellectual property. Congress provided the United States Trade Representative (the USTR) with authority to self-initiate Section 301 investigations,[47] and also added annual reporting requirements that required the USTR to identify unfair trade barriers.[48] Although these reports played no legal role in United States trade policy under the 1984 Act, they were ultimately to serve as the basis upon which Congress sought to force executive action against the trade practices of other nations.

[41] S. 161(a). Formally, the status of Congressional member participation was changed from member of the US delegation to official adviser to the delegation.

[42] Pub. L. No. 96–39, 93 Stat. 144 (1979).

[43] See Jackson, 'United States law' at 166.

[44] S. 1101. The Act did make some relatively minor changes to the advisory committee structure. See s. 1103.

[45] Pub. L. No. 98–573, 98 Stat. 2948 (1984).

[46] S. 401(a) (amending s. 102 of the 1974 Act).

[47] S. 304(d)(1) (amending s. 302 of the 1974 Act.)

[48] S. 303 (adding s. 181 to the 1974 Act, codified at 19 USC s. 2241).

6.2.1.3 Negotiating authority for the Uruguay Round: the Omnibus Trade and Competiveness Act of 1988

The Omnibus Trade and Competitiveness Act of 1988[49] ('the 1988 Act') contains the President's negotiating authority for the Uruguay Round Agreements, although it was enacted nearly two years after the Uruguay Round was officially launched.[50] This Act has been described as 'unprecedented in scope and process'.[51] Although judgements differ about the overall protectionist nature of the legislation,[52] it clearly represented a new era in Congressional activism. At a broad level, it emphasized two themes. One, reflected in the Act's full name, is the perceived link between competitiveness and trade, and the implicit notion that the Government had a role to play in achieving competitiveness. The second theme was fairness and reciprocity, and the continuing notion that America's inability to compete abroad was in significant part due to the unfair trading practices of other nations.[53] Although the 1988 Act acknowledged the largely macro-economic causes of the United States trade deficits, it also sharpened United States unilateralism. Congress once more completely rewrote the Section 301 provisions of the 1974 Act, transferring from the President to the USTR the responsibility for taking 'mandatory' action under Section 301.[54] Super 301 and Special 301 required the USTR to identify 'priority foreign countries.' Super 301 further required the USTR to undertake an investigation of such countries,

[49] Pub. L. No. 100–418, 102 Stat. 1107 (1988).

[50] For more comprehensive treatment of the background to the 1988 Act, see Schwab, 'Trade-offs'.

[51] R. J. Ahearn and A. Reifman, 'Trade legislation in 1987: Congress takes charge', in R. E. Baldwin and J. D. Richardson (eds.) *NBER Conference Report: Issues in the Uruguay Round* (1988), 74.

[52] See Note, 'The Omnibus Trade and Competitiveness Act of 1988—the Section 301 amendments: insignificant changes from prior law?', (1989) 7 B.U. Int. LJ 115, 115 n.5 (relating reaction of other countries); Ahearn and Reifman, 'Trade Legislation in 1987' at 80 ('The bills passed by the House and Senate in 1987 seem to be more protectionist than they have been since the 1930s.'); J. H. Bello and A. F. Holmer, 'The 1988 Trade Bill: is it protectionist?' in H. Applebaum and L. M. Schlitt (eds.), *The New Trade Law: Omnibus Trade and Competitiveness Act of 1988* (1988), 329:

'Those who persist in claiming that the Act is protectionist should be condemned to read it. . . . [T]he final bill signed by the President clearly continues rather than contorts traditional US trade policy; and renews rather than reneges on the US commitment to the multilateral trading system. It does not legislate barriers at our borders to close the US market and create a Fortress America, but rather simply provides better trade remedy tools to use judiciously to open foreign markets.'

[53] For a marvellous analysis of the notion of unfairness in US trade policy, see K. W. Abbott, 'Defensive unfairness: the normative structure of Section 301', J. Bhagwati & R. Hudec, *Fair Trade and Harmonization* (1996). See also J. M. Finger, 'The meaning of "Unfair" in United States import policy' (1992) 1 Minn. J. Global Trade 35.

[54] S. 1301(a) (amending s. 301 of the 1974 Act).

and to impose sanctions in the case of an affirmative determination. These provisions helped Section 301 become the darling of American protectionist interests and the *bête noire* of its trading partners.

The 1988 Act provided three kinds of authority to negotiate trade commitments. As with the 1974 Act, the President was authorized to negotiate tariff cuts (but only up to 50 per cent rather than 60 per cent) and to implement those negotiated tariffs through proclamation without further legislative action. Unlike under the 1974 Act and the Trade Agreements Act of 1979 ('the 1979 Act'), the President was not provided with any authority to raise tariffs through proclamation. (Because tariffs were increased as the result of the tariffication under the Uruguay Round Agreement on Agriculture, those tariffs had to be specifically approved in the implementing legislation.)[55] Secondly, the President was granted fast-track treatment for agreements on non-tariff barriers (and on bilateral agreements) if certain requirements were met. Thirdly, the President technically had negotiating authority under the 1988 Act to negotiate on virtually any trade barrier, although it might not benefit from the fast-track procedure.[56] Each of these authorizations of negotiations was limited to five years (until 1 June 1993), except that the fast-track authority was limited to three years unless renewed.

The President also has some trade negotiating authority outside the specific provisions of the 1988 Act. Other statutory provisions, such as Section 301 of the 1974 Act, provide ongoing negotiating authority. Even in the absence of clear statutory authority to negotiate on a matter, the President could negotiate and enter into certain agreements pursuant to his general foreign relations powers. The prevailing view is that without Congressional action, the President does not have authority on his own to override earlier conflicting legislation.[57] If implementation of an agreement requires such legislation, it would be according to the usual rules for the adoption of legislation (unless approved by the Senate as a treaty).

6.2.2 Implementation of trade agreements

6.2.2.1 General overview of implementation

The process by which the President is authorized to negotiate and accept an international agreement must be distinguished from its implementation

[55] S. 111 URAA.

[56] Congress did, however, purport to limit the authority under the 1988 Act to agreements that make 'progress in meeting the applicable objectives described in s. 1101' (s. 1102 (b) (2)). See n. 84.

[57] See *United States* v. *Guy W. Capps, Inc.*, 204 F.2d 655 (4th Cir. 1953), affirmed on other grounds, 348 US 296 (1955); R. E. Hudec, 'The legal status of GATT in the domestic law of the United States', in M. Hilf *et al*, eds., *The European Community and GATT* 187 at 194–5 (1986); Restatement (Third) s. 115 n. 5 (1986).

in domestic law. United States law treats international agreements, or portions thereof, as either self-executing or non-self-executing. A self-executing agreement may be applied directly in domestic law, for example as a defence to a civil or criminal action or perhaps as the basis of a cause of action for declaratory, injunctive or monetary relief. This is a determination made by the courts both on the basis of the treaty itself (the nature of the language and the intent of the parties) and Congressional intent.[58] Even if the Senate approves a treaty, or Congress approves an international agreement as part of implementing legislation, that treaty or agreement might have no direct application in United States law. Congress has increasingly adopted the position that the treaties it approves are not self-executing.[59] In that event, if Congress and the President fail to fully transform the obligations flowing from an international agreement into domestic law, the United States will be in violation of those obligations.

The RTAA and subsequent legislation clearly authorized the President to implement, through Presidential proclamation, tariff reductions within specified limits. The GATT was never approved by the US Congress, either as a treaty or through the specific adoption of legislation implementing its provisions. Because the language of the RTAA was somewhat ambiguous, it is not clear as a legal matter whether the agreement is an authorized Congressional–executive agreement or a sole executive agreement.[60] In each extension of the RTAA (through to 1955), Congress provided that the legislation 'shall not be construed to determine or indicate the approval or disapproval by the Congress of the executive agreement known as the General Agreement on Tariffs and Trade.'[61] As a

[58] See generally J. H. Jackson, 'Status of treaties in domestic legal systems: a policy analysis' (1992) 86 AJIL 310; J. J. Paust, 'Self-executing treaties' (1988) 82 AJIL 760. Prof. Henkin has recently suggested that Senate declarations that treaties are not self-executing may be unconstitutional where the character of the treaty obligations are such that they otherwise would be self-executing (L. Henkin, 'U.S. ratification of Human Rights Conventions: the ghost of Senator Bricker' (1995) 89 AJIL 341 at 347.

[59] This unwillingness is not confined to international trade agreements. For example, in its recent ratification of several human rights covenants, the Senate expressly provided that the agreements were not self-executing. See, e.g., International Convention on the Elimination of all forms of Racial Discrimination, 140 Cong. Rec. S7634 (daily ed. 24 June 1994) (proposed resolution); The Covenant on Civil and Political Rights, 138 Cong. Rec. S4781, S4783 (daily ed. 2 Apr. 1992) (proposed resolution).

[60] See generally J. H. Jackson, 'The General Agreement on Tariffs and Trade in United States domestic law' (1967) 66 Mich. L. Rev. 249; Hudec, *The Legal Status of GATT*. Jackson and Hudec, in their very thorough and thoughtful analyses, come to slightly different conclusions regarding the status of GATT obligations in domestic law. See also R. A. Brand, 'The status of the General Agreement on Tariffs and Trade in United States domestic law' (1990) 26 Stan. JIL 479; T. W. France, 'The Domestic Legal Status of the GATT: The Need for Clarification' (Note) (1994) 51 Wash. & Lee L. Rev. 1481.

[61] Trade Agreements Extension Act 1955, Pub. L. No. 84–6 s. 3 (a) (1) (A), 69 Stat. 162, 163 (1955). The language of the 1974 Act was somewhat softened to provide, in conjunction with the permanent authorization of funding for the United States' share of GATT expenses,

result, the legal status of the GATT of 1947 (and its amendments prior to 1979) in United States law was uncertain. It has been given direct application in very few cases. Most state courts that have considered the issue have assumed that state laws inconsistent with the GATT cannot be applied.[62] By contrast, courts have never held GATT obligations to prevail over inconsistent federal law.[63] The GATT has, however, often played a significant role in interpreting federal law, particularly federal law intended to implement GATT obligations.[64]

Since 1974, multilateral non-tariff trade agreements and regional and bilateral free trade agreements have been negotiated under a structure that combines aspects of both *ex ante* and *ex post* Congressional approval. Congress authorizes the President to negotiate certain trade agreements to achieve certain objectives, subject to statutory implementation by the usual majority decision of both the House and Senate. This is basically a four-step process. Congress first authorizes the President to negotiate and enter into trade agreements. Pursuant to this authority, the President negotiates and signs the agreement. Congress then approves the agreements (perhaps under the fast-track procedure described below), adopts provisions implementing them into domestic law, and authorizes the President to accept the agreements (perhaps subject to conditions). The President then formally accepts the agreements on behalf of the United States. Tariff reductions are still implemented under the three-step procedure followed since the RTAA: Congressional provision of negotiation authority, Presidential negotiation, and Presidential proclamation of the tariff cuts (or increases).[65]

This was the basis on which the Tokyo Round agreements were authorized and implemented in the United States. It is noteworthy that the implementing legislation for those agreements did not approve the GATT itself, but only the specific agreements negotiated during the Tokyo

that the authorization 'does not imply approval or disapproval by the Congress of all articles of the General Agreement on Tariffs and Trade' (s. 121 (d)). When Congress approved the Tokyo Round Agreements, it still failed to explicitly approve of the GATT itself. Thus the 1994 Act marks the first time Congress has explicitly approved the GATT (in this case, the GATT 1994).

[62] See, e.g., *KSB Technical Sales Corp.* v. *North Jersey Dist. Water Supply Com.*, 381 A.2d 774 (1977). See Hudec, *The Legal Status of GATT*.

[63] Ibid., 210–11.

[64] Recently, however, several courts have failed to pay much heed to the GATT in construing US anti-dumping and countervailing duty legislation. See p. 217.

[65] In the Tokyo Round, the tariff authority and non-tariff authority were independent, so that in theory the President could implement the tariff cuts even if Congress failed to approve the non-tariff agreements. In the last renewal of negotiating authority in the Uruguay Round, Congress withdrew that option, and provided that the tariff cuts could be implemented only upon enactment of the implementing legislation for the non-tariff agreements. Pub. L. No. 103–49, 107 Stat. 239 (1993) (adding subsection (e) to s. 1102 of the 1988 Act).

Round.[66] That Congress 'approves' the agreements in the implementing legislation does not make them directly applicable in United States law. Indeed, as discussed below, despite Congressional approval of both the Tokyo Round and Uruguay Round Agreements, Congress clearly intended that those agreements were non-self-executing. Implementation of non-self-executing agreements is through a combination of specific legislative action and administrative action authorized either under the implementing legislation or the more general authority of the relevant administrative agencies.

Prior to the conclusion of the Uruguay Round,[67] free trade agreements were implemented, one of which (NAFTA) was pursuant to the negotiating authority in the 1988 Act. The North American Free Trade Agreement Implementation Act served more as the model for the URAA than did the 1979 Trade Agreements Act. Indeed, a comparison between the United States–Canada Free Trade Agreement Implementation Act of 1988 and the North American Free Trade Agreement Implementation Act of 1993 ('the NAFTA Act') reveals substantial evolution in the Congressional approach to the implementation of trade agreements since the authorization of the Uruguay Round negotiations (the same year as the United States–Canada Free Trade Agreement Implementation Act ('the USCFTA Act'). The NAFTA debate made clear that trade had become an extraordinarily contentious, public issue. Congress increasingly insisted not only on setting the terms of the President's negotiating authority and the implementing legislation, but also restraining and supervising future action by the executive and international organs. Ultimately, many of the general implementation provisions of the URAA were drawn from the NAFTA Act.

I examine in greater detail below the status of the Uruguay Round Agreements, including the GATT 1994, in United States law. At this point, it bears emphasizing that as a result of the URAA, Congress has for the first time explicitly approved the GATT and concomitantly specified its status in domestic law. The legislation substantially alters its status in respect of both federal and state law. Since, with one minor exception,[68] all the Tokyo Round agreements have been redrafted as part of the Uruguay Round, those agreements as well have a new, clearer status in domestic law.

---

[66] S. 2 (c), Trade Agreements Act 1979.

[67] One more piece of legislation is worthy of brief note, as it potentially played a strategic part in the Uruguay Round negotiations. In 1990 Congress passed the Agricultural Reconciliation Act, Pub. L. No. 101–508, 104 Stat. 1388 (1990). This Act provided for significant reductions in farm subsidies, but also called for a US$1bn. increase in agricultural export subsidies if the Uruguay Round negotiations failed.

[68] The exception is the Agreement on Trade in Civil Aircraft. Its status in US law continues to derive from the 1979 Act. The US is not a party to the International Dairy Arrangement.

6.2.2.2 The fast-track process: general principles and procedures

The so-called fast-track process for trade agreements was inaugurated in the 1974 Act, which authorized the Tokyo Round negotiations. Today the fast-track is widely perceived as essential to any complex trade negotiation with the United States. It applies both to non-tariff multilateral agreements and to bilateral trade agreements. The fast-track innovation was in large part a response to the diminished negotiating credibility that had resulted from the failure of Congress to implement certain agreements that had been concluded during the Kennedy Round. The 1979 multilateral trade agreements were the first agreements to be implemented through the fast-track process.[69]

The fast track consists of a set of expedited legislative procedures which are followed if certain conditions regarding trade agreements are met. The primary requirement is to notify and consult with both Congress and the private sector (through the advisory committee structure discussed below) on an ongoing basis during the trade negotiations. Prior to the 1988 Act, the fast-track authority to negotiate trade agreements on non-tariff barriers was extremely broad and not expressly conditioned on specific substantive objectives (although some such objectives were identified). Under Section 151 of the 1974 Act, the authority is available for implementing legislation that contains provisions approving both the trade agreements and the statement of administrative action proposed to implement those agreements, as well as any necessary or appropriate changes in law (including amendments and repeals). The President must notify Congress of his intent to enter into the agreement ninety days prior to signing the agreement, and thereafter transmit the final agreement and draft implementing legislation to Congress. Failure to comply with these requirements does not deprive the President of authority to negotiate trade agreements, but only the fast-track procedure to implement them. The President would retain the option of submitting a trade agreement as a treaty to the senate or as a Congressional–executive agreement to the Congress for adoption under the normal procedural rules of each House. The fast-track rules, although enacted by statute, have only the status of internal rules for each House of Congress.[70] Each House of Congress could revoke the fast-track process

---

[69] For a comprehensive description of the implementation process in the US, see Jackson, 'United States law', n. 22. See also J. E. Twiggs, *The Tokyo Round of multilateral trade negotiations: a case-study in building domestic support for diplomacy* (1987). For a more general overview of the Tokyo Round, see G. R. Winham, *International Trade and the Tokyo Round Negotiation* (1986).

[70] S. 151 (a), Trade Act 1974.

through its normal rules of procedure, which require a majority vote.[71]

The key elements of the fast-track procedure ensure that once the implementing bill is submitted by the President, it will be quickly voted on by both Houses of Congress without amendment. Immediately after introduction of the bill in both Houses, it is referred to the appropriate committees. The bill is discharged from those committees after forty-five days if they have not already reported the bill out, and a vote by both Houses follows within fifteen days of the committee report or automatic discharge. No amendments are permitted either in committee or on the floor. Debate is strictly limited to twenty hours, and any motion to recommit the bill is not in order. Thus, any implementing bill submitted by the President will be voted up or down within sixty days of its submission to Congress.

The adoption of the fast-track process can be thought of as a *quid pro quo* between Congress and the President. The President agreed to consult with Congress (and private sector interests) in the course of negotiating trade agreements, and Congress agreed to an up or down vote on the legislation implementing those agreements. At the outset, however, it is critical to understand what the fast-track procedure is not. In its formal version, the fast-track might appear as a process in which the executive branch first drafts implementing legislation on its own, and then the President formally submits the implementing legislation to Congress, which must then vote on the entire package without amendment and within strict time limits. Such a process would give Congress, and perhaps also private interest groups, little influence over the contours of the legislation, except of course that the President would be constrained to submit legislation that could ultimately obtain the necessary Congressional approval.

In fact, the process closely resembles the typical complex process by which bills are drafted, elaborated, and ultimately submitted for a vote.[72] But under fast-track, this process takes place outside the formal rules of procedure, and the formal submission of the bill by the President marks the end, not the beginning, of the Congressional input into the content of the legislation. The USTR consults respective Congressional committees before preparing a draft bill. This bill does not officially exist, but is informally submitted to Congressional committees. The committees then

---

[71] See I. B. Nickels, 'NAFTA's passage through fast-track' (1993) 3 Mex. Trade & L. Rep. 7. As one commentator put it, 'The Fast Track "emperor" has no clothes'. H. H. Koh, 'The fast track and United States trade policy' (1992) 18 Brooklyn JIL 143, 151.

[72] Prof. Jackson reached a similar conclusion regarding the 1979 process. See Jackson, 'United States law', at 162–4.

engage in 'mock' mark-up sessions. After the House and Senate committees have each formulated a draft bill, they hold a 'shadow conference' session to reconcile the bills. The single bill that emerges from the shadow conference is then transmitted to the President, who in theory could make additional changes prior to submitting it formally to Congress.[73] It is during the informal process that hearings are generally held and various interests have an opportunity to influence the content of the legislation. In contrast to the agreement notification requirement and legislative enactment after the bill is officially submitted, there is no time limit on this stage of the fast-track process. In the Tokyo Round it lasted about six months; in the Uruguay Round about nine.

In some ways, the fast-track process reverses the strategic positions of the President and the Congress. With most legislation, even if submitted by the President, it is the Congress that determines the final form of the legislation. In addition to its own ability to formally enact that legislation, it is constrained only by the threat of Presidential veto. Thus the President can either approve or disapprove, trading off what are perceived as the negative aspects of a bill against the prospects for approval of a revised bill if a veto is cast. Under the fast-track, the President determines the final content of the legislation, and Congress must vote it up or down. In the context of multilateral trade agreements, however, there will generally be little prospect for a modified bill. Assuming the executive branch has its own agenda that might have trouble garnering sufficient Congressional support, its task is to draft a bill that will just achieve the necessary votes for passage, although this would be a somewhat risky strategy. Members of Congress recognize the President's dilemma, and thus are inclined to strategically oppose a draft bill until their particular concerns have been met. Once the formal bill has been introduced, the opportunities for strategic behaviour are limited.[74]

Where the necessary votes would not be assured through implementing legislation that strictly implements the negotiated agreements, the President ultimately has several avenues to secure additional support. He can add additional provisions that are not required by the agreements but do not violate them; he can include provisions that might violate the underlying trade agreements; and he can make promises regarding subsequent legislation or administrative actions, whether or not related to

---

[73] See P. H. Potter, 'Comments on the fast-track process for review of NAFTA' and J. A. Nuzum, 'Comments on the fast-track process for Congressional consideration of NAFTA' (1993) 1 US-Mex. LJ 343 at 343–44, and 339 at 339–40 respectively.

[74] As discussed below, Senator Dole was able to extract some additional concessions from the President after the bill was submitted, perhaps in part as a result of the huge Republican electoral gains. These concessions, however, were promised as future legislation or executive action, and not added to the implementing bill.

the trade agreements. The most common tactic has been the first of these. As two knowledgeable commentators put it, 'every fast-track bill enacted [prior to the Uruguay Round] contained provisions that were unnecessary to implement the agreement concerned, but nonetheless were useful to obtain the votes needed for passage.'[75] The Uruguay Round was no exception, and indeed included the latter two types of actions as well. Some of these provisions are an attempt to undercut or soften the impact of these agreements,[76] whereas others are essentially unrelated to them. It could in theory be argued that there is no authority for applying the fast-track process to such unrelated provisions, but once the bill has been passed by the Congress and enacted into law, it possesses the full requirements, and hence constitutionality, of any statute.[77] The fast-track process thus does not completely avoid the process of hanging 'ornaments' on the trade bill 'tree'.

6.2.2.3 The Uruguay Round fast-track authority

The struggle to enact new fast-track authority had begun in 1985 as the foundations for a new negotiating round were being laid. The trade environment in the mid 1980s was quite different from that in 1979. The trade balance had ballooned from a slight surplus to over a US$150bn. deficit in 1987. The rise in the dollar to an all-time high in the spring of 1985 resulted in the perception of trade-induced misery being widespread rather than confined to a few sectors.[78] Imports as a share of US production of goods had risen dramatically, whereas the share of exports had fallen.[79] Congress largely remained unhappy with the executive, particularly more *laissez-faire* Republican, administration of trade remedies under United States law. Congress was in no mood simply to hand the Administration a blank cheque in the form of an extension of the fast-track authority. Indeed, contrary to earlier trade legislation, it was Congress and not the Administration that initiated the legislation.[80] Democrats had

---

[75] J. H. Bello and A. F. Holmer, 'The Post-Uruguay Round Future of Section 301' (1994) 25 Law & Policy Int. Bus. 1297 at 1299.

[76] As David Palmeter wrote of the URAA anti-dumping provisions, the Administration's strategy was to 'offset the required liberalizing changes with gratuitous restrictive changes'. D. Palmeter, United States implementation of the Uruguay Round Anti-Dumping Code' (1995) 29 J. World Trade 39, 41. Some of these changes are discussed at p. 236.

[77] See Jackson, 'United States law' at 168.

[78] To give but one example, in agriculture, a traditionally strong export sector, exports had declined from $44bn. in 1981 to $26bn. in 1986. See J. S. Hillman, 'Agriculture in the Uruguay Round: a United States perspective' (1993) 28 Tulsa LJ 761, 765.

[79] I. M. Destler, 'United States trade policy-making in the Uruguay Round', in H. R. Nau (ed.), *Domestic Trade Politics and the Uruguay Round* (1989), 191, 197.

[80] Ibid. at 191.

started working on a trade bill in 1985, but the Senate Republicans judged
it inexpedient to allow any bill that might receive a Presidential veto to be
passed before the fall 1986 elections.[81] By the time the Administration
submitted its trade legislation in early 1987, trade bills were already being
debated in the House and Senate.[82]

The basic fast-track provisions of the 1974 Act authority were
maintained, coupled with an attempt to further constrain executive
authority and exercise Congressional influence over the trade negotiation
process. This was done in two ways. The 1988 Act linked the fast-track
authority to certain negotiation goals, albeit weakly. The Act contained a
much more extensive statement of 'negotiating objectives' than either the
1974 or 1979 Acts. In addition to very broad negotiating objectives (which
had also been included in the 1974 Act), the 1988 Act identified sixteen
'principal trade negotiating objectives'.[83] These objectives were loosely
linked to the fast-track authority by requiring the President to provide,
along with the draft implementing bill, a statement 'asserting' that the
trade agreement makes progress on achieving the principles, policies and
objectives of the Act, and explaining how it makes such progress and to
what extent it does not. The Act further declared that the non-tariff
negotiating authority applied to a trade agreement 'only if such agreement
makes progress in meeting the applicable objectives described in Section
1101' of the Act.[84] These linkages, however, are not very substantial from
a legal (as opposed to political or rhetorical) point of view. The same
process that could be used to revoke the fast-track process without such
justification would probably have to be used even if the administration

---

[81] Ahearn & Reifman, 'Trade Legislation in 1987' at 82–83.

[82] See Destler, 'US trade policy-making' at 200. See also Ahearn & Reifman, 'Trade
Legislation in 1987' at 77 (Both the House and Senate bills 'were drafted by Congress without
much, if any, input from the executive branch'.)

[83] 1988 Act, s. 1101, 19 USC s. 2901 (1995). The objectives identified are: (1) more
effective and expeditious dispute settlement, (2) improvement of the GATT and multilateral
trade negotiation agreements, (3) broader application of the principle of transparency, (4)
ensuring that developing countries undertake appropriate trade obligations, (5) imposing
discipline on countries with persistent trade surpluses, (6) to develop mechanisms to assure
greater co-ordination, consistency and co-operation between international trade and
monetary systems and institutions, (7) liberalization and rationalization of trade in
agricultural products, (8) to improve discipline of 'unfair trade practices' (e.g., dumping,
subsidies, and actions of state trading enterprises), (9) eliminating barriers to trade in
services, (10) effective enforcement of adequate intellectual property laws, (11) to eliminate
barriers to foreign direct investment, (12) to develop rules on safeguard measures, (13)
elimination of specific barriers to obtain competitive opportunities for US products equivalent
to those provided to other states in the United States, (14) to obtain review of the relationship
between worker rights and the GATT, and to adopt a principle that denial of worker rights
should not be used as a means of obtaining competitive advantage, (15) to eliminate barriers
to access to high technology, and (16) to obtain GATT revision to eliminate disadvantage that
flows from border tax adjustment for indirect, but not direct, taxes.

[84] S. 1102 (b) (2), 1988 Act, 19 USC s. 2902 (b) (2) (1995).

failed to provide such explanations or to achieve sufficiently the stated objectives of the Act.

Congress intended to keep the executive on a tight leash during the negotiations. Ultimately, each of three Presidents (Reagan in 1988, Bush in 1991, and Clinton in 1993) was obliged to seek fast-track authority for the Uruguay Round negotiations from Congress. The initial fast-track authority was only for three years (compared to the original five years in the 1974 Act and eight years in the 1979 Act). This could be renewed for an additional two years (until 1 June 1993) if the President submitted a request for an extension and neither House of Congress adopted a disapproval resolution before the expiration of the initial period (1 June 1991). This was yet another device to ensure that the President kept the Congress fully informed. The President was required to submit, along with the request for an extension, a description of any agreements that had been negotiated and the progress made in the negotiations in achieving the purposes set forth in the 1988 Act. Furthermore, a report from the advisory committee for trade negotiations was also required. The extensions of authority in 1991 and 1993 were ultimately unconditional, but in each instance, Congress took the opportunity to remind the President of its trade negotiation agenda and extract certain commitments from the administration.[85]

In the 1993 extension, which was not provided for in the 1988 Act, Congress also made two slight changes to the implementation process. It extended the pre-signing notification requirement from 90 days to 120 days, thus providing Congress with greater opportunity to comment on provisions of the draft agreements.[86] Congress also, for the first time, made the President's tariff proclamation authority dependent on the implementation by Congress of the non-tariff agreements.

In addition to the renewal provision, Congress also included in the 1988 Act an ongoing option to terminate the fast-track authority if, within any sixty-day period, 'procedural disapproval' resolutions were adopted by both Houses. These resolutions would provide that the fast-track provisions shall not apply because 'the President has failed or refused to consult with

---

[85] In the debate over the statutory extension in 1991, most of the concerns were directed at NAFTA, not at the Uruguay Round negotiations. NAFTA was submitted to Congress under that extension, and the extension of fast-track authority in 1993 was only for the Uruguay Round agreements. The Administration promised it would renew Super 301 and not enter into agreements that would undermine US anti-dumping and countervailing duty laws.

[86] Pub. L. No. 103–49, 107 Stat. 239 (1993) (codified at 19 USC s. 2902 (e) (3) (A) (1995)). Congress also extended the time for private sector advisory committees to submit reports to 30 days after notification by the President. Both extensions were partly due to timing, and the expectation that the President would make the notification around the time Congress recessed. See Sen. Rep. No. 66, 103d Cong., 1st Sess. 3 (1993).

Congress on trade negotiations and trade agreements in accordance with the provisions of the [1988] Act.'[87] Some aspects of the fast-track process applied to consideration of these resolutions. Certain procedural requirements for such resolutions made it unlikely that they would pass both Houses,[88] but this provision again served to ensure that the President would fully comply with the procedural consultation provisions as well as the most important substantive Congressional objectives.

In sum, the fast-track procedure has served as the fulcrum for Congressional leverage on trade negotiations. This influence is exercised throughout the negotiating process, through public hearings, participation (usually through staff members) in the trade negotiations, contacts with administration officials, and even on occasion contact with the officials of other countries and the GATT.[89]

Since implementation pursuant to the fast-track authority is only a particular procedure for the adoption of a statute, the ordinary rules for such adoption, namely a majority vote by both Houses, apply. However, the 'pay-as-you-go' provisions of the Budget Enforcement Act of 1990 added an additional procedural hurdle. Those rules require that all statutes be 'scored' by the Congressional budget office for their budgetary impact. If they do not meet certain budget balancing requirements, a point of order may be raised, and a super majority vote is required to proceed.[90] Although this apparently had no effect on the trade negotiations, it had two effects on the implementing legislation. First, in order to meet the budget balancing requirements, it was necessary to include as part of the bill 'revenue provisions' that had nothing whatsoever to do with either the Uruguay Round Agreements or, for that matter, trade.[91] Secondly, since

---

[87] S. 1103 (c) (1) (E), 19 USC s. 2903 (1995).

[88] Under the provisions of the Act, the resolution was required to be introduced in the House of Representatives by the chairman or ranking minority member of the Committee on Ways and Means or the Rules Committee, rather than any member, and in the Senate was required to be an original resolution of the Senate Finance Committee. The mandatory discharge provision also does not apply. In short, only the 'floor' provisions of the fast-track procedure applied, and the only basis of such a disapproval resolution was the failure to consult. See House Conf. Rep. No. 576, 100th Cong., 2d Sess. 535 (1988), reprinted in 1988 USCCAN 1547 at 1568.

[89] One reported example was telephone calls by Senate Finance Committee Chairman Lloyd Bentsen and House Ways and Means Committee Chairman Dan Rostenkowski to Arthur Dunkel before the 1991 Dunkel Draft was formulated to indicate that Congress would not accept liberalizing changes in US anti-dumping law. See G. N. Horlick and E. C. Shea, 'The World Trade Organization Anti-dumping Agreement' (1995), 29 J. World Trade 5, 18.

[90] The Congressional Budget Office followed a relatively 'static', rather than 'dynamic', process of determining budgetary impact. Thus the Uruguay Round tariff cuts were determined to result in a substantial loss of revenue (approximately US$12bn. over five years), and increased trade and other positive economic effects were not counted in determining the overall impact.

[91] The bulk of these concerned pension reform. One revenue provision which was opposed in part on trade grounds would have changed the tax sourcing rules for certain export

the bill still did not meet the Senate requirements (which required balancing over a ten-year, rather than five-year, period), a 60 per cent vote would be needed to overcome a point of order that was certain to be raised.

6.2.3 Private sector involvement

The process of negotiating and implementing trade agreements in the United States is characterized by the substantial influence of non-governmental actors. The 1974 Act required that the President seek advice from the private sector before entering trade agreements, and established the basic advisory committee structure for obtaining that advice.[92] The major comprehensive advisory committee is the Advisory Committee for Trade Policy and Negotiations, which consists of up to forty-five individuals representing 'non-federal governments, labour, industry, agri-culture, small business, service industries, retailers, non-governmental environmental and conservation organizations, and consumer interests.'[93] In practice, the committee has been overwhelmingly dominated by industry representatives. Of the thirty-seven members comprising the ACTPN at the conclusion of the Uruguay Round, only one, the labour representative, dissented from the report endorsing the Uruguay Round Agreements.

In addition, the President is authorized to establish general policy, sectoral, and functional advisory committees. Seven policy committees and over thirty technical advisory and functional committees have been established. The number of members on each committee ranges from eight (certain of the agricultural technical advisory committees) to ninety-five (the labour advisory committee). There are about 1,000 individuals directly involved in the trade advisory committee structure,[94] collectively representing numerous firms, industries, unions and non-governmental

transactions. Another provision which attracted considerable attention on the television talk-show circuit was a settlement of litigation with the *Washington Post* and others regarding so-called 'pioneer preferences' for certain FCC licences. Although these provisions led to some additional rhetoric, some opposition, and perhaps some support, they played little role in the Congressional process and do not affect the future implementation of the US Uruguay Round commitments. Still, budgetary rules raise a potential additional hurdle for future trade agreements involving tariff or fee reductions. In the course of the process, some participants expressed the view that future trade agreements should not be subject to 'pay-as-you-go' budget rules.

[92] A more informal advisory committee system had been used in the Kennedy Round, but the system was not regarded as satisfactory by the advisers. See Twiggs, 'The Tokyo Round' at 35.

[93] S. 135, Trade Act 1974, 19 USC s. 2155 (b) (1), as added by s. 128, URAA. (The reference to environmental and conservation groups was added by URAA, and the reference to non-federal governments by the 1988 Act.)

[94] Cohen, *United States International Economic Policy*, 57.

groups.[95] These advisory committees are exempted from requirements relating to open meetings, public notice, public participation, and public availability of documents if it is determined that this would compromise the United States' negotiating objectives or bargaining position. The vast majority of the meetings of these committees are in fact closed to the public.[96] Although the USTR is not bound by recommendations it receives in consultations with the advisory committees, it must inform them of significant departures from such recommendations. At the conclusion of trade negotiations, each of these committees is obliged to submit a report to the President, Congress and the USTR indicating whether the agreements achieve the statutory negotiating objectives.

Individuals serving on these advisory committees, and the interests they represent, have a distinct advantage in influencing trade policy. They are given high level briefings and confidential information, and have ongoing access to officials involved in the negotiation process. Since the legislation calls for the advisory committees to submit reports that take positions on the agreements, the USTR must be concerned with securing their ultimate approval if at all possible. As these reports are to be submitted very shortly after the President notifies Congress of his intent to enter into an agreement, the committee members must be fully informed throughout the process.

Opportunities for influence extend beyond these required formal mechanisms. As the domain of trade law has expanded and the American economy has become more internationalized, international trade agreements have attracted greater attention both from various interest groups and the public in general. There is a broad range of participation in the negotiation and implementation process. The participation takes three primary forms: public political (for example, Congressional testimony, petitions for delivery to political actors), private political (lobbying), and public non-political (press releases, public papers, and other attempts to influence public opinion).

Although many industry representatives and organizations had direct access to the Office of the USTR, much of the private influence on the process is channelled through members of Congress. In addition to direct Congressional participation as part of the United States delegation, Congress also exercises its influence through ongoing hearings as well as

[95] Technically, of course, the individuals on the advisory committees do not represent their companies or individual groups. But '(. . . reality did not completely reflect the law.) The barrier that was supposed to exist between the advisers and the companies that employed them probably didn't exist in all instances'; interview with Richard Rivers, in Twiggs, 'The Tokyo Round' at 108 (speaking of the Tokyo Round negotiations).

[96] Indeed, just prior to the formal completion of the Uruguay Round, the USTR directed that all meetings of 21 of the advisory committees would be closed to the public for the period from 1 Mar. 1994–1 Mar. 1996; 59 Fed. Reg. 26,686 (1994).

through direct contacts between Congressmen (or, in most cases, their staff) and the USTR and other federal agencies potentially involved in trade policy-making. These connections thus make available to various private firms and interest groups two channels of potential influence outside the advisory committee structure. Industry representatives might have direct access to various levels of the USTR or other involved departments such as agriculture, state, and commerce. If these channels of access prove unsatisfactory, they may be able to obtain information or influence through the office of a senator or representative, particularly if that person occupies a position on one of the relevant Congressional committees.

There were numerous hearings throughout the period during which the Uruguay Round Agreements were being negotiated. The Senate Finance Committee alone held twenty-five such hearings. Members of Congress or their staff and representatives of private interests were often on site at crucial stages of the negotiation in order to ensure that their voices were heard. Although Congress had rejected a proposal that private sector interests be directly represented in the negotiations, they had endorsed the notion that such representatives could participate right up to the door of the negotiation room. In the Uruguay Round, the promulgation of the Dunkel Draft of the agreements in December of 1991 probably served to intensify the role played by private interests. Industry and other organized groups focused on the draft and quickly made their specific complaints known to the administration and Congress.[97] In particular, the anti-dumping provisions of the Dunkel Draft were severely criticized by many, and this criticism escalated until the draft was substantially revised in December of 1993.[98]

As a result of both formal and informal access, few organized interests could claim at the conclusion of the Uruguay Round that they did not have some access to information and some opportunity to present their views. In

---

[97] In public letters to the USTR's office and accompanying press statements, the US Chamber of Commerce, the National Foreign Trade Council, the US Council for International Business, the Labor–Industry Coalition for International Trade, the International Intellectual Property Alliance, the Retail Industry Trade Action Coalition and the MTN Coalition expressed their individual objections to the Dunkel Draft. See, e.g., 'US Chamber of Commerce cites flaws in draft GATT Accord; other reaction mixed', 9 Int. Trade Rep. (BNA) 110 (15 Jan. 1992).

[98] See, e.g., 'US industries criticize provisions in Dunkel text on Anti-dumping, services', 9 Int. Trade Rep. (BNA) 198 (29 Jan. 1992); 'Attorney Says Uruguay Round Draft Text Would Eviscerate US Anti-dumping Law', 9 Int. Trade Rep. (BNA) 362 (26 Feb. 1992) (reporting lecture from a National Association of Manufacturers trade forum). There was, however, considerable support for the Dunkel Draft anti-dumping provisions among American importing and exporting interests. See 'Few Changes Seen Required in US Anti-dumping Law Under GATT Plan', 9 Int. Trade Rep. (BNA) 276 (12 Feb. 1992) (reporting views of the American Association of Exporters and Importers).

the course of the negotiating process, USTR staff conducted thousands of meetings with Congress and various interest groups. Access, information, and influence were not limited to sectoral industrial interests and labour organizations. Organized 'public interest' groups participated in the debate over trade liberalization as never before. Protectionist interests (representing both management and labour) secured new allies from environmentalists, and to a lesser extent from consumer organizations.[99]

The battle for public opinion in the Uruguay Round was certainly a new phenomenon as regards multilateral trade agreements, although it did not quite reach the feverish pitch of the debate over NAFTA. The protagonists often attempted to reduce the debate to simplistic issues or catch-phrases in an attempt to mobilize the public. Media attention was often attracted by a punchy phrase, such as Ross Perot's description of the 'giant sucking sound' that would supposedly result (at least metaphorically) as jobs fled the United States for Mexico in the wake of NAFTA. In the Uruguay Round debates, much attention was focused on child labour and the fact that the GATT would ostensibly prohibit nations from restricting the import of products made with child labour. The willingness to seize upon any argument in support of one's position helped even less politically influential groups achieve at least nominal support for their arguments, and on occasion generated unusual alliances. One of the not-so-new lessons of the NAFTA near-fiasco was that opposition to trade liberalization coalesces quickly and strongly, whereas support tends to be diffuse and unorganized. Industry interests in support of the Uruguay Round results created such organizations as Alliance For GATT Now. This and other pro-trade organizations undertook public polling and public campaigning, and presented testimony before Congress.

The Uruguay Round saw the emergence of a powerful new voice in the trade debate, namely that of environmentalists. Environmental interests first played a major role in trade agreements in the context of NAFTA. In the 1991 renewal of fast-track authority, Congress expressed its strong views that environmental concerns should be taken into account. The election of President Clinton in the fall of 1992 brought an increased emphasis by the Administration on environmental issues, particularly as related to the two major trade negotiations then under way: the Uruguay Round and NAFTA. In each, environmental groups played a significant role in mobilizing public opposition and exercising sufficient political influence to assure some 'greening' of the agreements. With regard to the Uruguay Round, the Clinton administration quickly moved to establish a number of 'green' modifications. Although the United States was

---

[99] Ralph Nader's organization, Public Citizen, was among the most vociferous opponents. Consumers' Union, on the other hand, supported the Uruguay Round Agreements.

apparently the only country strongly pushing for modification of the draft Uruguay Round Agreements to reflect greater concern for the environment, the European Union co-operated with the efforts. A number of changes were obtained, notably in the agreements on sanitary and phytosanitary measures, technical barriers to trade, trade related aspects of intellectual property, and services.

A number of major environmental organizations eventually supported the ratification of NAFTA, but none supported the implementation of the Uruguay Round agreements. This was in large part due to the success of these groups and others in obtaining a more significant recognition of environmental concerns in the conclusion of the NAFTA negotiations, notably in the so-called environmental side-agreement. The NAFTA provisions set the minimum standard for judging the Uruguay Round Agreements from the perspective of environmental groups. They achieved some small victories in the implementing legislation, including the addition of an environmental group representative to the ACTPN and a clause restricting any interpretation of the URAA as modifying US environmental laws. Despite these provisions, environmental groups announced their virtually unanimous opposition to the legislation.[100] How influential this opposition was is unclear, but those who opposed the pact for other reasons lent their support to the environmentalists.[101]

---

[100] Opposition from environmental groups resulted from two distinct concerns. There was a cosmopolitan objection that trade was not linked to environmental concerns and as a result would potentially cause widespread degradation of the environment. This was coupled with a more nationalist sovereignty–oriented objection that the ability of the US to set its own environmental priorities and laws would be compromised, either as a legal or political matter. Some of the opposition to trade agreements no doubt also derives from the diminished political influence wielded by environmental organizations in the context of trade negotiations. To some degree, the position of environmentalists reflects the federalism issues discussed below. Although to a large extent environmental regulation has been centralized, much of this regulation remains at the state level, and the availability of state regulation provides an alternative forum when power at the federal level is less hospitable to environmental concerns. Regulation of disposable containers, for example, has primarily been at the state level. The Supreme Court has been tolerant of such regulation, even when it has a somewhat protective effect. Since it was clear that the agreements themselves could not be renegotiated, the debate focused largely on those elements of the implementing legislation that were at least in some sense 'optional'. The debate over trade and the environment was largely fought over the issue of renewing fast track authority.

Some of the arguments of the environmentalists were undermined late in the process by the GATT panel decision on certain United States automobile taxes; United States—Taxes on Automobiles, DS 31/R (1994) (unadopted), reprinted at (1994) 33 ILM 1397. The panel released its report to the parties on 29 Sept. 1994 and the USTR immediately announced the results to the public. Whether the panel or the GATT Secretariat was influenced in the timing of its decision remains a matter of speculation. Ordinarily, GATT panel decisions are restricted, and not for public distribution, until the report has been adopted by the GATT council.

[101] Sen. Hollings, for example, invited environmental organizations to testify before the Commerce Committee after the implementing bill had been formally submitted, and made reference to environmental arguments in the debates.

6.3 THE URUGUAY ROUND AGREEMENTS ACT

6.3.1 Formulation and adoption of implementing legislation

The President notified Congress of his intent to enter into the Uruguay Round Agreements on 15 December 1993, the last possible date under the fast-track authority of the 1993 extension. This was, as required, 120 days prior to the formal signing of the agreements in Marrakesh on 15 April of the following year. Administration discussions with Congressional staff members regarding implementing legislation began in January of 1994, advisory committee reports were submitted by 15 January, and general hearings on the agreements began in early February.

Primary responsibility for trade agreements, the fast-track process, and relations with the executive branch has fallen in recent years on two powerful Congressional committees, the Finance Committee in the Senate and the Ways and Means Committee in the House. The great scope of the Uruguay Round led to an expansion in the number of Congressional committees with significant jurisdictional claims. In the end, the legislation was formally referred to six Senate committees[102] and eight House committees.[103] Still other committees held hearings on particular aspects or consequences of the agreements. As noted above, these hearings provided an opportunity for the private sector and various interest groups to make their views known regarding both the substance of the agreements and the content of implementing legislation.

The USTR prepared the initial draft of the implementing legislation, and the House commenced its informal mark-up sessions in May. Controversy was already developing over a number of issues, including the extension of fast-track authority and the link between labour rights and trade. By mid July, attention had focused also on the failure of the Administration to present a funding or budget proposal. Indeed, the controversies during the drafting phase generally concerned matters not required by the Uruguay Round Agreements. The President sought to include a number of such items in the legislation. These included renewal of fast-track authority, certain changes in anti-dumping and countervailing duty law regarding former socialist economies, and adjustment of benefits for Caribbean Basin Initiative countries. In general, the President's attempts to include such items on the implementing bill did not fare well.[104]

---

[102] Finance; Agriculture, Nutrition, and Forestry; Commerce, Science, and Transportation; Governmental Affairs; the Judiciary; and Labor and Human Resources.

[103] Ways and Means; Agriculture; Education and Labor; Energy and Commerce; Foreign Affairs; Government Operations; Judiciary; and Rules.

[104] The Generalized System of Preferences programme, however, was extended for 10 months, s. 601, URAA, amending s. 505 (a), Trade Agreements Act 1974, codified at 19 USC. s. 2465 (a).

The most visible casualty of the informal phase of the legislative process was the extension of fast-track authority. The Republicans had already been incensed by the Administration's insistence on placing labour rights on the agenda of the preparatory committee, and strongly opposed any link between trade and either workers' rights or the environment as a condition to the President's negotiating authority. They were supported in this view by industry. Most Democrats, by contrast, insisted on such a link. The House was able to reach a compromise version with somewhat ambiguous language, but the Senate was not. The extension of the fast-track negotiating authority was eventually dropped.

Although the fast-track process is flexible, it is ultimately less open to participation and public debate than the normal legislative process. Although some of the mark-up sessions were public, most were not. Senators and representatives not on the key committees were limited in their ability to influence the process. One response to these aspects of the fast-track procedure was the introduction of related bills during the course of the implementation process. These were primarily a combination of public posturing and signalling to the Administration of substantive concerns and demands. For example, in July and August of 1994, several members of the House introduced the Trade and Environment Reporting Act,[105] and in the Senate, Senator Kerry proposed the Trade and Environment Harmonization Act of 1994.[106] In a similar vein, Senator DeConcini introduced a separate bill entitled the Trade-related Aspects of Intellectual Property Rights Implementation Act, ostensibly for the purpose of generating comment on the aspects of the implementing legislation which related to the Agreement of that name.[107]

On the other hand, the fast-track process presented ample opportunity for the influence of private interests, particularly at the level of Congressional staff charged with the responsibility for the detailed mark-up of the implementing legislation. The steel industry, for example, was unhappy with certain judicial decisions which had held that an arm's length sale of an enterprise terminated the benefits of subsidies that had been bestowed on the entity prior to the sale. The Uruguay Round Agreement on Subsidies and Countervailing Measures certainly did not require any change in this rule, and the draft implementing legislation submitted by the Administration contained no provision on such changes in ownership. An amendment was introduced as part of a package of Congressional staff recommendations that appeared to give the Commerce Department

---

[105] 140 Cong. Rec. 1447 (1994).

[106] 140 Cong. Rec. S9180, S9181 (1994).

[107] S2368, 103rd Cong., 2d Sess. (1994). See Sen. DeConcini's remarks at 140 Cong. Rec. S10878–05, S10883–84 (1994).

greater leeway to find that such subsidies continued after sale and could therefore be countervailed. Supported by the steel industry, the new provision was adopted as part of the implementing legislation.[108] The fast-track process meant that last-minute deals struck just prior to the submission of the final implementing bill were not subject to any Congressional or public discussion.[109]

The House and Senate completed their respective mark-ups of implementing legislation in August, and convened conference committees later that month. The House Ways and Means Committee and the Senate Finance Committee concluded their joint conference on the implementing bill on 20 September. To this were added the results of other committee conferences, and a single bill was transmitted to the President on 23 September. There remained a few controversial items which the conference was unable to resolve, and these were left to the President to decide.[110] The President formally submitted the implementing legislation (which was the Congressional conference text plus the Presidential resolution of a few issues which the conference could not resolve), together with the statement of administrative action, on 27 September. The finality of this action (subject only to a Congressional up-or-down vote) was illustrated by the prompt action of the Senate Finance Committee, which reported the bill favourably by unanimous vote within two days. House committees were mandated to report within six days. Plans to expedite consideration of the bill, which in any event could not be amended, were thwarted when Senator Hollings (a staunch defender of the textile industry and opponent of the agreements) insisted that his committee have the full forty-five days before mandatory discharge. An agreement was eventually reached that would allow a vote in an unusual lame-duck session of Congress after the fall elections, without requiring that Congress remain in session for the 45-day-period.

[108] See D. A. Codevilla, 'Discouraging the practice of what we preach: *Saarstahl I*, *Inland Steel* and the implementation of the Uruguay Round of GATT 1994' (1995), 3 Geo. Mason Ind. L. Rev. 435. In similar fashion, the steel industry was able to obtain the reversal of a 1993 International Trade Commission ruling that 'captive production' could not be excluded in determining whether domestic industry is injured by the import of subsidized products. See Alan F. Holmer, Gary N. Horlick, and Terence P. Stewart, 'Enacted and rejected amendments to the Anti-Dumping Law: in implementation or contravention of the Anti-Dumping Agreement?' (1995), 29 *Int. Law* 483, 490.

[109] See, e.g., Horlick's description of the provision requiring an adjustment for profit in determining export price in Holmer *et al.*, 'Enacted and rejected amendments to the anti-dumping law' at 497 (reporting deal struck at 12:20 a.m. the day the implementing bill was submitted, in order to obtain Sen. Hollings' agreement not to block the entire bill).

[110] None of these were items required to implement the results of the Uruguay Round. They included the re-authorization of Super 301, the schedule for any change in the rule of origin for textile imports, increased tariffs on tobacco imports, and the extension of certain benefits to countries under the Caribbean Basin Initiative ('CBI parity').

This resolution was further complicated by the huge Republican victory in the Congressional elections held on 2 November. The anti-GATT voices pressed anew their view that consideration of the bill should be delayed at least until the newly elected Congress was in session.[111] The effects of the change were muted by the fact that Republican Congressional leaders in both Houses, Robert Dole in the Senate and Newt Gingrich in the House, were in general strong supporters of free trade. Still, after the election Senator Dole continued to express misgivings about some aspects of the WTO and the implementing legislation, and indicated support for the view that consideration of the implementing legislation should be delayed.[112] The Administration entered into an agreement with Senator Dole to support legislation addressing these concerns after the implementing legislation was passed.[113] The House held its floor debate and voted on 29 November. The Senate debated for the following two days, and passed the legislation on 1 December. From notification of intent to enter the agreements to legislative approval had taken eleven and a half months, compared to six months for the Tokyo Round agreements and fifteen months for NAFTA.

6.3.2 Basic structure and overview of the Act

The implementing legislation is complex, and spans over 650 pages of text in its official printed format.[114] We cannot in this context examine the details of the substantive implementation, particularly on such issues as anti-dumping, countervailing duties and intellectual property protection. The implementing legislation is divided into seven titles. The first, Title I, contains general provisions relating to the approval and implementation of

[111] See, e.g., 140 Cong. Rec. H10957, H10958 (Rep. Burton); 140 Cong. Rec. H10957, H10960 (Rep. Dreier).

[112] 11 Int. Trade Rep. (BNA) 1742 (16 Nov. 1994), 11 Int. Trade Rep. (BNA) 1699 (9 Nov. 1994), and 11 Int. Trade Rep. (BNA) 1715 (9 Nov. 1994).

[113] The most important aspect of the agreement was the WTO review commission, discussed infra at 223. In addition the agreement provided for assessment of the auction of pioneer preference licences, agreement to review the length of patents, and assurances on the funding for various agricultural programmes including EEP, CRP and 'green box subsidies'. It also confirmed that there was no link between changes to the capital gains tax and the Uruguay Round.

[114] Of this, the non-trade related revenue provisions occupy about one quarter (159 pages). To give some idea of the relative complexity of the provisions and extent of reform of present law on various issues, the following indicates the number of pages occupied by various provisions: general provisions (70 pages); modifications to anti-dumping and countervailing duty law (249 pages); implementation of the Agreement on Safeguards (17 pages); foreign trade barriers including amendments to S. 301 (14 pages); reform of S. 337 (10 pages); implementation of Agreements on Textiles and Clothing (12 pages), Government Procurement (11 pages), Technical Barriers to Trade (5 pages), Agriculture, including Sanitary and Phytosanitary Measures (43 pages), TRIPs (53 pages).

the Uruguay Round Agreements, and most of the discussion here will focus on those provisions. Title II, the most extensive section of the Act, contains the anti-dumping and countervailing duty provisions. These provisions constitute a massive rewriting of that law, in part to conform it to the Uruguay Round Agreements but also to make changes otherwise desired by Congress (usually at the behest of certain industries). Title III implements other Agreements, notably those on safeguards, textiles, government procurement and technical barriers to trade. In general, these represent comparatively slight modifications of United States statutory law, albeit in some cases with substantial effect. Title III also contains certain reforms of US unfair trade remedy laws, some required by GATT dispute settlement findings and others intended to strengthen certain US remedies. Title IV implements the agreements on agriculture and on the application of sanitary and phytosanitary measures. Title V conforms United States law to the provisions of the agreement on trade-related aspects of intellectual property. Title VI contains certain trade provisions and changes in customs procedures and fees not required by the Uruguay Round Agreements. Titles VII and VIII are revenue provisions, unrelated to either the Uruguay Round or international trade, but intended to offset the calculated loss to the budget caused by the Uruguay Round tariff reductions.[115]

The Uruguay Round did not present some of the difficult acceptance problems that the Tokyo Round had.[116] By the time Congress acted, all of the basic agreements were complete,[117] although concessions in some areas (notably services and government procurement) remained to be negotiated. In addition, there seemed much less concern that other countries would fail to accept the agreements once the United States had. And perhaps most important, all of the agreements other than the four specified plurilateral agreements were required to be accepted by all members of the new WTO. The implementing legislation provided simply that at such time as the President determined that a 'sufficient number' had accepted the agreements in order 'to ensure the effective operation of, and adequate benefits for the United States,' the President was authorized to accept the agreements.[118] Interestingly, the URAA did not distinguish between the obligatory multilateral agreements and the two amended plurilateral agreements (the Agreement on Government Procurement and the

---

[115] See discussion of the 'pay-as-you-go' rules p. 196.

[116] See Jackson, 'United States law' at 160.

[117] Congress had specifically amended the 'fast track' procedures in 1979 to require that the 'final legal text' of the agreements accompany the implementing legislation. This wording was carried over to the 1988 Act (s. 1103 (a) (1) (B)).

[118] SAA and the legislative reports identified the European Union, Japan, Canada and Mexico as the critical countries. See SAA, 12, 1994 USCCAN 4040, 4049.

International Bovine Meat Agreement), and the language suggested that the President was to accept all the agreements, including the plurilateral agreements, as a package. On 23 December 1994, the President directed the USTR to accept the Uruguay Round Agreements. On the same date, the President exercised his authority under the 1988 Act and the URAA to modify customs duties in accordance with those agreements.[119] For the most part, these modifications were effective from 1 January 1995.

Implementation of commitments under the Uruguay Round Agreements falls into four categories. Some commitments, notably most of the tariff reductions, can be implemented pursuant to authority previously delegated by Congress to the President, although the 1993 extension made that authority conditional on the enactment of implementation legislation regarding non-tariff barriers. Many of the specific commitments contained in the Uruguay Round Agreements necessitated corresponding changes to United States statutory law. This was the primary purpose of the URAA. These changes included (in a few instances) conforming United States law to prior adverse findings by GATT dispute settlement panels.[120] A number of commitments required no change in United States law, but only possible forbearance of any action in violation of those commitments by administrative agencies or judges. One example, discussed below, is action under Section 301 of the 1974 Act. Finally, in many instances mandatory US law already complied with the Uruguay Round Agreements. For example, the US legislation already provided for a phase-down of agricultural subsidies that meets the requirements of the agreement on agriculture, and most provisions of US intellectual property law already met the requirements of the Agreement on Trade-related Aspects of Intellectual Property Rights.

Most of the provisions (other than the revenue provisions) simply implement the Uruguay Round Agreements. But where Congress was unhappy with those agreements, it generally took some measure to encourage or force executive action, or narrow the scope of provisions that it did not like. It also imposed stringent reporting and consultation requirements in such contexts. A good example of this approach concerns the so-called 'green light' subsidies for regional development, basic

---

[119] In addition, in order to comply with Agricultural Agreement, the President terminated all quantitative limitations on agricultural products under s. 22(f) of the Agricultural Adjustment Act.

[120] See, e.g., s. 321, URAA, amending s. 337 Tariff Act 1930, 19 USC s. 1337, to conform to the GATT panel ruling in United States; s. 422, URAA, amending s. 106(g) Agricultural Act 1949, 7 USC s. 1445(g), to comply, or permit the President to comply, with United States—Measures Affecting the Importation, Sale and Use of Tobacco (adopted 4 Oct. 1994); s. 137, URAA, codified at 19 USC s. 3556, implementing results of United States—Denial of Most-Favoured-Nation Treatment as to Non-Rubber Footwear from Brazil, 39th Supp. BISD 128 (adopted 19 June 1992).

research, and adaption of facilities to meet the requirements of environmental protection laws. As discussed below,[121] Congress made such subsidies subject to special investigatory procedures that would result in triggering Section 301 procedures and, possibly, remedies. Furthermore, rather than provide that the provisions under which these subsidies were exempted from countervailing duties would expire if those provisions of the Subsidies Agreement were not renewed as provided in the Subsidies Agreement, Congress insisted that any such extension be made through new legislation.[122] By mid 1999, the Secretary of Commerce must submit a comprehensive review of the operation of the Subsidies Agreement. In a similar vein, Congress explicitly provided that compliance with the provisions of TRIPs would not prevent a determination that a country was engaged in an unfair trade practice for purposes of Section 301.[123]

The bill contains a number of additions to present law intended to provide additional protections for domestic industry that are consistent with, but not required by, the Uruguay Round Agreements. The use of special provisions to blunt opposition to the trade bill is well illustrated by the case of the textile industry. As always, textiles remained a critical political pressure point. Most of the United States industry vociferously opposed the Uruguay Round liberalization, strongly supported by influential legislators from states with significant textile production. They had been persuaded to support NAFTA through the adoption of rules of origin that served more to raise barriers to non-North American imports than to liberalize trade between the three signatory countries. Again it was rules of origin that were used to counteract some of the liberalization mandated by the agreement on textiles. URAA requires certain changes in the rules of origin for textiles, shifting the place of origin for clothing from the place where the fabric is cut to where the garment is assembled.[124] Similarly, the amendments to the anti-dumping and countervailing duty laws contain numerous changes not required by the new agreements, and some that may be in violation of them. These are discussed in greater detail below.

Unlike the Tokyo Round legislation,[125] the Uruguay Round legislation was not accompanied by any significant reorganization of executive branch administration of United States trade laws and remedies. The legislation, like virtually every major Trade Act since the 1974 Act, implicitly

---

[121] See p. 220 infra.

[122] S. 282, URAA. Congress did, however, provide fast-track authority for such an extension. S. 282 (c) (4), URAA, amending s. 151 Trade Act 1974, 19 USC s. 2191.

[123] S. 313 (2) (B), URAA, amending s. 182 Trade Act 1974 ('Special 301'), codified at 19 USC s. 2242 (d) (4); s. 314 (c), URAA, amending s. 301 (d) (3) Trade Act 1974, codified at 19 USC s. 2411 (d) (3).

[124] S. 334, URAA, codified at 19 USC s. 3592.

[125] See Jackson, 'United States law'.

enhances the authority and pre-eminence of the USTR in trade matters. In a new development, the USTR is given the authority to make certain critical determinations in matters that affect the application of United States law.[126] Although the accretions to the authority of the USTR are small, they represent important additional steps in the concentration of trade policy authority.[127]

As discussed above, the attempt to renew the fast-track authority failed as a result of conflicting views regarding the linkage of trade to environmental and labour rights issues. Yet the legislation contains something for these groups as well. Section 131 of the URAA requires the President to seek the establishment of a working party on the relationship of workers' rights to the trade agreements, and environmentalists won a permanent place in the advisory committee system, as well as a number of indications that the legislation and the agreements should not be allowed to undercut environmental protection laws.[128]

6.3.3 The issue of sovereignty

As with the implementation of any trade liberalizing agreement, much of the debate focused on the particular sectoral interests that would be benefited or harmed by the agreements.[129] Two issues, however, were prominent in the consideration of the Uruguay Round Agreements: sovereignty and federalism.[130] As noted above, these issues together

[126] E.g., the implementing legislation grants the USTR the authority to designate which countries are 'developing' and 'least developed' for purposes of applying certain provisions of countervailing duty law. S. 267, URAA, amending s. 771, Tariff Act 1930, 19 USC s. 1677.

[127] Examples of these additions include an enhanced role in intergovernmental consultations and domestic enforcement of the Uruguay Round obligations (see s. 102, URAA, 19 USC s. 3512); role in implementation of dispute settlement panels adverse to the United States (see s. 123 (g), URAA, 19 USC s. 3533(g), and s. 129, URAA, 19 USC s. 3538); authority to determine whether to allow anti-dumping petitions on behalf of third countries (see s. 232, URAA, 19 USC s. 1677n, amending s. 783, Trade Act 1930); an enhanced role in issues regarding foreign subsidies (see p. 220); and the designation of developing and least developed countries (see note 126 supra). If Congress passes certain proposals to abolish the Department of Commerce, USTR would become an even more important and powerful agency in matters relating to trade policy.

[128] See discussion p. 213.

[129] In the debates, many Senators and Representatives referred to how particular industries in their states would be affected by the agreements. See, e.g., Senators Roth (Delaware), Feinstein (California) and Durenberger (Minnesota) at 140 Cong. Rec. S15287, S15347 and S15361 (1994) respectively. To some extent, the votes against the implementing legislation were largely from states with concentrations of an industry that was viewed as most adversely affected by the agreements.

[130] See 'Documents relating to the Clinton Administration's Agreement with Sen. Dole (R-Kan) concerning the Uruguay Round Agreement', issued by the White House, 23 Nov. 1194, 11 Int. Trade Rep. (BNA) 1865 (30 Nov. 1994). In a letter to Sen. Dole, Mickey Kantor stated that '[s]overeignty has been the central issue in the debate on the WTO throughout this year.'

sparked an important constitutional question, namely whether the Uruguay Round Agreements could be approved as a Congressional–executive agreement, or were required to be ratified by the Senate as a treaty. Although these issues were no doubt employed by those who sought to protect various economic interests, they also clearly reflect both the greater scope of international trade agreements and the expansion and heightened publicity of the domestic debate.

Two Agreements in particular were at the heart of the sovereignty and federalism concerns, namely the Agreement on Sanitary and Phytosanitary Measures and the Agreement on Technical Barriers to Trade. Not only did these Agreements strengthen the obligations to assure that product standards do not serve as trade barriers, but they also increased the extent of the obligations regarding state and local governments.[131] These changes were against the background of the enhanced dispute settlement process, which would no longer leave the United States (or any other country) with an effective veto. This meant that sanctions (suspension of trade concessions) would be more easily available should the United States be found in violation of its WTO obligations and fail to comply with the recommendations of a Dispute Settlement Panel.

Sovereignty is a complex value,[132] but the primary aspect of sovereignty at issue seems to have been autonomy. In the Congressional and public debates over the Uruguay Round results, both federal (United States) and state sovereignty concerns were urged. These concerns significantly affected the implementing legislation, and as a result the way in which the WTO obligations will be implemented by the United States, particularly regarding dispute settlement. The impact of sovereignty can be usefully divided into two areas: concerns regarding federal regulatory autonomy and concerns regarding state regulatory authority. The latter is addressed below in the section on federalism issues.

As with the Congressional opposition to the ill-fated international trade organization following the 1947 provisional implementation of the GATT, the sovereignty concerns focused largely on the creation of a new multilateral institution, namely the WTO. Within this context, the greatest misgivings were expressed in regard to three elements. First was the virtually automatic approval of Dispute Settlement Panel decisions, and to some extent the imposition of 'sanctions' for failure to comply with them. Secondly, the new agreements expressly set forth rules of decision that, although urging the continuance of consensus-based decision-making, also explicitly provided for majority votes on various matters. Both these elements had the consequence of eliminating any United States veto over

---

[131] See p. 226.
[132] L. Henkin, *International Law: Politics and Values* (1995), 8–12.

WTO decision-making.[133] Thirdly, many objected to the lack of openness or transparency in the GATT dispute settlement process.

These institutional and procedural concerns were accompanied by substantive objections, which focused on product standards, and in particular on sanitary and phytosanitary measures. The provisions in the Agreements on Technical Barriers to Trade and on Sanitary and Phytosanitary Measures were regarded as potentially undercutting the ability of the United States to set its own health, safety and environmental standards.

Although many of the sovereignty concerns had little basis in either domestic or international law or practice,[134] as a political matter they still had to be addressed in the legislation. The institutional and substantive concerns were resolved in three ways. First, the role of the Uruguay Round Agreements themselves in United States law is extremely circumscribed. The potential impact of the implementing legislation, particularly with regard to possible implications for environmental protection and consumer safety, is also carefully delimited. Secondly, the results of any WTO dispute settlement proceedings will not be incorporated into United States law without following a specified domestic implementation process. Thirdly, the legislation, and planned legislation, imposes some constraints on United States participation in the WTO, and allows Congress to maintain ongoing supervision of such participation. For the most part, these provisions followed evolving United States practice, although the Uruguay Round implementing legislation takes these principles to a more stringent level.

6.3.4 The status of the Uruguay Round Agreements in United States law

In a sense, the text of the legislative implementation of the Uruguay Round Agreements is in three parts: the agreements themselves, the statutory language, and the statement of administrative action that accompanied the President's submission of the bill. We can thus pose the question of the role of each of these texts in determining future United States actions. The ultimate issue is of course the extent to which, as a matter of domestic law, the United States must act in accordance with the Uruguay Round Agreements.

---

[133] Sen. Jesse Helms expressed this concern, and attempted to capitalize on widespread antipathy toward the UN, by labelling the WTO 'a UN of world trade, without the veto' (Testimony of Sen. Jesse Helms before the Senate Foreign Relations Committee, 14 June 1994).

[134] As Robert Bork put it, 'The opponent's charge is simply false' (140 Cong. Rec. S15271, S15295 (1994))

As noted above, recent United States practice has generally been to declare treaties not to be self-executing. As with the Tokyo Round implementing legislation, the language of the statute in this regard is somewhat oblique, but the SAA makes it absolutely clear that the Uruguay Round Agreements are not self-executing.[135] Thus of the three texts, the agreements themselves have the least direct application in United States law. Although Congress specifically approved the agreements, it simultaneously provided that 'no provision of any of the Uruguay Round Agreements, nor the application of any such provision to any person or circumstances, that is inconsistent with any law of the United States shall have effect.'[136] Furthermore, Congress mandated that no person other than the United States 'shall have any cause of action or defence under any of the Uruguay Round Agreements' or challenge 'any action or inaction . . . of the United States, any state, or any political subdivision of a state on the ground that such action or inaction is inconsistent' with one of those agreements.[137]

In short, the Uruguay Round Agreements themselves are unlikely to be directly applied in any proceeding other than a proceeding brought by the United States for the purpose of enforcing obligations under the agreements. To the extent that the agreements are fully implemented by the statutory language, this is not a matter of concern, but many aspects of the agreement were not explicitly implemented by the legislation. The agreements, including authoritative interpretations by the WTO or decisions of dispute settlement panels, might still be applied either by a court to resolve ambiguities in the language of a statute or by administrative agencies in promulgating rules and regulations. But such applications could not lead to an interpretive result that was contrary to any clearly expressed intent of Congress.[138]

---

[135] SAA, at 14, 20. See Jackson, 'United States law' at 170.

[136] S. 102, URAA, 19 USC s. 3512. This language is nearly identical to that in the Trade Agreements Act 1979.

[137] S. 102 (c) (1), URAA, 19 USC s. 3512 (c) (1). This language was considerably broader than the corresponding provisions in the Trade Agreements Act 1979 (s. 3(f), 19 USC s. 2504), although it is unclear whether the effect was any different since under both Acts the agreements were non-self-executing.

[138] See, e.g., *Mississippi Poultry Ass'n, Inc.* v. *Madigan*, 31 F.3d 293 (5th Cir. 1994). Under applicable principles of administrative law, the courts will defer to any interpretation of a statute by an administrative agency so long as it is reasonable. See p. 216. However, a greater burden would fall on the agency to justify any interpretation that was clearly in violation of US international obligations under the agreements. Moreover, courts will if possible construe a statute to avoid bringing the US in violation of its international obligations (see *Murray* v. *The Charming Betsy*, 6 US (2 Cranch) 64 (1804)). Indeed, in some instances they are willing to overlook substantial legislative history to the contrary (see n. 139). Such a statutory construction would in turn limit agency discretion in enforcing the legislation and promulgating implementing legislation.

These restrictive aspects of United States implementation are consistent with United States practice since the Tokyo Round. What is newer is the attempt to circumscribe the effect of the statute itself. Generally speaking, statutes later in time take precedence over both earlier statutes and treaties.[139] Although every effort will be made to construe statutes in order to avoid conflicts, implementation of the language and purpose of the later statute will prevail when two statutes cannot be reconciled. A critical question is how broadly a statute should be interpreted when it arguably conflicts with previous legislation. This was a matter of considerable concern in the implementation of the Uruguay Round Agreements, particularly regarding environmental protection and product standards. Congress included provisions intended to limit the potential effects of not only the Uruguay Round Agreements, but also the implementing legislation itself. Section 102 (a) (2) of the URAA provides:

> Construction.—Nothing In This Act Shall Be Construed—
> (A) To amend or modify any law of the United States, including any law relating to—
>> (i) the protection of human, animal, or plant life or health,
>> (ii) the protection of the environment, or
>> (iii) worker safety, or
> (B) To limit any authority conferred under any law of the United States, including Section 301 of the Trade Act of 1974,
>> Unless specifically provided for in this Act.

The effect of this provision[140] is to greatly limit the extent to which the Act may be interpreted as altering any laws (which for this purpose include administrative regulations). The statement of administrative action also contains a fairly extensive illustrative list of environmental and health-related statutes that are declared not to be modified by the URAA.[141]

If any statutes of the United States not specified in the implementing legislation need to be amended to conform to the Uruguay Round Agreements (whether as a result of dispute settlement or a voluntary

---

[139] However, courts will sometimes go to extraordinary lengths to avoid construing a statute in a way that would bring the US into violation of its obligations under international law, including treaties. See, e.g., *United States* v. *Palestine Liberation Organization*, 695 F. Supp. 1456 (SDNY 1988), where the court construed the Anti-terrorism Act as not requiring the closure of the PLO's Permanent Observer Mission to the UN despite substantial evidence that many in Congress intended precisely that result. The court found that since Congress did not explicitly indicate its intention to violate the UN Headquarters Agreement, the statute should be construed to avoid that result, despite the legislative history and its arguably plain meaning.

[140] This is another example of the evolution of Congressional implementation between 1988 and 1993. The provision is drawn from s. 102, NAFTA Act, but there is no corresponding provision in the USCFTA Act.

[141] SAA, 31–32, 1994 USCCAN 4040, 4063.

determination by the United States), the normal legislative process would have to be followed. This is in stark contrast to the 1979 Act, which explicitly provided a fast-track procedure for any bills submitted by the President to amend a statute to conform to one of the trade agreements approved by Congress.[142] That provision apparently applied not only to any statute that might have been overlooked during the implementation process, but also to changes necessary to comply with dispute settlement rulings or amendments to any of the covered agreements. In short, instead of choosing to grease the path to compliance, Congress to a considerable degree chose to put stones on it.

One significant change from the Tokyo Round implementing legislation is the status of the SAA. The 1979 Act, like the URAA, provides that Congress approves the SAA. But the 1979 Act left unclear the role of that statement in the interpretation and application of the Tokyo Round agreements, and the House Report at least suggested the statement should not be given primary weight as legislative history and a source of administrative authority.[143] In contrast, the URAA provides that 'The statement of administrative action shall be regarded as an authoritative expression by the United States concerning the interpretation and application of the Uruguay Round Agreements and this Act in any judicial proceeding in which a question arises concerning such interpretation and application.'[144] This is not surprising in that the SAA was as much subject to negotiation with Congress as the implementing bill, and became a means by which the Administration could assuage Congressional concerns without incorporating the provisions into the implementing legislation.[145] It might be thought that giving the President's statement of his intentions such authority was an enhancement of executive influence in trade policy, but just the opposite is the case. By insisting that the President spell out in some detail the plans for administrative implementation, and making those plans authoritative, Congress in effect imposed additional restraints on such administrative actions.[146] The SAA is intended to guide not only future administrative actions by the President and executive agencies and any judicial interpretations of the URAA, but also the United States' position regarding its international obligations under the Uruguay Round

---

[142] S. 3(c), Trade Agreements Act 1979, 19 USC s. 2504. It is unclear whether this omission was the result of deliberate decision not to include this type of fast-track authority, or the failure to provide any general extension of fast-track authority.

[143] See Jackson, 'United States law' at 167.

[144] S. 102(c), URAA, 19 USC s. 3512 (c). There is no corresponding provision even in the most recent implementing legislation prior to the URAA, the NAFTA Implementation Act.

[145] See D. A. Codevilla, 'Discouraging the Practice' at n. 14.

[146] See n. 150.

Agreements.[147] Thus the statement contains numerous interpretations of the provisions of those agreements, some of which might be disputed by other parties.[148]

Several provisions of the Act provide authority for administrative agencies to implement the Uruguay Round Agreements. Section 103 provides broad authority for the President and administrative agencies to implement the URAA. That section was 'intended to ensure full implementation of US obligations under the Uruguay Round Agreements upon their entry into force.'[149] Although the wording of the statute is somewhat ambiguous, an agency would have to justify such action either on the basis of the pre-existing statute which provided its authority, specific provisions of the URAA, or the SAA.[150] Also, despite the fact that the agreements cannot be invoked by a private person as the basis of a cause of

---

[147] SAA, 1, 1994 USCCAN 4040 explicitly provides:

[T]his Statement represents an authoritative expression by the Administration concerning its views regarding the interpretation and application of the Uruguay Round agreements, both for purposes of US international obligations and domestic law. Furthermore, the Administration understands that it is the expectation of the Congress that future Administrations will observe and apply the interpretations and commitments set out in this Statement. Moreover, since this Statement will be approved by the Congress at the time it implements the Uruguay Round agreements, the interpretations of those agreements included in this Statement carry particular authority.

[148] The SAA devotes a separate section to each of the Uruguay Round Agreements being implemented. That section generally consists of two subsections: a 'Summary of Provisions' of the particular agreement, and 'Action required or appropriate to implement the Agreement'. Interpretations of the provisions of the Uruguay Round agreement might appear in either of the sections, and they pervade the document. Although many of the descriptions of the agreements are noncontroversial, others would probably be disputed by other parties. For example, the SAA asserts that the Decision on Anti-Circumvention 'constitutes a recognition of the legitimacy of anti-circumvention measures and does not preclude members from maintaining, modifying, or enacting anti-circumvention measures at this time' (SAA, 149, 1994 USCCAN 4040, 4160). Similarly, the language in the Agreement on Anti-Dumping is somewhat ambiguous as to whether the requirement that exporters be allowed 60 days to adjust their prices to changes in exchange rates applies only to investigations or also to reviews, but the SAA explicitly asserts that it does not apply to reviews (SAA, 140, 1994 USCCAN 4153).

[149] House Report 103–826(I), at 27.

[150] The following passage (SAA, 14, 1994 USCCAN 4050), indicates that no additional regulatory authority can be derived from general approval of the Uruguay Round agreements:

The Administration has made every effort to include all laws in the implementing bill and identify all administrative actions in this Statement that must be changed in order to conform with the new US rights and obligations arising from the Uruguay Round agreements. Those include both regulations resulting from statutory changes in the bill itself and changes in laws, regulations and rules or orders that can be implemented without change in the underlying US statute.

Accordingly, at this time it is the expectation of the Administration that no changes in existing federal law, rules, regulations, or orders other than those specifically indicated in the implementing bill and this Statement will be required to implement the new international obligations that will be assumed by the United States under the Uruguay Round agreements. Should it prove otherwise, the Administration would need to seek new legislation from Congress or, if a change in regulation is required, follow normal agency procedures for amending regulations.

action or defence, government agencies are free to consider (and hear argument on) the consistency of any proposed action with the Uruguay Round Agreements in undertaking any action.[151]

Congress's assignment of the details of the implementation to executive agencies did not eliminate opportunities for political influence and protectionist action. Under the Agreement on Textiles and Clothing, for example, each country is required to integrate textiles subject to import quotas into the GATT over a ten-year period. The URAA provides that the department of commerce shall publish the integration schedule within 120 days of the Uruguay Round Agreements entering into force.[152] But the textile industry was not disappointed by the results of this delegation. The products integrated in the earlier years were generally of little or no significance.[153]

With respect to administrative implementation, a critical issue is whether Congressional approval of an agreement limits administrative discretion to violate that agreement. In other words, if statutory law is unclear, and if in the absence of WTO obligations the administrative agency's interpretation or application of the statute would have been upheld, would the fact that the agency's action violates the Uruguay Round Agreements cause the Court to strike down the agency action as not being within its discretion? There appears to be only one provision of the implementing legislation which specifically directs an agency not to act in violation of the agreements. Section 411 directs the commodity credit corporation to administer and carry out the export enhancement programme 'in a manner consistent, as determined by the President, with the obligations undertaken by the United States set forth in the Uruguay Round Agreements.' Without such explicit direction, maxims of statutory construction and administrative agency discretion potentially collide. Although Congress can, under the 'later in time' rule, enact statutes that put the United States in violation of its international agreements, courts will avoid such a construction unless the intent of Congress is clear.[154] Under the rule of *Chevron* v. *NRDC*,[155] the courts must defer to an agency interpretation of a statute if it is reasonable. Although one could argue that an agency interpretation is not reasonable if it causes the United States to be in violation of its international obligations, this argument might seem less apt where the statute was enacted prior to the international agreement. Ordinarily, the later-in-time rule could resolve that conflict, but the

[151] SAA, 20, 1994 USCCAN at 4055.
[152] S. 331, URAA, codified at 19 USC s. 3591.
[153] See P. Passell, 'Phasing out protection for textiles may take a silver bullet' *NY Times*, 4 May 1995, s. D, at 2, col. 1.
[154] See p. 215.
[155] *Chevron USA, Inc.* v. *Natural Resources Defense Council, Inc.*, 467 US 837 (1984).

URAA limits the application of that rule to changes specifically provided by the Act.

Several recent decisions in the anti-dumping and countervailing duty context raise the concern that the courts will not seriously limit administrative discretion in order to assure compliance with the United States' multilateral trade obligations.[156] In one case several years ago, the Court broadly pronounced:

[e]ven if we were convinced that commerce's interpretation conflicts with the GATT, which we are not, the GATT is not controlling. While we acknowledge Congress's interest in complying with US Responsibilities under the GATT, we are bound not by what we think Congress should or perhaps wanted to do, but by what Congress in fact did. The GATT does not trump domestic legislation; if the statutory provisions here are inconsistent with the GATT, it is a matter for Congress and not this court to decide and remedy.[157]

These words have been seized upon by other courts to virtually ignore GATT compliance as an issue in reviewing domestic agency action.[158] In the most notorious case, the Court struck down an agency poultry standard regulation where the agency itself argued that its interpretation of the statute was necessary to assure compliance with the GATT. The Court concluded that the 'flawless reasoning' of the above passage required it to 'give effect to Congress's intent, even if implementation of that intent is virtually certain to create a violation of the GATT.'[159] The Court further explicitly cast doubt on the notion that the maxim that statutes be construed to avoid bringing the United States into violation of international law applied with respect to multilateral trade agreements.[160] In a very

---

[156] As Peter O. Suchman, a representative of the American Association of Exporters and Importers testified before the Committee on Ways and Means Subcommittee on Trade on 8 Feb. 1994:

In the past, the Department of Commerce, the ITC and the federal courts have, unfortunately, been reluctant to pay deference to the GATT Anti-Dumping Code when interpreting US law. Despite a clear statement in the Trade Agreements Act of 1979 that its purpose was to implement Tokyo Round agreements, including the GATT Code, the US courts have frequently allowed the Department of Commerce in administering the statute to interpret ambiguous provisions of US law in a manner contrary to the Code. For example, in the *Suramerica* case, the Federal Circuit expressly refused to follow a GATT panel ruling on the standing provisions of the Code, and instead upheld as a reasonable exercise of the agency's discretion Commerce procedures which were clearly contrary to the Code.

[157] *Suramerica de Aleaciones Laminadas, C.A.* v. *United States*, 966 F.2d 660 (Fed. Cir. 1992) (Judge Plager).

[158] See, e.g., *Torrington Co.* v. *United States*, 1995 WL 549113 (Ct. Int. Trade 1995) ('This Court's finding that Commerce's construction of the anti-dumping duty statute is reasonable eliminates any need to discuss Torrington's assertion that the challenged regulation conflicts with the GATT.')

[159] *Mississippi Poultry Association* v. *Madigan*, 992 F.2d 1359, 1366 (5th Cir. 1993). The court ruled that the 'plain language' of the statute compelled a meaning contrary to that adopted by the agency, so the agency was not entitled to deference under the principles of *Chevron.*   [160] Ibid. at 1367.

recent decision, however, the judge who wrote the above passage explicitly applied the maxim to the GATT.[161]

At the time the Uruguay Round Agreements came into force, ambiguity remained regarding the status of the GATT in domestic United States law and in particular its role in constraining both statutory interpretation and federal agency action. No decision has as yet addressed the new agreements. On the one hand, the Uruguay Round Agreements have been explicitly approved by Congress, and thus courts may regard those agreements as having a greater role in statutory interpretation than the GATT of 1947 had. On the other hand, some of the explicit provisions in the implementing legislation that limit the role of those agreements could be interpreted also as limiting their effect in the context of judicial review of agency action.[162] This should not be the favoured interpretation of those provisions, but it cannot be completely foreclosed.

6.3.5 Conduct and implementation of Dispute Settlement proceedings

Many of the provisions regarding the dispute settlement process were also aimed at protecting aspects of the United States' autonomy. These provisions addressed both consultation regarding an ongoing dispute settlement proceeding and implementation of the results of such a proceeding. Not only will any decisions finding the United States in violation of its WTO obligations not have any direct effect in US law, but the Congress required that certain procedures be followed in order to

---

[161] *Federal Mogul Corp.* v. *United States*, 63 F.3d 1572 (Fed. Cir. 1995) (panel opinion by Judge Plager). In reversing the lower court's decision striking down the Commerce Department's interpretation, the Court stated: 'For the Court of International Trade to read a GATT violation into the statute, over Commerce's objection, may commingle powers best kept separate.' Thus in this case the maxims of deference to agency interpretations and avoiding conflict with international obligations were in accord rather than conflict. Judge Plager characterized the *Suramerica* decision as involving 'a conflict between a GATT obligation and a statute' (63 F.3rd at 1581). The decision in *Footwear Distributors and Retailers of America*, 852 F. Supp. 1078 (Ct. Int. Trade 1994), discussed at n. 180, also found that the *Chevron* deference principle yielded to the maxim of construing statutes to avoid conflict with international law, but ultimately held that the flexibility of the remedy provided by the GATT dispute settlement process meant that the United States was not necessarily in violation of its GATT obligations.

[162] E.g. s. 102 (a), URAA, 19 USC s. 3512 (a), could be read to preclude the use of the Uruguay Round agreements to overcome any apparent conflict with US law, and s. 102 (c) (1) (B), URAA, 19 USC s. 3512 (c) (1) (B), could be interpreted to preclude any argument that an agency abused its discretion by bringing the US into violation of its Uruguay Round commitments. However, the statement in the SAA that the latter provision 'does not preclude any agency of government from considering, or entertaining argument on, whether its action or proposed action is consistent with the Uruguay Round agreements,' suggests not only that the agency is free to consider that, but also that it might be an abuse of discretion not to (1994 USCCAN at 4055).

implement any such decision, even if ordinarily an administrative agency might have had discretion to change its regulations to comply with the decision.

It was never seriously considered that a WTO dispute settlement decision would directly apply in US law. The sovereignty issue in the dispute settlement context focused on whether the choice of complying with a WTO ruling, offering 'compensation', or having other parties authorized to suspend trade concessions, was sufficient for the maintenance of some notion of sovereignty. In the debate, these GATT concepts became quite distorted, and references to 'fines' (unknown in GATT or WTO parlance or practice) became commonplace.[163] Few seemed to recall, or wanted to acknowledge, that compensation meant no more than the voluntary offering of alternative trade concessions and that sanctions in the context of the GATT meant only the authorized withdrawal of benefits by one country in an equal measure to the benefits that had been denied by another party.

The implementing legislation requires that the USTR keep Congress and other groups informed about WTO dispute settlement proceedings, and that it provide certain opportunities to participate in those proceedings.[164] Once a Dispute Settlement Panel is established to consider the consistency of any United States (federal or state) law or practice with any of the Uruguay Round Agreements, the USTR must notify Congress of the nature of the dispute, the members of the Dispute Settlement Panel, and whether those members were appointed by consensus.[165] Similar obligations apply regarding any appeal of the Panel Report to the Appellate Body, and the USTR must consult with appropriate Congressional committees regarding any appeal or implementation of a Panel Report.[166]

Private sector and non-governmental organizations must also be given an opportunity to make their views known. Whenever the United States is

---

[163] See, e.g., 140 Cong. Rec. S15077, S15105 (1994) (Sen. Byrd); 140 Cong. Rec. S15271, S15362 (1994) (Sen. Smith); 140 Cong. Rec. S15271, S15318 (1994) (Sen. Cohen); 140 Cong. Rec. S15077, S15125 (1994) (Sen. Heflin). See also Ralph Nader, 'Reject this flawed Treaty' *USA Today*, 22 Nov. 1994, 140 Cong. Rec. S15271, S15314. (Mr Nader made the same comments in testimony on 18 Oct. 1994 before the Senate Commerce Committee, on 14 June, 1994 to the Senate Foreign Relations Committee, on 26 Apr. 1994 to the House Small Business Committee, and on 16 Mar. 1994 to the Senate Finance Committee). Bruce Fein referred to fines in his testimony to the Senate Foreign Committee on 14 June 1994.

[164] S. 127, URAA, codified at 19 USC ss. 2155 and 3537. S. 7 of the proposed WTO Dispute Settlement Review Commission Act, S. 16, 104th Cong., see p. 223, would require additional rights of participation for any person 'that is supportive of the United States government's position before the panel or appellate body and that has a direct economic interest in the panel's or appellate body's resolution of the matters in dispute shall be permitted to participate in consultations and panel proceedings.'

[165] S. 123 (d), URAA, 19 USC s. 3533 (d).

[166] S. 123 (e) and (f), URAA, 19 USC s. 3533 (e) and (f).

a party to a dispute settlement proceeding, the USTR must consult not only with appropriate Congressional committees, but also the relevant private sector advisory committee and any appropriate private sector and non-governmental organizations.[167] In addition, the USTR must publish a notice regarding the proceeding in the federal register seeking written comments from the public.[168] The USTR is required to make its own submissions public (except to the extent they contain proprietary or confidential information), and request that other parties make their submissions available to the public as well. If another party does not make its submissions public, the USTR is directed to request non-confidential summaries of its submissions. All of this material, along with any panel decisions, is to be maintained in a public file.[169] In short, even if the WTO fails to move toward openness and transparency in its processes, the United States will.

As for situations in which the United States may be a complaining party, Section 301 continues to provide the basic procedural elements for launching the dispute settlement process. The USTR may self-initiate investigations of possible violations of trade agreements, or such investigations may be initiated by private petition. No changes were made in Section 301 in this regard, except to conform the time limits to those in the dispute settlement understanding.[170]

Also noteworthy are special provisions regarding complaints about subsidies of other WTO Members. The Uruguay Round Agreement on Subsidies and Countervailing Measures shifts the remedial emphasis to some extent from countervailing duties to complaints under the dispute settlement process. Section 281 of the URAA provides that an 'interested party' may petition the International Trade Administration for a determination whether merchandise from a WTO member country is benefiting from either prohibited or actionable subsidies. If the ITA determines that a subsidy is prohibited or actionable, it must notify the USTR. This notification in effect triggers the Section 301 procedure with regard to those subsidies.[171] Where a 'green light' subsidy has been notified under Article 8 of the Subsidies Agreement, and the USTR determines that it does not satisfy the criteria for non-actionable subsidies under that Article, USTR must invoke the special dispute settlement procedures contained in Articles 8.4 and 8.5 of the Agreement.[172] Similarly, the USTR must invoke

[167] S. 127, URAA, 19 USC s. 3537.
[168] S. 127 (b), URAA, 19 USC s. 3537 (b).
[169] S. 127 (c), (d) and (e), URAA, 19 USC s. 3537 (c), (d) and (e).
[170] S. 314 (d), amending s. 304 (a) Trade Act 1974, URAA, 19 USC s. 2414 (a). See additional discussion of s. 301 TAN p. 232.
[171] S. 281 (d), URAA, 19 USC s. 3571 (d).
[172] S. 281 (e) (1), URAA, 19 USC s. 3571 (e) (1).

the procedures of Article 9 of the Subsidies Agreement if the ITA finds that an Article 8 subsidy is resulting in 'serious adverse effects,' and that determination is supported by the facts.[173] If the subsidizing country prevents the Subsidies Committee from making a final determination, or the Subsidies Committee fails to act within 120 days, the USTR must determine what action to take under Section 301.[174]

The implementation process for dispute settlement decisions is complex, and there are distinctions for federal statutory law, federal administrative regulations and rulings, and state law. (State law is discussed in the following section.) If a federal statute is found to violate the United States' obligations, only the Congress can act to change the statute, and the normal legislative processes apply. There is no fast-track or similar procedure available for legislation intended to implement dispute settlement decisions. If agency regulations or practices are found to violate the WTO agreements, the practice may not be modified until Congressional committees are consulted, private sector advice is sought, the agency follows certain procedural requirements, and the USTR has submitted reports on any proposed modifications to appropriate Congressional committees. Both the USTR and the head of the agency must in addition consult with those committees regarding any proposed final rule. That rule may not ordinarily go into effect until sixty days after such consultations have begun. During that time the House Committee on Ways and Means and the Senate Committee on Finance may vote their approval or disapproval of the proposed change, although this does not bind the agency.[175] Nevertheless, an agency will be keenly aware that its decision will be subject to such a vote, and hesitant to adopt a rule if the Committees oppose it. The probable effect of the provision is to give members of the Committees increased leverage in their discussions with agency staff.

These provisions do not apply to regulations and practices of the International Trade Commission.[176] If a Dispute Settlement Panel finds that some action by the ITC in a particular proceeding violates the agreements on anti-dumping, safeguards, or subsidies and countervailing measures, the USTR may request an advisory report from the ITC on whether the ITC would be permitted under United States law to bring its action into conformity with the WTO dispute settlement ruling. As in other contexts, the USTR must notify Congressional committees if it makes such a request, and consult with them if the ITC determines that it could

---

[173] S. 281 (e) (2), URAA, 19 USC s. 3571 (e) (2).
[174] S. 281 (e) (2) (B), URAA, 19 USC s. 3571 (e) (2) (B).
[175] S. 123 (g), URAA, 19 USC s. 3533 (g).
[176] S. 123 (g) (4), URAA, 19 USC s. 3533 (g) (4).

conform to its decisions. In that case, the USTR is authorized to request that the ITC make a determination that would bring its action into compliance with the dispute settlement ruling, and the ITC is required to do so.[177] Similar provisions apply to determinations of the Department of Commerce regarding countervailing and anti-dumping duties.[178]

The implementing legislation thus makes clear that WTO dispute settlement rulings are not self-executing, and thus could not be used in judicial action directly to invalidate federal statutes or administrative regulations or actions. The URAA is less clear, however, regarding the potential impact of the substance of a dispute panel ruling on agency rule-making or adjudication. As discussed above, the general rule is that statutes are to be construed, and agency discretion constrained, to avoid bringing the United States in violation of its international obligations. Presumably this would include rulings of Dispute Settlement Panels. However, in a recent decision, the Court of International Trade refused to invalidate a countervailing duty order that was found by a GATT Dispute Settlement Panel to be in violation of the United States' obligations.[179] The basic reasoning of the Panel was that in the wake of such a ruling the United States could in effect choose which of several alternative remedies would be offered to the prevailing party, including alternative trade concessions by the United States or the suspension of equivalent concessions by the prevailing party.[180] Because compliance with the ruling was only one such alternative remedy, the United States was not necessarily in violation of the GATT. This is doubtful reasoning, but if accepted by other courts would further limit the effect on United States law of WTO dispute settlement rulings.[181]

Finally, as a result of the last minute compromise with Senator Dole, a

---

[177] S. 129 (a), URAA, 19 USC s. 3538 (a).

[178] S. 129 (b), URAA, 19 USC s. 3538 (b). The USTR is only required to consult with Commerce rather than request and receive an advisory report (as it must from the ITC) before requesting the Department of Commerce to comply with the dispute settlement ruling.

[179] *Footwear Distributors and Retailers of America* v. *United States*, 852 F. Supp. 1078 (Ct. Int. Trade 1994). In an important and interesting aspect of the case, the United States proceeding was stayed pending two GATT dispute settlement panel rulings.

[180] Ibid. at 1096. The court stated 'However cogent the reasoning of the GATT panels reported above, it cannot and therefore does not lead to the precise domestic, judicial relief for which the plaintiff prays. That is, that relief simply does not attach. Rather, a party in Brazil's position, having sought and obtained a favourable panel ruling, has and has had relief available to it via suspension of its obligations to the offending party pursuant to Article XXIII of the General Agreement.' This decision was under the GATT dispute settlement procedure, but the court indicated in a discussion of the provisions of the Uruguay Round agreements that the same result would prevail with regard to a ruling under the Uruguay Round Dispute Settlement Understanding.

[181] A provision of the WTO Agreements does, however, provide futher support for the view that there is in fact an obligation to comply with the WTO agreements and dispute settlement rulings. Art XVI: 4, Agreement Establishing the World Trade Organization.

bill to establish a WTO Dispute Settlement Review Commission is now pending in Congress and may eventually pass in some form.[182] The Commission will consist of five federal appeals court judges appointed by the President after consultation with Congressional leaders. The Commission is charged with reviewing all reports of Dispute Settlement Panels and the Appellate Body of the WTO which are initiated by other parties against the United States and are adverse to the United States.[183] In any such case, the Commission must determine whether the panel or Appellate Body:

(a) . . . exceeded its authority or its terms of reference;
(b) . . . added to the obligations of or diminished the rights of the United States under the Uruguay Round Agreement which is the subject of report;
(c) . . . acted arbitrarily or capriciously, engaged in misconduct, or demonstrably departed from the procedures specified for panels and appellate bodies in the applicable Uruguay Round Agreement; and
(d) . . . deviated from the applicable standard of review, including an anti-dumping, countervailing duty, and other unfair trade remedy cases, the standard of review set forth in Article 17.6 of the Agreement on Implementation of Article VI of the General Agreement on Tariffs and Trade 1994.

The Commission is required to make these determinations within 120 days after any Dispute Settlement or Appellate Body report is adopted, and report them to the House Ways and Means Committee and the Senate Finance Committee. If, after any such report, both Houses approve a joint resolution, the President must undertake negotiations to amend or modify the rules and procedures of WTO Dispute Settlement. Under the 'three strikes and we're out' provision, following three such determinations by the Commission within a five-year period, Congress's direction to the President to seek reform of the Dispute Settlement rules and procedures is coupled with a resolution withdrawing approval of the WTO agreement and requiring the United States to withdraw from WTO membership. These resolutions are subject to Presidential veto. The critical element of this legislation is the application of fast-track procedures to the resolution of withdrawal.

Both the meaning and constitutionality of many of these provisions is uncertain.[184] It is also unclear whether the effect of this legislation will be to stabilize or destabilize United States participation in the WTO. It seems

[182] The Senate Bill is S. 16, 104th Cong., 1st Sess. (1995), introduced on 4 Jan. An identical House Bill, H.R.1434, 104th Cong., 1st Sess. (1995), was introduced in April.
[183] The bills also provide that the Commission shall review dispute settlement reports, whether or not initiated by other parties or adverse to the US, upon the request of the USTR.
[184] The legislation raises several Constitutional questions, including whether the use of sitting federal judges violates the separation of powers, and whether Congress has Constitutional power to compel the President to withdraw from the WTO.

somewhat unlikely that a group of five federal court of appeals judges would in fact find that a WTO Panel failed in one of the respects enumerated. In the absence of such a finding, it might be more difficult for Congress to attempt to withdraw from the WTO on the basis that the dispute settlement resolutions are objectionable. On the other hand, those Dispute Settlement Panels are now on notice that their decisions will be reviewed by an ostensibly independent commission, and the criteria that will be applied.

6.3.6 Federalism issues in implementation and dispute settlement

As noted above, the GATT of 1947 was, in the relatively few cases in which the issue arose, given direct application in State courts. As the Uruguay Round Agreements impose greater obligations regarding product standards, and also potentially address business regulation more generally in the area of services, federalism issues were much more prominent in the Uruguay Round than in the Tokyo Round. This was one of the arguments offered in support of the view that the Uruguay Round Agreements required approval as a treaty rather than as a Congressional–executive agreement.[185] There is little doubt that Congress has the authority to restrict or preclude state regulatory action in areas such as insurance or product safety, but the voice of federalism or state sovereignty still carries substantial weight in American political debates.

Both the federal government and the states have the power to regulate commerce.[186] The states, however, are forbidden from imposing duties on imports or exports[187] or discriminating against foreign or interstate commerce.[188] The states thus have no authority to impose protectionist border measures such as quantitative restrictions, countervailing or anti-dumping duties, or safeguard measures.[189] But the states retain substantial

---

[185] See discussion p. 179.

[186] The federal government's power derives from the Commerce Clause, which grants to Congress the power 'To regulate Commerce with foreign Nations, and among the several States, and with the Indian Tribes.' Art. III, s. 8, cl. 3, US Const. The power of the states derives from their general police powers.

[187] Art. I, s. 10, US Const.

[188] For an excellent overview of the limitations on the power of the states to regulate commerce, see V. Blasi, 'Constitutional limitations on the power of states to regulate the movement of goods in interstate commerce', in T. Sandalow and E. Stein (eds.), *Courts and Free Markets: Perspectives from the United States and Europe* (1982), 174.

[189] Perhaps surprisingly, states do have the power to regulate prices within their jurisdiction, including the establishment of minimum price regulations. See, e.g., *Milk Control Board* v. *Eisenberg Farm Products*, 306 US 346 (1939); *Parker* v. *Brown*, 317 US 341 (1943); *Cities Service Gas Co.* v. *Peerless Oil & Gas Co.*, 340 US 179 (1950). Less clear, perhaps, is the ability of states to impose quantitative restrictions of the sort permitted by certain exceptions to GATT Article XI.

regulatory authority over products, businesses, and markets, particularly regarding matters of consumer protection and safety. In many ways, the United States today is, at least from a legal point of view, less a single market than the European Union.[190] Although under the Commerce Clause there are limits to such authority, the Supreme Court has by and large taken a deferential approach so long as the measures are not discriminatory.[191] However, the federal government possesses very broad powers to enter into international agreements, and ordinarily those agreements 'trump' state law even if they concern matters traditionally regulated by states.[192] With the possible exception of some aspects of government procurement, there is no doubt the courts would sustain the federal government's entering into agreements that imposed significant obligations on states regarding non-tariff barriers. The constitutional division of sovereignty between the federal and state governments thus poses little in the way of a legal constraint on the power of the federal government to enter into international commitments and enforce those commitments.[193]

The political stature of federalism in the United States today countervails to some extent the broad legal powers of the federal government. Federalism, in the sense of the value of more localized state regulatory power over centralized federal regulatory power, enjoys widespread support in the United States. It is a strong value professed not only by the Republicans who now dominate Congress, but in light of that very domination also by some environmentalists and consumer activists who see states today as more likely to act upon their agendas. Although ultimately state officials strongly supported the implementation of the Uruguay Round Agreements, they made their voices heard in the process.[194]

[190] See generally T. Bourgoignie & D. M. Trubek, *Consumer Law, Common Markets and Federalism in Europe and the United States* (1987); A. D. Tarlock (ed.), *Regulation, Federalism, and Interstate Commerce* (1981); B. Friedman, 'Federalism's future in the global village' (1994) 47 Vand. L. Rev. 1441; D. A. Farber and R. E. Hudec, 'Free trade and the regulatory state: a GATT's eye view of the dormant commerce Clause' (1994) 47 Vand. L. Rev. 1401.

[191] Compare, e.g., *Minnesota* v. *Clover Leaf Creamery Co.*, 449 US 456 (1981) (upholding Minnesota restrictions on milk containers) with *Commission* v. *Denmark*, Case 302/86, [1988] ECR 4607 (Danish bottles case, striking down Danish law on recyclable containers).

[192] See *Missouri* v. *Holland*, 252 US 416 (1920).

[193] Panel Report–United States measures affecting alcoholic and malt beverages. BISD 39th Supp., 206 (Adopted 19 June 1992). There may, however, be significant constraints on the means by which the federal government may enforce those commitments. At least in some contexts, the federal government might not be able to simply compel state government officials to fulfill obligations created by international treaty. Cf. *New York* v. *United States*, 505 US 144 (1992). It seems unlikely, as well as unwise, that the principle of *New York* v. *United States* would be applied when the federal government is acting under its various foreign relations powers.

[194] See, e.g., Letter from Michael S. Carpenter, Attorney-General of Maine, to President Clinton (6 July 1994), printed in 140 Cong. Rec. S8847–01 (daily ed. 13 July 1994).

The Uruguay Round Agreements pose a number of potential challenges to state law. The most important of these relate to product safety (particularly food), and thus most of the concern was focused on the Agreements on Technical Barriers to Trade and on the Application of Sanitary and Phytosanitary Measures. The General Agreement on Trade in Services also poses potential obligations in traditional areas of state regulation (notably banking and insurance), and the Agreement on Subsidies and Countervailing Measures could result in challenges to state subsidy practices, including tax breaks which have become a common means of inducing investment. More generally, the Uruguay Round Agreements go further than both the GATT of 1947 and the Tokyo Round agreements in imposing responsibility on central governments for compliance by regional and local governments.[195]

Additionally, for the first time, certain items in the schedules of commitments impose direct obligations on the states. The agreement on government procurement now applies (on a positive list basis) to some state procurement as well, and thus states may be forced to reform their procurement practices.[196] According to the SAA, these commitments voluntarily undertaken by states are 'codified' by Section 101 of the URAA.[197] Similarly, the failure to include a most-favoured-nation or

---

[195] GATT Art. XXIV:12 provides that 'Each contracting party shall take such reasonable measures as may be available to it to ensure observance of the provisions of this Agreement by the regional and local governments and authorities within its territory.' The Uruguay Round Understanding on the Interpretation of Article XXIV of the GATT elaborated on this obligation:

13. Each Member is fully responsible under the GATT 1994 for the observance of all provisions of the GATT 1994, and shall take such reasonable measures as may be available to it to ensure such observance by regional and local governments and authorities within its territory.
14. The provisions of Articles XXII and XXIII of the GATT 1994 as elaborated and applied by the Understanding on Rules and Procedures Governing the Settlement of Disputes may be invoked in respect of measures affecting its observance taken by regional or local governments or authorities within the territory of a Member. When the Dispute Settlement Body has ruled that a provision of the GATT 1994 has not been observed, the responsible Member shall take such reasonable measures as may be available to it to ensure its observance. The provisions relating to compensation and suspension of concessions or other obligations apply in cases where it has not been possible to secure such observance.

The Agreements on Technical Barriers to Trade and on the Application of Sanitary and Phytosanitary Measures impose similar obligations regarding the specific matters which they cover. The agreements also require the central government to 'formulate and implement positive measures and mechanisms in support of the observance' of the provisions by state and local governments.

[196] The Agreement lists 37 out of 50 states as being covered. The entities and scope of coverage for each state varies substantially. See Agreement on Government Procurement, Appendix I, Annexe 2 of the United States.

[197] SAA, 374–75, 1994 USCCAN at 4327. The SAA states that 'S. 101 (a) of the implementing bill approves the 1996 Code (as well as other Uruguay Round agreements covering state measures), and in doing so codifies the commitments that particular states voluntarily undertook to be covered by the 1996 Code. Title I of the bill requires the President

national treatment exception for a state in the schedule of services commitments would also bind the states with regard to any practices that might violate those obligations.

Professor Laurence Tribe, testifying before Congress, suggested five ways in which the Uruguay Round Agreements might have an adverse impact on the states. First, particular states might be targeted by foreign government sanctions (that is, suspension of concessions) if the United States failed to implement an adverse panel decision. Secondly, states would be dependent on the USTR to defend challenged state laws which the federal government and the USTR might not have much interest in upholding. Thirdly, the USTR faces a potential conflict in being required both to defend state law before a WTO Panel and then challenge it if the panel declares the law in violation of the WTO agreements. Fourthly, the USTR might be inclined to offer changes in state rather than federal law in the context of Dispute Settlement. Fifthly, the Uruguay Round requirements, particularly those that the federal government takes measures to insure compliance by states, might have a 'chilling effect' on state regulatory activity.[198]

Similarly, a letter on behalf of state attorneys-general expressed concerns about whether private parties could challenge state law in federal court on the basis that it violated the WTO agreements, and how state laws would fare in the WTO Dispute Settlement process. The letter inquired, for example, whether the implementing legislation would adequately guarantee states 'that the federal government will genuinely consider accepting trade sanctions rather than pressuring states to change state laws which are successfully challenged in the WTO'.[199] Wisconsin Governor Thompson, the National Governors' Association representative for trade, argued in his testimony before Congress that states should play a large role in the dispute settlement process when state laws are challenged.[200] State

---

to consult with the states for the purpose of achieving conformity of state laws and practices with the 1996 Code.' The use of the term 'codify' apparently means only that states are bound by their commitments as a matter of federal law. Presumably, the general provisions of the URAA still prevent a private party from directly asserting a claim that state procurement practices are in violation of a scheduled commitment under the Government Procurement Agreement. See p. 212.

[198] See Prepared Statement of L. Tribe, 18 Oct. 1994, to Senate Committee on Commerce, Science, and Transportation. See also State Groups, Law-makers Oppose Pre-emption of State Law Under GATT, 11 Int. Trade Rep. (BNA) 1136 (20 July 1994) ('If the USTR staff cannot force GATT-related changes in federal laws, but can force such changes on state and local laws, the latter will become the preferred bargaining chips in trade negotiations for both USTR and foreign governments').

[199] 140 Cong. Rec. S8847, S8853 (1994).

[200] Testimony of Gov. Thompson on 10 June 1994 to the House Ways and Means Committee.

tax authorities expressed concern about the impact of the WTO agreements on various state tax practices.[201]

In late July of 1994, an agreement was reached between the USTR and state representatives regarding safeguards to be included in the implementing legislation to protect state sovereignty.[202] The URAA incorporated many of the recommendations made by state officials, and reflected federalism concerns in three ways.[203] First, as with federal law, it precluded the agreements from having any direct effect, and indeed required an action by the United States Government for the purpose of striking down a state law. Secondly, it required a consultation process with state officials regarding the implementation of Uruguay Round commitments. Thirdly, state officials were provided an opportunity to participate in virtually every aspect of any WTO Dispute Settlement proceeding that challenges state law.

State compliance with Uruguay Round obligations is initially to be sought on a voluntary basis through consultations by the President with the intergovernmental policy advisory committees on trade. The URAA also requires the USTR to establish an expanded federal–state consultation process for addressing issues relating to the Uruguay Round that affect state interests. States are given an opportunity to express their views on such matters, and the USTR must take those views into account in formulating its positions.[204] For this purpose, the USTR will designate a 'WTO co-ordinator for state matters.'[205] In order to simplify matters, the USTR expects the Governor's office in each state to designate a single contact point for USTR relations, and the Governors to collectively designate one or two Governors to serve as contact points for matters generally affecting state interests.[206]

No state law, or its application, may be declared invalid on the basis that it violates the Uruguay Round Agreements except in an action brought by the federal government specifically for that purpose.[207] In sweeping

---

[201] 11 Int. Trade Rep. (BNA) 901 (8 June 1994).

[202] See 11 Int. Trade Rep. (BNA) 1165 (27 July 1994).

[203] Comparable provisions were not included in the Trade Agreements Act 1979. They built on similar provisions in the NAFTA Implementation Act, but were considerably stronger. This is another instance in which the evolution primarily occurred between the implementation of USCFTA in 1988 and NAFTA in 1993.

[204] S. 102 (b), URAA, 19 USC s. 3512 (b).

[205] See SAA, 15, 1994 USCCAN at 4051.

[206] SAA, 16.

[207] S. 102 (b) (2) (A), URAA. The decision to bring such an action would rest with the Department of Justice, not the USTR. In deciding whether to bring such an action the SAA, at 18 states:

The U.S. Attorney-General will consider the advice of the Trade Representative as to whether a WTO member government has objected to the state measure in question and the extent to which any WTO

language, Congress made it clear that this was the exclusive means for challenging state law.[208] Congress elaborated several procedural requirements for such actions. First, USTR must provide a report to Congress describing the proposed action and any efforts to resolve the matter by other means thirty days before bringing such an action. (The more extreme suggestion that any pre-emption of state law require specific future Congressional action was not incorporated in the implementing legislation.)[209] A decision by a WTO Dispute Settlement Panel is not entitled to deference in such a proceeding, and the burden is on the United States to prove that the state action is inconsistent with one of the Uruguay Round Agreements. The effect of these provisions is to require a court to make a *de novo* determination whether the state law violates the agreement.[210] In practice, courts are likely to accord the United States substantial deference in any challenges to state law. Any law found to be invalid on this basis

---

member complaining of the measure is taking necessary measures to ensure the conformity of its subnational government measures with the relevant Uruguay Round agreement. The Attorney-General will be particularly careful in considering recourse to this authority where the state measure involved is aimed at the protection of human, animal, or plant health or of the environment or the state measure is a state tax of a type that has been held to be consistent with the requirements of the US Constitution. In such a case, the Attorney-General would entertain use of this authority only if consultations between the President and the Governor of the state concerned failed to yield an appropriate alternative.

[208] S. 102 (c) (2) provides:

INTENT OF CONGRESS.—It is the intention of the Congress through para. (1) to occupy the field with respect to any cause of action or defence under or in connection with any of the Uruguay Round Agreements, including by precluding any person other than the United States from bringing any action against any State or political subdivision thereof or raising any defence to the application of State law under or in connection with any of the Uruguay Round Agreements—
(A) on the basis of a judgment obtained by the United States in an action brought under any such agreement; or
(B) on any other basis.

Clause (A) precludes the use by a private party of a judgment obtained by the US in an action under s. 102 (b) (2). If this is a correct reading of this provision (a reading supported by the SAA and the Senate Report on the bill), it is unclear what purpose is served by the s. 102 (b) (2) action. It is presumably an action to compel state officials to conform their law, but if the state fails to do so, and its officials continue to enforce the law which violates the Uruguay Round agreements, a private party would be without a defence. There may also be constitutional limits on the ability of the federal government to compel a state to enact law. Cf. *New York* v. *United States*, 505 US 144 (1992). The SAA also precludes any use of the Uruguay Round agreements as part of an argument that the state regulation is precluded by Congress' authority under the Commerce Clause (SAA, 20). Indeed, it now seems a matter of federal law that state courts may not, as they have occasionally done in the past, strike down state action under the supremacy clause because it violates the law of the GATT. The underlying premise, expressed in the House report, was 'that it is the responsibility of the federal government, and not private citizens, to ensure that federal or state laws are consistent with US obligations under international agreements' (H.R. Rep. 103–826 (I)).

[209] 11 Int. Trade Rep. (BNA) 1136 (20 July 1994).

[210] S. 102 (b) (2) (B), URAA, 19 USC s. 3512 (b) (2) (B). See also SAA, 19, 1994 USCCAN at 4054. Indeed, the Administration undertook not to 'seek to introduce into evidence in federal court any panel or Appellate Body report issued under the DSU with regard to the state measure at issue'.

may only be declared invalid prospectively.[211] The result of these provisions may be a paradox. Although Congress has for the first time fully approved the GATT, it is now more difficult than prior to the Uruguay Round to assert GATT obligations to challenge the application of state law.[212]

Again, the evolution in trade agreement implementing legislation from 1979 through to 1994 is substantial. The 1979 Act contains no provision specifically limiting the effects on state law or assuring states a right to participate in the implementation or dispute settlement process. The USCFTA Act explicitly provided that the free trade agreement prevailed over any conflicting state law,[213] although the reach of that provision was greatly limited by the provision excluding private remedies. The NAFTA Act dropped the explicit supremacy clause and instituted an elaborate consultation process regarding any impact of the agreement on state law. It also added a provision stating that no state law could be declared invalid on the ground that it is inconsistent with the agreement except in an action explicitly brought for that purpose.[214] The URAA takes this several steps further by clarifying the burden of proof, prohibiting retrospective effect of any determination of state law invalidity, and most importantly, requiring consultation with Congress before such an action is brought.

Technically, these restrictions apply only to claims that a state is in violation of one of the Uruguay Round Agreements, not to a claim that the state is in violation of the URAA. But as a general matter, Congress failed to specify state obligations in the implementing legislation. Thus, the reluctance to impinge on state activity resulted in inaction in cases where implementing provisions were arguably required. For example, although the Uruguay Round Agreement on Technical Barriers to Trade imposes greater responsibility than the Tokyo Round standards agreement on the United States Government for compliance by state and local governments, the implementing legislation did not amend Section 403 of the 1979 Act, which was more hortatory in nature and did not directly pre-empt inconsistent state law.[215] In effect, there is no provision in the implementing legislation which directly provides that state laws which violate the requirements of the agreement are invalid. The provisions on the

---

[211] S. 102 (b) (2) (B) (iv), URAA, 19 USC s. 3512 (b) (2) (B) (iv).

[212] At least two state courts had recognized that the GATT pre-empted inconsistent state law provisions. See *Hawaii* v. *Ho*, 41 Haw. 565 (1957) (at the time, Hawaii was a territory) and *KSB Technical Sales Corp.* v. *North Jersey Dist. Water Supply Comm.*, 381 A.2nd 774 (NJ 1977).

[213] Pub. L.No. 100–449, 102 Stat. 1851 (1988), s. 102, 19 USC s. 2112.

[214] Pub. L.No. 103–182, 107 Stat. 2062 (1993), s. 102 (b) (2), 19 USC s. 3312 (b) (2).

[215] See R. Hudec, 'The legal status of GATT in the domestic law of the United States', in Meinhard Hilf *et al.* (eds.), *The European Community and GATT* (1986), 187.

implementation of the Agreement on Sanitary and Phytosanitary Measures are similarly silent with regard to state laws. Thus the procedures described above are the only means to secure state compliance with these two agreements. Federalism concerns regarding the GATS were directly reflected in the United States' schedule of commitments. Many of those commitments, particularly in the financial sector, specifically exclude various state practices. Nothing in the implementing legislation specifically mandates states to abide by the commitments which apply to them in the schedules to the GATS or the Agreement on Government Procurement. Thus in each of these contexts, a private litigant would appear unable to raise a claim that the state action violated the Uruguay Round Agreements.

The URAA also sets forth rights of participation for states in dispute settlement proceedings that challenge state laws or otherwise affect their interests.[216] Within seven days of receiving a request for consultations under the WTO dispute settlement proceedings that suggest a state law is inconsistent with the obligations of the United States under the WTO agreements, the USTR must notify the Governor of the state. The USTR must consult with state representatives, keep them informed of the status of dispute settlement proceedings, and provide them with an opportunity to assist in the preparation of the case. Furthermore, the USTR will invite state representatives or officials to attend panel and Appellate Body hearings as part of the US Delegation, and possibly make presentations to the panel. The USTR will work with state representatives in fashioning any settlement.[217] If the United States government wishes to challenge the action of foreign political subdivisions (for example, states, länder, provinces, or local government units), it must ordinarily notify representatives of each such subdivision thirty days before requesting consultations under Article 4 of the Dispute Understanding, and solicit their views.[218]

6.3.7 Future unilateral actions: Section 301

In a number of circumstances, the President arguably retains authority to act in violation of the Uruguay Round Agreements. The most important of these is the unilateral imposition of sanctions under Section 301. Congress explicitly preserved Section 301 authority, and indeed made a number of enhancements to that and related provisions. These included a somewhat modified version of super 301, which had expired in 1990 and been

---

[216] S. 102 (b) (1) (D), URAA, 19 USC s. 3512 (b) (1) (D).
[217] S. 102 (b) (1) (C), URAA, 19 USC s. 3512 (b) (1) (C).
[218] S. 102 (b) (1) (D), URAA, 19 USC s. 3512 (b) (1) (D).

renewed by Presidential Order in 1994.[219] Nothing, however, in those provisions requires the President or the USTR to act in violation of the Uruguay Round Agreements. But the USTR was quite clear in his testimony that the United States remained willing to invoke unilateral sanctions to open foreign markets, and the recent negotiations between Japan and the United States on automobile parts bear out that willingness. In the Congressional debates, supporters of the implementation bill generally took the position that Section 301 and its hybrids remained intact, whereas opponents generally indicated that the Uruguay Round Agreements precluded the United States from using Section 301 to undertake unilateral action.

In the SAA, the administration made assurances that it intends to use Section 301 to pursue vigorously unfair trade barriers that violate United States rights or deny benefits to the United States under the Uruguay Round Agreements. The administration has also stated its intention to use Section 301 to pursue foreign unfair trade barriers that are not covered by the WTO Agreements.[220] The administration has remained strongly committed to the continued use of US trade remedy laws unilaterally when deemed necessary. In the SAA, the USTR had this to say:

Just as the United States may now choose to take Section 301 actions that are not GATT-authorized, governments that are the subject of such actions may choose to respond in kind. That situation will not change under the Uruguay Round Agreements. The risk of counter-retaliation under the GATT has not prevented the United States from taking actions in connection with such matters as semiconductors, pharmaceuticals, beer, and hormone-treated beef.[221]

The only concession made in the implementing legislation regarding Section 301 was to conform the Section 301 time-frames so that the results of WTO dispute settlement proceedings are available before any trade sanctions are imposed.[222] If a Panel decision or Appellate Body recommendation is not implemented, the statute provides for the USTR to take action within thirty days of the expiration of the 'reasonable time' period provided in the WTO agreement.[223]

Indeed, in several respects the Uruguay Round implementation legislation 'enhances' Section 301. It makes clear, for example, that actions which

---

[219] The original Super 301, Section 1302 of the 1988 Omnibus Trade and Competitiveness Act, adding s. 310 to the Trade Act 1974, was according to its terms applicable only to 1989 and 1990. An executive order was issued by the President on 3 Mar. 1994, that was a scaled-down version of Super 301. Exec. Order No. 12 901, 59 Fed. Reg. 10 727, reprinted in 19 USC s. 2420 (1994).

[220] SAA, 364, 1994 USCCAN 4040, 4319.

[221] SAA, 367, 1994 USCCAN at 4321.

[222] S. 314 (d), URAA, amending s. 304 (a), Trade Act 1974, 19 USC s. 2414 (a).

[223] S. 314 (b) (2), URAA, amending s. 301, Trade Act 1974, 19 USC s. 2411.

'deny the provision of adequate and effective protection of intellectual property rights' are subject to action under Section 301 even if the country is in full compliance with its obligations under TRIPs.[224] It further makes Section 301 available for cases in which market access opportunities that rely on intellectual property rights are denied.[225] This is an important distinction, since the TRIPs only mandates the protection of intellectual property rights; it does not require the liberalization of their trade. And the amendments to Section 301 clarify that denial of market access opportunities might be the result of state or private firms, not just private firms.[226]

The amendments also contain a one-year extension of what we might term the 'strong' rather than 'super' 301 provision. Former Super 301, which lasted for only two years, has been replaced by a provision modelled on President Clinton's administrative extension of Super 301 issued in March 1994.[227] The provision eliminates the requirement that 'priority foreign countries' be identified. Now only 'priority foreign country practices' must be identified. The section also contains an 'early warning' provision, providing that the USTR may describe in its report foreign country practices that 'may in the future warrant identification as priority foreign country practices.'[228]

The result of these and other provisions is the continued 'legalization' of the process for challenging actions by trade partners of the United States.[229] This stands in sharp contrast to the 'de-legalization' of the United States' trade obligations in its domestic law which was described above.

6.3.8 Compliance with substantive terms of the WTO agreements

The above discussion has indicated a number of potential problems regarding United States compliance both with the terms of the WTO agreements and the implementation of subsequent WTO decisions,

---

[224] S. 314 (c) (1), URAA, amending s. 301 (d) (3), Trade Act 1974, 19 USC s. 2411 (d) (3).

[225] S. 314 (c), URAA, amending s. 301 (d), Trade Act 1974, 19 USC s. 2411 (d).

[226] S. 311 (a) (1) (C), URAA, 19 USC s. 2241 (b) (2), amending s. 181 (b) (2), Trade Act 1974, and s. 314 (c) (1), URAA, 19 USC s. 2411 (d) (3), adding subparagraph (B) (i) (IV) to s. 301 (d) (3), Trade Act 1974.

[227] S. 314 (f), URAA, amending s. 310 Trade Act 1974 in its entirety, codified at URAA, 19 USC s. 2420. In the first application of the administrative version of this provision, the USTR 'decided not to identify any priority country practices at this time'. 59 Fed. Reg. 51664–04 (1994). It did, however, identify Japanese market access for wood and paper as possibly warranting such identification in the future.

[228] S. 310 (a) (3) (A), Trade Act 1974, as amended by s. 314 (f), URAA, 19 USC s. 2420 (a) (3) (A).

[229] See J. H. Jackson, 'Perspectives on the jurisprudence on international trade: costs and benefits of legal procedures in the United States' (1984) 82 Mich. L. Rev. 1570.

including in particular dispute settlement proceedings. For the most part, the United States took a minimalist approach to implementation: if the provisions of its law were not clearly in violation of the WTO agreements as the United States interpreted them, the United States took no legislative action. Particularly with regard to federalism problems, and sensitive areas of legislation not directly related to international trade, the approach was one of 'wait and see': wait to see if in fact violations develop and whether they are challenged by other parties to the WTO. Thus, there was no general legal mandate to assure full WTO compliance by either the federal government or the states. Still, in most contexts the United States took the steps required to bring it into compliance with its WTO obligations.

There are, however, a number of provisions in the implementing legislation which appear not to be in full compliance with the WTO agreements. I cannot in the context of this overview comprehensively review the detailed implementation by the United States of each of the eighteen agreements implemented by the URAA. One area, however, worthy of some more focused discussion is the anti-dumping and countervailing duty provisions. These provisions are the clearest source of doubts regarding compliance with the Uruguay Round Agreements, and they illustrate ongoing problems in the United States implementation process.

Anti-dumping was one of the most controversial and difficult issues in the Uruguay Round.[230] The practices of countries that make frequent use of anti-dumping actions, such as the United States, have been the subject of severe criticism in international discussions. The anti-dumping provisions are perhaps the most vociferously defended of the United States' trade remedies. The release of the so-called Dunkel Draft in December of 1991 galvanized those sectors of industry that were frequent petitioners in anti-dumping cases. No other agreement in the Dunkel Draft was as controversial. Although these industry sectors did not consider the final Uruguay Round Anti-Dumping Agreement as quite the disaster it regarded the Dunkel Draft, they made their dissatisfaction with the results clear at an early stage and insisted that the implementing legislation should offset the unfavourable provisions of the agreement with other changes in

---

[230] Originally, anti-dumping was not on the Uruguay Round agenda as set forth in the Punta del Este Ministerial Declaration. The primary reason for this is that the agenda was, for the most part, formulated by the US. The demand for tighter rules on anti-dumping came largely from developing countries, and the proposals offered by GATT members ranged from those of the US and the EC, which aimed at increasing the scope and availability of anti-dumping actions, to those of Hong Kong and other countries, suggesting a fundamental re-examination of the use of anti-dumping. See G. N. Horlick and E. C. Shea, 'The World Trade Organization Anti-Dumping Agreement', (1995) 29 J. World Trade 5.

the anti-dumping law.[231] These industries lobbied both for an absolutely minimalist implementation of the agreement, and for additional changes in the anti-dumping law not required by the agreement but which would tend to enhance its efficacy against imports and counterbalance the limitations imposed by the agreement.

By and large the protectionist forces had their way.[232] At every turn, the implementing legislation gave a very restrictive reading to the provisions of the anti-dumping agreement, effectively tilting the law back in favour of the petitioner.[233] For example, in order to mitigate the artificial appearance of below-cost pricing resulting from unusually high start-up costs, the agreement required in fairly vague terms that cost calculations (such as the cost of production and constructed value) be adjusted for start-up operations. The implementing legislation gave this a very restricted reading,[234] allowing commerce to make such an adjustment only if:

1. the investigated company is using new production facilities or is producing a new product that requires substantial additional investment; and

2. production levels are limited by technical factors associated with the initial phase of commercial production.[235]

---

[231] See, e.g., Testimony of Robert E. Heaton, Chariman of the Board of Directors of Specialty Steel Industry of the United States, '[T]he implementing legislation must re-balance US trade law to add provisions that improve the opportunity for American industries to obtain redress from unfair trade practices'; Statement on Behalf of Clifton L. Smith, President & CEO Corning-Asahi Video Products '[the Anti-Dumping Agreements] should be implemented in fashion so as to minimize their adverse consequences on domestic petitioners. Furthermore, where the new code gives the United States some flexibility, it should use that flexibility to strengthen the current law'; Statement by Clarence C. Comer, President & CEO of Southdown, Inc., 'While the legislative changes needed to implement the Uruguay Round Agreement will necessarily weaken some aspects of US antidumping and countervailing duty remedies, those changes can and should be counter-balanced by legislation to strengthen other aspects of existing law in ways that do not contravene the new Codes'; all before the Committee on Ways and Means, Subcommittee on Trade, 8 Feb. 1994, 1994 WL 212964, 212961 and 212956 (FDCH).

[232] The lobby for anti-dumping is strong not only for the traditional public choice reason that their interests are concentrated (and they are politically very well connected), but also because anti-dumping laws receive a broad range of support. Both labour and industry support them. Not just old industry such as steel, but also newer high-tech industry such as semiconductors, support strong anti-dumping laws. There is some domestic opposition, namely from potential users of imports that are most likely to be subjected to anti-dumping duties (e.g., computer manufacturers) and from exporters concerned that if the US aggressively applies anti-dumping measures, other countries will do so as well.

[233] See D. Palmeter, 'United States implementation' 39 at 41 ('the Administration's strategy: offset the required liberalizing changes with gratuitous restrictive changes').

[234] See the debate in A. F. Holmer et al., 'Enacted and rejected amendments to the anti-dumping law'.

[235] S. 224, URAA, amending s. 773 (f) (1) (C), Tariff Act 1930, codified at 19 USC s. 1677b (f) (1) (C).

The SAA put an additional narrowing gloss on these provisions, further reducing the Commerce Department's discretion in applying the principle.[236] It directed Commerce not to consider an expansion of an existing production line's capacity to be a start-up operation unless the expansion constitutes such a major undertaking that it requires the construction of a new facility. Mere improvements to existing products or facilities will not qualify, according to the SAA, for a start-up adjustment. Moreover, the Administration limited the costs eligible for the adjustment to production costs, thereby excluding sales and marketing costs, although the agreement itself made no such distinction.

One loophole in the code that the drafters of the implementing legislation took full advantage of was the distinction between investigations and reviews, and the fact that some of the stringent requirements regarding investigations arguably did not, according to the literal wording of the agreement, apply to reviews.[237] For example, the *de minimis* rules regarding dumping margins and the volume of dumped imports do not apply to reviews,[238] nor do the provisions requiring average-to-average or transaction-to-transaction price comparisons,[239] nor those allowing sixty days to adjust prices for changes in exchange rates.[240]

In addition, the implementing legislation contained many changes in the anti-dumping laws not required by the agreement that tend to tilt the dumping playing field back in favour of petitioners. These included measures providing for the deduction of United States profit from constructed export price,[241] excluding 'captive production' from the

---

[236] SAA, 166–67, 1994 USCCAN 4040, 4172–74.

[237] Art. 11 of the Anti-Dumping Agreement governs reviews of anti-dumping duties. Art. 11.4 provides: 'The provisions of Art. 6 regarding evidence and procedure shall apply to any review carried out under this Article.' The *de minimis* provisions are contained in Art. 5, which governs the initiation of proceedings to impose anti-dumping duties.

[238] S. 213 (a), URAA, amending s. 733 (b), Tariff Act 1930, 19 USC s. 1673b (b), applies the 2% *de minimis* dumping margin only to investigations. In contrast, and very possibly in violation of the Anti-dumping Agreement, s. 752 (c) (4), Tariff Act, 19 USC s. 1675a, added by s. 221 (a), URAA, provides that a zero or *de minimis* dumping margin shall not by itself require the termination of an anti-dumping order under review.

[239] S. 229 (a), URAA, amending s. 777A, Tariff Act 1930, (19 USC s. 1677f–1). Subsection (d) (1) requires weighted average to weighted average, or transaction to transaction, price comparisons for investigations under Subtitle B, but subsection (d) (2) contemplates that the Commerce Department will compare individual export transaction prices to weighted average foreign prices. The SAA further makes it clear that this latter methodology will be 'the preferred methodology' in reviews (SAA, 173, 1994 USCCAN 4040, 4178).

[240] S. 773A (b), Tariff Act 1930, 19 USC s. 1677b–1, added by s. 225, URAA, applies only to investigations under Subtitle B of the Tariff Act. The provisions on reviews are in Subtitle C.

[241] S. 223, URAA, adding s. 772 (d) to the Tariff Act 1930, 19 USC s. 1677a (d). This controversial provision will likely be challenged in the WTO as a violation of the fair comparison requirement in the Agreement. See G. N. Horlick, in Holmer *et al.*, 'Enacted and rejected amendments to the anti-dumping law' at 496.

United States industry in determining injury,[242] and enhancing the anti-circumvention provisions.[243] Many of these optional provisions in the URAA raise new questions about whether US anti-dumping law complies with its obligations under the anti-dumping agreement.

Finally, in a number of cases the URAA fails to make changes that are arguably required to bring United States anti-dumping law into compliance with the agreement. For example, prior to the conclusion of the Uruguay Round, the court of appeals for the federal circuit had held that cross-cumulation of imports subject to anti-dumping and countervailing duty investigations was required.[244] The anti-dumping agreement apparently does not permit this. However, neither the implementing legislation nor the SAA addresses the issue.[245]

Additionally, the United States' much disputed approach in determining causation of material injury in anti-dumping and countervailing duty proceedings has remained unchanged by the implementing legislation. The URAA fails to ensure that Commerce will discontinue its practice of attributing injury caused by other factors to the dumping violation in determining the extent of injury despite Article 3:5 of the code, which prohibits such attribution.[246]

Similar approaches are found on the subject of countervailing duties, representing a combination of grudging readings of the Uruguay Round Agreement on Subsidies and Countervailing Measures, enactment of new provisions with greater protectionist effect, and failure to correct existing practices that may violate the agreement. For example, although nothing in the Uruguay Round Agreements required it, the implementing legislation overturns several judicial decisions which found that the benefit of a subsidy did not continue after an arm's length sale of an enterprise.[247] The SAA also indicates that the United States will continue to treat as

---

[242] S. 222 (b) (2), URAA, amending s. 771 (7) (C) Tariff Act 1930, codified at 19 USC s. 1677 (7) (C) (iv). 'Captive production' refers to output used by the manufacturer in the production of downstream products. Anti-dumping petitioners had under prior law been unable to get the ITC and the courts to exclude this production in determining whether there was material injury, and the administration had initially opposed changing this policy. After vigorous lobbying by the US steel industry, '[t]he administration eventually caved to political pressure, however, and the captive production provision made its way on to the implementing legislation.' G. N. Horlick, in Holmer *et al.*, 'Enacted and rejected amendments to the anti-dumping law' at 490–491. Exclusion under the URAA is, nonetheless, subject to significant restrictions.

[243] S. 230 (a), URAA, amending s. 781, Tariff Act 1930, codified at 19 USC 1677j.

[244] *Bingham & Taylor Div., Va. Indus.* v. *United States*, 815 F.2nd. 1482 (Fed. Cir. 1987).

[245] See Palmeter, 'United States implementation' at 58. This raises the question as to whether a court could directly apply the Agreement to overrule its prior interpretation of a provision that was not changed.

[246] Ibid. at 59–63.

[247] S. 251 (a), URAA, amending s. 771 (5), Tariff Act 1930, codified at 19 USC s. 1677.

countervailable subsidies certain programmes that probably do not meet
the requirements of a countervailable subsidy under the agreement on
subsidies and countervailing measures.[248] Similarly, the *de facto* specificity
test adopted in the URAA also appears to be somewhat broader than that
contained in the agreement.[249]

This is only a sampling of the potential compliance problems with the
implementation legislation. They suggest that anti-dumping and countervailing duty proceedings will continue to be among the major sources of
complaints (along with unilateral action under Section 301) about United
States trade policy.

6.4 FUTURE NEGOTIATIONS AND WTO ACTIONS

6.4.1 United States participation in and implementation of future WTO actions

The Uruguay Round Agreements contain numerous mechanisms by which
the obligations of the parties under the agreements can be changed or
clarified. These include not only the formal power of amendment,[250] but
also the effect of dispute settlement rulings (whether or not a country is a
party to such a ruling), interpretations formally adopted by the WTO,[251]
waivers,[252] and the results of additional negotiations authorized either
under specific provisions of the agreements or by future decisions of WTO
bodies.[253] Normally, the President has power to enter into agreements
regarding the interpretation of a treaty or international agreement, but his
power to enter into amendments is limited unless such power is conferred
by Congress (or, in the case of a treaty, by the Senate) as part of its
approval of the agreement.

---

[248] See SAA, 256, 1994 USCCAN 4040, 4239–40, indicating inter alia that export restraints
would continue to be regarded as countervailable subsidies if they led to a reduction in
domestic prices. Canada specifically questioned this view in its equivalent of the SAA. See
Department of Foreign Affairs and Internal Trade, Agreement Establishing the World Trade
Organization–Canadian Statement on Implementation (31 Dec. 1994) at 4916.

[249] S. 251 (a), URAA, amending s. 771 Tariff Act 1930, codified at 19 USC s. 1677. The
relevant subsection, 5A, provides that the subsidy is specific if 'one or more' of the factors
identified in the Uruguay Round agreement are present. Art. 2 of the Agreement on
Subsidies and Countervailing Measures simply lists the factors that 'may be considered' in
determining whether a subsidy is specific in fact. Thus in cases in which the one factor suggests
the subsidy is specific and the others suggest that it is not, US law may be in violation of the
Agreement.

[250] Art. X, Agreement Establishing the WTO, 15 Apr. 1994,

[251] Ibid., art. IX.   [252] Ibid.

[253] There are a number of such provisions scattered throughout the Uruguay Round
Agreements.

The URAA contains no explicit approval of the President's power to agree to amendments or interpretations that alter the obligations of the United States, but such Presidential authority is clearly implicit both in the terms of the Uruguay Round Agreements themselves as well as in some of the provisions of the legislation. Congress's primary concern seemed to be the potential for decisions not made on the basis of consensus. In effect, if the United States agrees to changes, the Congress was willing to delegate substantial power to the President to enter into future agreements so long as they did not change statutory law.

Congress announced in the implementing legislation that it was 'the objective' of the United States that the WTO continue the practice of decision-making by consensus,[254] although that provision has very limited legal effect. In pursuit of this policy, Congress required the USTR to consult with appropriate Congressional committees before any vote is taken by the ministerial conference or general council that 'would substantially affect the rights or obligations of the United States under the WTO agreement or another multilateral trade agreement or potentially entails a change in federal or state law.'[255] This provision applies to any decision, including in particular the adoption of interpretations, the granting of waivers, any amendments of the Uruguay Round Agreements, any amendment of the rules or procedures of the WTO ministerial conference or general council, and the accession of any state or customs territory to the WTO. The legislation also imposed significant year-end reporting requirements on the USTR regarding all WTO actions, including specification of member votes in cases in which the decision was not taken unanimously.[256]

The implication of these explicit provisions regarding any WTO decisions that are not made by consensus is that the executive branch (through the USTR) is authorized to participate in such decisions and to accept the results of them if made by consensus rather than vote. Of course, as with the agreements themselves, the power to bind the United States in terms of its international obligations does not itself implement any such amendments or modifications into domestic law. The very detailed provisions on dispute settlement results are discussed above. Perhaps surprisingly, Congress put considerably fewer obstacles in the path of other processes. For example, an administrative agency that changed its rules or regulations pursuant to an interpretation adopted by the WTO or an amendment of one of the agreements would not have to follow the

---

[254] S. 122 (a), URAA, 19 USC s. 3532 (a) (1995).
[255] S. 122 (b), URAA, 19 USC s. 3532 (b).
[256] S. 122 (c), URAA, 19 USC s. 3532 (c). This provision applies to decisons taken by a vote. S. 124, 19 USC s. 3534, imposes more general annual reporting requirements regarding the WTO.

consultation procedures specified for changes pursuant to dispute settlement rulings. If a change in statutory law is required, this would have to be
done pursuant to normal legislative procedures without the benefit of the
fast-process rules. This is, as previously noted, in contrast to the special
fast-track rules provided in the 1979 Act for implementing such changes.

The legislation also mandates the United States to seek certain actions
by the WTO, although it attaches no particular consequences if the United
States fails in those attempts. These include the establishment of rules
governing conflicts of interest by persons serving on dispute settlement
panels or the appellate body,[257] and the creation of a working party 'to
examine the relationship of internationally recognized worker rights . . .
to the articles, objectives, and related instruments of the GATT 1947 and
of the WTO, respectively.'[258] In contrast, the President is prevented from
entering on his own authority into future agreements contemplated by the
Uruguay Round Agreements. For example, any agreement under the
WTO rules of origin programme,[259] or any extension of the 'green light'
subsidies provisions,[260] will require additional Congressional action.

The implementing legislation provides for a review every five years of
United States participation in the WTO.[261] It adopts 'reverse fast-track'
procedures for a joint resolution stating 'that the Congress withdraws its
approval . . . of the WTO agreement.' Any member of the House or
Senate can introduce such a resolution, and it will be automatically
discharged from committee consideration after forty-five days. The
resolution is subject to Presidential veto, in which case a two-thirds vote of
both Houses would be required to override it. As discussed above,
legislation pending in Congress as a result of the agreement between the
administration and Senator Dole would provide an additional review
mechanism for dispute settlement rulings adverse to the United States.[262]

These provisions together reflect extraordinary distrust by Congress for
the WTO. Still, because Congress explicitly restrained the ability of the
President to act on behalf of the United States in the WTO in only a few
instances, these provisions should have relatively little effect so long as no
changes in statutory law are required.

6.4.2 Future negotiations

As discussed above, the administration's efforts to obtain renewal of fast-
track authority foundered on the issue of linking such authority to

---

[257] S. 123 (c), URAA, 19 USC s. 3533 (c).
[258] S. 131 (a), URAA, 19 USC s. 3551 (a).
[259] S. 132, URAA, 19 USC s. 3552. See Art. 9, Agreement on Rules of Origin.
[260] See p. 220.   [261] S. 125 (a), URAA, 19 USC s. 3535 (a).
[262] See p. 223.

environmental protection and labour rights. Thus the United States is for the first time since 1974 without negotiating authority for trade agreements (other than the brief lapse in 1988).[263] The implementing legislation does, however, contain some explicit negotiating authority, and arguably some implicit negotiating authority.

Section 135 of URAA sets forth 'objectives for extended negotiations' regarding trade in financial services, telecommunications services, and civil aircraft. The legal effect of these provisions is unclear. At least implicitly, they extend the President's negotiating authority, or acknowledge negotiating authority in the absence of such legislation. The identification of 'principle negotiating objectives' tracks the language in Section 1101 of the 1988 Act, but one could not really argue that the language extends fast-track authority for those specific negotiations. Thus any agreement which required changes in United States law would require implementing legislation that, at least as of this date, would not benefit from fast-track procedures.

Implementation of the most-favoured-nation obligation under GATS may pose a particularly difficult problem. The schedule of commitments by the United States (Schedule XX) contains numerous exceptions for both most-favoured-nation and national treatment.[264] The former exceptions are, in principle, to be eliminated within ten years.[265] Many of these, however, are state laws.

6.5 CONCLUSIONS

The implementation of trade agreements in the United States remains a highly political process. Perhaps unlike earlier major trade enactments (with the recent exception of NAFTA), it has become a highly public process. Although both Congress and the President largely intended that the implementation comply with the Uruguay Round Agreements, the process also suggests a willingness to tread close to the limit (in part by

[263] The 'Trade Agreement Implementation Reform Act', S. 577, was introduced by Sen. Lugar on 17 Mar. 1995 (141 Cong. Rec. S4148–02). This bill would provide fast-track authority for regional, bilateral and multilateral trade agreements. The bill attempts to limit future implementing legislation benefitting from the fast-track procedure to 'necessary provisions', but the definition of that term is so broad that it is doubtful that any provision in the URAA would have been excluded on that basis. However, a point could be made by any senator against a provision that is not a 'necessary provision', and if the point were sustained by a majority, the provision would be stricken. Ibid., s. 4 (a). More recently, the 'Trade Agreements Authority Act of 1995' was introduced in the House of Representatives, H.R. 2371. 141 Cong. Rec. H9451–09 (daily ed. 21 Sept. 1995).

[264] Recently, the US withdrew from the negotiations on financial services and indicated it would invoke an exception to the most-favoured-nation obligation for that sector.

[265] Art. II:2, GATS, and para. 6, Annexe on Article II Exemptions. It is doubtful that this is an enforceable obligation subject to the dispute settlement procedures.

adopting disputable interpretations of the agreements) and to exploit any opening left by the agreements for protectionist interests. This is potentially problematic in light of the many questions left open by the agreement, and the interpretive authority granted to the WTO. As some of these questions are resolved, additional modifications may be necessary. In most cases, the legislation leaves the executive with sufficient authority to comply with future agreements. But Congress intentionally made it much more difficult to achieve compliance by inserting procedural hurdles to complying with dispute settlement decisions and by failing to provide expedited procedures for legislation.

The fast-track process seems again to have been an essential part of implementing the Uruguay Round. Perhaps ironically (or perhaps not), that process was at least a temporary casualty of the Uruguay Round. There is no doubt that the fast-track procedure is under attack on several fronts, and for several reasons. The formal conditionality of the process, although probably largely meaningless, has become the battleground for conflicting trade ideologies. One response may be to co-opt opposing forces into the process by creating additional advisory committees, as was done with trade and the environment.

Congress continued its policy of expanding the ability of United States enterprises to force the President and the USTR to take international action, while simultaneously closing United States courts to those wishing to challenge actions of the state or federal government as violative of international commitments. At every level, Congress made it more difficult to obtain changes to domestic law to conform it to international agreements. Ten years ago Jan Tumlir lamented that the 'proposal to enact the GATT code into domestic law binding on governments is impracticable'.[266] Although the implementation of the Uruguay Round results in the United States was a laudable advance in the mutlilateral trade régime, at the same time it moved the United States further away from the idealistic goal of direct application in domestic law. The consequence may be that disputes about the trade effects of laws and policies are necessarily resolved at the international level, rendering such disputes at least as much political as legal.

In sum, the URAA arguably represents a post-1930 highwater mark in Congressional assertion of influence in trade policy. Although the Act does implement the agreements, it constrains the authority of other governmental actors to apply those agreements beyond the precise terms Congress agreed to. Whether these constraints will constitute a serious obstacle to United States compliance with the agreements, or dispute settlement panel decisions interpreting them, remains to be seen.

[266] J. Tumlir, *Protectionism: Trade Policy in Democratic Societies* (1985) 65.

7

CANADIAN IMPLEMENTATION OF THE AGREEMENT ESTABLISHING THE WORLD TRADE ORGANIZATION

*Debra P. Steger**

7.1 INTRODUCTION

In Canada, the negotiation and implementation of international economic agreements requires delicate collaboration between the federal and provincial levels of government. The federal government has the power to negotiate and sign international agreements on behalf of Canada. Indeed, it is the federal executive, and not Parliament,[1] which has the authority to negotiate and conclude treaties. Within the last ten years, the federal government has developed an extensive, formal process for consultation and accommodation with the provincial governments and the private sector in the development of trade policy, including the negotiation and implementation of trade agreements. This is not decreed by the Constitution but results from the complex and fragile nature of Canadian federalism. The practice of federal–provincial relations in Canada is often characterized as the 'politics of accommodation'.

The Canadian Constitution provides for a division of powers between the federal and provincial governments. Legislative authority over specific subject-matter is divided between the federal and provincial levels of government in sections 91 and 92 of the Constitution Act.[2] The powers specified in section 91 are designated as exclusively within the authority of the federal government, and those specified in section 92 belong to the provincial governments. There are some matters for which both levels of government have shared jurisdiction.

* The author is indebted to D. Jeffrey Brown and Susan Hainsworth for their assistance in the preparation of this article. The views expressed in this article are those of the author, and not those of her present or former employers. At the time of writing of this article, the author was Hyman Soloway Professor of Business and Trade Law at the University of Ottawa Faculty of Law (Common Law). She is now Director, Appellate Body Secretariat, World Trade Organization.
[1] In Canada, 'Parliament' refers to the federal legislature, while its provincial counterparts are referred to as 'provincial legislatures'.
[2] 30 & 31 Vict., c. 3. It was originally called the British North America Act, 1867.

Since Confederation, the provinces have always had a great deal of autonomy over local matters. Subjects such as health, education, welfare and natural resources have long been recognized as being almost exclusively within provincial jurisdiction. Recent constitutional developments, including the failure to bring the province of Quebec fully within the new constitution in 1982, have resulted in enhanced sensitivities to the concerns of the provinces in the development of federal policy initiatives. It is simply a fact of Canadian political life that a delicate balancing of provincial and private interests must be taken into account, and that the provinces must be on side with any policy initiative of the federal government.

Although the federal executive has the exclusive power to negotiate and enter into treaties, the ability to implement aspects of international agreements into domestic law depends on the division of powers set out in sections 91 and 92 of the Constitution Act. In other words, authority to implement the provisions of an international agreement may rest with the federal government or with the provincial governments depending on who has the constitutional jurisdiction over the subject matter concerned. Determining which level of government has jurisdiction is the major question in implementing international agreements within the Canadian constitutional system.

Although the federal government's powers in this area were the subject of considerable controversy for almost one hundred years, recent Supreme Court of Canada jurisprudence appears to give the federal government sufficient powers to enact a general regulatory scheme designed to implement an international economic agreement that benefits and applies to the nation as a whole. As a matter of law, however, this question is far from settled.

The federal government has implemented three major international trade agreements in the last few years. The Canada–United States Free Trade Agreement Implementation Act[3] came into effect in 1989, the North American Free Trade Agreement Implementation Act[4] (NAFTA Act) in 1994 and the World Trade Organization Agreement Implementation Act[5] (WTO Act) in 1995. Each was implemented by means of an omnibus statute enacted by the Parliament of Canada. These statutes were drafted in a similar format. The first Part of each Act approves the Agreement, sets out its purposes and provides for general matters, such as the appointment of representatives to certain bodies under the Agreement and the powers of the Governor-in-Council to suspend concessions or obligations under the Agreement. Part II contains legislative amendments

[3] Stats. Can. 1988, c. 65.   [4] Stats. Can. 1993, c. 44.
[5] Stats. Can. 1994, c. 47.

necessary to bring existing Canadian legislation into conformity with the international obligations. Schedules to the Acts set out the amendments to the tariff schedules required to carry out the market access commitments of the Agreements.

In the case of each of these Agreements, the federal government selected the format of an omnibus bill designed to establish a general, national regulatory scheme in order to provide a sound constitutional basis for the implementing legislation. The bills introduced in Parliament have also been minimalist in character, that is, they contain only the amendments necessary to bring Canadian legislation into conformity with the obligations of the international agreement. The Government has avoided tacking on free riders or other major legislative changes that were not absolutely required to implement the treaty. This approach was perceived to be the most constitutionally defensible.

The negotiation and implementation of the Canada–United States Free Trade Agreement (CUSFTA) was extremely politically contentious in Canada. It was the major focus of the federal election campaign in 1988, and several provinces were opposed to it. Although political opposition to the North American Free Trade Agreement (NAFTA) was much less pronounced, some provinces, particularly Ontario and British Columbia, were also opposed to that agreement. Although all the provinces supported the Agreement Establishing the World Trade Organization (WTO Agreement) in principle, there were some aspects, such as the implementation of the tariffication requirements of the Agreement on Agriculture and some parts of the Agreement on Trade-Related Aspects of Intellectual Property Rights (TRIPs), which were controversial. Some of the provinces, most notably Ontario, Canada's largest province, threatened to challenge the federal government's actions in implementing the CUSFTA and the NAFTA in the courts, but to date, no formal constitutional challenge has been made.

Canada is a dualist state, following in the British legal tradition. International obligations, although binding on the federal government in international law, are not directly applicable or effective in domestic law. There must be an act of transformation in order for international treaty obligations to become applicable in domestic law. As a result of the doctrine of Parliamentary supremacy, Parliament or the legislatures of the provinces may legislate in contravention of Canada's international obligations; however, the courts will go to great lengths to interpret legislation in a manner which is consistent with the provisions of a treaty. Transformation may take place by the exercise of the Royal prerogative by the Governor-General or, in most instances, by federal or provincial legislative action, either primary or delegated. It is well-established law that the provisions of a treaty affecting the rights of private persons, requiring the expenditure of government monies or requiring changes in existing law, must be implemented by means of specific legislative action either by Parliament or by the provincial legislatures in order to become effective in Canadian law. As there is no specific provision in the Canadian Constitution giving the federal government power to implement treaties, the implementation of each new international agreement in Canada requires a careful co-ordination by the federal government with the provincial governments and private interests.

7.2 THE WORLD TRADE ORGANIZATION AGREEMENT IMPLEMENTATION ACT

7.2.1 General

The Uruguay Round of multilateral trade negotiations was the most extensive round ever in the history of the General Agreement on Tariffs and Trade (GATT). It resulted in over twenty agreements on a comprehensive range of subjects involving trade in goods, trade in services and trade-related intellectual property rights as well as institutional arrangements, including the establishment of the World Trade Organiza-tion (WTO), an integrated dispute settlement system[6] and the Trade Policy Review Mechanism.

The WTO Agreement represents a sea-change from the tariff and non-tariff barrier-reducing agreements that characterized previous multilateral trade negotiation rounds to a system comprised of numerous rules-based agreements. In the goods area, for example, there are twelve detailed agreements, in addition to the GATT 1994, which cover such diverse areas as trade in agriculture, textiles and clothing, subsidies and countervailing duty measures, anti-dumping, safeguards, technical barriers to trade, sanitary and phytosanitary measures, customs valuation, preshipment inspection, rules of origin, trade-related investment and import licensing. The General Agreement on Trade in Services (GATS) and the Agreement on Trade-Related Intellectual Property (TRIPs) are important new multilateral trade agreements. Some of the WTO agreements, such as the GATS, subsidies, anti-dumping, technical barriers to trade, sanitary and phytosanitary measures and TRIPs, include detailed substantive rules as well as procedural and due process requirements which require specific incorporation into domestic law.

The WTO Agreement was implemented in Canada by a single, omnibus statute enacted by the Parliament of Canada, the WTO Act.[7] It came into

---

[6] As a result of the Understanding on Rules and Procedures Concerning the Settlement of Disputes, Annex 2 to the WTO Agreement.   [7] See n. 5.

effect on 1 January 1995, and comprised some 145 pages, not including the Schedules implementing the tariff and other market-access commitments. The Governor-in-Council also promulgated delegated legislation or regulations implementing, in further detail, aspects of the WTO Agreement in early 1995. More regulations, particularly to implement the tariffication requirements of the Agreement on Agriculture and provisions of the Agreement on Textiles and Clothing are contemplated. This said, the Act is a minimalist statute that makes the amendments necessary to change previously existing statutes to ensure their compliance with the WTO Agreement. Numerous changes, for example to investment, services and intellectual property laws, had already been made to comply with the NAFTA in the NAFTA Act,[8] making the task of conforming to the WTO Agreement less onerous. However, some of the specific provisions relating to investment and services in the NAFTA Act were extended on a most-favoured-nation basis in the WTO Act.

Part I of the WTO Act contains a standard clause of approval of the WTO Agreement by Parliament, without giving the Agreement the force of law in Canada.[9] The purpose of the Act is to implement the Agreement.[10] Sections 5 and 6 prohibit a private party from bringing an action or proceedings of any kind to enforce or determine any right or obligation arising under Part I of the Act (which deals with implementation of the Agreement generally), or under the WTO Agreement itself, without the consent of the Attorney General of Canada. This effectively prevents private persons from bringing actions against federal or provincial legislative or administrative bodies to enforce rights or obligations under Part I of the Act or under the WTO Agreement, except for the usual type of actions under domestic law, including actions pursuant to amendments to specific legislation contained in Part II of the Act.

Section 4 provides that Her Majesty in Right of Canada is bound by the Act. Furthermore, Part I provides for Canada's participation in the new WTO institutions, in particular, it allows for the appointment of Canadian representatives to the Ministerial Conference and other committees, councils or bodies of the WTO; obliges the Government of Canada to pay its appropriate share of the expenditures of the WTO; and provides the mechanism for the Governor-in-Council to suspend the application of concessions or obligations, in accordance with Article 22 of the Under-standing on Rules and Procedures Governing the Settlement of Disputes for WTO Members, or otherwise for non-WTO Members.

Part II of the Act, which comprises 139 of the 145 pages, contains related and consequential amendments to twenty-three federal statutes necessary to bring existing Canadian legislation into conformity with the WTO

---

[8] See n. 4.   [9] S. 8, WTO Act.   [10] S. 3, WTO Act.

Agreement.[11] The most extensive and controversial changes were those made to implement the Agreement on Agriculture and TRIPs. Major amendments were made to the Special Import Measures Act[12], the Canadian International Trade Tribunal Act[13] and the Customs Tariff[14] in order to comply with the Agreements on Subsidies and Countervailing Measures, Anti-Dumping, and Safeguards. Significant changes were made to the Western Grain Transportation Act[15] to conform to Canada's commitments with respect to export subsidies pursuant to the Agreement on Agriculture.

Article 4.2 of the Agreement on Agriculture, which requires the conversion of non-tariff barriers such as quantitative import restrictions and discretionary import licensing into ordinary customs duties, necessitated major changes to the Canadian Wheat Board Act,[16] the Export and Import Permits Act[17] and the Customs Tariff.[18] The scheme developed to convert existing quantitative restrictions and other non-tariff barriers on agricultural products into tariff-rate quotas is complex. In addition to certain changes made to the three Acts mentioned above, changes were also made to the Regulations under those statutes and to administrative practice. The Meat Import Act was repealed,[19] and the Canadian Wheat Board Act, which previously gave the Canadian Wheat Board a monopoly on the importation and exportation of wheat, wheat products, barley and barley products, was changed to allow the importation of those products without an import licence.[20] The administration of the new tariff-rate quotas will be done under the revised Export and Import Permits Act.[21] A number of agricultural products were added to the Import Control List, and imports of those products within the tariff-rate quota will require an import permit granted on a discretionary basis by the Department of Foreign Affairs and International Trade. In order to facilitate the new scheme, that Department has established Tariff-Rate Quota Advisory Committees, consisting of producers, processors, retailers, wholesalers, distributors and importers of the products covered by the tariff-rate

[11] Section numbers in the following references refer to sections in Part II of the WTO Act setting out the amendments made to other pieces of legislation; except where specifically noted the section numbers are not those in the amended statutes themselves.

[12] Ss. 144–189, WTO Act.   [13] Ss. 27–47, WTO Act.
[14] Ss. 73–83, WTO Act.   [15] Ss. 212–19, WTO Act.
[16] Ss. 48–49, WTO Act. See also Dept of Foreign Affairs and International Trade, 'Agreement Establishing the World Trade Organization: Canadian Statement of Implementation' (Statement of Implementation), *Canada Gazette, Part I*, 31 Dec., 1994 at 4880–1.
[17] Ss. 100–14, WTO Act. See also Statement of Implementation at 4880–1.
[18] Ss. 73–83, WTO Act. See also Statement of Implementation at 4880–1.
[19] S. 140, WTO Act. See also Statement of Implementation at 4879–81.
[20] See n. 16.   [21] See n. 17.

quotas, to advise on matters related to the implementation and administration of the tariff-rate quotas.

Amendments were made to the Investment Canada Act to raise the thresholds for review of direct acquisitions for WTO Members to the same level as that for United States' and Mexican investors under the NAFTA Act.[22] In fact, the Canadian Government went beyond its obligations under the GATS and extended these new higher thresholds to acquisitions of goods-providers as well as services-providers. Other changes to effect compliance with the GATS included amendments to five statutes governing federal financial institutions. Amendments to the Bank Act,[23] the Cooperative Credit Associations Act,[24] the Insurance Companies Act,[25] the Investment Companies Act[26] and the Trust and Loan Companies Act[27] were required to implement the national treatment and most-favoured-nation commitments in the GATS and to eliminate discrimination against foreign-owned companies. These Acts had been partially liberalized as a result of the NAFTA Act, but the WTO Act amendments eliminated the remaining discrimination against all WTO Members.

Second only to the changes made to comply with the Agreement on Agriculture, the amendments required in the TRIPs area, particularly with respect to performers' rights, were the most controversial with private interest groups. The Copyright Act was amended to specifically provide protection for a performer's performance by prohibiting unauthorized fixation or subsequent reproduction of performances by other means, including sound recordings and broadcasting.[28] Criminal sanctions were added to prohibit infringement of the new performers' right,[29] and the Copyright Board was given the authority to determine the compensation payable for restoration of copyright or performers' rights.[30] The Patent Act,[31] the Industrial Design Act[32] and the Trade-marks Act[33] were amended to permit applications by WTO Members. Changes were also made to the Trade-marks Act to comply with the provisions of the TRIPs Agreement dealing with geographical indications.[34]

[22] Ss. 132–5, WTO Act. See also Statement of Implementation at 4933–4.
[23] Ss. 14–26, WTO Act. See also Statement of Implementation at 4933–4.
[24] Ss. 50–5, WTO Act. See also Statement of Implementation at 4933–4.
[25] Ss. 119–28, WTO Act. See also Statement of Implementation at 4933–4.
[26] Ss. 136–9, WTO Act. See also Statement of Implementation at 4933–4.
[27] Ss. 202–11, WTO Act. See also Statement of Implementation at 4933–4.
[28] S. 58, WTO Act. See also Statement of Implementation at 4938–9.
[29] S. 64, WTO Act. See also Statement of Implementation at 4938–9.
[30] S. 68, WTO Act. See also Statement of Implementation at 4938–9.
[31] S. 141, WTO Act. See also Statement of Implementation at 4938–9.
[32] S. 118, WTO Act. See also Statement of Implementation at 4938–9.
[33] Ss. 194, 199, WTO Act. See also Statement of Implementation at 4938–9.
[34] Ss. 190–2, WTO Act. See also Statement of Implementation at 4938–9.

7.2.2 Anti-dumping and Subsidies and Countervailing Measures Agreements

In order to implement its obligations under the Agreement on the Implementation of Article VI of the GATT 1994 (the Anti-Dumping Agreement) and the Subsidies and Countervailing Measures Agreement (the SCM Agreement), Canada made extensive amendments to the Special Import Measures Act (SIMA) and the regulations under that Act. Related amendments were also made to the Canadian International Trade Tribunal Act (CITT Act) and the Canadian International Trade Tribunal Rules. To gain insight into the interaction between international obligations and Canadian domestic law, this section examines in detail the Canadian implementation of the Anti-Dumping and SCM Agreements. The WTO Act amendments to SIMA are interesting for two reasons: (1) they were extensive, more extensive than necessary simply to implement the changes required by the WTO Agreement, and (2) they include specific mechanisms for executive action required to implement the results of dispute settlement rulings, Subsidies Committee determinations and arbitration findings in the future.

As noted above, the federal government implemented the WTO Agreement through the enactment of an omnibus statute, the WTO Act. The general approach was to make the amendments necessary to bring existing federal legislation into conformity with Canada's international obligations under the WTO Agreement, nevertheless, the revisions made to SIMA were more extensive than strictly necessary to conform with specific changes made in the Anti-Dumping and SCM Agreements. Canada's implementation of the 1979 Tokyo Round agreements on Subsidies/Countervail and Anti-Dumping[35] was effected in the SIMA of 1984.[36] However, that legislation did not replicate exactly the language of the Tokyo Round agreements. The language of the 1984 SIMA was less detailed, and in some aspects, the concepts were somewhat different, from the Tokyo Round agreements.

The WTO-related SIMA revisions achieve greater precision in the implementation of the Anti-Dumping and SCM Agreements by mirroring certain language and concepts contained in those Agreements. These amendments to SIMA can be separated into two types. First, certain revisions were made to incorporate precise language that had not changed since the Tokyo Round agreements. In particular, these included changes to the 'material injury' provisions and to the definition of 'domestic industry'. Second, other revisions were made to incorporate language and

---

[35] Agreement on Interpretation and Application of Articles VI, XVI and XXIII (1979) BISD 26S/56; and Agreement on Implementation of Article VI (1979) BISD 26S/171.
[36] R.S.C. 1985, c. S-15, as amended.

concepts which were new in the Anti-Dumping and SCM Agreements. These included the incorporation of the definition of 'subsidy', including the concept of 'financial contribution'; the addition of a 'standing requirement'; the *de minimis* threshold criteria; provisions on cumulation of injury from different sources; and new rules concerning undertakings.

Under the revised injury provisions, the Canadian International Trade Tribunal (the CITT) is required to determine whether the dumping or subsidizing of goods 'has caused injury or retardation or is threatening to cause injury.'[37] This replaces the former injury test of 'has caused, is causing or is likely to cause material injury or has caused or is causing retardation.'[38] The new section 42 explicitly separates 'injury' and 'threat of injury' into two distinct concepts. The changes make it clear that if the CITT makes a finding of injury, it is not necessary to proceed to an examination of whether threat of injury also exists. Formerly, due to the wording of the previous legislation, the CITT made a finding with respect to 'likelihood of future injury' after having made findings concerning past and present injury in every case. On one interpretation of the prior section 3 of SIMA,[39] it was believed that Revenue Canada did not have the authority to impose duties on dumped or subsidized goods imported after a CITT finding of injury unless there was also a finding of likelihood of future injury.

Other consequential changes to SIMA were required to implement this new injury test. Thus, an investigation may only be initiated where there is evidence disclosing a 'reasonable indication' that the dumping or subsidizing of goods 'has caused injury or retardation or is threatening to cause injury'.[40] 'Threat of injury' is defined as meaning that the circumstances in which the dumping or subsidizing of goods would cause injury are 'clearly foreseen and imminent', reflecting the language in the WTO agreements.[41] Furthermore, the SIMA definition of 'retardation' is now framed in terms of the 'domestic industry', rather than in terms of the 'production in Canada of like goods'.[42] Rules for injury determination, including the critical element of causation, are more fully fleshed out in the revised administrative regulations promulgated under SIMA.

The new 'standing' requirements for the initiation of an anti-dumping or subsidy investigation in SIMA follow the language in the Anti-Dumping and SCM Agreements.[43] This is an innovation in Canadian law, as there

[37] S. 169, WTO Act. See Art. 3 (fn. 9) Anti-Dumping Agreement, and Art. 15 (fn. 45) SCM Agreement.   [38] S. 42, SIMA. See n. 36.   [39] See n. 36.
[40] S. 160, WTO Act.
[41] S. 144 (4), WTO Act, (now s. 2 (1.5), SIMA); Art. 3.7 Anti-Dumping Agreement and Art. 15.7 SCM Agreement.
[42] See Art. 3 (fn. 9) Anti-Dumping Agreement, and Art. 15 (fn. 45) SCM Agreement.
[43] S. 160, WTO Act (now s. 31 (2), SIMA), based on Art. 5.4 Anti-Dumping Agreement and Art. 11.4 SCM Agreement.

was previously no explicit, statutory standing requirement except for the incorporation by reference of Article 4 of the Tokyo Round Anti-Dumping Agreement, which, in the definition of 'domestic industry', refers to 'a major proportion of the total domestic production of like products'.[44]

The new SIMA definition of 'domestic industry' expressly incorporates the language of Article 4 of the Anti-Dumping Agreement and Article 16 of the SCM Agreement, including the provisions relating to regional industries. Previously, these provisions were incorporated by reference in section 42 (3). In the SIMA definitions of 'injury' and 'retardation', the 'domestic industry' concept replaces the language in the former legislation which referred to the 'production in Canada of like goods'.[45]

The definition of 'subsidy', and the criteria and conditions for the determination of the 'specificity' of a subsidy in the SCM Agreement,[46] have also been incorporated directly into SIMA.[47] The revised SIMA now bases the concept of subsidy on 'the benefit to the recipient' rather than upon 'the cost to government', and defines 'financial contribution'[48] as it is defined in the SCM Agreement.[49] Following the approach in the SCM Agreement,[50] SIMA permits a certain degree of discretion in determining specificity, thus, even if a subsidy is not limited to a particular enterprise, the Deputy Minister of National Revenue (Deputy Minister) can determine that specificity nevertheless exists under certain enumerated circumstances.[51] These revisions are a welcome addition to Canadian law. Previously, although there was a very general definition of the term 'subsidy', in SIMA, there were no further detailed legislative or regulatory provisions setting out how the Deputy Minister determined what was a 'countervailable subsidy'. The SIMA definition of 'prohibited subsidy' also corresponds to the criteria set out in the SCM Agreement.[52] The WTO Act has included the SCM Agreement definition and criteria for so-called 'green light' or 'non-actionable subsidies'.[53]

Reflecting the *de minimis* criteria in the Anti-Dumping and SCM Agreements, SIMA now provides that an investigation may be terminated in respect of goods from a country where the margin of dumping or the amount of subsidy is 'insignificant' or the volume of dumped or subsidized

[44] S. 42 (3), SIMA. See n. 36.

[45] Definitions of 'material injury' and 'retardation' in s. 2 (1), SIMA.

[46] Art. 2.1 (a)–(b).

[47] S. 144 (6), WTO Act, (now s. 2 (7.1–7.2), SIMA).

[48] S. 144 (4), WTO Act (now s. 2 (1.6), SIMA).   [49] Art. 14.

[50] Art. 2.1 (c).

[51] S. 144 (6), WTO Act (now s. 2 (7.3), SIMA).

[52] Art. 3, i.e. an export subsidy or a subsidy contingent on the use of local goods.

[53] See s. 144 (3), WTO Act (now s. 2 (1), SIMA); i.e., subsidies which are not actionable although they may be specific, as set out in Art. 8, Part IV of the SCM Agreement. See discussion below.

goods, actual or potential, is 'negligible'.[54] The definitions for 'insignificant' and 'negligible' are based upon those in the Anti-Dumping and SCM Agreements. The revised SIMA also includes new rules for the calculation of the margin of dumping and the amount of subsidy, allowing, *inter alia*, for the investigation to be terminated with respect to goods from a country whose exports have been determined to be *de minimis*.

For the first time, SIMA provides explicitly for the assessment of cumulative injurious effect where imports from more than one country are under investigation under certain circumstances.[55] Although the CITT, and its predecessors, the Canadian Import Tribunal and the Anti-Dumping Tribunal, have in practice usually cumulated the effects of imports from various sources under investigation, there was previously no express requirement in Canadian law to do so.

Changes in the Anti-Dumping and SCM Agreements concerning the acceptance of undertakings necessitated major revisions to the SIMA provisions on undertakings. Whereas previously in Canadian law, an undertaking could only be accepted before a preliminary determination by the Deputy Minister on the issue of dumping or subsidization had been made, SIMA now requires a prior preliminary determination as a prerequisite for the acceptance of an undertaking.[56] This amendment will add complexities to the domestic administrative process, as undertakings can now be accepted by the Deputy Minister during the injury inquiry by the CITT, up to the time when the final determination on dumping or subsidization by the Deputy Minister is made. The revised SIMA also contains an obligation to complete a subsidy investigation and injury inquiry where the government of the exporting country so requests,[57] new provisions on duty liability[58] and on the termination, review and renewal of undertakings.[59]

In addition to the amendments made to SIMA, changes were made to the SIMA regulations concerning such subjects as additional information

---

[54] See ss. 165, 167, WTO Act (now ss. 35, 41, SIMA).

[55] S. 169, WTO Act (now s. 42 (3), SIMA); Art. 3.3 Anti-Dumping Agreement, and Art. 15.3 SCM Agreement.

[56] S. 171 (3), WTO Act (now s. 49 (2)(b), SIMA).

[57] Ss. 171 (4), 172, WTO Act (now ss. 49 (3), 50 (a)(iii), and 50 (b), SIMA). See Art. 8.4 Anti-Dumping Agreement and Art. 18.4 SCM Agreement.

[58] Ss. 145–6, WTO Act (now ss. 3–4, SIMA).

[59] Ss. 174–5, WTO Act (now ss. 52–3, SIMA); Art. 11 Anti-Dumping Agreement and Art. 21 SCM Agreement. For example, except where the CITT has made an order or finding that the dumping or subsidizing of the goods to which a preliminary determination applies has caused injury or retardation or is threatening to cause injury and that order or finding has not been rescinded, the Deputy Minister must review the undertaking within 5 years of its acceptance. Where the Deputy Minister is satisfied that the undertaking continues to serve its intended purpose and is not subject to termination, the Deputy Minister shall renew it for a further period not exceeding 5 years.

to be included in properly documented complaints; the time period after which undertakings may no longer be accepted by the Deputy Minister; factors to guide the CITT in its inquiry into injury, threat of injury or material retardation, as well as factors establishing the requisite causal link between alleged dumping or subsidization and injury; and guidelines for calculation of a subsidy to reflect the change from the 'cost-to-government' to the 'benefit-to-recipient' basis.

As a result of Canada's dualist approach to international legal obligations, such obligations are binding upon the federal government in international law, but they are not directly effective in domestic law. International obligations must be directly implemented in domestic law in order to render them effective in the domestic legal order. SIMA contains three important mechanisms whereby the executive may act in future to implement the specific results of WTO dispute settlement proceedings, or of the WTO Committee on Subsidies and Countervailing Measures ('the Subsidies Committee') or arbitration decisions under the SCM Agreement, or to apply retaliatory measures allowed under the DSU.

The first illustration of the inter-relationship between domestic law and international legal obligations relates to 'non-actionable' subsidies. SIMA has incorporated the definition and criteria for so-called 'green light' or 'non-actionable subsidies' from Article 8 of the SCM Agreement. That Article requires the notification to the Subsidies Committee of any subsidy a WTO Member wishes to declare as 'non-actionable', providing it meets the specified conditions and criteria set out in Article 8.2 of the SCM Agreement. Where a notification has been made concerning one of an enumerated list of programmes, such a programme is free from challenge under the SCM Agreement or under domestic countervail legislation. However, because it would still be possible for private parties to file a complaint under domestic countervail legislation, it was necessary to provide a mechanism in SIMA precluding the investigation of subsidies which qualify as non-actionable under the SCM Agreement. Accordingly, under SIMA,[60] the Deputy Minister may not initiate an investigation relating to a subsidy which has been notified as being non-actionable.[61] However, upon request by a WTO Member, the Subsidies Committee must review a notification of a subsidy programme to determine its consistency with the criteria set out in Article 8. A WTO Member may refer such a determination by the Subsidies Committee, or its failure to make such a determination, or the alleged violation of the conditions of the notified programme, to binding arbitration.[62] Therefore, a domestic legal

---

[60] S. 161, WTO Act (now ss. 31.1 (1)–(3), SIMA).
[61] In accordance with Arts. 8.3, 10 (fn. 35) SCM Agreement.
[62] Arts. 8.3, 8.4, and 8.5 SCM Agreement.

procedure had to be devised to deal with the situation where a subsidy notified to the Subsidies Committee was found not to meet the non-actionable criteria either by the Subsidies Committee or as a result of binding arbitration. Accordingly, SIMA provides the Deputy Minister with the authority to initiate an investigation in respect of a notified subsidy which has subsequently been determined, or re-determined, by the Subsidies Committee or by binding arbitration, not to be non-actionable. A determination by the Subsidies Committee or an arbitration body that a subsidy is not 'non-actionable' does not automatically trigger an investigation by the Deputy Minister, rather he may, in his discretion, initiate an investigation or include that subsidy in an ongoing investigation.

SIMA also covers the situations where the Deputy Minister determines pursuant to an investigation that a subsidy not notified to the Subsidies Committee qualifies in fact as a non-actionable subsidy,[63] or that a subsidy determined by the Subsidies Committee or an arbitration body to be non-actionable is in fact actionable due to substantial modification in its nature.[64] In such situations, the Deputy Minister must notify the Deputy Minister of Finance and the domestic complainant. On receipt of this notification, the Deputy Minister of Finance must notify the Deputy Minister of International Trade and any other person who, in the opinion of the Deputy Minister of Finance, is interested.[65] In the case of a subsidy determined, in whole or in part, to be non-actionable, the Deputy Minister's notification to the Deputy Minister of Finance will terminate all further investigation with respect to that subsidy, or part thereof, on the part of the Deputy Minister.[66] On the other hand, where a subsidy is determined to be actionable, SIMA leaves some discretion to the competent authorities concerning whether and how the subsidy should be dealt with.

As a result of Canada's dualist approach to implementation of its treaty obligations, a legislative mechanism was also adopted in SIMA to enable the government to deal with the results of WTO dispute settlement proceedings in anti-dumping and in countervail cases. Under the Canadian Constitution, WTO Dispute Settlement Body (DSB) recommendations and rulings are not directly applicable in domestic law. A vehicle was therefore necessary to transform internationally-binding DSB rulings into Canadian domestic law. The new SIMA section 76.1 provides the Minister of Finance with the authority to request the relevant investigating

---

[63] S. 161, WTO Act (now s. 31.1 (4)(a), SIMA).
[64] S. 161, WTO Act (now s. 31.1 (4)(b), SIMA).
[65] S. 161, WTO Act (now s. 31.1 (5), SIMA).
[66] This must be read in conjunction with s. 159, WTO Act (now s. 30.4 (3), SIMA), requiring that 'an amount of subsidy shall not include any amount that is attributable to a non-actionable subsidy'.

authority, the Deputy Minister or the CITT, to review all or any portion of its decision, determination, order or finding in the light of a DSB recommendation or ruling concerning that authority's decision or order.

Any such review conducted by the CITT or the Deputy Minister is also potentially subject to judicial review in the courts or to NAFTA Chapter 19 binational panel review where one of the exporting countries is the United States or Mexico. It is interesting that the means chosen to implement DSB rulings and recommendations that are binding upon Canada in international law is discretionary in nature—first, in that the Minister of Finance *may* request the authority to review its decision; and secondly, in that the authority may decide, as a result of its review, to continue its original decision or to modify it as the authority deems appropriate, but it is not bound to follow the DSB ruling. As the DSB rulings and recommendations are not recognized as part of Canadian domestic law, it is questionable whether they alone could form the basis for an application for judicial review.

The third interesting illustration of the interaction between the domestic and international levels of legal obligation relates to executive action taken to suspend concessions or other obligations under Article 22 of the DSU, where another WTO Member has failed to implement a DSB recommendation or ruling within the terms of the DSU. As mentioned above, the WTO Act provides a general mechanism, not limited to anti-dumping and countervail cases, whereby the Governor-in-Council may suspend, pursuant to Article 22 of the DSU, concessions or obligations under the WTO Agreement. Section 13 of the WTO Act provides that the Governor-in-Council may suspend concessions or obligations in accordance with the WTO Agreement by suspending rights or privileges granted by Canada to another WTO Member or to its goods, service-suppliers, investors or investments under the WTO Agreement or any federal law. Section 13 (1) states that any such action may be taken 'for the purpose of suspending in accordance with the Agreement the application to a WTO Member of concessions or obligations of equivalent effect pursuant to Article 22' of the DSU.

The Statement of Implementation[67] emphasizes that the Government of Canada will be vigilant about the implementation by its trading partners of

---

[67] The Statement of Implementation (see n. 16) is an official government document prepared by the Dept of Foreign Affairs and International Trade and published in the *Canada Gazette*. According to its introduction, it 'sets out the Government of Canada's general interpretation of the rights and obligations contained within the [WTO] Agreement and reflected in the [WTO Act]' (at 4847). However, its status in domestic law is unclear; it has not been implemented as a regulation and does not have the force of law. In contrast to the domestic law and practice of the US where legislative history is an accepted aid to statutory interpretation, as a general rule, Canadian courts do not examine legislative history except where the wording of the legislation is ambiguous or unclear.

the Anti-Dumping and SCM Agreements. It states that Canada intends to use the enhanced surveillance and dispute settlement mechanisms available under the WTO Agreement to monitor, and if necessary, to challenge the legislation and policies of its major trading partners, particularly the United States, if they do not comply fully with the Agreement. The Statement highlights that Canada would pay particular attention to United States' implementation of the Agreement, and to the impact on Canadian exporters of certain provisions in the United States' implementing legislation and statement of administrative action relating to anti-dumping and subsidies and countervail. In the anti-dumping context, the issues of causality and determination of injury were highlighted. In the subsidies context, the 'effects' test under the definition of subsidy, the countervailability of export controls, the determination of specificity and the establishment of a causal link between subsidized goods and injury being suffered by the domestic industry were emphasized as potential problems in the United States' implementing legislation.

Within the Government of Canada, the Department of Finance is primarily responsible for development of policy and legislation relating to trade remedies, including the SIMA and the CITT Act. As is the usual practice with legislative proposals, there was a comprehensive inter-departmental process, involving other interested governmental departments (Department of Justice, Department of Foreign Affairs and International Trade, and Department of Industry) as well as the relevant administrative authorities (Revenue Canada and the Canadian International Trade Tribunal) in developing the WTO revisions to the SIMA and the CITT Act. The legislative proposals were worked up in this interdepartmental process over several months from the end of 1993 to mid-1994. A detailed drafting phase followed during the latter part of 1994.

Consultations with private sector and concerned interest groups, allowing public comments and input into the domestic implementation process, occurred in two distinct phases of the preparation of the WTO Act. The first involved statutory amendments to SIMA, while the second involved consequential amendments to the regulations under SIMA. There were informal consultations with the private sector during the government's preparation of Bill C–57, as well as more formal input after the bill was introduced in Parliament, during its review by the House of Commons Standing Committee on Foreign Affairs and International Trade and the Senate Standing Committee on Foreign Affairs.[68] In particular, testimony

---

[68] See House of Commons, Minutes of Proceedings and Evidence of the Standing Committee on Foreign Affairs and International Trade respecting Bill C–57, An Act to implement the Agreement Establishing the World Trade Organization, Issue Nos. 9–13, 5 Oct. and 3, 14–17 Nov., 1994; and Senate of Canada, Proceedings of the Standing Senate Committee on Foreign Affairs respecting Bill C–57, An Act to implement the Agreement Establishing the World Trade Organization, Issue Nos. 9–11, 13–15 Dec., 1994.

was heard concerning the amendments to SIMA and the CITT Act on 14, 16 and 17 November 1994 by the House Standing Committee on Foreign Affairs and International Trade, and by the Senate Standing Committee on Foreign Affairs from 13–15 December 1994. These hearings provided an opportunity for public comment, including testimony from representatives of business (for example, the Canadian Chamber of Commerce), industry (for example, the Canadian Steel Producers Association), and agriculture (for example, the Canadian Federation of Agriculture) as well as experienced trade lawyers and academics. During these Committee hearings, concern was expressed regarding the WTO dispute settlement process, including the composition of dispute settlement panels and the means by which the CITT and the Deputy Minister would review their decisions in the light of DSB rulings and recommendations. Considerable attention was paid to the US implementing legislation and the Dole Bill proposal for review of WTO Panel or Appellate Body Reports by a judicial commission. Witnesses emphasized the benefits of strengthened WTO disciplines relating to anti-dumping and subsidies and countervail, together with the more rigorous dispute settlement machinery. With respect to the second phase of domestic implementation, concerning revisions to the administrative regulations under SIMA and the CITT Act, public comment was accepted by means of written submissions from industry and academic participants up until March 1995.

In order to fulfil its obligations under NAFTA Chapter 19 concerning any proposed amendments to its trade remedy legislation, Canada consulted with its NAFTA partners on the draft amendments to the SIMA and the CITT Act prior to the enactment of the WTO Act,[69] as well as on the modifications to the regulations promulgated under those Acts.

Consistent with its notification obligations under the Anti-Dumping and the SCM Agreements,[70] Canada presented the full final texts of its relevant amended legislation and regulations to the WTO Committees on Anti-Dumping Practices and on Subsidies and Countervailing Measures in June, 1995. Canada's legislation was reviewed at a joint special meeting of those Committees in October 1995, as part of a process of oral and written inquiries and responses on certain aspects of the Canadian legislation of concern to other WTO Members.

Apart from the amendments to the SIMA and the CITT Act, the legislative changes made to ensure compliance of existing Canadian law with the WTO Agreement were not very extensive. Existing Canadian legislation, in many cases, already complied with the WTO Agreement's

---

[69] Art. 1902 NAFTA requires a NAFTA Party to give prior notice to, and allow comments from, other NAFTA Parties that will be affected by statutory amendments to dumping or subsidy and countervail legislation.

[70] Arts. 18.5 and 32.6, respectively.

obligations. Implementation of the CUSFTA in 1989 and the NAFTA in 1994 had already resulted in major changes to domestic legislation affecting trade in services, investment, government procurement practices, intellectual property and textiles and clothing. These prior changes made Canadian compliance with the WTO Agreement easier to effect, and less controversial politically.

7.3 THE CANADIAN CONSTITUTION

In Canada, the key constitutional issue regarding implementation of the WTO Agreement is identifying which level of government has authority to implement the Agreement or, more precisely, parts of the Agreement. Canada's Constitution provides for a 'division of powers' between the federal and provincial governments. The question of which level of government has authority to implement an aspect of the Agreement hinges on its subject matter, and whether it falls within the federal or the provincial powers in the constitution.

In its modern form, Canada originated in an Act of the Imperial Parliament in London. The British North America Act, 1867 (now called the Constitution Act, 1867)[71] created a union among four Canadian provinces and established the basis on which the remaining provinces later joined Confederation.[72] The Preamble to the Constitution Act stated that the provinces were 'federally united into One Dominion under the Crown of the United Kingdom of Great Britain and Ireland, with a Constitution similar in Principle to that of the United Kingdom.' Union on these terms ensured that the constitutional division of powers in Canada would have two aspects. First, having a 'Constitution similar in Principle to that of the United Kingdom' meant that Canada imported the British parliamentary form of government, including its allocation of powers between the executive and the legislative branches of government. In contrast, Canada's federal nature added a dimension to Canadian constitutional law that the United Kingdom, a unitary state, lacked. Accordingly, the Constitution Act contains a codified federal–provincial division of powers.

In the context of implementation of the WTO Agreement, this two-dimensional division of powers gives rise to two constitutional issues, namely the authority to negotiate and sign treaties[73] and the authority to

---

[71] See n. 2.

[72] The original participants in Confederation were Ontario, New Brunswick, Nova Scotia, and Quebec. Six additional provinces subsequently joined: Manitoba (1870); British Columbia (1871); Prince Edward Island (1873); Alberta and Saskatchewan (1905); and Newfoundland (1949).

[73] The term treaty is here used as it is generally understood, i.e., any international agreement which is binding upon the parties in international law. A. E. Gotlieb, *Canadian Treaty-Making* (1968), 20.

implement treaties into domestic law. Each involves the division of powers between the executive and the legislature, as well as between the federal and provincial governments.

Following in British constitutional tradition, Canada is a dualist state. Customary international law is directly applicable in domestic law, but a treaty is not applicable unless there is an act of transformation specifically implementing it into domestic law.[74] With respect to treaties, the federal executive has the power to bind Canada in its relations with other sovereigns. Implementation of these obligations requires additional executive or, most likely, legislative action. Where legislative action is required, the major Canadian constitutional dilemma is whether the federal Parliament or a provincial legislature has the requisite jurisdiction.

7.3.1 Authority to negotiate and sign treaties

It is well-settled in Canadian constitutional law that the power to negotiate and enter into treaties rests with the federal executive. This power derives from English constitutional law, in which the common law accorded certain 'prerogative' powers and privileges to the Crown.[75,76] Prerogative powers are displaceable by Parliament, with the result that there are few left. None the less, '[t]he conduct of foreign affairs, including the making of treaties and the declaring of war, continues to be a prerogative power in Canada.'[77]

At the time of Confederation in 1867,[78] Canada lacked international personality. The Imperial government in London conducted Canada's foreign affairs, while section 132 of the Constitution Act provided a means by which the Government of Canada and Parliament could implement international obligations entered into by the Imperial Government on behalf of Canada. Canada gradually attained international personality over the next half century,[79] resulting in all of the Royal prerogative powers,

[74] H. M. Kindred et al., International Law: Chiefly as Interpreted and Applied in Canada, (5th edn. 1993) 147 f. The primary authority for Canada's adoptionist position regarding customary international law is Reference as to Powers to Levy Rates on Foreign Legations and High Commissioners' Residences (Foreign Legations), [1943] SCR 208. See also Municipality of Saint John et al. v. Fraser-Brace Overseas Corp. et al., [1958] SCR 263.
[75] P. W. Hogg, Constitutional Law in Canada (3rd (supplemented) edn. 1992) 1-11; Gotlieb, Canadian Treaty-Making, 4.
[76] In practice, executive powers are exercised by the Governor-General on the advice of the Governor-in-Council, which is the federal executive. Gotlieb, Canadian Treaty-Making, 4-5.   [77] Hogg, Constitutional Law, 1-13.
[78] Pursuant to the British North America Act, 1867 (now called the Constitution Act, 1867) (see n. 2).
[79] Kindred et al., International Law, 162. According to the SCC in Re Offshore Mineral Rights, [1967] SCR 792, at 816, Canada acquired sovereignty 'in the period between its separate signature of the Treaty of Versailles in 1919 and the Statute of Westminster, 1931, 22 Geo. V, c. 4.'

including the power to make treaties, being transferred from the Imperial Crown to the Governor-General of Canada.[80,81]

Treaty-making is also an exclusively federal power. The provinces may, and often do, enter into arrangements with foreign states, but such arrangements are not binding in international law. International law would recognize a provincial treaty-making power if, as Professor Hogg puts it, the Canadian Constitution 'clearly accorded that capacity'.[82] The Canadian Constitution, however, is silent on the issue, and there is little support for the view that the provinces have a treaty-making power. The federal government has never accepted the existence of such a power, and it appears unlikely that the Supreme Court of Canada would do so.[83] In *Re Offshore Mineral Rights*, which dealt with whether property rights in the bed of territorial sea adjacent to British Columbia rested with the province or the federal government, the Supreme Court of Canada implied that the Canadian constitution does not include a provincial treaty-making power:

[T]he rights in the territorial sea arise by international law and depend upon recognition by other sovereign states. Legislative jurisdiction in relation to the lands in question belongs to Canada which is a sovereign state, recognized by international law and thus able to enter into arrangements with other states respecting the rights in the territorial sea.[84]

It is well-established, therefore, that the power to negotiate and enter into international agreements on behalf of Canada rests exclusively with the federal executive.

7.3.2 Application of treaties in domestic law

7.3.2.1 General principles

With respect to international agreements, Canada is a dualist state, which means that treaties are not self-executing or directly applicable.[85] Treaties entered into and ratified by Canada do not have status in domestic law

---

[80] Canada's formal head of state is Queen Elizabeth II, but she is represented in Canada by the Governor-General. The Governor-General is appointed, but, in practice, he or she acts on the advice of the Prime Minister and the Cabinet.

[81] Gotlieb, *Canadian Treaty-Making*, 28; Hogg, *Constitutional Law*, 11-22.

[82] Hogg, *Constitutional Law*, 11-18.

[83] Ibid.; Gotlieb, *Canadian Treaty-Making*, 27; see also Kindred *et al.*, *International Law*, 162–6.

[84] [1967] Sch 792, 817.

[85] In contrast, customary international law is directly applicable and enforceable by the courts without any act of transformation. See n. 74.

until there is an act of transformation.[86] Some aspects of treaties may be implemented by the federal executive as an exercise of the Royal prerogative, but aspects that are inconsistent with existing laws, affect private rights or require the expenditure of public monies must be implemented by legislation.

In *Francis* v. *The Queen*, an aboriginal person relied on a treaty to argue that he was not subject to customs duties or sales tax for articles he had purchased in the United States and brought back to Canada. Rand J, speaking for the Supreme Court of Canada, set out the following test:

Speaking generally, provisions that give recognition to incidents of sovereignty or deal with matters in exclusively sovereign aspects, do not require legislative confirmation: for example, the recognition of independence, the establishment of boundaries and, in a treaty of peace, the transfer of sovereignty over property, are deemed executed and the treaty becomes the muniment or evidence of the political or proprietary title . . . Except as to diplomatic status and certain immunities and to belligerent rights, treaty provisions affecting matters within the scope of municipal law, that is, which purport to change existing law or restrict the future action of the Legislature, including, under our Constitution, the participation of the Crown, and in the absence of a constitutional provision declaring the treaty itself to be the law of the state, as in the United States, must be supplemented by statutory action.[87]

In this case, the treaty had not been implemented or sanctioned by legislation, and therefore, it was not enforceable in the courts.[88]

---

[86] *In Re Arrow River and Tributaries Slide and Boom Co.* [1932] 66 OLR 577, 2 DLR 216 (OCA); rev'd, [1932] 2 DLR 250 (SCC) at 260. The SCC reversed an Ontario Court of Appeal decision in which Riddell JA had held that only clear and explicit language would permit a legislature to contradict a treaty obligation of the Crown. The case concerned whether a treaty between Great Britain and the US guaranteeing 'free and open' access to certain rivers separating Canada and the US barred Ontario from allowing a company to collect tolls on the side of the river within its jurisdiction. The majority agreed the treaty had no effect on the provincial legislation because it was unimplemented.

The SCC reaffirmed this principle in *Capital Cities Communications Inc.* v. *Canadian Radio-Television Commission* [1978] 2 SCR 141. In addressing the applicability of an international radio communications convention to a federal government agency, Laskin CJ, speaking for six of nine judges, said at 173 '. . . [a submission based on a convention] can only relate to the obligations of Canada under the Convention towards other ratifying signatories. There would be no domestic, internal consequences unless they arose from implementing legislation giving the Convention a legal effect within Canada.'

[87] [1956] SCR 618, at 625; (1956) 3 DLR (2d) 641, at 647.

[88] See also *Attorney-General for Canada* v. *Attorney General for Ontario* [1937] AC 326 (JCPC), (*Labour Conventions*) at 347 where Lord Atkin said: 'Within the British Empire there is a well-established rule that the making of a treaty is an executive act, while the performance of its obligations, if they entail alteration of the existing domestic law, requires legislative action.'

7.3.2.2 Implementation of treaties

7.3.2.2.1 The executive power

As noted in *Francis*, not all treaties require legislative action to be implemented.[89] Some treaties or parts of treaties may be implemented by the executive under its prerogative power,[90] although the modern prerogative power is relatively narrow. In *Francis*, the Supreme Court of Canada held that the executive implementation power is generally restricted to treaties concerning recognition of the incidents of sovereignty, while legislation is required to implement treaty obligations that affect individual rights, or require the expenditure of public monies or changes to existing legislation.[91] Thus, while the executive may implement some treaty provisions, legislation is necessary to implement most international obligations.

7.3.2.2.2 Legislative implementation

As Canada is a federal state, the issue of whether the federal or provincial government has the jurisdiction to implement aspects of an international agreement is complex. It is the most important and difficult constitutional question concerning the domestic implementation of the WTO Agreement. It is also an issue that has not been tested directly, because there has been no constitutional challenge or reference to the Supreme Court of Canada involving legislative implementation of an international trade agreement. Certain provinces threatened to bring constitutional challenges against federal implementation of the CUSFTA and the NAFTA, but they never materialized.

7.3.2.2.2.1 Division of powers generally
The importance of the federal–provincial division of powers in the Canadian Constitution was expressed by Lord Atkin of the Judicial Committee of the Privy Council in *Labour Conventions*:

No one can doubt that this distribution is one of the most essential conditions, probably the most essential condition, in the inter-provincial compact to which the British North America Act gives effect.[92]

This division is set out primarily in sections 91 and 92 of the Constitution Act,[93] under which Parliament and the provincial legislatures are each

---

[89] See n. 87.
[90] Some may also be implemented by the executive under the authority of a statute delegating certain powers to Cabinet, or to a government department or departmental agency. This is known as delegated legislation or regulations. In a constitutional sense, however, such implementation derives from the legislative power.
[91] See n. 87.   [92] *Labour Conventions*, 351.   [93] See n. 2.

allocated enumerated powers. Pursuant to section 91, Parliament has, subject to the provincial powers listed in section 92, exclusive legislative authority over, among other matters:

- regulation of trade and commerce;
- any form of taxation;
- statistics;
- defence;
- navigation and shipping;
- sea coast and inland fisheries;
- banking;
- weights and measures;
- patents and copyrights;
- naturalization and aliens; and
- criminal law.[94]

Section 92 enumerates a list of 'Classes of Subjects' within which the provinces have exclusive legislative jurisdiction. These include:

- direct taxation within the province;
- municipal institutions within the province;
- management and sale of provincial public lands and of the timber and wood on such public lands;
- local works and undertakings;
- property and civil rights within the province; and
- all matters 'of a merely local or private nature' in the province.[95]

While both Parliament and the provinces have certain enumerated powers, Parliament has two additional sources of legislative authority. In the event of an apparent conflict between the enumerated powers in sections 91 and 92, the federal power is paramount.[96] Furthermore,

---

[94] Section 91 has also been interpreted by the courts as giving Parliament legislative jurisdiction over: tariffs and the movement of goods into Canada, *Citizens Insurance Company of Canada* v. *Parsons*, (1881) 7 AC 96 (JCPC); competition law (*Proprietary Articles Trade Assn.* v. *A.-G. Canada* [1931] AC 310 (JCPC)), trade marks (*MacDonald* v. *Vapor Canada Ltd.* [1971] 2 SCR 134), telecommunications (*In re The Regulation and Control of Radio Communication in Canada* [1932] AC 304 (JCPC)), aeronautics (*In re The Regulation and Control of Aeronautics in Canada* [1932] AC 54 (JCPC)), and offshore mineral resources (*Re Offshore Mineral Rights* [1967] SCR 792, and *Re Newfoundland Continental Shelf* [1984] 1 SCR 86).

[95] The section 92 enumerated powers are supplemented by a recent amendment in s. 92A, which gives the provinces jurisdiction over non-renewable resources, forestry and electrical energy. S. 95 designates agriculture as a shared power of Parliament and the provincial legislatures.

[96] See *Caloil Inc.* v. *The Attorney General of Canada*, [1971] SCR 543, at 550. The concluding words of section 91 also provide that any enumerated power within section 91 'shall not be deemed to come within the Class of Matters of a local or private Nature'.

Parliament has a residual power, that is, it has legislative jurisdiction over any matter not within the enumerated subject matters in sections 91 and 92.[97]

In summary, the division of powers set out in sections 91 and 92 may be summarized as follows:

The Dominion Parliament has, under the initial words of s. 91, a general power to make laws for Canada. But these laws are not to relate to the classes of subjects assigned to the Provinces by s. 92, unless their enactment falls under heads specifically assigned to the Dominion Parliament by the enumeration in s. 91. When there is a question as to which legislative authority has the power to pass an Act, the first question must therefore be whether the subject falls within s. 92. Even if it does, the further question must be answered, whether it falls also under an enumerated head in s. 91. If so, the Dominion has the paramount power of legislating in relation to it. If the subject falls within neither of the sets of enumerated heads, then the Dominion may have power to legislate under the general words at the beginning of s. 91.[98]

Sections 91 and 92 are worded so generally that, even though the courts may try to be as definitive as possible, some powers inevitably overlap and conflict, particularly when the subject matter is complex. It is not always possible to define federal and provincial powers in a mutually exclusive manner. Lord Fitzgerald acknowledged this in *Hodge* v. *The Queen*, where he said: 'subjects which in one aspect and for one purpose fall within Sect. 92, may in another aspect and for another purpose fall within Sect. 91.'[99] In Canadian constitutional law, Lord Fitzgerald's observation is known today as the 'double aspect doctrine'.[100]

International trade obligations tend to be all-pervasive in the economy. The principle of national treatment, for example, cuts across areas of federal and provincial economic regulation. The double aspect doctrine enables the federal government to obtain jurisdiction over an international aspect of an otherwise wholly provincial or local subject-matter. However, it also means that the provinces retain their rights to legislate with respect to the same subject matter, as long as the legislation affects a local aspect. Thus, in many areas of complex, economic activity, the federal and provincial governments have shared jurisdiction. This is what makes

---

[97] Parliament's residual power is also called 'the POGG power', because it derives from the first part of s. 91, in which Parliament is given power to make laws for the 'Peace, Order and good Government of Canada, in relation to all Matters not coming within the Classes of Subjects. . . . assigned exclusively to the Legislatures of the Provinces.'

[98] Viscount Haldane, in *Toronto Electric Commissioners* v. *Snider*, [1925] AC 396 (JCPC), at 406. The Supreme Court of Canada has existed since 1875, but it only became Canada's highest court in 1949. Prior to that date, Canada's highest court was the Judicial Committee of the Privy Council (JCPC) in London.   [99] (1883), 9 AC 117 (JCPC) at 130.

[100] Hogg, *Constitutional Law*, 15–11.

federal–provincial relations so difficult, and why the practice in Canada has come to be known as the politics of accommodation.

The courts use several analytical tools to resolve conflicts between sections 91 and 92. Of particular significance are those used to characterize a contested provision or statute.

> The characterization of a statute is often decisive of its validity, and the Court will obviously be aware of that fact. . . . What are the criteria of importance that will control or at least guide this crucial choice? No doubt, full understanding of the legislative scheme, informed by relevant extrinsic material, will often reveal one dominant statutory policy to which other features are subordinate. No doubt, too, judicial decisions on similar kinds of statutes will often provide some guide. But in the hardest cases the choice is not compelled by either the nature of the statute or the prior judicial decisions. The choice is inevitably one of policy.[101]

7.3.2.2.2.2 The legacy of *Labour Conventions*

Under section 132 of the Constitution Act, Parliament and the Government of Canada have the power to implement all treaties entered into by the Imperial Government on Canada's behalf (so-called Empire Treaties). As the power to make treaties passed to the federal executive when Canada attained international personality, the question arose as to whether it was accompanied by a federal power to implement those treaties. This issue was addressed in the 1937 decision of the JCPC in *Labour Conventions*,[102] which remains the leading case on this question. *Labour Conventions* concerned the validity of federal legislation implementing Canada's obligations under conventions adopted by the International Labour Organization under the Treaty of Versailles, which Canada had ratified. The particular obligations in issue dealt with labour standards which would unquestionably have been within provincial jurisdiction as matters relating to property and civil rights within the province had they been implemented outside the scope of the treaty. The federal government argued that the existence of the treaty put the matter within its jurisdiction.

Speaking for the JCPC, Lord Atkin rejected the federal arguments and held that there was no federal treaty implementation power. While he confirmed that the power to make treaties was solely the prerogative of the federal executive, he held that the power to implement treaties was divided between Parliament and the provincial legislatures according to the enumerated powers in sections 91 and 92 of the Constitution Act. This is the so-called 'watertight compartments' doctrine. He interpreted section 132 strictly, concluding that it had no application to treaties entered into by Canada after she had attained international personality. It applied, in his

---

[101] Hogg, *Constitutional Law*, 15-18.1.   [102] See n. 88.

view, only to Empire Treaties entered into by the Imperial Crown on behalf of Canada.

Most significantly, Lord Atkin asserted the importance of the federal–provincial division of powers:

For the purposes of ss. 91 and 92 . . . there is no such thing as treaty legislation as such. The distribution is based on classes of subjects; and as a treaty deals with a particular class of subjects so will the legislative power of performing it be ascertained. *No one can doubt that this distribution is one of the most essential conditions, probably the most essential condition, in the interprovincial compact to which the British North America Act gives effect.*[103]

Lord Atkin did not think this decision would unduly hamper Canada's ability to participate in international affairs:

In totality of legislative powers, Dominion and Provincial together, she [Canada] is fully equipped. But the legislative powers remain distributed, and if in the exercise of her new functions derived from her new international status Canada incurs obligations they must, so far as legislation be concerned, when they deal with Provincial classes of subjects, be dealt with by the totality of powers, in other words by co-operation between the Dominion and the Provinces. While the ship of state now sails on larger ventures and into foreign waters she still retains the watertight compartments which are an essential part of her original structure.[104]

Although many commentators believe that the decision has become an anachronism as Canada has become a modern state afloat in a sea of international commerce,[105] *Labour Conventions* remains good law. Maintaining the integrity of the division of powers in sections 91 and 92, as Lord Atkin so strongly emphasized, remains a priority of the courts.[106] Although the Supreme Court has yet to review the question of a federal treaty implementation power directly, it is possible that the Court could

---

[103] *Labour Conventions Case* at 351 (emphasis added).

[104] Ibid, at 354.

[105] Hogg, *Constitutional Law*, 11–12, 11–15. See also Scott H. Fairley, 'Implementing the Canada–United States Free Trade Agreement', in Donald M. McRae and Debra P. Steger (eds.), *Understanding the Free Trade Agreement* (1988) 195; and R. St. J. Macdonald, 'International treaty law and the domestic law of Canada' (1975) 2 *Dal. LJ* 307.

[106] For a recent example of a decision in which the Supreme Court re-iterated the importance of safeguarding the integrity of the federal–provincial division of powers, see the minority decision of Dickson J in *Attorney General of Canada* v. *C.N. Transportation Ltd.*, [1983] 2 SCR 206 (C.N. Transportation) where Dickson J developed several indicia for applying the general branch of the federal trade and commerce power. While the criteria, which were subsequently endorsed by a majority in *General Motors of Canada Ltd.* v. *City National Leasing*, [1989] 1 SCR 641; (1989), 58 DLR (4th) 255 (all references to DLR) generally had the effect of expanding the federal power, Dickson J also warned in *C.N. Transportation*, at 277, 'it is still necessary even in the face of all these factors to consider the issue of constitutional balance, and whether a finding of validity under the trade and commerce power might not erode the local autonomy in economic regulation contemplated by the Constitution.'

recognize a limited power by narrowing, rather than overruling, *Labour Conventions*.[107]

Even without a specific treaty implementation power, there are two other constitutional pillars which the federal government can use to justify its legislative implementation of the recent international trade agreements, most notably, the federal trade and commerce power and the national concern doctrine.

7.3.2.2.2.3 The Federal Trade and Commerce Power

One of Parliament's enumerated powers in section 91 of the Constitution Act is the regulation of trade and commerce. Since the 1881 decision of the JCPC in *Citizens Insurance Co. of Canada* v. *Parsons* (Parsons),[108] there has been no doubt that this power gives Parliament 'exclusive jurisdiction over the setting of tariffs and the regulation of the movement of goods into Canada'.[109] Beyond this, however, the extent of the power is uncertain, because there is potential overlap with the provincial power respecting property and civil rights. For example, the ability of Parliament to establish, for the provinces, certain standards with respect to the treatment of foreign services providers, including professional services, is a matter of great uncertainty.[110] The same may be said of certain other areas covered by the WTO Agreement that have a local aspect, such as technical barriers to trade, sanitary and phytosanitary measures, trade-related intellectual property, subsidies, trade-related investment measures and provincial and municipal government procurement practices.

In the early 1900s, the federal trade and commerce power was interpreted extremely narrowly. After the Supreme Court of Canada replaced the JCPC as Canada's highest court in 1949, it began to expand the power. The key early case was the 1881 decision in *Parsons*.[111] In that case, the JCPC noted that the basic problem respecting the scope of the trade and commerce power was that, if broadly construed, it could be sufficiently wide to include every regulation of trade, 'ranging from political arrangements in regard to trade with foreign governments, requiring the sanction of parliament, down to minute rules for regulating particular trades.'[112] Their Lordships held that, insofar as federal trade and

---

[107] For example, Professor Hogg suggests that *Labour Conventions* might be confined to treaties concerned with the harmonization of policies in accordance with certain shared values, while those through which states make mutual commitments to one another would be subject to a federal treaty implementation power 11-14 to 11-16.

[108] See n. 94.

[109] J. G. Castel, *et al.*, *The Canadian Law and Practice of International Trade with Particular Emphasis on Export and Import of Goods and Services* (Toronto: Edmond Montgomery, 1991) (1991), at 314.

[110] Ibid.   [111] See n. 94.   [112] *Parsons* at 112.

commerce power overlapped with the jurisdiction of the provinces, it consisted of two branches:

Construing therefore the words 'regulation of trade and commerce' by the various aids to their interpretation above suggested, they would include political arrangements in regard to trade requiring the sanction of parliament, regulation of trade in matters of interprovincial concern, and it may be that they would include general regulation of trade affecting the whole dominion.[113]

Neither branch, the JCPC decided, entitled the federal government to regulate contracts of a particular business or trade, in this case insurance, within a single province.[114]

Although *Parsons* divided the trade and commerce power into two branches, subsequent cases have dealt primarily with the interprovincial branch. The JCPC began narrowing its interpretation of that branch in its 1916 *Insurance Reference* decision.[115] Whereas *Parsons* stated that Parliament could not regulate contracts of a particular business within a single province, the *Insurance Reference* extended this prohibition to a particular trade whether or not its business was carried on within a single province.[116]

The *Insurance Reference* was followed by other judgments which took the interprovincial trade branch in a similar direction. In *Re The Board of Commerce*,[117] the Dominion unsuccessfully appealed to an argument now known as the 'provincial inability test',[118] that is, that the federal scheme addressed a situation prevailing throughout Canada that the provinces alone or together could not regulate. Similar arguments by the federal government also failed in *Toronto Electric Commissioners* v. *Snider*[119] and *The King* v. *Eastern Terminal Elevator Co.*[120] in the 1920s. The trend toward increasingly restrictive interpretations of the trade and commerce power ended with the 1931 decision in *Proprietary Articles Trade Assn.* v. *Attorney-General for Canada*,[121] where the JCPC reversed its holding in *Re Board of Commerce* that the trade and commerce power was an ancillary power. However, it was only after the Supreme Court replaced the JCPC as Canada's highest court that expansion of the trade and commerce power began in earnest.

---

[113] Ibid. at 113.   [114] Ibid.

[115] *Attorney-General for the Dominion of Canada* v. *Attorney-General for the Province of Alberta*, [1916] 1 AC 588 (JCPC).

[116] Ibid. at 596.

[117] *In re The Board of Commerce Act, 1919, and The Combines and Fair Prices Act, 1919* [1922] 1 AC 191 (JCPC). These Acts established an anticombines Board.

[118] See Dickson J in *C.N. Transportation*, at 268; Dickson CJ in *General Motors* at 269; and *R* v. *Crown Zellerbach Canada Ltd.*, [1988] 1 SCR 401, at 96.

[119] See n. 98.

[120] [1925] SCR 434. This case dealt with trade in grain.

[121] [1931] AC 310 (JCPC).

In the *Farm Products Marketing Reference*,[122] the Attorney-General of Canada challenged the constitutionality of a provincial scheme for 'the control and regulation in any or all aspects of the marketing within the Province of farm products'[123] on the ground that the scheme infringed the federal trade and commerce power. Although the provincial scheme was upheld, this case is none the less important. While a majority of the court based their decisions on the finding that the Act applied only to intraprovincial transactions, they went on to suggest that if such transactions had other interprovincial or foreign trade purposes, they would be within the scope of the federal trade and commerce power.

In *Murphy* v. *Canadian Pacific Railway Co.*,[124] the Supreme Court dealt with a constitutional challenge to the Canadian Wheat Board Act in the context of an *inter*provincial transaction. Under the Act, the Canadian Wheat Board had a monopoly with respect to the importation and exportation of grain. In addition, it was the exclusive marketing agent for grain grown by Canadian farmers. Murphy challenged the Act after the Canadian Pacific Railway Company, in accordance with the Act, rejected his request to transport wheat, oats, and barley out of the province. Murphy alleged that the Act was *ultra vires* Parliament, because it interfered with the provincial power over property and civil rights.

The Supreme Court held, however, that it was 'too clear for argument' that the Act was valid under the trade and commerce power insofar as it related to exported grain.[125] The fact that this would interfere with property and civil rights was, according to Locke J, 'immaterial', owing to the provision in section 91 that once a subject matter is identified as falling within section 91 it is treated as being outside section 92.[126] While the Canadian Wheat Board Act also applied to intraprovincial transactions, the court upheld the Act because it applied to interprovincial and international transactions.

The opportunity to consider the Act in light of an intraprovincial transaction arose soon after in *R.* v. *Klassen*.[127] Klassen operated a mill and was charged under the Act for failing to enter a delivery of wheat in a permit book. Unlike in *Murphy*, the wheat in question was produced, purchased, sold, and used in Manitoba. Klassen never engaged in interprovincial or foreign trade, nor was he aware of products from his mill being exported from the province. The Manitoba Court of Appeal upheld the legislation even as it applied to an intraprovincial transaction.[128] The

---

[122] *In the Matter of a Reference Respecting the Farm Products Marketing Act*, [1957] SCR 198.   [123] Ibid. at 202.
[124] *Murphy* v. *Canadian Pacific Railway* [1958] SCR 626.
[125] Ibid. at 631–2.   [126] Ibid.
[127] (1959), 20 DLR (2d) 406 (Man. CA).   [128] Ibid. at 412.

entire court, however, accepted that the overall purpose of the Act fell within the scope of the federal trade and commerce power, and that to exempt intraprovincial transactions from its scope would undermine the Canadian Wheat Board's quota system, thereby frustrating the Act's purpose. By refusing leave to hear an appeal of the decision in *Klassen*, the Supreme Court of Canada effectively extended its holding in *Murphy* to intraprovincial transactions.

As Professor Hogg has observed:

The *Klassen* decision was a striking departure from the course of Privy Council decisions, which had consistently decided that federal regulation under the trade and commerce power could not embrace wholly intraprovincial transactions, even when the main object was to regulate the interprovincial or export trade.[129]

The Supreme Court further clarified the relationship between the trade and commerce power and the provincial power over property and civil rights in *Caloil Inc.* v. *Attorney-General of Canada*.[130] In *Caloil*, an oil importer challenged the validity of a federal regulation that prohibited the sale of imported oil east of the Manitoba border. The court unanimously upheld the legislation, finding that the prohibition was an 'integral part of a scheme for the regulation of international or interprovincial trade'.[131]

Professor Hogg points out that it is difficult to gauge the influence of the interprovincial trade and commerce cases, because they involved commodities moving in interprovincial commerce. Nonetheless, they lend some support for the existence of a federal power where the market for a commodity is national or international.[132]

In comparison with the interprovincial branch, the general branch of the trade and commerce power has received much less judicial attention. Indeed, it was virtually ignored until *MacDonald* v. *Vapor Canada Ltd.*[133] in 1977.[134] In that case, at issue was section 7(e) of the Trademarks Act, which created a civil remedy against unethical business practices. The plaintiff claimed that it was *ultra vires* Parliament, because Civil remedies were within the jurisdiction of the provinces. Laskin CJ considered whether section 7(e) could be upheld as valid federal legislation under the

---

[129] Hogg, *Constitutional Law* at 20-6.   [130] See n. 96.   [131] Ibid. at 550.
[132] Hogg, *Constitutional Law*.   [133] See n. 94.
[134] In *General Motors*, Dickson CJ said (at 265): 'So far as I can gather, legislation has been upheld under the second branch by a final appellate court on only two occasions. In 1937, the Privy Council upheld a federal scheme creating a national trade mark to be used in conjunction with federally established commodity standards under the general trade and commerce power: *A.-G. Ont.* v. *A.G. Can.* [1937] 1 DLR 702, 67 CCC 342, [1937] AC 405 (PC). . . . The second occasion was in *John Deere Plow Co.* v. *Wharton* (1914), 18 DLR 353, [1915] AC 330, 7 WWR 635 (PC), where the Privy Council located the regulation of federally incorporated companies within the general branch of s. 91(2), although they also upheld the legislation under the "peace, order and good government" power.'

general branch of the trade and commerce power. He began by criticizing narrow interpretations of *Parsons* and said he was prepared to take a broad reading of that decision.[135] He then enunciated three criteria for determining whether a federal provision could be saved under the general trade and commerce power:

1. Is the provision part of a national regulatory scheme?
2. Is there continuing oversight by a regulatory agency? and
3. Is the legislation concerned with trade as a whole rather than a particular industry?[136]

Laskin CJ's comments about the general trade and commerce power in *Vapor* were *obiter dicta*. In 1983, Dickson J wrote a minority opinion in *Attorney-General* of *Canada* v. *Canadian National Transportation Ltd*.[137] that proved to be a major turning point. Dickson J expanded on Laskin CJ's approach in the context of anti-combines legislation. The specific issue in this case was whether Parliament could provide for federal prosecutors to prosecute a charge of conspiring to lessen competition. In resolving the issue, Dickson J relied on the three criteria set out by Laskin CJ in *Vapor* and added two additional indicia, which he regarded as being even more important:

4. Inability of the provinces to regulate together or alone; and
5. Ability of one province to undermine the scheme by opting out.[138]

This approach was entrenched in *General Motors of Canada Ltd*. v. *City National Leasing*,[139] where Dickson CJ applied the principles enunciated in *Vapor* and *C.N. Transportation*. The challenge here was to the provision of a civil cause of action in the federal Combines Investigation Act. The Supreme Court upheld the provision under the general trade and commerce power, applying the test set out by Dickson J, as he then was, in *C.N. Transportation*.[140] In *General Motors*, the Chief Justice added a further refinement to the test: the standard for determining whether the measure is sufficiently integrated into the regulatory scheme depends on the seriousness of the encroachment on provincial powers.[141] The purpose of the five criteria was to 'ensure that federal legislation does not upset the balance of power between federal and provincial governments'.[142] The five

---

[135] *Vapor* at 160. [136] Ibid. at 164–5. [137] See n. 106.
[138] Ibid. at 268. [139] See n. 106. [140] See n. 106.
[141] *General Motors* at 276 and 285.
[142] Ibid. at 269. More specifically, Dickson CJ said: 'Each of these requirements is evidence of a concern that federal authority under the second branch of the trade and commerce power does not encroach on provincial jurisdiction. By limiting the means which federal legislators may employ to that of a regulatory scheme overseen by a regulatory agency, and by limiting the object of federal legislation to trade as a whole, these requirements attempt to maintain a delicate balance between federal and provincial power.'

factors were to be used, furthermore, as a 'preliminary checklist' only; Dickson CJ said 'a careful case-by-case analysis remains appropriate' in any situation 'where the general trade and commerce power is advanced as a ground of constitutional validity'.[143]

General Motors is a significant decision, because it raises 'the possibility of a broader reading of the general trade and commerce power and possibly of the ambit of the power to regulate international trade.'[144] However, it is a long way from opening the door to major federal incursions into provincial jurisdiction. As Dickson CJ emphasized, the purpose of the *General Motors* analysis is to maintain a balance between sections 91 and 92.[145] He also emphasized that in complex subject matters, there would inevitably be shared jurisdiction between the federal and provincial governments:

competition is not a single matter, any more than inflation or pollution. The provinces, too, may deal with competition in the exercise of their legislative powers in such fields as consumer protection, labour relations, marketing and the like. The point is, however, that Parliament also has the constitutional power to regulate interprovincial aspects of competition.[146]

The trade and commerce power is the principal basis on which a constitutional defence of federal legislation implementing an international trade agreement could be made. While its two branches, as set out in *Parsons*,[147] were once restrictively applied or ignored altogether, after the recent Supreme Court of Canada decisions in *C.N. Transportation* and *General Motors*, it is clear that the trade and commerce power now holds much greater potential for asserting federal jurisdiction in the implementation of international economic agreements. At the same time, the courts remain committed to protecting the integrity of the division of powers in sections 91 and 92, and are wary of federal encroachments on provincial powers. Therefore, the federal government when designing legislation to implement an international trade agreement must take into account both the criteria and the careful approach set out in the recent decisions. It is also apparent that the provinces continue to enjoy legislative jurisdiction to

---

[143] Ibid. at 270.

[144] Castel, *Canadian Law and Practice of International Trade*, at 314.

[145] *General Motors* at 269.

[146] Ibid. at 284. This statement parallels closely that of Rand J in the *Farm Products Marketing Reference*, where he said:

Although not specifically mentioned in s. 92 of the British North America Act, there is admittedly a field of trade within provincial power . . . The power is a subtraction from the scope of the language conferring on the Dominion by head 2 of s. 91 exclusive authority to make laws in relation to the regulation of trade and commerce, and was derived under an interpretation of the which was found necessary in order to preserve from serious curtailment, if not from virtual extinction, the degree of autonomy which, as appears from the scheme of the Act as a whole, the provinces were intended to possess.

[147] See n. 85.

implement those aspects of international agreements that are traditionally within their powers.

Under the interprovincial trade branch, the federal government appears to have the authority to regulate the marketing, and probably the manufacture and processing, of products where the market for such products is national or international in scope.[148] While a modern court would probably agree generally with Rand J's view that the federal government has 'responsibility for promoting and maintaining the vigour and growth of trade beyond Provincial confines', it is doubtful a court would go so far as to say that the discharge of this responsibility 'must remain unembarrassed by local trade impediments'.[149]

As for the general branch, *General Motors*[150] has been praised for expanding the scope of the trade and commerce power. The overall effect of *General Motors* may have been to broaden the power, but one must not overlook Dickson CJ's caution that the purpose of the criteria set out for applying the general branch was to 'maintain a delicate balance between federal and provincial power'.[151]

7.3.2.2.2.4 The National Concern Doctrine

The third basis on which the federal government could defend its implementation of the WTO Agreement is the national concern doctrine, which is a particular aspect of the federal government's residual (or peace, order and good government (POGG)) power in section 91 of the Constitution Act. This doctrine provides that, in certain circumstances, matters that would otherwise be within provincial jurisdiction may attain such national importance that they transcend the enumerated powers in section 92, and become subject to Parliament's residual power to govern for the peace, order and good government of Canada.[152]

Like the trade and commerce power, the national concern doctrine has enjoyed a recent resurgence. In *R. v. Crown Zellerbach Canada Ltd.*,[153] Le Dain J, in a majority decision, reviewed the case law on the doctrine and set out the test for its application. Crown Zellerbach was charged under the federal Ocean Dumping Act with dumping· waste from its logging operations in inland marine waters, but it resisted the charge on the ground that inland waters were within provincial jurisdiction. Although the Act did not expressly say so, the court accepted that it implemented an international convention on ocean dumping.[154] The Supreme Court

---

[148] *Farm Products Marketing Reference*; *Murphy*; *Klassen*; and *Caloil*.
[149] *Farm Products Marketing Reference* at 210.
[150] See n. 106.   [151] Ibid. at 268.
[152] See Lord Watson's decision in *Attorney-General for Ontario* v. *Attorney-General for the Dominion*, [1896] AC 348 (JCPC) at 361.   [153] See n. 118.

acknowledged that the statute did not come under any of the federal government's enumerated powers in section 91, but it upheld the provision under the national concern doctrine. After characterizing the Act, 'viewed as a whole', as being 'directed to the control or regulation of marine pollution',[155] the Court held that marine pollution was primarily an extraprovincial and an international problem, as evidenced by the existence of a treaty on the subject, and therefore was of national concern to Canada as a whole.[156]

In reaching this conclusion, Le Dain J reviewed the case law on the doctrine and summarized it in this way:

1. The national concern doctrine is separate from the national emergency doctrine, the latter of which only provides a constitutional basis for legislation of a temporary nature.
2. The doctrine applies to matters that did not exist at Confederation as well as to matters that were once matters of a local or private nature but have since become matters of national concern.
3. To qualify under the doctrine, a matter must have a singleness, distinctiveness and indivisibility that clearly distinguishes it from matters of provincial concern, as well as a scale of impact on provincial jurisdiction that is reconcilable with the fundamental distribution of legislative power under the Constitution.
4. In determining whether a matter has sufficient singleness, distinctiveness and indivisibility, it is relevant to consider the effect on extra-provincial interests of a provincial failure to deal effectively with the control or regulation of intra-provincial aspects of the matter.[157]

He emphasized the particular importance of the last factor, namely the 'provincial inability' test, which he considered 'the most satisfactory rationale' of the doctrine, because it involved 'a limited or qualified application of federal jurisdiction' in areas otherwise within provincial jurisdiction.[158] Le Dain J, however, was careful to state the doctrine in a way that would protect the integrity of the constitutional division of powers. Even where the doctrine applies, he noted that: '. . . the entire problem would not fall within federal competence in such circumstances. Only that aspect of the problem that is beyond provincial control would do so.'[159]

In the last few years, it is thus apparent that there has been an expansion of both the federal trade and commerce power and the national concern doctrine. Obviously, where a court is willing to uphold federal legislation under the trade and commerce power, based on the approach taken in the

---

[155] Ibid. at 419.   [156] Ibid. at 436.   [157] Ibid. at 431–2.
[158] Ibid. at 432.   [159] Ibid. at 432–3.

recent *C.N. Transportation* and *General Motors* cases, it is not necessary to have recourse to the national concern doctrine. However, where all of the requirements set out in *General Motors* are not met, or they are met only marginally, then the national concern doctrine could become an additional basis for asserting federal jurisdiction to legislate in implementation of an international trade agreement. Although the trade and commerce power appears to be a stronger basis for federal jurisdiction, the national concern doctrine could be a useful alternative or supplementary argument.

7.4 RELATIONSHIP BETWEEN INTERNATIONAL AGREEMENTS AND DOMESTIC LAW

7.4.1 Status of treaties in domestic law

It has been well-established since *Labour Conventions*[160] that a treaty is an agreement binding on Canada in international law, but its provisions do not, without legislative implementation, have the force of domestic law.[161] Neither ratification of the treaty by the government nor its approval by Parliament alter its status, unless it is specifically implemented in domestic law. As stated by Smith J in *R. v. Canada Labour Relations Board*:

a treaty is a contract between States creating rights and obligations that enure to, and are binding on, the executive Governments which are parties to it. The common law recognizes this rule, but it has long been settled law that a treaty binding the Government does not, *ipso facto*, become part of our law and enforceable in the Courts.[162]

Treaty provisions affecting matters within the scope of domestic law, which require changes to existing law or intend to restrict the action of Parliament, must be implemented by legislation. Where there is a conflict between a statute and a treaty provision which has not been specifically implemented, the statute prevails.[163]

However, the courts will go a long way to avoid finding a conflict between a statute and a treaty. In *Re Arrow River and Tributaries Slide and Boom Co. Ltd.*,[164] three Justices of the Supreme Court struggled to find that there was no conflict between a provincial statute and the Webster–Ashburton Treaty of 1842. Lamont J (concurred with by Cannon J) also held that, as the treaty had not been implemented by legislation, it was not enforceable by the courts. He stated:

---

[160] See n. 88. [161] Ibid. at 347.
[162] (1964), 44 DLR (2d) 440 (Man. QB) at 453–4.
[163] *Francis*, per Rand J, at 625. See also *Canada Labour Relations Board*, per Smith J.
[164] See n. 86.

The treaty in itself is not equivalent to an Imperial Act and, without the sanction of Parliament, the Crown cannot alter the existing law by entering into a contract with a foreign power . . . Where, as here, a treaty provides that certain rights or privileges are to be enjoyed by the subjects of both contracting parties, these rights and privileges are, under our law, enforceable by the Courts only where the treaty has been implemented or sanctioned by legislation rendering it binding upon the subject . . . In the absence of affirming legislation this provision of the treaty cannot be enforced by any of our Courts whose authority is derived from municipal law.[165]

7.4.2 Treaty interpretation

Where an international agreement has been implemented by legislation, the question arises as to whether the agreement should be used as an aid to interpreting that legislation. The courts, in the past, took the position that if the legislation was clear and unambiguous, it was not appropriate to have resort to the treaty, because the treaty itself was not effective as domestic law. However, recent decisions of the Supreme Court of Canada demonstrate a greater willingness to look to the provisions of a treaty in interpreting a statute, even where the implementing legislation is not ambiguous on its face.

Schavernoch v. *Foreign Claims Commission*[166] set out the principle that only where there is an ambiguity in the legislation should the court refer to extrinsic aids to interpretation, such as treaties. Estey J said the following:

If one could assert an ambiguity, either patent or latent, in the regulations it might be that a court could find support for making reference to matters external to the regulations in order to interpret its terms. Because, however, there is in my view no ambiguity arising from the above-quoted excerpt from these regulations, there is no authority . . . entitling a court to take recourse either to an underlying international agreement or to textbooks on international law with reference to the negotiation of agreements or to take recourse to reports made to the Government of Canada by persons engaged in the negotiation referred to in the regulations.[167]

In *Re Regina and Palacios*,[168] where the provisions of a treaty had been implemented specifically by legislation, the Ontario Court of Appeal held that the principles of public international law, and not domestic law, govern its interpretation. Blair JA, speaking for the court, interpreted the treaty in light of the 'effectiveness principle' by reading the treaty as a whole to ascertain its purpose and intent and to give effect to it.[169]

A major turning point, but a case which has resulted in some confusion among commentators, was the 1990 Supreme Court of Canada decision in

---

[165] Ibid. at 260.   [166] (1982), 136 DLR (3d) 447 (SCC).
[167] Ibid. at 451–2.   [168] (1984) 45 OR (2nd) 269 (CA).
[169] Ibid. at 277–8.

National Corn Growers Association v. *Canada (Import Tribunal)*.[170] One of the issues the court had to decide in that case was whether it was unreasonable for the Canadian Import Tribunal to have made reference to the Tokyo Round Agreement on Subsidies and Countervailing Measures for the purpose of interpreting a provision of the Special Import Measures Act, which all parties agreed was domestic legislation designed to implement the Subsidies Code. The Court held that it was not unreasonable for the Tribunal, in the face of an uncertainty, to have examined the underlying agreement in interpreting the legislative provision. However, Gonthier J, speaking for the majority, went further by suggesting:

Indeed where the text of the domestic law lends itself to it, one should also strive to expound an interpretation which is consonant with the relevant international obligations . . . Second, and more specifically, it is reasonable to make reference to an international agreement at the very outset of the inquiry to determine if there is any ambiguity, even latent, in the domestic legislation. The Court of Appeal's suggestion that recourse to an international treaty is only available where the provision of the domestic legislation is ambiguous on its face is to be rejected.[171]

In its most recent statement on the subject, *Thomson* v. *Thomson*,[172] the Supreme Court of Canada applied both an international agreement and the provincial statute implementing it. The Court took great pains to arrive at an interpretation of the domestic legislation that gave full effect to the purpose of the treaty. In effect, the Court applied the presumption that the provincial legislature did not intend to violate the international agreement, and gave effect to an interpretation which would respect Canada's international obligations.[173]

7.5 COMPARISON BETWEEN IMPLEMENTATION OF NAFTA AND WTO AGREEMENT

There are two major differences in the general approaches taken in the implementation of Canada's obligations under the NAFTA and the WTO Agreement. While it remains to be seen whether these differences are recognized, or prove to be significant, they are none the less interesting in that they touch upon some of the constitutional issues addressed in this paper. Both differences concern a general provision in the first part of the

---

[170] [1990] 2 SCR 1324. [171] Ibid. at 1371. [172] [1994] 3 SCR 551.
[173] This case dealt with an application under the Hague Convention on the Civil Aspects of International Child Abduction and the Manitoba Child Custody Enforcement Act, which implemented the Convention. It is not clear whether this analysis would necessarily be applied to legislation implementing an international trade agreement.

NAFTA Act that was specifically omitted in the corresponding part of the WTO Act. One can only speculate as to the reasons why these provisions were not repeated in the WTO Act.

7.5.1 Interpretation of legislation

The first such provision is section 3 of the NAFTA Act. It states that 'This Act, any provision of an Act of Parliament enacted by Part II and any other federal law that implements a provision of the Agreement or fulfils an obligation of the Government of Canada under the Agreement *shall be interpreted in a manner consistent with the Agreement*'.[174]

No similar provision appears in the WTO Act. This distinction is interesting, because the NAFTA Act provision goes considerably further than the jurisprudence expounded by the courts to date. It imposes an obligation on any administrative agency or court, in interpreting the NAFTA Act or any other federal law that fulfils an obligation under the NAFTA, to interpret that law in a manner consistent with the NAFTA. Thus, section 3 elevates to the status of a mandatory obligation what was previously only a suggestion or an inclination of the courts.

As noted earlier, there has been considerable confusion over the language of Gonthier J concerning this issue in *National Corn Growers*.[175] In that case, Gonthier J questioned a reading of the previous jurisprudence that there had to be an ambiguity in the legislation before the courts could look to an international agreement to aid in interpretation. He suggested, although it was not essential to the finding in that case and therefore was *obiter dicta*, that an administrative agency or a court in interpreting implementing legislation should look to the treaty to determine whether, indeed, an ambiguity exists. The *ratio decidendi* in *National Corn Growers* was that it was not unreasonable for an agency, in the face of uncertainty, to review the underlying international agreement in interpreting implementing legislation. Gonthier J did not go so far as to say that an agency or a court *must* interpret a legislative provision in a manner consistent with the international obligations.

In the most recent Supreme Court of Canada decision on the issue, *Thomson*,[176] the Court deliberately chose an interpretation of the provincial statute that was consistent with the international convention, but it did not go so far as to state a new principle that domestic legislation must always be interpreted in a manner consistent with the international agreement. The doctrine of parliamentary supremacy makes it possible for Parliament or the provincial legislatures to legislate in conflict with Canada's international obligations, if that is the legislature's intent.

---

[174] See n. 4 (emphasis added).   [175] See n. 170.   [176] See n. 172.

Thomson stands for the proposition that the courts will presume that the legislature did not intend to violate Canada's international obligations. Viewed in that light, section 3 of the NAFTA Act could be seen as an expression by Parliament of its intention to be bound by its international obligations under NAFTA. Therefore, it has expressly stated that the NAFTA Act and any other federal law implementing NAFTA must be interpreted in a manner consistent with the NAFTA.

The question then arises whether, in fact, the omission of a similar provision in the WTO Act is significant. Section 3 of the WTO Act states that '[t]he purpose of this Act is to implement the Agreement'. Section 4 states, furthermore, that the 'Act is binding on Her Majesty in right of Canada'.[177] Corresponding provisions appeared in sections 4 and 5 of the NAFTA Act.[178] Although they express Parliament's intention to implement the terms of the international agreements, they do not directly address the duality of domestic law and the international obligations in Canadian constitutional law.

As there is no provision in the WTO Act stipulating how it is to be interpreted, recent jurisprudence would seem to apply. However, as a result of section 3 of the NAFTA Act, it and other federal laws applying NAFTA must be interpreted in a manner consistent with that Agreement.

7.5.2 Federal assertion of jurisdiction

In section 9 of the NAFTA Act, there is an assertion that nothing in that Act limits the right of Parliament to enact legislation or to fulfil any of Canada's international obligations under the NAFTA. It states as follows:

For greater certainty, nothing in this Act, by specific mention or omission, limits in any manner the right of Parliament to enact legislation to implement any provision of the Agreement or fulfil any of the obligations of the Government of Canada under the Agreement.[179]

Although there was an identical provision in section 6 of the CUSFTA Act,[180] it does not appear in the WTO Act. It is not clear what it means in the context of the NAFTA Act or the CUSFTA Act. It appears to be a hortatory statement, because obviously Parliament cannot give itself, by statutory decree, jurisdiction that it does not have. Thus, the statement seems to be nothing more than Parliament asserting that it did not intend to limit its own jurisdiction by enacting those Acts. The issue of Parliament's jurisdiction to implement the aspects of an international trade agreement remains to be determined by the courts in accordance with Canadian constitutional law.

---

[177] See n. 5.   [178] See n. 4.   [179] S. 9, NAFTA Act.
[180] See n. 3.

Consequently, the omission of a similar provision in the WTO Act does not seem to be significant. Whether, and to what extent, Parliament has jurisdiction to implement all relevant aspects of the NAFTA or the WTO Agreement is a matter ultimately for the courts to decide. Parliament's views on the matter would presumably be taken into consideration, but they would not be definitive of the issue.

7.5.3 Private rights

All three statutes implementing Canada's obligations under the recent international trade agreements, namely the WTO Act, the NAFTA Act and the CUSFTA Act, include provisions making it clear that those Acts do not create private rights entitling persons to enforce the provisions of the Agreements directly in the courts.[181] These provisions reinforce the duality and distinctiveness of the implementing legislation and the treaties. To the extent that private parties have rights under Canadian legislation, including the statutes amended by the WTO Act, the NAFTA Act and the CUSFTA Act, to enforce Canadian law, those rights are maintained. These provisions, however, clarify that no additional rights to bring proceedings in Canada accrue to private persons by virtue of the international agreements themselves.

7.6 CONCLUSION

As noted earlier, Canada is a dualist state, which means that treaties must be transformed to become applicable in domestic law. Transformation may be effected by executive or legislative action, but treaties whose subject-matter affects private rights, requires the expenditure of public monies or purports to change existing law require legislative implementation. When legislation is required, the constitutional division of powers between the federal and provincial governments becomes critical in determining which level of government has the power to enact such legislation.

In implementing the WTO Agreement, there are three constitutional arguments that can be used to support the federal government's assertion of jurisdiction: the possible existence of a federal treaty–implementation power in the wake of *Labour Conventions*,[182] the federal trade and commerce power and the national concern doctrine.

---

[181] S. 5, CUSFTA Act; s. 6, NAFTA Act; and s. 5 and 6, WTO Act read similarly:
No person has any cause of action and no proceedings of any kind shall be taken without the consent of the Attorney-General of Canada, to enforce or determine any right or obligation that is claimed or arises solely under or by virtue of Part I or (under or by virtue of) the Agreement.

[182] See n. 88.

However, the first argument is very weak. In *Labour Conventions*, the JCPC rejected the existence of a federal treaty implementation power under sections 91 or 132 of the Constitution Act. While that decision has been subject to much criticism, it has never been directly reconsidered. The Supreme Court has hinted on several occasions that such a reconsideration might eventually occur, and Laskin CJ went so far as to suggest that it might result in the decision being overruled.[183] However, for now, the decision in *Labour Conventions* remains good law. Therefore, the trade and commerce power and the national concern doctrine are obviously much sounder arguments on which to base federal jurisdiction.

The strongest federal claim of constitutional authority to implement an international trade agreement is the trade and commerce power in section 91 of the Constitution Act. Since *Parsons*,[184] the trade and commerce power has consisted of two branches: the interprovincial branch and the general branch. The interprovincial branch provides a credible basis for assertion of federal jurisdiction over the regulation of the marketing, and probably the manufacture and processing, of commodities where the market for the commodities is national or international. How that branch might apply to trade in services, trade-related intellectual property, trade-related investment or government procurement practices, however, has not been tested.

The general branch of the trade and commerce power justifies a claim of federal jurisdiction concerning a regulatory scheme dealing with trade as a whole, as opposed to regulation of a particular commodity or trade. The recent decision in *General Motors*[185] that upheld federal jurisdiction to enact a general regulatory scheme relating to competition within the economy as a whole clearly provides a strong precedent for a statute the purpose of which is to implement an international trade agreement for the benefit of the nation as a whole. While *General Motors* opened the door to an expansion of federal jurisdiction over general trade regulation, its potential is far from unlimited. Dickson CJ highlighted the importance the Supreme Court continues to place on maintaining the integrity of the federal–provincial division of powers in sections 91 and 92.[186] He also expressly acknowledged that complex subject matters inevitably give rise to shared jurisdiction between Parliament and the provincial legislatures.[187]

Finally, the national concern doctrine may apply if there is no applicable enumerated head of power in section 91. The doctrine applies where, notwithstanding the lack of a specific federal power, the subject matter of the legislation is of such national importance that it transcends being

---

[183] *Vapor* at 169.   [184] See n. 94.   [185] See n. 106.
[186] Ibid. at 269.   [187] Ibid. at 284.

simply a local concern under section 92 and falls instead within Parliament's residual power in section 91. Like the general branch of the trade and commerce power, the national concern doctrine has enjoyed a recent resurgence.[188] It may be useful where the trade and commerce power would not apply, for example, where there is no comprehensive, federal regulatory scheme. However, the WTO Act would likely meet the approach set out in *General Motors*. Therefore, reliance on the national concern doctrine would not likely be necessary.

Clearly, the federal government enjoys broader latitude in the legislative implementation of an international trade agreement than it did a few decades ago. Most interesting is the rise of the provincial inability test in the recent jurisprudence relating both to the federal trade and commerce power and the national concern doctrine. Whereas the inability of the provinces, alone or together, to implement a particular regulatory scheme was either ignored or rejected in early cases like *Re Board of Commerce*,[189] *Snider*,[190] and *Eastern Terminal Elevator*,[191] recent Supreme Court of Canada judgments have relied on this criterion to support federal jurisdiction.[192] This said, the integrity of the division of powers remains a central feature of Canadian constitutional analysis, and it is likely that in many areas, such as trade in services, government procurement, technical barriers to trade, TRIPs, sanitary and phytosanitary measures and trade-related investment, the federal government and the provincial governments would both have to take steps to implement Canada's international obligations.

With respect to the WTO Agreement, to date, only the federal government has enacted implementing legislation. In the future, if the WTO were to reach into subjects such as the regulation of professional services, labour standards or the environment, implementation might also have to be effected concurrently by the provinces where they have inconsistent existing legislation.

---

[188] *Crown Zellerbach* (see n. 118).   [189] See n. 117.   [190] See n. 98.
[191] See n. 120.
[192] *General Motors* (see n. 106) and *Crown Zellerbach* (see n. 118).

IMPLEMENTATION OF THE WORLD TRADE ORGANIZATION AGREEMENT IN AUSTRALIA*

Professor Jeffrey Waincymer[‡]

8.1 INTRODUCTION

An analysis of the functions, problems and prospects of international economic regulation should not be undertaken without attention being given to domestic implementation issues. These include the domestic legal and constitutional constraints on the development of trade policy, the domestic legal requirements for the applicability of international economic norms and the optimal political, legal and administrative structures for those purposes. It is particularly inappropriate to debate the respective merits of domestic and international solutions to legal problems without fully analysing the relationship between the two.

Within each country these matters need to be considered to ensure that completed international agreements can more closely meet their intended aims. It is also desirable to analyse the variations between countries in their domestic legal and constitutional features, and consider what if any adverse effect this has on the international negotiating and rule-making process itself and how such negative features may be minimized in the future. Other questions to consider include variations between countries in the basic attitudes to law, the role and ambit of administrative law and administrative review, the relative powers of bureaucrats versus parliament and the resources that have been and can be expected to be allocated to domestic implementation.

In a comparative study such as this, the Australian perspective is a valuable adjunct to an analysis of the major players on the world trading scene. As a small developed country with a major role in the agriculture

---

* Commentary on the process of negotiations and the outcomes as compared to Australia's negotiating aims are largely based on discussions with Mr Graham Thomson, Principal Adviser, Trade and Negotiations and Organizations Division, Department of Foreign Affairs and Trade, Canberra, and have also drawn heavily on Mr Thomson's paper 'What the Uruguay Round means for Australia', presented to a conference 'Challenges and Opportunities for East–Asian Trade', Australian National University, 13–14 July 1994.

‡ Professor, School of Law, Deakin University, Melbourne, Australia.

sector, a strong commitment to the rule of law and transparent systems and procedures, it provides a valuable case study for an analysis of key processes to promote openness and accountability in decision-making. The two main ways in which this is achieved are through the role of the Industries Commission which is an independent review body which imposes limits on the power of government to impose new tariff levels and through an elaborate system of administrative law and administrative review. Apart from the Commission, legislative constraints on governmental trade policy are limited to international economic rules that have been derived through the General Agreement on Tariffs and Trade/World Trade Organization system. There are no constitutional constraints in the trade policy field.

8.2 INTERDISCIPLINARY PERSPECTIVES

After considering the variations between countries we can then address a number of important hypotheses such as whether protectionism is more likely in some constitutional structures rather than others. How important are domestic courts and legal methods? What is the role of the bureaucracy in facilitating or preventing trade? What are the rights and obligations of bureaucrats and traders when there are disputes? How can an international organisation such as the WTO promote optimal domestic structures and procedures?

These questions have recently been addressed by a number of scholars. Valuable work has been done in analysing domestic implementation in the field of international economic law, initially through the work of Professors Jackson, Louis and Matsushita[1] and more recently by Professors Hilf and Petersmann.[2] Some have been influenced by work in other disciplines, particularly philosophy, economics, and political science. For example, the underlying issues considered in this symposium are very much allied to the field of public choice theory. The central question is what institutional arrangements are appropriate to foster certain economic goals. Many public choice theorists have pointed out that it is important to consider institutional issues separately from substantive areas to foster a consensus in favour of reform.[3]

---

[1] J. H. Jackson, J.-V. Louis and M. Matsushita 'Implementing the Tokyo Round: legal aspects of changing international economic rules' (1982) 82 Mich. L. Rev. at 267; J. H. Jackson, J.-V. Louis and M. Matsushita, *Implementing the Tokyo Round: National Constitutions and International Economic Rules* (1984).

[2] M. Hilf and E.-U. Petersmann (eds.) *National Constitutions and International Economic Law* (1993).

[3] On the other hand, without considering the problems and prospects within specific areas, it is often difficult to identify just how important institutional reform actually is.

Perhaps the greatest lesson we can learn from public choice theory is that domestic trade policy formulation will tend to bias itself towards the interests of producers over that of consumers. Those with most to gain from political pressure are more inclined to exercise it. In the trade arena this takes the form of protectionist policies applied for the benefit of domestic industry. This in turn promotes a decrease in net welfare by skewing resources away from their most efficient use and by increasing the price of goods and services. The main focus of institutional reforms should then be aimed at constraining governments and bureaucrats from behaving in this way and promoting greater involvement of consumers. Many commentators advocate greater transparency as a crucial reform. For example, the Leutwiler Report[4] proposed bringing the making of trade policy into the open and analysing costs and benefits through a 'protection balance sheet.'

A study of public choice and implementation issues may raise doubts and problems as well as provide options for reform and promotion of multilateral trade. One of the difficulties of utilising public choice theory to promote an organisation such as the WTO, is that to some public choice theorists, all institutions are captured by vested interest groups. Their theories are used to argue against the viability of the institutions themselves. Certainly the presence of GATT rules did not stop the development of regional initiatives, the Multifibre Agreements, voluntary export restraints, protectionist use of anti-dumping duties and other discriminatory measures such as procurement and standards rules.[5] Some authors are particularly critical. For example, Finger argues that the GATT rules are essentially protectionist in nature and has on a number of occasions highlighted the administered protectionist approach of the United States in particular.

Some scholars also question the potential for major domestic reform and raise the question of whether the essential function of international economic law is to promote domestic application of international norms or to overcome domestic biases through the establishment of a viable international rule-making and dispute resolution body. Thus while political economists may call for constitutional restraints to stop vested interest groups skewing the political process, the ability of the same vested interest groups to prevent such constitutional change is a major problem.[6] Roessler

---

[4] Trade Policies for a Better Future, Proposals for Action, GATT 1985, 35.

[5] C. H. G. Grubel 'Does the world need a GATT for services?' and J. M. Finger 'Protectionist rules and internationalist discretion in the making of a national trade policy', both in H.-J. Vosgerau (ed.), *New Institutional Arrangements for the World Economy* (1989), at 257 and 310 respectively.

[6] F. Roessler 'The constitutional function of international economic law' in *National Constitutions*, 53.

also points out that governments can often avoid domestic constraints if they want to and uses as an example, voluntary export restraints that on any legal analysis would offend against separation of powers, equality before the law and the right to judicial review in most western democracies.[7]

Part of the problem of putting GATT law into the domestic environment, is that in most countries, this environment is largely given in terms of philosophy and policy choices. Those choices may favour some policies over others which may not necessarily be the most conducive to free trade. For example, in Australia, customs laws are within the administrative law framework which includes substantial merits review, comprehensive judicial review and an ombudsman. The philosophy of this is to give government broad powers over trade, subject to certain standards of behaviour such as the right to natural justice. This philosophy, valuable in itself, may at times operate counter to one of the aims of GATT/WTO, namely, to constrain governments and encourage them to make only economically efficient policy choices. Administrative courts do not pursue this except indirectly in extreme cases of ultra vires or in cases where internal ambiguities are resolved by choosing the most purposive approach to interpretation. Even then they only do so within the confines of the given statutes. For these reasons it is particularly important to be aware of the basic features of each jurisdiction before evaluating the extent and methodology of implementation of international rules.

8.3 THE AUSTRALIAN CONSTITUTIONAL SYSTEM

With the exception of the federal nature of its political system, Australia has none of the intricate and complex politico/legal features of the three main players in the trade arena, the United States, the European Union and Japan. It has neither the full separation of powers of the United States, the importance of the bureaucracy in both Japan and the European Commission, nor direct legal effect of international agreements as in Europe.

Australia is a federal nation state within the Commonwealth. The Head of State is the Queen of England in her capacity as Queen of Australia and Her other Realms and Territories, Head of the Commonwealth.[8] She acts through her local representative, the Governor-General. Because of the intended federal structure, there was a need at the outset to delineate

---

[7] Roessler, in *National Constitutions*, 472.
[8] Royal Style and Titles Act 1973.

power between central and State governments. The Commonwealth Constitution[9] deliberately follows the pattern of the US Constitution[10] by providing specific powers to the central government and leaving all residual powers with the state governments. The Canadian model which adopts the converse approach, was specifically rejected.[11]

Chapters I, II and III of the Constitution deal respectively with the legislature (being the Commonwealth Parliament), the executive (being the Federal Government) and the judiciary (in particular, the High Court of Australia). Section 51 of Chapter I lists the specific law making powers given to the central government.

The Federal Parliament comprises two Houses, a House of Representatives and a Senate. Voting is compulsory. The House of Representatives is elected on the basis of population in designated geographical areas. Where the Senate is concerned, the States are equally represented regardless of differences in population size. The Executive Government is drawn from the party or parties which control the majority in the House of Representatives.

8.4 TREATY-MAKING

The Constitution makes no specific reference to treaties or treaty-making powers. This silence was due in part to the lack of intent at the time of Federation in 1901, for Australia to be an international actor separate from the United Kingdom on matters of international policy.[12] In fact an express mention of legislative power over treaties was dropped from an early draft of the Constitution at the Constitutional Convention's 1898 session.[13]

Prior to Federation, treaties negotiated by the United Kingdom covered the colonies in certain circumstances. Initially, the application of those treaties was automatic through the inherited law. In 1894, Australia was given permission to negotiate its own tariff arrangements.[14]

In the late 1880s, the United Kingdom shifted to a situation where commercial treaties only applied to colonies after their consent was obtained. Over time, colonies were given the right to separately adhere to

---

[9] The Commonwealth of Australia Constitution Act 1900 (IMP), 63 & 64 Vict. c.12.

[10] Hunt, *American Precedents in Australian Federation* (1930); P. H. Lane, *A Manual of Australian Constitutional Law* (5th edn. 1991), 5.

[11] British North America Act 1867, 30 & 31 Vict. c.3.

[12] H. Burmester, 'The Australian states and participation in the foreign policy process', (1978) 9 Fed. L. Rev. 257 at 260.

[13] Ibid. 260.

[14] D. P. O'Connell and J. Crawford, 'The evolution of Australia's international personality' in K. W. Ryan (ed.), *International Law in Australia* (2nd edn. 1984), 5.

or denounce particular treaties. The Colonial Conference in 1902 passed a formal resolution to the effect that colonies should be consulted in the negotiation stage.[15]

While Federation occurred on 1 January 1901, there is no clear agreement on the date at which Australia realized full international status. This is relevant in terms of identifying the nature and extent of treaty making powers. Certainly by the Second World War this was seen as complete but whether it operated from Federation or a subsequent date has been debated by judges and scholars.[16] Because Australia commenced its status as a dominion of the United Kingdom, even after Federation, a question still arose as to the status and power of the dominions, given that their legislative powers derived from the United Kingdom Acts of Parliament.

The Balfour Declaration of 1926 indicated that the dominions were 'autonomous communities within the British Empire'.[17] This position was confirmed by the Statute of Westminster 1931. This indicated that Acts of the Imperial Parliament would not extend to the dominions without their own legislative consent. This Act was adopted retrospectively by Australia in 1942.[18] Because the dominions all had the Crown as Head of State, a belief in the indivisibility of the Crown meant that in the early days it was not felt possible for the dominions to enter into treaties between themselves.

Eventually British courts came to accept the divisibility of the Crown. In *R* v. *Secretary of State for Foreign and Commonwealth Affairs; ex parte Indian Association of Alberta*,[19] Lord Denning MR acknowledged that usage and practice led to divisibility whereby the Crown was a separate and divisible monarch for each self-governing entity.

After Federation on 1 January 1901, a question also arose as to the effect this event had on pre-existing treaties of Australian colonies. There was significant debate for a number of years as to whether these treaties remained in force and if so who had responsibility for them. O'Connell and Crawford described the result as a form of 'functional succession' whereby

---

[15] O'Connell and Crawford, 'Evolution of Australia's international personality', 8.

[16] Murphy J suggested that independence from UK legislative authority should be taken as dating from 1901. *Bistricic* v. *Rokov* (1977) 51 ALJR 163 at 169. In *Commonwealth* v. *Tasmania* (1983) 46 ALR 625 one of the judges indicated that the shift to Dominion status and independent international personality resulted from the removal by the Statute of Westminster of restrictions upon extra territorial legislative effect or on legislation inconsistent with Imperial legislation.

[17] Cmd. 2768, cited in O'Connell and Crawford, 'Evolution of Australia's international personality' at 17.

[18] Statute of Westminster Adoption Act 1942 (Cth).

[19] [1982] 2 All ER 118 at 127–8.

the treaties remained in force with functional authority taken over by the Commonwealth Government.[20]

In due course the government saw itself as having a comprehensive and independent treaty-making role. While there is no express treaty power in the Constitution, Australia inherited the English common law which deals with the prerogative powers of the Crown. These include foreign affairs and treaty-making powers. Section 61 of the Constitution indicates that the executive power of the Commonwealth is vested in the Queen and provides further that this executive power 'is exercisable by the Governor-General'.

The initial narrow view of section 61 was to the effect that it should be limited to powers expressly conferred by the Constitution or domestic legislation.[21] Others have argued that section 61 is wide enough to include all the executive prerogatives that existed prior to Federation. In *Commonwealth* v. *Tasmania*,[22] Dawson J indicated that the exact basis of the external affairs power is largely academic because such power is clearly recognized by the international community, and because no cases have centred on the exact site of such power.[23] Nevertheless the predominant view, for example, as accepted by Mason J in *Barton* v. *Commonwealth*[24] is that the treaty-making power does in fact emanate from section 61. This is supported by modern commentators.[25]

Australia also follows the English system of responsible parliamentary government which requires that foreign affairs be conducted consistent with policies of the parliamentary majority.[26] Because of these principles of responsible government, the executive powers of the Governor-General in relation to treaty-making are exercised on the basis of the advice of the Federal Executive Council and administered under Section 64 of the Constitution by the Minister of State for Foreign Affairs.[27] This Ministry has now been combined with the Ministry of Trade.

Before a treaty is brought before the Federal Executive Council, it must be approved by Cabinet or the responsible minister. Unless the treaty is to

---

[20] O'Connell and Crawford, 'Evolution of Australia's international personality' at 16.

[21] Promoting the narrow view of s. 61 on the basis of the strict wording of the Constitution begs the question, as Hanks has pointed out, in that the breadth of the Commonwealth legislative power depends upon the way judges interpret external affairs powers that flow from treaty commitments made by the Commonwealth. P. J. Hanks, *Australian Constitutional Law Materials and Commentary* (4th edn. 1990), 757.

[22] (1983) 46 ALR 625.   [23] Ibid. 562.   [24] (1974) 131 CLR 477.

[25] L. Zines (ed.), *Commentaries on the Australian Constitution: a tribute to Geoffrey Sawer* (1977) 24–25; G. Winterton, *Parliament, the Executive and the Governor-General* (1983) Chs. 2 and 3.

[26] G. Sawer 'Australian constitutional law in relation to international relations and international law' in *International Law in Australia*, 35.

[27] N. D. Campbell 'Australian treaty practice and procedure' in ibid., 54.

be signed by the Head of State, Head of Government or the Foreign Minister, an instrument of full powers must be prepared showing authority in the signatory.[28] If the treaty must also be ratified, separate approval for this must be obtained from the Governor-General in Council. The same applies if the treaty is acceded to at a date after the time for signature.

The administrative responsibility for treaty negotiations is in the Department of Foreign Affairs and Trade regardless of the subject matter of the treaty. That Department prepares all recommendations for the minister to submit to the Federal Executive Council. If the substance of the treaty relates to the responsibilities of another ministry, the submissions are generally prepared in consultation with officers of those departments.[29] If legislation is required, the Attorney-General's Department is also consulted. If the substance of the treaty is not within existing Cabinet policy, approval of Cabinet would also be sought. As of 1948, the text of all Australian treaties are published by the Department in the Australian Treaty Series and in addition are published in the United Nations Treaty Series.

Because the Departments of Trade and Foreign Affairs have now been merged in Australia, both the substantive and general treaty functions in the Uruguay Round were found within one Ministry. A separate Ministry for Trade Negotiations was also established to which was delegated the primary negotiating role in the Uruguay Round. Other relevant ministers included the Minister for Industry, Technology and Commerce, the Minister for Primary Industries and Energy, the Minister for Transport and Communications, the Minister for Science, Customs and Small Business, and the Treasurer.

One of the key issues is the extent to which Parliament should be involved in the treaty process. As a general principle of constitutional law, Australia does not need to ratify a treaty to make it binding simply because there is no separation between the executive and the legislature. Where multilateral treaties are concerned, because some parties do need to ratify a treaty to make it effective, the norm is that all parties are asked to do so. While a number of parliamentary bills have purported to approve treaties, this is not required for the treaties to have binding effect on Australia.[30] Australia in fact passed the International Trade Organization Act 1948 that sought to give formal approval to depositing instruments of acceptance of the GATT and the Havana Charter for an International Trade Organization with the Secretary-General of the United Nations. Like virtually all other

---

[28] A. Twomey, *Procedure and Practice of Entering and Implementing International Treaties* (1995), (PRS Background Paper No. 27) 4.
[29] Campbell, 'Australian treaty practice', at 55.
[30] Campbell, 'Australian treaty practice', at 54.

countries, however, Australia applied the GATT under the Protocol of Provisional Application.

In 1961 a practice developed whereby the then Prime Minister promised to table the text of treaties already signed in both Houses of Parliament and would in most cases not ratify or accede to treaties for at least twelve sitting days so that there would be an opportunity to comment.[31] This practice had been eroded over time. The Department of Foreign Affairs and Trade then began to table treaties in bulk every six months.[32] Many treaties were therefore only tabled after they had been ratified or were otherwise in force. On 21 October 1994 the Minister for Foreign Affairs and Trade and the Attorney-General announced that in addition to bi-annual tabling, the Government's intent was to table wherever possible all treaties other than sensitive bilateral ones before action is taken to adhere to them.[33] However in a statement to the Senate Estimates Committee, the Minister for Foreign Affairs and Trade also indicated that the tabling of treaties was not intended to be an exercise in ascertaining Parliament's views about whether or not Australia should become a party.[34]

Because the strict legal position is that the executive has sole power to negotiate treaties, many critics have from time to time sought to alter that situation by proposing some legislative requirement to involve parliament. In a paper published in 1994, the Department of Foreign Affairs and Trade supported the *status quo* partly by suggesting that Parliament has the opportunity to debate a treaty prior to action because of the usual practice of passing the legislation before agreeing to the treaty.[35] The Australian practice is generally to pass legislation before finally ratifying a treaty, based on the somewhat technical view that the Government would otherwise be temporarily in breach of the treaty from the time of ratification until the time of implementation and also because there can be no presumption that Parliament would necessarily pass the implementing legislation.[36] Certainly for those jurisdictions where the mere ratification of a treaty has immediate domestic effect, there is no such possible hiatus.

In any event, the tabling of enabling legislation before the treaty is ratified is not an adequate protection for Parliament if it is thought that this body should have meaningful input. This is because the enabling legislation

---

[31] Ibid.

[32] A. Twomey, *Procedure and practice*, at 8.

[33] 'Government slams Opposition hypocrisy on Treaties', Joint Statement by the Minister for Foreign Affairs, Sen. Gareth Evans and the Attorney-General, Michael Lavarch, 21 Oct. 1994.

[34] Australia, Senate Estimates Committee, Hansard, DFAT, 29 Nov. 1994, 158.

[35] DFAT, *Common Concerns about Australia's Participation in Treaty Regimes—Questions and Answers*, Oct. 1994.

[36] See A. Twomey, *Procedure and Practice*, 12.

is only drawn when Australia has agreed at the negotiation stage on the text of the treaty. Consequently, Parliament could not make any meaningful changes to the legislation or recommend renegotiations at that stage without putting Australia in breach of international law. Parliament is also unable to make any input where no enabling legislation is necessary or contemplated.

A number of commissions and conventions have recommended giving Parliament a greater role in the treaty-making process.[37] Individual politicians have also sought to effect changes. In 1983, an independent senator attempted to establish a standing committee on treaties which would analyse and report on treaties tabled in the Senate. This motion has not been moved by the Parliament. Another senator introduced the Parliamentary Approval of Treaties Bill 1994 into the Senate which, if enacted, would require the tabling of treaties in both Houses of Parliament. It would also stipulate that a treaty could not enter into force until either approved by both Houses or alternatively, if not approved, disapproved of within a set time period. Nothing is likely to come from this in the short term, although the important modern feature of the Australian political scene is that the Senate is never likely to be controlled by either the government or the main opposition party. Hence a greater number of 'deals' tend to be struck which can incorporate such legislative trade-offs. On a more general level, experience with the International Trade Organization and GATT does not inspire confidence that prescribing greater control by legislatures at the negotiation stage is a reform that would increase the equity and efficiency of the process. In particular, if Parliament is to have a role, it is important to prevent undue vested interest influence. One way is to provide for a fast-track approval system on an all or nothing basis as now occurs in the United States and as occurred with the WTO Agreement itself.

8.5 IMPLEMENTATION AND DOMESTIC EFFECT

For the vast majority of treaties, a transformation doctrine applies, requiring domestic legislation before there is any municipal application of the treaty norms. The corollary of this is that from a constitutional point of view, if there is an inconsistency between domestic legislation and the international treaty, the former will prevail. Similarly, a subsequent Act of Parliament prevails over the provisions of a prior treaty.[38]

---

[37] Constitutional Commission Advisory Committee on the Distribution of Powers, Report, 6 June 1987; Constitutional Commission, Final Report, 1988, Vol. 2, 731.
[38] *Woodend Rubber Co* v. *CIR* [1971] AC 321.

The traditional view in Australia was as expressed by the Privy Council in *Attorney-General for Canada* v. *Attorney-General for Ontario*[39] and is known as the rule in *Walker* v. *Baird*.[40]

> Within the British Empire there is a well-established rule that the making of a treaty is an executive act while the performance of its obligations, if they entail alteration of the existing domestic law, requires legislative action. Unlike some other countries, the stipulations of a treaty duly ratified do not within the Empire, by virtue of the treaty alone, have the force of law.

Similar views were expressed in *R* v. *Barger*,[41] *Chow Hung Ching* v. *the King*[42] and *Dietrich* v. *The Queen*.[43]

A more complex debate revolves around the place of customary international law in the domestic system. While this would not normally be expected to have an impact upon a domestic trade dispute, the nature and extent of customary law is always debatable and evolving, so the legal status should at least be identified. The approach to customary international law in Commonwealth courts is described as 'incorporation', 'adoption', or 'transformation'. These rules are considered part of municipal law in so far as they are not inconsistent with legislation or prior and binding judicial decisions.[44] Some cases are seen as supporting a narrower principle of transformation whereby customary rules will only be considered part of domestic law if they have been clearly adopted by legislation, precedent or established usage.[45] Brownlie concludes that the authorities taken as a whole support the doctrine of incorporation.[46]

Theoretical issues about the relation of municipal law and international law are spoken of by international law scholars as a conflict between a dualist and a monist view of international legal jurisprudence. This in turn relates to attitudes to the State and to individuals and the question of whether the latter should be the essential subject matter of any legal system. For proponents of this view, a monist system is supported.[47] Kelsen argued that national legal systems derived their validity from the international legal order which in turn supports a monist approach.[48] The traditional monist/dualist debate was more understandable in the early days of international law and international obligations where there was a clear delineation between the normative prescriptions for states and

---

[39] [1937] AC 326 at 347.   [40] [1892] AC 491.   [41] (1908) 6 CLR 41
[42] (1948) 77 CLR 449.   [43] (1992) 109 ALR 385
[44] *Polites* v. *The Commonwealth* (1945) 77 CLR 60; *International Tin Council Appeals* [1989] 3 WLR 969; *Chow Hung Ching* v. *the King* (1948) 77 CLR 449.
[45] See the discussion in I. Brownlie, *Principles of Public International Law* (4th edn. 1990) 43 ff.   [46] Ibid. 47.
[47] See e.g. H. Lauterpacht, *International Law and Human Rights* (1950).
[48] H. Kelsen, *General Theory of Law and the State* (1945) 363 ff.

individuals. We now have broad fields of private international law, protection of human rights, conflict of laws and the like which make the borderline somewhat blurry.

Nevertheless, because direct application is the exception rather than the norm, it is important that positive obligations in the area of implementation are added to general specific international commitments. The Permanent Court of International Justice has recognized the general duty to bring municipal law into conformity with international legal obligations. The WTO Agreement does not leave this issue to be resolved by general principles of law but rather in Article IX:4 requires that each member's laws, regulations and administrative procedures be in conformity with the annexed agreements. Similar sentiments are expressed in Article X of GATT 1947.

A further question is the extent to which a convention or treaty that has not been implemented should affect the behaviour of administrators. The treaty may not have direct effect as a matter of law, but administrators who are often given a role in developing 'reasonable' principles and procedures, need to have an understanding of the constraints, if any, that international obligations seek to place upon them. The legal issue arose directly in the recent High Court decision of *Minister for Ethnic Affairs* v. *Teoh*.[49] Mr Teoh was a Malaysian citizen who had come to Australia in 1988 under a temporary entry permit. He subsequently married an Australian citizen and applied for resident status. While that application was still pending he was convicted of the importation of heroin and was sentenced to six years' imprisonment. His application for resident status was rejected on the basis of the conviction. After seeking reconsideration through the Immigration Review Panel and the Minister, he appealed to the Federal Court. The Full Federal Court held that the Minister's delegate had not fully considered the effect of the break up of the family on the children of the marriage in making the decision. Two of the judges also considered that the ratification by the Government of the United Nations Convention on the Rights of the Child required that the decision-maker should act on the basis that the 'best interests' of the children should be treated as 'a primary consideration', notwithstanding that there was no domestic implementing legislation for that convention. The decision was appealed to the High Court. A majority of the High Court dismissed the appeal.[50]

Mason CJ and Deane J in a point judgement stated:

Where a statute or subordinate legislation is ambiguous, the Courts should favour that construction which accords with Australia's obligations under a treaty or international convention to which Australia is a party, in at least those cases in

---

[49] (1995) 128 ALR 353.
[50] Mason CJ, Deane, Toohey and Gaudron JJ with McHugh J dissenting.

which the legislation is enacted after, or in contemplation of, entry into, or ratification of, the relevant international instrument. That is because Parliament, *prima facie*, intends to give effect to Australia's obligations under international law.

They went on to say that the fact that the provisions of the convention did not form part of Australian law was a less than compelling reason for ignoring its provisions.

Gaudron J agreed with Mason CJ and Deane J in relation to the status of the convention in Australian law. Toohey J also found that the convention gave rise to legitimate expectations in the circumstances.[51]

After this case, it was initially thought that where trade laws are discretionary in nature, such as anti-dumping, administrators needed to be aware of the treaty provisions as well as any implementing legislation. However, the Government was concerned with the decision and introduced legislation to overcome it.[52] Once the bill is passed the position will be that a decision-maker can take the treaty into account without thereby invalidating the decision, but the treaty will not be taken as creating any rights in individuals to have the treaty so considered. International practice can also affect the behaviour of bureaucrats. For example, in the customs field, the work of the World Customs Organisation in the areas of tariff classification and valuation is particularly influential in preparing conventions but also has influence on administrators through the provision of persuasive interpretations.

8.6 CONSTITUTIONAL POWERS AND TRADE LAW

Because of the federal system, not only must an international treaty be given effect to by domestic legislation but that legislation must be within the constitutional power of the relevant parliament. Where international economic law is concerned, the relevant parliament will almost always be the Commonwealth Parliament, although private commercial laws (such as the Vienna Convention on the Sale of Goods) have at times needed to be implemented through uniform state legislation.

While the Constitution does not specifically mention treaties, a number of provisions deal with the design and ambit of domestic import and export laws. Section 51 (i) of the Commonwealth Constitution indicates that the Parliament has power to make laws for the peace, order, and good government of the Commonwealth with respect to trade and commerce with other countries, and among the states. Because of this wording, the

---

[51] The decision in *Teoh* follows an earlier decision in *Gunaleela* v. *Minister for Immigration and Ethnic Affairs* (1987) 74 ALR 263.
[52] Administrative Decisions (Effect of International Instruments) Bill 1995.

High Court has taken the view that there is a distinction between international and inter-state trade on the one hand, which are the subject of express Commonwealth legislative power and intra-state trade on the other, which is left as a matter of state responsibility unless it comes within some other head of Commonwealth power. A number of decisions have in turn sought to argue that certain aspects of intra-state trade are sufficiently connected with inter-state and international trade to be proper areas for Commonwealth Government regulations.

Other heads of power are also relevant. Section 51 (ii) deals with taxation, which would encompass customs duties. Section 51 (iii) covers uniform bounties. Section 51 (xxix) provides the Commonwealth with power to enact laws in relation to 'external affairs'. Section 90 indicates that the Commonwealth has exclusive power over duties of customs and bounties. Section 92 indicates that trade and commerce between the States shall be absolutely free. Section 51 (xx) provides ancillary powers to the express heads of power.

Where international economic law is concerned, these powers cumulatively make clear the ability to enter into agreements such as GATT and the WTO Agreement although the ambit of the General Agreement on Trade in Services and the Standards Agreement cover some areas which are traditionally the jurisdiction of State governments. Where services are concerned, other specific heads of Commonwealth power include postal, telegraphic, telephonic and other like services, banking, insurance, copyrights, patents, trade marks, and designs and corporations.

When questions arise as to the constitutional validity of specific laws, one issue is whether a constitutional power can be used for some ulterior motive. Such an aim will be upheld as valid if it is truly a law about an express head of power and does not offend against any express limitation on power. In *Fairfax* v. *FCT*[53] Menzies J indicated that neither the economic effect nor motivation are relevant to determining the basis of power for any law. Instead the court must look at the 'true character' of the law, although no criteria were articulated to indicate how this is to be determined. Based on these principles, the High Court has upheld health regulations imposed on a slaughter house where the meat was for export,[54] a dried fruits board to control exports,[55] and a tariff of charges for international charter flights.[56]

While the courts have interpreted the constitutional grounds for international trade laws widely, they are not without limits. In *Mather* v.

[53] (1965) 14 ATD 135.
[54] *O'Sullivan* v. *Noarlunga Meat Ltd (No 1)* (1954) 92 CLR 565.
[55] *Crow* v. *Commonwealth* (1935) 54 CLR 69.
[56] *R.* v. *Halton; ex parte Aus. Students Travel Pty Ltd* (1978) 138 CLR 201.

Classic Radio & Television Pty Ltd[57] Hudson J indicated in the Victorian Supreme Court that regulations concerning prohibited imports which purported to include conditions that imported goods not be disposed of within a two year-period were invalid because the relevant characteristics that make goods prohibited cannot depend upon events that may occur after the time of importation.

8.7 FEDERALISM AND INTERNATIONAL ECONOMIC LAW

Particular tensions arise when considering international law norms and responsibilities in the context of a federal system, particularly where residual legislative power is left to the states and not the central government. This tension has forced commentators and judges to take sides in a general debate about state rights versus central government authority in the field of international relations. In any federation, judges are inevitably forced to consider how expansively they wish to interpret the constitution to either promote states' rights or the rights of the central government.

As with the US Constitution, state powers are maintained unless inconsistent with the Commonwealth Constitution.[58] One major distinction is that the Australian Constitution has no express Bill of Rights. There are a limited number of guarantees within the Constitution and in recent times, the High Court has grappled with the concept of implied rights, discernible within constitutional provisions.

Thus in the Federation there are two separate questions; first whether the Commonwealth may enter into an international treaty, and secondly whether the Commonwealth has legislative competence to implement the terms of the treaty. The Court has long accepted the broad external affairs power to enter into treaties. The States themselves have no external affairs power. Barwick CJ in *Seas and Submerged Lands*[59] indicated that while external affairs was not expressed to be an exclusive power vested in the Commonwealth, only the Commonwealth has international status and the states are not international persons.

Quite distinct views emerged on the question of Commonwealth legislative competence to implement treaty provisions in cases where broad external affairs powers or treaty making powers are used to enter areas that were not otherwise mentioned in the Constitution. The key question was whether the Commonwealth should have the full power to implement international obligations or whether States should be the appropriate

---

[57] [1960] VR 595.   [58] Ss. 107 and 109.
[59] *NSW* v. *Commonwealth* (1975) 135 CLR 337.

parties where the substantive area of law was traditionally within their jurisdiction. In *Koowarta* v. *Bjelke Petersen*,[60] Mason J argued strongly against dividing legislative power in this way.

In *R.* v. *Burgess; ex parte Henry*,[61] the Court began the debate as to whether the external affairs power was such as to give the Commonwealth power to legislate implementation of any international treaty fully, save where this was a device to procure additional domestic jurisdiction. A wide view was suggested by Evatt and McTiernan JJ and Latham CJ. Narrower comments were made by Starke J and were suggested by aspects of the decision of Dixon J. Narrower views were also expressed by Barwick CJ in *Airlines of NSW Pty Ltd* v. *New South Wales (2)*.[62] One commentator suggests that the more traditional literalism of the Australian High Court is a result of the more detailed and wider list of specific powers given to the central government in the Australian Constitution when compared to the American Constitution.[63]

The question was left unresolved for some time while the Commonwealth adopted the practice of leaving implementation of many treaties to State Parliaments.[64] As and when litigation ensued, particularly when States have not been willing to implement legislation or have queried aspects of proposed legislation, the trend has been for the High Court to determine an increasing ambit of power in the central government merely through its international relations power.

The leading case was that of *Commonwealth* v. *Tasmania* (the *Tasmanian Dams Case*)[65] where the external affairs power was used to sign an international convention on world heritage listing that then gave the central government constitutional power to legislate in respect of conservation, an area which was not specifically granted to it under the Constitution. After a more narrowly constructed decision in *Koowarta* v. *Bjelke-Petersen*,[66] the *Tasmanian Dams Case* saw the majority hold that the Commonwealth could legislate to implement international obligations assumed under a bona fide international treaty. The subject-matter was not relevant for this proposition, but the Commonwealth law must be reasonably appropriate in terms of giving effect to the treaty and the power is subject to any express or implied limitations contained in the Constitution.[67] Brennan J indicated that if there was no legislative obligation contained in the treaty, the subject-matter would have to be of international concern to justify domestic legislation in an area where the Commonwealth does not have express power.

---

[60] (1982) 153 CLR 168.   [61] (1936) 55 CLR 608.
[62] (1965) 133 CLR 54.   [63] See Lane, *Manual*, 6.
[64] See Hanks, *Australian Constitutional Law*, 764.
[65] (1983) 57 AL JR 450; 46 ALR 625.   [66] (1982) 153 CLR 168.
[67] See Hanks, *Australian Constitutional Law*, 799.

The next question is to determine how a court would identify when the subject-matter of a treaty is truly international in character. Mason J in *Tasmanian Dams* indicated that these questions were ones on which 'the court cannot substitute its judgment for that of the executive government and parliament'. They were 'issues involving nice questions of sensitive judgement which should be left to the executive government for determination.'[68]

The next question is the extent to which the domestic legislation implementing such a treaty must conform to that treaty where the treaty itself, through the external affairs power, is the only basis for legislative power. While the domestic legislation does not have to mirror the treaty on a word for word basis and can deal with reasonable ancillary matters, the judges in *Tasmanian Dams* considered that the legislation must be reasonable for the performance of the treaty obligations. The expansive view as per *Tasmanian Dams* was confirmed in *Richardson* v. *Forestry Commission*.[69] Deane J's test of 'reasonable proportionality' in *Tasmanian Dams* was accepted by the majority in *Richardson*. Parliament may adapt the treaty to local conditions. Secondly, it may choose the means that it thinks best carries out the aims. Thirdly, the legislative provision should not be narrowly compared to the treaty.[70]

Regardless of the ultimate legal position, consultation in a federation is an important goal and mechanism for coherent reform. A number of initiatives have aimed to promote such consultation. At the State Premiers' Conference in 1982, procedures were set out dealing with consultation and co-operation between the Commonwealth and the states where international matters were concerned.[71] The procedures are outlined in a document entitled 'Principles and Procedures for Commonwealth–State Consultation on Treaties' a document which has been revised from time to time. The agreed principles do not require prior agreement of all states and territories before the Commonwealth will enter into a treaty obligation.

In addition, the Standing Committee of Attorneys-General, comprising the Attorneys-General and Ministers of Justice of the Federal Government, the States, the Northern Territory, the Australian Capital Territory and New Zealand is the body that works towards uniform or harmonized legislative reforms. Implementation of the UN Convention on Contracts for the International Sale of Goods (the Vienna Sales Convention) was handled through the Standing Committee and implemented by State and Territory legislation.

---

[68] (1983) 57 ALJR 450 at 525.   [69] (1988) 164 CLR 261.
[70] See Lane, *Manual*, 142.
[71] ACC External Affairs Report (1984), 255–8 reprinted in ACC Proc., Brisbane 1985, vol 2.

8.8 DOMESTIC COURTS AND THE INTERPRETATION OF TREATIES
AND TRADE LAWS

When examining the behaviour of domestic courts, there are a number of levels to consider. To some, questions of interpretation raise particularly fundamental philosophical perspectives.[72] At the practical level, the first question is the constitutional validity of any treaty or enabling domestic legislation. This was outlined above. The second is the way such provisions will be interpreted and the extent to which international treaties can be used as aids to interpretation. The third issue involves the constraints, if any, that the court will impose on bureaucratic decision-making where trade laws involve elements of discretionary protection such as anti-dumping or safeguards regimes. A fourth issue is the approach to questions of evidence. Here the main subsidiary issues include the role for traditional rules of evidence, the use of expert witnesses, onus and burden of proof and use of economic witnesses in injury determinations.

In addition, where an international convention has been entered into which is binding on Australia, it may be a legitimate source of guidance on the development of common law.[73] In this respect and when gap-filling in legislation, the court has both a substantive and procedural function.[74]

Where treaty interpretation is concerned, we have already said that international law rules cannot override domestic legislation in breach of the international law, although the interpretational issue is that courts will not readily conclude that there is such intentional departure where more than one interpretation is possible.[75] Here the presumption is that Parliament intended to give effect to the international treaty.[76] Where discrepancies are found between the domestic legislation and the international convention, it is more appropriate to see these as an inevitable corollary of translating the convention into domestic language and law rather than Parliament's intent to depart from the treaty obligations.[77]

While domestic legislation that aims to alter a treaty provision will

---

[72] See, e.g., M. S. McDougal, H. D. Lasswell and J. C. Miller, *The Interpretation of International Agreements and World Public Order; Principles of Content and Procedure* (1994).

[73] Toohey J in *Dietrich* v. *The Queen* (1992) 109 ALR 385.

[74] R. E. Hudec, 'The role of judicial review in preserving liberal foreign trade policies' in *National Constitutions*, 503.

[75] *Polites* v. *Commonwealth* (1945) 77 CLR 60.

[76] *Salomon* v. *Commissioners of Customs and Excise* [1967] 2 QB 116.

[77] See, e.g., Megaw LJ in *The Bankco* [1971] 1 All ER 524, 537 and Diplock LJ in *Post Office* v. *Estuary Radio Ltd* [1967] 3 All ER 679 at 682. In the latter case, Diplock LJ pointed out that international agreements do not seek to use terms of art from domestic legal systems so some modifications are often inevitable.

prevail, in cases of ambiguity, the clearer the reference to the international treaty and a legislative purpose of giving effect to it, the more likely a court will be influenced by treaty provisions that are not directly incorporated in the legislation. For example, in early anti-dumping cases, importers relied on the then section 14 of the Customs Tariff (Anti-Dumping) Act which stated that the Minister was not to take action inconsistent with Australia's international obligations under any international agreement relating to tariffs and trade. A number of importers sought interim injunctions against provisional securities called for under the legislation. The perverse result was that after the first case, the provision was repealed.[78]

One interpretation issue that may undermine harmonization is that under a system of transformation, transformed rules could be interpreted according to municipal approaches which in turn could differ from the rules of international law.[79] In *Shipping Corporation of India Ltd* v. *Gamlen Chemical Co.* (A/Asia Pty Ltd),[80] the High Court discussed the means of interpreting expressions in conventions. The Court indicated that the rules formulated by an international convention should be construed in a normal manner appropriate for the interpretation of an international convention unconstrained by technical rules of English law or by English precedent, but on broad principles of acceptation. Recourse could also be made to municipal law for the purpose of elucidating the meaning of conventions.[81]

In *Salomon* v. *Commissioners of Customs and Excise*,[82] Diplock LJ said:

If the terms of the legislation are not clear but are reasonably capable of more than one meaning the treaty itself becomes relevant for there is a *prima facie* presumption that parliament does not intend it to act in breach of international law, including therein specific treaty obligations; and if one of the meanings which can reasonably be ascribed to legislation is consonant with the treaty obligations and another or others are not, the meaning which is consonant is to be preferred.

Section 15AA and 15AB of the Acts Interpretation Act now require a court to give effect to the purpose of legislation where there is an ambiguity and also indicate that material not forming part of the Act, which is capable of assisting in ascertaining the meaning of a provision, can be

---

[78] The case was *Feltex Reid Rubber Ltd* v. *Minister for Industry and Commerce* (1983) 46 ALR 171. Anecdotal evidence suggests two conflicting reasons for the repeal of s. 14. The first view was that the Department was merely concerned that it was used against it in litigation. The second was to ensure that the US could not use it to challenge s. 10A and 10B, which removed an injury test if such test was not applied by US authorities.

[79] K. J. Partsch, 'International law and municipal law' in R. Bernhardt (ed.), *Encyclopaedia of Public International Law*, 10 (1987) 246.

[80] (1980) 147 CLR 142.

[81] The Court expressly approved the English approach as indicated in *James Buchanan & Co Ltd* v. *Babco Forwarding & Shipping (UK) Ltd* [1978] AC 141.

[82] [1967] 2 QB 116.

considered to confirm that the meaning is the ordinary meaning as conveyed by the text, or to determine the meaning when the provision is ambiguous or obscure or where the ordinary meaning leads to a result that is manifestly absurd or is unreasonable. Section 15AB (2) sets out certain types of material that can be relied upon and in paragraph (b) specifically refers to any treaty or international agreement referred to in the Act. Even if the treaty was not specifically mentioned, it is likely that Australian courts would not look at *travaux preparatoires* quite readily.

8.9 ADMINISTRATIVE LAW AND THE COURTS

The next question relates to the general role and ambit of administrative law, particularly where trade and customs disputes are involved. Administrative law issues also raise the design question of the extent to which discretions are or should be incorporated in international trade rules. Are the discretions appropriately circumscribed? What guides could reasonably be placed in the WTO Agreements to constrain discretionary decision making?

Where administrative aspects of the trade regime assume importance, which is often the case, much depends on the nature, style and attitudes of judicial and administrative review in the domestic system. In Australia we have an elaborate system of review, primarily through three avenues. The bulk of classification and valuation disputes are handled through the Administrative Appeals Tribunal. The Administrative Appeals Tribunal Act established a tribunal which undertakes a full merits review of disputes. Thus the tribunal stands in the shoes of the decision-maker and may come to a contrary decision notwithstanding that it believes that there was nothing unreasonable in the decision-maker's thought processes or conclusions.

One of the aims of the legislation has been to reduce the cost and formality of disputes. The Tribunal is also not bound by the formal rules of evidence and may, for example, accept hearsay evidence as a matter of course. The tradition, however, is for a more conservative approach and for a strong preference to be indicated for traditional and acceptable forms of evidence. The most important issue is the role of onus and burden of proof, particularly if a tribunal is looking at complex questions of injury and the like. The legislation makes no specific comment in this regard but the tribunal has long held that there is no general onus on any party.[83] On the other hand, a number of cases have indicated that it depends on the

---

[83] *Re Ladybird Children's Wear Pty Ltd* v. *Department of Business and Consumer Affairs* (1976) 1 ALD 1.

statutory formulation as to who has an the effective onus before a tribunal.[84]

Other than providing that the Tribunal is not bound by the formal rules of evidence, the legislation does not indicate how litigation should be conducted. Perhaps inevitably because of the general nature of the Australian legal system and the growing involvement of lawyers in customs disputes, AAT litigation has become more adversarial in nature. Whilst some tribunal members take a strong controlling approach, the norm is to allow parties to present their own cases in their own way.

The legislation also indicates that persons whose interests are affected may also be joined as parties. While this at first sight has appeal, recent trends are of grave concern because of the adversarial approach and the lack of power to award costs against the losing party. Thus in a typical tariff concession or classification case, there may be representation by the aggrieved importer, other importers, domestic manufacturers and the decision-maker. If all parties have the right to an opening and closing address and cross-examination, the potential for unnecessarily lengthening the hearing is obvious.

Another issue is the role taken by the decision-maker before the Tribunal. One former Tribunal member considered that the preferred role of the decision-maker is not as an adversary but rather 'to assist the Tribunal in reaching the right or preferable decision.'[85] On the one hand it is desirable for the decision-maker to keep an open mind and be willing to advise the Tribunal when he or she thinks their decision was wrong. On the other hand, a non-adversarial approach should not be an excuse for failing to prepare fully but instead rely on the joined parties to present the complete picture. The latter is another disconcerting trend of late.

The second tier of administrative review is through the Federal Court under the Administrative Decisions (Judicial Review) Act. This legislation provides for direct Federal Court review of any decision taken under an enactment where that decision is of an administrative nature. ADJRA aims to simplify and codify and to some extent reform common law aspects of judicial review of Commonwealth administrative actions. It overcomes a number of the common law distinctions on grounds of review, for example indicating that a general error of law is a ground for review whether or not that error appears on the record of the decision. The Act does not affect judicial review in the High Court's original jurisdiction as this is provided for in section 75 of the Constitution and cannot be excluded by Parliament.

Both ADJRA and the AAT Act allow the person whose interests are

---

[84] *McDonald* v. *Director-General of Social Security* (1984) 6 ALD 6.
[85] Senior Member Hall cited in R. C. Davey 'The new administrative law: a commentary on costs' (1983) 22 AJPA (2) 263.

affected to request a statement of reasons for the decision and an outline of the material evidence upon which the decision was reached. The AAT Act gives rights of standing to any 'person whose interests are affected'. ADJRA gives standing to 'a person aggrieved'. In *Tooheys Case*[86] this was a purchaser from the importer.

Decisions leading to the making of duty demands are specifically exempted from review under ADJRA. This is to support the requirement in the legislation that where there is a dispute as to duty, the amount in dispute must be paid under protest and an action commenced within a six-month time period.[87] Without such an exemption, some litigants might challenge each step along the way of a complex assessment process.

The Federal Court has interpreted the basis of jurisdiction widely. It considered the case of a refusal to make a discretionary section 273 by-law determination in *Tooheys Ltd* v. *Minister for Business and Consumer Affairs*,[88] prohibited imports where classification was an issue in *Peacock* v. *Zyfert*,[89] and securities called for under anti-dumping legislation in *Tasman Timber Ltd* v. *Minister of Industry and Commerce*.[90] After the latter decision, the Administrative Decision (Judicial Review) Regulations then exempted from the operation of ADJRA decisions under section 42 of the Customs Act 1901 to take securities in respect of duty payable under the then sections 8, 9, 10 or 11 of the Customs Tariff (Anti-Dumping) Act 1975. Similar amendments were made to the Act under the Customs Securities (Anti-Dumping) Amendment Act 1982. Schedule 1 (d) was also included in the Act to stop challenges to such interim decisions but all that happened was that in *Re Hayes ex parte J Wattie Canneries Ltd*,[91] the importer merely switched its claim to the Judiciary Act 1903 to avoid this exemption. Because the Constitution specifically grants citizens the right to bring actions before the High Court, a mere statutory exemption cannot preclude that power. Under the Judiciary Act, High Court powers are delegated down to the Federal Court in certain circumstances. Section 39B of the Judiciary Act 1903 invests the original jurisdiction of the Federal Court with jurisdiction in respect of any matter in which a writ of *mandamus* or prohibition or an injunction is sought against an officer or officers of the Commonwealth. This change was introduced in 1983 to help shift some of the heavy workload from the High Court to the Federal Court. The amendment does not preclude an applicant seeking such remedies directly from the High Court.

A number of Federal Court challenges have been taken in the customs area, particularly where anti-dumping duties are concerned. Unlike the

[86] (1982) 42 ALR 260.   [87] S. 167 Customs Act.
[88] (1982) 42 ALR 260.   [89] (1983) 48 ALR 549.
[90] (1983) 46 ALR 149.   [91] (1986) 70 ALR 65; (1987) 74 ALR 202.

United States, Australia's anti-dumping legislation is general in nature without any specific regulations or statements of administrative action detailing the way many of the subsidiary questions are resolved. This in turn has necessitated greater resort to litigation to fill in the gaps left by the legislation. These and other court decisions in the customs field have made important comments about the Court's role in trying to balance the rights of the individual, the rights of the bureaucracy and the general needs of the commercial and importing communities. The Court has consistently tried to combine principles of administrative accountability with the need for reasonable rather than precise and expensive decision-making in order to facilitate commerce.

The third tier of administrative review is the Commonwealth Ombudsman. The Ombudsman cannot review decisions of ministers but ombudsmen have from time to time taken the view that they can review recommendations to ministers from departmental officers. The Ombudsman has a discretion to refuse to be involved in a complaint if there is an adequate alternative remedy. As is the general norm, the Ombudsman has no powers to compel bureaucrats to behave in a particular way. In the late 1980s, tensions arose between the Commonwealth Ombudsman and the Australian Customs Service with the latter refusing to follow certain recommendations. In the 1989–90 annual report the then Commonwealth and Defence Force Ombudsman said there was a 'tendency for certain kinds of agency to be inward-looking and to display a narrow appreciation of administrative issues. I do not think it unfair to say that in my view this description applies to the Australian Customs Service.' Particular concerns were the alleged excessive willingness to litigate, reluctance to accept views of courts contrary to its own, reliance on highly technical legal interpretation, harshness in administration of penalty policies and unwillingness to hear representations or reconsider decisions.[92] After these critical comments, a meeting was held between the Comptroller-General of Customs and the then Ombudsman. A number of measures were agreed upon to improve their working relationship including formal annual meetings, quarterly meetings for senior officers, participation by the Ombudsman's office in Australian Customs Service training programmes and its in-house newsletter, and establishing central contact points in both organizations.

The lack of a clear blue print as to the rights and obligations of importers and customs officials is likely to lead to significant unnecessary transaction costs in some jurisdictions at least, although it is not suggested that GATT negotiators should themselves spend significant time on these issues. One issue that is dominant in the thinking and actions of Australian Customs

[92] *1989–90 Annual Report*, 40.

officials which is almost never discussed in GATT/WTO and rarely discussed in the Customs Co-operation Council is the problem posed by transactions aimed at avoiding customs duty or customs duty fraud. In a society that witnessed epidemic proportions of tax avoidance in the 1970s, this is a reasonable concern of government, which in turn has led to very widespread powers of investigation, search, seizure, and both administrative and criminal penalties. Inevitably, such powers are used from time to time against innocent parties which leads to justifiable outrage by the importing and legal communities. At worst, this can grossly interfere with the liberty of individuals and be a significant non-tariff barrier to trade. For example, at the recommendation of the Commonwealth Director of Public Prosecutions, the Customs Department instigated a high profile conspiracy trial against a group of importers and a leading consultant in the late 1980s. After many years, the case was proved ill-founded and a Parliamentary Committee recommended A$23m. be paid in compensation.

8.10 TRANSPARENCY IN POLICY-MAKING AND DECISIONS

Transparency includes identification of the costs to government and the adverse effects on other industries as a result of any policy proposal.[93] In addition to the review avenues described above, the main transparency mechanisms are the Freedom of Information Act 1982 and the role of the Industry Commission. The Freedom of Information Act allows for certain non-confidential documents of government to be obtained by the public. The Industry Commission is an advisory body that has received strong recommendations as a model for all governments by many economic commentators. Australia's Commission and New Zealand's Economic Development Commission were commented upon favourably both by the Organization of Economic Co-operation and Development and the Trade Policy Research Centre Special Report on Public Scrutiny of Protection.[94] Another aspect of openness is the Senate Standing Committee for the Scrutiny of Bills whose terms of reference include analysing the effect of legislation on various individual rights.

The Industry Commission was established in 1990 to review and advise government on industry matters. Its primary function is to conduct public enquiries and report on matters referred to it. In addition, the Industry Commission Act 1989 requires the Commission to report annually on the

---

[93] For an analysis of these issues of transparency, see O. Long et al. Public Scrutiny of Protection, Domestic Policy Transparency and Trade Liberalisation, Trade Policy Research Centre Special Report No. 7.
[94] Ibid; OECD, Transparency for Positive Adjustment, 1983.

performance of Australian industry and developments in assistance and regulations of industry. The Commission has within it an Office of Regulation Review which analyses regulations in sectors under review in its programme. Secretariat and research functions are also provided by the Commission. The Commission provides some research for a Steering Committee on National Performance Monitoring of Government Trading Enterprises which was established at the July 1991 special Premiers' Conference. The July 1993 Premiers' Conference established a Steering Committee for the Review of Commonwealth and State Service Provision.

The main work is in the area of assistance. Section 8 of the Industry Commission Act indicates that the following general policy guidelines should inform the work of the Commission:

(a) to encourage the development and growth of Australian industries that are efficient in their use of resources, self-reliant, enterprising, innovative, and internationally competitive: and

(b) to facilitate adjustment to structural changes in the economy and to ease social and economic hardships arising from those changes; and

(c) to reduce regulation of industry (including regulation by the States and Territories where this is consistent with the social and economic goals of the Commonwealth Government); and

(d) to recognize the interests of industries, consumers, and the community, likely to be affected by measures proposed by the Commission.

Section 10 indicates that the Minister shall not take certain action relating to industry without a report by the Commission. Section 11 indicates that the actions which require an Industry Commission report as a preliminary measure include, the imposition, removal, increase or reduction of duties on goods imported into Australia, the prohibition or restriction of the importation of goods into Australia, the removal, extension or reduction of a prohibition or restriction, the provision of financial assistance for over two years to an industry or additional finance to an industry which has already received financial assistance for greater than that period and the suspension, withdrawal, increase or reduction of such financial assistance.

Section 12 exempts actions from the section 10 requirement if they are necessary to correct anomalies, errors or ambiguities in the Customs Tariff Act 1987 or to correct an error in the implementation of a decision of the Government and where the minister considers that a decision of a court or tribunal has altered the intended rate of duty. Section 12 is a contentious provision with the legal profession, given that it provides scope for the bureaucracy to have the legislation changed after a court decision adverse to it has been tendered. Furthermore, defining what is truly an anomaly or ambiguity is a problematic issue.

The Commission may summons persons to attend to give evidence and produce documents and there are significant fines and jail terms for failure to do so. To promote transparency, the Commission makes a draft report available to the public before finalizing a report on any particular enquiry. Hearings are open to the public, as are transcripts and material provided to the Commission. As well as public hearings, the Commission utilizes workshops and round table discussions from time to time where appropriate.

There are a number of advantages of using a body like the Industry Commission. First it helps to shield politicians from vested interest groups by requiring them to present an objective case to an independent expert body. Secondly, by providing a forum for open discussion of issues, it raises the chance that competing groups, including consumers, will counter the efforts of rent seekers. Thirdly, it should promote rationality in debate and consistency in decision-making.

One difficulty with such an approach to tariff setting is that it may lead to a more fragmented tariff Act simply because specific duty rates are identified for each industry rather than across the board. This in turn leads to complex classification disputes between importers and Government. Circumstances may also change so rapidly that quick responses cannot be made by Government and the Commission.

8.11 AUSTRALIAN TARIFF POLICY-MAKING

Protection for Australian industry arises in a number of ways through tariffs, licensing, subsidies, anti-dumping, tax concessions, price stabilization schemes and the like. It has been described by one commentator as piecemeal in fashion and arising from a disparate collection of economic influences.[95] In that sense it is dissimilar to the discretionary and litigious protectionism of the United States and the suggestions of a managed trade partnership between bureaucracy and government in Japan or the regional-oriented protectionism of the European Union. Nevertheless, the major feature of Australian protectionism has been the central role of the tariff. Within the GATT context, because there is no direct binding obligation to reduce tariffs but merely an obligation not to raise bound tariffs and an obligation to offer tariffs on a most favoured nation basis, Australia has been slow to openly liberalize its trade regime, but has done so within its GATT rights. Anderson and Garnaut highlighted the fact that tariffs rose reasonably steadily in Australia for seventy years after

---

[95] J. Nieuwenhuysen 'Towards freer trade for Australia' in J. Nieuwenhuysen (ed.), *Towards Freer Trade between Nations*, (1989), 115.

Federation.[96] The following section involves a brief history of Australia's tariff policy. This helps put the Uruguay Round negotiating aims and domestic political views in better perspective.

Prior to Federation, the two largest states in Australia, Victoria and New South Wales had quite distinct attitudes to protection, Victoria being strongly protectionist whilst New South Wales was principally free-trade-orientated.[97] The first Federal Government was primarily a coalition of protectionist forces, although some compromise with the free traders was inevitable. The first Federal tariff was enacted in 1902 and was primarily revenue-raising in focus.[98] A Royal Commission was established which operated between 1905 and 1907[99] and which made largely protectionist recommendations.

Initially, much protectionist rhetoric related to the rights of workers and the need for protection to protect jobs and wage rates. For example, the Royal Commission led to a number of changes including the Excise Tariff (Agricultural Machinery) Act 1906, which linked the tariff to awards under the Conciliation and Arbitration Act and provided that labour remuneration should be fair and reasonable in order to obtain exemptions. While economists would consistently challenge any positive relationship between protection and employment levels, such popular misconceptions abound in the trade arena. To understand Australian attitudes, it is important to realize that until relatively recently in its federal history, no government could expect to survive for very long in office if unemployment rates were at any significant level. One of the two main political parties, and the one in power throughout the Uruguay Round, the Australian Labor Party, has had consistent links with the union movement.

The Lyne tariff was introduced in 1908. In 1912 the then Labor government established the Interstate Commission, an independent body with both judicial and advisory powers over trade and commerce.[100] This began a long traditional of transparent and independent bodies operating in the trade field. In 1915, the High Court ruled that the judicial powers granted to the Interstate Commission were unconstitutional as only courts could exercise judicial functions. This left it with merely an advisory role. When the term of office of the then Commissioners expired in 1920, the Commission was left to lapse.

In 1921, tariffs were raised through the Greene tariff and anti-dumping provisions contained in the Customs Tariff (Industry Preservation) Act

---

[96] K. Anderson and R. Garnaut, *Australian Protectionism—Extent, Causes and Effects* (1987), 6.
[97] L. Glezer, *Tariff Politics: Australian Policy Making 1960–1980* (1982), 4.
[98] See Nieuwenhuysen, 'Towards freer trade', 115.
[99] Royal Commission on Customs and Excise Tariffs.
[100] Interstate Commission Act (No 33) 1912.

1906 were strengthened. A new body, the Tariff Board was established under the Tariff Board Act 1921. Section 15 (1) of the Act provided a list of matters which were required to be referred to the Board. These included 'the necessity for new increased or reduced duties and the deferment of existing or proposed deferred duties'. It was initially established on a two-year trial period. Changes to the Act in 1924 gave it a permanent existence. At that time, a further amendment was made to require all enquiries to be held in public.

Protectionist pressures were high in the mid 1920s and two further tariff increases occurred through the Pratten tariff. Some tensions also began to appear between the views of the Board and that of the Government. In 1927 a Committee was appointed to review and report on the effects of the tariff.[101] The Committee provided a mildly protectionist conclusion, but indicated that increasing protection would not be advisable and sought to quantify the cost. As the Depression took hold, the new Labor government bypassed the Board and increased tariff levels significantly.

The importance and role of the Board was strengthened by the Ottawa Agreement of 1932 which established the system of British Commonwealth preferences.[102] In addition to the reciprocal promises of lower duty rates, Australia also agreed to limit protection to industries 'reasonably assured of sound opportunities of success'. The Tariff Board was to review duties on the basis of such an approach. No duties on British goods could be imposed before a Board recommendation and no new duty could apply to such goods in excess of the recommendation of the Board. British manufacturers were also given rights of representation before the Board. The Ottawa Agreement also required that UK producers be given full opportunity of reasonable competition on the basis of the relative cost of economical and efficient production. Following the Ottawa Agreement, the Board saw its role as being to 'provide a marginal advantage in favour of the Australian manufacturer'.[103]

Thus where British imports were concerned, the Board moved from an advisory body to a regulatory one.[104] As one commentator put it:

The Board now had the formal power of setting limits on Australian protection which, to all appearances, were binding on the Government. In that limited sense, it was above Parliament. Parliament had thus renounced control over a crucial option of tariff-making.[105]

---

[101] The Brigden Committee whose Report was published as J. B. Brigden et al., The Australian Tariff: an Economic Enquiry.

[102] The United Kingdom–Australia Trade Agreement, CPP, Sessions 1932–4, IV, 1043–5. The Ottawa Agreement lapsed in 1937 and was then continued on a six-monthly basis. It was renegotiated in 1938.

[103] Tariff Board, Annual Report 1932–3, 12; see Glezer Tariff Politics, 18.

[104] Ibid. 17   [105] Ibid. 17–18.

The next key event was the establishment of the GATT. While Australia was an original signatory to the GATT[106] and has generally been seen as a complier with GATT obligations, its initial aims in entering the Agreement were far removed from the promotion of liberal international trade. Commentators assert three reasons for Australia adopting the GATT. The first was the freedom to protect domestic industry through the tariff and to protect for balance of payments problems. The second was the wish to maintain the tariff preferences under the Imperial Preference System which emanated from the Ottawa Agreement, unless compensating concessions were received. While some modifications were made to British preferences at the establishment of GATT, these were largely left intact, leaving the Tariff Board to warn of possible conflicts between the Ottawa and GATT Agreements.[107] The GATT schedules originally adopted merely set out maximum margins of preference for pre-GATT preferential arrangements. Thirdly, it sought stability in commodity prices and some limits on agricultural protectionism.[108] Australia has also been a party to international commodity agreements such as the International Wheat Agreement 1942 which sought to fix minimum and maximum prices.

The failure of the United States to convince Great Britain to dismantle the Commonwealth Preference System at the time of the establishment of GATT placed Australia on the outer of liberal and non-discriminatory trading relationships from the outset. In the period leading up to the establishment of GATT, Australia relied primarily on import licensing and quotas for protection rather than the tariff. The 1950s and 1960s then saw further increases in protectionism. The collapse of wool prices in the early 1950s led to a deterioration in Australia's balance of trade.[109] In March 1952, import controls and quotas were established under the direction of the Department of Trade and Customs. These were introduced as a temporary measure because of these balance of payments difficulties. Licensing operated from 1952 to 1960 and was established under the principles of Article XII of the GATT. Other import controls were justified on the basis of the Grandfather clause, Article XX and XXI exceptions. Prior to 1952, import restrictions were applied to goods of US

[106] Australia signed the GATT as one of 23 countries on 30 Oct. 1947. It came into effect for Australia on 1 Jan. 1948 through the Protocol of Provisional Application. Not only was Australia one of the original signatories of the GATT but it was also one of the 14 countries invited by the US to join in negotiations to that end in Dec. 1945. K. Kock, *International Trade Policy and the GATT 1947–1967* (1969), 38.

[107] Tariff Board, *Annual Report 1950*, 20; see Glezer *Tariff Politics*, 22. See also J. G. Crawford (ed.), *Australian Trade Policy (1942–1966)*, 127–37.

[108] K. W. Ryan, 'Australia and international trade law' in *International Law in Australia*, 279.

[109] A. D. Woodland, 'Trade policies in Australia' in D. Salvatore (ed.), *National Trade Policies: Studies in Comparative Economic Policies* (1992), 241.

dollar area origin pursuant to Article XIII and to goods of Japanese origin through the use of Article XXXV, when Japan became a contracting party. During the 1950s, a number of other measures were introduced to assist primary industry. These included tax concessions, financial grants, preferential credit, research and advisory programmes, and price stabilization schemes.[110] During the 1960s, greater use was made of production quotas and government subsidies to industries such as dairy, tobacco, and wheat.[111]

Problems with the Commonwealth Preference System also prevented tariff cuts between Commonwealth countries and the United States at the Torquay Conference in 1950–51.[112] The Ottawa Agreement was replaced in 1957 by a trade agreement. The intent was to renegotiate this agreement after a five-year period but this was deferred while the United Kingdom negotiated to accede to the European Economic Community. Renegotiation was then overtaken by the Kennedy Round. The Agreement was ultimately terminated on 31 January 1973 after the United Kingdom had entered the EEC.

Australia was a strong advocate of the 1955 Revision of the GATT and in particular sought to incorporate the Havana Charter Articles dealing with employment and economic activity.[113] At the GATT review session in 1955, Australia sought to make an amendment to allow immediate increase of bound rates subject to compensatory concessions where delay would be likely to damage an Australian industry in a way that would be difficult to overcome. Article XVIII of GATT was amended to this effect.

In 1966, Australia received a waiver to establish a preference system in relation to developing countries. This predated the 1971 general GATT waiver establishing generalized system of preference schemes. Where development issues were concerned, Australia saw itself in a midway position between developed and developing countries arguing that it has had a similar orientation to less developed countries and needed high tariffs to protect domestic infant industries.[114] Being a high tariff country with an interest in a relatively small number of primary products, Australia was singled out as a country requiring special treatment in the Kennedy Round negotiations. Along with Canada, New Zealand, and South Africa, Australia was to be provided with a 'balance of advantages based on trade concessions by them of equal value'.[115]

For obvious reasons, Australia has been particularly concerned with the agricultural policies and rules incorporated within GATT at the outset. At

---

[110] Industries Assistance Commission, *Annual Report 1973–74* (1974), 8.
[111] See A. D. Woodland, 'Trade Policies in Australia' at 242.
[112] Kock, *International Trade Policy*, 71   [113] Ibid. 81.   [114] Ibid. 221.
[115] Ibid. 105–6.

the 1955 review session, Australia was unsuccessful in seeking to completely ban export subsidies. The introduction of Article XVI (3) was a compromise which worked satisfactorily in the *Wheat Flour Case* but not the subsequent *Sugar Case*.[116] The next important stage was the publication of the Haberler Report in 1958. The Report was criticized in some circles[117] but led to the establishment of a Committee on agricultural protection.

The 1958 GATT panel on French Government Subsidies on the Export of Wheat and Wheat Flour found in favour of the Australian complaint which in due course resulted in an agreement between the two governments.[118] The 1976 GATT panel dealing with Australia's complaint about EEC Export Refunds on Sugar gave rise to a more equivocal conclusion holding that the refunds were a subsidy and that serious prejudice had been caused to Australia but that it was not possible to conclude that the EEC thereby had a more than equitable share of world trade. Ryan argues that the reasoning was inappropriate because the panel looked to see whether Australian exports were displaced and whether there was a causal link between the replacement and the export subsidy. If, however, the Australian exporters reduced their prices and profit margins to maintain share, this methodology would not be satisfied notwithstanding clear injury.[119] Other concerns in the agricultural arena included the use of the variable levy by the European Community, the US Agricultural Waiver, voluntary export restraints and numerous other forms of quantitative restrictions.

Considerable use was made of Article XIX actions under the GATT. In the 1950s, Article XIX was invoked twice, in the 1960s fifteen times, seventeen times during the 1970s and four times between 1980 and 1983. No such safeguard actions have been taken since then.[120] In the 1960s and 1970s, after import licensing was removed, legislation was introduced to allow for temporary import restrictions while references were being considered by the Tariff Board.[121] That was replaced by the powers given to the Temporary Assistance Authority under the Industries Assistance Commission Act 1973. At least in this sense there was an open and

---

[116] *French Assistance to Exports of Wheat and Wheat Flour*, GATT Panel Report, adopted 21 Nov. 1958, BISD, 7S/46; *European Community—Refunds on Exports of Sugar*, Report of GATT Panel adopted on 6 Nov. 1979, BISD, 26S/290.

[117] e.g. G. Curzon, *Multilateral Commercial Diplomacy* (1965), 182.

[118] See Ryan, 'Australia and international trade laws' at 282.

[119] See also G. Thomson, 'The legal framework for international trade: a current perspective on the GATT', 9th International Trade Law Seminar, Canberra 1982.

[120] GATT, *Trade Policy Review, Australia 1989* (1990), 264.

[121] See Ryan, 'Australia and international trade law' at 279.

transparent system, although one without the guidelines that an elaborate safeguards and structural adjustment regime might require.

During the 1970s, liberal trade attitudes became more influential. A 25 per cent across-the-board tariff cut in 1973 occurred when the then Labor Government decided to open the economy to greater international competition. With hindsight, this was seen as too much of a cut in too short a time.

A recession followed the across-the-board tariff cut. The Government introduced tariff quotas in 1974 in the areas of textiles, clothing, footwear and the passenger-motor-vehicle industry. A new local contents scheme for passenger motor vehicles was set up in 1974. In 1974, the Tariff Board was replaced by the Industries Assistance Commission.

In 1978, the Export Expansion Grants Scheme was established to provide grants to companies able to increase exports. Because of the concern that this scheme would constitute an actionable subsidy under GATT rules, it was changed to an Export Markets Development Grant scheme where grants were no longer tied to actual exports but rather to the identification and pursuit of foreign markets. In 1978 an additional import duty of 12.5 per cent was added to goods subject to licensing or tariff quotas. In May 1972 a 2 per cent revenue tariff was imposed on previously duty-free goods. A seven-year phase-out of tariff quotas for textile clothing and footwear was introduced in January 1982. Phased tariff reductions were introduced in May 1988. The 2 per cent revenue duty was removed on 1 July 1988.

In addition to Commonwealth preferences, Australia has also entered into a free trade area with New Zealand. This commenced on 1 January 1966 via a New Zealand–Australia Free Trade Agreement which sought to establish free trade within a ten-year period. It was very narrow in its initial scope and the contracting parties of GATT were cautious in their conclusion on its validity under Article XXIV, inviting the parties to give serious consideration to a more comprehensive plan as soon as possible.[122] This was then replaced by the Closer Economic Relations Trade Agreement which now provides for duty-free trade between the two countries.

In recent times, both the government and business have sought to be more export oriented. In 1993–94 exports of goods and services comprised about 22 per cent of gross domestic product in volume terms. This compares with 14 per cent ten years earlier.[123] After a severe recession in the 1980s, Australia has emerged with strong growth and low inflation levels although unemployment remains much higher than OECD averages.

---

[122] BISD 14S 1966 22–3 and 115 ff.
[123] Industry Commission, *Annual Report 1993–94*, 1.

Assistance to industry has declined to an average effective rate of 10 per cent in the manufacturing sector and 11 per cent in the agricultural sector.[124] The 1991 proposals to reduce tariffs were supplemented by an announcement in 1994 that tariffs were to be phased down to 5 per cent in 1996 and would be maintained thereafter at that level. The key exceptions are in relation to passenger motor vehicles and the textile clothing and footwear industries. Tariffs on passenger motor vehicles will be 15 per cent by the year 2000 and up to 25 per cent in the textile clothing and footwear industries by that date.

Under the Trade Policy Review Mechanism, the GATT Council undertook two reviews of Australia's trade policy and regime. The first review occurred in December 1989. The second occurred in February 1994. The latter noted the key reforms in the Australian trading system and raised a small number of residual concerns in relation to tariff peaks and escalation in the area of passenger motor vehicles and textile clothing and footwear, the higher than average tariff levels, quarantine requirements and sanitary and phytosanitary regulations, restrictive purchasing practices of state marketing boards, preferential procurement policies and Australia's non-participation in the Government Procurement Code, amendments to anti-dumping legislation in 1991 and 1992, and support schemes for telecommunications and pharmaceuticals. United States Trade Representative Annual Reports have also alleged that customs valuation rules dealing with royalties and buying commissions were inconsistent with GATT although there seems little basis for this allegation.

8.12 NEGOTIATING PROCEDURE AND ARRANGEMENTS

The promotion of a new GATT Round was a matter of Government policy from soon after the end of the Tokyo Round because the latter was seen as being a failure from Australia's perspective, both in terms of outcomes and generally in terms of the influence Australia had.

The development of Australia's negotiating position for the Uruguay Round was primarily through the Department of Foreign Affairs and Trade and its liaison with industry groups, state governments, unions, and academics. The Trade Development Council has been the principal advisory body for the Ministry of Foreign Affairs and Trade. The formal industry group was the Trade Negotiations Advisory Group, a process which had been followed by Australia in the Tokyo Round and which was similar in nature to an industry advisory group utilised by the United States. In addition to the Trade Negotiations Advisory Group, there was a

[124] Ibid, 13.

Trade in Services Group, a Commodities Trade Advisory Group and the Industrial Property Advisory Committee which has an ongoing function in relation to reform of industrial property legislation.

As indicated above, while the Departments of Foreign Affairs and Trade had been merged some time ago, a separate Ministry for Trade Negotiations was established, primarily for the purposes of the Uruguay Round. The carriage of the negotiations was left to that Minister. Because of the wide-ranging nature of the Uruguay Round agreements, there also needed to be involvement from a number of other ministers. Stoeckel and Cutherbertson[125] have asserted that the inclusion of various departments in the process lead to a fragmented approach to trade policy formulation in Australia. It would certainly be a worthy topic for analysis to question whether a body such as the United States Trade Representative (USTR) is better able to develop and promote a coherent trade policy package.

While a number of ministers were consulted, Cabinet was only involved on an *ad hoc* basis. While Cabinet does not need to become involved in the treaty negotiating process, in fact approximately twenty reports were made to Cabinet and about four or five action submissions calling for actual decisions. At the end of the Round, the Minister for Trade Negotiations wrote to each of those ministers that had been consulted and received confirmation that the final decision on the package did not need to go to Cabinet.

If new legislation is required, Parliamentary Counsel is briefed by relevant departments to draft the provisions. If there is only a need to amend existing legislation, the Attorney-General's Department normally performs this function. The drafting and development of the Uruguay Round implementing bills was ultimately the responsibility of the Attorney-General whose Department co-ordinated the determination of what changes were necessary. In practice, there was an inter-departmental process. The Australian Customs Service did drafts of amendments to Customs legislation which required it. The Department of Prime Minister and Cabinet also acted as legislation manager. The Australian amending legislation only sought to implement the necessary changes and was not used as an excuse to add other legislative reforms.

The package of legislation to implement the results of the Uruguay Round comprised the Customs Tariff (World Trade Organization) Amendments Act (1994) which amended the Customs Tariff Act 1987 to give effect to Australia's tariff binding commitments, the Customs Tariff (Anti Dumping) (World Trade Organization Amendments) Act 1994, the Patents (World Trade Organization Amendments) Act 1994, the

---

[125] Stoeckel and Cuthbertson *The Game Plan: Successful Strategies for Australian Trade*, (1987).

Trademarks Act 1994, the Dairy Produce (World Trade Organization Amendments) Act 1994 and the Sales Tax (World Trade Organization Amendments) Act 1994. The day on which the World Trade Organization Agreement entered into force in Australia was the day declared by the Governor-General by Proclamation under paragraph 2 (5) (B) of the Copyright (World Trade Organization Amendments) Act 1994.

8.13 URUGUAY ROUND NEGOTIATIONS AND RESULTS

In some respects it is difficult to evaluate the outcomes of the Uruguay Round. One reason is because in the most troublesome areas such as agriculture and services, the results are only a tentative first step in an ongoing process. Thus future developments in that process are of paramount importance.

It is also difficult to assess the outcome of negotiations without considering something about the process of negotiation and politics itself. The USTR at the time of the Tokyo Round, Mr Strauss, said:

We must be wary of well-meaning purists. Their measure of progress is not the giant step forward we take from where we stand, but the gap still remaining to achieve the ideal. Although I admire their intelligence and dedication, I do not have much patience with their position. Their tactical thrust is often to attack the 'politics of the deal' and the process of developing a political consensus that can assure national support . . . They imply that politics is something dirty and improper rather than recognising that progress in a democracy is built on accommodating different views from all sections of society.[126]

Of course a contrary argument equally valid is the economic theory of second best that reminds us that a reform initiative that moves us closer to but not fully at an ideal position, will not necessarily be more equitable and efficient. Nevertheless we would be foolish not to seek to assess outcomes with a healthy acceptance of *realpolitik* and a consideration of the likely scenarios if the Round had completely broken down.

Another question is where to focus attention in analysing results. For example, one possible Australian approach is to look at the likely effect on opening Asian markets to growth in trade rather than looking at how the negotiations sought to overcome restrictive policies of the three major players.

Perhaps the major coup in the Round for Australia was the establishment

---

[126] R. S. Strauss 'The achievements of the Tokyo Round', *Washington Post*, 20 Mar. 1979, quoted in J. E. Twiggs, *The Tokyo Round of Multilateral Trade Negotiations: a Case Study in Building Domestic Support for Diplomacy* (1987), 48.

of the Cairns Group of agricultural 'fair trading' countries.[127] The group was named after the site of the first meeting which was held in August 1986. It is particularly remarkable that the Cairns Group comprises developed, developing, and centrally planned economies all working together to promote a single issue.

The role of the Cairns Group was particularly important on a number of levels. The obvious level is the immediate influence it had in the agriculture negotiations. More general interest relates to the reasons why the majors allowed the group to have that influence and what lessons can be learned for the future for smaller nations to band together and develop enough influence to have a meaningful reciprocal negotiation with the key players.

The Cairns Group is the most important but only one example of the greater role and involvement of Australia in the Uruguay Round. First, Ambassador Oxley was made Chair of the GATT Council for part of his time in Geneva. His successor, Ambassador Hawes, chaired the Services negotiations and was one of three designated 'Friends of the Chair'. Mr Duthie chaired the Textiles and Natural-Resource-Based Products Group and in due course the entire Market Access Negotiating Group. Mr Robertson was one of the so called 'Seven Samurai' who provided comments on reform of the subsidies rules. In addition, Australia was part of a number of key informal groups including the Rolle group which worked in the services area, the De la Paix group which steered the early phases of negotiations, and the Bœuf Rouge group and the Friends group dealing with intellectual property matters. Australia was also part of the G4 on agriculture along with the United States, the European Community, and Japan.[128]

In spite of this greater involvement, size and power remain important in negotiations and Thomson suggests that a major disappointment was the bilateral focus between the United States and the European Economic Community and the eventual down-sizing of the overall package once the likely lessening of the agriculture agreement became clear.[129] He suggests that efforts in the final days of negotiations were primarily aimed at 'halting the backsliding rather than enlarging the package'.[130]

Australia's major complaint about the GATT throughout its history has been its failure to deal effectively with liberalization of the agriculture sector. In addition to the normal vested interest group problem that promotes protectionism, the agriculture area is beset by other policy aims

---

[127] The Cairns Group comprised Argentina, Australia, Brazil, Canada, Chile, Colombia, Fiji, Hungary, Indonesia, Malaysia, The Philippines, New Zealand, Thailand and Uruguay.
[128] The above material is drawn from G. Thomson, 'Legal framework for international trade' at 3.   [129] Ibid. 5.   [130] Ibid. 5.

that are a significant barrier to fair and liberal trade. Most governments see food production as an important strategic issue. Farmers, particularly small farmers, are often seen as having an important role in promoting rural ambience. Agricultural produce is also affected greatly by weather patterns with severe cyclical price fluctuations. In addition, the United States had obtained a waiver in respect of agriculture early on in GATT history. When the EEC was established, promotion of the Common Agricultural Policy was seen as the central means of achieving successful integration of the European economies.

Protectionism per se in the agricultural area is bad enough, but history has shown a most perverse form of self-perpetuating protection through the use of the least efficient types of protectionist devices that in turn call for further and further protection levels. For example, both the EEC and USA have traditionally used domestic price supports and other devices to promote production in the first place, and then when excess production results, they utilize market access controls and export subsidies to help producers make sales. Total annual expenditure by developed countries on various forms of subsidies to agricultural producers was estimated at a staggering US$335b. per annum in 1993.[131]

In previous Rounds, US rhetoric has tended to be to the effect that as the EEC is not willing to budge on agriculture, the US must retaliate. Demands for reform are heard loudly at the beginning of each Round and fizzle out in the face of alleged EEC intransigence. Some cynical commentators even assert that the US is not entirely unhappy for this outcome as it can keep its protectionist policies but argue it has the high moral ground in having offered to liberalize trade on a reciprocal basis.

Whatever the reality, as the cost of promoting excess production and subsidising sales has grown astronomically, governments with severe budget deficit problems have had to take notice. In addition, the Uruguay Round, by bringing in new areas such as services, trade-related aspects of intellectual property rights and trade-related investment measures, necessitated real trade-offs, otherwise there would simply have been no movement in the new areas. Because the new areas were of particular interest to the US and EU, there was for the first time an environment where real change might be expected in the agriculture area. Thus the concept of the Cairns Group was developed at just the right time. Because the real negotiations in GATT Rounds occur in private meetings, it is up to the majors to decide who they will 'deal in'. From early on the US chose to include the Cairns Group in agricultural negotiations which gave it real status from the outset. Little has been written about the establishment of

---

[131] Ibid. 6, citing OECD, *Monitoring an Outlook Report on Agricultural Policies, Markets and Trade 1994.*

the Cairns Group. One theory is that the United States was not getting anywhere in the services negotiations in the early stages and decided to bring the Cairns Group in on agriculture to develop more leverage.

Australia's negotiating objectives in the agriculture area were for comprehensive coverage and tariff-based protection only. There was a realization, however, that the extent of protectionist measures would require some phasing-out entitlements, particularly where subsidies were concerned. The Cairns Group stepped up the pressure as the Round proceeded with little movement up to and including the mid-term review in Montreal in December 1988. In the Ministerial Statement from the Cairns Group meeting in Budapest on 12 November 1988 the group stated that 'failure to reach positive results on agriculture in Montreal would mean failure of the mid-term review'. At the meeting in Chiangmai in Thailand on 23 November 1989, the ministers agreed on a comprehensive proposal for agricultural trade reform. In addition, they emphasized that without a substantial outcome on agriculture the Round cannot and will not be successfully concluded.

Through the course of the negotiations, the Cairns Group and the United States and others had firstly to fight EU suggestions to re-balance protection levels between commodities, which would have increased the protection in some areas, and secondly to utilize an overall aggregate measure of support as the only measure of liberalizing commitments. The latter would have been virtually impossible to police and would also have allowed protection levels on individual products to move up and down as it suited the European Community.

The meeting in Geneva on 5 November 1990 pointed out the crisis state of negotiations prior to the intended conclusion of the Round in Brussels in December of that year. The Cairns Group ministers singled out the European Community in allocating blame for the crisis through the latter's failure to table offers or information following the Chairman's text. In its communiqué from Geneva on 18 October 1993, with fifty-eight days to run, the group rejected the possibility that agriculture could be set aside in order to conclude an interim or partial agreement. The group reiterated that 'the Round must be concluded on the basis of a multilaterally agreed, balanced global package'.

The Cairns Group held firm and the Round dragged on. While it continued to perform a major role, the Group was not part of the Blair House Accord and was in some ways unable to prevent the effects this had on the final negotiating package. The final agreement on agriculture includes a commitment to reduce domestic support measures by 20 per cent on an aggregate basis. Exemptions are allowed for special problems such as disaster relief, research, environmental protection, and the like. The worst aspect of this outcome was the move to an aggregate measure rather than a commodity by commodity commitment as had been proposed in the Draft Final Act of December 1992 (the Dunkel Draft).

Where market access is concerned, the major agreement was to convert existing protectionist measures to tariff equivalents. Thus quantitative restrictions, variable import levies, minimum import prices and the like are to be converted into tariffs. There is then a commitment to cut tariffs on average by 36 per cent over the six-year implementation period. The minimum cut on any tariff line is 15 per cent and these tariffs are bound. Where retariffication is concerned, the European Union included a 10 per cent Union preference over and above the internal Union prices rather than merely calculate the difference between internal and import price. This raises tariff equivalents well above that needed to support domestic prices.[132]

One of the key reform issues was the way to deal with non-tariff barriers to agriculture trade in a system that utilizes reciprocal bargaining. There are a number of problems with a retariffication exercise. First there is no obvious means of converting non-tariff barriers to tariffs. There will always be divergence amongst economists in making such assessments. For example, utilizing the difference between the import price and the selling price in the domestic market would only be appropriate in certain circumstances.[133] A further problem arises with this approach if voluntary export restraints are involved, as in that case import prices already are affected by the restriction.[134]

If tariff rates are set too low, structural adjustment would face more rapid problems than intended. This in turn might lead to balance of payments problems or other side effects that would in turn reduce the interest in trade liberalization. If tariffs are set too high then tariffication would in fact be a greater barrier to trade than the non-tariff barrier. Furthermore, setting them too high might lead to ongoing problems if it is unlikely that future negotiations will rapidly reduce tariffs.[135]

Because of these problems of devising appropriate tariff levels, some commentators advocate the use of tariff quotas on an increasing basis to dismantle quantitative restrictions over time. Auction quotas, as the term implies, involve licences being sold by the Government to the highest bidder. This occurred in the textile clothing and footwear industries in Australia. The premium in the bidding process gives the Government

---

[132] N. Andrews, R. Roberts and S. Hesta, *The Uruguay Round Outcome: Implications for Agricultural and Resource Commodities*, paper delivered to ABARE Outlook '94 Conference Canberra 1–3 Feb. 1994; cited in Industries Commission Annual Report, 242.

[133] J. Bhagwati, 'The non-equivalence of tariffs and quotas', in R. E. Baldwin *et al.* (eds.), *Trade, Growth and the Balance of Payments* (1965), quoted in Takacs, 'Transitional measures in trade liberalisation', in C. S. Pearson and J. Riedel (eds.), *The Direction of Trade Policy* (1990), 161.   [134] Ibid. 161.   [135] Ibid. 160.

information about tariff equivalents of the quota regime. A tariff quota could be used on a phase-in basis by slowly reducing the penalty rate applicable. One problem with this approach is that there is no guarantee that the bidding process is sufficiently open and broad-based to be an accurate reflection of true market demand.

Where export subsidies are concerned, there was greater success in getting a commodity based commitment. The European Union had argued for a mere commitment on total money expenditure. The promise was to reduce direct export subsidies to 36 per cent below that in a base period of 1986 to 1990. The quantity of subsidized exports was to be reduced by 21 per cent. While the inclusion of the base period as the starting point rather than the position at the end of the Round diminishes the total commitment, it is important to realize that export subsidies were escalating year by year. Consequently any significant decrease is a major shift in approach, although at a rate less than was desired by the Cairns Group and the USA.

In addition, the Andriessen commitment not to subsidize into Australia's key Asian markets was reiterated as part of the negotiations. The removal of the meat import law in the United States, the reduction of subsidised skim milk powder by the United States, greater access to Association of South East Asian Nations and the US dairy markets and the gradual opening of the Japan and South Korea rice markets are also important initiatives. Indirectly, the phasing out of the Multi Fibre Arrangement will assist Australia's prospects in the area of cotton and wool. The Agreement on the Application of Sanitary and Phytosanitary Measures should also assist Australia's agricultural exports by making the procedures more open and requiring them to be based on objective and accurate scientific data.

Australia has had to make amendments to the support arrangements for the dairy industry and to tariff measures on cheese and tobacco as well as certain processed agricultural products. Differential sales taxes on fruit juices with 25 per cent or more Australian content, which had been protected under the grandfather provisions of the GATT Agreement, were removed through the Uruguay Round.

How then do we assess the final outcome in this area? On the positive side the mere fact of an agreement and the commitments outlined above were never assured and must be appreciated. Analysts have used different models to assess the value of the Uruguay Round for the agriculture sector. The Industry Commission estimated that the Round could result in a A$1.1b. increase in annual income of the agriculture sector.[136] Andrews, Roberts and Hesta assess similar levels under a different model.[137] While results will be slow to emerge, Australia was prepared to accept

---

[136] Bhagwati, 'The non-equivalence of tariffs and quotas', 327.
[137] N. Andrews *et al.*, *The Uruguay Round Outcome*.

retariffication even though it occurred at rates clearly higher than necessary, in return for real bound minimum access commitments and growth commitments. Australian officials were aware, however, that the actual barriers to trade in the short term are probably higher than at the commencement of the Round through the retariffication process.

On the negative side, there has only been a small decrease in the rate of protection and the actual effects for exporters may not be felt for many years. In addition it is not clear what bilateral unstated promises have been made for those countries who are tentatively opening new markets. Here a particular concern is the growing bilateral trade dispute between the United States and Japan. Another problem with the developments in agriculture is that the style of promise has a decidedly anti-legalist flavour if for no other reason than the inevitability of phase-out arrangements rather than an immediate commitment to tariff protection alone. While it certainly may not be appropriate to force GATT/WTO dispute settlement functions to deal with areas of 'soft' law, nevertheless, this writer at least is concerned at a small reduction in the level of export subsidies in return for a promise not to contest these before WTO dispute settlement panels.

One of the key issues is the extent to which certain of the vaguer provisions will ultimately be seen as 'soft' law even after the period where Article XXIII cannot be brought. This depends in part on the attitude that panels might take. For example, the Australian complaint on subsidies on sugar discussed above foundered on the basis that the panel was not able to conclude that the European Community had gained more than an equitable share of world trade. The new Agriculture Agreement, with its complex accounting elements and its mandated protection levels over time periods, will be particularly difficult to challenge through the dispute settlement system. If the forms of protection are allowed but only the amount is limited, the rules may not be effective if parties adversely affected cannot get timely information that would indicate whether the rules are being complied with.

Some take a different approach and see the move to legalism as a problem. Teese asserts that the organization's strength has rested on co-operation. In his view, the GATT rules were merely intended as guidelines. He asserts that as co-operation has diminished, reliance on legalism has increased, including the demand for new rules when existing rules are transgressed.[138] He also asserts that as the other key players have not shouldered the burden of increased importation from developing countries to assist the United States, the latter has turned more and more to adversarial dispute settlement to try and force the opening of markets.

---

[138] C. Teece, 'Australia after Uruguay and the crisis in international trade' (Mar. 1994) *Quadrant*, 505.

This is not necessarily a bad thing as those rules may be a means of getting reluctant players to shoulder needed responsibilities.

Another important area where Australia is concerned is services. More than three-quarters of Australia's total employment occurs in the services sector.[139] Approximately 20 per cent of Australia's exports are in this sector. This figure is growing by about 7 per cent per annum.[140] Services currently account for 73 per cent of gross domestic product.[141] Because of Australia's isolated position, efficient transport and communication regimes are particularly important.

Common barriers to trade in the Australian services sector and recent reform initiatives include local content rules in television and advertising, diversified and local ownership and control rules under the Broadcasting Act, aviation regulation through international conventions such as the International Air Transport Association and the domestic dual airlines policy, banking and finance reform where sixteen foreign banks were allowed to establish operations in 1985, the float of the Australian dollar in 1983 and the removal of most exchange controls at that time, and the decision in 1985 to allow full fee places to overseas students in Australian education. Export of health care services are affected by local ownership rules and recognition of foreign qualifications. Australian films are subsidized through the tax system. Where shipping is concerned, Government procurement and general regulation of coastal shipping are the main barriers.

A problem with the Uruguay Round services negotiations was the failure to conclude agreements in the areas of telecommunications, maritime transport and professional services. Much will obviously depend on the next round of GATS negotiations in five years' time. The GATS itself is certainly a 'primitive' legal document both in detail and in coverage given the amount that remains to be negotiated and the decision to only include lists of positive commitments rather than general liberalizing norms subject to limited exemptions.

Australia maintained its position on local content requirements in the audio-visual industry notwithstanding strong US pressure. Impressionistically at least, this sector provides some support for infant industry arguments. A significant number of Australian film directors now work full time in the United States, many of who received their start in the Australian advertising industry doing commercials. Of course from an economic point of view, that may not have been the most efficient from the consumer's point of view, but in terms of developing a culturally significant

---

[139] DFAT, *Australian Traded Services: An Introduction*, (1987).
[140] DFAT, *Uruguay Round: Outcomes for Australia*, 15 Dec. 1993, 29.
[141] G. Thomson, 'Legal framework for international trade' at 16.

local film industry, that, alongside preferential tax treatment, is likely to have been influential.

The TRIPs Agreement necessitated only minor changes to Australian law. Because Australia has been a member of the Paris Convention for many years, major changes have not been required in the patents area. The bill introduced to amend the patent law increases the term of Australian patents from sixteen to twenty years. It removes the separate provisions that allowed for extensions of the term for pharmaceutical products and shifts the burden of proof for alleged infringement of a patent. It provides for compulsory licences if a person made a substantial investment anticipating a patent expiring on its sixteen-year term when that investment occurred before 1 October 1994. In addition, a patent licensee may obtain a compulsory licence covering an extra four-year term where the existing licence was worded to expire at the end of the sixteen-year term. Most of the amendments were due to commence on 1 July 1995.

While TRIPs has a number of things to say about enforcement, no amendments have been made in the Australian system, presumably because the Government believes we meet those requirements.

The dumping negotiations were important for Australia given that it is one of the big users of this form of protection. The GATT Secretariat's second report on Australia presented in January 1994 noted that over the previous few years, approximately one-third of the world's anti-dumping actions were initiated by Australia. These actions concentrated heavily in the areas of chemicals and processed agricultural products.

A number of domestic reviews have been undertaken in relation to anti-dumping over recent years. In 1986, a leading economist was commissioned to review the provisions, which lead to some reduction in assistance and a recommendation against an overriding national interest criterion.[142] A Department of Industry and Commerce review in 1991 lead to two stage changes introduced on 10 July 1992 and 1 January 1993.[143] The 1991 Review took into account findings of a Senate Standing Committee on Industry, Science and Technology which investigated the workings of the anti-dumping system in 1991. The 1 January 1993 amendments introduced an interim duty system along the lines of that employed in the European Union which uses the export price at the time of the anti-dumping action to determine interim duty regardless of the actual export price of individual importers. Importers who are exporting at higher prices must then seek six-monthly refunds. Other amendments also extended injury to suppliers of

[142] F. H. Gruen, *Review of the Customs Tariff (Anti-Dumping Act) 1975: Report* (1986).
[143] Button J 'Ministerial Statement on anti-dumping Legislation' Hansard Vol. 22, Senate, Dec. 1991 pages 4288–94.

inputs that are used in domestic products that compete with dumped goods.[144]

Uruguay Round changes incorporated in local legislation include the following:

- in addition to determining dumping margins based on a comparison of individual export prices with individual normal values, weighted averages may now also be used;
- guidelines are now included for determining an appropriate third country and for determining a constructed value;
- the right to cumulation is now formalized;
- the Minister must now reject or terminate if margins are *de minimis* or volumes are negligible based on quantified thresholds;
- greater openness and requirements of non-confidential summaries of confidential information are required;
- industry proportion requirements are now defined;
- end-users, consumer and trade organizations are now within the ambit of investigation;
- parties can require completion of an investigation even after an undertaking is accepted;
- reasons must be given if an undertaking is refused;
- company specific duties and residual rates are allowed;
- anti-dumping securities can be held for six months;
- guidelines have been developed for identifying subsidies; and
- preferential thresholds are incorporated for subsidy investigations of developing countries.

The reforms will do much to provide certainty and guidance as the Australian regime has not had the elaborate guidelines of the US system. More fundamental reform was not achievable in the Round, however.

In assessing the outcomes of the tariff negotiations, the major concern was the failure to agree on a tariff-reducing formula, in particular one which would redress the problems of tariff escalation and tariff specialization. The Australian Government proposed that each contracting party determine a measure of the effective rate of assistance under both tariff and non-tariff measures to support the negotiations during the Round.[145]

Where particular industries are concerned the major problem was the failure to conclude any agreement on steel through negotiations that were

---

[144] See 1990–91 Dept. of Industry and Commerce *Annual Report.*
[145] Comm. from Australia: Market Access Negotiations, Multilateral Trade Negotiations, the Uruguay Round, GATT Group of Negotiations, 16 Nov. 1987, 1, cited in Nieuwenhuysen, *Towards Freer Trade*, 136.

run in parallel to the Round. One major outcome was the commitment by the European Union to reduce subsidized coal production.

Where tariff bindings are concerned, Australia has generally made its bindings higher than the level at which the Government has already agreed to cut tariffs. The average actual tariff on 30 June 1996 should be 6 per cent while the average bound tariff for that date will be 11 per cent.[146] Australia did, however, agree to reduce tariffs on certain medical equipment and light beer below the 5 per cent level. Negotiations in the Round will lead to 95 per cent of Australian tariff lines being bound.

Average tariff reductions on Australia's exports with its major trading partners have been calculated at 53.5 per cent on a trade-weighted basis.[147] Average cuts were Japan 75 per cent, the United States 57 per cent, Republic of Korea 68 per cent, the European Community 49 per cent, India 27 per cent and Thailand 33 per cent.[148]

Reform of domestic customs law has also been considered independently of the Uruguay Round negotiations. The Australian Law Reform Commission commenced a reference in 1987 and tabled a draft bill in 1992. The Government has yet to decide what action to take in relation to that bill although recent amendments have been proposed in the area of search and seizure.

Where dispute settlement is concerned, Australia's traditional approach has been to favour a rule-based multilateral trading system and it is hence a strong supporter of the dispute settlement process. While Australia has not been a party to a great number of Article XXIII disputes, it has been involved in a number of particularly important ones from a legal perspective at least, being the first non-violation complaint heard under the GATT and the key agricultural subsidies cases against France and the European Community respectively. Australia has been particularly pleased at the automaticity of reports' outcome but was neither a strong proponent or opponent of the Appeals Review mechanism that was needed to get agreement on adoption.

One issue that has not been fully addressed is the relationship between WTO dispute settlement and dispute settlement domestically under WTO-inspired rules. The anti-dumping area raises a number of issues when comparing domestic with international dispute resolution mechanisms. If a panel is asked to look at matters of domestic administration, one question is what style of review they should adopt or whether they should merely start afresh and see if the action conforms to GATT/WTO law. There still needs to be overriding principles of review for example, where the question is whether there is enough evidence of material injury. Other issues would be whether the panel could hear new evidence and how they

---

[146] Ibid. 237.   [147] G. Thomson.   [148] Ibid. 2.

would test the veracity of evidence in general. A problem of relying on GATT law in domestic settings is that some judges may be mercantilist or deferential to governmental discretions or bureaucratic decision-making.

A related question is whether a panel should hear an anti-dumping dispute before domestic appeal processes have been exhausted. One reason that this should be allowed is that the WTO panel can raise questions of legal validity that many domestic tribunals simply cannot consider.

Another issue is the debate about private rights of action. Australia has not had a strong position on this question as it has not been pushed in the negotiations. Commentators have been divided. For example, Tumlir argued against the suggestion of Professors Jackson, Louis and Matsushita that private rights of action before GATT tribunals should be considered. Tumlir argued that it would bring diplomacy into conflict with the national judicial process. He argued instead, that effort should be made to use international law to promote justiciable personal rights at the national level.[149]

8.14 FUTURE PROSPECTS AND CONCLUSIONS

A particularly important outcome from Australia's perspective, although one which in part reflected some of the failures of the Round, was to incorporate ongoing negotiation commitments in the final agreement. Australia's position has certainly been that reform of the rules should not be left to Rounds but should instead be an ongoing process. Thus as soon as the Tokyo Round ended, Australia immediately began working towards the establishment of a further Round to deal with perceived problems, particularly in the area of agriculture.

One problem with GATT Rounds is that they inevitably deal with long standing problems that may not necessarily be the most important ones for the future. While the key issues addressed in the Uruguay Round were certainly important, it is worth noting that immediately upon the Round concluding, there was a major bilateral dispute between the United States and Japan which dealt with domestic structural issues, competition law, and questions of managed versus free trade. Another concern is that some officials take the view that regionalism may be worth promoting in the short to medium term as a more likely way of achieving consensus and harmonisation on trade related issues such as competition and investment. A cynic might question whether the Round will effectively lead to an

---

[149] J. Tumlir 'Conceptions of the international economic and legal order' (1985) 9 *The World Economy* 85.

implied multi-agriculture agreement and multi-auto agreement under the same power politics that led to the Multi Fibre Agreements.

Where domestic implementation issues are concerned, Australia at least provides a valuable model for the development of transparent and consistent advisory and review processes. Such analysis and this symposium may hopefully inspire more multilateral and unilateral attention to these issues on an ongoing basis.[150]

---

[150] While scholars well understand the importance of domestic transparency, little specific agreement was possible under the Uruguay Round.

SWITZERLAND: THE CHALLENGE OF DIRECT DEMOCRACY

Thomas Cottier* and Krista Nadakavukaren Schefer[†]

9.1 INTRODUCTION

On 1 January 1995, when eighty-one countries were celebrating the end of the Uruguay Round with the coming into effect of the World Trade Organization, Switzerland was preparing for yet another political trade battle. This time, though, it was fought on the home front: direct democracy made it necessary to convince the Swiss citizens that they should endorse the new trading regime with all its implications.

Switzerland's Federal Constitution requires that there be an opportunity for a popular referendum to be held before the country can become a member of an international organization. Waiting to see if this opportunity would be taken delayed Switzerland's joining the WTO. It was five months after the WTO came into effect, on 1 June 1995, that the Swiss executive branch, the Bundesrat, was finally able to ratify the results of the Uruguay Round.[1] Due to WTO transitional arrangements, this delay did not adversely effect Switzerland's trading relations. But it does serve as a reminder that direct democracy is at odds with the pace set by, and potentially with the very fact of, the increasing internationalization of law-making.

Indeed, the internationalization of economic activities is a challenge to traditional democracy in many countries, not only in Switzerland. This internationalization shifts rule-making away from the national level, resulting in a loss of influence for national legislatures' constitutional

---

* Professor of Law, Institute of European and International Economic Law, University of Berne; formerly a member of the Swiss delegation to the Uruguay Round 1986–94 with responsibilities in particular in dispute settlement, subsidies and intellectual property; member of several GATT panels.
† Assistant in the Institute of European and International Economic Law, University of Berne; J.D., Georgetown University (1994); attorney-at-law.

[1] The ratification took effect 30 days later, on 1 July 1995, published in the official Swiss reporter *Amtliche Sammlung* 1995 II 2117.

procedures. The role of parliaments in economic law is increasingly reduced to approving international agreements and to enacting implementing legislation. In many instances, this role does not leave room for policy-making by elected representatives. At the same time, domestic power shifts to the executive branch, diplomats, and those organized interests that have access to the administration in power. Negotiating processes such as the Uruguay Round take centre stage in framing new approaches in domestically important areas such as agriculture and textiles.

The process of internationalization of law-making offers many economic advantages to producers and consumers. It allows the opening of markets and the overcoming of trade barriers in goods and services that national processes often are not able to bring about on their own. Constitutional and international law, however, need to balance substantive developments in trade law with the procedures by which these results are achieved in international relations. Specifically, it is necessary to explore how the values of democracy and self-determination can be preserved and promoted in the new global environment. Current complaints about the lack of democratic rule and transparency in the context of integration in Europe will inevitably be extended to matters regulated within the realm of the WTO.

It is in this context that a case study of Switzerland is of particular interest. The country's economy is dependent on world markets, but sits within the strong controls of direct democracy. Switzerland's experience in negotiating and implementing the Uruguay Round lends insight into both the potentials and the limitations of democracy in international economic regulation. While in many respects Switzerland's experiences are the same as that of other countries, with respect to direct democracy's effects on implementation they are unique. Looking at the country's process of garnering public support for the Uruguay Round is thus of general interest to all those concerned with the democratic legitimacy of multilateral trade rules.

In this article we first address the political and legal structures peculiar to Switzerland within which the Swiss implementation of the Uruguay Round took place. Then we study the areas influencing the implementation process that are common to many countries. In Section 2 we look at the impact of legal constraints on developing international trade rules. We examine the constitutional effects of the Round on the Swiss domestic political process in Section 3. In Section 4, we look at the role of law and the judiciary in the domestic enforcement of WTO obligations. Finally, in Section 5, we draw conclusions on how the democratic implementation process improved the legitimacy of the resulting legislative framework.

9.2 THE POLITICAL AND ECONOMIC STRUCTURE OF SWITZERLAND

Switzerland has one of the most outward looking economies in the world trading system, but domestically the country's political constitution looks inward. The combination of these traits set the stage for Switzerland's role in the Uruguay Round and for the implementation of its results.

9.2.1 Outward-looking economy

Ranking eighty-ninth in population and 127th in area of the world's nations,[2] Switzerland occupies position ten in total merchandise exports (2.2 per cent of world trade) and imports (2.1 per cent) (counting the European Community as a single entity and excluding intra-EC trade). In 1994, the country held position six in exports of services (2.1 per cent) (counting the EC as a single entity).[3] On average, approximately 36 per cent of the Gross National Product is earned abroad, mainly in the areas of mechanical engineering, chemical production, and services.[4] While export-oriented industries are fully subjected to global competition, domestic operators are often organized in protective cartels which contribute to the country's high price levels.[5]

While a member of neither the European Union nor the extensive association agreement on the European Economic Area, Switzerland is dependent on the European economy, being the European Union's second largest export market[6] and its third largest source of imports.[7] Swiss trading relations that exist with the WTO's non-EC Member States, however, are important and growing stronger.[8] Reliant on market access

---

[2] See *1994 Information Please Environmental Almanac* (1994).

[3] 10 *WTO Focus* (1996) at 7–8. For previous data see WTO, *International Trade: Trends and Statistics 1995*, 13–14.

[4] Unlike the stereotype of Switzerland as a nation dependent on its chocolate, watch, and banking industries, small- and medium-sized exporters are the main contributors to the Swiss economy. For a statistical breakdown of Swiss imports and exports by industry and destination, see *Statistisches Jahrbuch der Schweiz 1996* Table G 6.3 at 170.

[5] Legislation to reinforce anti-trust laws and to abolish still existing intra-cantonal trade barriers were recently enacted. See BBl 1995 IV 516, AS 1996 I 546 (effective 1 July, 1996) (Revised Anti-trust Law); BBl 1995 IV 548, AS 1996 1738 (effective 1 July, 1996) (Intra-cantonal Trade Law).

[6] See, *Kommission der Europäischen Gemeinschaft, Europäische Wirtschaft, Die EG als Welthandelspartner 1993: Zweiter Aussenhandelsbericht*, No. 52 Table 88 (1993) (showing that 18.2% of all EC exports go to the United States, and 9.8% go to Switzerland; citing Eurostat as the source of the statistics).

[7] Ibid. 11 at n. 3 (reporting that in 1990, 7.4% of the EC's imports come from Switzerland); ibid. at Table 82 (showing that US products ranked first with 18.4% of EC imports, and Japan's were second with 10.0% in 1990).

[8] See, e.g., H. Hauser and K.-U. Schanz, *Die Wirtschaftliche Bedeutung der Uruguay-Runde für die Schweiz—Gutachten* (1993) 9 (in 1992, almost 35% of Swiss exports went to countries not members of the EEA).

for its exports to both Europe and beyond, Switzerland shares an interest with many small- and medium-sized nations in reinforcing the rule of law in international economic relations. Due particularly to its contemporary position in Europe, Switzerland was eager to defend its trading interests in the Uruguay Round and contribute to the Round's successful conclusion. In its report on the Round's proceedings, the Bundesrat, the Swiss executive branch, set out its reasoning:

For the Swiss economy, earning almost every second franc abroad, the results of the negotiations are of decisive importance. Switzerland is able to maintain and build up her position in international trade only to the extent that multilaterally agreed rules and disciplines are observed. A small country like Switzerland, that has become an important world trading partner, fully depends on reliance on international law for the preservation of her interests.[9]

9.2.2 Inward-looking political system: the referendum

Switzerland's international economy is accompanied by an inward-looking political system and a seldom-found level of direct democracy.[10] Structurally, the government is decentralized, shaped in a three-layered federal system of twenty-six cantons with extensive horizontal and vertical separations of power.[11] While the federal legislative branch (Bundes-versammlung) with its two chambers (Nationalrat and Ständerat) is formally the most powerful of the three federal branches, the executive branch is the most influential in determining foreign policy. However, compatible with the system of direct democracy, in Switzerland the citizen—as the Sovereign—has an instrument of direct and final control over what will become law: the referendum.

Together with the initiative,[12] the referendum is one of the characteristic

---

[9] Schweizerischer Bundesrat, *Botschaft zur Genehmigung der GATT/WTO-Überein-kommen vom 19. September 1994*, BBl 1994 IV 1 at 2 (authors' translation).

[10] For an overview of the Swiss political system, see generally W. Linder, *Swiss Democracy: Possible Solutions to Conflict in Multicultural Societies* (1994); J.-F. Aubert, *Traité de droit constitutionnel suisse*, vols. I–III (1967–82).

[11] While the structure of federalism is very similar to that set out in the US Constitution, the horizontal separation of powers on the federal level and the interplay of the three branches is very different. In Switzerland, the legislative branch possesses a relatively high degree of influence. For instance, unlike the American system, the Swiss legislative branch appoints the members of the executive body. This naturally changes the dynamic of the relationship between the two branches. Further, the federal court system does not have the oversight that the US Supreme Court does, as there is no extensive judicial review of Switzerland's federal statutes.

[12] The 'initiative' is another instrument available to the Swiss citizens to influence the law directly. The initiative, unlike the referendum, allows for positive control; that is, by collecting 100,000 signatures, a change to the Constitution can be proposed and put to popular vote. One of the most dramatic and controversial uses of this instrument was the

features of Swiss governance. Final decisions in treaty-making, including those regulating foreign economic relations, are subject to either compulsory or facultative (non-automatic) popular referendums to nearly the same extent as is internal legislation.[13] This has an impact on the formulation of negotiating positions, the negotiations themselves, and the ultimate implementation efforts.

According to paragraphs (2) and (3) of Article 89 of the Federal Constitution, all international agreements providing for accession to an international organization are subject to a *facultative* referendum. This means that if, within three months of Parliament's approval of a treaty, 50,000 signatures (a mere 1.09 per cent of today's electorate) can be collected in favour of a referendum, the treaty must be submitted to the Swiss people for a popular vote. Any treaty approved by Parliament that has an indefinite duration and is irrevocable, that results in membership to an international organization, or that brings about a multilateral harmonization of the law, is therefore subject to a moratorium for three months while the signature-gathering can be attempted.[14] The referendum can be used against either the treaty or the implementing legislation, or against both. The system therefore runs the risk of producing inconsistent results: a

successful Alpine Transit initiative, resulting in the requirement that as of 2004, trucks carrying cargo across Switzerland be transported on trains when crossing alpine territory—a position at odds with the official policies at the time. Art. 36^{sexies}, Federal Constitution; AS 1994 1101. See also *Bundesratsbeschluss über das Ergebnis der Volksabstimmung vom 20. Februar 1994*, BBl II 1994 at 696 (21 April, 1994) (Art. I(4)).

[13] Although there has been a referendum requirement for treaties with foreign states since 1921, Art. 89 was revised in 1977, broadening the pool of treaties subject to the possibility of a facultative referendum. See G. Kreis, *Der lange Weg des Staatsvertragsreferendums: Schweizerische Aussenpolitik zwischen indirekter und direkter Demokratie* (1995) 9.

[14] Art. 89 of the Constitution (SR 101) reads as follows:
1) Für Bundesgesetze und Bundesbeschlüsse ist die Zustimmung beider Räte erforderlich.
2) Bundesgesetze sowie allgemeinverbindliche Bundesbeschlüsse sind dem Volke zur Annahme oder Verwerfung vorzulegen, wenn es von 50,000 stimmverechtigten Schweizer Bürgern oder von acht Kantonen verlangt wird.
3) Absatz 2 gilt auch für völkerrechtliche Verträge, die
   a. unbefristet und unkündbar sind;
   b. den Beitritt zu einer internationalen Organisation vorsehen;
   c. eine multilaterale Rechtsvereinheitlichung herbeiführen.
4) Durch Beschluss beider Räte können weitere völkerrechtliche Verträge Absatz 2 unterstellt werden.
5) Der Beitritt zu Organisationen für kollektive Sicherheit oder zu supranationalen Gemeinschaften untersteht der Abstimmung des Volkes und der Stände.
   Art. 89 bis:
1) Allgemeinverbindliche Bundesbeschlüsse, deren Inkrafttreten keinen Aufschub erträgt, können durch die Mehrheit aller Mitglieder in jedem der beiden Räte sofort in Kraft gesetzt werden; ihre Gültigkeitsdauer ist zu befristen.
2) Wird von 50,000 stimmberechtigten Schweizer Bürgern oder von acht Kantonen eine Volksabstimmung verlangt, treten die sofort in Kraft gesetzten Beschlüsse ein Jahr nach ihrer Annahme duch die Bundesversammlung ausser Kraft, soweit sie nicht innerhalb dieser Frist vom Volke gutgeheissen wurden; in diesem Falle können sie nicht erneuert werden.
3) Die sofort in Kraft gesetzten Bundesbeschlüsse, welche sich nicht auf die Verfassung stützen, müssen innert Jahresfrist nach ihrer Annahme durch die Bundesversammlung von Volk und Ständen genehmigt werden; andernfalls treten sie nach Ablauf dieses Jahres ausser Kraft und können nicht erneuert werden.

treaty may be approved and the implementing legislation rejected; or vice versa.

Once the necessary signatures are collected, public debate on the issue is necessary before the vote can occur, further delaying ratification. Past experience with the refusal on 6 December 1992 to adopt the EEA Agreement after only six months of public debate has shown that supplying the public with the relevant facts and issues in contention takes at least nine months if the final vote on such a complex issue is to truly represent the views of an informed citizenry.[15]

For accession to supranational organizations, such as the European Community or the North Atlantic Treaty Organization, Article 89 (5) of the Constitution sets out that a *compulsory* referendum is to be held. The compulsory referendum, as its name indicates, requires that a treaty be put to a popular vote before it can become law. Such a treaty is only approved if both a majority of the voting electorate and a majority of the cantons agree. The procedure favours the small, mostly rural cantons, as the voting power of their inhabitants in such cases considerably exceeds that of the densely populated industrialized centres.[16]

The referendum, in its different forms, has a significant influence on politics in Switzerland in both internal and external affairs. This is true because even a potential use of referendum can be—and is—wielded to force the Administration to reconsider its proposals. Thus, the instrument often has profoundly conservative effects. It slows adaptability to new circumstances and, together with the traditional neutrality of Switzerland, impedes extensive foreign policy initiatives and handicaps pro-active leadership.

The last three decades have witnessed an increased recourse to referendums. Since 1866, the Swiss have voted on 434 issues. Exactly half of the referendums, 217, occurred between June 1965 and 1995.[17] Since

---

[15] See generally, *Botschaft zur Genehmigung des Abkommens über den Europäischen Wirtschaftsraum*, BBl 1992 IV 1(A) and BBl 1992 IV 668(B) (detailed account of the effort to bring Switzerland into the EEA, including proposals for the necessary changes to the national laws. The commentary, complete with index, runs to 1,881 pp.).

[16] The Canton of Appenzell Ausserrhoden, for example, having a population of 13,714 has one representative in the *Nationalrat* and one in the *Ständerat*, thus enjoying a 1:13,714 ratio of representation in each Chamber. The canton of Zürich, on the other hand, with a population of 1,159,080 is represented by 35 *Nationalrat* members and 2 *Ständerat* members, giving representation ratios of 1:33,926.6 and 1:579,540 respectively. However, in popular votes for which a double affirmative is required, e.g. a compulsory referendum, each full canton receives one equally weighted vote. Thus, the entire population of Zürich is represented by a voice no louder than the 84.5 times smaller population of Innerrhoden. Statistics from Bundesamt für Statistik, *Taschenstatistik der Schweiz* (1993) 2, 23 (population figures as of 31 Dec., 1991).

[17] See Federal Government, *Reform der Bundesverfassung: Erläuterungen zum Verfassungsentwurf* (1995), 208.

1921, when the referendum requirement on federal legislation was introduced, there have been 120 referendums on federal legislation. Of these, fifty-nine affirmed and sixty-one dismissed the proposed bills and decisions—often with implications for foreign relations. Only six referendums, however, directly focused on multilateral agreements. Three of them were approved, and three were rejected.[18] The three agreed to were in support of the accession to the League of Nations in 1920, the Swiss–EC Free Trade Agreements in 1972, and accession to the Bretton Woods institutions in 1992. The others negated a decision by Parliament to give concessionary aid to the International Development Agency in 1976,[19] rejected full United Nations membership in 1986, and rejected the EEA Agreement in 1992.

The record shows that both in domestic and foreign affairs, the test of a referendum is not easy to pass; indeed, in Switzerland, the electorate assumes a role of loyal opposition to the Government. As a result, the executive branch and Parliament are eager to avoid the challenges of the referendum, and seek to foster consensus by major political interests in advance. This important anticipatory effect of the referendum right works to satisfy pressure groups most of the time.[20]

9.3 JURISDICTION TO NEGOTIATE AND CONSTITUTIONAL CONSTRAINTS ON THE DEVELOPMENT OF INTERNATIONAL TRADE LAW

9.3.1 The authority to conduct negotiations and submit offers

While foreign policy is constitutionally a joint matter for the executive branch (Bundesrat) and the two chambers of Parliament (Nationalrat and Ständerat), the executive's constitutional and statutory powers are stronger in practice. In international and economic relations, the executive branch can take protective measures if necessary and is allowed to provisionally apply agreements that have not yet been approved by Parliament.[21] Unlike in the United States, no authorizing legislation from the Parliament was necessary to define the goals of the Uruguay Round. Neither did the legislature provide a framework of negotiations as the United States Congress did, nor adopt a formal mandate as was done in the European Community.

---

[18] Ibid.
[19] See J. P. Müller & L. Wildhaber, *Praxis des Völkerrechts* (2nd ed. 1982) 58, 389.
[20] Since 1874, some 1,800 federal Acts have been subject to referendum requirements. Of those, 1,776 were enacted without a popular vote.
[21] Bundesgesetz über aussenwirtschaftliche Massnahmen, SR 946.201 (25 June, 1982).

At the beginning of the Uruguay Round negotiations, formal proposals by the Ministry of Economics in collaboration with related Ministries[22] and the private sector[23] defined the Swiss positions. These positions were co-ordinated by the Chief Negotiator and the Division of GATT–World Trade in the Department of External Economic Relations.[24]

As the Uruguay Round progressed, the Bundesrat adopted basic negotiating mandates. The mandates, or guidelines, were developed by the same process as were the formal proposals. Unlike the earlier proposals, however, the mandates remained confidential documents for internal use, defining goals and possible concessions. Within the ranges defined by the Bundesrat, the negotiating teams enjoyed flexibility to put forth creative proposals in all areas of offensive interest. In the areas of agriculture and the liberalization of a number of domestic services (often regulated by the cantons), by contrast, the negotiators were constrained by tightly framed instructions.

9.3.2 Anticipatory effects of the referendum right

Perhaps the most important constraint on shaping international trade rules is the electorate's right to seek a referendum, discussed above.[25] In the context of the Uruguay Round, the referendum requirement not only played a major role in Switzerland's negotiating behaviour at the Uruguay Rounds, it also furthered an evolution in internal Swiss politics. Political compromises made to avoid subjecting proposed legislation to a referendum are much more difficult to achieve on the international level than on the national level. Because such legislation is no longer influenced solely by domestic players, solutions achieved through international trade diplomacy may not satisfy powerful domestic interest groups. Consequently, recourse to the referendum is likely to become more frequent. Thus, at the same time as the influence of the foreign relations on the daily life of the Swiss citizen is increasing, the opportunity to control this influence is also growing. One author characterized this two-sided development as follows:

First, relations to the so-called 'outside world' show less and less a truly foreign relations character; due to a growing interdependence and level of integration it

---

[22] The Ministry of Economics (EVD/DFEP) includes the Dept. of External Economic Affairs (BAWI/OFAEE) and the Dept. of Agriculture (BLW/OFAC).

[23] The private sector was mainly represented by the Swiss Association of Trade and Industry ('Vorort') and the Swiss Farmers' Association (Bauernverband).

[24] In particular, the Foreign Office was consulted for proposals on financial services, the Ministry of Justice was the partner agency for intellectual property platforms, and the Ministry of Finance was responsible for government procurement proposals.

[25] See Section 2.2.

actually comes to a flooding of the domestic political arena with foreign policy issues.

Second, we are experiencing a further flooding of the same domestic arena through the use of direct-democratic instruments of participation in decision-making. Clearly, direct democracy these days very much enjoys a level of vitality never experienced before. Or restated in the negative: the readiness of the sovereign to relinquish decision-making to the executive or legislature is today in all areas particularly small.[26]

Given this trend and the record of referendums in the past, in particular the 1992 rejection of the EEA Agreement by a small majority of the Swiss people and a substantial majority of cantons, it is evident that the constitutional right to seek a referendum was one of the most substantial constraints on the executive branch and Parliament in the development of liberal international trade rules during the Round. The possibility of a referendum—either compulsory or facultative—was a constant companion to Swiss negotiators in the Uruguay Round from the cycle's official launching in Punta del Este in 1986 to the Marrakesh Ministerial Meeting in March 1994. Just as the referendum requirement heavily influenced the negotiating procedures and positions of the Administration's team during the Round, by the final stages, Parliament too had to consider the possibility of such a public vote.

Constraints from the threat of referendum were felt both in substantive and in structural issues. With regard to substantive law, agricultural trade regulation with its extensive implications on domestic law was the most sensitive issue.[27] Another area which might have triggered a referendum was the relationship between the trade regime and international environmental protection. The absence of specific negotiations on this subject was widely felt to be a serious omission and created resistance to GATT. The elaboration of an initiative on trade and environment sponsored by Switzerland and her European Free Trade Association partners at the 1990 Brussels Ministerial Meeeting,[28] which became the basis of the post-Uruguay Round work programme in this respect,[29] was partly motivated on the Swiss side by efforts to deter a referendum.

The patenting of life forms was another example of anticipatory effects of the referendum. Given the industrial structure of the Swiss economy,

[26] Georg Kreis, *Der lange Weg des Staatsvertragsreferendums: Schweizerische Aussenpolitik zwischen indirekter und direkter Demokratie* (1995), 5–6 (authors' translation, fn. omitted).
[27] See Section 3.3.
[28] MTN.TNC/W/47; see generally GATT, Trade and the Environment: Factual Note by the Secretariat (L/6896 Feb. 1992).
[29] See Ministerial Decision on Trade and Environment in WTO, *The Results of the Uruguay Round of Multilateral Trade Negotiations: The Legal Texts* (1994), 469–71.

enhanced protection of intellectual property rights became one of the prime goals of the negotiators. From the point of view of the chemical and pharmaceutical industries, improved protection of biotechnological inventions became important. Swiss industry therefore pressed for strengthening the present, somewhat unclear, levels of protection contained in the European Patent Convention.[30] This aim was shared by the United States, while the European Community sought to introduce the standards existing in the European Patent Convention. These attempts to achieve enhanced protection via the Trade-Related Aspects of Intellectual Property Agreement met fierce opposition not only from developing countries, but also from international non-governmental organizations and Swiss pressure groups dedicated to sustainable development and Third World interests. Public campaigning and threats to oppose the results of the Round on this particular issue led to a modification of ambitions among industrialized countries, including Switzerland. In the end, a compromise was found with a level of protection less than that in the European Patent Convention's protection, but with a review clause.[31] The experience taught governments and negotiators that sensitive issues take consensus-building at home before they can be successfully brought to the international level.

Similarly, it was the latent referendum power of the groups defending the interests of developing countries that forced the negotiators to seek balanced results with developing countries and to substantially improve market access for products from these countries.[32]

Anticipatory effects of the referendum requirement are also noticeable in the procedural law and the institutional structure of the WTO. To prevent the compulsory referendum, discussed above, the Swiss negotiating team was particularly anxious to avoid any supranational elements in the WTO structures. Proposals by other delegations, such as automatically binding treaty revisions upon majority approval by a Ministerial Meeting or the General Council, would have increased the coherence of the international trading system and avoided a two-tiered WTO as it existed in the earlier GATT. Yet these efforts were strongly opposed by Switzerland's team because they would have obliged Parliament to submit the results of the Round to a compulsory referendum by both the people and the cantons. In partnership with the United States, but for her own reasons, Switzerland therefore supported the exclusion of all supranational characteristics from the WTO's structure. After rejection of the EEA Agreement,

---

[30] Art. 53 (b), Conv. on the Grant of European Patents Munich, 5 Oct. 1973, entry into force 7 Oct. 1977, 13 (1974) ILM 270–351. This Convention does not form part of EC law. It enjoys an independent status and is equally open to non-EC states.

[31] Art. 27, TRIPs in *The Legal Texts* at 379.

[32] See C. Häberli, 'Das GATT und die Entwicklungsländer,' in T. Cottier (ed.), *GATT–Uruguay Round: Nine Papers* (1995), 123–34.

the Government could not risk making adoption of the Round more difficult.

9.3.3 Constitutional obligations to support agriculture

Switzerland enjoys a long tradition of free trade in industrial goods, but agriculture has been heavily protected since the end of the Second World War. When the land-locked country was surrounded by belligerents, necessary self-reliance entrenched the farmers' political influence. In 1947, foundations of the system were introduced into the Constitution with broad support. The post-war support system was further elaborated by the 1951 Farm Act.[33] Albeit formulated in broad terms, Article 31[bis] (3) of the Constitution set forth a combination of goals of the agricultural policy: high quality, low cost food; assurance of a food source in case of emergency; environmental protection; and decentralized, rural settlements.[34]

The 1947 constitutional requirements help explain why farm policies were responsible for belated accession under the favourable but costly terms of the 1966 Protocol of Accession to GATT.[35] They were also responsible for Switzerland's defensive positions on trade in agriculture in the early stages of the Uruguay Round. The Constitution also explains the successful Swiss effort to have the idea of agricultural 'multifunctionality' and the safeguard clauses accepted by the other signatories of the Agreement on Agriculture.[36]

9.3.4 Other areas

It is safe to say that in virtually all areas other than agriculture and a number of service sectors, it was the outward-looking, on-the-offensive

---

[33] Bundesgesetz über die Förderung der Landwirtschaft und die Erhaltung des Bauernstandes (3 Oct. 1951) in SR 910.1 (SR vol. 9, s. 91).

[34] Art. 31bis (3) Federal Constitution states: 'Wenn das Gesamtinteresse es rechtfertigt, ist der Bund befugt, nötigenfalls in Abweichung von der Handels- und Gewerbefreiheit, Vorschriften zu erlassen: . . . b) zur Erhaltung eines gesunden Bauernstandes und einer leistungsfähigen Landwirtschaft, sowie zur Festigung des bäuerlichen Grundbesitzes; . . .' These goals were characterized as 'economic goal', 'strategic goal', 'ecological goal' and a 'socio-political goal'. R. Horber, *Die schweizerische Agrareinfuhrordnung* (1987), 15. In the Government's Farm Report of 1992, however, there is a recognition that in the whole population, the importance of the environmental/ecological goal now overshadows the others. Thus, the agriculture policy is changing to fit these new values. See *Schweizerischer Bundesrat, Siebter Landwirtschaftsbericht* (1992), 393–4. For the 1996 constitutional amendments to the Agriculture Law, proposed in the wake of the Uruguay Round, see n. 68 and accompanying text.

[35] 'Die Liberalisierung des Agrarhandels' in T. Cottier (ed.) *GATT-Uruguay Round*, 55.

[36] Art. 5 (Special Safeguard Provisions) Agreement on Agriculture in *The Legal Texts* 43.

trading interests that prevailed in the internal debate on ratification of the Uruguay Round. Interests in an open trading system also prevailed in systemic issues such as the reinforcement of the rule of law, dispute settlement, and improvements relating to the GATT and its instruments, as well as to substantive improvements in the fields of services and intellectual property. While negotiating positions sought to maximize the compatibility with existing domestic law, few if any legal or political constraints hindered the efforts undertaken to improve the legal and business security of foreign markets. With the exception of patenting life forms, none of these items carried a serious risk of triggering major opposition—nor therefore of a referendum. There was broad consensus that all measures improving market access abroad would be of vital interest to the Swiss economy. A study undertaken in 1993 showed that for six out of seven different industries in Switzerland, the benefits of the WTO would be substantial, and a decision to remain outside the Agreement would have had 'catastrophic consequences'.[37]

9.4 THE IMPACT OF THE ROUND ON THE GOVERNMENTAL SYSTEM

For Switzerland, the Uruguay Round reflected the process of globalization more than it did a deepening of the country's commitment to the international trade system. One effect of the Round, for example, was a domestic shift in the governmental power structures. First, interagency co-operation improved and real legislative powers further shifted from Parliament to the executive branch and its negotiators, all primarily responsible for, and active on, the international stage. Secondly, the relative influence of the Federal Government and the cantons changed. Finally, non-governmental organizations (besides those defending traditional producers' interests) developed into a source of credible influence.

9.4.1 Enhanced interagency co-operation

In its final stages, the Uruguay Round benefited from the Administration's experience and the improvements in interagency co-operation during the 1989–92 negotiations on the EEA. Wider than the Round in its subject

---

[37] H. Schöchli, 'GATT: Nabelschnur für die Schweizer Wirtschaft' *Der Bund*, 30 Oct. 1993 2; see also 'GATT fördert den Wohlstand' *Neue Zürcher Zeitung* 20 June 1994 27 (reporting that *Regierungsrat* Eric Honegger warned that if Switzerland refused to ratify the GATT, the Swiss economy would go into a 'free fall'); *Neue Zürcher Zeitung*, 7 Dec. 1994 (quoting Rosmarie Bär, Congresswoman from Berne as saying that staying outside of the WTO system would be 'suicidal').

matter, the EEA negotiating process compelled improvements in consultation and co-operation among the concerned agencies. While tensions and bureaucratic infighting were frequent in the beginning, the traditional distances between the different departments was largely overcome. Oral consultations and internal negotiating processes became more frequent than before. As a result, while no formal changes were made in existing interagency procedures, the practice of co-operation in interagency teams and task forces began to emerge as a model for making decisions within the Federal Administration. In fact, new policy-making within the Administration very much resembles international negotiations—the system now seeks compromise and consensus rather than a voting out of diverging views from other departments. In the future, negotiating techniques applied in the WTO and elsewhere could also be applied in a domestic context, and officials should be trained to make use of the experience of the Uruguay Round.[38]

9.4.2 The changing role of Parliament

The Uruguay Round, like the EEA negotiations, greatly enhanced the awareness that traditional Swiss patterns of political power-sharing in foreign policy no longer fulfil the needs of democratic processes and legitimation. While foreign policy is constitutionally a joint responsibility of the executive branch and both Chambers of Parliament, in treaty-making the traditional role of Parliament was limited to general debate and approval of major agreements with a view to ratification, with little or no input given to the Administration before and during negotiations. Foreign policy was not considered an important vote-catching domain, although there has long been an instrument available that could have been developed to steer the process.[39] Consequently, negotiations were only

---

[38] One example where such negotiating techniques were deliberately used was in the elaboration of an executive branch policy paper on patenting life forms. A paper was necessary for achieving a common position for the TRIPs negotiations and the UN Conference on Environment and Development in Rio de Janiero. Instead of written interagency consulations, an oral negotiating process was developed within a working group. In case of blockage, clearance was sought with the highest levels of the department or ministeries concerned. It is only through such techniques that a common policy in this complex matter could be achieved. See Eidgenössische Justiz- und Polizeidepartement, Biotechnologie und Patentrecht, 'Die Patentierbarkeit von Erfindungen betreffend Organismen' (EDMZ Doc. 407.761d, 1993).

[39] This instrument is called the Motion. See Art. 22 GVG vol. 1, p. 171.11. It is, however, not entirely clear whether the legislature could have legitimately used it. Art. 22 only authorizes the use of a Motion in areas of legislative competence. See Arts. 22[bis] and 22[ter] GVG. Under present law, it is agreed that Parliament cannot give binding instructions in foreign policy matters, and thus must use means that are less severe, such as the postulate or interpellation. For more on the various legislative instruments to influence the executive in foreign policy-making, see B. Ehrenzeller, *Legislative Gewalt und Aussenpolitik* (1993), 566–97. For more on the legislative Motion, ibid. at 571–8.

rarely prepared in formal consultation with members of Parliament or political parties. In contrast, in economic matters there is a tradition of extensive informal consultation with interested industry and labour associations, as well as with other lobbies and pressure groups.

The situation in the first stages of the Uruguay Round was typical of the traditional method of determining foreign policy: the executive branch analysed Swiss economic interests and developed proposals in close consultation with the private sector, and the Parliament stood back uninterested. This benign neglect prevailed until the preparations for the 1991 meeting in Brussels. When the Uruguay Round began receiving broad press coverage in the run-up to the meeting—the interest mainly focused on agriculture—Parliament awoke. It was only then that the parties and politicians began to realize that the city in which fundamental decisions about Switzerland are made is no longer Berne, it is Geneva.[40]

Sensing a similar shift of power in the contemporaneous negotiations on the EEA, Parliament attempted to re-establish a position of influence in both sets of negotiations. Within a package of procedural reforms, Parliament required the executive to consult with the respective Committees of both Chambers. Article 47bis (a) of the Parliament Act (Geschäftsverkehrsgesetz) requires the executive to inform and consult with Parliament on foreign affairs affecting legislative functions.[41] Although positions taken by legislative committees are not legally binding, they do have political influence on the Administration's adopted positions.

The reform amendment has been in place for two years, and early

---

[40] See in particular the lengthy and lively debate in Parliament in early Oct. 1990, two months before the Brussels Ministerial Meeting. The debate took place upon request of the party representing main farming interests, 'Dringliche Interpellation der Fraktion der Schweizerischen Volkspartei, Schweizerische Agrarpolitik, GATT', Amtl. Bull. NR 1990 at 1705–24, 1725–27. The interpellation, urgently submitted, argued that, *inter alia*, the Government had misjudged the effects of the Declaration of Punta del Esta, and the question was put to the Government how it intended to assure the realization of established and domestically agreed goals of national agricultural policies. The debate shows both conservative and progressive views, but both of them leave little doubt that main decisions are no longer reserved to domestic politics but are being mainly shaped in international negotiations.

[41] Bundesgesetz über den Geschäftsverkehr der Bundesversammlung sowie über die Form, die Bekanntmachung und das Inkrafttreten ihrer Erlasse, Art. 47bis (a) (as amended) (23 Mar. 1962):

3) Bei Verhandlungen in internationalen Organisationen, die zu Beschlüssen führen, durch die in der Schweiz geltendes Recht geschaffen wird oder geschaffen werden muss, konsultiert der Bundesrat die aussenpolitischen Kommissionen zu den Richt- und Leitlinien für das Verhandlungsmandat, bevor er diese festlegt oder abändert.

. . .

5) Die Absätze 3 und 4 gelten sinngemäss auf Verlangen der zuständigen Kommissionen auch für Verhandlungen mit auswärtigen Staaten oder internationalen Organisationen über völkerrechtliche Verträge.

(SR, vol. 1, p. 171.11).

experiences have shown the procedures to be in need of refinement. In particular, it will be necessary to define more precisely the scope of issues the executive branch must submit to the Committees for consultation. Such issues should be limited to strategy and rule-making, which fall within the realm of Parliament. Still, the instrument has already improved not only the awareness of issues related to foreign policy, but it also has made a considerable contribution to preparing members of Parliament for the task of bringing foreign policy issues into the domestic political debate—an achievement of major importance in the context of a direct democracy. While reluctant to make full use of the instrument, the Administration has increasingly recognized the amendment's importance in building foreign relations expertise in Parliament and in fostering acceptance of foreign policy results in the public at large.

9.4.3 The changing role of the cantons in external economic relations

Another impact of the Uruguay Round on internal constitutional processes was on the position of the cantons in negotiations and treaty-making. Most subject-matter dealt with in the Round pertains to federal law.[42] Government procurement, the granting of important subsidies, and a considerable number of services, however, are regulated by cantons, and the subjects were therefore of direct interest to them as well as to municipalities.[43] Though the Administration consulted little if at all with the cantons during the first stages of the Round, this situation changed in later stages. Efforts by the cantons to increase the flows of information and participation in the negotiating process were mainly driven by the EEA negotiations because these affected cantonal prerogatives much more than did the Uruguay Round, but the structures resulting from the EEA-directed efforts helped improve participation of the cantons in the Uruguay

---

[42] The making of international trade agreements, the setting of tariffs and determination of federal subsidies, the setting of sanitary and phytosanitary standards, and the protection of intellectual property rights, for instance, are all matters for the national policy-makers in Switzerland. Cantons, like states in the US, are formally given all powers not reserved by the federal government Art. 3 BV. However, in practice, the cantons are restricted in the scope of their exclusive authority. While they can decide most matters of education and have considerable discretion in the use of their land (they may make zoning regulations and decide certain matters having to do with natural resources), in most areas they share their powers with the federal government. One aspect of this power-sharing is the cantons' execution of federal laws. See generally, P. Saladin, 'Art. 3' and 'Art. 2 ÜeB' (1986) in J.-F. Aubert *et al.* (eds.), *Kommentar zur Bundesverfassung der Schweizerischen Eidgenossenschaft vom 29. Mai 1874* (1986).

[43] The services regulated directly by cantonal governments include: education, the legal profession, and the hotel and restaurant industry.

Round as well. Regular meetings between the responsible officials of the Administration and representatives of the governments of the cantons assured that information was transmitted in matters of direct concern to these bodies.[44]

Today, the governments of the cantons are organized in a body called the Konferenz der Kantonsregierungen. This organization meets periodically to co-ordinate policy positions with the federal government and to protect the cantons' areas of competence. In 1996, legislation is being proposed to preserve and reinforce the cantons' foreign policy prerogatives. It remains to be seen how the interaction between the cantons and the federal government will evolve and whether new constitutional structures of decision-making will emerge to reinforce representation of the cantons in the light of the internationalization of law-making.[45]

9.4.4 The role of non-governmental organizations

Some of the tensions observed in Switzerland and elsewhere during the years of negotiations can be traced back to unequal access to the process by non-governmental actors. Switzerland's administrations have a long tradition of informal consultation with the private economic sector. In the Uruguay Round a special joint committee of the negotiating team and the private sector was established (*groupe de liaison*), and negotiating teams and representatives of the private sector conducted in-depth consultations with each other. Sometimes, for instance in tariffication issues, these consultations amounted to fully-fledged internal negotiations.

Standard procedures assured that industry and farmers' associations would have an influence on the outcome of the Swiss positions taken to the negotiations. The same holds true for labour unions, although they used the forums to a lesser extent. However, new actors, namely public interest groups defending Third World interests and particularly the environmental pressure groups, were not systematically included in consultations prior to 1991.

Increasing opposition to the Uruguay Round, particularly that from environmental protection and development groups, backed by the power

---

[44] In order to reinforce their impact on federal politics and law-making, the cantonal governments constituted the standing Conference of Cantonal Governments (*Konferenz der Kantonsregierungen*) with the purpose of co-ordinating policy positions *vis-à-vis* the federal level, and protecting their areas of competence from erosion. The Cantonal Conference was partially successful. In the field of domestic legislation, the Conference enjoyed a greater level of influence. In foreign economic affairs, with efforts focused on Europe, the main impact of concerted actions on the Uruguay Round can be found in the field of government procurement.

[45] *Bericht über die grenzüberschreitende Zusammenarbeit und die Mitwirkung der Kantone an der Aussenpolitik*, BBl. 1994 II 620–95 (10 May 1994).

to call for a referendum, forced the Administration to adjust its decision-making practices to include the non-industrial organizations in discussions on areas sensitive to their various interests.[46] Such integration efforts ran parallel to the preparations for the 1992 United Nations Conference on Environment and Development, and the new contacts formed in this arena spilled over into the Uruguay Round. This incorporation of views was important to the building of a national consensus.

9.5 THE IMPLEMENTATION OF THE RESULTS OF THE ROUND

9.5.1 Parliament and implementing legislation

The Bundesrat, having signed the Uruguay Round's Final Act in Marrakesh on 15 April 1994, submitted the package to Parliament on 19 September 1994.[47] It was accompanied by all the necessary implementing legislation.[48] The submission consisted of three types of decisions. The first decision related to the Agreement Establishing the World Trade Organization. It contained all the Agreements that form the mandatory package. The second submission related to the plurilateral trade agreements, to all of which Switzerland is a party. The third submission contained all the legislative changes necessary for the implementation of the Round. A total of sixteen federal bills, most of them relating to intellectual property, tariffs, and agriculture needed modification. In addition, an entirely new bill on federal government procurement was introduced.[49]

Both chambers of Parliament discussed the submissions during the two weeks of winter term of 1994.[50] To be able to pass the new legislation and consent to the Final Act before the end of the year, an exception was made to the practice of consecutive deliberation of treaties and bills in both chambers.

The bulk of implementing legislation was directly related to treaty provisions, so Parliament was not offered much opportunity to make modifications. This was partly due to the fact that the Administration,

---

[46] For the role of the interest groups in the referendum process, see Section 4.4.

[47] See *Botschaft zur Genehmigung der GATT/WTO Übereinkommen (Uruguay-Runde) (GATT-Botschaft 1)*, BBl 1994 IV 1 (24 Oct. 1994).

[48] See *Botschaft zu den für die Ratifizierung der GATT/WTO-Uebereinkommen (Uruguay Runde) notwendigen Rechtsanpassungen (GATT-Botschaft 2)*, BBl 1994 IV 950. For the changes as adopted 16 Dec. 1994 and implementing regulations enacted by the Bundesrat see AS 1994 1773–2111.

[49] AS 1996 508, 518 (bill and Government regulation).

[50] For the debates in Parliament see official transcripts in *Amtliches Bulletin Nationalrat* at 2149–2204, 2209–24, 2244–59, 2276–2307, 2311–16, 2356–57 (official reporter Winter 1994) and *Amtliches Bulletin Ständerat* 1096–1121, 1129–37, 1140–44 (official reporter Winter 1994).

fearing that an expanded package would increase the risk of referendum, had decided to limit legislative adjustments to only the most important. This left Parliament with a difficult problem still to be settled. The main issue of discussion in the Committees focused on the financial guarantees to the farming community. While most of the major political parties stood solidly behind accepting the WTO packages,[51] many did express concern about the future of the farmers,[52] and as was to be expected, the parties representing mainly agricultural interests were far from enthusiastic.[53] The environmentally-oriented Green Party was split, but neither side was happy with the WTO rules.[54]

The National Farmers' Association (Schweizerischer Bauernverband) requested that losses stemming from obligations to reduce export subsidies—both in terms of financial support and quantity—and from reducing domestic product-related supports be compensated for by direct payments allowed under the 'Green box' of the Agreement on Agriculture.[55] In strongly-worded announcements, the farming community

---

[51] See 'Zustimmung bei den Parteien' *Neue Zürcher Zeitung*, 9 Sept. 1994 14 ('Für eine rasche Ratifizierung der Abkommen treten die FDP und die CVP ein . . . [Die FDP] sieht in den GATT-Botschaften ihre Forderung erfüllt. Für die Landwirtschaft seien die Umstellungen tragbar').

[52] See, e.g., ibid. (While supporting the GATT/WTO effort, the CVP found that '[d]as Abkommen habe aber auch negative Folgen für die Landwirte. Die CVP fordert deshalb eine Agrarpolitik, die den Bauernfamilien eine eigenständige und existenzsichernde Tätigkeit ermöglicht'); Generalsekretariat des SVP, 'Abkommen der Uruguay-Runde/GATT-WTO: Vernehmlassung der Schweizerischen Volkspartei (SVP)' at 1, 2 (18 Aug. 1994) ('Die Schweizerische Volkspartei unterstützt die Ratifizierung der aus der Uruguay-Runde resultierenden Abkommen. Die Teilnahme der Schweiz an diesen Vertragswerken ist für unsere Volkswirtschaft von entscheidender, existentieller Bedeutung . . . [Aber] Vor der Ratifikation des GATT-Abkommens verlangen wir deshalb Klarheit über die Ausgestaltung der Auswirkungen des GATT auf die schweizerische Landwirtschaft'); Pressedienst der Liberalen Partei der Schweiz, 'Das liberale Profil Nummer 30' (29 Sept. 1994) ('Wir unterstützen [the GATT–WTO Agreement], die der Grundhaltung und Tradition unseres Landes gegenüber dem Freihandel entsprechen. Für die Exportwirtschaft zeichnen sich echte Auswirkungen ab. Demgegenüber weiss man, dass die Landwirtschaft wird Opfer bringen müssen. Wir werden uns also dafür einzusetzen haben, dass die Wiederentfaltung des Primärsektors durch finanzielle und gesetzgeberische Massnahmen unterstützt wird').

[53] H. Bravo, *Auswirkungen des GATT-Abkommens auf die schweizerische Landwirtschaft* (1994), 1, 2: ('Der Druck auf die Landwirtschaft ist heute gross, allein in den letzten drei Jahren sind die landwirtschaftlichen Einkommen um rund 30% gesunken. Dieser Prozess wird durch die Resultate der Uruguay-Runde des GATT noch beschleunigt und verstärkt. [Es] ist schon heute klar, dass das GATT massive negative Auswirkungen auf die schweizerische Landwirtschaft zeigen wird').

[54] See 'Die Grünen im Gatt-Dilemma', *Neue Zürcher Zeitung*, 29 Aug. 1994 13 (reporting that the Greens party's decision on GATT was a difficult one. 'Darin wurde einerseits festgehalten, dass die Ergebnisse der Uruguay-Runde als negativ zu beurteilen seien. Anderseits rang sich der Vorstand zur Positions durch, dass die Schweiz trotz aller Mängel des Vertragswerks auf dessen Ratifizierung nicht verzichten könne').

[55] Annex 2 (7), Agreement on Agriculture in *The Legal Texts*, supra note 29, at 59–60.

informed the Government that short of legal assurances of financial aid, a referendum would be attempted.[56]

Assessing the possible implications of a nation-wide popular referendum in a highly complex and sometimes confusing subject matter, Parliament yielded after farmers and industry had informally concerted their positions and officially announced mutual support. Parliament legally assured the farmers that during the transitional period of six years, the reductions in export and production subsidies would be offset by direct payments.[57]

The second matter which fostered some debate in Parliament in winter 1994 was government procurement. The main controversial points concerned the social and ecological 'dumping' that might occur if foreign firms, unencumbered by strict labour and environmental regulation, could compete equally with the regulatory-cost laden Swiss firms. A majority in Parliament supported such a requirement, as proposed by the Government and potentially inconsistent with the agreement, that all foreign suppliers are obliged to honour existing social and labour standards as well as the ecological regulations.[58]

One should note that not all subject-matter contained in the WTO Agreements was subject to transformation into national law. Switzerland does not have legislation on countervailing dumping and unlawfully subsidized imports. Unlike in the United States or the European Union, so far there has not been any need for this type of protection. The Anti-Dumping Agreement[59] and the Subsidy Agreement[60] are not implemented

---

[56] H. Bravo, *Auswirkungen des GATT-Abkommens auf die schweizerische Landwirtschaft*, 6:
Wer also heute den Agrarteil des GATT definitiv zu beurteilen vorgibt, der tut dies in Unkenntnis der ganzen innenpolitischen Umsetzung. Dies bedeutet zwingend, dass erst dann definitiv zum GATT Stellung genommen werden kann, wenn feststeht, wie der Bund den GATT-Rahmen im Interesse der Landwirtschaft ausschöpft . . . Die Landwirtschaft is nicht bereit, auf blosse Versprechungen hin auf die vom GATT gewollten Veränderungen in der Agrarpolitik einzutreten . . .
'GATT/WTO ohne Kompensation nicht tragbar', *Bauernzeitung* (25 Nov. 1994) ('Beim GATT verlange die NBKS eine volle Kompensation der Eindommensausfalle, sonst werde sie sich den Referendumskreisen anschliessen').

[57] cf. the Administration's original proposal in the *Bundesblatt* with the implemented form of the legislation. The final form of the law provides for direct payments to farmers for the first 6 years in order to compensate for lost production subsidies. AS 1995 II 1841 (Landwirtschaftsgesetz, Übergangsbestimmung). The proposal for the Agriculture laws had no such reference. BBl 1994 IV 1099 (24 Oct. 1994).

[58] Bundesgesetz über das öffentliche Beschaffungswesen, Article 8(b), AS 1996 508 at 511. For the draft legislation introduced by the Bundesrat see BBl 1994 IV 950 at 1209. It is interesting to observe that a similar requirement was denied by a majority in internal relations under the internal market law (*Binnenmarktgesetz*). See T. Cottier & M. Wagner, 'Das neue Bundesgesetz über den Binnenmarkt (BGBM)' (1995) 12 *Aktuelle Juristische Praxis* 1582 at 1587.

[59] Agreement on Implementation of Art. VI of GATT 1994 in *The Legal Texts*, supra note 29 at 168.

[60] SCM Agreement, Agreement on Implementation of Art. VI of GATT 1994 in *The Legal Texts*, supra note 29, at 264.

either by statute or executive regulation. This will be of particular importance in discussing the self-executing nature of WTO agreements.[61]

In the final votes on 16 December 1994, the GATT/WTO package passed with overwhelming majorities in both houses of Parliament.[62] With the implementing legislation's promised direct agriculture payment provisions, and the backing of commercial interests, support came in as expected from every major political party.

Upon approval of the statutes by Parliament, the executive branch undertook work to adjust all the relevant regulations (Verordnungen) which fall under its delegated authority. A total of seventeen regulations were adjusted, most of them in agriculture, and in place when the WTO agreement came into force in July 1995. Subsequent adjustments, most of them in implementing tariffication in agriculture, followed in due course according to agreed schedules.[63]

The Uruguay Round's impacts extended beyond the mere technical adjustment of particular legislative provisions on tariffication and import restrictions. The process of the Round influenced long term thinking and shook the foundations of agricultural policies in Switzerland. The fundamental change from product-dependent payments to direct payments began under the shadow of the Round and appeared in the Seventh Agricultural Report in 1992,[64] before the Round had been concluded. Moreover, the Round stimulated reform of the Constitution. After two

[61] See Section 6.

[62] On 16 Dec. 1994, the *Ständerat* unanimously approved the Uruguay Round agreements in their final vote. With the exception of the votes on the Agriculture, Sugar, and Government Procurement proposals, which had 2, 2, and 5 votes against them, respectively, the implementing legislation votes were also unanimous. See Ständerat/Conseil des Etats, *Ämtliches Bulletin der Bundesversammlund*, Wintersession 1994 at 1356–60. Later that same day, the *Nationalrat* passed the Uruguay Round agreements. In that Chamber, there were 171 votes for the agreements, 2 against, 10 withheld, and 16 absent representatives. The President of the Chamber did not vote. In the votes on the implementing legislation, the results varied more than they did in the *Ständerat*, but again the agriculture and government procurement proposals received much opposition, with 54 and 35 votes against, accompanied by 47 votes against the inventor's patent rule-change. See Nationalrat/Conseil national, *Amtliches Bulletin der Bundesversammlung*, Wintersession 1994 at 2532–42.

[63] E.g., Tariffs: Verordnung über die Inkraftsetzung der im Rahmen des Uebereinkommens GATT/WTO vereinbarten Zollansätze des Generaltarifs (zweite Abbaustufe), AS 1995 5367; Agricultural Products: Verordnung über die Festsetzung der Zollsätze und Zollkontingente für landwirtschaftliche Erzeugnisse, AS 1995 5520. For a survey see *Bericht über die zolltarifarische Massnahmen im 2. Halbjahr 1995*, BBl 1996 I 1134–40.

[64] See, e.g., *Siebter Landwirtschaftsbericht* at 397 (setting out the 'new orientation' of farm policy for Switzerland, including a more market-oriented pricing and world price view, looking toward a long term goal of EU-compatible prices); R. Horber, *Die schweizerische Agrareinfuhrordnung* at 12, n. 3 ('Since the beginning of the 1980s, the calls for "more competition" have been increasing, even in Agriculture') (authors' translation).

early initatives by the farmer and the environmental organizations[65] were withdrawn, and a counter-proposal by Parliament[66] failed, Parliament submitted a new compromise proposal to the cantons and the people in June 1996. This time the proposal succeeded, and was adopted to replace Article 31bis (3)(b) of the Federal Constitution.[67] The new provision, Article 31^{octies}, emphasizes direct payments and environmentally-sound production methods, including labelling for the protection of extensive (ecological) production, controls against excessive use of fertilizers, and the support of agricultural research, education, and investment.[68] While the fundamental change toward supporting ecological production stems from domestic and continental environmental movements, the Uruguay Round certainly stimulated the changes toward the system of direct payment. This system is vital to realizing less intensive production which had formerly relied on product-related support. Without the Uruguay Round (and parallel efforts within the European Community's agricultural policies before the conclusion of the Blair House Accord), it would not have been possible to bring around the necessary change of attitudes within a decade.

[65] See Botschaft zu den Volksinitiativen 'für eine umweltgerechte und leistungfähige bäuerliche Landwirtschaft' (Initiative des schweizerischen Bauernverbandes) and 'Bauern und Konsumenten—für eine naturnahe Landwirtschaft' (Bauern und Konsumenten–Initiative, BBl 1994 III 798.

[66] BBl 1995 II 1362 (49.1% yes, 50.9% no, 8 cantons and two semi-cantons in favour, 12 cantons and 4 semi-cantons against). The refusal of the fairly open constitutional text was mainly induced by a simultaneous refusal of specific measures in milk regulation (refusal to render milk quotas tradable) and legislation to continue compulsory support of marketing efforts by agricultural associations.

[67] See n. 34. The amendment, Art. 31^{octies}, was ratified on 6 June 1996 with a vote of 77.6% of the votes cast in favour of the reform. See 'Glanzergebnis fur Agrarartikel nach Strafrunde' *Neue Zurcher Zeitung*, 10 June 1996 at 17.

[68] Art. 31^{octies}:

Der Bund sorgt dafür, dass die Landwirtschaft durch eine umweltgerechte und auf die Absatzmöglichkeiten ausgerichtete Produktion einen wesentlichen Beitrag leistet zur:

    a. sicheren Versorgung der Bevölkerung;

    b. nachhaltigen Nutzung der natürlichen Lebensgrundlagen;

    c. Pflege der Kulturlandschaft;

    d. dezentralen Besiedlung des Landes.

    2. In Ergänzung zur zumutbaren Selbsthilfe der Landwirtschaft und nötigenfalls in Abweichung von der Handels- und Gewerbefreiheit trifft der Bund Massnahmen zur Fürderung der bodenbewirtschaftenden bäuerlichen Betriebe. Er hat insbesondere folgende Befugnisse und Aufgaben:

    a. Er kann die landwirtschaftliche Forschung, Beratung und Ausbildung fördern sowie Investitionshilfen leisten.

    b. Er kann Bestimmungen über die Allgemeinverbindlicherklärung von Vereinbarungen über die Selbsthilfe erlassen.

    c. Er kann Vorschriften zur Festigung des bäuerlichen Grundbesitzes erlassen.

    d. Er ergänzt das bäuerliche Einkommen durch Direktzahlungen zur Erzielung eines angemessenen Entgelts für die erbrachten Leistungen.

    e. Er fördert mit wirtschaftlich lohnenden Anreizen Produktionsformen, die besonders naturnah, umwelt- und tierfreundlich sind.

    3. Er setzt dafür zweckgebundene Mittel aus dem Bereich der Landwirtschaft und allgemeine Bundesmittel ein.

9.5.2 The referendum movement

While many members of Parliament were far from enthusiastic supporters of the new trade agreements in 1994, there was an overwhelming sense that there was no real chance that a referendum would prevent joining the WTO after the basic deal between agriculture and industry had been achieved in Parliament. Then, in early September 1994, an ad hoc committee, spearheaded by three men, decided to challenge the WTO package.[69] Although an unlikely alliance when viewed from their various interests, the triumvirate agreed on the need to bring 'GATT Before the People' ('*GATT vors Volk*'). Recognizing that the WTO Agreement is not a 'simple trade agreement', but rather one of a far-reaching new world order', the small but vocal referendum committee particularly criticized the secrecy in which the agreement was negotiated. The GATT Before the People committee, knowing that the WTO would be approved at some point, wanted an open debate before that time.[70] Their main purpose was to bring to the attention of the public at large what they considered to be 'undemocratic, unsocial and environmentally damaging agreements'.[71]

In early December, the GATT Before the People committee announced they would attempt a referendum if Parliament passed the WTO legislation. At that time, they were supported by the Union of Small and Middle-sized Farmers, the Western Swiss Union of Producers, and the East- and Inner-Switzerland's New Farmer Co-ordination, besides garnering international support from consumer protectionist Ralph Nader and international farmer and environmental concern groups. What is more significant, however, is that none of the major parties, associations, or interest groups—not the National Farmers' Association, nor the Green Party, nor the Small Farmers, nor the Union of Organic Farming Organizations—supported the referendum attempt.

---

[69] The triumverate was composed of the environmentalist Luzius Theiler, President of the Swiss Green Party; the Bernese farmers' leader Werner Salzmann; and the journalist Christopher Pfluger. None of them, however, was acting in an official capacity for his respective organization.

[70] 'Schweiz: Gatt soll vor das Volk; USA: Kongress stimmt dem GATT zu', *Basler Zeitung*, 3 Dec. 1994.

[71] 'Wir sind keine Strohmänner', *Der Bund*, 3 Dec. 1994 ('Die Chance winkt, das politikverdrossene Volk endlich über die antidemokratischen, unsozialen und umweltschädlichen Folgen der Abkommen aufzuklären'). Questions of the degree to which workplaces would be lost to foreign labour, the concern for maintaining control over Switzerland's high level of environmental protection and the ability to impose ethically-motivated limitations on the freedom of Swiss scientists to do research in genetic technologies, remained issues removed from direct public input during the Uruguay Round. This lack of transparency in the diplomatic decision-making process not only caused much suspicion during the Uruguay Round, it remains a matter for concern in all of today's international institutions.

As mentioned previously, a referendum could target either treaty consent and implementing legislation together, or either treaty consent or single acts of implementing legislation alone. A successful referendum against any one of the major implementing bills would have held up ratification of the acts necessary to implementing tariffication in agriculture.[72] The GATT Before the People committee decided to target the entire package.

The referendum movement did not lose time. The clock on the collection of 50,000 signatures having started on 1 January 1995, the WTO package was open for challenge until the end of March. The efforts of the GATT Before the People organizers focused on those aspects of the WTO that allow for decision-making on the supranational level. The changes in the dispute settlement process for instance, making silence on panel decisions equal to acceptance, was particularly criticized as a loss of national sovereignty. With such a rule, they pointed out, international corporations could easily avoid adhering to Switzerland's national laws.[73]

Although nervous, the Government was fairly certain that in the end, the referendum would occur but be soundly defeated by the Swiss popular vote. After all, despite the referendum's outcry of the democracy-deficit of the negotiations, the political parties in Parliament had been heavily influenced by their constituencies, and had voted for implementation accordingly.

What the executive branch and Parliament had hardly dared to hope for, much less expect, is the news they received at the end of March 1995. With the end of the three month moratorium, the referendum had failed with a total of only 29,181 validated signatures.[74] The path for ratification was open.

The reason for the public's strong support of WTO membership remains a matter of speculation. To our knowledge, no official in-depth polls were taken. The following reasons may have been relevant:

- It was widely felt that upon rejection of the EEA Agreement in 1992 and given the present state of relative isolation in Europe, Switzerland could not afford to stay outside the world trading system and prosper without market access rights (in particular for markets outside Europe).
- Since the nineteenth century there has been a long and uninterrupted tradition of free trade policies in Switzerland, with the single exception

---

[72] Other bills in the field of intellectual property and in particular those relating to controversial issues of patenting life forms, for instance, would not necessarily have such an effect.   [73] See n. 70.

[74] *Referendum gegen den Bundesbeschluss vom 16. Dezember 1994 über die Genehmigung der in der Multilateralen Handelsverhandlungen unter der Aegide des GATT (Uruguay Runde) abgeschlossenen Abkommen: Nicht Zustandekommen*, BBl 1995 II 669, AS 1995 II 2115.

of the post-Second World War agriculture sector. As Switzerland joined the GATT provisionally in 1955 and fully in 1966, adherence to the WTO system is an expression of continuity in this open market ideology.

- Despite the WTO's considerable expansion beyond the classical domain of trade in goods, none of the sensitive issues found in the context of European integration and the EEA Agreement arises: free movement of persons and capital still are in the very beginning stages in the General Agreement on Trade in Services and the Agreement on Trade-Related Aspects of Intellectual Property Rights; the Agreement Establishing the WTO does not formally contain elements of supranationality; unlike EEC law, amendments and new agreements will be subject to approval and ratification; and adopted panel and Appellate Body reports do not directly affect individuals.

- Despite fundamental shifts in the instruments that regulate trade in agriculture, the level of protection will be reduced only gradually. Commitments are largely compensated for by direct payments, legally guaranteed by Parliament at least for the transitional period. The farming community leaders were well aware that direct payments depend on full integration of the economy into the world markets and that market access rights are essential to that effect.

- WTO law being a complex matter, it is likely that a large part of the population was not in a position to grasp all of the major and long-term implications of the Uruguay Round results within a period of three months. Lack of support for the referendum therefore may also have been caused by lack of information.

9.5.3 Entry into force and compliance expected

Throughout the moratorium, the executive branch continued its internal work, making the necessary adaptations to governmental regulations. With entry into force of the WTO membership for Switzerland on 1 July 1995, all implementing legislation and most regulations were in place. None of the transitory periods provided for in the different agreements and Article XIV:2 WTO Agreement was required. The policy of simultaneous motions for treaty consent and submission of necessary implementing legislation and regulations removed the insecurity which could result from *ex post* implementation and transitional arrangements for the various agreements.

Standard policy in Switzerland is to seek to pass legislation and government ordinances with ratification and to have all the necessary instruments in place with the entry into force of international obligations. The policy, again, is induced by the threat of referendum, as people want to know what they are getting when international agreements subject to the referendum are being passed in Parliament. This standard policy is not without drawbacks,[75] but it also reflects another mainstay in Swiss attitudes: tough negotiations and hard bargaining, accompanied by the Government's will to honour the principles of *pacta sunt servanda* and the legitimate expectations of trading partners.

9.5.4 The right to referendum as supporting democratic legitimacy of WTO law

Despite the negotiating difficulties posed by the threat of a public vote occuring after the finalization of the text resulting from the Uruguay Round, the referendum requirement should not be viewed as merely a burden, totally at odds with globalization, slowing down participation in the trade system and risking political isolation. The requirement also had the effect of fostering debate and democratic control among an informed citizenry. Due mainly to the fear that there would be a referendum, the executive branch undertook a broad public information campaign throughout the later stages of the negotiating process. During this campaign, considerable efforts were made to explain Switzerland's national interests, those of Switzerland's main trading partners, and the resulting platforms. Much effort was given to commenting on and explaining the results of the negotiations in a series of brochures, publications, numerous lectures, media events, and academic literature.[76] The negotiating team was as active domestically as it was in Geneva. The detailed informing of the press and media, co-ordinated by a special press office of the Ministry of Economics, was vital to enhancing the public's understanding of the Round.[77]

The referendum requirement thus heightened the legitimacy of the treaties subject to, and approved under, these procedures. Upon acceptance and ratification, the results will be felt positively, in the facilitated implementation of the Agreement, in compliance with the results, and in contributing to the law-abiding reputation of Switzerland in international relations. Moreover, the legitimacy gained through direct democratic processes facilitates the direct application of justiciable treaty provisions.[78]

---

[75] See Section 5.5.

[76] The potential referendum stimulated a number of books on WTO matters in Switzerland. See H. Hauser & K.-U. Schanz, *Wirtschaftliche Bedeutung*; D. Thürer and S. Kux (eds.), *GATT 94 und die Welthandelsorganisation: Herausforderung für die Schweiz und Europa* (1996); R. Senti, *GATT-WTO*, (1994); T. Cotter (ed.) *GATT-Uruguay Round* (1995).

[77] The efforts of private organizations to shape public opinion were also considerable as well. See, e.g., Eidgenössisches Volkswirtschaftsdepartement, *GATT 1947–WTO 1994: Grundlagendokumentation*, (1994); Département Fédéral de l'économie Publique, *GATT APERÇU*, (1994); Schweizerischer Bankverein, *GATT WTO: Der Schlüssel zur neuen Welthandelsordnung*, (1994). [78] See Section 6.

9.5.5 Proposed adjustments in referendum procedures

While the referendum requirement adds to the legitimacy of the acceptance of those treaties subject to it, the standard policy of simultaneous submission of legislative changes does put some strain on internal law-making processes. The primary problem with immediate implementation is that it does not leave Parliament sufficient time to reflect on the bills proposed. In the case of the WTO Agreement, Parliament received the 959-page report containing the executive's proposals in the second half of September 1994. As the votes were due in December for a timely ratification, that left only three months for the Nationalrat and Ständerat members to consider whether to accept or reject the proposals. Credibility of the internal political process may suffer if large numbers of legislative changes are undertaken without thorough debate.

The experience of the Uruguay Round brought to light problems of adequate timing of the international agenda and direct democracy. As discussed above, treaties are submitted to Parliament together with their implementing legislation.[79] While Swiss constitutional law basically follows monist traditions, the package of implementing legislation is submitted with the treaty so as to allow citizens to assess precisely the rights and obligations incurred under the treaty. The treaty itself and its implementing legislation are subject to separate votes, running the risk of creating a split vote. Alternatively, this simultaneous submission of an independent package of implementing laws may delay or even prevent ratification and adherence to an approved treaty because a majority does not like a particular mode of implementing rights and obligations.

The rapid pace of change in the increasingly complex international legislation arena has made the dual approval system too burdensome. There are attempts to adjust referendum rights to fit the new conditions in international law-making. In present constitutional reforms, there are proposals to avoid this splitting and to allow for the exclusion of such statutory provisions from the referendum which are necessary to implement approved treaty provisions.[80] Another idea, not contained in the proposals submitted, would allow separate referendums on implementing legislation only after entry into force and a trial period. Instead of simply striking down an act, proposals would be submitted in an initiative (constructive

---

[79] See Section 5.1.
[80] See Art. 125, Draft Constitution ('Untersteht der Genehmigungsbeschluss eines völkerrechtlichen Vertrags dem obligatorischen oder fakultativen Referendum, so kann er die Bundesversammlung ermächtigen, die Gesetzeänderungen, die aufgrund des Vertrages notwendig sind, unter Ausschluss des Referendums anzunehmen').

referendum) to change problematic areas without impairing international rights and obligations. The numbers required for a referendum would be increased to 100,000 signatures, but the type of treaties subject to it would no longer be limited to multilateral instruments. Instead all bilateral treaties would also be subject to a referendum.[81] Whether these adjustments will succeed in accommodating modern treaty-making needs remains to be seen.

9.6 The future role of private litigation and the judicial branch

Among Swiss lawyers—as is also true elsewhere—GATT/WTO law still is far from familiar. It is not an instrument utilized daily by most, and as a result is unlikely to spark an interest beyond general ones brought out in times of extensive press coverage of the subject. The Swiss legal community has shown little interest in absorbing the legal fruits of the Round—less than the Swiss economists and businesses have shown, and much less so than lawyers have expressed in the context of European law.

The lack of GATT knowledge is due at least in part to *Maison G. Sprl* v. *Direction Générale des douanes*, a 1986 judgment by the Swiss Federal Court refusing to accept the objectives set out in the Preamble of GATT and Article III of GATT as self-executing.[82] It therefore *seems* to many lawyers that GATT is without any direct impact in Swiss law. This impression is reinforced by the fact that extensive implementing legislation was enacted, the consultation of which suffices when dealing with ordinary import and export issues.

The situation, however, is more complicated than no direct impacts of GATT and WTO law. First, some of the agreements emanating from the Tokyo Rounds were never transformed into domestic law. The Government at the time expressed the view that rights and obligations under these agreements would be met this way and that no implementing legislation was necessary. Anti-dumping and countervailing duties may be imposed

---

[81] See Art. 124, Draft Constitution:

1. Auf Verlangen von *100,000* Stimmberechtigten oder acht Kantonen werden dem Volk die Genehmigungsbeschlüsse der Bundesversammlung zu völkerrechtlichen Verträgen zur Abstimmung unterbreitet, die:

. . .

c) rechtsetzende Normen enthalten oder zum Erlass von Bundesgesetzen oder allgemeinverbindlichen Bundesbeschlüssen verpflichten.

[82] Federal Court Reporter (BGE) 112 Ib 189: '. . . il faut cependant constater que [Preamble and Art. III GATT] constituent de simples déclarations à caractère de programme et ne contiennent aucune obligation juridique que le juge administratif se doit d'appliquer. S'adressant exclusivement à l'autorité politique, elles ne présentent en l'espèce aucune utilité pour la recourante.'

directly based upon these agreements in Switzerland.[83] More importantly, procedural rights in anti-dumping investigations and countervailing duty investigations are exclusively found in these agreements. The same is true under the revised agreements of the Uruguay Round.[84] Except in the field of government procurement, it was felt that more specific procedural and substantive rules in these other areas would be unnecessary.

Secondly, many provisions of agreements relating to intellectual property are generally considered to be suitable for direct effect in Swiss law.[85] With respect to the Paris and Berne Conventions, as incorporated in the TRIPs agreement, this view is equally shared by the Government.[86] It is difficult to see why there should be a different evaluation of the same norms within the TRIPs Agreement—especially since rights and obligations under the new agreement are even more specific.

Thirdly, the self-executing nature of Article III of GATT was denied by the Federal Court without substantive reasoning. No explanation exists as to why precise rules of most favoured-nation and national treatment are not justiciable in the light of GATT panel practice.[87] This is the reason the Government insisted that the direct effect of WTO law not be ruled out.[88]

Finally, under an explicit rule in case law, the Swiss Constitutional Court must construe national laws to be compatible with international law obligations to avoid divergences between the two levels of law.[89] Thus, it is likely that the courts will have an opportunity to adjudicate the issue of direct effect and interpretation in accordance with international obligations under WTO law in the coming years.

In the light of the explicit denial of the Uruguay Round results' direct effect in United States' implementing legislation[90] as well as indications to similar effects in preambular language of implementing acts[91] and the case

---

[83] The self-executing nature of the agreement was a main reason to abstain from the introduction of implementing legislation after the Tokyo Round, see 1988 *Amtliches Bulletin Nationalrat* 693 at 694–5; T. Cottier, 'Die Bedeutung des GATT im Prozess der europäischen Integration', in O. Jacot-Guillarmod *et al.*, (eds.), *EG-Recht und schweizerische Rechtsordnung* (1990), 143 at 177.

[84] See Part V, Arts. 10–23 SCM Agreement in *The Legal Texts*, supra note 29 at 278–96.

[85] See M. J. Lutz and W. Heizelmann, 'Staatsverträge im Immaterialgüterrecht', in R. von Büren and L. David (eds.), 1 *Schweizerisches Immaterial- und Wettbewerbsrecht: Allgemeiner Teil* (1995) 39 at 65–71.   [86] See Botschaft, BBl 1994 IV 287–88.

[87] See n. 82.   [88] See Botschaft, BBl 1994 IV 418.

[89] *Frigero* v. *EVED*, BGE 97 I 669 at 678 ('Im Zweifel muss innerstaatliches Recht völkerrechtskonform ausgelegt werden; d.h. so, dass ein Widerspruch mit dem Völkerrecht nicht besteht. Diese Auslegungsregel erlaubt es, Konflikte zwichen den beiden Rechtsordnungen meistens zu vermeiden . . .')

[90] See 19 USC 3512 s. 102(c):

(1) LIMITATIONS.—No person other than the United States–
    (A) shall have any cause of action or defence under any of the Uruguay Round Agreements or by virtue of congressional approval of such an agreement . . .
See also Chap. 6.

[91] Council Dec. 94/800/EC, 22 Dec. 1994, [1994] OJ L336/2; see also Chap. 2.

law of the European Community,[92] it is likely that mercantilist and trade policy arguments against the direct effect of even sufficiently precise rules, such as non-discrimination, will be addressed in Swiss courts. Some will argue that interpretation by national courts and direct effect in national jurisdictions will necessarily impair the homogeneity of trading rules in different jurisdictions and create conditions of uneven playing fields.

Such arguments are supported by case law relating to the application of the Swiss–EC Free Trade Agreement of 1972 to which direct effect was denied by the Swiss Federal Court on the grounds that it amounts to a mere trade agreement, short of economic integration.[93] The criticism voiced against this doctrine both with respect to the application of the Free Trade Agreement and the GATT[94] is equally valid for WTO law.

A general denial of self-execution of suitable provisions by the courts arguably amounts to judicial protectionism. More importantly, it fails to recognize that direct effect is in the interest of the economy concerned.[95] It is often necessary to offset the political processes that naturally tend to favour domestic economic interests at the expense of imports. Under the framework of open markets, direct effect therefore becomes a core element of checks and balances and separation of powers in the trade constitution of monist countries. A judicial policy of direct application will finally bring about the necessary legal interest in WTO rules beyond the circles of government, diplomacy, and large enterprise. Only direct effect can bring international trading rules to the attention of the legal

---

[92] See *Federal Republic of Germany* v. *Council of the European Union*, Case C–280/93 [1994] ECR I 4973; *International Fruit Company* v. *Produkteschap voor Groenten en Fruit*, Cases 21–24/72 [1972] ECR 129; *Società Italiana per l'Oleodotto Transalpino* v. *Italy*, Case 266/81 [1983] ECR 731; *Amministrazione delle Finanze dello Stalo* v. *Società Petrolifera Italiana SpA and SpA Michelin Italia* Cases 267–9/81 [1983] ECR 801. For a critical view see, e.g., Cottier, 'Die Bedeutung des GATT' at 171–8; S. Griller, 'Direct effects of WTO rules within the Community legal system?' (on file with authors).

[93] *Bosshard Partners* v. *Sunlight*, (1979) BGE 105 II 49; *Adams* v. *Staatsanwaltschaft des Kantons Basel-Stadt*, (1978) BGE 104 IV 179; *Association pour le recyclage du PVC*, (1992) BGE 118 Ib 367.

[94] O. Jacot-Guillarmod, *Le juge national face au droit européen* (1993) 128–40, 175–8; Cottier 'Die Bedeutung des GATT' at 172–8; T. Cottier, 'Constitutional trade regulation in national and international law: structure and substance pairings in the EFTA experience' in M. Hilf and E.-U. Petersmann (eds.), *National Constitutions and International Economic Law* (1993) 409–42; T. Cottier, 'Das Problem der Parallelimporte im Freihandelsabkommen Schweiz-EG und im Recht der WTO-GATT' in *Revue suisse de la propriété intellectuelle* (1995) 37, 44–52. Unlike the courts, the Government favours direct application of the FTA: see *Bericht des Bundesrates über die Stellung der Schweiz im europäischen Integrationsprozess*, BBl 1988 III 249, 348 ff.

[95] See in particular E.-U. Petersmann, 'National constitutions and international economic law', in M. Hilf & E.-U. Petersmann (eds.), *National Constitutions and International Economic Law* (1993), 3; E. U. Petersmann, 'Limited government and unlimited trade policy powers? Why effective judicial review and a liberal constitution depend on individual rights' *National Constitutions*, 537–62.

community and trigger a genuine interest within the profession to deal extensively with WTO law.

The avoidance of mercantilist trade policy arguments based on reciprocity is particularly attractive for small and medium trading nations that do not engage in trade wars and power play. Their markets are too small to threaten effectively a denial of market access in case of unfair trade policies by foreign nations. In small countries, the interest in direct effect is primarily an interest in assuring open markets and efficiency within the bounds of agreed trade rules.

Finally, but importantly in the context of this paper, WTO rules enjoy the same legitimacy as do statutory rules in the case of Switzerland. As they were subject to the right of referendum just as any other statute would be, the acceptance of the WTO rules by positive or implied referendum (absence of a vote due to no campaign or insufficient signatures) produces the same type of legitimacy as enjoyed by the domestic statutory rights and obligations. It is at this point that the disadvantages of the referendum in terms of complicated procedures and risks of rejection are compensated for and matched by enhanced legitimacy. Thus, they enjoy a greater potential for compliance than elsewhere. Direct democracy can considerably enlarge the basis of direct application in the interest of the majority of voters concerned, once the hurdles of treaty approval are successfully overcome. Switzerland, in our view, is therefore an excellent candidate to use direct application of WTO law to its own advantage—to enhance political checks and balances, to improve the competitive environment, and to achieve an optimal allocation of resources within the country.

9.7 CONCLUSION

As the Uruguay Round implementation process in Switzerland proves, direct democracy does not provide quick or easy decisions and results. Prior to and during negotiations with other states, time and resources must be spent on measuring and developing official government positions in accordance with those interests having the means and power to bring about a referendum campaign and a potential to win the vote. After the negotiations, more time and more resources must be expended on ensuring domestic acceptance of the resulting laws. At all stages of law-making, the transaction costs of direct democracy are higher than in the political processes of other governments.

Yet, in the words of US Supreme Court Chief Justice Warren Burger, 'Convenience and efficiency are not the primary objectives—or the hallmarks—of democratic government.'[96] Direct democracy's primary

---

[96] *INS* v. *Chadha*, 462 US 919, 944 (1983).

virtues are legitimacy, the consideration of all interests concerned, and the bringing about of stable and fair results. Once results are adopted in accordance with the constitutional procedures in a direct democracy, they enjoy a high degree of stable and democratic legitimacy. This is equally true for international law adopted under such procedures. Implementation will not run into major difficulties and the direct application of international law within a state is encouraged by prior consent of the citizens to be governed by that law. Ultimately, direct democracy in the field of international trade can lend an efficiency of a different but more fundamental quality to the WTO and world trade law.

10

IMPLEMENTATION OF THE RESULTS OF THE URUGUAY ROUND AGREEMENTS: KOREA

*Moon-Soo Chung**

10.1 INTRODUCTION

The Uruguay Round has never been popular in Korea and the Korean Government was a reluctant participant throughout the negotiations. The results of the Uruguay Round, in particular those concerning agricultural products, were met by a national uproar and demonstrations against ratification. The Government was blamed for poor negotiations.[1] Partly due to the Government's all-out campaign, but arguably due more to the reality of a *fait accompli*, the Uruguay Round agreements passed through the National Assembly on 16 December 1994, followed by the Presidential ratification on 23 December 1994.

On 1 January 1995, the Uruguay Round Agreements became effective in Korea as part of its domestic law. Implementing arrangements, legal and administrative, are being put in place. Given the magnitude of preparatory work necessary to implement the Uruguay Round Agreements fully, however, it is not surprising that details of many implementing measures are still to be worked out. Accordingly, it is too early at this stage to present a comprehensive picture of Korean implementation of the Uruguay Round results and analysis thereof. Overall, full implementation of the Uruguay Round Agreements is expected to encounter no major difficulties in spite of the initial backlash noted above. There are none the less quite a few potential issues and weaknesses which may hamper smooth implementation unless adequately remedied. These will be taken up below; but first, a brief introduction to Korean political and legal systems.

* Associate Professor of Law, Inha University, Inchon, Korea. Preparation of this Chapter was partly assisted by a research grant from the Inha University in Korea.
[1] In an effort to soothe the hostile national mood, the Government had to sack the Minister of Agriculture, Forestry, and Fisheries, the chief negotiator for the agricultural sector. It is ironic that the Minister was in fact a staunch opponent against opening of the agricultural market and is largely credited with the success in deferring the opening of the rice market until after 2004.

10.2.1 Presidential system

The Government of the Republic of Korea is based on a presidential system but mixed with some parliamentary features. The President, elected for a five-year single term, is the Head of State representing the country to foreign countries and at the same time the head of the executive branch of the Government. As the Head of State, the President is authorized, *inter alia*, to enter into, and to ratify, treaties with foreign countries.[2] The executive branch of the Government consists of the President, the Prime Minister, the Cabinet Council, and various ministries. The Prime Minister is appointed by the President with the consent of the National Assembly. The Cabinet, comprising the President, the Prime Minister and all ministers, deliberates on and formulates all important legislative proposals, presidential decrees and other major policy matters. The executive branch also has the constitutional right to present bills to the National Assembly.[3]

Legislative power rests with a unicameral directly-elected National Assembly (the Assembly), that passes all laws. The Assembly possesses broad powers to introduce and pass laws, to investigate and audit the executive branch, and to approve the national budget. Members of the Assembly may also serve in the executive branch, although ministers need not be members of the Assembly. Laws are constitutionally required on all matters bearing on rights and obligations of citizens. Once a law is passed by the Assembly, the law goes to the President for signature and proclamation within fifteen days. The latter may veto the law, which may in turn be overridden by a two thirds vote of the Assembly. Subsequent to the proclamation of a law, the President issues a presidential decree and the minister concerned issues implementing regulations. It may be noted in this regard that most proposals of law originate from the executive branch. Laws are general with broad delegation from laws to presidential decrees, and from the latter to implementing regulations. However, this long-standing practice raises three important issues:

● First, it runs the risk of violating the constitutional principle that any measure restricting citizens' rights or imposing obligations can only be taken by the Assembly, in the form of a law.

---

[2] Constitution, Art. 73.
[3] In fact, most bills passed by the National Assembly originate from the executive branch.

- Secondly, the Constitution is quite explicit that no delegation can be on *carte blanche*, but must have specific limits.[4]
- Thirdly, such broad delegation, coupled with wide discretion on the part of delegatees, while largely serving bureaucratic convenience, makes it almost impossible for ordinary citizens outside the bureaucracy to find out what the law really is. Most ministerial regulations are not well published and are amended with short notice.

The judiciary, the third branch of the Government, consists of the Supreme Court, the Constitutional Court and lower courts. The Chief Justice of the supreme court is appointed by the President, with the consent of the Assembly, for a single term of six years. Thirteen other Supreme Court justices are appointed by the President upon nomination of the Chief Justice. Lower court judges are appointed by the Chief Justice for ten year renewable terms. The Supreme Court is the final arbiter of all cases except for questions of constitutionality of laws passed by the Assembly. The latter belongs to the exclusive jurisdiction of the Constitutional Court, which is composed of nine justices: three elected by the Assembly, three nominated by the Chief Justice and the remaining three appointed by the President.[5]

10.2.2 International treaties

As noted above, the power to enter into international treaties and to ratify them rests with the President.[6] There are two requirements to be met for the President exercising this power. The Cabinet Council should deliberate on all proposals of treaties.[7] Further, the Assembly must consent to major treaties. Major treaties are those concerning mutual assistance, mutual security, major international organizations, friendship, commerce and navigation, peace treaties, treaties restricting sovereignty, treaties imposing significant financial burden on the country or citizens, or other treaties concerning legislative matters.[8] Legislative matters means here any matters affecting rights and obligations of a citizen, thus requiring amendment of an existing law or enactment of a new law.[9] Other treaties and international agreements not enumerated here, such as agreements

---

[4] Constitution, Art. 75.

[5] The Constitutional Court is also responsible for adjudication of impeachments, dissolution of political parties, and jurisdictional disputes amongst governmental agencies and local autonomous bodies. It may be noted, however, that the constitutionality or legality of presidential decrees and implementing regulations is decided by the ordinary courts, with the Supreme Court having the final authority.   [6] Constitution, Art. 73.

[7] Constitution, Art. 89.   [8] Constitution, Art. 60 (1).

[9] Constitution, Art. 37 (1).

concerning matters delegated by major treaties, implementing details of a treaty or executive agreements, need not go to the Assembly. Is it possible for the Assembly to approve the treaty on a selective basis, that is to say with its own amendments? As yet, there is no case, but the majority view is that such amendments would not be allowed.[10] This means that all approvals or consents of the Assembly are always on a 'fast track'.

Unlike its counterparts in some other countries, such as the United States, the Assembly has not been a major player in conducting diplomacy and trade negotiations, aside from exercising its constitutional consenting power as noted above. Formulating trade-related policies and conducting trade diplomacy remains almost exclusively in the hands of the executive branch. Lately, however, it has been observed that the Assembly has become more assertive in foreign trade matters and in overseeing of the executive branch's operations. This is a welcome change, which it is to be hoped may lead to a more rule-based trading regime and improved transparency.[11]

Input of the Assembly into trade policy formulation is also provided indirectly through periodic party–Government consultative meetings, held regularly between the executive branch and the ruling Government party. In fact, all major policies, whether international or otherwise, are cleared through this process before they are submitted to the Assembly for formal legislation. There is no such established channel between the executive branch and the opposition party.

The role of civic groups outside the Government has been minimal in the past, but this has been changing lately. There are now several non-governmental organizations active in such areas as environmental protection, consumer protection and economic justice.[12] Pursuant to the Government's newly initiated policies of transparency, government agencies are required to issue advance notice of not less than twenty days for all legislative proposals directly affecting citizens' livelihoods, and, in the case of major legislation, to hold an open hearing inviting civic groups to participate.[13] In such hearings, concerned civic groups may present their views, while Government officials and representatives of the Government-owned research institutions defend the Government position.[14]

---

[10] C. Kim, *Heonbeobhak Kairon* (*The Constitutional Law*) (1994), 752.

[11] For a similar view, see, GATT, *Trade Policy Review: Republic of Korea 1992*, Vol.1, 39.

[12] In particular, the Association of Citizens for Realization of Economic Justice, as well as several environment-oriented organizations, with wide membership of intellectuals and academicians, has recently become very prominent. They periodically put out alternative policy options on major current issues.

[13] Pres. Dec. Advance Publication of Draft Laws and Regulations (1983), Art. 3.

[14] Government-owned research institutions like the KDI and the KIIEP act as the Government's think-tank and play a significant role in international trade policy formulations.

The President's power to negotiate treaties and international agreements is largely exercised by his ministers. Generally speaking, the Minister of Foreign Affairs is largely responsible for such negotiations. When it comes to economic and trade-related matters, however, the Ministry of Foreign Affairs' role becomes secondary to that of the ministry which has jurisdiction over the subject-matter (the competent ministry). Thus, if negotiations are about an Organization for Economic Co-operation and Development code on shipbuilding, it is handled by the Ministry of Trade, Industry and Natural Resources, which is responsible for regulating the shipbuilding industry. If it concerns duty on textiles, on the other hand, it may require a joint action between that Ministry and the Finance and Economics Board. The competent ministry would normally prepare a position paper and clear it with other concerned ministries, as well as the Office of the Prime Minister and the Presidential Secretariat, before engaging in formal negotiations. In the event that there is no consensus, or objections or reservations are raised during this working-level consultation, the matter goes up to higher level co-ordination for resolution. Such forums include the International Co-operation Committee, the Economic Ministers' Meeting or the full Cabinet Council Meeting, depending on the importance of the issues.[15]

10.2.3 Negotiation of Uruguay Round Agreements

The negotiation of Uruguay Round Agreements has been conducted by the executive branch under the broad treaty-making authority of the President. However, it may be noted in this regard that, concerning tariff concessions, the Tariff Law already has a provision granting broad delegation to the executive branch: the executive branch is authorized to enter into negotiations with an international organization or a particular

---

[15] The EMM was established in 1964 to promote co-operation between economic ministries. The EMM used to be presided over by the Deputy Prime Minister and Minister of the Economic Planning Board with participation by all the ministers having portfolios dealing with economic affairs, e.g., that of Finance; Trade, Industry and Natural Resources; Agriculture, Forestry and Fisheries; Construction and Transportation; Health and Welfare; Labour; Posts and Telecommunications; Environmental Protection; and the Chief Economic Secretary to the President. All agendas to this Meeting are cleared beforehand by the Economic Vice-Ministers' Meeting. These two forums act to co-ordinate the diverse views and interests of different ministries. The International Co-operation Committee, formed by a presidential decree in 1986, examines matters relating to both bilateral and multilateral aspects of Korea's international trade relations. It used to be chaired by the Deputy Prime Minister and Minister of Economic Planning Board, and consisted of all economic ministers, the Ministers of Foreign Affairs and the Environment, the Chief Economic Secretary to the President, and the Assistant Minister to the Prime Minister. As noted below in s.10.2.4, there have been some changes in designations and portfolios of these Ministries.

country where deemed necessary to promote foreign trade;[16] and in such negotiations, tariff concessions of up to 100 per cent of the basic tariff may be granted *vis-à-vis* international organizations, but of only up to 50 per cent to a particular country.[17]

As noted above, while it is the President who is authorized under the Constitution to enter into treaties, Korea's negotiations in the Uruguay Round were carried out by his ministers and authorized deputies. In the absence of a specialized organization like the Office of the Trade Representative in the United States, such negotiations have been carried out by representatives of the Ministry of Foreign Affairs, and various other ministries with jurisdiction on the subject-matter under negotiation. For example, the general tariff reduction and opening of the financial sector has been by and large handled by the Finance and Economics Board (formerly the Ministry of Finance), the opening of the agricultural market by the Ministry of Agriculture, Forestry and Fisheries, and the opening of the telecommunications sector by the Ministry of Posts and Tele-communications. Overall co-ordination of negotiating positions was attempted at several levels: initially at interdepartmental working-level meetings, and for major matters, at the International Co-operation Committee and the Economic Ministers' Meeting.

In retrospect, the Korean Government's overall performance at the Uruguay Round negotiating tables may be rated poor. Up until early 1993, when the Uruguay Round negotiations moved toward their last stage, the Government appears to have been ill-prepared. When the negotiations suddenly picked up and moved toward conclusion in 1993, the Government finally awoke to their significance and tried to make the best out of them with little success. According to the newpapers, the Government officials were not only ill-prepared but, worse, were embroiled in interdepartmental turf-fighting and rivalries.[18]

10.2.4 Restructuring of economic ministries

The Government issued a formal apology to the nation for the poor results of the Uruguay Round negotiations; in particular, for the opening of the

---

[16] Art. 43–8, the Tariff Law.   [17] Ibid.

[18] There were at one point three would-be-heads for the Korean delegation despatched to Geneva to negotiate the Uruguay Round: one from the Economic Planning Board, presiding over all economic affairs, one from the Ministry of Foreign Affairs, the official representative of the Government, and one from the Ministry of Commerce, Industry and Natural Resources, with jurisdiction over trade matters. According to the report, the Ministry of Finance did not care much as they believed most important matters are in their hands anyway. See daily newspapers, the *Dong-A Ilbo* and *Chosun Ilbo*, 2 Dec. 1993.

agricultural market.[19] However, the Government quicky reeled back and launched a nation-wide campaign to overturn this mood. This campaign was waged under the new catch phrase of *Segyehwa* (Globalization): hitherto self-centered norms and institutions, be they economic or cultural, should give way to those which were more open-ended and compatible with the world generally. In economic terms, this was interpreted as meaning that all economic activities and institutions should be based on the norm of world-wide competition and most, if not all, restrictive regimes and regulations on economic activities should be removed.

The first visible action of Globalization was announced and implemented with little notice: the Government ministries responsible for economic affairs were to be restructured and down-sized. The restructuring was carried out at a lightning speed in less than one month in December 1994. The Economic Planning Board and the Ministry of Finance were merged into one entity called the Finance and Economics Board; the Ministry of Construction and the Ministry of Transportation into a single Ministry of Construction and Transportation; the Ministry of Commerce, Industry and Natural Resources was down-sized by one-third and renamed as the Ministry of Trade, Industry and Natural Resources; and other economic ministries were similarly down-sized though to a lesser extent. The Prime Minister's Office was, on the other hand, strengthened in its co-ordinating role by taking over from the Economic Planning Board the Fair Trade Commission. The measure appears to have been taken for multiple reasons, political as well as economic. One account justified it as the most effective, if not the only, action available against the entrenched bureaucracy which was viewed by many as the root cause of all overly restrictive regulations. Whatever merits the measure might have had, however, were largely lost due to the way it was handled. Swift as it was, it lacked clear rationale and gave rise to more questions and confusion than it answered and solved. It remains to be seen whether this drive for downsizing of the Government will continue with other ministries with non-economic portfolios, or Government-owned institutions and corporations.[20]

It is also as yet too early to assess the consequences of the above measures. As regards their impact on future trade-related negotiations, no major change is expected; but to the extent there are now fewer ministries

---

[19] The President issued a statement of apology. See, *Dong-A Ilbo*, 9 Dec. 1993. As noted in fn. 1, the then Minister of Agriculture, Forestry and Fisheries had to resign over the nation-wide uproar against the opening of the rice market.

[20] Consistency and logic would call for similar measures concerning other ministries and agencies with non-economic portfolios. Against growing criticisms, however, the Government has announced that the exercise is over.

to be co-ordinated, more highly co-ordinated negotiations and enforcement are anticipated.[21] A more strengthened co-ordinating role of the Office of the Prime Minister may be expected, but it remains to be seen to what extent it would be exercised.[22]

A proposal to set up a separate entity like the US Trade Representative had apparently been considered as part of the restructuring, receiving substantial support as possibly the best way to handle future trade negotiations. However, the idea did not materialize.[23]

10.3 DOMESTIC LEGAL EFFECT OF URUGUAY ROUND AGREEMENTS

International treaties and agreements entered into and promulgated pursuant to the Constitution, as well as generally recognized international laws, have equal status with domestic law in Korea.[24] There is no need for a separate domestic legislation except in the cases where such international treaties or agreements themselves clearly anticipate subsequent domestic legislation.[25] In other words, such treaties, agreements and international laws are self-executing in principle. An exception to this general recognized principle of self-execution occurs where the particular treaty provision at issue is too broad or ambiguous to be legally enforceable or merely more in the nature of a recommendation or declaration of policies.[26] It should, however, be noted that having equal status with domestic law does not necessarily mean that such treaties or international

---

[21] The recent episode concerning the US complaint against Korean phytosanitary measures on the oranges from US does not seem to bear proof to such an effect. According to the US claim, about one-third of the imported oranges putrefied while in customs quarantine, apparently due to the overly strict enforcement of quarantine measures. The US filed a complaint to the WTO. In a knee jerk reaction the Korean Government hastily removed the requirement for the test to be performed prior to customs clearance of oranges from the US. It is not clear whether the same treatment will apply to imports of oranges from other countries or to those of other fruits. The ministerial turf fighting and lack of co-ordination has been cited as two of the causes for the overall poor handling of this matter. Another problem raised with the new FEB is that it has now become a 'super ministry' with all the powers of budget, finance and banking, tax and economic management rolled into one. The checks and balances which used to be exercised by the Economic Planning Board and the Ministry of Finance are now gone, with one single minister; and other ministries are no longer a match for this dinosaur.

[22] Traditionally, a too strong Prime Minister has not been favoured either by the President or by other ministers.

[23] The Government instead announced a system of incentives to encourage government officials to specialize in international trade matters.

[24] Constitution, Art. 6 (1).   [25] C. Kim, *Constitutional Law*, 212.

[26] In a case involving the issue of constitutionality of a labour rights provision in the Private School Law, the Constitutional Court affirmed the constitutional principle of direct application of treaty provisions but found the Human Rights Declaration adopted by the UN to be merely a declaratory nature. The Const. C. Decn. No. 89 *hunga* 106 (1991).

laws will rank with domestic laws in the narrow sense of laws passed by the Assembly. Treaties without the Assembly's consent may rank with a presidential decree, or an implementing regulation, as the case may be.[27]

In case of conflicts between domestic laws, a newer law will prevail over an older law, and a special law with more specific coverage will override a general law.[28] Inasmuch as treaties have equal status with domestic law, then it is not impossible that some provisions of a treaty duly consented to by the Assembly may subsequently be nullified or impaired by subsequently passed laws, whether by intention or by accident. However, potential conflicts between domestic and international laws are in practice avoided by the executive branch, either on its own initiative or following a Supreme Court decision, through necessary amendments to domestic legislation for conformity with international agreements.

The Uruguay Round Agreements were approved by the National Assembly as a single package under the title of the Marrakesh Agreement Establishing the World Trade Organization, and subsequently ratified by the President in December 1994. They thus became part of the law of the country. This holds equally true with the provisions of the General Agreement on Tariffs and Trade. The Supreme Court affirmed the direct applicability of the GATT provisions in several cases.[29]

What would be the legal status of a Panel Report adopted by the World Trade Organization under its dispute settlement procedure? There is as yet no case nor any academic discussion on the question. A Panel Report duly adopted by the Dispute Settlement Body of the WTO would stand in terms of its legal authority as a resolution of the WTO, binding the Government of Korea in accordance with the norms of the WTO dispute settlement provisions. Obviously, however, such a report would not enjoy the same status with the provisions of the WTO Agreements themselves, a treaty duly approved by the Assembly. It is most likely that such panel decisions would be treated like a decision of the Supreme Court. While there is strictly speaking no *stare decisis* recognized in Korea, decisions of the Supreme Court are closely followed by lower courts.

---

[27] This is the majority view in Korea. Ibid. at 215.

[28] In a case concerning enforcement of an arbitration award, the Seoul Civil District Court found that the New York Convention on the Recognition and Enforcemnet of Foreign Arbitral Awards constitutes a treaty under the Constitution and as such takes precedence over the provisions of the domestic Arbitration Law (Seoul Civil District Court Decn. No. 83 *kahap* 7051 (1984). It is, however, not quite clear what was the specific basis of such a finding as the court opinion is silent on that point. It may be said that the Convention is a special law to the Arbitration Law.

[29] See, the Sup. C. Decn. Nos. 85*nu* 448 (1987) and 91*nu* 10763, both concerning tariff asssessments.

10.4 IMPLEMENTING URUGUAY ROUND AGREEMENTS

As discussed above, the provisions of the various Uruguay Round Agreements are, as a matter of principle, already effective as a part of domestic law in Korea, and as such prevail over existing domestic laws in conflict therewith. Some provisions in the Uruguay Round Agreements, however, necessitate certain domestic legislation before they can be domestically implemented, if only for the purpose of providing the procedures for exercising rights and obligations thereunder. While Uruguay Round Agreements are deemed to override existing domestic laws under the Constitution, such conflicting domestic laws need to be amended to avoid the confusion and uncertainty almost certain to follow otherwise. Further, actual implementation of many provisions of the Uruguay Round Agreements need to be translated into appropriate affirmative executive actions, besides the legislation noted above.

Along with the ratification of the WTO Agreement, the Government quickly moved to amend the relevant laws, decrees and regulations, with a view to implementing the results of the WTO Agreement. Given the scope and the magnitude, however, such legislative action is bound to be a continuing process taking several years. It is as yet too early to take stock of all such measures being taken to implement the Uruguay Round Agreements. Before discussing specific measures for implementing various WTO Agreements, it is in order to discuss briefly one special law.

10.4.1 Special Implementation Law

Besides granting its consent to the Uruguay Round Agreements, the Assembly took one further step and passed a special law titled the Special Law Implementing the World Trade Organization Agreement (the Special Law). As noted above, this type of separate law implementing the Uruguay Round agreements was not required under the Constitution and in fact it was the first under the constitutional history of Korea. It should, however, be noted that in spite of the similarity in its name, this law is distinguishable from its counterpart in the US. While the latter is a comprehensive legislation covering all the domestic measures necessary to implement the Uruguay Round agreements and replacing the latter as the source of domestic law, the Special Law does not replace the WTO Agreement which has itself become part of the domestic law, but only stipulates certain additional implementing matters on a selective basis. The full text of the law follows this chapter as Appendix A.[30] The Special Law

---

[30] The translation is unofficial, done by the author.

gives a mandate to the executive branch to take various measures for the protection of farmers and fishermen, who were perceived by the law-makers as being most vulnerable to the adverse consequences of the WTO.

In terms of consistency with the Uruguay Round regime, the Special Law appears largely innocuous. While it mandates the executive branch to take certain remedial actions, such actions are required to be taken *'in accordance with the provisions of the WTO Agreement as well as those of the relevant laws of the country'*.[31]

However, the law may be more interesting for what was struck out from the original bill, as the original bill did contain several provisions whose compatability with the Uruguay Road Agreements was questionable. One provision stated that the WTO Ageement would not be effective against existing domestic laws.[32] Another provision proclaimed that any provision of the WTO Agreement shall not be construed to impair or nullify the *economic sovereignty* of the country. Yet another provision would have required mandatory retaliatory trade measures in the fashion of section 301 of the US's Trade Act 1974. Not surprisingly, law-makers who were against the WTO Agreement must have wondered why they could not do the same as their counterparts on Capitol Hill. Subsequently, however, those troublesome provisions have been either deleted or diluted to the present form, largely as a result of concerns about unconstitutionality.[33]

The Special Law as passed also has several provisions of interest: first, the trade between North Korea and South Korea is to be considered as internal and as such not subject to the regime of the WTO.[34] It is not entirely clear, however, how this fits in with the existing GATT/WTO rules.[35] While the question may have to be dealt with as part of the broader question of the status of the two Koreas and their unification under general

---

[31] Arts. 4, 6, 8, and 9 Special Law (emphasis added).

[32] Art. 3 of the original bill read as follows: 'The WTO Agreement shall not be effective against existing unamended domestic laws in absence of a special provision to that effect in this Law'.

[33] As noted above, the Korean Constitution expressly provides that duly entered into treaties, the WTO Agreement being one of them, are of equal force with domestic laws. See *Report of the Committee of Foreign Affairs and National Unification on the Special Law* (Dec. 1994) 9.

[34] Art. 5 Special Law. This declaration is in line with the provisions of the Agreement Between the South and the North Concerning Reconciliation, Non-Agression, Exchange and Co-operation, 13 Dec. 1991, between the two Koreas, which came into effect on 19 Feb. 1992. The Government also legislated the Law Concerning Exchange and Co-operation between South and North, Law No. 4239, 1 Aug. 1990 to allow tax-free importation of goods from North Korea.

[35] In this regard, the US had complained to the Korean Government in March 1991 that the despatch of 5,000 tons of rice by the South to the North and the import of certain goods from the North without tariff were in violation of the obligations under the GATT. The US had suggested that Korea seek a waiver under Art. XXV:5 of the GATT 1947.

international laws, and the above provision of the Special Law is generally considered to be merely declaratory in nature, it may as well be viewed as making it incumbent upon the executive branch to make appropriate arrangements with the WTO.[36] The executive branch will then have to initiate negotiations within the framework of GATT, now the WTO, to obtain a general waiver for its trade with North Korea.

10.4.2 Tariff reduction

Korea actively participated in the tariff reduction negotiations for industrial and marine products. Over 90 per cent of the total number of items, and 85 per cent in value of all industrial and marine products were agreed to be bound and the average tariff rate was reduced from 17.9 per cent in 1986 to 8.2 per cent. In particular, Korea participated in 68 items out of the total of 76 earmarked for zero tariffication[37] and in 193 out of 196 petrochemical products for tariff harmonization. New rates pursuant to those of zero tariffication and tariff harmonization are already effective as of 1 January 1995. Further, an overall review and modification of the entire Tariff Schedule annexed to the Tariff Law was carried out to generally lower the levels of tariff during 1995.

10.4.3 Agriculture

For many countries, the agricultural sector was, the toughest area to be negotiated throughout the whole negotiations of the Uruguay Round; but this was particularly true for Korea. Korea has traditionally been agriculture-based and Koreans have lived on rice for thousnds of years. Rice means to most Koreans not just food but a whole livelihood. Self-sufficiency in food, that is, rice, has been the catch-phrase successive Korean governments held high for the last fifty years. Most Koreans, whether living in cities or in the countryside, are still strongly attached to their rural home town. Despite the much reduced significance of agriculture in the national economy and the fact that most Koreans now live in urban areas, Korean culture, and to a large extent, Korean politics

---

[36] A good precedent would have been that of Germany. When acceding to the GATT in 1951, West Germany made an express reservation and GATT approved that West Germany's accession to GATT should not affect intra-German trade. When Korea was joining the GATT in 1967, Korea did not make such explicit reservation on intra-Korean trade. A good opportunity may have been lost when Korea deposited with WTO its acceptance of WTO Agreement in 1994 without making a similar reservation.

[37] The items are steel, construction equipment, agricultural equipment, pharmaceuticals, electronics, paper, toys, and non-ferrous metals, excluding, however, beer, distilled spirits, and wood.

as well, is still deeply rooted in the countryside. This probably explains why the Korean Government fought to the last minute against the pressure to open the rice market.

The final results were that tariffication on rice will be deferred for ten years, to be renegotiated at the end thereof, but guaranteeing that the mimimum market access of one per cent of national consumption in 1995 will gradually be increased to 4 per cent in 2004. Import of fourteen other sensitive agricultural items which Korea sought to exclude from tariffication were all made open: immediately from 1995 (barley, corn, beans, potatoes, and sweet potatoes); by 1997 (oranges, pork, and chicken); by 2000 (beef) or 1997 (others). Increasing annual quantities of minimum market access and/or current market access was guaranteed for the intervening period as appropriate. Imports of these products were made open, subject to tariffication. Imports of twenty-three fresh fruits hitherto subject to restrictions were also made free.

Implementation of the above market opening makes it necessary to amend various special laws dealing with the respective regulations restricting import of such products. These include the Foodgrains Control Law, the Livestock Law, the Sericulture Law, and the Agricultural Seedlings Law. The Tariff Law and presidential decree need to be revised to incorporate the concept of tariff equivalents into the tariff system, as well as the special safeguard tariff for agricultural products allowed under the Uruguay Round. Management of the import of the minimum access/current access quantities presents vexing problems as well. Who should be allowed to handle them, and under what procedure? What should be done with any excess profits that are realized? The Foreign Trade Law and relevant special laws dealing with the specific products will have to provide for them. The Foodgrains Control Law, which subjected import of most grains to the permission of the Minister of Agriculture, Forestry and Fisheries, was revised in December 1994 to make importation of grains other than rice subject to recommendation of the Minister, instead of subject to his permission.[38] The Foodgrain Control Law was also revised to authorize the Minister to issue orders concerning sale prices and usage of such imported grains. Pending issuance of the relevant implementing regulations, the intention of the Govenment is not yet clear, but it appears to be that the import of the minimum access quantity of rice will be entrusted to the Office of Supplies, and the profits therefrom will be used

---

[38] This relaxation from the requirement of *permission* to *recommendation* does not mean much in reality. While it may be said that the latter authority is more administerial in nature and usually delegated to lower entities like relevant producers' associations, such distinction becomes negligible when the Minister or the bureaucracy under him keeps a tight hand on such recommendations.

to make up for any losses in the Grains Management Special Account.[39] Similarly, imports of other agricultural products are going to be handled by various government corporations and producers' associations concerned with the respective products. On the other hand, for some minor products, the Government is reportedly also considering the sale of import rights to private trading houses in an open bidding, with any excess profits that are generated (differences of the import price and domestic resale price) to be collected as tax. Such tax proceeds are in turn earmarked to be put into the Grains Management Special Account or to the Special Account for the Agricultural and Marine Products Price Stabilization, both being Government-operated statutory funds.

A new provision was also added to the Tariff Law to incorporate the special safeguard provisions. From 1 January 1995, special safeguard tariffs are leviable on seventy-six agricultural products out of the total of 111 products being newly liberalized under the Uruguay Round Agreement, for quantities exceeding certain pre-set levels of imports; and for thirteen other products, in the event that the import price falls 10 per cent or more below the bench-mark level.[40]

Concerning subsidies, the Government conducted a comprehensive review of various measures with subsidy features like the grain purchase programme, the agricultural products price stabilization programme, and other assistance programmes, to determine whether each of them is permissible, actionable or prohibited under the new Uruguay Round norms, and also to determine what to do with them. Legislative action in this regard is expected to follow completion. Separately, the Government has announced policies to undertake overall structural adjustment and deregulation of the agriculture sector with a view to making it a smaller but more viable industry.

10.4.4 Sanitary and phytosanitary measures

The Agreement on Sanitary and Phytosanitary Measures seeks to harmonize the sanitary and phytosanitary measures of members, and requires such measures not to be applied as a disguised restriction on trade.

Implementation of this Agreement, together with that of the Agreement on Technical Barriers to Trade, appears to constitute the biggest challenge

---

[39] This special account is used for the Government's grain purchase programmes. Every year, the Government purchases from farmers certain selected grains, most notably rice, up to a predetermined quantity at a predetermined price, to encourage production of those products.

[40] The rate of tariff was set at one-third of the Tariff Equivalent or the difference in price, respectively.

to the Korean Government. Present rules and regulations on sanitary and phytosanitary measures are obsolete, primitive and deficient, and by and large lack proven scientific basis. Such regulations are increasingly criticized by exporting countries as arbitrary non-tariff barriers.[41] There is as yet no national institution competent to come up with the necessary rules based upon scientific facts, nor to effectively enforce such rules. At present, sanitary and phytosanitary measures are handled by both the Ministry of Health and Welfare (previously the Ministry of Health and Social Affairs) and MAFF. There is, however, no clear delineation of responsibilities, nor close co-ordination between them. For example, testing of marine products destined for export is conducted by the Marine Products Inspection Centre under MAFF but that for imported marine products falls under the jurisdiction of MHW. Neither MHW nor MAFF at present possess the expertise and equipment necessary to adequately enforce such measures. The situation is indeed alarming.[42] In the past, this did not matter much since agricultural products and foodstuffs were mostly not allowed to be imported at all and the limited instances of import came from countries with stricter sanitary standards, such as the United States, Canada, and Australia. The situation is very different now, with the fast pace of import liberalization. Increasing amounts of imported agriculural products are coming from developing countries such as China, the Philippines, Thailand, Argentina, and Malaysia, which have generally lower or laxer sanitary and phytosanitary standards. Against this rush of imported agricultural products from both developed and developing countries, due to the liberalization under the new WTO regime, Korean

[41] An example is the recent controversy concerning the sale of sausages imported from the US. The Korean Government prohibited sale of certain sausages imported from the US on the ground that it exceeded the statutory distribution period. The US Government complained that setting of such periods or expiration dates must be left to self-regulation by manufacturers. Such mandatory distribution period had been justified in the past because self-regulation by private manufacturers could not be expected, given the rather low self-discipline of the industry and also in view of the still below-standard refrigerated storage facilities available in Korea. One may still question whether it is realistic to leave the matter entirely to the private manufacturers, many of which in Korea are small and would not have many qualms about making money at the expense of people's health. The Korean Government announced a phasing-out of the mandatory period by 1997, but the US Government is reportedly pressing for an immediate repeal. The US complaint concerning oranges, discussed at fn. 21, is another good example.

[42] According to the audit report of the Audit Commission on the Ministry of the Health and Social Affairs dated 27 Sept. 1993, the Ministry did issue regulations for testing meats for residues of geranol and 5 other growth hormones, but, due to its failure to provide for the method of testing, all meat imported from Jan. 1991 to May 1992 (other than beef, pork, and chicken) was allowed in after mere visual inspection by the quarantine officials, without any test for potentially harmful substances like antibiotics, growth hormones and bactericites. During the same period, out of 106 unprocessed or dried agricultural products, 79 minor products were imported without any test for residual pesticides.

authorities appear helpless at the moment. The situation is aggravated by the worsening congestion at Pusan and other ports, where ships often have to wait at least five to six days for berthing.

Given the expected continued increase in imports of various agricultural products and livestock from all over the world, it is imperative, and indeed already overdue, for the Government to overhaul all existing sanitary and phytosanitary measures; quickly put in place new rules and regulations which are based on currently available scientific evidence and international practices, train border officials on such new regulations and procedures, and equip them with modern testing equipment. In so doing, the Government will have to ensure that those rules and measures are either in harmony with corresponding international rules and norms or sufficiently justifiable on their own from a scientific point of view. In the same vein, such rules and measures will have to be enforced in accordance with reasonable procedures.[43]

The Korean Government is reportedly in the process of strengthening the related laws and regulations: the list of quarantine pests is to be expanded, and additional residual substances like hormones, pesticides and heavy metals are to be monitored. Existing quarantine organizations are to be expanded and other measures strengthening institutions are also going to be taken. In this connection, the Government announced that an agency similar to the US Food and Drug Administration would be established.[44] It will, however, take a considerable time before the expertise, equipment, and regulations required for adequate SPS measures are built up in Korea. In the meantime, Korean authorities are likely to be forced to take one of two unenviable alternatives; to enforce whatever rules they have now and face the many trade disputes sure to follow, or to allow importation with few sanitary and phytosanitary safeguards, at the risk of the general public health.

10.4.5 Subsidies

The Uruguay Round Agreement on Subsidies and Countervailing Measures categorizes subsidies in three groups: prohibited subsidies, actionable subsidies, and non-actionable subsidies. Prohibited subsidies are those contingent upon export performance or use of domestic over imported goods. Actionable subsidies are those on specific regions, industries, or

---

[43] The sausages incident (see fn. 34) was initially triggered by a surprise announcement reducing the statutory distribution period for refrigerated sausages from 90 days to 30 days, made effective immediately without any grace period. In the face of the US complaint, the Korean government agreed to go back to 90 days again. All along, there was no explanation at all as to what is the appropriate period from a scientific point of view.

[44] The agency was subsequently established in 1996 under the MHW and made responsible for all SPS measures for food and drug products.

enterprises which are not contingent upon export or use of domestic goods. While these subsidies are not prohibited, they are subject to countervailing measures by the importing countries. Non-actionable subsidies are those without specificity or certain qualified subsidies for research activities, or those to disadvantaged regions. To comply with the Uruguay Round Agreement, Korea, as a developing country, has to abolish export subsidies in eight years and subsidies on use of domestic goods in five years.[45] Korea will also have to review all practices constituting actionable subsidies for eventual removal. What are those subsidies and practices, and what are the actions needed to be taken to make them acceptable to the WTO? It would be useful first of all to briefly review subsidy practices in Korea.

Korea's strong growth performance has been based on an outward-oriented, high investment strategy starting in the early 1960s. In the mid 1960s, a system of export incentives was first introduced to offset the anti-export bias inherent in then existing import restrictions, and to encourage exports, which stood at a neglible level. Such incentives have been instrumental in boosting Korean exports and economic development. The amount of exports grew from less than US$100m. in the early 1960s to over US$10bn. in the 1980s. Starting from the second half of the 1980s, however, Korea adopted policies toward a gradual trade liberalization and disengagement of the Government in line with the changing environment, that is, the growing protectionist sentiment world-wide and increasing pressure from outside, particularly the United States and the European Union, to liberalize its economy.

Support to industries in Korea may be broken into four types: tax incentives, financial incentives, preferential sale or lease of Government-owned property, and preferential procurement.[46] Tax incentives are provided for in the Law Regulating Tax Reduction and Exemption and other special laws. As regards financial incentives, the Government merged seven industry-based laws providing for assistance to specific industries into the Law on Industrial Development. Sale and lease of Government-owned property is governed by the Government-owned Property Law and the procurement by the Budget Accounting Law. Under these laws, assistance is available to industries and individual enterprises

---

[45] Concerning the grace period, the US Congress is reportedly against Korea's status as a developing country in relation to this provision. In the event the US formally raises the issue, the issue may have to go to the WTO Dispute Settlement Body for resolution. One further complication: Korea applied for membership of the OECD in March 1995 and is expected to formally join it soon. It remains to be seen whether or to what extent this expected OECD membership would affect Korea's status as a DMC.

[46] A detailed discussion on the concept and types of subsidy in Korea is provided in J. Oh, Y.-K. Shin, and J. Kim, *Current Status of Laws Related to Subsidies and Recommendation for Reform* (1994). The book, written in Korean, also contains an exhaustive list of all kinds of subsidies currently provided in various laws.

satisfying certain statutory criteria to support various policy objectives like increased export, development of technology, structural adjustment, environmental protection, or increased investment. Small and medium enterprises are eligible for special assistance.

In line with the requirement for reporting of all the subsidies being maintained to WTO by the end of March 1995, the Government reportedly reviewed all existing subsidies for classification: out of the total of 133 subsidies currently maintained, sixteen were found to be prohibited and thirty-two others actionable. Those found prohibited include: (1) export subsidies like export loss provisions, tax exemption and reduction for foreign-invested enterprises in the free export zone, provisions for overseas market development, export financing, and preferential loans to small and medium enterprises, and (2) import substitution subsidies like preferential loans to small and medium enterprises, support for distribution of domestically manufactured mainframe computers, and tax exemptions for structural adjustment investments and investments by small and medium enterprises.

A comprehensive overhaul of these incentives is under way by the Government, with a broad view to redirecting the overall industrial policies. In line with, and as a major element of, the Globalization drive, the Government has announced that past industrial policies, ranging from entry barriers to industries,[47] from industry rationalization[48] to diversification of import sources,[49] would be completely overhauled in favour of pro-competitive policies.[50]

[47] Entry into many industries in Korea used not to be free and was subject to the tight control of the Government. The Government is never short of weapons and tools in enforcing this policy. Various regulatory and incentive measures provided in various laws are at the disposal of the Government. For example, when Samsung, the biggest conglomerate in Korea, wanted to engage in automobile production with technology from Nissan of Japan, it had to fight an ongoing battle with the Government for more than four years. The only requirement officially required for Samsung was to report or notify its arrangements with Nissan to import the technology. The Government simply refused to accept Samsung's notification of the import of the technology. The Chairman of Samsung made a big cover story by openly criticizing the fact that Samsung had to obtain no fewer than one thousand seals (signatures) for its licence for automobile production.

[48] A certain selected industry (or one or more enterprises making up that industry) satisfying certain criteria may be designated by the Government as elegible for industrial rationalization, which entitles them to various incentives and assistance (Art. 5 Law on Industrial Development).

[49] This used to be specifically targeted at the excessive imports from Japan. Korea has a long history of huge running deficits in its current accounts with Japan, largely due to industrial imports of machinery and components. In an effort to rectify such huge deficits, which have become worse over the years, the Government has adopted a policy of restricting imports of machinery and other industrial products from Japan in favour of other sources. The measure is inconsistent with the MFN principle of GATT. The Government has announced that the policy will be gradually phased out for complete removal by the end of 1998.

[50] See *Seoul Economic Daily*, 18 Jan. 1995, p. 1.

Upon completion of the above review, it is expected that those incentives forbidden under the Uruguay Round Agreement will gradually be reduced and abolished during the grace period allowed.[51] Remaining incentives and subsidies to be maintained are expected to be restructured to subsidies which are compatible with the Uruguay Round Agreements: those for research and development, for regional development or for environmental protection, and others without specificity. In the meantime, the Law on Industrial Development, the basic law providing support to industries, had already been revised. A new law, called the Law Concerning Build-Up of Base for Development of Technology for Industry and Energy was enacted to redirect governmental assistance away from direct support to enterprises and towards indirect assistance for the build-up of infrastructure for technological development, such as technical education and training, establishment of research facilities, and utilization of industrial information.

Small and and medium-sized enterprises[52] are eligible under the statutes for certain special protection against competition from big enterprises. Various laws and regulations on small and medium enterprises have recently been integrated into three laws, which were approved by the Assembly in December 1994. They are: the Basic Law Concerning Small and Medium Enterprises, the Law Concerning Protection of the Areas of Business Reserved for Small and Medium Industries and Increased Cooperation between Enterprises, and the Law Concerning Provision of Assistance to Small and Medium Industries. They require the executive branch, among others, to implement measures needed to rationalize small and medium industries, to upgrade their technology and product quality, and to standardize their production.[53] Further, they require necessary measures to be taken to increase the productivity of small and medium enterprises, and to modernize their facilities for production and information systems.[54] Certain specific industries are reserved exclusively for SMIs, into which big enterprises and their affiliates are forbidden to enter. Various facilities are to be in place to assist the launching of new businesses by SMIs. Thus, it is incumbent upon the executive branch to come up with concrete measures to help them. Any such measures will, however, need to be devised as non-specific and neutral as possible, to stay clear of the rules of the Uruguay Round regime.

---

[51] Besides concern for compliance with the Uruguay Round agreements, the call for abolition of subsidies will also be coming from the OECD which Korea is scheduled to join soon (see, fn. 37).

[52] Enterprises with 300 or less permanent employees are considered as small and medium under the Basic Law for the Small and Medium Enterprises.

[53] The Basic Law Concerning Small and Medium Enterprises, Law No. 1840, revised Dec. 1994, Art. 6 (1).   [54] Ibid., Art. 6 (2).

10.4.5 Safeguard, anti-dumping and countervailing duties

The rules for the safeguard, anti-dumping and countervailing duties provided in the GATT 1947 have been significantly strengthened during the Uruguay Round. How have these rules been implemented so far in Korea, and how are the strengthened rules going to be implemented from now on? To answer these queries, it is necessary first to look briefly at the way those measures are incorporated into Korean domestic laws.

Measures for safeguard, anti-dumping and countervailing duties are covered in Korean laws under the broad concept of 'relief of industrial injuries' and are found in two laws: the Foreign Trade Law and the Tariff Law. The FTL is administered by the MTINR and the TL by the Finance and Economics Board. Anti-dumping duties and countervailing duties are provided for in the TL, together with other special duties like emergency duty, international co-operation duty, retaliatory duty and tariff quota. On the other hand, safeguard measures, as well as measures against imports infringing on intellectual property rights are found in the FTL. As regards institutional set-up, the role of the International Trade Commission is noteworthy. It is an autonomous body similar to the International Trade Commission in the United States. The TC does not, however, make a final decision, but submits its findings in the form of a recommendation to the competent ministers for action. The TC's findings and determinations are, however, rarely disturbed. The present TC consists of the Chairman and six members. Cases involving safeguards and infringement of intellectual property rights are handled by the TC in their entire phases. In the cases of anti-dumping and countervailing duties, only determination of injuries to domestic industries are made by the TC, and the findings of anti-dumping and existence of subsidies are made by the Office of Investigations under MTINR.

Statutory provisions in the FTL and the TL are largely in line with those of the relevant articles of the GATT, except possibly for the fact that they very much take the broad brush approach, lacking specifics on criteria and procedural requirements. These laws and implementing regulations are expected to be revised shortly to incorporate the results of the Uruguay Round Agreements.[55] Several measures need to be taken as part of such revision, to make the overall system more efficient, transparent and equitable. One is to consolidate and streamline the FTL and TL into one, thus dispensing with the confusion and waste inherent in the present bifurcated system. Secondly, the statutory provisions need to be made

---

[55] Some revisions were already instituted: The Decree to the TL was revised in Dec. 1994 to incorporate the results of the negotiations on anti-dumping as it did not require revision of the TL itself.

more specific, with detailed criteria and procedures provided in the law and the presidential decree, instead of leaving them to ministrial regulations or the discretion of officials. This will not only enhance overall transparency but also make them more amenable to judicial review. Thirdly, the TC should be strengthened as a fully autonomous body and be made responsible for all the import relief cases.

Have these measures for relief from import been widely utilized in the past? Not yet. During the period of 1987 to 1993, there were twenty-two complaints for safeguard actions, out of which fifteen were found affirmative and seven were withdrawn. During the same period, there were fifteen anti-dumping complaints, out of which four were dismissed for lack of injury, five were in the affirmative, and the rest were subsequently withdrawn by agreement of the parties.[56] There has been as yet no case involving claims for countervailing duties. This scarcity of cases may be attributable in part to the relatively heavy dependency of the Korean industries on imports for their parts and technologies, which gives rise to conflicting interests among the concerned parties. While resort to anti-dumping in the developed countries has been largely by enterprises in the declining industries, the pattern in Korea shows that most claims were from small and medium-sized enterprises; with new technologies competing with imports.[57] Many of them, however, are still not very knowledgeable on the availability of the relief, and have little expertise nor resources to undertake the costly and time-consuming procedures for relief.[58]

10.4.7 Technical barriers to trade

Generally speaking, barriers to international trade have taken the generic development from tariff barriers to non-tariff barriers, and within non-tariff barriers from price-related ones like dumping and subsidies to those not related to prices, and in the nature of technical regulations and procedural requirements. The history of negotiations in the GATT shows

[56] For a more detailed information on the actual cases, see, Korea Chamber of Commerce, *New Directions for Import Management System in an Era of Internationalization*, (1994) (written in Korean).
[57] This creates a difficult question determining incidence of injury to the domestic industry. In a typical situation where a new domestically-manufactured product is introduced in the market, it tends to replace imports, against which the foreign exporter responds with dumping to compete with and outnumber the domestic goods. A traditional affirmative finding of injury usually requires an incidence of reduced sale or market share. In the above situation, however, the amount of sale or the market share of the domestic producer tend to increase rather than decrease despite the dumping, at least initially. The situation would not easily meet the traditional requirement for 'retardation of development of the domestic industy' in as much as the domestic industry is already there.
[58] Korea Chamber of Commerce, *New Directions* at 248.

rather clearly that the focus of negotiations has correspondingly shifted; from reduction of tariff to removal of price-based non-tariff barriers (Kennedy and Tokyo Rounds) to technical and procedural barriers (Uruguay Round). From this perspective, the Uruguay Round Agreement on Technical Barriers to Trade, together with that for sanitary and phytosanitary measures, will take on increasing significance in the future.

The provisions of the Agreement on Technical Barriers to Trade concern both (1) preparation, adoption, and application of technical regulations and standards and (2) procedures for assessment of conformity with such regulations and standards. They require member governments[59] to provide national treatment; to adopt or maintain technical regulations or standards only to the extent necessary to fulfil legitimate objectives, and not as disguised trade barriers; to use relevant international standards to the extent appropriate; and to recognize, whenever possible, the results of conformity assessment procedures undertaken in other member states. There are also additional provisions for purposes of transparancy and fairness in procedures.

Regulations related to standardization and other technical requirements in Korea are found in the Industrial Standards Law, the Quality Management Promotion Law, and forty-seven other individual laws for specific industries.

The provisions of the Industrial Standards Law (ISL) provides for use of the Korean Standard mark. Use of the KS mark is voluntary. Depending on the products, however, the mark may be essential for acceptance thereof by consumers in general, or for procurement thereof by government agencies. KS marks are available to products produced in factories approved by the Office of Industrial Promotion. Such approval is based on inspection of the factory concerned, rather than on the products themselves.[60] Use of the KS mark is open to foreign manufacturers. However, the ISL includes two mandatory provisions: The Head of the Office of Industrial Promotion may, when deemed necessary for purposes of promoting use of KS marks on certain designated products, limit production of certain products to those with the KS mark. He may also issue an order to simplify or standardize technical specifications of a product when deemed necessary to enhance its interchangeability or inter-operability.

---

[59] TBT is applicable directly to central government bodies but only indirectly to local government bodies. While Korea introduced local autonomy starting in the latter half of 1995, it is not likely that these local governments would play a significant role in TBT areas in the foreseeable future.

[60] Japan takes the same approach. See, J. H. Jackson, J.-V. Louis and M. Matsushita, *Implementing the Tokyo Round* (1984), 113.

The Quality Management Promotion Law deals with non-mandatory quality marks and assessment of quality control process on the one hand, and mandatory requirements of safety tests for designated products involving risks to consumers, or damages to property and environment.

The individual special laws cover diverse areas of industry comprising, for example, the Pharmaceuticals Law, the Food Sanitation Law, the Harzardous Chemical Substances Law, the Pesticides Management Law, the Electrical Appliances Law, the Measurement Law, the Environmental Conservation Law, the Wastes Management Law, the Movie Law, the Petroleum Industry Law, and the Communications Law.[61] Various measures provided in these laws are for the purposes of protecting human, animal, and plant life or health, and public safety; and as such appear to be excepted under the GATT general exceptions. None the less, these provisions need to be closely scrutinized in the light of the requirements of the Uruguay Round Agreement, particularly their procedural aspects. Many of them lack detailed procedures for compliance and merely authorize the government agency concerned to make appropriate rules and regulations. Most of these laws, when they were made, were prepared with little concern for the possibility of them being applied to foreigners. They have no explicit provisions applicable directly to foreign suppliers, and simply require that the requirements applicable to domestic manufacturers be complied with by Korean importers as well. Procedures to be followed by foreign exporters and manufacturers need to be clearly provided. Regulatory standards are often archaic, with little regard to the ever developing state of technology in producing, distributing and testing the products.

Another important issue to be raised in this regard is whether or to what extent the results of various tests conducted abroad should be accepted. Again, no clear provisions are found in those laws and regulations. The recent controversy concerning approval of the type (specifications) for communications equipment and medical equipment between US and Korea forebode what is to come in the future. A complaint was made that the type-approval requirement is being abused as non-tariff barriers and should be waived for those which already carry equivalent overseas approval like Underwriters Laboratories or Food and Drug Administration approval. Korean officials claimed in defence that requirements for Korean approvals should not necessarily be the same as those in other countries with different conditions. In general, as far as any requirement is applicable equally to both domestic products and imported ones, and

---

[61] The complete list of the 47 individual laws identified by the Government as relating to TBT is found in KIIEP, *Current Status and Suggestions for Improvement of Trade-Related Policies and Institutions* (1992), 121 (written in Korean).

supported on sufficient technical grounds, there would be little ground to challenge them. Nevertheless,if such approvals take two to three years and the required technical tests are available only in Korea, such requirements may in fact constitute substantial competitive disadvantages for imported products. Several improvements have been suggested to remedy the situation: the approval requirements may be made more specific and published in advance so that foreign parties are prepared for them; results of relevant tests by authoritative foreign agencies may be accepted on a reciprocal basis, provided sufficient documentation is submitted;[62] as regards a new product based on an old model previously approved, tests may be limited to those aspects related to the new improvements; and fast-track test procedures may be introduced, with the additional costs borne by the applicant.

It is likely in this regard that the historical legislative tradition of broadly delegating everything to the executive agency concerned without any clear criteria or procedures will be increasingly subject to criticism. Not only for the purpose of complying with the Uruguay Round provisions, but also for meeting the increasing internal demand for transparency, the Government will have to conduct a critical review of all these laws to make them more transparent, equitable, compatible with the Uruguay Round Agreements, and user-friendly.

An effective review and reformation of such laws will need to be accompanied by the requisite institutional set-up. At present, the agency mainly involved in TBT matters is the Office of Industrial Promotion under the Ministry of Trade and Industry. Many individual laws, however, are under the jurisdiction of other ministries such as the MHW, the Ministry of Information and Communications, MAFF, and the Ministry of Environment. These ministries have, by and large, been laggards in the negotiations and their bureaucrats generally have little interest in change of the present system, which will no doubt reduce their discretionary powers and subject them to stricter scrutiny. In this regard, an inter-departmental entity or committee comprising all the concerned ministries would be useful to co-ordinate and monitor implementation of TBT provisions.

10.4.8 Services

Korea made commitments on seventy-eight services in eight fields out of the total of eleven fields and 155 services as classified by the GATT

---

[62] Out of the total of 38 tests, 28 are now waived on cars from the US and 15 on cars from the EU on this basis.

Secretariat. Fields agreed to be open are various professional services, engineering and architectural design, communications, construction, distributions, environmental services, financial services, sightseeing, and transportation; while excepted from concessions are the three fields of education, health and social services, and cultural and recreational services. Most of the services committed are those already agreed to under bilateral negotiations; and individual commitments are also subject to various market access and national treatment limitations, closely following existing restrictions in existing domestic laws.

The domestic implications and consequences of opening of the services market are none the less bound to be broad and immense, and necessitate adjustments in the entire regulatory and institutional set-up. In this regard, it should be noted that the General Agreement on Trade in Services is only the beginning of a continuing process which will eventually bring about the opening of all service sectors. Secondly, unlike trade in goods, the trade in services cannot be confined to border measures, and is intertwined with the country's broader institutional and regulatory regime; and the opening of one sector cannot be contained in that sector alone but is bound to have consequences over many other related sectors and systems. This also means that an opening of a services sector will not be meaningful unless necessary changes to all related regulatory and institutional regimes are in place. In other words, even if a particular sector is nominally made open, it would be of little significance unless accompanied by appropriate changes outside that particular sector. This is why the GATS requires each member to publish all relevant measures of general application, and to inform the WTO of the introduction of any new laws, regulations, or administrative guidelines, or of any changes to existing ones, which affect trade in services.

It is not surprising at all that the Korean Government entered into the GATS negotiations with much reluctance and apprehension. Second only to agriculture, the services sector was generally considered weak and vulnerable. Indeed, compared with the rather impressive growth in the industrial sector, most service sectors in Korea are still very much lagging behind and under-developed. Korean negotiators were naturally very guarded about revealing such a national mood.

Thanks to the Globalization drive noted above, however, there has been a significant change in the thinking of the people, if not in their philosophy. Most people now appear to have accepted as inevitable the opening of the internal services market to international competition, and are willing to face it as a challenge to be overcome. This change of heart, if one might so call it, will undoubtedly prove the biggest underpinning of a smooth and quick real opening of various service sectors in Korea. Against the backdrop of this overall development, the Government has now commenced the process of revising individual laws and regulations to make them in line with the provisions of the Uruguay Round Agreement.[63]

Service industries in Korea are generally subject to more restrictions and reservations, compared with the industrial sector. Further, these restrictions are not clearly provided in the law but broadly delegated to the executive regulations.[64] Even these regulations fail to provide for objective criteria or clear procedures, but leave them to wide discretion of the government officials. This provide plenty of room for arbitrariness and abuse, at the cost of transparency and equity.

The Govenment apparently intends to go beyond the minimum requirements of GATS and to conduct a critical review of all existing barriers to entry and operation of various service industries, and to push for an overhaul of the whole system for delivery of services, dismantling most, if not all, artificial restrictions.[65]

10.4.9 Intellectual property rights

Largely due to successive bilateral trade negotiations with the US and other countries in the past, protection of intellectual property rights in Korea has been substantially strengthened during the last decade. Computer programs, layout designs of integrated circuits, and business secrets are under statutory protection, as well as more traditional industrial property rights and copyrights. Accordingly, there is little need for fresh legislation to incorporate the results of the WTO Agreement on Trade-Related Aspects of Intellectual Property Rights, except for several minor points mostly relating to the longer period of protection. Relevant domestic laws are being revised to incorporate them. They include the

[63] The Architect Law and the Tax Accountant Law were first to be revised to allow domestic practice of foreigners.

[64] e.g., among the Korean commitments in the financial services sector including gradual increase of ceilings for foreigners' investment in the stocks; relaxation in the ratio of the mandatory underwriting of the Currency Stabilization Fund by trust accounts; increased foreign participation in the investment consulting business; relaxed requirements for permission of new branches of foreign financial institutions; raised ceiling for issue of certificates of deposit by foreign banks; freer introduction of new financial products by foreign financial institutions; and other measures expanding the scope of business of foreign financial institutions, none are found in the laws enacted by the National Assembly, or even in the related presidential decrees. All of them are issued as part of ministry-level regulations or guidelines. As a case in point, concerning the limit on foreigners' stock investment, Art. 203 Securities Transaction Law, broadly provides that such limitation may be imposed pursuant to the provisions of the Presidential Decree. The latter in turn passes the authority to the Securities Management Committee, a statutory committee under the supervision of the Minister of Finance. Formality aside, the whole power is exercised by the Minister of Finance.

[65] Recently at the occasion of the Annual Meeting of the Asian Development Bank, a series of measures opening the financial services sector, including an increased ceiling for foreigners' investment in stock markets and the setting up of branches by foreign banks in Korea, have been announced by the Government much ahead of market expectations.

Patent Law,[66] the Trade Mark Law,[67] the Copyright Law,[68] the Computer Program Protection Law,[69] and the Law Concerning Protection of the Layout-Designs of Integrated Circuits.[70] This had already been revised in December 1994 and other laws are expected to follow.[71]

There is one development on the enforcement side as well, which may prove significant in terms of effectiveness of enforcement in the coming years. Customs officials are now vested with an authority to initiate, on their own, criminal investigation into border offences involving violations of intellectual property rights; while such authority belonged exclusively to the Office of Public Prosecutors in the past.[72] From 1 January 1995, the customs officials have been armed with the authority to initiate criminal investigation into suspected border offences provided in the TRIPs.[73]

10.4.10 Government Procurement

Korea is a signatory to the Uruguay Round Agreement on Government Procurement. The Agreement will come into effect for Korea starting 1 January 1997. In preparation, a new law was enacted in December 1994. The Law Concerning Contracts with the Government as a Party completely replaces the old law.[74] In line with the provisions of the Agreement, this law, known as the Contract Law, requires international bidding for procurements by government agencies of goods, construction, and services, and expressly adopts the principle of national treatment. Certain

---

[66] To incorporate Art. 31 (use without authorization of the right holder) ands Art. 33 (term of protection) of TRIPs.

[67] To expand the definition of the trade mark to include colour and other combinations and to give protection to geographical indications.

[68] To extend the term of protection of copyrights to 50 years.

[69] To extend the term of protection to 50 years and to allow protection to compilations of data.

[70] Protection of the undisclosed information is provided in the Law on Prevention of Unfair Competition, Law No. 3897, as amended Dec. 1991.

[71] In line with the provisions of TRIPs, restrictions on the amount of damages recoverable have been removed and the procedure and criteria for granting authorization to use have been provided.

[72] Such investigative authority used to be reserved exclusively for the public prosecutors. Police officers and certain other government officials enumerated in the Law Concerning the Officials Authorized to Carry Out Judicial Police Power and the Scope of Their Job ('The Judicial Police Law'), Law No. 380, as amended, may carry out criminal investigations, but only under the direction of public prosecutors. Without the authority to do more, customs officials had merely filed a complaint to the Office of the Public Prosecutors, or more commonly to the police officers for investigation in the event they suspected an offence; and it was up to the police officers to initiate investigation.

[73] The Judicial Police Law was amended, as from 1 Jan. 1995, to grant customs officials the judicial police power.

[74] Old procurement regulations were found in Chapter 6 of the Budget and Accounting Law, Law No. 4102, as revised.

kinds of procurement are, however, excepted from an international bidding requirement. They are: (1) procurement of goods and services for production destined for sale or resale; (2) procurement of products of small and medium enterprises pursuant to the provisions of the Law Concerning Promotion of Procurement of Products of Small and Medium Enterprises; (3) procurement of agricultural, marine and livestock products pursuant to the provisions of the Grains Management Law, the Law Concerning Distribution and Price Stabilization of Aricultural and Marine Products and the Livestock Law, and (4) such other procurement as is excepted under the Agreement.[75] Pursuant to the requirement of Article XX of the Agreement, the Contract Law establishes the International Contracts Claims Settlement Committee to hear and settle claims. Before lodging the claims with the Committee, however, the claimant must first file his complaint with the head of the government agency. The decision of the Committee is subject to judicial review.

However the enactment of the law would be only the first step toward implementation of the Agreement. This is particularly so because provisions of the Contract Law itself are very broad, and, as usual, delegates many critical details to the presidential decree and implementing regulations. For example, it provides, without clear definition, four types of procurement mode: general competitive bidding, limited competitive bidding, competitive bidding among nominated bidders, and direct negotiations. It remains to be seen what each of them means, and how they relate to the three procurement modes under the Agreement, namely, open tendering, selective tendering, and single tendering. The newly-introduced concept of procurement of services, as distinguished from that of goods or construction services, would require special substantive and procedural rules. Also needed are clearer rules regarding related institutions like prequalification, rules of origin, technical evaluation, and so on.

10.5 LEGAL REMEDIES

What are the legal remedies available to foreign business enterprises and citizens when the Korean Govenment fails to implement any provision of the Uruguay Round Agreements? And can a foreign enterprise use as a defence the provisions of the Uruguay Round Agreements when it is

---

[75] The Law Concerning Contracts with the Government as a Party, Law No., Art. 4 (1). Besides, the Law on Promotion of New Technology, Law No. 8941, as revised, provides that the Government may accord preferential treatment for local products produced with new technology. However, this provision is due to be revised or abolished soon.

accused of violating a Korean law or regulation that is contrary to the Uruguay Round provisions?[76]

Inasmuch as the provisions of the WTO Agreements are already a part of the domestic laws in Korea, non-compliance therewith by a government agency or by a government official would be unlawful. An individual's right to recover damages sustained due to the wrongful conduct of a government official is recognized under the Constitution.[77] It follows then, that a person who incurred a loss because a government official has violated one of the Uruguay Round provisions is allowed to recover damages, in accordance with the provisions of the law. The question is whether this constitutional remedy is equally available to a foreigner or a foreign enterprise when their property is wrongfully injured due to an action of a Korean official that is held to be in violation of the Uruguay Round provisions. The relevant law, the State Redress Law provides that the remedies under the law are applicable to foreigners, subject to the principle of reciprocity. This means that a foreign person could recover damages if his own country allows Korean citizens to recover similar damages. As applied in the Uruguay Round context, provided that the reciprocity condition is met, a foreign citizen or a foreign enterprise can thus bring a suit against the Korean Government or a local public entity in the event his business interests have been adversely affected by a governmental action, for example, by a refusal to issue a licence to sell a product in Korea against provisions of the Uruguay Round to the contrary. As was explained, all Uruguay Round agreements have been ratified by the President after obtaining the consent of the National Assembly, and as such are part of the domestic law of Korea. In accordance with the principles of the Constitution, they will override provisions of other pre-existing laws that are in conflict, as well as any provisions of administrative regulations or actions to the contrary.

Procedures for challenging wrongful governmental actions for cancellation are provided in the Administrative Cases Litigation Law. Can a foreigner bring a suit under this law? The Law is silent on this point. The Civil Procedure Law, the basic law for civil procedures and the provisions of which are supplementarily made applicable to administrative case litigation, does, however, allow foreigners to avail themselves of litigation

---

[76] These were the questions posed and answered by Prof. Matsushita in his article on multilateral trade negotiations in Japan. I find his analysis and conclusions on these questions under then Japanese laws are very much valid for the current Korean laws. See Jackson *et al.*, *Implementing the Tokyo Round* at 123–129. Relevant constitutional and other legal provisions are identical in Korea and Japan in this regard. The discussion in the text accordingly closely follows Prof. Matsushita's.

[77] Art. 29 (1) of the Constitution provides: 'Any person may request the State or a public body for indemnification of damages when he has sustained such damages by a tortious act of a public official, in accordance with the provisions of a law.'

and specifically provides that a foreigner may become a party in litigation pursuant to the provisions of the relevant Korean laws.[78] It appears clear from this provision that a foreigner can bring a suit against the Korean Govenment and its officials as long as he has the power to be a party to the litigation. The Administrative Cases Litigation Law allows a person who possess a legal interest to challenge an action taken by, or a failure to act by, a governmental agency or official in their exercise of the governmental authority. Such a suit may seek either cancellation of a governmental action wrongfully taken or confirmation as wrongful of a governmental failure to act. Thus, for example, if a foreigner was denied a licence which he is entitled to under the Uruguay Round provisions, he may seek cancellation of the action. On the other hand, if the government official fails to act upon his application in violation of his legal obligation to take action within a reasonable period, he may seek the court's confirmation that the failure to act is wrongful. To be qualified as plaintiff in a suit, a party must have some legal interest in the litigation. This is a question of standing. It should also be noted that some kinds of administrative actions are discretionary in nature and generally not subject to the court's review. Most actions involving foreign trade, like issue or non-issue of licences, assessment of duty, and product approvals may, however, be regarded as ministerial and subject to review. Even in the case of discretionary actions, the court may intervene if the action is found to have exceeded the limit of discretion allowed or abused.[79]

When a foreign enterprise is accused of violating a Korean law or regulation that is contrary to the provisions of the Uruguay Round agreements, it may defend its action on the basis that the law or regulation under which it is being accused is null and void as violating the provisions of the Uruguay Round. The defending party must of course prove that the law or regulation is contrary to the provisions of the Uruguay Round.

APPENDIX

SPECIAL LAW ON IMPLEMENTATION OF WORLD TRADE ORGANIZATION AGREEMENT

Article 1 Purpose

The purpose of this law is to ensure the rights and interests of the Republic of Korea (hereinafter called ROK) as a member of the World Trade

---

[78] Art. 53, Civil Procedure Law, Law No. 547, as amended.
[79] Art. 27, Administrative Cases Litigation Law, Law No. 3754, as amended.

Organization (hereinafter called a member) in implementing the Marrakesh Agreement Establishing the World Trade Organization (hereinafter called the Agreement), and to secure sound development of the national economy by minimizing the injuries which may be caused by implementation of the Agreement.

Article 2 Protection of Economic Sovereignty

Any article of the Agreement shall not be construed to allow impairment of the legitimate economic rights and interests of ROK as member of the global free trade regime.

Article 3 Security of Rights and Interests under the Agreement

1. The Government shall exercise its rights and comply with its obligations, in accordance with the basic principles of the Agreement.
2. The Government shall enter into renegotiatiations in accordance with the procedures provided in the Agreement, in the event the results of any trade negotiations are in contravention of the basic principles of the Agreement, or in the event the implementation of any obligations under the Agreement results in material injury to any specific product in the domestic market.

Article 4 Measures against Subsidies

The Government shall take appropriate measures deemed necessary in accordance with the provisions of the Agreement and/or applicable laws of the country, in the event any member exports to ROK any product with subsidies not permissible under the Agreement.

Article 5 Intra-Nation Transaction

The trade between South Korea and North Korea constitutes an internal trading within a nation and as such shall not be regarded as that between countries.

Article 6 Special Emergency Tax

The Government may, in accordance with the provisions of the Agreement and the applicable laws of the country, levy a special emergency tariff at a level in excess of the bound tariff schedule for that product, in respect of any agricultural/forest/fisheries product, the import of which increases sharply, or the international prices thereof fall substantially.

Article 7 Use of Tariff Proceeds and Import Profits of Agricultural/Forest/Fisheries Products

The proceeds of tariff and the profits from import of agricultural/forest/fisheries products resulting from implementing the Agreement shall be used for the purpose of increasing income of the farmers and fisheries people and development of the rural/fisheries areas.

Article 8 Protection of Health

In the event there is reasonable ground to believe that any foodstuff, any container thereof or any other imported product contains bacteria, germs, viruses, diseases or any other harmful substances as provided in the quarantine laws, foodstuff sanitation laws, plant quarantine laws or domestic animal contagious disease prevention laws, thus causing or threatening to cause public national health problems, the Government may, in accordance with the provisions of the Agreement and/or the applicable laws, prohibit or restrict the importation of the said product, products manufactured or transformed therefrom, or other similar products from the manufacturer or transformer of the said product.

Article 9 Protection of Environment

In the event there is danger of environmental pollution causing damage to human, animal or plant life, the Government may, in accordance with the provisions of the Agreement and the applicable laws, prohibit or restrict the importation of the said product and/or the products manufactured or transformed therefrom.

Article 10 Designation of Import Agency

In the event the importation of a certain agricultural/forest/fisheries product is found liable to cause retardation of the relative domestic industry, the Government may, in accordance with the provisions of the Agreement and the applicable laws, designate an agency of the Government, a local autonomous body, a Government-invested corporation or a producers' association to import said product(s).

Article 11 Implementaion of Domestic Support Policy

1. Promptly after the effectiveness of the Agreement, the Government shall implement measures facilitating export market exploration including provision of credit guarantee for export products or provision of information related to export markets to the extent permissible under the Agreement.
2. Promptly after the effectiveness of the Agreement, the Government shall, to the extent permissible under the Agreement, institute the following support measures:
   (a) direct payment to control production,
   (b) support to marginal farmers,
   (c) support to farmers engaged in organic farming and other environmentally beneficial farming,

(d) support against calamities in agriculture/forestry/fisheries,

(e) income support not related to production.

Article 12   Support to Producers' Association for Moderation of Supply and Demand of Agricultural/Forest/Fisheries Products

The Government shall, in accordance with the provisions of the applicable laws, provide support to the producers' associations engaged in moderating the demand and supply of agricultural/forest/fisheries products in respect of their facilities for procurement, storage and processing.

Article 13   Implementation of Agricultural/Forestry/Fisheries Industry Structural Adjustment

The Government shall implement the structural adjustment of the agricultural/forestry/fisheries industry in connection with the implementation of the Agreement, and shall annually report to the National Assembly the status thereof.

Article 14   Implementing Regulations

Necessary details for implementing this law shall be provided in the Presidential Decree.

THE URUGUAY ROUND AGREEMENTS: CONSTITUTIONAL AND LEGAL ASPECTS OF THEIR IMPLEMENTATION IN COSTA RICA

Roberto Echandi*

11.1 INTRODUCTION

If one studies the implementation of the Uruguay Round Agreements in Costa Rica, two aspects immediately attract attention. One is the readiness of the Costa Rican legal system to incorporate international law prescriptions into the domestic order, and the existence of effective legal means by which individuals and moral entities can seek the enforcement of those prescriptions. The other aspect, and one more directly related to the result of the General Agreement on Tariffs and Trade multilateral trade negotiations which concluded in 1994, is the straightforward approval the Uruguay Round Agreements were given by the Costa Rican Legislative Assembly. As this chapter will explain, it took only one session (approximately forty minutes long) for the Special Congressional Commission dealing with bilateral and multilateral trade matters to recommend approval of the Uruguay Round Agreements. Further, on the floor of the Congress, the agreements won virtually unanimous approval. The obvious question arising here is: what are the political and economic factors that explain the positive attitude of the Costa Rican legislature towards the Uruguay Round package?

Having said that, this chapter aims to present a twin-faceted analysis. Thus, it will examine not only the constitutional/legal issues related to the negotiation, approval and incorporation of international trade agreements into the Costa Rican domestic legal system, but also the role of the main political actors in each of these phases. This chapter is divided into four

* Senior adviser, Department of International Trade Negotiations, Ministry of Foreign Trade, San José, Costa Rica. Professor of International Trade Law at the Manuel María Peralta Diplomatic Institute, Ministry of Foreign Affairs, and at the University of San José, Costa Rica. The author wishes to express his gratitude to Francisco Chacón and Anabel González for their valuable comments on this paper.

sections. Section 2 presents a brief profile of Costa Rica and its legal system. The idea is to provide the reader with the elementary information needed to place the rest of the analysis in its proper context. Section 3 focuses on the constitutional and legal issues related to the negotiation, approval and ratification of international treaties in Costa Rica. Because, under Costa Rican constitutional law, international trade agreements do not receive different treatment from treaties dealing with other matters, the analysis presented in Section 3 is applicable to the Uruguay Round Agreements as well as any other international agreement. Finally, Section 4 addresses the issues arising from the implementation of the Uruguay Round in particular. The analysis here will also have two dimensions. In addition to explaining the legislative approval and the reforms of domestic legislation entailed by the Uruguay Round Agreements, this section will attempt to provide a brief explanation for the smooth and rapid approval of the new rules governing the multilateral trade system of the World Trade Organization.

11.2 COSTA RICA: AN ELEMENTARY PROFILE

Costa Rica is one of the countries with a strong tradition of respect for the rule of law in the Latin American region. This small nation, with little more than three million inhabitants and geographical dimensions similar to those of the US state of West Virginia, has come to provide an exceptional example of strong democratic institutions and political stability in Latin America. Having abolished the army in 1948, Costa Rica definitely constitutes a *sui generis* case in the turbulent Central American isthmus.

As Costa Rica has limited weight in the world economic order, its governing élites have long been aware of the country's vulnerability *vis-à-vis* external political and economic variables. Costa Rican policy-makers have gradually become convinced of the need to use the limited instruments at their disposal—international law among them—to face the numerous challenges posed by an unpredictable international environment. This is even more evident in the 1990s, when an increasingly interdependent world economy is blurring national boundaries.

For the reasons mentioned, Costa Rican policy-makers have traditionally been keen to promote the effectiveness of and respect for international law, both within and beyond the national borders. The fast and smooth implementation of the Uruguay Round Agreements illustrates this point. Not only were the agreements on the GATT multilateral trade negotiations approved almost unanimously by the Costa Rican Legislative Assembly; but Costa Rica's constitutional law also provides the required instruments to enable individuals as well as moral entities—both Costa Rican and foreign—to enforce the Uruguay Round obligations effectively at the domestic level.

As in the case of the great majority of the countries in the West, the 1949 Costa Rican Constitution provides for separation of powers between the legislative, executive and judicial branches of government. There is a fourth, independent power in charge of the electoral process, the Tribunal Supremo de Elecciones. The government follows a presidential scheme. The president is elected by universal suffrage for a four-year term and is not eligible for re-election. Together with the ministers, whom he freely appoints and removes, the president is vested with executive power.

The Legislative Assembly, a unicameral body, comprises fifty-seven representatives (*Diputados*) who are also elected for a four-year term, and who cannot be re-elected for consecutive terms. The seats are allocated on a territorial basis, according to the population density of each of the seven Costa Rican provinces.

The judicial branch includes the Supreme Court of Justice and the lower tribunals it has established. The Supreme Court comprises 22 Justices, who are traditionally elected by a consensus of the Legislative Assembly for an eight-year term. The Justices are automatically considered re-elected, unless they are removed by a two-thirds majority voting in the Legislative Assembly. Within the judicial branch, the most relevant body for the application of international law is the Constitutional Tribunal. Established in 1989, this tribunal is one of the four sections which form the Supreme Court of Justice of Costa Rica. The Constitutional Tribunal has become a pivotal factor; not only in ensuring the real effectiveness of the constitutional provisions, but also for the incorporation of international law into the Costa Rican domestic legal system. Despite following a civil law system, previous court decisions play an important role in the interpretation of the Constitution and ordinary legislation. Further, as will be explained in detail in Section 11.3.2 and 11.3.3 below, the decisions of the Constitutional Tribunal have *ergo omnes* effects[1] (that is, these decisions are binding beyond the particular case in which they were enacted). Thus, despite the civil law nature of the Costa Rican legal system, in the particular case of the Constitutional Tribunal, the *stare decisis* principle is followed.

Costa Rica is divided into seven provinces, which in turn are subdivided into eighty-one cantones (counties) and 415 districts. Each cantón has a municipal government elected by popular vote for a four-year term. Because Costa Rica is not a federal republic, laws, regulations, and international treaties are applicable and implemented on a national basis.

---

[1] Art. 13, Ley de Jurisdicción Constitucional, No. 7135, 11 Oct. 1989.

11.3.1 Trade policy formulation and treaty negotiation

11.3.1.1 Constitutional stipulations

In Costa Rica international trade policy is the exclusive prerogative of the executive branch of government. Article 140 (12) of the Constitution states that the President and the relevant Minister of the Cabinet have the duty of conducting 'the international relations of the Republic'.[2] Although this provision does not imply that the other branches of government do not have a say in foreign policy matters, in fact participation by the legislative and the judicial branches is limited to reacting to the initiatives of the executive.

The prerogative to conduct international relations granted by the Constitution is general. That is, the executive branch has the exclusive power to formulate the foreign policy of the nation and to deal with all the international affairs affecting the country, regardless of their political, economic, social or environmental nature. With this general constitutional mandate, the executive branch does not require, at least from a legal point of view, any authorization from any other branch of government to formulate the international trade policy of the nation. This explains why in Costa Rica the executive branch, represented by the President and the ministers of the Cabinet, have the exclusive capacity to negotiate international agreements, with almost no constitutional and legal limitations, and do not require any previous delegation of authority from Congress or the courts to do so. In this respect, the Constitution states in its Article 140 (10):

Duties and attributions which correspond jointly to the President and the relevant Minister are:

. . .

10) To conclude agreements, public treaties and concordats, and promulgate and execute them once they have been approved by the Legislative Assembly or by a Constitutional Assembly, when this (latter) approval is required by this Constitution. The Protocols derived from those public treaties or international agreements which do not require legislative approval, will enter into force once promulgated by the Executive Power.[3]

Despite the great degree of discretion given to the executive branch to negotiate international agreements, that prerogative has to be exercised

---

[2] Art. 140 (12), Constitución Política de la República de Costa Rica, San José, 7 Nov. 1949.   [3] Art. 140 (10), Constitución Política.

within the limits of the existing constitutional order. This entails two kinds of limitations. First, although the Constitution does not limit the abstract capacity of the executive to negotiate, in order for those negotiations to culminate in a treaty which is valid under Costa Rican law, the agreement has to be approved by the Legislative Assembly and revised by the Constitutional Tribunal, in accord with the procedures established by the Constitution, the Internal Congressional Regulations and the Law of the Constitutional Jurisdiction. Thus, the executive branch cannot act individually and assume an international obligation in the name of the Costa Rican republic. Secondly, the President and the Ministers also have constitutional limitations regarding the substantive obligations which can be assumed through international agreements.

11.3.1.1.1 Procedural limitations to the negotiation of treaties

The procedure for approving treaties already negotiated will be explained in the following section. Our concern here is to analyse the procedural limits to the capacity of the executive branch to negotiate international agreements. In this respect, the main implication of Article 140 (10) of the Constitution, quoted above, is that it grants the executive branch the power to negotiate, ratify and execute an international agreement. It should be noted that these are three distinctive prerogatives. First, the power to negotiate implies the capacity to reach an agreement with another state(s) or any other subject of international law; an agreement which, however, will not be valid until it is approved by Congress. As will be explained in the following section, the role of the legislature is limited to approving or rejecting the international agreement negotiated by the executive branch; it cannot introduce amendments to the text submitted for discussion. In practical terms, this means there is a permanent 'fast track' in favour of the President and relevant minister undertaking international negotiation on any matter.

Secondly, the power to ratify an international agreement refers to the exclusive capacity of the executive branch to assume—provided there is previous legislative approval—an international obligation on behalf of the Costa Rican republic. This prerogative is consistent with the constitutional provision which reserves the direction of international relations to the President and the relevant minister, and stems from the distinction that Costa Rican jurisprudence has distinguished between the act of legislative approval of a treaty and the ratification of an international agreement. Interestingly, this distinction is often overlooked, even by numerous Congressmen. The ratification is the final act by which the executive branch assumes, on behalf of the state, the international obligation entailed by the treaty. This act has the double effect of binding the Costa Rican state internationally, whilst incorporating the treaty into the internal legal system. Legislative approval, however, is just an act of domestic law which allows the executive branch to ratify the international agreement.[4] The legislature's approval of an international agreement does not bind the executive to ratify it. It is legally possible that, owing to a change of circumstances, the President and the relevant minister decide to abstain from ratifying a treaty already approved by Congress. In this case, the international agreement does not become binding on Costa Rica, nor part of its internal legal system, until ratification and official publication of the treaty takes place. In sum, although the legislature's approval is absolutely necessary to make the treaty have any effect on both the domestic and international plane, Congress's participation is conceived as a prerequisite for a process which, in the end, is initiated and completed by the executive.

This scheme has produced a balanced outcome, which reconciles required flexibility of the executive branch to manage the nation's international affairs with the Legislative Assembly's democratic control over its acts. While is true that the executive branch enjoys great discretion in the treaty-making process, under Costa Rican constitutional law the President and the relevant Minister cannot bind the Costa Rican state acting solely on their own.

An important limitation arising from Article 140 (10) of the Constitution is that, unlike other legal orders, international agreements cannot be concluded by the Costa Rican President alone. This is true in a double sense. For one thing, the President himself cannot negotiate or sign any treaty. That power resides in the President and the relevant ministers of the Cabinet acting jointly. Given the presidential nature of the Costa Rican political system, this distinction may not be of great significance. Indeed, as the President has the power to appoint and remove Cabinet members, it is difficult to foresee a situation under which the President could not impose authority because the relevant minister refused to sign a treaty.[5]

The only kind of international agreements which the Executive branch can sign without any subsequent Congressional or judicial approval are the derived 'protocols' cited by Article 140 (10). Although in a loose sense

---

[4] Sala Constitucional de la Corte Suprema de Justicia, Vote No. 738–90, 16:45 hrs, 28 June 1990.

[5] It would be misleading to think of the President as an authoritarian figure in Costa Rica, however. One should not underestimate the capacity of the Cabinet to influence the behaviour of the President. In practice, given the particular consensual trends predominant in Costa Rican politics, presidents have rarely taken decisions on their own. Further, the opinions of individual ministers as well as the Cabinet as a whole have on some occasions prevailed over the original views of the President. Thus, the Constitutional provision requesting the joint action of the President and the relevant minister to negotiate and sign treaties is not, after all, irrelevant.

these protocols could be considered as international agreements, strictly speaking they are not. They are just accessory instruments to a pre-existing treaty, which in the end constitutes the source of law within the domestic legal order. In fact according to Costa Rican jurisprudence, a protocol is considered to be part of the domestic legal system only to the extent that the executive branch has not exceeded the limits of the authority granted by the relevant treaty.[6]

The Constitutional Tribunal has ruled that including clauses of provisional application in international agreements cannot be acceptable under Costa Rican law since it would undermine the spirit of the Constitution, which aims to ensure the participation of the Legislative Assembly in the treaty making process. This would also violate Article 9 of the Constitution which states that 'none of the Powers can delegate the exercise of their functions'.[7] In fact, the impossibility of signing treaties with provisional application clauses was one of the reasons why the Costa Rican Government did not ratify the Vienna Convention. Although the Costa Rican courts recognize that the Vienna Convention codifies some principles of international customary law which are binding on Costa Rica,[8] in 1980 the executive refused to ratify it, arguing that Articles 11, 12, and 25 of the Convention were unconstitutional.

The provisional application of treaties, that is, the possibility that a treaty could generate effects before the internal [legislative] approval and ratification process are implemented, is not possible according to our Constitution. Provisional application clauses cannot apply to treaties nor to lower rank protocols or derived agreements, because even in this latter case, ratification by the Executive branch and the subsequent publication in the *Official Journal* is required . . . Regarding articles 11 and 12 [of the Vienna Convention] . . . the Costa Rican constitutional order does not authorize any form of consent without the approval of the Legislative Assembly. [Thus] article 25 [is also unconstitutional because] . . . Costa Rica does not admit the provisional application of treaties.[9]

---

[6] The Constitutional Tribunal of Costa Rica has ruled that the validity of these 'supplementary agreements' is limited to the extent that they do not exceed the legal frame provided by the treaties, which in these cases are considered as 'basic agreements', and the sources of the international obligations. Sala Constitucional de la Corte suprema de Justicia, Vote No. 682–90, 17:15 hrs, 19 June 1990.

[7] Art. 9, Constitución Política. This point has been developed by the Constitutional Tribunal: Sala constitucional de la Corte Suprema de Justicia, Vote No. 557–91, 14:12 hrs, 20 Mar. 1991.

[8] Sala constitucional de la Corte Suprema de Justicia, Vote No. 835–90, 15:30 hrs, 18 Jul. 1990.

[9] Veto Presidencial al proyecto de Ley que aprueba la Convención de Viena sobre el Derecho de los Tratados, Casa Presidencial, Zapote, 20 May 1980.

11.3.1.1.2 Substantive limitations to treaty-making negotiations

Although in principle the executive branch can negotiate any matter, there are constitutional limitations to the substantive commitments which can be assumed through an international agreement. In trade-related areas, the primary limitations are the following Articles 46 and 121 (14).

Article 46 would forbid any agreement which granted a private monopoly or led to restrictive practices (in the territory of the republic) which affected 'the freedom of trade, agriculture or industry'.[10] This clause is quite general, however. In practice, no treaty has been declared unconstitutional on these grounds.

A constitutional provision which in practice has generated some trade-related controversies is Article 121 (14), which states:

[the following] will not be able to leave definitively the dominion of the State: a) the energy which could be obtained from public domain waters in the national territory; b) coal and oil deposits and any other hydrocarbon substances, as well as deposits of radioactive minerals existing in the national territory; c) the wireless services; the mentioned resources will be able to be exploited only by the public administration or by particular agents, according with the law and through special concessions granted by limited periods and according to the conditions and stipulations established by the Legislative Assembly. The national railways, ports and airports—the latter while being in service—will not be able to be, directly or indirectly, sold, leased or burdened, and will not be able to leave the control or domain of the State.[11]

As can clearly be seen, this constitutional provision limits the discretion of the executive branch to negotiate international trade agreements in areas such as natural resources and electric, telecommunication and transportation services. In the last two years, this constitutional limitation has generated some trade tensions between the Costa Rican Government and the World Bank and the US Government. The latter entities have objected to the state monopoly in telecommunications, a sector in which some foreign companies consider they could obtain significant profits.[12] Without doubt, this will be one of the most politically sensitive aspects of any future trade negotiation in services. In fact, some of the state-provided

---

[10] Art. 46, Constitución Política.

[11] Art. 121 (14), *ibid*.

[12] A case in point was the controversy generated when Millicom, a telecommunications enterprise controlled by Dutch and Belgian capital, attempted to sell cellular telephone services in Costa Rica. A concession was granted on the basis of an old radio-telecommunications law. The Constitutional Tribunal considered that the cited law, Law No. 1758 of 19 June 1954, did not envisage the use of cellular phones, which at that time did not exist, and consequently, could not be used as a legal basis to grant the concession. After that decision, Millicom could no longer operate in Costa Rica. Currently, a new telecommunications bill is being prepared to avoid this kind of situation.

services are provided efficiently, at a relatively low cost, and thus some of these state monopolies enjoy considerable political backing from Costa Rican public opinion. The situation is even more complex because, far from being costly for the state, monopolies such as telecommunications and oil refining are important sources of public revenue.

11.3.1.2 Institutions involved in policy formulation and treaty negotiation: the legal view

From a constitutional or legal perspective, the power to formulate international trade policy in Costa Rica resides exclusively in the President and the relevant minister.[13] In principle, that 'relevant minister' is the head of the Ministry of Foreign Trade, which by law is 'the organ of the Executive Power in charge of conducting and co-ordinating the external trade policy . . .'.[14] Given the generic constitutional mandate of managing the international relations of the republic, the President and the Minister of Foreign Trade do not have any limitations on pursuing international trade negotiations either at a bilateral or multilateral level.

How does the Ministry of Foreign Trade (COMEX from its initials in Spanish) operate and implement its functions? The Ministry is one of the most flexible and efficient public entities of the Costa Rican government. It is the Ministry with the least employees in the public administration. The international negotiation department has less than thirty officials and fewer than ten negotiators. This fact is misleading, however, because despite its general mandate, the Ministry of Foreign Trade is not the only entity which participates in the formulation of international trade policy in Costa Rica.

Besides COMEX, Costa Rican law also entrusts other ministries and autonomous institutions with the formulation of policies in specific trade-related areas under their domain. Thus, Ministries such as Agriculture, Health, Treasury, Economics, Trade and Industry, Natural Resources, Energy and Mines, Tourism, Transportation, Culture, etc., have a say in the formulation of Costa Rican international trade policy in relation to their particular areas of competence. Autonomous institutions such as the Central Bank and other public entities, especially those which enjoy a monopoly in the provision of particular services, such as the Costa Rican

---

[13] 'Formulation' is understood here in a strict sense, that is, the identification of the objectives to be pursued in the international trade arena and the selection of the appropriate means to pursue those goals. Legislative and judicial involvement may be required in subsequent stages of implementation of the policy which has previously been formulated by the executive branch.

[14] Art. 6, Ejecución de los Acuerdos de la Ronda Uruguay de Negociaciones Comerciales Multilaterales, Law No. 7473, 9 Dec. 1994.

Institute of Electricity (communications and electrical services), also participate in the formulation of Costa Rican policy in the international trade arena.

As the reader may already have realized, with this great number of public entities, their prerogatives frequently overlap, and interministerial conflicts of competence are not unusual. This is particularly true considering the resistance of the bureaucracy to the consequences arising from the 'rolling back' of the State, entailed by the market-oriented economic reforms initiated in Costa Rica in the 1980s. Attempting to justify their very existence, the bureaucracy in several ministries has tended to furiously defend their participation either in areas which it is no longer necessary to regulate, or in fields in which other institutions are more efficient at delivering the particular service. Indeed, as will be explained in Section 4 of this chapter, domestic interbureaucratic disputes have been one of the sources of controversy regarding the implementation of the Uruguay Round Agreements in Costa Rica. There have been conflicts within the executive branch as to which ministry will be in charge of implementing particular obligations arising from these trade agreements.

11.3.1.3 The main political actors involved in trade policy formulation and treaty negotiation

To explain in detail the political dynamics behind the formulation of international trade policy in Costa Rica is a titanic task beyond the scope and length of this chapter. However, so that the reader does not get an incomplete image of trade policy-making in Costa Rica, we will briefly depict some elementary aspects of the political dimension of this process. First of all, one has to differentiate between international trade policy-making and the political practices involved in the negotiation and legislative approval of treaties.

Regarding trade policy formulation, interest groups in Costa Rica (that is, unions, public institutions, non-governmental organizations, rural organizations, and the multiple chambers representing the private entre-preneurial sectors) have at their disposal the institutional channels that any democratic system provides for the defence of their interests. The vote is the most powerful instrument the interest groups have for influencing Government policies. Although in theory, according to Costa Rican law, Deputies should not be subject to Congressional lobby, in practice interest groups find a way to make Congressmen consider their grievances. However, it is through the political parties that most of the political bargaining takes place.

More interesting is the political consultation that takes place during the negotiating stages of an international trade agreement. Before any negotiation takes place, the established practice is that COMEX officials have to undertake two preliminary steps. First, an evaluation of the existing domestic legislation regulating the matter subject to negotiation is carried out. If the content of the potential treaty is likely to conflict with the domestic legal status quo, then the next step is to explore whether the international agreement meets with the required political support for its Congressional approval. Secondly, although the executive branch has great discretion in exercising its constitutional prerogative to negotiate international agreements, from a political perspective COMEX rarely—if ever—initiates international negotiations without a previous consultation with the interest groups most likely to be affected. Further, representatives of the private sector, as well as other public bodies, usually participate, in the negotiations directed by COMEX through so-called 'side room' practice. The idea of these practices is that by the time an international agreement is reached at the international level, the executive branch has already ensured the required support for its legislative approval. Thus, COMEX's policy aims at avoiding a situation in which, after dedicating significant resources to a particular negotiation, the Legislative Assembly or the Constitutional Tribunal do not approve the proposed treaty, either on political or constitutional grounds.

The actors who usually participate indirectly in international trade negotiations are the chambers of industry, agriculture, exporters, commerce, and the union of chambers of the private sector. Recently, given the negotiations on professional services under the aegis of the Uruguay Round and the Costa Rica–Mexico Free Trade Agreement, professional organizations have also begun to show increasing interest in international trade negotiations. From the public sector, representatives of the Ministry of Foreign Affairs, and the relevant area (agriculture, industry etc.) also join COMEX negotiators at the negotiating table.[15]

Finally, an important point to stress is that, once an international agreement is approved, interest groups lose practically any chance of influencing the content of an international agreement. This is for two reasons. First, because in Costa Rica treaties take precedence over ordinary legislation, interest groups cannot aspire to override the effects of a treaty by influencing the Legislative Assembly to enact a subsequent law. Secondly, given the autonomous character of the Constitutional Tribunal, interest groups cannot expect to influence the Judiciary to 'mutate' the reach of an international agreement via interpretation either. In sum, once a treaty is approved, provided that it is constitutional, it is a strait-jacket not only for interest groups, but also for the Government itself, which can

---

[15] Unlike the representatives of the private sector, the delegates of other Ministries, being part of the executive, can get directly involved in the negotiation process.

only override the treaty by denouncing it or requesting the other party to re-negotiate the terms of the international agreement.

11.3.2 The approval of international trade agreements

Despite the lack of participation by the Legislative Assembly in the formulation and negotiation of international trade agreements, its role in the treaty-making process is pivotal. Indeed, without Congressional approval, no international agreement can have any effect in the Costa Rican legal order. Further, it is the discussion in the Assembly that provides the diverse interest groups, from the public as well as the private sector, with the opportunity to subject the proposed international agreement to their scrutiny. This is particularly important given the fact that, once approved and ratified, the treaty will have higher authority than ordinary domestic legislation. Thus the provisions of international agreements become immune from subsequent influence that interest groups could potentially exert through the legislature.

The other entity that plays an important role in the approval of an international agreement is the Constitutional Tribunal, one of the four sections making up the Supreme Court. Its functions will be explained in further detail in the following section. Although the main role played by the judiciary regarding international agreements is to ensure the effective incorporation of the treaty into the domestic legal system, the Constitutional Tribunal also has to be consulted about the constitutionality of the proposed agreement before it is approved by Congress.

11.3.2.1 Constitutional parameters

Article 121 (4) of the Constitution of Costa Rica states:

In addition to the other attributions conferred by this Constitution, the Legislative Assembly has the sole prerogative:

. . .

4) To approve or reject the international agreements, public treaties and concordats. The public treaties and international agreements which confer or transfer particular competencies to a communitary legal order, with the purpose of fulfilling regional and common objectives, will require the approval of the Legislative Assembly, by no less than two thirds of the total of its members.

Lower rank protocols derived from public treaties or international agreements approved by the Assembly will not require legislative approval, when these instruments (the latter) authorize explicitly such derivation.[16]

---

[16] Art. 121 (4), Constitución Política.

An initial aspect to clarify is that the distinction between 'public treaties' and 'international agreements' is doctrinal, and not juridically relevant. This differentiation does not originate, as under US constitutional law,[17] from the existence of different procedures for approving international agreements. The distinction in question stems from doctrinal considerations which differentiate 'general international law' from 'particular international law'.[18] Thus, in Costa Rica there is only one general procedure for approving treaties.

As the Constitution explicitly states, the power of the Legislative Assembly is limited to approving or rejecting the international agreement submitted by the executive. In Costa Rica, the Congress does not have the authority to propose treaties nor to amend the terms of international agreements. Thus, the approval procedures are like a permanent 'fast track' in favour of the executive branch. The juridical rationale for this norm resides in the fact that what the Legislative Assembly approves is not an ordinary law, but the treaty itself. This is done through the enactment of a legislative decree which follows a procedure practically the same as that followed by ordinary legislation. However, it is not a law that the legislature approves. Therefore, the Congress does not have at its disposal the same prerogatives it enjoys in approving ordinary bills. Because it is a treaty, and not an ordinary law, what the Legislative Assembly approves or rejects entails several important implications.

First, as Article 7 of the Constitution explicitly states, treaties have higher status than ordinary laws.[19] Secondly, unlike common legislation, in

---

[17] Under US constitutional law a distinction is usually made between 'treaties', 'congressional–executive agreements', and 'presidential sole agreements'. Although under international law they may all be considered as treaties, this distinction entails different domestic procedures by which the US can assume an international obligation.

[18] The term 'public treaty' is used by some sectors of Latin American international law doctrine to refer to those multilateral agreements, usually signed by a great number of countries, which deal with a general matter. Treaties establishing an international organization, like the UN Charter, or those codifying general principles or international customary law, such as the Vienna Convention on the Law of Treaties, are examples of what this sector would consider 'public treaties'. The term 'international agreement', on the other hand, tends to refer to international accords which regulate more specific matters and are signed by just two or a small number of signatories. This controversial doctrinaire distinction is juridically irrelevant, since under international law, as well as under Costa Rican legislation, the differentiation does not entail different juridical effects. This fact explains why the most recent Costa Rican doctrine simply uses both terms indiscriminately to refer to international agreements. A similar case occurs with the 'concordats'. However, at least the formal distinction here is more concrete, since this denomination is used to refer to those treaties signed between the Roman Catholic Church acting as a subject of international law and a State. However, even in this case, the distinction is more formal than juridically relevant. For further details, see Edmundo Vargas Carreño, *Introducción al Derecho Internacional* (2nd edn.) 29.

[19] This point will be developed in more detail in S. 3.3, which deals with the incorporation of international agreements into the Costa Rican domestic legal order.

order to become incorporated into the domestic legal system, international agreements require, in addition to approval by the Legislative Assembly, ratification by the executive. Since the ratification of a treaty is at the discretion of the President and the relevant minister, the mere fact that an international agreement has been approved by the Congress does not mean that it has become part of the Costa Rican legal order.[20] Even after the treaty has been approved by the Legislative Assembly, the executive can reconsider its ratification inappropriate and decide not to continue with the ratification process. The proposed international agreement would not, then, become part of the Costa Rica legal system.

Furthermore, even after the ratification and publication of an international agreement has taken place, it may still not become part of the domestic legal order. The other signatories may not have completed their ratification procedures, or the treaty itself may indicate a subsequent date for its entry into force. In these cases, the international agreement cannot generate any legal effect in the internal order, given the fact that what is approved by Congress is the treaty itself, and not an ordinary law. If the treaty is not enforceable, then its effects would be pending at the international as well as the internal level. In this respect, the Constitutional Tribunal has stated that when the legislative decree approving an international agreement states that it is in force from its publication onwards,

it has to be understood that such an indication refers only to the legislative act which expresses Congress's conformity with the content of the convention, and not to the treaty itself, of which the entry into force is subject to the subsequent ratification or promulgation by the Executive Power and the provisions established by the convention itself.[21]

Although the Constitution states that the Legislative Assembly will only be able to approve or reject international agreements negotiated by the executive branch, the Constitutional Tribunal has ruled that this does not preclude Congress from introducing interpretative declarations.

The effect of these declarations consists in determining the reach that the signatory State purports to recognize for the treaty, and the particular manner in which the obligations implied by it will be complied with.[22]

---

[20] It should be noted that ordinary legislation is also required to be published and receive the approval of the executive branch before it can become binding. However, this kind of approval is totally different from the act of ratification of treaties. While in the first case, a Presidential veto can be overridden by the Legislative Assembly, in the case of international agreements the Congress cannot force the executive branch to ratify a treaty.

[21] Sala Constitucional de la Corte Suprema de Justicia, Vote No. 647–90, 15 hrs, 12 June 1990.

[22] Sala Constitucional de la Corte Suprema de Justicia, Vote No. 835–90, 15:30 hrs, 18 July 1990.

Interpretative declarations can be made either by the executive branch when ratifying a treaty, or during the approval procedure in the Legislative Assembly, either by the Congress's own initiative or at the suggestion of the Constitutional Tribunal. In the latter case, the declaration could be added to the text of the legislative decree which approves the treaty, by adding to the latter an extra article. The possibility for the legislature to use such declarations has great practical significance. Indeed, without them, international agreements containing clauses with dubious constitutional status would often have to be rejected on those grounds. In practice, these devices have saved several treaties from legislative rejection, and the Constitutional Tribunal has played an important role in suggesting the particular wording such declarations should have in order to avoid any conflict with the norms, principles and spirit of the Constitution.[23]

11.3.2.2 Institutions involved in the treaty-approval process

In Costa Rica, there are two entities that participate in approval of an international agreement. First, there is the Legislative Assembly, which is the branch of government with the prerogative to approve or reject the treaty proposed by the executive branch. Secondly, there is the Constitutional Tribunal. Strictly speaking, the latter's role is not to judge the political, economic or social suitability of the agreement for the interests of the nation—that is the legislature's and the executive branch's task. The Constitutional Tribunal examines whether the proposed international agreement fits the letter and spirit of the Constitution, which is, in the end, the supreme law of the land.

The approval of an international treaty follows practically the same procedure used to enact ordinary laws. Once presented to the Legislative Assembly, the proposed agreement is sent to a Commission for study and public discussion, passing afterwards to the floor of the Congress, where it is subject to three debates on different days. After the second debate, the Directory of the Legislative Assembly has to send the text of the proposed treaty to the Constitutional Tribunal, where its constitutional status is analysed. Finally, the 'bill' is returned to Congress, with the pertinent observations, for the final vote.

In the Costa Rican Legislative Assembly there is no permanent commission to deal with international trade matters. Since the accession of Costa Rica to GATT in 1990, special commissions have been established to study those international commercial agreements and proposals considered by the Government to be vital to the interests of the nation. Thus, a special commission was established to deal with the accession to the GATT in

---

[23] *Ibid.*

1989–90. The same occurred in 1992, with the establishment of a special commission to study the Enterprise for the Americas Initiative, and lately, in 1994, another special commission was set up to deal with Uruguay Round Agreements and the Costa Rica–Mexico Free Trade Agreement.[24]

These study commissions, which comprise Deputies from the different parties, perform an important legal and political task. From a legal perspective, they allow the Deputies of the Legislative Assembly to examine in detail all the legal implications the approval of the treaty may have. This is particularly important since, due to its higher status, the treaty, once approved and ratified, will automatically derogate any contradictory domestic law. From a political perspective, these commissions also play a significant role, since they allow representatives of the different sectors to present their views and advice regarding the proposed international agreement. All the sessions of the commissions are public, and in the particular case of international trade agreements, the Deputies have had the good sense to invite not just the representatives of the diverse interest groups from the public and private sectors; there has also been great interest in inviting predominant academic experts to give their technical advice. This was particularly true in the case of the 1994 commission established to study the Uruguay Round Agreements.

As far as voting is concerned, in principle, international agreements (regardless of their nature) are approved by an absolute majority of the Deputies present at the debates.[25] There are four exceptions to this rule. Those treaties referring to the territorial integrity or political organization of the country require approval by no less than three quarters of all members of Congress, plus two-thirds of a special Constitutional Assembly established to address the matter.[26] Secondly, international agreements negotiated with countries which purport to allow their citizens to have double nationality have to be approved by two-thirds of the total members of the Legislative Assembly.[27] The same applies with any international agreement dealing with external public borrowing.[28] Finally, the Constitution establishes that,

---

[24] Asamblea Legislativa de la Republica de Costa Rica, Acta de la Sesión Plenaria No. 40, 16:00 hrs, 6 July 1994.

[25] This is based on the stipulations of Art. 119 of the Constitution which states: 'The resolutions of the Assembly will be taken by an absolute majority of the present [Deputies], except in the cases in which this Constitution requires qualified majority voting.'

[26] Art. 7, 2nd para.

[27] Art. 16 (1) of the Constitution states:
'Costa Rican nationality is lost: 1) by adoption of another nationality, except in those cases stipulated by international agreements. These agreements will require for their approval a favourable vote of two thirds of the total members of the Legislative Assembly, and will not be able to authorize the simultaneous exercise of nationalities, nor modify the laws of the republic regarding immigration, professional exercise and ways to acquire nationality. The execution of these agreements does not oblige [the citizen] to renounce his/her original nationality' (translation from Spanish).

[28] Art. 121 (15), Ibid.

The public treaties and international agreements which ascribe or transfer particular competencies to a communitary legal order with the purpose of realizing regional and common objectives, will require the approval of the Legislative Assembly by no less than two-thirds majority of its total members.[29]

The Constitutional Tribunal has interpreted that the norm cited above calls for qualified majority voting in the approval of all those treaties, regional or not, which contain dispute settlement procedures that would address matters which otherwise would be solved by national tribunals.[30] Considering that the new WTO establishes a 'rule-oriented' dispute settlement procedure, and that the Uruguay Round has extended the scope of the areas regulated by the multilateral trading system, one could question whether the resolution of the Constitutional Tribunal cited above is relevant for the approval of the Uruguay Round Agreements in Costa Rica. Thus, would the latter instruments require qualified majority voting to be properly approved by the Legislative Assembly? The answer would be no. Several reasons justify this view.

First, the WTO is not, clearly, a regional community legal order. Secondly, one could hardly argue that the WTO dispute settlement procedures will deal with matters which would otherwise be solved by national tribunals. The WTO dispute settlement provisions are designed to enable the contracting parties—most of them states—to solve conflicts among them. Domestic tribunals, on the contrary, deal with conflicts of a different nature: those which arise from conflicts among individuals, moral entities and between them and the administration. Thus, it could hardly be argued that the Uruguay Round Agreements would require qualified majority voting to be properly approved in Costa Rica. However, even if that was the case, the incorporation of the Uruguay Round Agreements into the Costa Rican domestic legal system could not be contested. Indeed, as mentioned before, these agreements were approved in the Legislative Assembly practically by unanimity.

Besides the Congress, the other institution involved in the approval of international agreements is the Constitutional Tribunal. This special section of the Supreme Court exercises a pre-emptive constitutional control of international agreements before they are approved in the third Congressional debate. The Congress Directorate is obliged to consult the Tribunal before the third debate is held.[31] Because this inquiry does not have to be justified on particular grounds, the Constitutional Tribunal is free to examine any aspect of the treaty it considers appropriate. The

---

[29] Art. 121 (4), Constitución Política.
[30] Sala Constitutional de la Corte Suprema de Justicia, Vote No. 1079, 14:48 hrs, 2 Mar. 1993. Similar views were expressed in resolution No. 10–92, 16:30 hrs, 7 Jan 1992.
[31] Art. 96, Ley de la Jurisdicción Constitucional.

opinion of the Tribunal will be delivered within one month, and it will be binding only if it reveals a violation of the approval procedures established by the Constitution. It is important to state that, in any case, the opinion of the tribunal does not preclude future potential constitutional challenges to the validity of the international agreement.[32] Thus, rather than being a definitive constitutional test, the preliminary revision of the international agreement by the Tribunal is intended to act as a screening device to avoid deviation from the procedural rules for treaty-making, and at the same time, prevent the Legislative Assembly from approving, and the executive branch from assuming, international commitments which clearly violate the letter and spirit of the Constitution. After the Constitutional Tribunal has presented its opinion, the proposed international agreement is returned to the floor of Congress to be discussed for the last time, and to be referred to the executive branch for its ratification and publication.[33]

11.3.3 Incorporation of international trade agreements within the domestic legal order

11.3.3.1 Status of international trade agreements within the domestic legal system

The status of international law within the Costa Rican domestic legal system has evolved over the years. Originally, the Constitution of 1949 did not explicitly deal with the numerous issues deriving from the relationship between the different sources of international law and the domestic legal system. Perhaps due to fervour for the dogma of national sovereignty among the constitutional founding fathers, there was not a single general provision, like that in the Spanish Constitution of 1931, which recognized the general and higher validity of international law.[34] Several provisions in the text of the Constitution, such as those establishing the national territorial boundaries, made reference to international law principles, however. Although the Constitution established the procedures for

---

[32] Art. 101, Ibid.

[33] When the content of an international agreement deals with matters which fall within the competencies of an autonomous institution, the Constitutional Tribunal has interpreted Art. 190 of the Constitution as requiring the Legislative Assembly to request the advice of these entities before the treaty is approved. These opinions are not binding, however. Sala Constitucional de la Corte Suprema de Justicia, Vote No. 3–92, 14:30 hrs, 7 Jan 1992.

[34] For a detailed analysis of the original provisions of the 1949 Constitution regarding the interaction between domestic and international law (before the 1968 and 1989 reforms), as well as for the views expressed in the Constitutional Assembly in 1949 on this matter, see: R. Piza Escalante, 'Régimen de tratados internacionales en el derecho de la República de Costa Rica', *Revista de Ciencias Jurídicas*, December 1967.

approving treaties, recognizing them as a soure of law within the domestic constitutional order, the Constitution did not contain an explicit general clause indicating the status of the different sources of international law within the domestic legal order, nor the legal ranking of the treaties *vis-à-vis* ordinary legislation.

This situation not only generated numerous problems regarding the applicability and implementation of international agreements, but also led to an incoherent and inconsistent national jurisprudence on this matter. Although the Supreme Court consistently stated its respect for international law, its position regarding the hierarchy of international agreements and principles *vis-à-vis* the national Constitution and the domestic laws varied, depending on which particular source of international law it was being attempted to implement. Regarding particular principles of international law, such as the *ius cogens* and the principles of diplomatic immunity, the Supreme Court granted them superior status, even over the provisions stated in the Constitution.

There [are] principles which [are] universally accepted by International Law, which take precedence even over Constitutional precepts, even if the Constitution does not recognize this explicitly, because these principles are, among other things, the base for the validity of the Constitutional norms and all internal law of the member States of the international community.[35]

The jurisprudential position regarding the status of the treaties within the domestic legal order, as opposed to principles of international law, was quite different. Since the procedure for approving a treaty is by a Legislative Decree with the characteristics of ordinary legislation, the Supreme Court used to consider that treaties had the same status as domestic laws. This view had several important implications. One is that treaties, unlike the *ius cogens*, could not prevail over the Constitution. In addition, if the provisions of an international agreement clashed with a domestic law, the situation was resolved as an ordinary conflict of laws. According to Costa Rican legislation, the later norm would prevail over the earlier, and particular provisions would prevail over the general. This meant that a treaty could be overridden by the enactment of either a subsequent or more specific ordinary law.

Thus, the effectiveness of international law within the Costa Rican legal system was quite limited. Not only did international agreements not enjoy

---

[35] Resolution of the Supreme Court, cited in Vargas Carreño *Introducción al Derecho Interntional*, 257. Despite these radical statements favouring international law over the domestic constitutional order, in practice the Supreme Court has never found any conflict between the Constitution and the interpretation of these fundamental principles of international law.

privileged status, but also, although international treaties had the same legal status as ordinary legislation, the national tribunals were inconsistent regarding the question of their direct applicability within the domestic legal order. In some cases the tribunals explicitly followed a dualist approach, stating that an 'act of transformation' was required before a treaty could be applicable in the Costa Rican domestic order, but others considered that no act of transformation was necessary if the text of the treaty was clear and precise enough as to be directly applicable. However, in practice the cases where treaties were found to be precise enough to render direct effects within the domestic order were rare.

The status and relevance of international law was considerably improved by Constitutional amendment No. 4123 of 31 May 1968, as well as by the establishment of the Constitutional Tribunal and the enactment of the Law for Constitutional Jurisdiction in 1989. The amendment of 1968 explicitly solved the issue of the rank of the treaties within the domestic order, granting these international agreements higher status than ordinary legislation. Thus, at present, in Costa Rica no treaty can be overridden by an ordinary law, regardless of the latter's date of promulgation or degree of specificity. Article 7 of the Costa Rican Constitution was reformed as follows:

The public treaties, international agreements and concordats properly approved by the Legislative Assembly, will have from the date of their promulgation, or from the day stated by them, superior authority to [domestic] laws.[36]

This Constitutional reform in 1968, despite explicitly recognizing the precedence of international agreements over ordinary domestic legislation, did not make Costa Rican judicial decisions entirely consistent. There was no specific procedure for challenging an ordinary law on the grounds that it contravened a valid treaty. The only possible argument one could use for this purpose was to argue the unconstitutionality of the challenged law on the grounds that, since it contravened a treaty, it was violating Article 7 of the Constitution. In fact, this argument was used on several occasions with mixed results. In some cases the unconstitutionality of a law was declared;[37] in other cases, the Justices considered that such an argument was not valid. Justices considered that laws would be unconstitutional only if they contravened the text and spirit of the Constitution, rather than an international agreement. Treaties were not, then, considered parameters of constitutionality. Thus, if Costa Rican judges applied domestic legislation to the detriment of the stipulations of an international

---

[36] Art. 7, Constitución Política.
[37] CORTE PLENA, sesión extraordinaria, 27 Nov. 1980, cited in M. Ramirez & G. Trejos, *Jurisprudencia Constitucional: 1979–1982* (1982) 39.

agreement, the Justices considered that such an act would be a problem of poor interpretation of the laws; that is, an issue of legality and not a constitutional one.[38]

With the promulgation of the Law of Constitutional Jurisdiction establishing a specialized tribunal, the old interpretation problems related to the incorporation of international treaties into the Costa Rican legal system were solved. Article 2 (b) of the Law of Constitutional Jurisdiction explicitly states:

It falls within the constitutional jurisdiction:

. . .

b) to exert control over the constitutionality of the [legal] norms of all kinds and all actions subject to Public Law, as well as the conformity of the internal order with International or Communitary Law, through the action of unconstitutionality and other questions of constitutionality.[39]

With the cited provision, international agreements have become, *de facto* and *de jure*, parameters of constitutionality in the Costa Rican legal order. Indeed, the Law of Constitutional Jurisdiction explicitly states in article 73 (d):

The action of unconstitutionality will proceed:
(d) when any law or general provision infringes the first paragraph of article 7 of the Constitution, for contravening a public treaty or international agreement.[40]

In principle, international agreements have direct effect in Costa Rica. In this respect, the Constitutional Tribunal has stated that when the provisions of the treaties are clear enough and do not require other norms to make them operative, domestic laws contravening the international agreements 'should be taken simply as abrogated by virtue of the superior rank of the treaties. Thus, the conflict between law and treaty . . . has to be solved, as far as possible, by the *automatic abrogation* of the former. However, this does not impede an action of unconstitutionality that could be presented subsequently against the law which conflicts with the treaty.'[41]

Thus treaties will be presumed to have direct effect, provided the following conditions apply:

1. the wording of the treaty is clear and precise enough to identify without doubt the obligation assumed by the Costa Rican state;

---

[38] CORTE PLENA, sesión extraordinaria, 27 Nov. 1980, cited ibid., 39–40.
[39] Art. 2 (b), Ley de la Jurisdicción Constitucional (emphasis added).
[40] Art. 73 (d), Ibid.
[41] Sala Constitucional de la Corte Suprema de Justicia, Vote No. 288–90, 17:hrs, 13 Mar. 1990.

2. the wording of the treaty is precise enough to identify clearly the rights granted to individuals, institutions or corporations; and
3. the Costa Rican internal legal order provides the institutional and procedural organization required to enable those individuals, institutions or corporations to exercise the rights provided by the international agreement in question.[42]

11.3.3.2 International trade agreements and private subjects

Owing to the characteristics of the Costa Rican constitutional system, and in particular to the establishment of the Constitutional Tribunal in 1989, private subjects—regardless of their nationality—have access to international law to defend their interests in the Costa Rican legal system. There are three main avenues through which citizens and/or moral entities can ensure the application of international agreements in Costa Rica. First, by virtue of Article 7 of the Constitution and its interpretation by the Constitutional Tribunal, treaties which comply with the characteristics stated in the last section are self-executing. Because treaties are incorporated into the Costa Rican legal system once properly ratified and published in the *Official Journal*, they *automatically* abrogate any other contradictory law. Thus, citizens are legally able to invoke the direct application of the treaty in any ordinary court, without necessarily having to challenge the law in question through an action of unconstitutionality before the Constitutional Tribunal.

A second means which individuals and moral entities (public or private) have at their disposal to ensure the application of an international agreement is through a claim of unconstitutionality. As mentioned before, this action would proceed when there is an attempt to apply a law which is contrary to the provisions of a treaty. In this respect, Article 75 of the Law of Constitutional Jurisdiction states:

To present an action of unconstitutionality, a trial must be pending to be resolved at the courts . . . and the unconstitutionality must be invoked as reasonable means to protect the right or interest which is considered to be impaired. The pending case will not be necessary when by the nature of the matter, no individual and direct injury may exist, or the case deals with the defense of diffused interests, or concerns the society as a whole.[43]

If the Constitutional Tribunal declares a law unconstitutional, this act has a declaratory effect. That is, the act will recognize a pre-existent

---

[42] Ibid.
[43] Art. 75 , Ley de la Jurisdicción Constitucional.

juridical situation, and as a result, it will have a retroactive effect as far back as the date when the unconstitutional law was promulgated. This would be the case if the law in question had been promulgated after the treaty invoked was already part of the Costa Rican legal order. In those cases where the ratification of the invoked treaty was subsequent to the promulgation of the law being challenged, the effects would be retroactive back to the date when the treaty in question was published. In any case, the resolution nullifying the effects of a particular law can graduate and limit the retroactive effect of the unconstitutional declaration, either on a territorial or temporal basis.[44]

The last avenue private individuals have under Costa Rican constitutional law for enforcing the provisions of international agreements, is the writ of *amparo* (a term which means 'protection' in Spanish). This writ entails a summary procedure aimed at protecting the fundamental rights and liberties of individuals. Fundamental rights are those provided by the Constitution and international law—human rights in particular. Although this procedure might not seem closely related to international trade accords, there is a fundamental right granted by the Costa Rican Constitution which would be of great significance in international trade matters: equality between nationals and foreigners.

Article 19 of the Constitution states:

Foreigners have the same individual and social rights and duties as Costa Ricans, with the exceptions and limitations this Constitution and the laws establish. [Foreigners] cannot interfere in the political affairs of the nation, and are subject to the jurisdiction of the tribunals of justice and authorities of the Republic, and cannot request diplomatic protection except in those cases covered by international agreements.[45]

The Constitutional Tribunal's interpretation of this clause is almost as important as the clause itself, and illustrates the enthusiasm of the Costa Rican Supreme Court for protecting individual rights and international law—a trend especially evident since 1989. This tribunal has opined that:

the phrase 'with the exceptions and limitations that this Constitution and the laws establish' contained in article 19 [of the Constitution], allows recognition of the logical differences between nationals and foreigners, but not so far as to deprive the rights of foreigners of Constitutional protection . . . Thus, those limitations should have an exceptional character and be interpreted restrictively. Consequently, regarding rights which could be subject to limitation, the legislator is not

---

[44] Art. 91, Ibid. This provision also states that the resolution nullifying a law on constitutional grounds will dictate rules necessary to avoid serious dislocation of the security, justice or social peace of the nation.

[45] Art. 19, Constitución Política.

completely free, since those rights continue to be constitutional . . . *thus, regarding foreigners, the only possible exceptions to the equality principle are those explicitly allowed by the Constitution.*[46]

On the basis of this interpretation of Article 19, any foreigner could use the writ of *amparo* to defend the fundamental principle of equality between aliens and Costa Rican nationals. The principle of national treatment is thus constitutionally ensured in Costa Rica.

The unique character of the Costa Rican legal system regarding the respect for international law does not end there. The Law of the Constitutional Jurisdiction establishes an incredibly straightforward procedure for the writ of *amparo*, enabling the individual to present the writ personally, not requiring a lawyer nor needing any formality.

In the writ of amparo . . . it will not be necessary to cite the Constitutional norm violated, provided that the violated right has been clearly determined, except when an international instrument is invoked. The writ will not require any other formality nor will require authentication. It can be presented by a memo, telegram or another written communication, in the latter case it will be post-free.[47]

In practice, the Constitutional Tribunal has interpreted Article 19 in a manner which is even more favourable to the interest of individuals. As an illustration, the Tribunal has accepted writs of *amparo* presented in foreign languages, in ordinary paper and even submitted by children!—who otherwise would need to act through a legal representative.[48]

Lastly, one of the most striking aspects of the Costa Rican writ of *amparo* is that it can be presented against the public body which committed the violation of the right, as well as against the public officer who was the author of the infringement. In the latter case, if the public servant violated the individual's right either intentionally or negligently, he or she would respond with his or her own personal patrimony to compensate for the damage caused.[49] Thus, according to Costa Rican constitutional law, a public officer could be personally responsible for the violation of an international agreement, if by doing this, a fundamental right of a citizen or a foreigner was impaired.

---

[46] Sala Constitucional de la Corte Suprema de Justicia, Vote No. 1282–90, 15:00 hrs, 16 Oct. 1990 (emphasis added).

[47] Art. 38, Ley de Jurisdicción Constitucional (emphasis added).

[48] The Constitutional Tribunal has even accepted writs of *amparo* presented in napkin paper by jail prisoners. R. Piza Escalante, '*La Justicia Constitucional*', lecture delivered to the Costa Rican Law Association, July 1995.

[49] Art. 51, Ley de la Jurisdicción Constitucional states that if the Tribunal finds that the fundamental right of the individual has actually been violated, the verdict, '. . . will be against the State, or respectively, against the entity from which the condemned depends, and also personally against the latter, if it is considered that he or she acted intentionally or negligently, this without prejudice of the other administrative, civil or criminal responsibilities the officer may have incurred.'

11.3.3.3 Interface between national law and the WTO Dispute Resolution Process

The readiness of the Costa Rican jurisprudence to incorporate international law into the country's domestic legal order raises the question of the effects which a Panel Report rendered under the WTO dispute settlement procedures would have in Costa Rica. Could these resolutions be directly applicable? Could private subjects, attempting to defend their interests *vis-à-vis* damaging trade practices of another WTO Member, force the Costa Rican Government to accuse that contracting party and request the application of the Organization's dispute resolution mechanisms?

Up to August 1995, no complaint has ever been brought to GATT or the WTO against Costa Rica. This fact prevents a determination of what the status of GATT or WTO panel reports within the Costa Rican domestic legal order has been in practice. Nevertheless, at least in theory, it is possible to state that the effects of a WTO Panel Report in Costa Rica would vary, depending on whether the panel had been based on a violation or non-violation complaint.

In the first case, if it was found that Costa Rica had infringed a WTO obligation and the Panel Report required this country to comply with an obligation included in the Uruguay Round Agreements, that report could be, in principle, directly applicable within the Costa Rican internal order. The basis for this would be that, in a report based on a violation complaint, *what the Panel probably would demand would be the effective compliance with an already existing obligation under the WTO agreements*. Because the Uruguay Round Agreement became part of the Costa Rican legal order on 1 January 1995, what a Panel Report would demand in a violation case would be then, in fact, the compliance with Costa Rican law. However, it has to be noted that, for a WTO Panel Report to be directly applicable within the Costa Rican domestic legal system, it would have to fulfil the same requirements with which International agreements need to comply in order to be invocable in Costa Rican courts. Thus, the wording of the Panel Report would have to be clear and precise enough to identify, without doubt, the obligation infringed on by Costa Rica and the rights of individuals or corporations violated by that infringement. Further, the Panel Report could be directly applicable, provided that the Costa Rican Government could have at its disposal the necessary institutional and procedural organization required to comply with the panel recommendations. Being a specific interpretation of a binding international agreement, that Panel Report would prevail over any conflicting ordinary legislation.

Based on the aforementioned considerations, an example of a Panel Report which could be directly applicable in Costa Rica would be one which requested the Government to dismantle new import quotas unlawfully established in detriment of a particular kind of product. In this case, any affected private subject, Costa Rican or foreign, could use the domestic courts to demand that the Government comply with that particular WTO Panel Report.

The situation would be different if a Panel Report were based on a non-violation complaint. In that case, Costa Rica would not be violating any WTO agreement incorporated into its domestic law. In this kind of case, the dispute between the contracting parties transcends the legal sphere. Thus, because there would not be any breach of any obligation, the possibility of using the domestic legal remedies to implement the Panel Report would not be present.

Regarding the possibility of private parties encouraging and participating in WTO complaints brought by the Costa Rican Government, from a merely legal perspective, their chance of forcing the executive branch to defend their particular interests would be negligible. As mentioned in Section 3.1.1, according to Article 140 (12) of the Constitution, in Costa Rica the executive branch enjoys full discretion in the management of the foreign affairs of the republic. Therefore, private parties would not have any legal argument with which to force the executive branch to request a panel under the WTO dispute settlement procedures.

From a political point of view, the situation is totally different. Given the close inter-relationship between COMEX and the private sector—national or foreign—operating in Costa Rica, in practice the entrepreneurs do have an important role in encouraging the executive branch to assume particular positions in international forums.[50]

11.4 IMPLEMENTATION OF THE URUGUAY ROUND IN COSTA RICA

11.4.1 The legal perspective

The legislative approval, ratification and implementation of the Uruguay Round Agreements in Costa Rica has gone so smoothly that it is hard to believe. In fact, it took the Deputies in Congress less than thirty minutes in the Special Congressional Commission to reach a consensual pronounce-ment recommending approval of the Uruguay Round package.[51] Although there were some questions regarding the domestic applicability of some of the declarations of the Marrakesh Ministerial Meeting, in the end the

---

[50] This point was developed in Section 3.1.3 above.
[51] See *Actas de la Ley que Aprueba los Acuerdos de la Ronda de Uruguay*, No. 7475, 20 Dec. 1994, Expediente No. 12049, Asamblea Legislativa, San José, Costa Rica.

Uruguay Round Agreements were almost unanimously approved in a vote on the floor of the Legislative Assembly.[52]

Two aspects are striking. The first is that the Uruguay Round Agreements enjoyed such a smooth ride in the usually turbulent Costa Rican legislative discussions. Secondly, the Deputies did not object to enacting a general law which authorizes the executive to implement, through executive branch regulations, most of the commitments of the accords which call for the internal legal system to be adapted according to the terms of the Uruguay Round agreements. This extremely favourable attitude of the Costa Rican Legislative Assembly towards approval and implementation of the Uruguay Round Agreements can be better explained from the perspective of political economy. I will attempt to present a brief analytical view of the process by which the Uruguay Round Agreements were approved and implemented. And then, in section 4.1.2 I will briefly analyse the political-economic context.

11.4.1.1 The legislative approval process

The Uruguay Round Agreements have been implemented in Costa Rica through the approval of two legislative decrees: firstly, the package of international agreements themselves,[53] and secondly, a general law enacted to implement those obligations of the agreements which, due to their generic nature, cannot have a direct effect on the Costa Rican legal system.[54] Although closely related, these two instruments constitute two different legislative actions. The process of approval of each of these instruments raises different issues and therefore, they deserve a separate examination.

Regarding the approval of the Agreements themselves, after being signed in Marrakesh on 15 April 1994, the Uruguay Round Agreements were submitted to the Costa Rican Legislative Assembly for their approval. On 6 July 1994, the Congress established, unanimously, a special commission whose mandate was:

to study and make recommendations regarding economic treaties, bilateral and multilateral, especially those signed with Mexico [a free trade area] and those of the GATT Uruguay Round. This Commission will be made up by five Deputies chosen by the President of the Assembly and will have three months to make the recommendations it considers appropriate. It will be able to propose the bills and legal reforms considered appropriate to fully comply with those accords.[55]

---

[52] Ibid. [53] Decreto Legislativo No. 7475, 20 Dec. 1994.
[54] Ley de Ejecución de los Acuerdos de la Ronda de Uruguay.
[55] Asamblea Legislativa de Costa Rica, Acta de Sesión Plenaria, Sesión No. 40, 16:00 hrs, 6 July 1994.

The scope of this mandate clearly illustrates the perceptions prevailing in 1994 among the Deputies, and in national public opinion in general, regarding the main initiatives of interest for Costa Rica in the field of international trade. As can be seen, the purpose of the Commission was to study not only the Uruguay Round Agreements, but also the Costa Rica–Mexico Free Trade Agreement, signed in April 1994 and expected to come into force on 1 January 1995.[56] To a great extent, the smooth ride the Uruguay Round had in the Legislative Assembly stems from the fact that, compared with the Mexico–Costa Rica free trade area project, the Uruguay Round Agreements came to be perceived as toothless, and as an instrument to establish the *minimum* regulatory framework in which world trade relations would take place, at least until the beginning of the 21st century.

It was the Costa Rica–Mexico Free Trade Agreement which attracted most of the attention of the Deputies, interest groups and press in 1994, deflecting the focus from the Uruguay Round Agreements. This explains why, although established in July 1994, and starting weekly sessions in that month, the Commission's public discussions, as well as the attention of the mass media, focused on the proposed Costa Rica–Mexico bilateral treaty for more than three months. In contrast, the Uruguay Round Agreements were discussed and approved in just one session.

An interesting issue raised during the discussion of the Uruguay Round Agreements in the Legislative Assembly was the question of the identification of the texts which would be binding for Costa Rica. The Uruguay Round package presented by the executive branch for its approval contained not only the Agreements establishing the WTO (and the annexes for trade in goods; services; intellectual property rights; dispute settlement procedures and the trade policy review mechanism), but also the fourteen decisions and Ministerial declarations approved at Marrakesh in April 1994. The question that arose was, then, whether the latter decisions would be considered part of the general Uruguay Round package, and as such, whether they would be incorporated into the Costa Rican legal system with a superior status to ordinary laws. Since the decisions dealt with other issues which are still politically sensitive in Costa Rica—for example, telecommunications and some financial services—clarifying this particular issue was of pivotal importance.

---

[56] The Costa Rica–Mexico Free Trade Agreement, a project enthusiastically promoted by the then Presidents Salinas of Mexico and Calderón of Costa Rica, was described as the 'most advanced' free trade agreement ever signed between two Latin American countries. This description stems from its similarity with NAFTA, and in particular, for the inclusion of chapters regulating 'new' topics such as trade in services, intellectual property rights, investment and government procurement. See 'Central America's model accord', *Financial Times*, 9 Mar. 1994.

Trying to prevent the development of an unfavourable atmosphere in Congress, the executive branch promptly informed the President of the Legislative Assembly that:

Although all those instruments [the accords and the decisions] constitute the whole documents resulting from the multilateral trade negotiations and all of them were addressed in the Ministerial Meeting at Marrakesh, the truth is that not all of these instruments have the same juridical value . . . The instrument signed by the Executive Power on 15 April 1994 with a binding character and which constitutes, consequently, the international treaty which would bind the country . . . is the only Agreement by which the World Trade Organization is established. This Agreement comprises the text through which this new international organization is created, plus several agreements denominated 'Multilateral Trade Agreements' incorporated in the Annexes 1, 2 and 3, which, according to Article II:2 of the WTO Agreement, are an integral part of the latter, and are binding for all the countries. The same does not occur with the 'Plurilateral Trade Accords' included in Annexe 4 of the WTO Agreement, which, according to Article II:3 of the latter, are binding only for those countries which have signed them—which is not the case for Costa Rica, as it has not signed any of them . . . The same is the case for the 'Ministerial Decisions and Declarations', which, like the Final Act, constitute juridical instruments in which all the participants of the Uruguay Round express their will, but owing to their content and wording, do not have a binding character and therefore, are not international treaties.[57]

Once this aspect was clarified, the legislative approval as well as the Constitutional Tribunal's examination proceeded smoothly. As the Constitutional Tribunal did not consider that the Uruguay Round Agreements conflicted with the Constitution, these instruments became part of the Costa Rican domestic legal system by 1 January 1995.

Because under Costa Rican constitutional law treaties are self-executing, at least in principle, the executive branch does not always have to present additional Bills to Congress in order to implement the commitments of international agreements. However, several of the obligations under the Uruguay Round Agreements are generic, and call for the adaptation of domestic legislation according to the negotiated standards. Cases in point would be the obligations regarding the Agreement on Trade-Related Aspects of Intellectual Property Rights, the Agreement on Trade-Related Investment Measures, unfair trade practices and safeguards, among others. Thus, in those areas where Costa Rican legislation did not comply with the newly agreed international standards, and given the generic character of some clauses of the accords—which impede their direct effect—they would have to be further implemented through the enactment of ordinary legislation.

---

[57]Communication of the President and the Ministry of Foreign Trade to the President of the Legislative Assembly, 29 Nov. 1994.

Thus, COMEX prepared several bills which would be presented to Congress for their approval—separately from the international accords themselves. COMEX officials initially proposed the enactment of the following laws:

1. A general law which, by stating compliance with the Uruguay Round Agreements on trade in goods, would eliminate still existing import licenses; establish 'tariffication' procedures; and also harmonize national standards with the agreement reached at the negotiations.
2. A law which would concentrate in COMEX most of the prerogatives required to manage the international trade policy of the nation, including the power to appoint the Ambassador to the WTO.
3. A general law which would implement the accords on TRIMs.
4. Legislation on unfair trade practices and safeguards.
5. Two laws to implement the Agreements on TRIPs, that is, the Law on Inventions, Utility Models and Industrial Drawings; and the Law for the Protection of Industrial Secrecy.[58]

Although most of the substantive obligations implied by the Uruguay Round package were not controversial at all, it would be inaccurate to say that there were no disagreements as to the most appropriate way to implement them. An interesting aspect, however, is that most of these discussions took place among the various ministries of the executive branch, rather than in the legislative forum. Various ministries were concerned that under the new laws proposed by COMEX, several of their competencies would be transferred to the latter. In fact, COMEX, as the government department in charge of the management of the nation's international trade policy, wanted to bring together several trade-related competencies that had traditionally been dispersed among various governmental agencies.[59]

Because COMEX officials intended to secure a smooth and timely approval of the Uruguay Round Agreements—that is, before 1 January 1995—they decided to follow a pre-emptive strategy: instead of presenting the original five different bills which would implement the various Uruguay Round Agreements, only a single project was presented to the Legislative Assembly. The idea was, then, to withdraw from the list of bills which were originally intended to be submitted to Congress, those which could generate controversy, either from other public agencies or from particular interest groups.

Thus, the bills relating to TRIMs, TRIPs, and unfair trade practices

---

[58] Ministry of Foreign Trade (COMEX), International Negotiations Dept., Dec. 1994.
[59] e.g. the Ministry of Foreign Relations objected to the Foreign Trade Ministry's proposal to make the Costa Rican Ambassador to GATT exclusively responsible to COMEX.

were filed temporarily, waiting for a politically opportune moment to be submitted to the legislature. The justification for the withdrawal of these particular bills is threefold. Regarding the TRIPs legislation, COMEX officials feared that some clauses, in particular those obligations related to patents, could lead the Costa Rican pharmaceutical sector to delay the approval of the whole WTO package.[60] Given that TRIPs provides developing countries with a five-year long transitional period to adapt their domestic legislation to TRIPs' standards,[61] COMEX officials decided to postpone momentarily the submission of these bills, and avoid placing the whole WTO package at risk.

Secondly, the bills implementing the Agreements on unfair trade practices and safeguards were also temporarily withdrawn from the original list of proposals to be presented to Congress. In this case, the motivations were different. In Costa Rica, unfair trade practices and safeguards are matters which are currently regulated by an executive regulation which was enacted in co-ordination with the other Central American countries,[62] an initiative taken under the aegis of the Central American Common Market programme. Whether this policy of co-ordination will continue in this area is an issue which is currently being discussed among the different Central American governments. Within this context, COMEX officials considered that the inclusion of the bills relating to unfair trade practices and safeguards could also delay the approval of the whole WTO package. Indeed, those sectors advocating a common Central American policy in these areas could have objected to an attempt of the Government of Costa Rica to enact, individually, its own laws on unfair trade practices and safeguards.

Lastly, given the inter-bureaucratic conflicts, the bill which purported to provide COMEX with a comprehensive legal framework was also withdrawn. In the end, COMEX presented just one bill to supplement the approval of the whole Uruguay Round Agreements. In that project, although COMEX could not concentrate all the competencies it originally pursued for itself, it devised a very flexible mechanism to ensure rapid implementation of most of the Uruguay Round package. The general law approved by Congress explicitly authorizes COMEX to implement the Uruguay Round obligations through Executive Decrees. The only exceptions to this rule were the proposed laws related to TRIMs and TRIPs, which, by the nature of the subject, cannot be regulated by executive decree. These are the two areas, together with the provisions regarding unfair trade

---

[60] This point is developed in S. 4.1.2.2 below.

[61] In this respect, see Art. 65:4 of the TRIPs Agreement.

[62] *Reglamento Centroamericano sobre Prácticas de Comercio Desleal y Cláusula de Salvaguardia*, Decreto Ejecutivo No. 21984MEIC, 8 Feb. 1993.

practices and safeguards, which by January 1995 were still pending implementation. Although the accords themselves granted countries like Costa Rica a five-year period to adapt their domestic legislation to the terms of the TRIPs and TRIMs, it seems very unlikely that the Costa Rican executive branch will require such a long period to comply with these commitments. As mentioned before, the bills are already prepared, and COMEX is just waiting for an opportune political moment to submit them to the Legislative Assembly.

Regarding the implementation already in place, Law No. 7473 of 20 December 1994, entitled Execution of the Uruguay Round Accords of the Multilateral Trade Negotiations enables COMEX to

represent the Government of the Republic before the General Agreement on Tariffs and Trade (GATT) or the succeeding organization, *and enact the norms and regulations required to execute the accords of the Uruguay Round of multilateral trade negotiations, without prejudice to the faculties of other competent Ministries according to the following articles.*[63]

The other Ministries involved in the implementation of the Uruguay Round Agreements are the following:

1. The Ministry of Agriculture and the Ministry of Health: these entities will execute the agreement on Sanitary and Phytosanitary Measures;
2. The Ministry of Economy, Trade and Industry and the Ministry of Health: each will, in their respective fields, execute the obligations on technical standards and measurements mentioned in the Agreement on Technical Barriers to Trade.

11.4.1.2 The main domestic legal reforms resulting from the Uruguay Round Agreements

The main reforms in the domestic legal system resulting from the Uruguay Round Agreements have already been roughly suggested. Before explaining them in more detail, it is important to stress that, being an international agreement, any legislation conflicting with a provision of the Uruguay Round Agreements, precise enough to be directly applicable, was automatically abrogated by the latter. The programmatic norms which resulted from the GATT multilateral negotiations and are not directly applicable, have already been implemented through the general law mentioned before. This law, in addition to regulating some of the obligations related to market access, authorized the executive branch to enact the regulations required to comply with the Uruguay Round

---

[63] Art. 6, Ley de Ejecución de los Acuerdos de la Ronda Uruguay de Negociaciones Comerciales Multilaterales (emphasis added).

Agreements. The only obligations still pending implementation are those related to TRIMs, TRIPs, unfair trade practices and safeguards, which require approval of the three bills already prepared by COMEX.

The Uruguay Round did not entail a significant modification of the legal status quo of Costa Rica. Having joined GATT in 1990, and more particularly, having implemented a significant economic reform programme from the mid-1980s, Costa Rica had already begun to adjust its legislation to international standards before the Uruguay Round ended. However, in Costa Rica, the prevailing political consensus for the new export-led economic model does not automatically extend to a completely passive concept of the state in economic affairs. Despite this, the Costa Rican trade system conformed quite closely with the pre-requisites of the Uruguay Round Agreements. The reforms implemented, with a few exceptions, were not substantial. The main revisions in domestic legislation resulting from the Uruguay Round were the following.

11.4.1.2.1 Market access

The most significant reform to be implemented was the abolition of all remaining import licences in several agricultural and other primary products. Thus commodities such as pork products, poultry and derived meats, seeds, rice, wheat, beans, tobacco, sugar cane, sugar and its derived products, natural salt, dairy products, and coffee, will no longer be subject to import licences.[64] The elimination of import licences does not mean total liberalization of these sectors. What it implies is that the protection granted will have to be implemented through tariffs, according to the procedures agreed in the Uruguay Round's accord on agriculture.[65]

The other main reform, although only indirectly related to the liberalization programme entailed by the approval of the Uruguay Round Agreements, was the abrogation of all export taxes—an exemption which was not, however extended to Costa Rica's traditional export products of coffee, bananas, beef and cattle.[66] The latter issue caused a group of Congressmen approving the Uruguay Round Agreements to ask the Constitutional Tribunal whether this differentiation made the proposed treaty unconstitutional, given the violation of the principle of legal equality protected by Article 33 of the Constitution.[67] The Constitutional Tribunal recognized that there was different treatment, to the disadvantage of traditional export products. However it also observed that these export taxes were an important source of fiscal revenue. In addition, considering

---

[64] Art. 1, Ibid.   [65] Art. 4, Ibid.   [66] Art. 3, Ibid.
[67] *Consulta de Constitucionalidad planteada sobre el Proyecto Legislativo No. 12049 'Ley de Implementación de los Acuerdos de la Ronda de Uruguay de Negociaciones Comerciales Multilaterales*, 15 Nov. 1994.

that the rationale of the GATT (and now the WTO) is, among other things, to enhance competitiveness in world production, if Costa Rica decided to tax its exports, it might be to the detriment of its interests, but would not affect any other country's benefits. Further, with very elaborate reasoning, the Constitutional Tribunal judged that the aforementioned discrimination on export taxes would not make the law that executes the Uruguay Round Agreements unconstitutional. The tribunal recognized that the discrimination objected to by the legislators may indeed exist. Nevertheless, that discrimination would be derived from omission and not commission. Thus, what the proposed law would do—that is, eliminate export taxes for some products—was constitutional. What might be unconstitutional would be the continuing imposition of taxes on traditional exports. However, this was another matter independent of the Uruguay Round Agreements.

The faults of legislative omission are not those which occur when legislating, but those resulting from not doing so; thus, if an unconstitutionality did exist, it would not be of the proposed treaty, but of the conduct or lack of legislative action. From this perspective the article [challenged] does not deserve the criticism presented against it. All this without prejudice that the Tribunal, when considering . . . actions of unconstitutionality . . . against export or production taxes, determines whether those duties are constitutional or not.[68]

This resolution of the Constitutional Tribunal shows the interest of the judicial branch in making the Uruguay Round Agreements and the law implementing it compatible with the existing legal order.

11.4.1.2.2 Normative topics

Regarding normative topics, existing Costa Rican legislation was not in open conflict with the Uruguay Round Agreements. Although Costa Rica still used to confer some export subsidies, a general law abrogated these privileges unilaterally in 1992.[69] The regulations which will be implemented by executive decree, that is standards and sanitary and phytosanitary measures, are (with some minor exceptions) intended to modernize previously obsolete legal provisions, or to regulate procedural matters not yet covered by Costa Rican laws, rather than to adjust previously incompatible legislation to the parameters set up by GATT 1994.

Legislation on unfair trade practices and safeguards will also require to

---

[68] Sala Constitucional de la Corte Suprema de Justicia, Vote No. 7403–94, 9:12 hrs, 16 Dec. 1994.

[69] Ley No. 7293, 31 Mar. 1992. Despite the fact that this law meant the immediate abrogation of most of the fiscal exemptions granted by the Government, it also established a phase-out period for certain export subsidies which will end in 1999.

be adjusted to the more specific norms and procedures included in the Uruguay Round Agreements. There are some provisions of the current legislation which are incompatible with the new WTO commitments. For example, countervailing duty law will have to adopt the 'traffic light' approach followed by the new subsidies agreement. However, the reforms entailed by the Uruguay Round Agreements in the areas of unfair trade practices and safeguards will not represent a radical transformation of the current legislation regulating these matters in Costa Rica. The sensitive issue regarding the implementation of the WTO Agreement in these areas is not, then, the substance of the obligations entailed by the accords. The controversial aspect has rather a procedural—and political—connotation. That is, whether or not Costa Rica will delegate the design and administration of its countervailing duty, anti-dumping and safeguards laws to the Secretariat of Central American Integration, as other member states of the Central American Common Market desire. This is an issue yet to be resolved. However, extra-official sources confirm the view that Costa Rica will not delegate these competencies to any 'quasi' supra-national entity.[70] Thus, the most likely outcome will be that the original bills that COMEX was going to present with the Uruguay Round package in December 1994, will probably be submitted and approved by the Legislative Assembly in 1996.

11.4.1.2.3 New topics

The new topics are areas where Costa Rican legislation was somewhat behind the parameters established by the Uruguay Round Agreements. Although the liberalization of trade in services is one of the most sensitive issues in Costa Rican politics, given the 'positive list approach' followed by the Uruguay Round Agreements, the commitments in this area did not conflict with the Costa Rican constitutional *status quo*. The situation would have been different if sectors such as telecommunications, electrical energy, insurance, and some financial services had been required to be liberalized. The Costa Rican constitution establishes clear rules ensuring the state control over these sectors, and in some cases, public monopolies. However, in the Uruguay Round negotiations, Costa Rica's offer in this matter comprised sectors already operating within a liberal regime: education, computing services, tourism, and some health services.[71] Thus, in the services sector the Uruguay Round did not entail any reform to the Costa Rican domestic legal order.

---

[70] Confidential sources. Ministry of Foreign Trade and Ministry of Economy Trade and Industry (MEIC) August 1995.
[71] Ministerio de Comercio Exterior, *La Ronda de Uruguay de Negociaciones Comerciales Multilaterales y sus implicaciones para Costa Rica* (1994).

The situation is different when it comes to TRIMs and TRIPs. As far as trade-related intellectual property rights are concerned, the proposed Law on Inventions, Utility Models and Industrial Drawings, as well as the Law for the Protection of Industrial Secrecy represent significant advances relative to the existing legislation in these matters. From a constitutional perspective, there is no conflict with the Uruguay Round Agreements. In fact, Article 47 of the Constitution establishes that:

Every author, inventor, producer or trader will enjoy, for a limited time, exclusive ownership of his work, invention, trade mark or commercial name, according to the laws.[72]

At the level of legislation, the only areas where Costa Rican laws will be significantly modified are in those relating to patents as well as matters of procedure. According to the Uruguay Round Agreements, patents would have a twenty-year long protection, while Costa Rican laws establish twelve years for most products and only one year for pharmaceutical, chemical and nutritional products.[73] However, the previously cited bills which will regulate these matters, that is the Law on Inventions, Utility Models and Industrial Drawings and the Law for the Protection of Industrial Secrecy, are intended to adjust domestic legislation to international standards.

Apart from the two laws on intellectual property rights awaiting approval, the only other Uruguay Round Agreements which will require implementation through the enactment of further legislation is the TRIMs. Unlike other Latin American countries, Costa Rica never had a general law restricting foreign investment in the country. In fact, it could be affirmed that with minor exceptions—such as those sectors controlled by the State—Costa Rican legislation on foreign investment has historically been quite open. With the initiation of the market-oriented economic reforms in the early 1980s, several laws were enacted to promote non-traditional exports. Various incentives were offered for promoting these sectors, usually conditional on export performance and local content requirements. However, even before the end of the Uruguay Round, and mainly owing to the heavy fiscal burden they represented for the Government, most of these incentives were eliminated. Within this context, compliance with TRIMs, which among other things calls for the elimination of performance and local requirements for foreign investment, does not represent a significant political burden for the Costa Rican government. Despite this, several incentive laws still containing certain TRIMs will have to be reformed. This is the case for laws in sectors such as tourism, *maquila*, and poultry, banana, and pork production.

---

[72] Art. 47, Constitución Política.   [73] Ley 6867, 12 Dec. 1983.

11.4.2 The political perspective: why did approval of the Uruguay Round package proceed so smoothly?

From a political point of view, the two main questions concerning the implementation of the Uruguay Round Agreements in Costa Rica are the following. Why did their legislative approval go so smoothly? And what does this tell us about general perceptions in Costa Rica of GATT and the WTO and their impact on national interests and sovereignty? The key to answering these questions lies in the profound process of economic reform which, as in other Latin American countries, has been implemented in Costa Rica since the early 1980s.[74]

11.4.2.1 General background

Since 1981, with the eruption of the debt crisis, the inward-oriented import-substitution industrialization model was brought into question. Since then, significant market-oriented reforms have gradually been implemented. Broadly speaking, these reforms have aimed, in the internal sphere, at a redefinition of the role of the state and its participation within the economy; while on the external front, they have aimed for an efficient and favourable insertion of Costa Rica into the world economy.

Since the early 1980s, an export-led growth model has been implemented, emphasizing the diversification of the national export supply as well as of its export markets. In order to remove the anti-export bias of the old protectionist policies and create a pro-export environment throughout the economy, the Costa Rican government gradually began a process of trade liberalization. Tariffs and non-tariff barriers began to be dismantled unilaterally, and in 1990 Costa Rica became a contracting party of GATT. Tariffs decreased from a nominal average of approximately 80 per cent in the early 1980s, to a nominal tariff average of 11.2 per cent in 1994.[75]

In order to diversify exports and markets, trade liberalization was originally complemented by a generous system of fiscal incentives, aimed at promoting non-traditional exports[76] to markets outside Central America.

---

[74] As in most Latin American countries, the debt crisis, which erupted in Costa Rica in 1981, brought the old state-led import-substitution model into question. In May 1982 President Monge, a Social Democrat, replaced President Carazo, who had won the 1978 elections with the social Christian coalition. In that year, annual inflation reached 120%; the budget deficit was of proximately 14% of GDP; and the national currency had to be devalued by more than 100% (source: Central Bank of Costa Rica, Statistical Dept.).

[75] WTO, *Trade Policy Review: Costa Rica*, Report from the Secretariat, Doc. No. WT/TPR/1, 9 May 1995.

[76] Free trade zones, tax drawbacks, and direct export subsidies through tradable income tax certificates (*Certificados de Abono Tributario*) were some of the main incentives granted by the Costa Rican Government during the 1980s. The great burden these incentives placed

The results were extremely positive. Non-traditional exports began to rise sharply, reaching an average annual growth rate of nearly 28 per cent between 1985 and 1992. By 1993, non-traditional exports represented 26.4 per cent of the Costa Rican total, surpassing traditional exports, such as sugar, cattle, and coffee, as a source of foreign exchange.[77] Further, the Costa Rican industrial sector, which had developed under the protection of the high common external tariff of the Central American Common Market since the 1960s, although still representing a minor share of Costa Rican exports,[78] showed itself able to adapt to international market competition.[79]

The economic reforms undertaken since 1982 have had two significant effects on the Costa Rican economy. First, they have converted Costa Rica into one of the most open economies in Latin America;[80] and secondly, so far, economic reform has, in fact, had a positive effect on Costa Rica's economic growth. Between 1987 and 1992, the real gross domestic product has grown at an average of 4.4 per cent annually.[81]

These facts partly explain the general consensus prevailing in Costa Rican politics about the basic features of the new export-led development model.[82] Despite some differences, mostly confined to fiscal discipline and

on the Government led to the abolition of most—except the free zones and drawback schemes—in early 1993. For the purposes of the export-incentive programmes, 'non-traditional' exports were all those apart from bananas, coffee, sugar and cattle; and 'third markets' were all those apart from the Central American Common Market.

[77] Calculation based on data from the Central Bank of Costa Rica, Dept. of Statistics.

[78] In 1991, industrial exports represented approximately 7.71% of total Costa Rican exports. The relative importance of this sector in national exports has been increasing in the last couple of years. In 1992 industrial exports reached 10.24% (approx) of the total, and in 1993, 10.54%. These shares only include exports of the main industrial export products: medicines; apparel; and rubber. The total contribution of industry to exports increases slightly if other minor products, mainly foodstuffs, are considered (source: Central Bank of Costa Rica, Dept. of Statistics).

[79] 'The Costa Rican industrial sector has shown a great capacity to penetrate new markets. In the last ten years it has been able to shift its export markets totally. In the past, 80% of industrial production went to Central America, and only 20% to third markets. In 1994, the proportions are inverted.'

Testimony of M. Schyfter, President of the Costa Rican Industrial Chamber, before the Special Commission of Congress to discuss the Costa Rica–Mexico free trade agreement and the Uruguay Round agreements. Asamblea Legislativa de Costa Rica, Minutes of Sess. No. 10, 7 Sept. 1994, File No. 11.948, 13.

[80] In 1993, the share of trade in goods and services to GDP reached 93% (source: WTO, see n. 75).

[81] R. Dallas, *The Economist: Pocket Latin America and the Caribbean* (1994), 32.

[82] As far as economic policy is concerned, the divergences between the two major political parties are not profound, tending to focus on the speed of economic liberalization and the extent to which the state should withdraw from economic management and social welfare programmes. In Costa Rica, unlike other Latin American countries, ideological conflict has not tended to polarize: e.g. despite the national consensus in favour of market-oriented

privatization, there is general agreement that, given its limited international economic significance and the globalization of the world economy, the future of Costa Rican development depends on its ability to adapt its productive structure in order to penetrate increasingly diversified foreign markets,[83] and attract international flows of capital and technology. This perception has prevailed particularly among top and medium-ranking government officials and private sector leaders, most of them well-trained technocrats, who have become very alert to the effects that international dynamics may have on the Costa Rican economy.[84]

In this context, COMEX has become crucial for the success of the new development strategy implemented in Costa Rica. A relatively new institution, COMEX was originally established in the mid 1980s as the Ministry of Exports. Its main function then was to promote the diversification of exports and markets for Costa Rican products. As the process of economic reform progressed, and Costa Rica got increasingly involved in bilateral and multilateral trade negotiations, Costa Rican policy makers became aware of the need for a specialized unit, comprising well-trained negotiators, capable of co-ordinating, in a more coherent manner, the international commercial relations of Costa Rica. This led in the late 1980s to the establishment of COMEX, which co-ordinated Costa Rica's accession into GATT in 1989–90, and since then has become the Ministry in charge of directing the bilateral and multilateral foreign trade negotiations of the country.

COMEX has become the Costa Rican Government's main tool for taking advantage of the increasing legalization of the international trade system. Indeed, in an increasingly interdependent world where economic and political power tends to concentrate in a limited number of states, international agreements—both at the bilateral and multilateral level—are one of the scant instruments small economies have at their disposal to defend their interests.

---

reform, there is also general agreement on maintaining state participation in several sectors considered essential for the social and economic development of Costa Rican society. That is the case for several public enterprises in strategic sectors, such as electricity, telecommunications, oil refining and some health services.

[83] The concept of 'market niches' is spreading widely among Costa Rican economic policy-makers and exporters: the small scale of the Costa Rican economy relative to most export markets allows substantial increases in exports without necessarily reaching an important market share in the recipient country. This has been perceived as a great potential advantage, as it means less problems with local protectionist interest groups in the main world markets, i.e. the US, Europe, and Asia.

[84] This perception is based on the testimony of representatives of the chambers of industry, commerce, agriculture, finance and sugar producers before the Special Congressional Commission on the Uruguay Round.

11.4.2.2 General perceptions of GATT and the WTO: national interests and sovereignty

In Costa Rica, unlike other GATT contracting parties, the establishment of the WTO and a new multilateral régime to regulate international commercial relations does not seem to be perceived as a threat to national sovereignty. The rapid and almost unanimous approval of the Uruguay Round Agreements in the Costa Rican Legislative Assembly clearly supports this perception. Rather than being seen as a threat to national sovereignty, the multilateral trade system of GATT (and now the WTO) tends to be perceived among policy-makers and the private sector as the very opposite: that is, that to be part of the WTO is an advantage, and not a burden, for Costa Rica. This view stems from the fact that signing the Uruguay Round Agreements has been considered as an extra element within a broader economic strategy; which aims at incorporating Costa Rica into an international economic order which is not only increasingly interdependent, but also poses serious potential threats to Costa Rican commercial interests. Being a small country, Costa Rica is particularly vulnerable to unilateral protectionist practices implemented by those developed countries where Costa Rican exports are marketed, in particular the United States and the European Union. Thus, the increasingly rule-oriented trade system entailed by GATT and the WTO—a forum where Costa Rica can also aspire to build alliances with other contracting parties with similar concerns—is clearly perceived as one of the scant instruments available for defending national interests in the international trade arena. This perception prevails despite the sour experience of the so-called *Banana Case* against the European Union. Although two panel reports favoured Costa Rica's claims and declared restrictions on banana imports into the European Union to be inconsistent with GATT, these reports have not been adopted by the GATT Council. This has been due to the Europeans' insistence on blocking the consensus required for adopting both panel reports.

As GATT and the WTO entail an increasing dismantling of barriers to trade, Costa Rican policy makers have become aware that, rather than access to export markets, the real challenge for a small export economy like Costa Rica will be to attract increasing flows of investment, both national and foreign. Considering the prevailing patterns of international production and global sourcing,[85] the establishment of regional trade blocs

---

[85] For further detail on the various patterns of international production, and the significance of regional integration in this respect, see R. Van Whiting, 'The dynamics of regionalization: road map to an open future?', in P. Smith (ed.), *The Challenges of Integration: Europe and the Americas* (1993).

also poses the implicit risk for Costa Rica of being excluded from the international capital and technology flows it requires for its long-term development. Thus, regionalism, and, in particular, potential accession into an expanded North American Free Trade Agreement, has become one of the topics which has attracted the attention of Costa Rican policymakers and public opinion since President Bush's announcement, in June 1990, of the Enterprise for the Americas Initiative.

Costa Rica's insertion into the world economy is, then, increasingly perceived by policy-makers as a double-track process: at a multilateral level through GATT and the WTO, and at a regional level, through the establishment of free trade areas with those countries which, representing important or potential markets for Costa Rican exports, agree to do so.[86] Thus, in 1994 Costa Rica signed a free trade agreement with Mexico. This treaty follows the fundamental features of NAFTA, and consequently, entails obligations which 'bite' much more than any of the commitments agreed in the Uruguay Round. As is widely recognized, it is easier to agree on substantial liberalization commitments on a bilateral level, than under the aegis of an organization where the interests of more than one hundred countries have to be reconciled. Because the Costa Rica–Mexico Free Trade Agreement contains obligations which are substantially more intrusive than those of the Uruguay Round, it should not be surprising that the former agreement became much more politically sensitive than the GATT accords. This explains why most of the discussions of the special legislative commission studying both accords centered on the bilateral free trade area. Compared with the Costa Rica–Mexico Free Trade Agreement, the Uruguay Round looked like a 'soft' agreement which did not generate any reaction from any organized interest group. It also explains why the Legislative Assembly approved the Uruguay Round Agreements without delay.

---

[86] Costa Rica is one of the Latin American countries anxiously expecting free trade negotiations with the US, which is Costa Rica's main trade partner. In 1990 46% of Costa Rican exports were sold in the US, and 40.8% of Costa Rican imports came from there. (Source: UN Statistical Office, UN COMTRADE data base, New York.)

12

THE RESULTS OF THE URUGUAY ROUND IN BRAZIL: LEGAL AND CONSTITUTIONAL ASPECTS OF IMPLEMENTATION

*Paulo Borba Casella**

12.1 CONCEPTUAL REMARKS

The implementation of the results of the Uruguay Round, in Brazil, as elsewhere, is an ongoing process and an open-ended task. The reasons for this include the depth and breadth of necessary measures as well as the fact that a constitutional revision is under way in the country. Implementation remains open-ended for many other relevant reasons, internal and external, legal and economical, and structural. Other factors include the regional economic agreements, such as those between Brazil and its partners within the framework of the Common Market of the South, with Argentina, Paraguay and Uruguay.[1]

Although it is hard to describe a building when you can only see an empty construction site, this is the right time for such a conceptual effort: to the extent that the complete building can be envisaged, a better evaluation of ongoing implementation measures can be attempted. This, nevertheless, is more easily said than done.

My goal is not only to describe the internal legal environments as they stand today, and into which the outcome of the Uruguay Round of

---

* University of São Paulo Law School & partner CASELLA, CUNHA & MARQUES Advogados, São Paolo.
[1] As this will be emphasized to differing levels and extent by various contributors to this volume, it is not necessary to divert the focus away from Brazil, as the specific country in question, except for a few hints at the relevance for law of the international trade issues related to the Mercosul Agreement.

The Mercosul Agreement (Treaty of Asunción, 26 Mar. 1991 and subsequent Protocols, especially the Protocol of Ouro Preto, 17 Dec. 1994) provides for a common market among Argentina, Brazil, Paraguay and Uruguay. After completion of most of a free trade zone, within the scheduled transition period (1991–94), the Mercosul countries are paving the way for a customs union (to be completed in two phases, by 2001 and 2006) and thereafter opening up the prospect of a (so far not clearly drawn) full common market. Such joint effort unavoidably has a bearing on issues related to the implementation of the results of the Uruguay Round, in the case of a country like Brazil.

The Mercosul–European Union agreement, 15 Dec. 1995, provides an interesting interregnal perspective for analysis.

multilateral trade negotiations will be inserted and have to operate, but also to indicate, tentatively, what should or could be. The law of international trade is a new and creative legal field, and its international framework is being consolidated.[2]

The relevance of such evaluation does not make it any less difficult; and at this point in time, it not only seems hard to be achieved, but will have to face the test of subsequent developments, in order to have its adequacy ascertained. But, the evolution of international trade in the last decades— and the growing legal framework to regulate such activities—together with the trading behaviour of countries should allow a sufficient basis for evaluation of both short and medium term perspectives.[3]

12.2 THE LEGAL PERSPECTIVE

Law has a vital role to play in the new world context. The view needs no further emphasis when placed against the background of world events in the last few years. There is no need to push the focus too far into the past, provided we consider the substantial, and, up to a very significant scale, quite unexpected changes which have occurred since 1989.

An extraordinary example is the outcome of the Uruguay Round of multilateral trade negotiations, the eighth round of General Agreement on Tariffs and Trade negotiations, the most extensive of its kind. It is noteworthy for its duration, but also for the number of states involved, for the list of matters discussed and subject to regulation, and last—but not least—the completion of the institutional framework, with the World Trade Organization replacing the former 'provisional' GATT structure, and all the complexities resulting therefrom.

This institutional framework, which the GATT 'provisional' structure has lacked since it was signed in 1947, has eventually been set up, under the

---

[2] D. Kennedy 'The international style in post-war law and policy: John Jackson and the field of international economic law' (1995) 10 AUJIL&P 671 evidences how much the consolidation of the law of international trade, as a legal discipline, owes to a single individual legal scholar.

The invitation made by Professors John H. Jackson and Alan Sykes to review the matter in this truly international perspective was most stimulating.

As recently as 1995, Patrick Juillard still inquired 'existe-t-il des principes généraux du droit international économique?' (in *L'internationalité dans les institutions et le droit: convergences et défis—études offertes à Alain Plantey* (1995), 243–52).

[3] Although projected to a wider and still more complex context, the conceptual framework and most of the analysis done by J. H. Jackson, J.-V. Louis and M. Matsushita (eds.), in *Implementing the Tokyo Round: national constitutions and international economic rules* (1984) is and remains both valid and inspiring, notwithstanding that more than a decade has elapsed since then.

new World Trade Organization (WTO). Whole new areas, not included before, are now regulated by WTO rules, while new and hopefully better dispute settlement mechanisms have been set up and will be ready to operate as well. Gaps persist, and will have to be progressively filled in, by both common WTO and domestic rules and practices, but the results achieved as stated in the Final Act embodying the results of the Uruguay Round of Multilateral Trade Negotiations, signed in Marrakesh on 15 April 1994, are quite impressive. We will all have to learn how to operate within this new framework.

Law has a vital role to play in the new system; and its role will depend on the effective implementation of the rules within the legal systems of each signatory state. After completion of the negotiation round, there is a considerable amount of work yet to be done to ensure effective implementation. To that effect, it is both extremely timely as well as challenging to address the issue and dwell on the legal and constitutional aspects of the implementation of the results of the Uruguay Round in Brazil.

12.3 NEW CONTEXT FOR WORLD TRADE

We now have the opportunity to operate in, and to develop a world trade context, that is simultaneously liberalized and regulated to levels never experienced before, yet in which considerable areas remain and necessarily will remain under the control of each state. International law, notwithstanding the existence of general rules of *jus cogens*—as acknowledged, *inter alia*, by the Vienna Convention of 1969, in Article 53—and extensive unregulated trade practice, due to its incompleteness as a system,[4] combines the obligation to observe international rules with a lack of mechanisms to ensure effective implementation of most of these rules. In short, international law does exist; but in order to ensure its effect, states all have to play a vital role in enforcing it.[5] The implementation by each

---

[4] 'Le droit international, si on le compare au droit interne, reste un droit incomplet, comportant des lacunes et soumis comme tel à l'arbitraire et à l'action discrétionnaire de l'État dans les zones encore soustraites à la règle de droit', C. Rousseau, *Traité de droit international public* (2nd. ed., 1970) vol. I, sec. 35.A.b, 53. See also C. Fitzmaurice 'The problem of non-liquet: prolegomena to a Restatement' in *La communauté internationale: mélanges offerts à Charles Rousseau* (1974), 89.

[5] B. Conforti, *International Law and the Role of Domestic Legal Systems* trans. R. Provost; C. D. de A. Mello, *Direito internacional econômico* (1993); id., *Direito constitucional internacional—uma introdução* (Constituição de 1988, revista em 1994; 1994); P. B. Casella, *Comunidade Européia e seu ordenamento jurídico* (1994); id., *Verfassungsrechtliche Hindernisse der wirtschaftlichen Integration* (1997); id., *MERCOSUL: exigências e perspectivas—integração e consolidação de espaço econômico* (1996); id., *Instituições do MERCOSUL* (1997).

state within its own legal system may lead to different results and quite a few new legal issues, such as in the case of the Federative Republic of Brazil. International legal scholarship dwelt extensively on the matter, both abroad and in Brazil.[6]

12.4 STATE SOVEREIGNTY AND INTERNATIONAL
ECONOMIC INTERDEPENDENCE

States, according to their needs, are led to create devices for co-operation, whose extent, competence and powers will be determined by the nature and level of co-operation required in each area of activity. This is not to be viewed as detrimental to the existence and the (at least theoretically unbound extension of) sovereignty of the state; but may be better assessed in a strategic analysis of costs and benefits between prerogatives relinquished and comparative advantages obtained.

[6] Rousseau, *Droit international public*, vol. I, sec. 35. A.b, 53; Fitzmaurice, 'Problem of non-liquet'; A. Cassese, *International law in a divided world* (1984); id., *Modern Constitutions and International Law* (RCADI, 1985–III, t. 192, 476); Conforti, *International Law*; and M. N. Shaw, *International Law* (3rd edn., 1991). For a Brazilian approach to this matter, see *inter alia*. C. D. de A. Mello, *Curso de direito internacional público* (7th rev. edn., 1982); id., 'Constituição e relações internacionais' in J. Dolinger (ed.), *A nova Constituição e o direito internacional* (1987) 19–37; id., *Direito internacional econômico*; id., *Direito constitucional internacional*; id., *Direito internacional americano—estudo sobre a contribuição de um direito regional para a integração econômica* (1995); id., Direito internacional da integração (1996); V. M. Rangel, *Do conflito entre a Carta das Nações Unidas e os demais acordos internacionais* (1954); id., 'La procédure de conclusion des accords internationaux au Brésil, (1960) 55 Rev. FDUSP 253; id., 'Os conflitos entre o direito interno e os tratados internacionais' (1967) 23 Bol. SBDI 45–46, 29); id., 'Solução pacífica de controvérsias no MERCOSUL: estudo preliminar' (ILAM, 1993); id., 'Solução de controvérsias após Ouro Preto', in P.B. Casella (ed.) *Contratos internacionais e direito econômico no MERCOSUL* (1996) 692–701; J. F. Rezek, *Direito dos Tratados* (1984); id., *Direito internacional público: curso elementar* (5th edn., 1995); J. G. Rodas, *Alguns problemas de direito dos tratados*, relacionados com o direito constitucional, à luz da Convenção de Viena (Coimbra, vol. XIX of the Law School Bull., 1972); id., 'The doctrine of non-reactivity of international treaties', 68 (1973) II Rev. FDUSP 341; id., 'Os acordos em forma simplificada' 68 (1973) I Rev. FDUSP 319; id., 'Jus cogens em direito internacionale' 69 (1974) II Rev. FDUSP 125; id., 'Depositário dos tratados internacionais' (Coimbra, vol. LI of the Law School Bull., 1976); id., *A publicidade dos tratados internacionais* (S. Paulo, Ed. RT, 1980); id., (ed.), *Contratos internacionais* (2nd edn., 1995); J. Dolinger & K. S. Rosenn (eds.), *A Panorama of Brazilian Law* (1992); J. Dollinger, 'Brazilian Supreme Court solutions for conflicts between domestic and international law: an exercise in eclecticism' (1993) Cap. U.L. Rev., 22.1993, 1041; id., *Direito internacional privado: parte geral* (3rd. edn., 1994); J. Dollinger & C. Tiburcio, *Vade-mecum de direito internacional privado: direito positivo nacional e estrangeiro—tratados e convenções internacionais* (1994). Evidence that this is a controversial issue in Brazil is given by reference to some of the authors who have dealt with the matter reaching differing conclusions. Legal scholarship and case law differ conceptually on the matter. While case law reflects actual view, legal doctrine holds the more appropriate conceptual view of the matter, rejecting the possibility of changes resulting from subsequent internal legislation.

This is neither the place nor the time to dare to resolve issues such as the confrontation between monism and dualism, or the issue of sovereignty *vis-à-vis* co-operation/integration imperatives, but these are matters that have to be noted for their implications in the matter of implementation of GATT/WTO rules. They are and have to remain as a backscreen against which a bundle of 'minor' or 'technical' hurdles may be viewed more adequately as a whole.

The existence, participation and operation of international organizations, since the end of the nineteenth century but especially after the end of the Second World War, has brought the issues of state sovereignty, the existence of an international legal order, and the need for co-ordinated action and co-operation to the foreground. This context is not to be viewed simplistically as just a 'loss' of the independence and the sovereignty of each state, as it actually—and unavoidably—also is. At the same time, a higher level of common regulation also implies an extension in the level of co-ordinated action; and the possibility for a state to influence commercial policies and trade practices of other states—leading to the possibility of taking action against trade partners who adopt trade practices that might be considered unfair and/or inconsistent with common rules.

As a founding member of GATT which has been very active over the years—much more extensively than in most other areas of international law—Brazil has been chosen as a case, significant enough to be picked up for separate review in this collective study. The country does not seem to be faced with insurmountable obstacles, but open areas remain to be filled in.

Great concern must be devoted to nationalistic opinions. These are voiced more often than might be desired: in Congress, in the media, and also in the academic milieu. They include objections to the extent to which a country like Brazil has let itself be bound by such common regulations, both in the case of the integration process taking place within the Common Market of the South (MERCOSUL), as well as within the new institutional and legal WTO framework. There are also interesting interactions between the two projects or processes.

The MERCOSUL integration project has already reached the level of a free trade zone, implementing, in the coming years, a customs union (for the majority of products until 2001, and for the areas subject to exceptions, until 2006).[7] But in order to have its features as a common market achieved—the free flow of goods, services, persons, and capital combined with co-ordinated policies and supranational, directly applicable and uniformly interpreted rules—the four States will have to decide whether and to what extent they are ready and willing to create supranational

---

[7] The Protocol of Ouro Preto (see n. 1), marked the completion of the transition period.

institutions. Determination of the extent of the powers to be ascribed to such institutions remain as open issues, which are crucial to the future of the whole integration process.[8]

12.5 FUNDAMENTAL ASPECTS OF THE BRAZILIAN LEGAL SYSTEM AND THE 1988 CONSTITUTION: THE TREATY-MAKING POWER

The negotiation and ratification of the Marrakesh Final Act of the Uruguay Round multilateral trade negotiations has been performed in accordance with, and under the provisions of, Brazilian constitutional law and practice.

The Brazilian Constitution of 5 October 1988, was revised in 1993–94, and was still undergoing revision as of late 1995.[9] Such revision aims to provide more structured guidelines and a clearer focus than the previous heterogeneous ensemble of non-constitutional provisions which had been pushed into the constitutional text. The proliferation of non-constitutional matters in the Constitution is one reasonable explanation for the need of revision; this was acutely felt shortly after the present Constitution came into force as of 5 October 1988.

As it stands, the Brazilian Constitution of 1988, now undergoing revision, may be categorized as a *dirigiste*-type constitution; adopting a presidential, rather than a parliamentary system of government, and embodying a whole title—Title VII—regulating 'economic and financial order'. It is the most hotly debated and controversial part of the constitutional text. Specifically, this new part of the Constitution is under more substantial revision. Once the revision is completed, a better assessment will be possible. For now, the following can be said. The political and administrative organization of the Federative Republic of Brazil (Title III, Articles 18–43) sets up a three-level federation,

---

[8] For a review of some issues related to the integration processes see extensive bibliographical references on the EU, NAFTA, the Andean Pact and Mercosul, and specifically in connection with constitutional and legal issues see references in P. B. Casella, *Comparative Approach to Competition Law in the European Communities and the MERCOSUL* ('Vortrag vor dem Europa-Institut der Universität des Saarlandes, Saarbrücken, den 20. Juli 1993', VRBEI, vol. 301, 1993); id., *Comunidade Européia e seu ordenamento jurídico* (1994); id., *Verfassungsrechtliche Hindernisse der wirtschaftlichen Integration* (1997); id., *MERCOSUL: exigências e perspectivas—integração e consolidação de espaço econômico* (1996); id., *Instituições do MERCOSUL* (1997). For a different perspective with interesting results, see also APEC, *Achieving the APEC Vision: free and open trade in the Asian Pacific* (1994) (2nd Rep. of the Eminent Persons' Group).

[9] Republica Federativa do Brasil *Constituição* ('texto constitucional de 5 de outubro de 1988 com as alterações adotadas pelas Emendas constitucionais nos. 1/92 a 4/93 e pelas Emendas constitucionais de revisão nos. 1 a 6/94', Brasília, Senado Federal, 1994).

comprising the union, the states, the federal district and the counties (*municípios*).

The very idea of this *dirigiste* constitutional model is that the Constitution does more than organize power, being a programme for shaping society. It sets out goals, and traces plans and programmes to achieve them. It has a prescriptive character, and it is precisely through these prescriptions that it tries to direct governmental action. As the supreme law, the constitution defines a 'permanent political direction' to be imposed upon governments constituted in accordance with its rules, making any 'governmental political direction' only a 'contingent political direction'.

The Constitution thus ceases to be merely 'procedural law' or an 'instrument of government' that allocates powers, regulates procedures and sets up limits; it becomes instead 'substantive law' that rigidly preordains goals, objectives and means. All governmental activity should be tied to this 'substantive law'. But as pointed out by Ferreira Jr., the Constitution remains 'ineffectual, and therefore unenforceable', and he adds, 'when the Constituent Assembly completed the Constitution and became only the Congress, it appears to have lost all interest in completing its work, particularly in completing the novel measures it adopted. None of the non-self-executing norms that abound in the Constitution have yet been regulated. Consequently the only provisions currently in force are those that are self-executing'.[10]

To the conceptual problems contained in the Brazilian Constitution of 1988 should be added implementation lacunae as well, especially in connection with the economic and financial order (Title VII, Articles 170–192) and the social order (Title VIII, Articles 193–232). Against such lacunae are to be held the 'general principles', as providing guidelines for the whole, such as, for example, Article 4, listing principles regulating Brazilian foreign relations, among which peaceful dispute settlement and co-operation for the progress of mankind are listed (Paragraphs vii and ix).

The Republic is the holder of the legal personality of international law, and its prerogatives are exercised by the Union through joint action of the executive and the Congress. According to Article 21, listing competences of the Union, the first item stipulates 'relations with foreign states and participation in international organizations'. Among exclusive competencies of the Union for legislation, listed in Article 22, is mentioned in Item I, *inter alia*, trade law (*direito comercial*).

---

[10] M. G. Ferreira Jr. Gonçalves, 'Fundamental aspects of the 1988 Constitution' in Dolinger & Rosenn, *Panorama of Brazilian Law*, 11.

Legislative power is exercised by the National Congress, composed of the Deputy Chamber and the Federal Senate, as stated in Article 44. Prerogatives of the Congress are listed (Articles 48 ff.), among which is mentioned in Article 49, Item I, as an exclusive competence of the Congress, the prerogative 'to decide definitively about treaties, agreements or international acts creating charges or commitments pledging national estate'.

Treaties, agreements and international acts are forwarded by the Ministry for Foreign Affairs (Ministério das Relações Exteriores) to the Deputy Chamber. If the text is not approved by the Deputy Chamber, the text will not go further. Nevertheless, the President may repeat the submission of a previously rejected text. Amendments may not be inserted to the text of a treaty but reservations may, either upon signature or forwarded jointly with the ratification instrument.

Among competences of the President of the Republic, stated in Article 84, are listed in Items VII and VIII, 'relations with foreign states and agreement to their representatives' as well as power to 'sign treaties, conventions and international acts, subject to referendum of the National Congress'. The signature is authorized or carried by the Presidency or a representative, diplomatic or other, but the approval of the text is incumbent upon the Congress, and is made by a legislative decree. Thereafter, promulgation of the treaty, 'becoming law' for internal effect, is made by presidential decree. Publication of the law in the *Official Gazette* (*Diário Oficial da União*) is mandatory to ensure that its contents are made known to the public, and are the reference for quotation of the legal text.

A relevant distinction is to be made between international effect of a treaty, following its ratification, and the internal effect of a treaty, 'becoming law' for internal effect through its publication by presidential decree. Therefore ratification necessarily precedes internal effect, but does not automatically imply that it will result.

In trade matters like the GATT/WTO rules, implementation goes beyond the formal requirements listed. The relevant test will be its effective interpretation and application.

12.6 WTO NEGOTIATION AND RATIFICATION FROM THE BRAZILIAN PERSPECTIVE

The new WTO framework is contained in the Message No. 498/1994, from the Presidency to the Congress, which thereafter approved the Uruguay Round agreements. The Federal Republic of Brazil's ratification of the Final Act of the Uruguay Round was deposited in Geneva with the

General-Director of GATT on 21 December 1994, being in force for Brazil as of 1 January 1995. The contents of the Final Act of the Uruguay Round, with Annexes I to IV, were published by Decree No. 1355, dated 30 December 1994, in the *Federal Official Gazette* (*Diário Oficial da União*).[11]

The Final Act of Multilateral Commercial Negotiations, as stated in the Presidential Message to Congress, includes 'two sets of instruments, the most relevant being the series of multilateral agreements, declarations and decisions, bound together in a sole indivisible package, which has to be accepted or rejected as a whole'. The second set refers to specific plurilateral instruments which shall be binding only for the countries adopting them: Agreement on Trade in Civil Aircraft, Agreement on Government Procurement, International Dairy Agreement, International Bovine Meat Agreement, 'of which only this last one has been signed by Brazil', as specified in the message.

The successful conclusion of the Uruguay Round, as stated in the Presidential Message,

before every other consideration, is a guarantee of preservation and strengthening of the multilateral trade system, setting aside the risk of breaking up international trade in self-contained blocs. Its impact will bring new drive for international economic activity, making it possible, through increase in trade and fostering investments, to resume growth, and improve employment levels.

It is worth quoting the following extracts from the Presidential Message, as they focus on the relevance of implementation of the results of the Uruguay Round:

I stress that those general benefits, as well as those specifically resulting from specific sector or subject negotiations have as their natural counterpart, the obligation for each GATT contracting party, to adapt, to the extent necessary, its policies and legislation to the results of the Uruguay Round, as a corollary of the necessity of maintaining the multilateral trade system and its agreement foundations.[12]

The agreements signed constitute tools for the liberalization and standardization of the most varied sectors related to international trade. The main advances towards trade liberalization within the Uruguay Round are situated in the areas of market access, where, as estimated, an average global reduction of about 40 per cent is expected, within the six years following the coming into force of the results of the negotiation.

Additionally, the Presidential Message points out that:

(1) agriculture is re-incorporated into the general GATT rules, to which is added the freezing and start of reversing subsidy schemes;

---

[11] See n. 23.
[12] In the original version in Portuguese: 'preservar o sistema multilateral de comércio e sua base consensual'.

(2) non-tariff barriers to textile products—a sector subject to old unfair discriminatory quota practices against developing countries—is re-integrated to GATT discipline; and

(3) the agreement brings regulation of so-called new areas, that is, services, intellectual property, and investment.

From an institutional point of view, still according to the Presidential Message to Congress, there were also relevant advances. 'With the setting up of the WTO and the improvement of dispute settlement regulation, anti-dumping, subsidies, and countervailing measures are regulated in a clearer and firmer way, as is the performance of countries in international trade; thereby reducing the capacity of arbitrary and non-discriminating protection measures by the great trade powers, for sectors not efficient in their economies'.

Let me now elaborate on these points, indicating what Brazil has perceived as the important gains from the Uruguay Round, justifying ratification.

12.6.1 Market access

It is estimated that the average tariff on Brazilian products will be reduced 36 per cent by the European Union, 24 per cent by the United States and 57 per cent by Japan, which means a relevant improvement of market access of our exports to those markets.

'Some relevant products of our export agenda had their tariffs reduced to zero, with the exception of pulp, paper, wood, beer, and metals not including iron. As a result of hard negotiations, the country also obtained profits in sectors such as shoes and orange juice, which traditionally had a high level of protection in third markets.' In the case of orange juice, the reduction was 20 per cent in the European Union and 15 per cent in the United States.

The Presidental Message stressed that 'In order to obtain such results, Brazil did not have to make any additional concessions to the import liberalization process unilaterally started in 1987'; and it went on to stress that the Brazilian offer for freezing a global average of 35 per cent, and a specific level of 55 per cent for some more sensitive agricultural products leaves a wide margin for subsequent adaptations eventually necessary in our commercial policy.

12.6.2 Agriculture

The Agreement on Agriculture sets up, for the first time at multilateral level and under the aegis of GATT, specific rules for the production and trade of agricultural products. Additionally, it freezes and starts reversion of a growing tendency towards protectionist policies, which implied heavy schemes of subsidies to production and to export, as well as import quotas and prohibitions. The Agreement on Agriculture sets up specific rules for subsidies and countervailing duties for this sector, not included in the Agreement on Subsidies.

An important innovation for Brazil was the tariffication agreement, whereby all non-tariff barriers applicable to trade in agricultural products were turned into tariffs, to which is added minimum level of market access, according to which between 3–5 per cent of supply is to be met by imports. Similarly, the understanding reached for reduction, within six years, to 36 per cent of budget value and 21 per cent of the total amount, of agricultural exports benefiting from subsidies, will have a positive impact on access of our exports to the markets of Brazil's main trading partners, and reduce unfair competition with Brazilian products in third markets.

12.6.3 Textiles

The Agreement on Textiles and Clothing stipulates the breaking up of restrictions to textile exports, made under the Multifiber Agreement, for a period of ten years. After the lapse of such period, considered as a transition, textile trade will be totally reintegrated to the general rules of GATT. 'This agreement represents the achievement of a long-term objective for Brazil, of wider access to developed markets (i.e., markets of developed countries). Contingent factors have led the Brazilian export efforts to slow down, such as obsolescence of equipment and the reduction of investments in this sector. Notwithstanding, basically, the country has a great potential to compete in an international market liberalized by GATT rules.'

12.6.4 Services

The General Agreement on Trade in Services is explained by the Presidential Message to Congress as 'a master agreement containing principles and rules that shall regulate, in a flexible way, trade in this sector, aiming at its liberalization. Once the results of the Uruguay Round are in force, a dynamic negotiating process will have started, giving a more concrete dimension to the provisions of the General Agreement.'

In 1992, services already contributed to more than 57 per cent of the total gross domestic product, but nevertheless they represent only 10 per cent of Brazilian exports. The reduced competitiveness which characterizes many Brazilian activities in services inspired a cautious position along the negotiations of the Uruguay Round. The liberalization of world markets should be seen from the perspective of the contribution it will bring to the growth of our exports in services.

'The text of the master agreement maintains the necessary flexibility to allow the country to undertake internationally only commitments compatible with the legal status in each sector. The list of the commitments initially undertaken by Brazil contains a limited number of sectors. In those areas, the country agreed to be bound maintaining the status quo. In most cases, such commitment refers only to the installation of service suppliers in the country (commercial presence), which tends to foster direct investment.'

12.6.5 Intellectual property

The Agreement on Trade-related Aspects of Intellectual Property Rights, according to the Presidential Message to Congress is to viewed favourably, 'to the extent the agreement sets up multilaterally agreed rules for protection of intellectual property rights. The agreement limits the capacity for arbitrary action by signatories, concerning unilateral interpretation of commercial defense measures.'

12.6.6 Institutional aspects

One of the most relevant innovations for Brazil in the Uruguay Round refers to strengthening multilateral trade rules, of which the setting up of the WTO is the most visible instrument. Among its main functions, the WTO will provide multilateral administration of an integrated dispute settlement system, more efficient and more transparent, that is to contribute to restricting the margin for arbitrary measures and unilateralism by major trading powers in bilateral dispute settlement.

The new anti-dumping and countervailing duties codes, as well as a new agreement on safeguards—areas where ambiguities have led to sometimes serious distortions in the use of trade defence measures—henceforth have clearer and firmer rules. Such rules, in addition to representing greater multilateral safety, will impart more efficiency to dispute settlement mechanisms.

The Presidential Message to Congress also stressed that signatory states were bound, as agreed in the Ministerial Meeting in Marrakesh, to have completed internal ratification procedures within a term, and in order to enable the WTO to operate as of 1 January 1995; it commented:

I am convinced that the approval of this series of agreements constitutes a relevant Brazilian contribution to strengthening the multilateral trade system, a *sine qua non* condition for the preservation and promotion of Brazilian external trade, and a progressively better insertion of the country in the world economic system, which are inseparable elements of its economic and social development.

Because of ratification, the implementation of the results of the Uruguay Round and the new WTO framework may be viewed as a settled matter in Brazil. At the same time it is and remains an open issue in Brazil, from both legal and technical viewpoints, and to the extent that it is yet to be experienced, through strict observance, thus testing the limits of its effective implementation.

12.7 GATT RULES IN BRAZIL AND THE NEW WTO FRAMEWORK

GATT rules are in force and subject to regular interpretation and application in Brazil. Extensive case law may be quoted applying GATT rules to tax exemptions.[13] For example, according to Federal Supreme Court consolidated case law (*Súmula* 575) 'to goods imported from a GATT signatory or a LAFTA [Latin American Free Trade Association eventually replaced by LAIA (Latin American Integration Association)] member state is extended the exemption of tax on circulation of goods granted to its national equivalent'.[14]

While Brazilian legislation already followed GATT parameters strictly, and the 'new' WTO rules have accordingly been enacted for internal effect,[15] it is now dawning in the mind of local operators that such legal tools, far from being hindrances, may be used as strategic weapons to operate in the fierce competition of freer international trade, as stipulated, for example, by anti-dumping and anti-subsidy codes.[16]

Another issue is to make rules more widely known.[17] This is not only a question of legal measures but also of making the average entrepreneur aware of their existence, contents and effects, both for internal and for external use.

Yet another more delicate and politically harder task is to ensure the

---

[13] See A. de A. Mercadante's *Acordo Geral sobre Tarifas Aduaneiras e Comércio (GATT): instrumentos básicos* (1988) 1–99.

[14] *Súmula* 575. 'A mercadoria importada de país signatário do GATT, ou membro da ALALC, estende-se a isenção do imposto de circulação de mercadoria concedida a similar nacional.'

[15] Leg. Decr. no. 30, 15 Dec. 1994, approved the text of the Uruguay Round, and this has been enacted by Decr. no. 1335, 30 Dec. 1994, in force as of 1 Jan. 1995.

[16] Anti-Dumping and Anti-Subsidy Codes were enforced in Brazil in accordance with Decr. nos. 93.941/1986 & 93.962/1987, with corresponding Administrative regs.
Changes to the Anti-dumping Agreement required a new law, viz. Law no. 9019, 30 Mar. 1995, resulting from approval of the results of the Uruguay Round. In turn, Decr. no. 1602, 23 Aug. 1995, regulated rules concerning administrative procedures related to application of anti-dumping measures.

[17] To that effect timely and necessary are initiatives such as the present volume, J. H. Bourgeois, F. Berrod & E. Gippini-Fournier (eds.), *The Uruguay Round results: a European lawyer's perspective* (1995), and P. B. Casella & A. Mercadante (eds.), *Guerra comercial: OMC e o Brasil—aspectos de direito internacional* (1996).

adequacy of the implementation through a balanced and correctly interpreted application by national courts, in the face of interpretations tending to give priority to supervening national rules. For example, although the Brazilian Supreme Court has formulated the above quoted rule according to which goods imported from a GATT signatory or a LAFTA/ LAIA member state are extended the ICMS (tax on circulation of services and goods) tax exemption applicable to an equivalent national product, a subsequent constitutional amendment brought a controversial element to that interpretation. Without going into the details, it may fairly be said that the later rule may have disrupting effects on a framework regulated by treaties and conventions such as GATT/WTO.

12.8 FINAL REMARKS

The viability and the necessity of co-ordinated regulation of economic matters is becoming more and more clear and imperative. To this should be added the possibility of exploring and developing comparative advantages to be reached through co-ordination. In order to reach such levels it is imperative to ensure that legal rules play their desired regulatory role, through implementation within each country, as well as through the operation of dispute settlement panels, ensuring the uniformity of interpretation and application for all countries concerned.

For all of the above discussed reasons, any attempt to evaluate WTO implementation in Brazil, at this point in time, is bound to be held as a strictly preliminary overview of the matter, and will require amendment as the implementation procedures are carried further. The uncertainties result from:

- internal changes connected to the constitutional revision still under way, and the corresponding changes in ordinary legislation to result from such constitutional revision;
- regional changes related to and resulting from the consolidation of integration process within the MERCOSUL framework and also the conceptual adequacy of the regional agreement under the general free trade zone and customs union concepts outlined by GATT/WTO rules; and
- general international change in circumstances.

The basic elements for implementation are present and have been laid down. How far these will be worked down to the last detail remains yet to be seen, in the next few years.

Clearly enough, Brazil is not an isolated case. Greater consciousness of the need for a comprehensive regulatory system for world trade is becoming unavoidable. This is and will remain a necessity for all countries engaged in foreign trade, which paradoxically leaves ever fewer out of this category—very few, if any, countries could possibly survive estranged from international trade—as isolationist models literally go bankrupt. What remains yet to be seen is what shall be the model for 'the regulation of international trade'[18] in the next few years.

What also remains yet to be seen is how the greater level of international co-operation will be integrated into institutions and legal systems.[19]

A new and broader frame of mind seems required to that effect. Such a frame of mind is yet to be developed, adding a specifically human challenge to the regulatory framework of the law of international trade.

---

[18] See *inter alia*. M. J. Trebilcock & R. Howse, *The regulation of international trade* (1995); G. Sacerdoti & S. Alessandrini, *Regionalismo economico e sistema globale degli scambi* (1994).

[19] In that sense some of the issues had already been discussed in *Les moyens de pression économiques et le droit international* ('Actes du colloque de la Société belge de droit international; Palais des Académies de Bruxelles, 26–27 octobre 1984') (1985); see also P. B. Casella, 'O advogado brasileiro e o desafio da internacionalização na prestação de serviços', in L. O. Baptista, H. M. Huck & P. B. Casella (eds.), *Direito e comércio internacional: tendências e perspectivas—estudos em homenagem a Ireneu Strenger* (1994); Plantey, *L'internationalité dans les institutions et le droit*; J. H. F. van Panhuys, *Relations and interactions between international and national scenes of law* (RCADI, 1964–II, t. 112, 1).

13

QUESTIONS AND COMPARISONS

John H. Jackson and Alan O. Sykes

Each of the papers in this volume reflects a different perspective on the relationship between national legal systems and international economic law. Although the authors considered a common set of questions, the resulting papers exhibit considerable diversity on many fronts. For example, in some of the papers, issues relating to federalism and 'subsidiarity' receive great attention. In others, the relationship among branches of government at the central government level were more important. Some of the papers exhibit much concern for the status of the international accords in domestic law and the question of 'direct applicability' or 'invocability'. For still others, the focus is more one of administration, and with the massive task of conforming domestic law to the detailed requirements of the World Trade Organization. A common theme in many of the papers concerns the role of interest groups in the negotiation and implementation process, and their impact on both the international agreement and on the domestic implementation process.

Despite the heterogeneity among the papers and their emphasis, we hope that readers will not find them unconnected and parochial. Rather, we believe that the papers in this volume raise a host of broader issues that deserve further consideration and research. In this concluding chapter, we identify some of these issues in the hope that we may encourage other scholars to pursue them.

13.1 THE VERTICAL AGENCY PROBLEM: FEDERALISM, SUBSIDIARITY, AND NEGOTIATING COMPETENCE

Particularly in Europe, Canada and the United States, the relationship between the federal government and subsidiary governments (or between Brussels and the European capitals) has had and will continue to have an important impact on the WTO system. During the negotiation process, these relationships created both obstacles and opportunities from the perspective of the negotiators. For example, the need for France to accept the WTO accords before Europe as a whole could accept them ensured that agricultural interests would have a considerable say about the final bargain. And in the United States, the prospects for eventual ratification of the WTO depended importantly on the support of a sufficient number of state legislatures (because of their influence on their Congressional representatives).

Individual states, provinces, and countries within a larger political entity are likely to tend to embody somewhat narrower constituencies than the larger group. One might reasonably speculate, therefore, that a federal structure of government may enhance the power of interest groups and their ability to constrain the outcome of negotiations. This hypothesis seems worthy of additional exploration.

The other side of the issue, however, relates to the agency problems that arise in the negotiation process. Because central governments do the negotiating, subsidiary governments must depend on their central government representatives to represent their interests faithfully. Subsidiary governments with limited sway over their central political figures may thus have their interests sacrificed under circumstances where they have no power to veto the outcome, or where a threat of a veto is not credible. Anticipating this problem, the subsidiary governments may then seek to limit the negotiating competence of their central governments. Nowhere has this type of battle been more prominent than in Europe, where the negotiating competence of Brussels representatives remains unsettled and subject to complex political and legal manœuvering.

These and no doubt other considerations suggest that the outcome of negotiations (or the set of feasible outcomes) can depend very much on the legal rules that govern the relationship between central and subsidiary governments. The delegation of negotiating competence, the information flow during the course of negotiations, and the power of subsidiary governments to block acceptance of the final package can all affect the degree to which the interests of subsidiary governments and their constituencies are pursued effectively.

Federalism and subsidiarity issues also enter at the implementation phase. Many of the issues that are the subject of the WTO accords—technical barriers, phytosanitary and sanitary regulations, and subsidies, for example—involve policies that are administered at least in part by subsidiary governments. The task of ensuring faithful implementation at that level is not an easy one. Indeed, the very existence of such policies that may be at odds with the WTO can reflect the political equilibrium of interest groups at the subsidiary government level that favours their retention. The response to this problem has evolved through the years in the General Agreement on Tariffs and Trade system, with the Uruguay Round achieving apparent convergence on the principle that central governments must do everything in their constitutional power to ensure compliance by subsidiary governments, to avoid violation of international law. But even this principle leaves room for considerable slippage, as perhaps it should. For in many areas, there may be great virtue in allowing certain matters of domestic regulatory policy to be resolved locally in accordance with varying tastes, incomes and other factors. The problem of WTO implementation by subsidiary governments is thus inextricably bound up with the internal problem of how to allocate powers over commerce, health and safety, consumer welfare and the like between central and subsidiary governments. Further study of these issues should do much to help us understand the normative and positive aspects of federal structures.

13.2 THE HORIZONTAL AGENCY PROBLEM:
AUTHORITY AND CREDIBILITY

The horizontal structure of central governments raises a set of related concerns. In one manner or another, all nations within our study have at least a *de facto* division between legislative and executive authorities. And within the executive domain lies a division between politically accountable officials and career bureaucrats.

Without exception, the power to take the lead in Uruguay Round negotiations was entrusted to the executive authority, from which we may infer that any alternative structure would have raised transaction costs unacceptably. The political officials of the executive authority were typically assisted by bureaucrats with sectoral or topical expertise in conducting the detailed negotiations. But this structure raises a multiplicity of agency issues—how does the legislative authority ensure that the executive will pursue its concerns? And how does the executive ensure that bureaucrats do not pursue an agenda of their own, perhaps by controlling the information flow to political officials in such a way as to make unattractive options appear more attractive? These twin problems raise doubts about the ability of the negotiators to serve various interest group constituencies effectively, as well as doubts about the democratic legitimacy of the negotiated outcome.

Partial answers to these problems seem to lie in various devices that ensure ongoing legislative and interest group involvement in the background of the negotiating process. Concerned legislative officials and interest groups work hard to ensure that they remain informed of proposals and counter-proposals. An open flow of information to these entities allows them to mobilize sooner and thus perhaps more effectively their opposition to certain possible outcomes. Likewise, familiar devices for the discipline of bureaucrats—such as the 'revolving door' that leads bureaucrats to seek to please their industrial constituencies—may also be in play to a great extent. And most importantly, it is common for legislative powers to retain in one capacity or another the power to reject altogether the final negotiated package.

But these devices for ensuring faithful interest-group representation by national negotiators carry a price. It is in the nature of trade agreements to liberalize trade in various ways, a process that inevitably creates interest group losers as well as winners. A system that gives too much power to individual interest groups will ensure that negotiations never succeed. Political officials as a whole will wish to go forward with trade agreements, however, whenever the winners gain on balance more than the losers, so that the agreement provides the officials with a net increase in political support. The need to be faithful to constituent interests during negotiations, therefore, must be delicately counterbalanced against the need to prevent disaffected interest groups from scuttling what is a valuable deal on balance.

Here, part of the response seems to be one of limiting the power of individual interest groups to block acceptance of the negotiated package after negotiations are concluded. The fast-track system in the United States may serve that purpose in certain respects, for example, as may the system in Europe where the WTO package was ultimately presented to national parliaments for up or down assent in their areas of competence. It is also a mistake to overlook the possibility of side payments in the political process—a properly-located new public works, project may do much to quiet the opposition of an otherwise hostile legislator.

Yet another opportunity to dampen hostilities to the negotiated outcome may lie in the implementation process. Delayed or imperfect implementation of the international obligation in domestic law may soften the blow to certain groups. If no one abroad complains in the end, one might even argue that such slippage may be valuable to the trading community on balance. Such possibilities lead to another set of issues—the status of international obligations in domestic law.

13.3 THE DOMESTIC EFFECT OF INTERNATIONAL LAW

The domestic implementation of international commitments may be facilitated by the direct incorporation of those commitments into domestic law. Where international obligations become a part of domestic law *automatically*, they are said to be 'directly applicable' or to have 'direct effect'. Their 'priority' is also important—even where direct applicability exists, it may be possible to avoid the international obligation in domestic law through subsequent, inconsistent domestic legislation. This will not be possible where the international obligation has priority over ordinary statutes. A further distinction is often drawn between direct applicability and 'direct invocability', the latter concept meant to capture certain issues of standing. An international obligation may be directly applicable in domestic law, for example, yet certain parties (such as private parties or foreigners) may be prevented from invoking it to their advantage in the domestic legal system. Similar issues arise at the international level—with few exceptions, private parties have no standing to pursue dispute resolution in the WTO.

The papers in this volume reflect a range of attitudes toward the incorporation of international obligations in domestic law. At one end of the continuum, international obligations are not only directly applicable, but international law is superior to ordinary domestic law in the event of a conflict between them (even if the domestic law is subsequent in time—the situation in Costa Rica is particularly striking in this respect). At the other end, international commitments have no direct domestic 'statute-like' effect, and their implementation in domestic law depends entirely on subsequent domestic legislation (for example, in Canada). In between are numerous jurisdictions where the domestic legal effect of the international obligation is subject to considerable uncertainty (such as the European Union and Japan).

Similarly, we see considerable heterogeneity in the extent to which various parties have standing to invoke the international agreement in domestic legal proceedings. In the United States, for example, only the Attorney-General can invoke the WTO accords to strike down inconsistent state legislation. Elsewhere, domestic private parties may have recourse to international law in a domestic court, but foreigners may not (for example, the reciprocity rule in Korea).

The variety in approaches is quite intriguing. It is intriguing, first of all, that international law does not compel direct applicability, either in general or with respect to the WTO agreements in particular. This fact suggests that some advantage is to be gained from its absence. But the source of that advantage is not obvious. The great advantage of direct applicability, of course, is the savings in transaction costs in the legislative process—once the international obligation is accepted, its text becomes the law of the land and further domestic legislation is unnecessary (except where compelled by the international obligation). Anyone familiar with the interstices of Title 19 of the United States Code will immediately appreciate this virtue of direct effect.

Another advantage of direct applicability is that it allows nations to make a firmer commitment to following the international rules. Although domestic judicial interpretations of international rules may depart from the interpretation put forward by other nations, at least there is no chance for slippage through inconsistent implementing legislation. The greater commitment to playing by the rules that may attend direct applicability can, in turn, increase the joint gains from international accords.

Related, an absence of direct applicability seemingly opens the door to greater levels of strategic behaviour. For domestic implementation of international accords can then depart from their requirements, yet no remedy under domestic law will arise. Aggrieved nations must incur the costs of proceeding under international dispute settlement mechanisms, which do not guarantee compliance with the international obligation in the end. And depending on the political situation, private sector interests may be unable to persuade their governments to pursue international dispute resolution, an important consideration given that private parties generally have no direct access to the dispute resolution mechanism of the WTO.

Why should the system tolerate such problems, and sacrifice the apparent benefits of direct applicability? Answers to this question are not obvious, but we offer some possibilities. In some government structures, international treaty obligations lack legitimacy because democratic or representative constitutional procedures for approval of such obligations are lacking. The implementing legislation process thus becomes a form of democratic approval. Another possibility is that some treaties (especially broad-based treaties such as the WTO agreements) have considerable ambiguity in their texts, which would be too difficult to resolve during the negotiation process. Implementing legislation may then be essential to making the obligations concrete enough to have legal force (despite the opportunities for self-serving construction that may arise). A third possibility is that treaties may be exceedingly difficult to change, and slow to adapt to changing circumstances due to the need for consensus or supermajority to modify them. Accordingly, direct applicability (unless modified by the rule that subsequent domestic legislation trumps) might make it impossible for governments to adapt their policies to new developments.[1] Closely related, the absence of direct applicability may stem from the political virtues of appropriate *ex post* adjustments in the terms of the bargain, and the related benefits of entrusting the ultimate enforcement of the agreement to a more political process. Suppose, for example, that France or California has a powerful interest group that wishes its government to proceed in a manner that may be in tension with a WTO agreement. If the WTO agreements were directly applicable and private litigants had standing to invoke them, a court might well stand in the way of the desired measures. Yet, it is possible that the detriment from those measures to potent interest groups abroad is minimal, so that deviation from the letter of the WTO accords (or a self-interested

---

[1] See J. H. Jackson, 'Status of Treaties in Domestic Legal Systems: A Policy Analysis' (1992) 86 AJIL 310–40.

interpretation of them in the face of ambiguity) may allow governments to reap great political benefits at home with little detriment to politically effective interest groups abroad. Under such conditions, a politically savvy agreement would allow deviation—the joint benefits would exceed the joint costs (in modern contract law, this idea is often referred to as 'efficient breach').

The WTO system facilitates such adjustment of the bargain by allowing for renegotiation at times, and by allowing for the possibility that a violation of the agreement need not always be corrected. Although the Understanding on Rules and Procedures Governing the Settlement of Disputes makes clear that compliance with the results of dispute proceedings is strongly preferred, as a practical matter the parties to a dispute are always free to reach a mutually satisfactory settlement (as long as no one else complains about it because of some other violation that it entails). Indeed, the Dispute Settlement Understanding explicitly provides for the possibility of compensatory concessions by a violator, or for a form of measured retaliation if negotiations over compensation break down. The dispute settlement process thus permits the modification of obligations, or even outright violation of them, in cases where the benefits are great and the aggrieved nations can be more or less made whole through substituted concessions.

These opportunities for mutually advantageous adjustments could well be thwarted by direct applicability, especially if private parties could invoke the international obligation. For instead of reaching a valuable accommodation at the international level, domestic courts might then compel nations to behave in a manner that was politically foolish. Perhaps these observations explain why the rights of private parties to invoke WTO obligations are so restricted. They may also explain why nations are free, if they so desire, to implement their obligations through separate implementing legislation that takes precedence over the international text. For here, once again, the possibility arises that a particular self-serving interpretation or even outright deviation may be valuable for domestic political reasons, but impose little cost abroad. Finally, the subsequent-in-time rule also facilitates adjustment, for if the international obligation took precedence over all ordinary legislation it would not be possible to implement a sensible adjustment in the bargain through ordinary legislative processes.

Not all countries will choose this route, however, because of the above-noted virtues of direct applicability. Both the transaction cost savings and the possible reputational advantage of incorporating the international obligation directly into domestic law may counsel in favour of direct effect. Smaller countries, for example, without the legal expertise and bureaucratic resources to write detailed implementing legislation may prefer to avoid the bother.

13.4 IMPLEMENTATION THROUGH DELEGATION

Whether the international text has direct applicability or the initial implementation is accomplished through additional legislation, the degree of adherence to international commitments will depend greatly on the way that courts, administrative agencies and other government bureaucrats carry out their day-to-day activities. Corruption, politicization, incompetence, and good-faith bottlenecks in these lower level entities can do much to hinder faithful implementation.

These difficulties arise at some level in all countries in the study. The developing countries sometimes tend to have less judicialization generally, and thus to lack the infrastructure for implementation that exists in some of their developed trading partners. And even within the larger trade bureaucracies of the developed world, the sheer magnitude of the WTO undertakings ensures that it will take some time to digest and codify them.

In some instances, a tradition of deference to bureaucratic discretion means that much will depend on the willingness of career bureaucrats to follow the law carefully (Japan is a notable example here). Virtually everywhere, the concern exists that courts and bureaucrats will permit domestic politics to influence their decision-making. The extent of the problem may tend to be greater, the greater the degree of decision-making authority entrusted to officials who are sensitive to political pressures. Administrative agencies headed by political appointees, for example, may be more subject to influence than life tenure judges.

Of course, for the reasons given earlier, the possibility that courts and bureaucrats may be sensitive to domestic political pressures may not be entirely a bad thing from the perspective of WTO Members' governments. Savvy political officials may wish to preserve such flexibility under international accords to allow them to maximize their political support when the opportunities arise. And as long as the political costs abroad are modest, member governments on average can benefit. But the problem of opportunism is present as well, and self-serving decisions by lower level government entities can assuredly frustrate important expectations under the WTO bargain. One device for reducing this problem may be to use the WTO texts as an aid to construction of domestic law (in the United States, for example, the Supreme Court's *Charming Betsy* doctrine requires consistency between international obligations and the construction of domestic statutes where possible). But this device is imperfect, as infidelity to the WTO texts can result from political pressures even if they are nominally accorded deference.

Hence, the real check on opportunistic departures from the bargain by courts and bureaucrats is the international dispute resolution process. Its importance in this respect was dramatically highlighted by the US–Canada Free Trade Agreement, in which Canada insisted on bi-national panel review of administrative agency decisions in preference to national judicial review. No such process was incorporated into the WTO, but its dispute resolution procedures nevertheless represent a substantial step forward over those of the GATT.

13.5 THE WTO DISPUTE SETTLEMENT PROCESS AND ITS NATIONAL CONSEQUENCES

The WTO Dispute Settlement Understanding creates for the first time in the GATT system an environment in which a member nation accused of violating its obligations cannot thwart the dispute settlement process. It ensures not only that aggrieved nations can secure dispute panels, but that recalcitrant violators will be subject to WTO-approved sanctions.

The effectiveness of this process will turn on a number of the same variables that influence whether the WTO texts themselves will be faithfully implemented. For example, what will be the status in domestic law of an adverse finding by a WTO dispute panel (or the appellate body)? Will it directly lead to correction of the violation in question, or will its domestic legal effect depend on the enactment of conforming legislation, or on the discretion of politically-sensitive courts or bureaucrats? In most instances, the answer seems to be that WTO dispute findings have less status in domestic law than the WTO agreements (which may themselves have little status), because the dispute findings are not treaties accepted by the national process for the creation of binding international obligations.

Hence, the prospect arises that disputes may drag on for years, with a cycle of decisions against member states, first finding that they have violated their obligations, then finding that they have failed to correct their violations, and so on. The essential problem results from the fact that WTO dispute settlement can do little more than send matters back to the national government found to be in violation of its commitments, with a mandate that it correct matters, while leaving all the imperfections in place that may have led to the violation in the first place. Only time will tell whether the impediments to domestic implementation of dispute findings undo much of the apparent progress toward effective centralized dispute resolution.

13.6 SOME CONCLUDING THOUGHTS ON 'SOVEREIGNTY'

The 'sovereignty' debate appeared under various rubrics in a number of countries during the WTO ratification process. As the WTO pushes the envelope of substantive international economic law in the years to come, perhaps in areas such as investment policy, service sector licensing, environment issues, competition policy, and labour standards, we may expect that the debate will remain vigorous. It may also stand in the way of progress in some areas.

The differing perspectives on 'sovereignty' in this volume are quite instructive. Smaller countries see themselves as having little control over international commercial policy, and thus see global rules more as a source of protection rather than constraint. Developing countries tend to see the implications of the WTO for 'sovereignty' as modest in comparison to other sources of intrusion, especially the World Bank and the International Monetary Fund, which have in some cases undertaken to restructure domestic fiscal and monetary policies in exchange for assistance. Thus, serious concern for 'sovereignty' arises mainly in the larger, more developed nations (and the European Union) which are used to greater flexibility in international economic relations and have faced little interference in the past from other international organizations.

In these nations, the prospect of a WTO decision holding that some politically popular domestic policy contravenes international law indeed raises nationalist hackles, and plays into the hands of interest groups that seek to avoid international constraints for other reasons. In our view, however, the resulting criticism of the WTO misses the mark widely because it fails to recognize the reciprocal nature of international commitments.

Any international agreement, whether a peace treaty, an extradition treaty, or a trade agreement, involves an exchange of promises. In this respect, such agreements are no different from private contracts. And as in the case of private contracts, promissory commitments impose some constraints on the promisor—the promisor must either perform or suffer some penalty for non-performance. Sometimes the only penalty is a loss of reputation, but more commonly it includes at least a reciprocal refusal to perform in whole or in part by the promisee. Additional penalties may come in the form of further unilateral retaliation or sanctions authorized by a third-party dispute resolution process.

The WTO has now embraced the third-party dispute resolution model, providing in the new trading system a credible threat of centrally authorized and calibrated sanctions for breach of agreement. Perhaps it is coherent to say that the threat of such sanctions intrudes on 'sovereignty', but no more so than that the rule of expectation damages may be said to intrude on the 'sovereignty' of private contracting parties. Private parties routinely enter contracts despite this burden, because what they get is more than what they give.

Precisely the same standard should be used to judge international agreements in general and international commercial agreements in particular. The question is not whether the agreement may prohibit something that a party might otherwise find expedient, thus presenting it with a choice between respecting the prohibition or incurring a penalty. By that standard, no international agreement would be desirable. Instead, the question is whether the benefits of the reciprocal promises made by other parties exceed the costs incurred to secure them. With respect to the WTO treaty, it is not difficult to conclude that the answer is yes. For the 'costs' incurred are in large measure simply a reduction in domestic impediments to the free flow of commerce, impediments that may be politically popular with some groups but that demonstrably reduce the aggregate well-being of the nation and the world as a whole. The occasional and likely minor affronts to legitimate domestic regulatory measures are a small price to pay for the benefits of this broader system of rules. The hard question is not whether the WTO system intrudes on 'sovereignty', therefore, but whether a continued focus on this silly question will prevent the effective implementation of existing rules and the negotiation of broader and better rules in the years to come.

INDEX